![Haynes THE BOOK ®]

FAULT CODES
Manual

Charles White and Martynn Randall

Systems covered:

Bosch KE-Jetronic
Bosch KE-Motronic
Bosch LH-Jetronic
Bosch Mono-Jetronic
Bosch Mono-Motronic
Bosch Motronic
Daihatsu MPi
Bosch EZ-K and EZ-L Ignition
Fenix
Ford EEC IV and EEC V
GM/Delco SPi
GM Multec

Isuzu I-Tec
Lucas 11CU and 14CUX
Lucas LH
Magneti-Marelli G5 and G6
Magneti-Marelli 8F and 8P
Mazda EGi
Mercedes HFM and PMS
Mitsubishi ECI-Multi
Nissan ECCS
Proton ECI-Multi and ECI-SEFi
Renix
Rover MEMS

Rover PGM-Fi
Saab Trionic
Siemens Bendix MPi
Siemens MS4.0
Simos
Simtec
Subaru MPFi
Suzuki EPi
Toyota TCCS
VAG MPi and MPFi
VW Digifant
Weber-Marelli IAW

A book in the **Haynes Service and Repair Manual Series**

© **Haynes Publishing 2004**

ISBN **978 0 85733 706 1**

British Library Cataloguing in Publication Data
A catalogue record for this book is available from the British Library.

Printed in the USA

Haynes Publishing
Sparkford, Yeovil, Somerset BA22 7JJ, England

Haynes North America, Inc
861 Lawrence drive, Newbury Park, California 91320, USA

Haynes Publishing Nordiska AB
Box 1504, 751 45 Uppsala, Sverige

(4175-328)

Contents

GENERAL INFORMATION

SYSTEM SPECIFICS (BY MANUFACTURER)

REFERENCE

Introduction

This book is devoted to the gathering of fault codes, and to the understanding and testing of the self-diagnosis element of the modern engine management system.

The book first gives a technical overview of self-diagnosis, including information concerning EOBD (European On-Board Diagnosis). Other Chapters describe test equipment and general test routines for individual components which may be indicated to be defective by the presence of a stored fault code. Finally, each vehicle manufacturer is given a specific Chapter with a comprehensive list of fault codes, details of how to obtain codes, and other relevant information. Even if the reader has no intention of actually attempting to investigate faults on his or her own vehicle, the book still provides valuable insight into self-diagnosis.

On the other hand, if you relish the task of electronic fault diagnosis, this book will provide you with much of the background knowledge necessary to test the components and circuits on your engine. Generally, we describe how to diagnose faults using simple tools and equipment, which will be available from most good automotive parts retailers. We also mention where the use of more specialised equipment is necessary, and describe some of the common routines used by the professional garage trade.

The vehicle manufacturers may not in fact specifically endorse a number of our tests and routines. In the main, this will be because the manufacturer's test routines are becoming more focused on their own dedicated test equipment which is not generally available outside of a main dealer network. In almost all instances, our own tests follow well-defined testing methods taught in independent training schools, and used by many modern vehicle technical specialists. We mainly describe simple testing methods that are possible with the aid of the ubiquitous digital multi-meter (DMM).

Our test procedures are necessarily generic. However, in many cases, following our procedures in conjunction with a good wiring diagram will reveal the reason for most faults.

The routine and test methods which we describe are perfectly safe to carry out on electronic systems, so long as certain simple rules are observed. These rules are actually no more than the observation of good electrical practice. Be aware that damage to highly-expensive electronic control modules can result from not following these rules. Refer to the Warnings section in the Reference section at the back of this book - these warnings will be repeated/referred to where necessary in the various procedures.

Throughout Europe, the USA and the Far East, the various manufacturers tend to use their own particular terms to describe a particular component. Of course, all these terms tend to be different, and the problem is exacerbated by translation into different languages. This often leads to confusion when several terms are used to describe essentially the same component. There have been several attempts to bring all the manufacturers into line, with a common naming standard for all. One such does now exist (J1930), but it seems unlikely that all manufacturers will adopt this particular standard, and we are not sure that the terms used are that meaningful anyway. Thus, the terms used in this book will follow those which are commonly used in the UK. To reduce confusion, we will apply these terms for the whole range of manufacturers covered in this book, and any commonly-used alternatives will be listed in the Reference section at the end.

Acknowledgements

We would like to thank all those at Sparkford and elsewhere who have helped in the production of this book. In particular, we would like to thank Equiptech for permission to use illustrations from the "CAPS" fuel injection fault diagnosis database, and for providing much of the technical information used. We also thank Kate Eyres, who compiled the lists and tables, John Merritt for his work on many of the Chapters, and Simon Ashby of RA Engineering for additional technical information. Sykes-Pickavant Ltd provided some of the diagnostic equipment used in our workshop.

We take great pride in the accuracy of information given in this book, but vehicle manufacturers make alterations and design changes during the production run of a particular vehicle of which they do not inform us. No liability can be accepted by the authors or publishers for loss, damage or injury caused by any errors in, or omissions from, the information given.

Working on your car can be dangerous. This page shows just some of the potential risks and hazards, with the aim of creating a safety-conscious attitude.

General hazards

Scalding

• Don't remove the radiator or expansion tank cap while the engine is hot.
• Engine oil, automatic transmission fluid or power steering fluid may also be dangerously hot if the engine has recently been running.

Burning

• Beware of burns from the exhaust system and from any part of the engine. Brake discs and drums can also be extremely hot immediately after use.

Crushing

• When working under or near a raised vehicle, always supplement the jack with axle stands, or use drive-on ramps. *Never venture under a car which is only supported by a jack.*
• Take care if loosening or tightening high-torque nuts when the vehicle is on stands. Initial loosening and final tightening should be done with the wheels on the ground.

Fire

• Fuel is highly flammable; fuel vapour is explosive.
• Don't let fuel spill onto a hot engine.
• Do not smoke or allow naked lights (including pilot lights) anywhere near a vehicle being worked on. Also beware of creating sparks (electrically or by use of tools).
• Fuel vapour is heavier than air, so don't work on the fuel system with the vehicle over an inspection pit.
• Another cause of fire is an electrical overload or short-circuit. Take care when repairing or modifying the vehicle wiring.
• Keep a fire extinguisher handy, of a type suitable for use on fuel and electrical fires.

Electric shock

• Ignition HT voltage can be dangerous, especially to people with heart problems or a pacemaker. Don't work on or near the ignition system with the engine running or the ignition switched on.

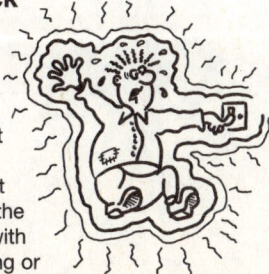

• Mains voltage is also dangerous. Make sure that any mains-operated equipment is correctly earthed. Mains power points should be protected by a residual current device (RCD) circuit breaker.

Fume or gas intoxication

• Exhaust fumes are poisonous; they often contain carbon monoxide, which is rapidly fatal if inhaled. Never run the engine in a confined space such as a garage with the doors shut.
• Fuel vapour is also poisonous, as are the vapours from some cleaning solvents and paint thinners.

Poisonous or irritant substances

• Avoid skin contact with battery acid and with any fuel, fluid or lubricant, especially antifreeze, brake hydraulic fluid and Diesel fuel. Don't syphon them by mouth. If such a substance is swallowed or gets into the eyes, seek medical advice.
• Prolonged contact with used engine oil can cause skin cancer. Wear gloves or use a barrier cream if necessary. Change out of oil-soaked clothes and do not keep oily rags in your pocket.
• Air conditioning refrigerant forms a poisonous gas if exposed to a naked flame (including a cigarette). It can also cause skin burns on contact.

Asbestos

• Asbestos dust can cause cancer if inhaled or swallowed. Asbestos may be found in gaskets and in brake and clutch linings. When dealing with such components it is safest to assume that they contain asbestos.

Special hazards

Hydrofluoric acid

• This extremely corrosive acid is formed when certain types of synthetic rubber, found in some O-rings, oil seals, fuel hoses etc, are exposed to temperatures above 400°C. The rubber changes into a charred or sticky substance containing the acid. *Once formed, the acid remains dangerous for years. If it gets onto the skin, it may be necessary to amputate the limb concerned.*
• When dealing with a vehicle which has suffered a fire, or with components salvaged from such a vehicle, wear protective gloves and discard them after use.

The battery

• Batteries contain sulphuric acid, which attacks clothing, eyes and skin. Take care when topping-up or carrying the battery.
• The hydrogen gas given off by the battery is highly explosive. Never cause a spark or allow a naked light nearby. Be careful when connecting and disconnecting battery chargers or jump leads.

Air bags

• Air bags can cause injury if they go off accidentally. Take care when removing the steering wheel and/or facia. Special storage instructions may apply.

Diesel injection equipment

• Diesel injection pumps supply fuel at very high pressure. Take care when working on the fuel injectors and fuel pipes.

⚠ *Warning: Never expose the hands, face or any other part of the body to injector spray; the fuel can penetrate the skin with potentially fatal results.*

Remember...

DO

• Do use eye protection when using power tools, and when working under the vehicle.

• Do wear gloves or use barrier cream to protect your hands when necessary.

• Do get someone to check periodically that all is well when working alone on the vehicle.

• Do keep loose clothing and long hair well out of the way of moving mechanical parts.

• Do remove rings, wristwatch etc, before working on the vehicle – especially the electrical system.

• Do ensure that any lifting or jacking equipment has a safe working load rating adequate for the job.

DON'T

• Don't attempt to lift a heavy component which may be beyond your capability – get assistance.

• Don't rush to finish a job, or take unverified short cuts.

• Don't use ill-fitting tools which may slip and cause injury.

• Don't leave tools or parts lying around where someone can trip over them. Mop up oil and fuel spills at once.

• Don't allow children or pets to play in or near a vehicle being worked on.

Notes

Introduction to Self-Diagnosis

1

1   Introduction

The objective of the Self-Diagnosis (SD) function (sometimes termed On-Board Diagnosis or OBD/EOBD) is to minimise pollutant emissions for motor vehicles. Self-diagnosis is the basis for controlling engine performance in order to provide the most effective conditions for efficient operation.

The chemical sequence of combustion

Fuels for spark ignition and diesel engines consist of various hydrocarbon compounds, which combine with the oxygen of the intake air. Nitrogen and other residual gases also combine during the combustion process. With perfect combustion, no toxic substances would be produced. Under actual operating conditions, non-toxic exhaust gases such as nitrogen (N_2), water vapour (H_2O) and carbon dioxide (CO_2) join the toxic products of incomplete combustion. Toxic substances in exhaust gases include carbon monoxide (CO), partially-unburnt hydrocarbons (HC), nitrogen oxides, sulphur dioxide (SO_2), lead compounds and soot *(see illustrations 1.1 and 1.2)*. The high concentration of pollutants resulting from vehicle emissions are known to be causing health problems, notably respiratory illnesses, and also have environmentally-damaging effects.

The idea that toxic emissions should be reduced while maintaining or improving the effective operation of vehicular engines was accepted and argued by the California Air

Resources Board (CARB). By 1968 regulations were introduced in California by Californian State Government under the "Clean Air Act" to restrict pollutant emissions for passenger cars.

Control functions, monitoring and diagnostic communication

By 1978 the first Engine Management Systems were developed, first appearing as the Bosch Motronic which was fitted to the BMW 732i. Engine management serves the purpose of enabling the engine components to operate effectively by means of an Electronic Control Module (ECM) which controls, monitors and in some cases adapts to ensure that the most efficient levels of engine operation can be expected.

The EMS soon evolved to include a Self-Diagnosis (SD) function which not only controls and monitors components of the engine system but also enables the driver or technician to identify faults that are otherwise difficult to detect. This was achieved by the invention and application of a data communication system, and the introduction of a computerised memory into the ECM. Faults could then be stored in ECM memory and retrieved at a later time. On some models, a self-diagnostic warning light illuminates to give warning of a fault, or the light can be used to display the stored faults as a series of flashes. A 1981 Cadillac was the first vehicle to which an ECM with self-diagnosis was fitted, and the system was Bendix Digital.

Chapter 1

Since the early 1980s, the evolution of the EMS has been relatively quick, and most vehicle manufacturers now equip their vehicles with an EMS that only bears some small resemblance to the early systems. Not only are the most recent Engine Management Systems almost universally fitted with a self-diagnosis capability, but many automatic transmissions, anti-lock braking systems (ABS) and supplementary restraint systems (SRS, typically airbags) controlled by ECMs have self-diagnosis. An adaptive capability has been introduced so that component operation is continually monitored and adjusted for optimum performance.

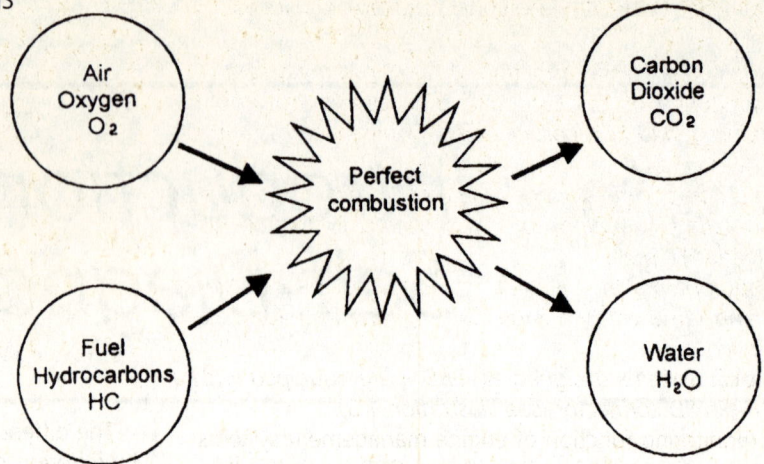

A brief definition of Self-Diagnosis (SD)

The Self-Diagnosis function checks the signals from the ECM circuits against a set of control parameters. If a signal does not lie within the bounds of the control parameters, or appears implausible, an internal fault is stored in ECM memory. The stored faults are represented in the main by codes termed "Fault Codes". When the fault codes are retrieved from the ECM they become an invaluable aid to diagnosis.

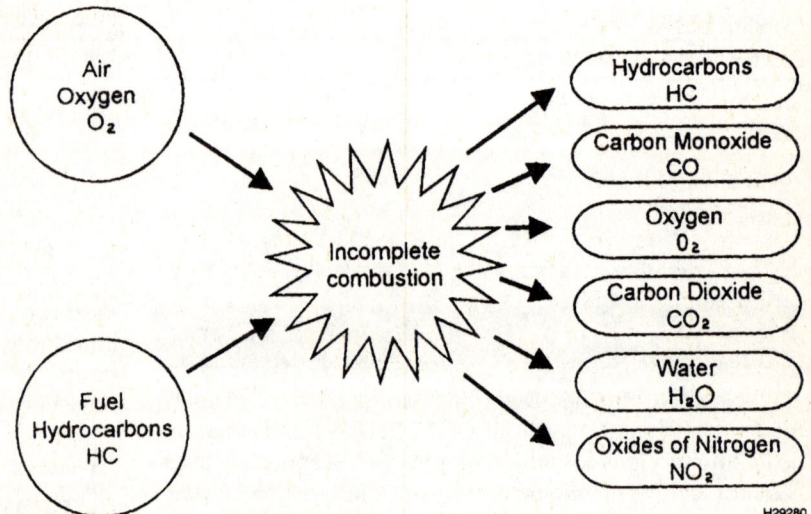

Standardisation of On-Board Diagnosis (OBD)

On-board Diagnosis established three essential criteria for manufacturers and vehicle technicians/engineers to ensure that vehicles conform from model year 1988. First, vehicles must be equipped with an electronic SD system. Second, any faults (malfunctions) relevant to exhaust emissions must be displayed by means of an SD warning light installed on the instrument panel. Third, the fault must be recorded in ECM fault memory, and may be retrievable with the aid of a Fault Code Reader (FCR), or via Flash Codes.

From 1988 to 1991 the International Standards Organisation drafted and updated ISO 9141 to ISO9141-2, which attempts to standardise:

The SD plug connection.
The diagnostic equipment and its range of diagnoses.
The contents of the protocols.
The extent of data to be exchanged.

These were based on the regulations for America. However, these agreed requirements were adopted by European governments and governments of all five continents in consultation with vehicle manufacturers.

More requirements were laid down by a second regulation, OBD II, which was applied from model year 1994. Diesel engines were also subject to the OBD requirements as

1.1 Combustion chart

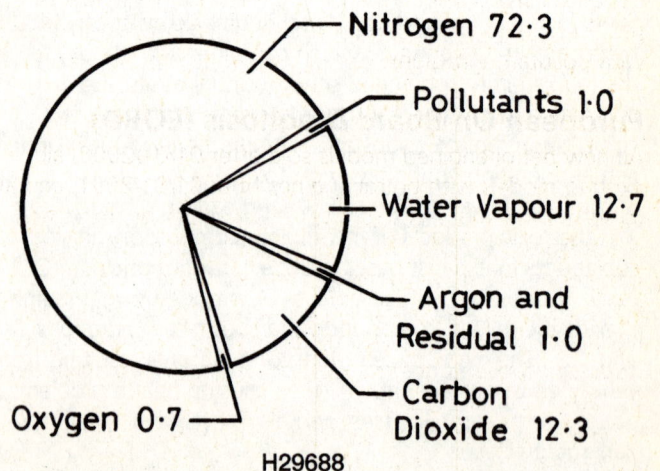

1.2 Pollutant chart showing the percentage of toxic emissions in 1.0% of exhaust gas

of model year 1996. The additional requirements are as follows:

> *Additional flashing function of the SD warning light.*
>
> *Monitoring of functions and components, not only for defects, but also for ensuring adherence to emission values.*
>
> *In addition to storing faults as a digital code, the operating conditions are also stored in the so-called "Freeze Frame".*
>
> *The contents of the fault memory must be capable of being retrieved by a Fault Code Reader instead of Flash Codes.*
>
> **Note:** *Systems designed to OBD II are equipped with a 16-pin SD connector (see illustration 1.3).*

The monitoring function of engine management systems has also been extended and regulated. OBD II calls for the continuous monitoring of the following components and areas:

> *Combustion.*
> *Catalytic converter.*
> *Oxygen sensor.*
> *Secondary air system.*
> *Fuel evaporation system.*
> *Exhaust-gas recirculation (EGR) system.*

Diesel engines are subject to the same regulations and objectives, but obviously different components, such as glow plugs, are monitored to interact with the relevant technology employed on each system.

The ISO, the SAE and a plethora of transport and environmentally-concerned non-governmental organisations have argued for further and consistent regulations. The US "Clean Air Acts" have adopted the CARB standards as a minimum level of protection for public health and well-being; similar legislation has been brought into being by many local and national governments since 1968. The introduction of catalytic converters, fuel injection systems, the increased use of vehicle diesel engines and of unleaded petrol engines during the past 30 years, has made further positive contributions to reducing the problems which arise with pollutant emissions.

European On-Board Diagnosis (EOBD)

All new petrol engined models sold after 01/01/2000, all existing models with petrol engines from 01/01/2001, and all diesel engined models sold after 2005 in Europe, must be equipped with EOBD. This is a higher standard of system monitoring, where any emission related faults must be notified to the driver by illuminating the MIL (Malfunction Indicator Light) in the instrument cluster, the fault (and the distance travelled since the fault occurred) must be recorded for later retrieval.

EOBD also attempts to standardise the type of diagnostic plug (16-pin J1962), the plug position, and the configuration of the plug terminals. The diagnostic plug must be within reach of the driver's seat; tools must not be required to reveal the plug, although it may have a removable cover.

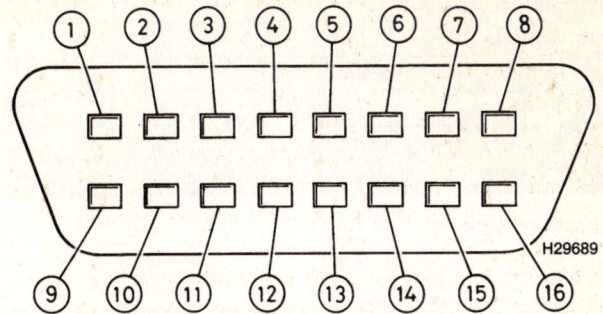

1.3 16-pin Self-Diagnosis connector

The different pins of the plug *(see illustration 1.3)* are used by different manufacturers in different ways, depending on which communication protocol is used. There are four protocols available:

Protocol	Connector pins used
J1850 VPW	2, 4, 5 and 16
ISO 9141 - 2	4, 5, 7, 15 and 16
J1850 PWM	2, 4, 5, 10 and 16
KWP2000 (ISO14230)	4, 5, 7, 15 and 16

Generally speaking, European and Asian manufacturers use ISO / KWP protocols, whilst General Motors (Vauxhall/Opel) use J1850 VPW, and Ford use J1850 PWM.

The plugs pins are configured as follows:

Pin	
2	J1850 BUS+
4	Chassis ground
5	Signal ground
6	CAN High (J-2284)
7	K-line
10	J1850 BUS
14	CAN Low (J-2284)
15	L-line
16	Battery power

Manufacturers may use additional pins for other purposes.

To a certain extent, EOBD standardises the fault codes generated by the self-diagnosis system. These five digit alphanumeric codes are made up as follows:

Letter	System
B	Body
C	Chassis
P	Powertrain
U	Network

The second digit determines whether the code is a generic EOBD code (where the definition of the code is stated in the EOBD regulations, and will be the same for all manufacturers), or a Manufacturer specific code (where definition of the code is determined by the vehicle manufacturer).

Chapter 1

Powertrain codes:

P0xxx - Generic	
P1xxx - Manufacturer specific	
P2xxx - Generic	
P30xx - Manufacturer specific	
P34xx - Generic	

Chassis codes:

C0xxx - Generic	
C1xxx - Manufacturer specific	
C2xxx - Manufacturer specific	
C3xxx - Generic	

Body codes:

B0xxx - Generic	
B1xxx - Manufacturer specific	
B2xxx - Manufacturer specific	
B3xxx - Generic	

Network communication codes

U0xxx - Generic	
U1xxx - Manufacturer specific	
U2xxx - Manufacturer specific	
U3xxx - Generic	

The third digit determines the specific system/sub-system within the vehicle that is associated with the recorded fault code:

Digit	System/sub-system
1	Fuel and Air metering
2	Fuel and Air metering (injector circuit only)
3	Ignition system or misfire
4	Auxiliary emission control system
5	Vehicle speed control and idle control system
6	Computer output circuits
7	Transmission
8	Transmission

Note: *Manufacturers are not obliged to adhere to the above table for their manufacturer specific codes.*

The forth and fifth digits of the code identify the section related to the code generation. The following is a list of the allocated codes beginning with P0 (Generic Powertrain). However, as all fault code readers/scanners identify the code and display the meaning in English, reference to a detailed list is not necessary.

Code	Fault description
P0000	No fault found
P0001	Fuel volume regulator control - open circuit
P0002	Fuel volume regulator control - circuit range/performance
P0003	Fuel volume regulator control - low circuit
P0004	Fuel volume regulator control - high circuit
P0005	Fuel shut-off valve - open circuit

Code	Fault description
P0006	Fuel shut-off valve - low circuit
P0007	Fuel shut-off valve - high circuit
P0008	Engine position system, bank 1 - engine performance
P0009	Engine position system, bank 2 - engine performance
P0010	Camshaft position actuator, intake/left/front, bank 1 - circuit fault
P0011	Camshaft position actuator, intake/left/front, bank 1 - timing over advance/system performance
P0012	Camshaft position actuator, intake/left/front, bank 1 - timing over retarded
P0013	Camshaft position actuator, intake/left/front, bank 1 - circuit fault
P0014	Camshaft position actuator, exhaust/right/rear, bank 1 - timing over advanced/system performance
P0015	Camshaft position actuator, exhaust/right/rear, bank 1 - timing over retarded
P0016	Crankshaft position/camshaft position, bank 1 sensor A - correlation
P0017	Crankshaft position/camshaft position, bank 1 sensor B - correlation
P0018	Crankshaft position/camshaft position, bank 2 sensor A - correlation
P0019	Crankshaft position/camshaft position, bank 2 sensor B - correlation
P0020	Camshaft position actuator, intake/left/front, bank 2 - circuit fault
P0021	Camshaft position actuator, exhaust/right/rear, bank 2 - timing over advanced/system performance
P0022	Camshaft position actuator, exhaust/right/rear, bank 2 - timing over retarded
P0023	Camshaft position actuator, exhaust/right/rear, bank 2 - circuit fault
P0024	Camshaft position actuator, exhaust/right/rear, bank 2 - timing over advanced/system performance
P0025	Camshaft position actuator, intake/left/front, bank 2 - timing over retarded
P0026	Intake valve control solenoid circuit, bank 1 - range/performance
P0027	Exhaust valve control solenoid circuit, bank 1 - range/performance
P0028	Intake valve control solenoid circuit, bank 2 - range/performance
P0029	Exhaust valve control solenoid circuit, bank 2 - range/performance
P0030	Heated oxygen sensor 1, bank 1, heater control - circuit fault
P0031	Heated oxygen sensor 1, bank 1, heater control - circuit low
P0032	Heated oxygen sensor 1, bank 1, heater control - circuit high
P0033	Turbo wastegate regulating valve - circuit fault
P0034	Turbo wastegate regulating valve - circuit low
P0035	Turbo wastegate regulating valve - circuit high
P0036	Heated oxygen sensor 2, bank 1, heater control - circuit fault
P0037	Heated oxygen sensor 2, bank 1, heater control - circuit low
P0038	Heated oxygen sensor 2, bank 1, heater control - circuit high
P0039	Turbo bypass valve, control circuit - range/performance
P0040	Oxygen sensor signals swapped, bank 1 sensor 1/bank 2 sensor 1
P0041	Oxygen sensor signals swapped, bank 1 sensor 2/bank 2 sensor 2
P0042	Heated oxygen sensor 3, bank 1, heater control - circuit fault
P0043	Heated oxygen sensor 3, bank 1, heater control - circuit low
P0044	Heated oxygen sensor 3, bank 1, heater control - circuit high
P0045	Turbo boost control solenoid - open circuit
P0046	Turbo boost control solenoid - circuit range/performance
P0047	Turbo boost control solenoid - circuit low
P0048	Turbo boost control solenoid - circuit high
P0049	Turbo turbine - over speed
P0050	Heated oxygen sensor 1, bank 2, heater control - circuit fault
P0051	Heated oxygen sensor 1, bank 2, heater control - circuit low
P0052	Heated oxygen sensor 1, bank 2, heater control - circuit high
P0053	Heated oxygen sensor, bank 1, sensor 1 - heater resistance
P0054	Heated oxygen sensor, bank 1, sensor 2 - heater resistance
P0055	Heated oxygen sensor, bank 1, sensor 3 - heater resistance
P0056	Heated oxygen sensor 2, bank 2, heater control - circuit fault
P0057	Heated oxygen sensor 2, bank 2, heater control - circuit low
P0058	Heated oxygen sensor 2, bank 2, heater control - circuit high
P0059	Heated oxygen sensor, bank 2, sensor 1 - heater resistance
P0060	Heated oxygen sensor, bank 2, sensor 2 - heater resistance
P0061	Heated oxygen sensor, bank 2, sensor 3 - heater resistance
P0062	Heated oxygen sensor 3, bank 2, heater control - circuit fault
P0063	Heated oxygen sensor 3, bank 2, heater control - circuit low

Code	Fault description
P0064	Heated oxygen sensor 3, bank 2, heater control - circuit high
P0065	Air assisted injector - range/performance
P0066	Air assisted injector - circuit fault/circuit low
P0067	Air assisted injector - circuit high
P0068	Manifold absolute pressure sensor/mass airflow sensor/throttle position correlation
P0069	Manifold absolute pressure sensor/barometric pressure sensor correlation
P0070	Outside air temperature sensor - circuit fault
P0071	Outside air temperature sensor - range/performance
P0072	Outside air temperature sensor - low input
P0073	Outside air temperature sensor - high input
P0074	Outside air temperature sensor - circuit intermittent
P0075	Intake valve control solenoid, bank 1 - circuit fault
P0076	Intake valve control solenoid, bank 1 - circuit low
P0077	Intake valve control solenoid, bank 1 - circuit high
P0078	Exhaust valve control solenoid, bank 1 - circuit fault
P0079	Exhaust valve control solenoid, bank 1 - circuit low
P0080	Exhaust valve control solenoid, bank 1 - circuit high
P0081	Intake valve control solenoid, bank 2 - circuit fault
P0082	Intake valve control solenoid, bank 2 - circuit low
P0083	Intake valve control solenoid, bank 1 - circuit high
P0084	Exhaust valve control solenoid, bank 2 - circuit fault
P0085	Exhaust valve control solenoid, bank 2 - circuit low
P0086	Exhaust valve control solenoid, bank 2 - circuit high
P0087	Fuel rail/system pressure too low
P0088	Fuel rail/system pressure too high
P0089	Fuel pressure regulator - performance
P0090	Fuel metering solenoid - open circuit
P0091	Fuel metering solenoid - short to earth
P0092	Fuel metering solenoid - short to positive
P0093	Fuel system leak - large leak detected
P0094	Fuel system leak - small leak detected
P0095	Intake air temperature sensor 2 - circuit fault
P0096	Intake air temperature sensor 2 - circuit range/performance
P0097	Intake air temperature sensor 2 - circuit low input
P0098	Intake air temperature sensor 2 - circuit high
P0099	Intake air temperature sensor 2 - circuit intermittent/erratic
P0100	Mass or Volume Air flow Circuit Malfunction
P0101	Mass or Volume Air flow Circuit Range/Performance Problem
P0102	Mass or Volume Air Flow Circuit low Input
P0103	Mass or Volume Air flow Circuit High Input
P0104	Mass or Volume Air flow Circuit Intermittent
P0105	Manifold Absolute Pressure/Barometric Pressure Circuit Malfunction
P0106	Manifold Absolute Pressure/Barometric Pressure Circuit Range/Performance Problem
P0107	Manifold Absolute Pressure/Barometric Pressure Circuit Low Input
P0108	Manifold Absolute Pressure/Barometric Pressure Circuit High Input
P0109	Manifold Absolute Pressure/Barometric Pressure Circuit Intermittent
P0110	Intake Air Temperature Circuit Malfunction
P0111	Intake Air Temperature Circuit Range/Performance Problem
P0112	Intake Air Temperature Circuit Low Input
P0113	Intake Air Temperature Circuit High Input
P0114	Intake Air Temperature Circuit Intermittent
P0115	Engine Coolant Temperature Circuit Malfunction
P0116	Engine Coolant Temperature Circuit Range/Performance Problem
P0117	Engine Coolant Temperature Circuit Low Input
P0118	Engine Coolant Temperature Circuit High Input
P0119	Engine Coolant Temperature Circuit Intermittent
P0120	Throttle Pedal Position Sensor/Switch A Circuit Malfunction
P0121	Throttle/Pedal Position Sensor/Switch A Circuit Range/Performance Problem
P0122	Throttle/Pedal Position Sensor/Switch A Circuit Low Input
P0123	Throttle/Pedal Position Sensor/Switch A Circuit High Input
P0124	Throttle/Pedal Position Sensor/Switch A Circuit Intermittent

Code	Fault description
P0125	Insufficient Coolant Temperature for Closed Loop Fuel Control
P0126	Insufficient Coolant Temperature for Stable Operation
P0130	O2 Sensor Circuit Malfunction (Bank 1 Sensor 1)
P0131	O2 Sensor Circuit Low Voltage (Bank 1 Sensor 1)
P0132	O2 Sensor Circuit High Voltage (Bank 1 Sensor 1)
P0133	O2 Sensor Circuit Slow Response (Bank 1 Sensor 1)
P0134	O2 Sensor Circuit No Activity Detected (Bank 1 Sensor 1)
P0135	O2 Sensor Heater Circuit Malfunction (Bank 1 Sensor 1)
P0136	O2 Sensor Circuit Malfunction (Bank 1 Sensor 2)
P0137	O2 Sensor Circuit Low Voltage (Bank 1 Sensor 2)
P0138	O2 Sensor Circuit High Voltage (Bank 1 Sensor 2)
P0139	O2 Sensor Circuit Slow Response (Bank 1 Sensor 2)
P0140	O2 Sensor Circuit No Activity Detected (Bank 1 Sensor 2)
P0141	O2 Sensor Heater Circuit Malfunction (Bank 1 Sensor 2)
P0142	O2 Sensor Circuit Malfunction (Bank 1 Sensor 3)
P0143	O2 Sensor Circuit Low Voltage (Bank 1 Sensor 3)
P0144	O2 Sensor Circuit High Voltage (Bank 1 Sensor 3)
P0145	O2 Sensor Circuit Slow Response (Bank 1 Sensor 3)
P0146	O2 Sensor Circuit No Activity Detected (Bank 1 Sensor 3)
P0147	O2 Sensor Heater Circuit Malfunction (Bank 1 Sensor 3)
P0150	O2 Sensor Circuit Malfunction (Bank 2 Sensor 1)
P0151	O2 Sensor Circuit Low Voltage (Bank 2 Sensor 1)
P0152	O2 Sensor Circuit High Voltage (Bank 2 Sensor 1)
P0153	O2 Sensor Circuit Slow Response (Bank 2 Sensor 1)
P0154	O2 Sensor Circuit No Activity Detected (Bank 2 Sensor 1)
P0155	O2 Sensor Heater Circuit Malfunction (Bank 2 Sensor 1)
P0156	O2 Sensor Circuit Malfunction (Bank 2 Sensor 2)
P0157	O2 Sensor Circuit Low Voltage (Bank 2 Sensor 2)
P0158	O2 Sensor Circuit High Voltage (Bank 2 Sensor 2)
P0159	O2 Sensor Circuit Slow Response (Bank 2 Sensor 2)
P0160	O2 Sensor Circuit No Activity Detected (Bank 2 Sensor 2)
P0161	O2 Sensor Heater Circuit Malfunction (Bank 2 Sensor 2)
P0162	O2 Sensor Circuit Malfunction (Bank 2 Sensor 3)
P0163	O2 Sensor Circuit Low Voltage (Bank 2 Sensor 3)
P0164	O2 Sensor Circuit High Voltage (Bank 2 Sensor 3)
P0165	O2 Sensor Circuit Slow Response (Bank 2 Sensor 3)
P0166	O2 Sensor Circuit No Activity Detected (Bank 2 Sensor 3)
P0167	O2 Sensor Heater Circuit Malfunction (Bank 2 Sensor 3)
P0170	Fuel Trim Malfunction (Bank 1)
P0171	System Too Lean (Bank 1)
P0172	System Too Rich (Bank 1)
P0173	Fuel Trim Malfunction (Bank 2)
P0174	System Too Lean (Bank 2)
P0175	System Too Rich (Bank 2)
P0176	Fuel Composition Sensor Circuit Malfunction
P0177	Fuel Composition Sensor Circuit Range/Performance
P0178	Fuel Composition Sensor Circuit Low Input
P0179	Fuel Composition Sensor Circuit High Input
P0180	Fuel Temperature Sensor A Circuit Malfunction
P0181	Fuel Temperature Sensor A Circuit Performance
P0182	Fuel Temperature Sensor A Circuit low Input
P0183	Fuel Temperature Sensor A Circuit High Input
P0184	Fuel Temperature Sensor A Circuit Intermittent
P0185	Fuel Temperature Sensor B Circuit Malfunction
P0186	Fuel Temperature Sensor B Circuit Range/Performance
P0187	Fuel Temperature Sensor U Circuit Low Input
P0188	Fuel Temperature Sensor B Circuit High Input
P0189	Fuel Temperature Sensor B Circuit Intermittent
P0190	Fuel Rail Pressure Sensor Circuit Malfunction
P0191	Fuel Rail Pressure Sensor Circuit Range/Performance
P0192	Fuel Rail Pressure Sensor Circuit Low Input
P0193	Fuel Rail Pressure Sensor Circuit High Input
P0194	Fuel Rail Pressure Sensor Circuit Intermittent
P0195	Engine Oil Temperature Sensor Malfunction
P0196	Engine Oil Temperature Sensor Range/Performance

Code	Fault description
P0197	Engine Oil Temperature Sensor Low
P0198	Engine Oil Temperature Sensor High
P0199	Engine Oil Temperature Sensor Intermittent
P0200	Injector Circuit Malfunction
P0201	Injector Circuit Malfunction - Cylinder 1
P0202	Injector Circuit Malfunction - Cylinder 2
P0203	Injector Circuit Malfunction - Cylinder 3
P0204	Injector Circuit Malfunction - Cylinder 4
P0205	Injector Circuit Malfunction - Cylinder 5
P0206	Injector Circuit Malfunction - Cylinder 6
P0207	Injector Circuit Malfunction - Cylinder 7
P0208	Injector Circuit Malfunction - Cylinder 8
P0209	Injector Circuit Malfunction - Cylinder 9
P0210	Injector Circuit Malfunction - Cylinder 10
P0211	Injector Circuit Malfunction - Cylinder 11
P0212	Injector Circuit Malfunction - Cylinder 12
P0213	Cold Start Injector 1 Malfunction
P0214	Cold Start Injector 2 Malfunction
P0215	Engine Shutoff Solenoid Malfunction
P0216	Injection Timing Control Circuit Malfunction
P0217	Engine Overtemp Condition
P0218	Transmission Over Temperature Condition
P0219	Engine Over Speed Condition
P0220	Throttle/Pedal Position Sensor/Switch B Circuit Malfunction
P0221	Throttle/pedal Position Sensor/Switch B Circuit Range/Performance Problem
P0222	Throttle/pedal Position Sensor/Switch B Circuit Low Input
P0223	Throttle/Pedal Position Sensor/Switch B Circuit High Input
P0224	Throttle/Pedal Position Sensor/Switch B Circuit Intermittent
P0225	Throttle/Pedal Position Sensor/Switch C Circuit Malfunction
P0226	Throttle/Pedal Position Sensor/Switch C Circuit Range/Performance Problem
P0227	Throttle/Pedal Position Sensor/Switch C Circuit Low Input
P0228	Throttle/Pedal Position Sensor/Switch C Circuit High Input
P0229	Throttle/Pedal Position Sensor/Switch C Circuit Intermittent
P0230	Fuel Pump Primary Circuit Malfunction
P0231	Fuel Pump Secondary Circuit Low
P0232	Fuel Pump Secondary Circuit High
P0233	Fuel Pump Secondary Circuit Intermittent
P0234	Engine Overboost Condition
P0235	Turbocharger Boost Sensor A Circuit Malfunction
P0236	Turbocharger Boost Sensor A Circuit Range/Performance
P0237	Turbocharger Boost Sensor A Circuit Low
P0238	Turbocharger Boost Sensor A Circuit High
P0239	Turbocharger Boost Sensor B Circuit Malfunction
P0240	Turbocharger Boost Sensor B Circuit Range/Performance
P0241	Turbocharger Boost Sensor B Circuit Low
P0242	Turbocharger Boost Sensor B Circuit High
P0243	Turbocharger Wastegate Solenoid A Malfunction
P0244	Turbocharger Wastegate Solenoid A Range/Performance
P0245	Turbocharger Wastegate Solenoid A low
P0246	Turbocharger Wastegate Solenoid A High
P0247	Turbocharger Wastegate Solenoid B Malfunction
P0248	Turbocharger Wastegate Solenoid B Range/Performance
P0249	Turbocharger Wastegate Solenoid B Low
P0250	Turbocharger Wastegate Solenoid B High
P0251	Injection Pump Fuel Metering Control "A" Malfunction (Cam/Rotor/Injector)
P0252	Injection Pump Fuel Metering Control "A" Range/Performance (Cam/Rotor/Injector)
P0253	Injection Pump Fuel Metering Control "A" Low (Cam/Rotor/Injector)
P0254	Injection Pump Fuel Metering Control "A" High (Cam/Rotor/Injector)
P0255	Injection Pump Fuel Metering Control "A" Intermittent (Cam/Rotor/Injector)
P0256	Injection Pump Fuel Metering Control "B" Malfunction (Cam/Rotor/Injector)

Code	Fault description
P0257	Injection Pump Fuel Metering Control "B" Range/Performance (Cam/Rotor/Injector)
P0258	Injection Pump Fuel Metering Control "B" Low (Cam/Rotor/Injector)
P0259	Injection lump Fuel Metering Control "B" High (Cam/Rotor/Injector)
P0260	Injection Pump Fuel Metering Control "B" Intermittent (Cam/Rotor/Injector)
P0261	Cylinder 1 Injector Circuit Low
P0262	Cylinder 1 Injector Circuit High
P0263	Cylinder 1 Contribution/Balance Fault
P0264	Cylinder 2 Injector Circuit Low
P0265	Cylinder 2 Injector Circuit High
P0266	Cylinder 2 Contribution/Balance Fault
P0267	Cylinder 3 Injector Circuit Low
P0268	Cylinder 3 Injector Circuit High
P0269	Cylinder 3 Contribution/Balance Fault
P0270	Cylinder 4 Injector Circuit Low
P0271	Cylinder 4 Injector Circuit High
P0272	Cylinder 4 Contribution/Balance Fault
P0273	Cylinder 5 Injector Circuit Low
P0274	Cylinder 5 Injector Circuit High
P0275	Cylinder 5 Contribution/Balance Fault
P0276	Cylinder 6 Injector Circuit Low
P0277	Cylinder 6 Injector Circuit High
P0278	Cylinder 6 Contribution/Balance Fault
P0279	Cylinder 7 Injector Circuit Low
P0280	Cylinder 7 Injector Circuit High
P0281	Cylinder 7 Contribution/Balance Fault
P0282	Cylinder 8 Injector Circuit Low
P0283	Cylinder 8 Injector Circuit High
P0284	Cylinder 8 Contribution/Balance Fault
P0285	Cylinder 9 Injector Circuit Low
P0286	Cylinder 9 Injector Circuit High
P0287	Cylinder 9 Contribution/Balance Fault
P0288	Cylinder 10 Injector Circuit Low
P0289	Cylinder 10 Injector Circuit High
P0290	Cylinder 10 Contribution/balance Fault
P0291	Cylinder 11 Injector Circuit Low
P0292	Cylinder 11 Injector Circuit High
P0293	Cylinder 11 Contribution/balance Fault
P0294	Cylinder 12 Injector Circuit Low
P0295	Cylinder 12 Injector Circuit High
P0296	Cylinder 12 Contribution/Balance Fault
P0300	Random/Multiple Cylinder Misfire Detected
P0301	Cylinder 1 Misfire Detected
P0302	Cylinder 2 Misfire Detected
P0303	Cylinder 3 Misfire Detected
P0304	Cylinder 4 Misfire Detected
P0305	Cylinder 5 Misfire Detected
P0306	Cylinder 6 Misfire Detected
P0307	Cylinder 7 Misfire Detected
P0308	Cylinder 8 Misfire Detected
P0309	Cylinder 9 Misfire Detected
P0310	Cylinder 10 Misfire Detected
P0311	Cylinder 11 Misfire Detected
P0312	Cylinder 12 Misfire Detected
P0320	Ignition/Distributor Engine Speed Input Circuit Malfunction
P0321	Ignition/Distributor Engine Speed Input Circuit Range/Performance
P0322	Ignition/Distributor Engine Speed Input Circuit No Signal
P0323	Ignition/Distributor Engine Speed Input Circuit Intermittent
P0325	Knock Sensor 1 Circuit Malfunction (Bank 1 or Single Sensor)
P0326	Knock Sensor 1 Circuit Range/Performance (Bank 1 or Single Sensor)
P0327	Knock Sensor 1 Circuit low Input (Bank 1 or Single Sensor)
P0328	Knock Sensor 1 Circuit High Input (Bank 1 or Single Sensor)
P0329	Knock Sensor 1 Circuit Input Intermittent (Bank 1 or Single Sensor)
P0330	Knock Sensor 2 Circuit Malfunction (Bank 2)

Code	Fault description
P0331	Knock Sensor 2 Circuit Range/Performance (Bank 2)
P0332	Knock Sensor 2 Circuit Low Input (Bank 2)
P0333	Knock Sensor 2 Circuit High Input (Bank 2)
P0334	Knock Sensor 2 Circuit Input Intermittent (Bank 2)
P0335	Crankshaft Position Sensor A Circuit Malfunction
P0336	Crankshaft Position Sensor A Circuit Range/Performance
P0337	Crankshaft Position Sensor A Circuit Low Input
P0338	Crankshaft Position Sensor A Circuit High Input
P0339	Crankshaft Position Sensor A Circuit Intermittent
P0340	Camshaft Position Sensor Circuit Malfunction
P0341	Camshaft Position Sensor Circuit Range/Performance
P0342	Camshaft Position Sensor Circuit Low Input
P0343	Camshaft Position Sensor Circuit High Input
P0344	Camshaft Position Sensor Circuit Intermittent
P0350	Ignition Coil Primary/Secondary Circuit Malfunction
P0351	Ignition Coil A Primary/Secondary Circuit Malfunction
P0352	Ignition Coil B Primary/Secondary Circuit Malfunction
P0353	Ignition Coil C Primary/Secondary Circuit Malfunction
P0354	Ignition Coil D Primary/Secondary Circuit Malfunction
P0355	Ignition Coil B Primary/Secondary Circuit Malfunction
P0356	Ignition Coil F Primary/Secondary Circuit Malfunction
P0357	Ignition Coil G Primary/Secondary Circuit Malfunction
P0358	Ignition Coil H Primary/Secondary Circuit Malfunction
P0359	Ignition Coil I Primary/Secondary Circuit Malfunction
P0360	Ignition Coil I Primary/Secondary Circuit Malfunction
P0361	Ignition Coil K Primary/Secondary Circuit Malfunction
P0362	Ignition Coil L Primary/Secondary Circuit Malfunction
P0370	Timing Reference High Resolution Signal A Malfunction
P0371	Timing Reference High Resolution Signal A Too Many Pulses
P0372	Timing Reference High Resolution Signal A Too Few Pulses
P0373	Timing Reference High Resolution Signal A Intermittent/Erratic Pulses
P0374	Timing Reference High Resolution Signal A No Pulses
P0375	Timing Reference High Resolution Signal B Malfunction
P0376	Timing Reference High Resolution Signal B Too Many Pulses
P0377	Timing Reference High Resolution Signal B Too Few Pulses
P0378	Timing Reference High Resolution Signal B Intermittent/Erratic Pulses
P0379	Timing Reference High Resolution Signal B No Pulses
P0380	Glow Plug/Heater Circuit "A" Malfunction
P0381	Glow Plug/Heater Indicator Circuit Malfunction
P0382	Glow Plug/Heater Circuit "B" Malfunction
P0385	Crankshaft Position Sensor B Circuit Malfunction
P0386	Crankshaft Position Sensor B Circuit Range/Performance
P0387	Crankshaft Position Sensor B Circuit Low Input
P0388	Crankshaft Position Sensor B Circuit High Input
P0389	Crankshaft Position Sensor B Circuit Intermittent
P0400	Exhaust Gas Recirculation Flow Malfunction
P0401	Exhaust Gas Recirculation Flow Insufficient Detected
P0402	Exhaust Gas Recirculation flow Excessive Detected
P0403	Exhaust Gas Recirculation Circuit Malfunction
P0404	Exhaust Gas Recirculation Circuit Range/Performance
P0405	Exhaust Gas Recirculation Sensor A Circuit Low
P0406	Exhaust Gas Recirculation Sensor A Circuit High
P0407	Exhaust Gas Recirculation Sensor B Circuit Low
P0408	Exhaust Gas Recirculation Sensor B Circuit High
P0410	Secondary Air Injection System Malfunction
P0411	Secondary Air Injection System Incorrect Flow Detected
P0412	Secondary Air Injection System Switching Valve A Circuit Malfunction
P0413	Secondary Air Injection System Switching Valve A Circuit Open
P0414	Secondary Air Injection System Switching Valve A Circuit Shorted
P0415	Secondary Air Injection System Switching Valve B Circuit Malfunction
P0416	Secondary Air Injection System Switching Valve B Circuit Open
P0417	Secondary Air Injection System Switching Valve B Circuit Shorted
P0418	Secondary Air Injection System Relay "A" circuit Malfunction

Code	Fault description
P0419	Secondary Air Injection System Relay "B" Circuit Malfunction
P0420	Catalyst System Efficiency Below Threshold (Bank 1)
P0421	Warm Up Catalyst Efficiency Below Threshold (Bank 1)
P0422	Main Catalyst Efficiency Below Threshold (Bank 1)
P0423	Heated Catalyst Efficiency Below Threshold (Bank l)
P0424	Heated Catalyst Temperature Below Threshold (Bank 1)
P0430	Catalyst System Efficiency Below Threshold (Bank 2)
P0431	Warm Up Catalyst Efficiency Below Threshold (Bank 2)
P0432	Main Catalyst Efficiency Below Threshold (Bank 2)
P0433	Heated Catalyst Efficiency Below Threshold (Bank 2)
P0434	Heated Catalyst Temperature Below Threshold (Bank 2)
P0440	Evaporative Emission Control System Malfunction
P0441	Evaporative Emission Control System Incorrect Purge flow
P0442	Evaporative Emission Control System leak Detected (small leak)
P0443	Evaporative Emission Control System Purge Control Valve circuit Malfunction
P0444	Evaporative Emission Control System Purge Control Valve Circuit Open
P0445	Evaporative Emission Control System Purge Control Valve Circuit Shorted
P0446	Evaporative Emission Control System Vent Control Circuit Malfunction
P0447	Evaporative Emission Control System Vent Control Circuit Open
P0448	Evaporative Emission Control System Vent Control Circuit Shorted
P0449	Evaporative Emission Control System Vent Valve/Solenoid Circuit Malfunction
P0450	Evaporative Emission Control System Pressure Sensor Malfunction
P0451	Evaporative Emission Control System Pressure Sensor Range/Performance
P0452	Evaporative Emission Control System Pressure Sensor Low Input
P0453	Evaporative Emission Control System Pressure Sensor High Input
P0454	Evaporative Emission Control System Pressure Sensor Intermittent
P0455	Evaporative Emission Control System Tank Detected (gross leak)
P0460	Fuel Level Sensor Circuit Malfunction
P0461	Fuel Level Sensor Circuit Range/Performance
P0462	Fuel level Sensor Circuit Low Input
P0463	Fuel level Sensor Circuit High Input
P0464	Fuel level Sensor Circuit Intermittent
P0465	Purge Flow Sensor Circuit Malfunction
P0466	Purge flow Sensor Circuit Range/Performance
P0467	Purge Flow Sensor Circuit Low Input
P0468	Purge flow Sensor Circuit High Input
P0469	Purge flow Sensor Circuit Intermittent
P0470	Exhaust Pressure Sensor Malfunction
P0471	Exhaust Pressure Sensor Range/Performance
P0472	Exhaust Pressure Sensor Low
P0473	Exhaust Pressure Sensor High
P0474	Exhaust Pressure Sensor Intermittent
P0475	Exhaust Pressure Control Valve Malfunction
P0476	Exhaust Pressure Control Valve Range/Performance
P0477	Exhaust Pressure Control Valve Low
P0478	Exhaust Pressure Control Valve High
P0479	Exhaust Pressure Control Valve Intermittent
P0480	Cooling Fan 1 Control Circuit Malfunction
P0481	Cooling Fan 2 Control Circuit Malfunction
P0482	Cooling Fan 3 Control Circuit Malfunction
P0483	Cooling Fan Rationality Check Malfunction
P0484	Cooling Fan Circuit Over Current
P0485	Cooling Fan Power/Ground Circuit Malfunction
P0500	Vehicle Speed Sensor Malfunction
P0501	Vehicle Speed Sensor Range/Performance
P0502	Vehicle Speed Sensor Circuit Low Input
P0503	Vehicle Speed Sensor Intermittent/Erratic/High
P0505	Idle Control System Malfunction
P0506	Idle Control System RPM lower Than Expected
P0507	Idle Control System RPM higher Than Expected

Code	Fault description
P0510	Closed Throttle Position Switch Malfunction
P0520	Engine Oil Pressure Sensor/Switch Circuit Malfunction
P0521	Engine Oil Pressure Sensor/Switch Range/Performance
P0522	Engine Oil Pressure Sensor/Switch Low Voltage
P0523	Engine Oil Pressure Sensor/Switch High Voltage
P0530	A/C Refrigerant Pressure Sensor Circuit Malfunction
P0531	A/C Refrigerant Pressure Sensor Circuit Range/Performance
P0532	A/C Refrigerant Pressure Sensor Circuit Low Input
P0533	A/C Refrigerant pressure Sensor Circuit High Input
P0534	Air Conditioner Refrigerant Charge Loss
P0550	Power Steering Pressure Sensor Circuit Malfunction
P0551	Power Steering Pressure Sensor Circuit Range/Performance
P0552	Power Steering Pressure Sensor Circuit Low Input
P0553	Power Steering Pressure Sensor Circuit High Input
P0554	Power Steering Pressure sensor Circuit Intermittent
P0560	System Voltage Malfunction
P0561	System Voltage Unstable
P0562	System Voltage Low
P0563	System Voltage High
P0565	Cruise Control On Signal Malfunction
P0566	Cruise Control Off Signal Malfunction
P0567	Cruise Control Resume Signal Malfunction
P0568	Cruise Control Set Signal Malfunction
P0569	Cruise Control Coast Signal Malfunction
P0570	Cruise Control Accel Signal Malfunction
P0571	Cruise Control/Brake Switch A Circuit Malfunction
P0572	Cruise Control/Brake Switch A Circuit Low
P0573	Cruise Control/Brake Switch A Circuit High
P0600	Serial Communication Link Malfunction
P0601	Internal Control Module Memory Check Sum Error
P0602	Control Module Programming Error
P0603	Internal Control Module Keep Alive Memory (KAM) Error
P0604	Internal Control Module Random Access Memory (RAM) Error
P0605	Internal Control Module Read Only Memory (ROM) Error (Module Identification Defined by SAE J1979)
P0606	PCM Processor Fault
P0608	Control Module VSS Output "A" Malfunction
P0609	Control Module VSS Output "B" Malfunction
P0620	Generator Control Circuit Malfunction
P0621	Generator Lamp "L" Control Circuit Malfunction
P0622	Generator Field "F" Control Circuit Malfunction
P0650	Malfunction Indicator Lamp (MIL) Control Circuit Malfunction
P0654	Engine RPM Output Circuit Malfunction
P0655	Engine Hot Lamp Output Control Circuit Malfunction
P0656	Fuel Level Output Circuit Malfunction
P0700	Transmission Control System Malfunction
P0701	Transmission Control System Range/Performance
P0702	Transmission Control System Electrical
P0703	Torque Converter/Brake Switch B Circuit Malfunction
P0704	Clutch Switch Input Circuit Malfunction
P0705	Transmission Range Sensor Circuit Malfunction (PRNDL Input)
P0706	Transmission Range Sensor Circuit Range/Performance
P0707	Transmission Range Sensor Circuit Low Input
P0708	Transmission Range Sensor Circuit High Input
P0709	Transmission Range Sensor Circuit Intermittent
P0710	Transmission Fluid Temperature Sensor Circuit Malfunction
P0711	Transmission Fluid Temperature Sensor Circuit Range/Performance
P0712	Transmission Fluid Temperature Sensor Circuit Low Input
P0713	Transmission Fluid Temperature Sensor Circuit High Input
P0714	Transmission Fluid Temperature Sensor Circuit Intermittent
P0715	Input/Turbine Speed Sensor Circuit Malfunction
P0716	Input/Turbine Speed Sensor Circuit Range/Performance
P0717	Input/Turbine Speed Sensor Circuit No Signal
P0718	Input/Turbine Speed Sensor Circuit Intermittent
P0719	Torque Converter/Brake Switch B Circuit Low

Code	Fault description
P0720	Output Speed Sensor Circuit Malfunction
P0721	Output Speed Sensor Circuit Range/Performance
P0722	Output Speed Sensor Circuit No Signal
P0723	Output Speed Sensor Circuit Intermittent
P0724	Torque Converter/Brake Switch B Circuit High
P0725	Engine Speed Input Circuit Malfunction
P0726	Engine Speed Input Circuit Range/Performance
P0727	Engine Speed Input Circuit No Signal
P0728	Engine Speed Input Circuit Intermittent
P0730	Incorrect Gear Ratio
P0731	ear 1 Incorrect Ratio
P0732	Gear 2 Incorrect Ratio
P0733	Gear 3 Incorrect Ratio
P0734	Gear 4 Incorrect Ratio
P0735	Gear 5 Incorrect Ratio
P0736	Reverse Incorrect Ratio
P0740	Torque Converter Clutch Circuit Malfunction
P0741	Torque Converter Clutch Circuit Performance or Stuck Off
P0742	Torque Converter Clutch Circuit Stuck On
P0743	Torque Converter Clutch Circuit Electrical
P0744	Torque Converter Clutch Circuit Intermittent
P0745	Pressure Control Solenoid Malfunction
P0746	Pressure Control Solenoid Performance or Stuck Off
P0747	Pressure Control Solenoid Stuck On
P0748	Pressure Control Solenoid Electrical
P0749	Pressure Control Solenoid Intermittent
P0750	Shift Solenoid A Malfunction
P0751	Shift Solenoid A Performance or Stuck Off
P0752	Shift Solenoid A Stuck On
P0753	Shift Solenoid A Electrical
P0754	Shift Solenoid A Intermittent
P0755	Shift Solenoid B Malfunction
P0756	Shift Solenoid B Performance or Stuck Off
P0757	Shift Solenoid B Stuck On
P0758	Shift Solenoid B Electrical
P0759	Shift Solenoid B Intermittent
P0760	Shift Solenoid C Malfunction
P0761	Shift Solenoid C Performance or Stuck Off
P0762	Shift Solenoid C Stuck On
P0763	Shift Solenoid C Electrical
P0764	Shift Solenoid C Intermittent
P0765	Shift Solenoid D Malfunction
P0766	Shift Solenoid D Performance or Stuck Off
P0767	Shift Solenoid D Stuck On
P0768	Shift Solenoid D Electrical
P0769	Shift Solenoid D Intermittent
P0770	Shift Solenoid E Malfunction
P0771	Shift Solenoid E Performance or Stuck Off
P0772	Shift Solenoid E Stuck On
P0773	Shift Solenoid E Electrical
P0774	Shift Solenoid E Intermittent
P0780	Shift Malfunction
P0781	1-2 Shift Malfunction
P0782	2-3 Shift Malfunction
P0783	3-4 Shift Malfunction
P0784	4-5 Shift Malfunction
P0785	Shift/Timing Solenoid Malfunction
P0786	Shift/Timing Solenoid Range/Performance
P0787	Shift/Timing Solenoid low
P0788	Shift/Timing Solenoid High
P0789	Shift/Timing Solenoid Intermittent
P0790	Normal/Performance Switch Circuit Malfunction
P0801	Reverse Inhibit Control Circuit Malfunction
P0803	1-4 Upshift (Skip Shift) Solenoid Control Circuit Malfunction
P0804	1-4 Upshift (Skip Shift) Lamp Control Circuit Malfunction

2 Function of the Self-Diagnosis system

Self-Diagnosis function

The Self-Diagnosis (SD) function (sometimes termed On-Board Diagnosis or OBD/EOBD) of the modern Engine Management System continually examines the signal values from the various engine sensors and actuators. The signals are then compared with pre-programmed control parameters. The control parameters may vary from system to system, and could include upper and lower measurement values, a specific number of erroneous signals within a pre-determined time period, implausible signals, signals outside of adaptive limits, and other parameters determined by the system designer or vehicle manufacturer. If the signal value is outside of the control parameters (for example a short-circuit or an open-circuit), the ECM determines that a fault is present, and stores a code in ECM fault memory.

Early SD systems were capable of generating and storing no more than a handful of codes. However, 15 years on, many of the more advanced systems can generate 1000 or more codes, and this may sharply increase over the next decade as engine management becomes capable of diagnosing many more fault conditions.

For example, in one SD system, a simple code may be generated to cover all possible fault conditions that could affect a particular circuit. In another SD system, several codes may be generated to cover various fault conditions, and this could pinpoint the reason for the fault in that particular sensor. If we use the Coolant Temperature Sensor (CTS) circuit as an example, the first code may be generated as a general CTS fault. Other codes may be generated to indicate an open or short-circuit. In addition, codes that indicate a weak or a rich mixture condition may be generated as a consequence of this particular component failure. Where the ECM practises adaptive control around the ideal mixture ratio, a fault may cause the adaptive limits to be exceeded, and even more codes may be raised. However, on determination of such a fault, the EMS will certainly move into LOS or "limp-home" mode - this will reduce the mixture problems and the probable number of different codes that could be generated.

As the EMS evolves, many more components will be controlled and monitored by the ECM, and the SD function will certainly extend to cover these additional components. This book is mainly concerned with testing areas that relate to the engine, although all codes generated by ancillary systems such as the air conditioning and automatic transmission will be listed in the Fault Code tables appearing in each Chapter.

Limitations to Self-Diagnosis

There are some limitations to Self-Diagnosis, and some sensor faults may not necessarily cause a code to be stored.

Faults in components for which a code is not available or for conditions not covered by the diagnostic software will not be stored. This also means that mechanical problems and secondary ignition circuit (HT) faults are not directly covered by the SD system. However, side-effects from, for example, a vacuum leak or faulty exhaust valve will create mixture and idle problems, which may cause appropriate codes to be stored. The trick then is to relate the fault code to the engine condition - engine checks may be necessary to aid diagnosis in this respect.

In addition, a fault code generally only points to a faulty circuit. For example, a code indicating a CTS fault may be caused by a faulty coolant temperature sensor, a wiring fault or a corroded connector.

Some vehicle systems are capable of storing faults that occur intermittently - others are not. In some instances, a fault code may be lost the moment that the ignition is switched off; care should be taken when retrieving codes or investigating faults in this kind of system.

The smart technician will use the fault code as a starting point, and as such, it can quickly point him in the right direction. On the other hand, absence of a code may not always be indicative of a fault-free system, and care should be exercised during diagnosis.

Spurious signal

Faulty HT signals or faulty electrical components can create Radio Frequency Interference (RFI) that may disrupt the EMS or cause spurious (erroneous) codes to be generated. A disrupted EMS may result in erratic ECM operation.

Limited range or out-of-range sensors

If the sensor remains within its design parameters, even if the parameters are incorrect for certain operating conditions, a fault code may not be stored. For example, a faulty coolant temperature sensor will cause a fault code to be generated if it is open-circuit or shorted to earth. However, if the sensor resistance does not change during a temperature change, a code may not be generated, although the engine will indeed run badly at some temperatures. The majority of current SD systems would not recognise a fault in this instance because the signal would remain within the control parameters. The next paragraph describes possible methods of overcoming this particular problem.

Implausible signals

The software in some newer systems is becoming more sophisticated, and will check for a change in voltage or current over a period of time. If the signal output does not change as expected, a fault will be stored. Also, earlier systems would generate a fault code if a particular circuit was outside of the control parameters without reference to other data or circuits. More modern systems will consider the output from several components, and relate one signal to another. A fault code will be generated based upon the plausibility of the signal when related to a number of other signals. For instance, if the engine speed (RPM) is increasing, the throttle position sensor (TPS) indicates a wide-open throttle, yet the airflow sensor (AFS) does not indicate an increase in airflow, the AFS signal could be considered implausible and a code would be generated.

SD warning light

Many vehicles are equipped with an SD warning light, usually located in the instrument panel on the facia (see illustrations 1.4 to 1.6). Alternatively, an LED may be set into the casing of the ECM. Once the ignition is turned on, the warning light or LED will illuminate. This serves as a check that the light circuit is functional. After the engine has started, the light should extinguish and remain off so long as the SD system does not detect a fault. If the ECM determines that a detectable fault is present, the warning light is turned on. The light remains turned on until the detectable fault is no longer present. If the fault clears, the light will usually turn off, although the code itself may remain stored until the ECM fault memory is cleared. A fault in some systems may be classified as a minor fault and although the ECM will log the presence of the fault, the light may not be turned on.

Not all vehicles utilise a warning light; systems without one will require interrogation by a FCR or Flash Code display by manual means to determine whether a fault is stored or not.

Fast and slow codes

Codes transmitted by an ECM may be designated as "slow codes" or "fast codes". Slow codes are fault codes which are emitted slowly enough to be displayed on an LED or on a facia-mounted warning light. Fast codes are digital fault codes that are too fast to be displayed on the LED or on the warning light. A digital FCR instrument is required for capturing fast codes. All vehicles to EOBD standard use fast codes.

Other SD functions

To a large degree, the format and type of data to be output is determined by the vehicle manufacturer (VM). The function of the FCR or manual code extraction routine is to initiate the VM's program and to make the best of what is actually available. In other words, if the VM does not make certain information available, then it is not possible to access such information through the diagnostic plug.

In addition to code retrieval and code clearing, a number of other functions are often available through SD, as listed below:

    Code retrieval.
    Code clearing.
    Actuator and component testing.
    Service adjustments.
    ECM coding.
    Obtaining Datastream.
    Flight recorder function.
Note: *Not all of the above functions are available in all systems, and an FCR will be necessary for many of the more advanced functions.*

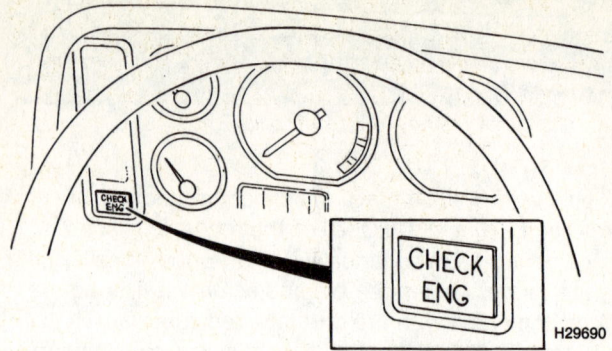

1.4 A typical SD warning light located in the instrument panel

1.5 A second typical SD warning light located in the instrument panel

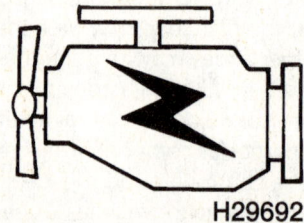

1.6 Typical appearance for a SD warning light

Fault code retrieval

Fault codes can be retrieved from the ECM via an SD output terminal (sometimes known as a diagnostic plug), by connecting a suitable Fault Code Reader or by triggering a manual retrieval routine. Although manual code retrieving (described below) is possible in most early systems, the practice has died out; all modern systems allow retrieval via an FCR alone.

FCR or Scanner ?

The professional tool used for retrieving codes from SD systems on motor vehicles in the UK is termed a Fault Code Reader. However another term sometimes used is "Scanner". The "Scanner" term originated in the USA, and defines a tool that "scans" data, as distinct from a tool whose sole function is to "retrieve" data. Realistically, the terms can be used interchangeably to describe code-retrieving equipment. Generally, we will use the term FCR to describe the code-reading equipment covered by this book.

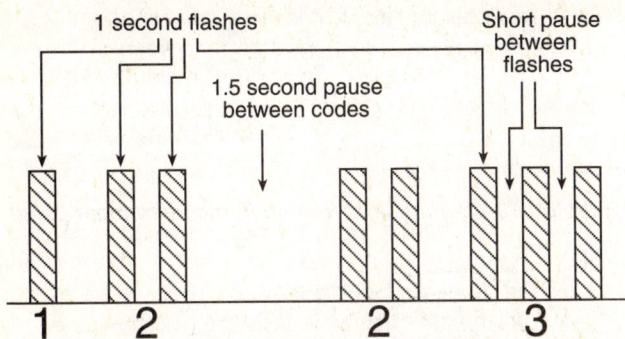

(Example of codes 12 and 23)   H29693

1.7 Representation of typical 2-digit flash codes as displayed on an SD warning light or LED. The duration of the flashes are the same for units and tens.

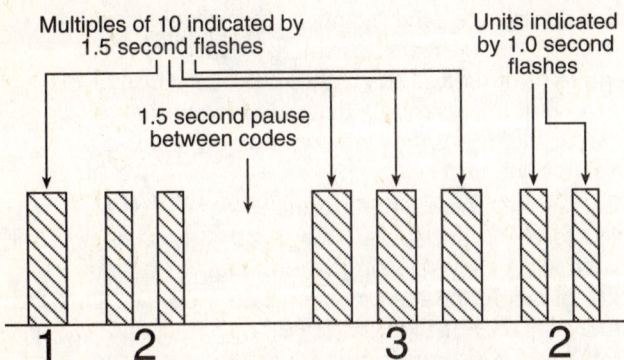

(Example of codes 12 and 32)   H29694

1.8 Representation of typical 2-digit flash codes as displayed on an SD warning light or LED. The flash duration is longer for the multiples of ten, and shorter for the single units

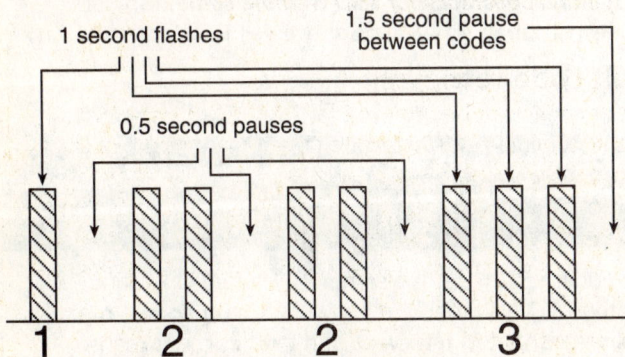

(Example of code 1223)   H29695

1.9 Representation of typical 4-digit flash codes as displayed on an SD warning light or LED

Manual fault code retrieval ("Flash Codes")

Some of the early SD systems allowed manual code retrieval. Although quite useful as a "quick-and-dirty" method of accessing codes without sophisticated equipment, manual code retrieval is limited, slow and prone to error. In addition, it is not possible to retrieve codes that are transmitted at the high transfer rates seen in modern systems. Typically, manual code retrieval is initiated by using a jumper lead to bridge certain terminals in the SD connector. The codes are then displayed by the flashing of the instrument panel warning light, or on the LED set into the ECM casing (where these components are fitted). Codes obtained in this fashion are often termed "Flash Codes" *(see illustrations 1.7 to 1.9)*. By counting the flashes or meter sweeps and referring to the Fault Code table in each Chapter, faults can thus be determined. Where an SD light or LED is not fitted, an LED diode or a voltmeter (see Warning No 5 in the Reference Section at the end of this book) can be used in some systems.

Fault code clearing

There are a number of methods used by the vehicle manufacturers to clear fault memory over the years. Mid-1980s systems did not retain codes, and were automatically cleared once the ignition was turned off. Soon the ECM fault memory was provided with a permanent battery voltage that allowed codes and other data to be retained after the ignition was turned off. Codes generated by these systems are normally cleared with an FCR (preferred method), although a manual routine is often possible. Removing a battery lead or the ECM multi-plug may also clear the codes from memory. Some of the latest types of systems utilise non-volatile memory. Non-volatile memory retains data even after the battery has been disconnected, and code clearing must be effected with the aid of an FCR *(see illustration 1.10)*.

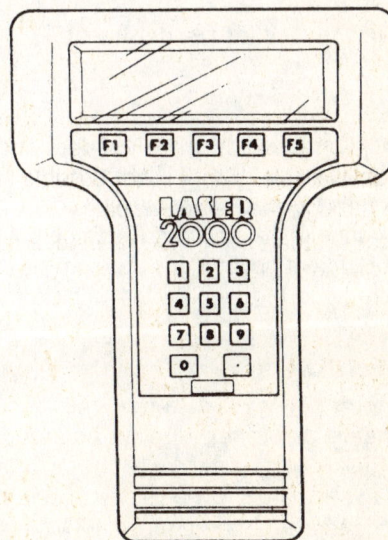

1.10 A common proprietary Fault Code Reader

Note: *Codes should always be cleared after component tests or after repairs involving the removal of an EMS component.*

Clearing codes manually

It is sometimes possible to clear fault codes by initiating a manual routine similar to that used to retrieve flash codes.

Actuator and component testing

The FCR can be used to test the wiring and components in certain actuator circuits. For example, the idle speed control valve (ISCV) circuit could be energised. If the valve actuates, this proves the integrity of that circuit. Depending on the system (it is not possible to test a particular actuator unless the routine has been designed into the SD system), possible circuits include the fuel injectors, relays, ISCV, and emission actuators amongst others. It may also be possible to test the signals from certain sensors. A common test is to check the signal from the throttle position sensor (TPS) as the throttle is moved from the closed to the fully-open position and then returned to the closed position. A fault will be registered if the potentiometer track is deemed to be defective.

Manual sensor testing and component actuation

Component actuation is normally the province of the FCR. However, in a very few systems, manual actuation and component testing is possible. Where appropriate, these routines will be described in the relevant Chapter.

Service adjustments

In most modern engines, any kind of adjustment to the idle mixture or ignition timing is not possible. However, some older systems are denied external adjustment, and an FCR is essential if certain adjustments are to be effected. Examples include some Ford vehicles with EEC IV, the Rover 800 SPi, and more recent Rover vehicles with MEMS. All of these vehicles require an FCR for various adjustments including ignition timing and/or idle mixture adjustment.

ECM coding

In some systems, an FCR may be used to code the control unit for certain applications. This function is normally reserved for the vehicle manufacturer's main agent, and allows a smaller range of control modules to be built for a large number of different applications. Coding the control unit would match the ECM to a particular vehicle.

Obtaining Datastream

Datastream information is live data from the various sensors and actuators that can be displayed on the FCR screen. This function is particularly useful for rapid testing of suspect sensors and actuators. Dynamic tests could be performed and the sensor response recorded. Where a component seems faulty, but a code is not generated, Datastream could be viewed over a range of engine speeds and temperatures. For example, the coolant temperature sensor signal could be viewed with the engine cold, and closely monitored as the engine is warmed up. Any irregularities in the signal should be obvious during the course of the time taken to warm the engine.

Although signals from the various components can be viewed by connecting an oscilloscope or digital multi-meter (DMM) to the relevant circuit, it is often quicker and more convenient to view the system data on the screen of the FCR. This function is only available with the aid of a FCR, and manual display of Datastream is not possible. Some FCRs can be connected to a standard personal computer (PC) and the data from all monitored components could be displayed simultaneously upon the screen. This overcomes the problem of displaying data from a small number of components on a small FCR screen. As dynamic tests are initiated, the response from each component could be more easily observed. In addition, with the aid of suitable software, the PC could chart and record each signal as various tests are performed. All of the signals (or a selection) could then be played back and reviewed at some later stage.

Flight recorder function

A facility that is available in some FCRs and/or SD systems is that of a "flight recorder" mode - more usually called a "snapshot" or "playback" function. Where a fault is intermittent or difficult to diagnose, the condition of the various components can be determined from the signal output at the moment of fault occurrence, and this could lead to a solution.

The FCR must be attached to the SD connector, and the vehicle taken for a road test. The snapshot function is usually initiated at an early stage in the run. Data will be gathered and recorded during the running period. However, since the memory capacity of the ECM or FCR is limited, data will only be retained for a short period. When the fault occurs, it is necessary to hit a button, then a pre-determined number of records before the occurrence and after will be stored. Back in the workshop, the data (usually presented as Datastream) can be played back one sample at a time, and frozen for evaluation where required. Reviewing all of the data from each sensor and actuator may then lead to the solution. However, not all SD systems or even all FCRs are capable of this function.

3 Limited Operating Strategy (LOS) - "limp-home" mode

All modern SD systems also have a Limited Operating Strategy (LOS) - otherwise known as "limp-home" mode. This means that in the event of a fault in certain sensor circuits (and usually where a fault code has been generated, although not all codes will initiate LOS), the ECM will automatically enter LOS and refer to a programmed default value rather than the sensor signal. This enables the vehicle to be safely driven to a workshop/ garage for repair or testing. Once the fault has cleared, the ECM will revert to normal operation.

LOS is a safety system, which allows the engine to operate at a reduced efficiency level. Some LOS systems are so smart, the driver may be unaware that a fault has occurred unless the warning light is illuminated (if fitted).

Since the substituted values is often that of a hot or semi-hot engine, cold starting and running during the warm-up period may be less than satisfactory. Also, failure of a major sensor, such as the airflow sensor or the MAP sensor, may cause the ECM to restrict engine performance. For example, if a Ford EEC IV system detects a major fault within the ECM, the engine will run with the timing set to 10° (no timing advance) and the fuel pump will run continuously.

In some systems, failure of a coolant or air temperature sensor (CTS or ATS) will cause the ECM to use the other component as a default. For example, if the CTS failed, the ECM would use the ATS value. In addition, the default value might be used when the engine is cold and then switched to a value that is close to that of a hot engine after the engine has run for 10 minutes. Unless the SD warning light comes on, it would thus be very difficult to recognise that a fault had actually occurred.

4 Adaptive control function

In many modern engine management systems, the ECM is adaptive to changing engine operating characteristics. Where the ECM software is adaptive, the data is constantly monitored from various engine functions, and the data is stored in memory so that over a fairly long monitoring period, signal averages can be built.

During normal engine operation, the ECM refers to several three-dimensional maps for timing, fuel injection, idle speed etc. Depending upon the changing signals from the various sensors (ATS, CTS, AFS or MAP, TPS, etc), the ECM constantly corrects the final output signals to the various actuators. By adopting the stored adaptive values as a correction to the basic map, the ECM is able to adapt much more quickly to almost any changed operating circumstances.

As the engine or its components wear or even if certain faults develop, the changed signals are added to the stored adaptive memory, and the signal averages gradually change. The ECM continually reacts to the adaptive memory and soon adapts to the changed conditions. If the adaptive value exceeds the control parameters, a fault code may be generated.

Adaptive control is applied typically to the following areas, and adaptation and correction of the various maps usually occurs during idle or part-load engine operation:

Idle operation.
Mixture adjustment.
Knock control.
Carbon filter solenoid valve (CFSV) operation.
Exhaust gas recirculation (EGR).

When the adaptive map is used in conjunction with the oxygen sensor (OS) in a catalytic converter system, the ECM is able to respond much more quickly and retain tighter control over the changing gases in the exhaust system. During closed-loop operation, the basic injection value is determined by the values stored in the map for a specific rpm and load. If the basic injection value causes exhaust emissions outside of the Lambda value (0.98 to 1.02 air-fuel ratio) the mixture would be too rich or too lean, and the OS would signal the ECM which in turn will correct the mixture. However, this response takes a little time, and so the ECM learns a correction value and adds this "adaptive" value to the basic map. From now on, under most operating conditions, the emissions will be very close to Lambda and so, after reference to the OS signal and adaptive map, the ECM will only need to make small corrections to keep it that way.

At idle speed, the system will settle down to idle at the best speed for each individual application. Operation of the CFSV introduces a combustible mixture to the engine that is compensated for by the fuel evaporation adaptive correction values after detection by the OS.

Adaptive values are learnt by the ECM over a period of time, and tend to be averaged over a great number of samples. This means that if the change in operating conditions is gradual, the adaptation will also be gradual. However, if a sudden and dramatic change occurs, the adaptive function may take some time to readapt to the changed conditions. The change in circumstances can occur when a fault occurs in the system, or even after a system component has been changed.

When one or more system components have been renewed, the ECM will need to relearn the new values, and this can sometimes create operating problems until the ECM has completed the process. This can create a temporary vehicle driveability fault that could certainly occur after proper repairs have been made to some part of the system. The driveability fault should gradually become less prominent as the EMS adapts.

For example, an injector may be leaking and the ECM will adapt to provide a leaner mixture. Once the faulty injector has been renewed or cleaned, the adaptation will err towards lean, and the engine may be hesitant until the ECM adapts to the correct mixture. In some systems, it is possible to use an FCR to reset the ECM adaptive memory to the original default value after a component has been renewed.

Most adaptive systems will lose their settings if the battery is disconnected. Once the battery is reconnected and the engine is restarted, the system will need to go through a relearning curve. This usually occurs fairly quickly, although idle quality may be poor until the adaptive process is completed.

Not all systems are affected by battery disconnection. Rover MEMS is an example of a system that uses non-volatile memory to retain adaptive settings when the battery is disconnected.

Rogue adaptive function

The danger with an adaptive function is that sometimes an erroneous signal may be adopted as a valid measurement, and this may create an operating problem. If the erroneous signal is not serious enough to generate a fault code, the fault may remain undetected.

In some instances the ECM can become confused and the adaptive values could become corrupted. This may cause operational problems, and a system check will reveal "no fault found". Disconnecting the vehicle battery may effect a cure, since the re-calibration will reset the ECM default base values. However, resetting values with an FCR is the preferred method, to avoid the loss of other stored values that will occur after disconnection of the battery.

Test equipment, training and technical data

2

1 Introduction

Testing the modern automobile engine is a serious business. To be good at it, you need to seriously invest in three areas. We can liken the three areas to the good old three-legged stool. In our automotive stool, the legs are equipment, training and information. Kick one leg away, and the others are left a little shaky. Those with serious diagnostic intentions will make appropriate investments in all three areas.

That is not to say that those without the best equipment, or the necessary know-how, or the information, are completely stuck. It will just require a little more time and patience, that's all.

Fault diagnosis then, and your method of diagnosis, will largely depend upon the equipment available. and your expertise. There is a definite trade-off in time against cost. The greater the level of investment in equipment and training, the speedier the diagnosis. The less investment, the longer it will take. Obvious, really!

2 Equipment

Within the confines of this Chapter, we will look at the Fault Code Reader and other equipment suitable for testing the various components of the Engine Management System. Some of this equipment is inexpensive, and some not.

Fault code reader (FCR)

A number of manufacturers market test equipment for connecting to the EMS diagnostic plug *(see illustrations 2.1 and 2.2)*. These general-purpose FCRs allow data to be retrieved on a wide range of vehicles and systems. The FCR could be used to obtain and clear fault codes, display Datastream information on the state of the various sensors and actuators, "fire" the system actuators, alter the coding

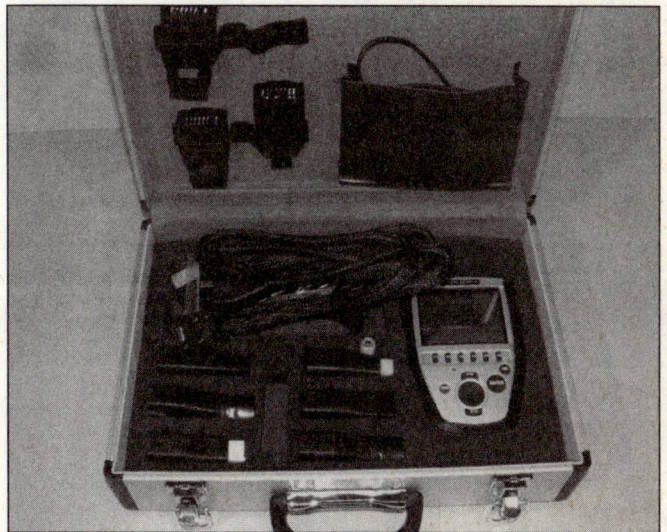

2.1 Fault code readers are normally supplied as a kit, including leads, pods, and instructions

2.2 One most code readers/scanners, a selection of software 'pods' are available for different applications, which simply slot into place in the FCR

of the ECM, make adjustments to the timing and/or idle mixture and provide a flight recorder function. However, not all of the FCRs available will fulfil all of these functions and in any case, some functions may not be possible in some systems.

The FCR is very useful for pointing the engineer in the direction of a specific fault. However, the faults detected

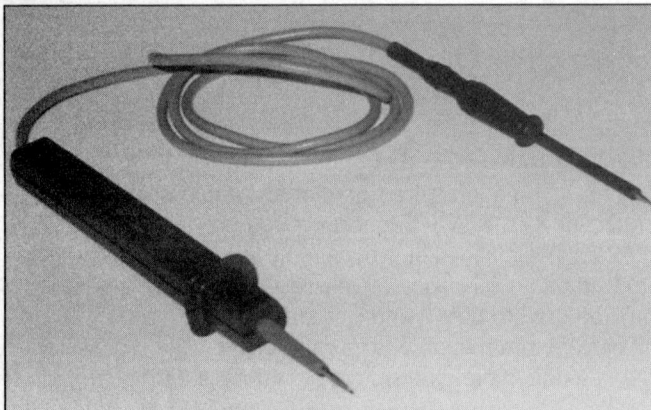

2.3 A typical diode test lamp

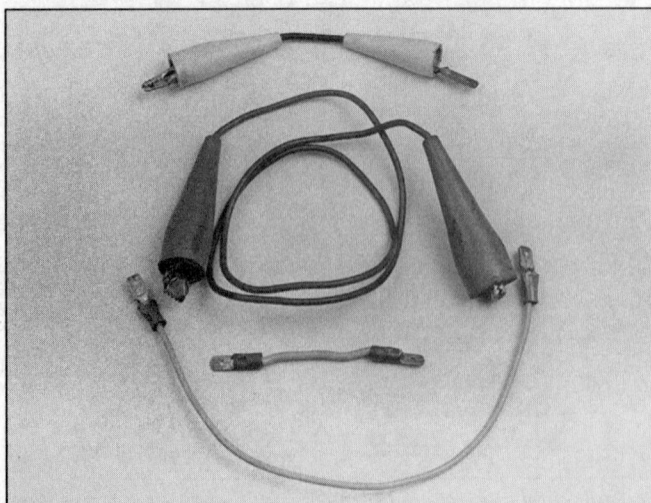

2.4 A selection of temporary jumper wires

may be limited by the level of self-diagnosis designed into the vehicle ECM, and other test equipment may be required to pinpoint the actual fault.

FCRs come in many shapes and sizes (and indeed in many price ranges) and could generally be divided into three levels. At the most basic level, the FCR may do little more than interface with the diagnostic plug and read codes as flash codes. A range of cables and connectors along with instructions on how to connect, retrieve and clear codes from the various vehicles and systems covered by the tool should be available. Flash code tables in an accompanying manual should be provided for interpretation purposes. The basic FCR will not be able to read fast fault codes, and will therefore be very limited in the number of vehicles that it can be used upon. Certainly, none of the advanced functions such as adjustment or actuator testing may be available.

FCRs at the second level are usually quite sophisticated, and will contain all of the functions available to the basic tool and a whole lot more. This FCR will probably display the code and a line of text describing the fault. Data for each range of vehicles or systems will usually be supplied on a removable pod or memory card, which makes the tester very upgradeable. Many of the more advanced facilities will be available, and interface with a PC and printer is often possible.

The more expensive FCRs offer more facilities than just a code reading function, and could more accurately be termed Electronic System Testers. These tools will test the widest range of vehicles, and often allow interface with a Break Out Box. Many additional test routines may be provided within the software, and the documentation and system data provided with the tool is likely to be extensive.

Some FCR manufacturers or suppliers may include a technical support hotline, and training courses may also be available.

Diode test light with LED

The diode test light with LED *(see illustration 2.3)* is particularly useful for obtaining manual flash codes where an SD warning light is not part of the system under test. The light must conform to minimum standards for tools to be connected to electronic circuits **(see Warning No 6 in the Reference Section at the end of this book)**. Additionally, the diode tester may be used for testing of digital signals at the ECM or ignition module.

Jumper wires

Useful for bridging terminals in the SD connector in order to obtain flash codes, or for checking out circuits, and bridging or "by-passing" the relay *(see illustration 2.4)*.

Franchised vehicle dealer

The franchised dealer will often use dedicated test equipment that relies on programmed test methods. The equipment will interface with the ECM, usually through the

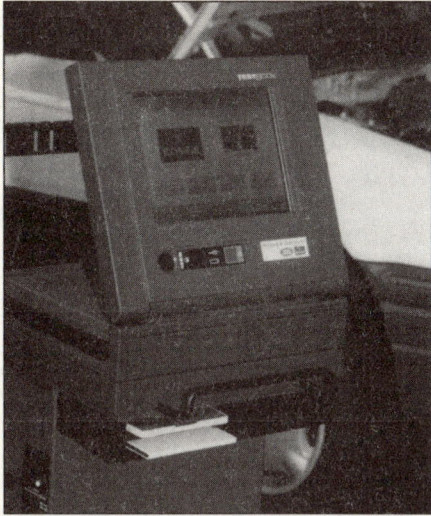

2.5 The Rover Testbook - a laptop computer-based piece of test equipment that contains a very sophisticated and interactive test programme

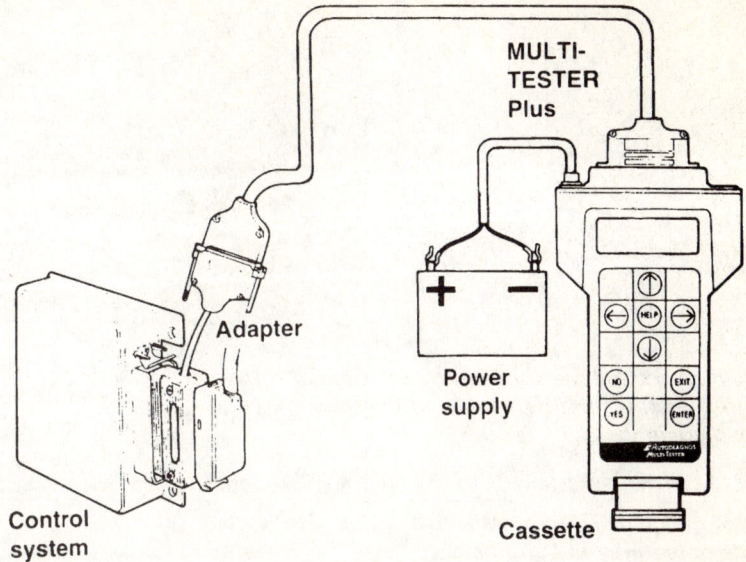

2.6 Programmed test equipment

diagnostic plug, and lead the engineer through a programmed test procedure. Depending on its sophistication, the test equipment may be able to test most circuits, or may refer the engineer to test procedures using additional equipment. This equipment is dedicated to one vehicle manufacturer, and may not be available to other workshops outside of the franchised network (see illustration 2.5).

Programmed test equipment

This kind of proprietary equipment will interface between the ECM and the ECM multi-plug, and is offered as an alternative to the serial port and FCR approach. This equipment checks the input and output signals moving between the ECM and its sensors and actuators. If one or more of the signals is outside of pre-programmed parameters, the equipment will display the erroneous signal as a fault. Once again, other test equipment may be required to pinpoint the actual fault (see illustration 2.6).

ECM testing equipment

Usually the province of those companies that specialise in the repair of the ECM, and not available for purchase by the garage or workshop. One company (ATP) offer an ECM test via a modem over the telephone network if the ECM is taken to one of their agents. Other ECM testing companies require that the ECM is sent to them by post for evaluation.

Multi-meter

This is the equipment required for the most basic approach. These days, the meter will probably be digital (DMM), and must be designed for use with electronic circuits. An analogue meter or even a test light can be used, so long as it meets the same requirements as the digital meter.

Depending on the sophistication of the meter, the DMM can be used to test for basic voltage (AC and DC), resistance, frequency, rpm, duty cycle, temperature etc. (see illustrations 2.7 and 2.8). A selection of thin probes and banana plugs for connecting to a break-out box (BOB) will also be useful (refer to illustration 2.13).

If the fault is a straightforward electrical fault, the meter will often be adequate. However, the drawback is that a DMM cannot analyse the complex electrical waveforms produced by many electronic sensors and actuators, and test results can sometimes be misleading.

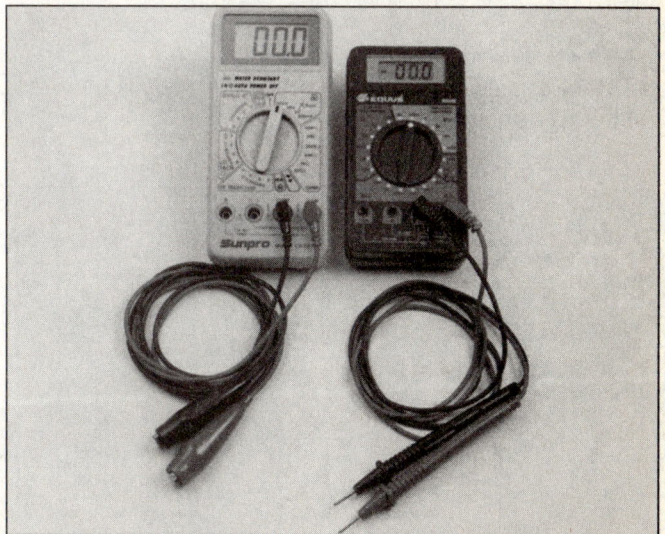

2.7 Two typical high-impedance DMMs with similar performance but different sets of leads and probes. The left unit is equipped with alligator clips and the right unit with spiked probes. Using the alligator clips frees your hands for other tasks, whilst the probes are useful for backprobing multi-plug connectors

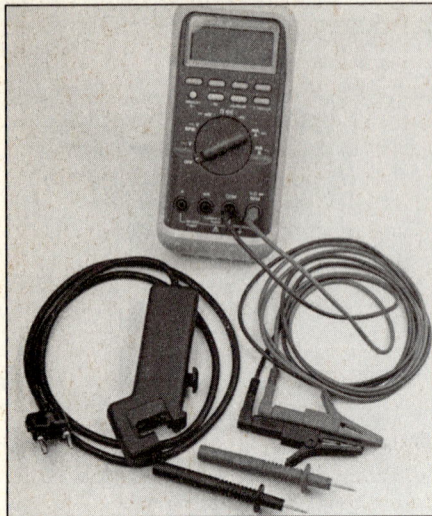

2.8 Top of the range Fluke DMM with a multitude of features and attachments

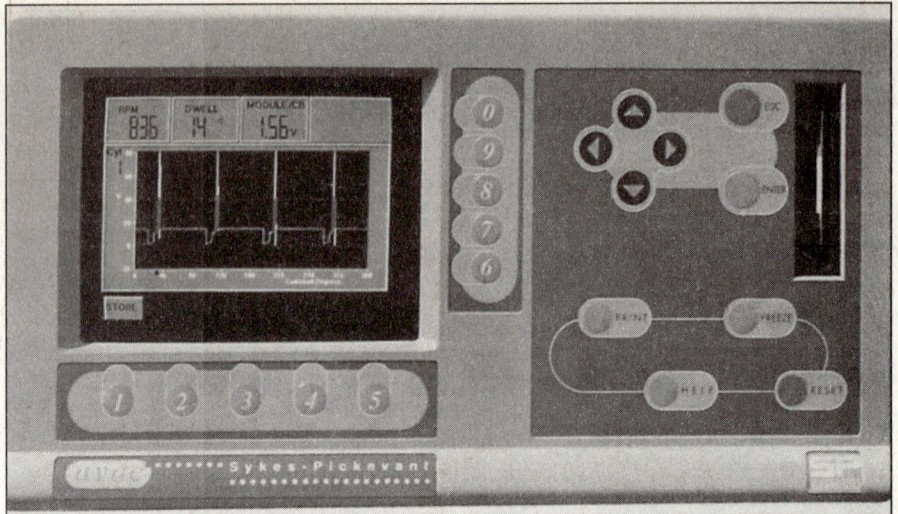

2.9 Oscilloscope

Oscilloscope (with or without DMM and engine analyser)

An oscilloscope (see illustration 2.9) is essentially a graphic voltmeter. Voltage is rarely still, and tends to rise and fall over a period of time. The oscilloscope (or 'scope) measures voltage against time, and displays it in the form of a waveform. Even when the voltage change is very rapid, the scope can usually capture the changes. Circuit faults can often be spotted much faster than when using other types of test instrument. Traditionally, the 'scope has been used for many years to diagnose faults in the primary and secondary ignition systems of conventional non-electronic vehicles. With the advent of electronics, the 'scope has become even more important, and when a labscope function is available, analysis of complex waveforms is possible. This equipment is often used in conjunction with other equipment, for speedy diagnosis of a wide range of problems. The large engine analyser and 'scope is now giving way to a plethora of smaller handheld 'scopes that pack great diagnostic power into portable form.

Exhaust gas analyser

These days the state-of-the-art gas analyser comes with the ability to measure four of the gases present in the exhaust pipe, and it also calculates the Lambda ratio. The gases are oxygen, carbon dioxide, carbon monoxide and hydrocarbons. Less-expensive gas analysers are available that will measure one, two or three gases. However, the better the gas analyser, the easier it gets. The gas analyser is now a recognised diagnostic tool. Faults in ignition, fuelling and various mechanical engine problems can be diagnosed from the state of the various gases present in the exhaust.

Fuel pressure test kit

Fuel pressure is vitally important to the well-being of the fuel-injected engine, and a proper test gauge that will measure fuel pressures up to 7.0 bar is essential. The pressure gauge is normally supplied with a kit of adapters to connect it to a wide range of disparate fuel systems (see illustration 2.10).

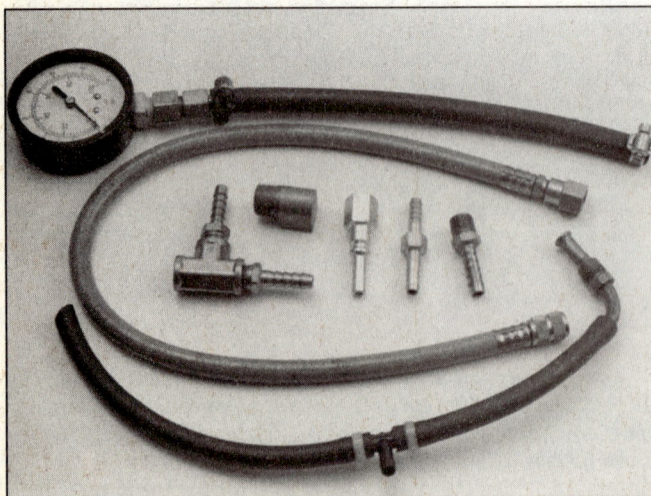

2.10 Fuel pressure gauge and adapter kit

Variable potentiometer

Because of the widespread use of the "limp-home" mode or LOS in the modern EMS, disconnecting a sensor such as the coolant temperature sensor (CTS) may have little effect on the running of the engine. The ECM will assume a fault, and place a fixed value as replacement for that sensor. However, it is useful to be able to vary the resistance sent to the ECM and note the effect. One answer is to use a potentiometer with a variable resistance. If this is connected in place of the CTS resistor, then ECM response, injection duration and CO may be checked at the various resistance values that relate to a certain temperature (see illustration 2.11).

Noid light

A noid light is a small inexpensive light for checking the signal to the injector. The injector harness is detached at the injector, and the noid light plugged into the injector harness. If the engine is then cranked, the light will flash if the injector is being pulsed by the ECM (see illustration 2.12).

Break-out box (BOB)

The BOB (see illustration 2.13) is a box containing a number of connectors that allows easy access to the ECM input and output signals, without directly probing the ECM pins. The BOB loom terminates in a universal connector. A multi-plug harness of similar construction to the ECM harness is interfaced between the ECM and its multi-plug, and the other end is connected to the BOB loom. The BOB will now intercept all signals that go to and from the ECM. If a DMM or an oscilloscope or any other suitable kind of test equipment is connected to the relevant BOB connectors, the ECM signals can be easily measured. The main drawback is the number of different ECM multi-plug connectors required for a good coverage of electronic systems. Small BOBs are also available for measuring values at components where it is difficult to connect the test equipment.

There are three main reasons why use of a BOB is desirable in order to access the signals:

1) *Ideally, the connection point for measuring data values from sensors and actuators is at the ECM multi-plug (with the ECM multi-plug connected). The ECM multi-plug is the point through which all incoming and outgoing signals will pass, and dynamically testing at this point is considered to give more accurate results.*

2) *In modern vehicles, the multi-plug is becoming more heavily insulated, and removing the insulation or dismantling the ECM multi-plug so that back-probing is possible, is becoming almost impossible. To a certain extent, the same is true of some components.*

3) *ECM multi-plug terminals (pins) are at best fragile, and frequent probing or backprobing can cause damage. Some pins are gold-plated, and will lose their conductivity if the plating is scraped off. Using a BOB protects the pins from such damage.*

Battery saver

Actually, "battery saver" is a misnomer, since the function of this device is to hold power to permanently live circuits whilst the battery is removed or changed. The live circuits may provide power to the radio security and station memory, and to the ECM adaptive memory, etc.

Jump leads with surge protection

It is possible to destroy an ECM if unprotected jump leads are used to provide emergency power to the battery. Rather than use jump leads, it is far safer to charge the battery

2.11 Using a variable potentiometer to vary the CTS resistance. Voltage change can be measured and the engine can be fooled into thinking it is cold or hot when the reverse is the case. This means that simulated cold running tests can be accomplished with the engine hot and without waiting for it to cool

2.12 Injector noid light

2.13 Using a Break-Out Box to obtain voltage at the ECM pins

before attempting to start the vehicle. A poor engine or chassis earth, flat battery or tired starter motor and unprotected jump leads are a recipe for total disaster.

Vacuum gauge

As useful as it always was. The vacuum gauge takes the pulse of the engine from a connection to the inlet manifold, and is useful for diagnosing a wide range of timing and mechanical faults, including a blocked exhaust system or vacuum leak *(see illustration 2.14)*.

Vacuum pump

The vacuum pump can be used to check the multitude of vacuum-operated devices that are fitted to many modern vehicles *(see illustration 2.15)*. A crude vacuum pump can be constructed from a bicycle pump. Reverse the washer in the pump, and the pump will then "suck" instead of "blow".

Spark jumper

Useful for attaching to an HT lead to check for a spark. If you hold the lead from a modern high-output ignition system whilst cranking the engine, you may get quite a shock when testing for spark. Apart from curling your hair, the ignition system may also be damaged.

Feeler gauges

Still useful for measuring the various clearances at the crank angle sensor, throttle switch, spark plug, valve clearances etc.

Hairdryer or cold spray

Useful for gently heating or cooling components during a test where heat may be contributing to failure.

HT lead puller

Ideal for safely breaking the HT lead-to-spark plug seal and then safely disconnecting the lead *(see illustration 2.16)*. How many times have you pulled at a lead to have it disintegrate into your hand?

Exhaust back-pressure tester

Useful for checking for exhaust back-pressure; screws into the oxygen sensor hole on catalyst vehicles. The presence of back-pressure indicates an exhaust blockage.

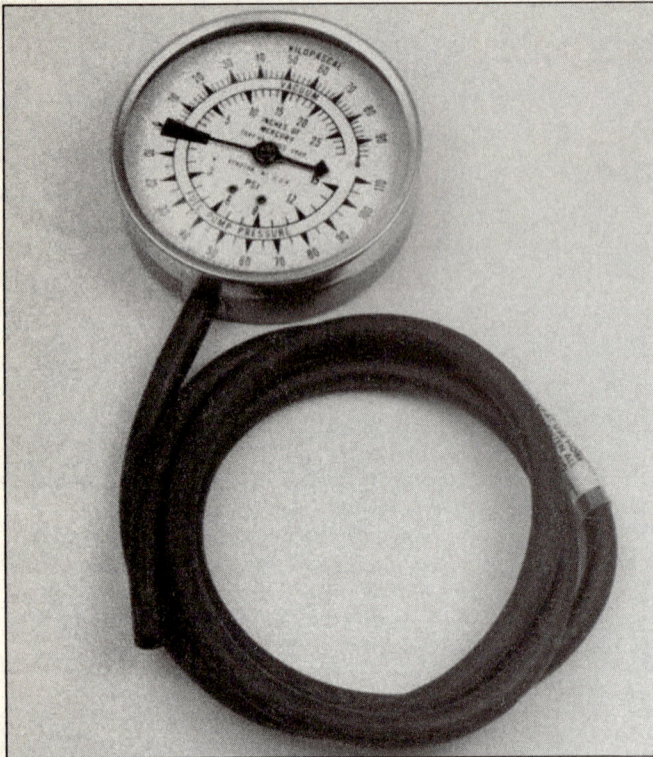
2.14 Vacuum gauge

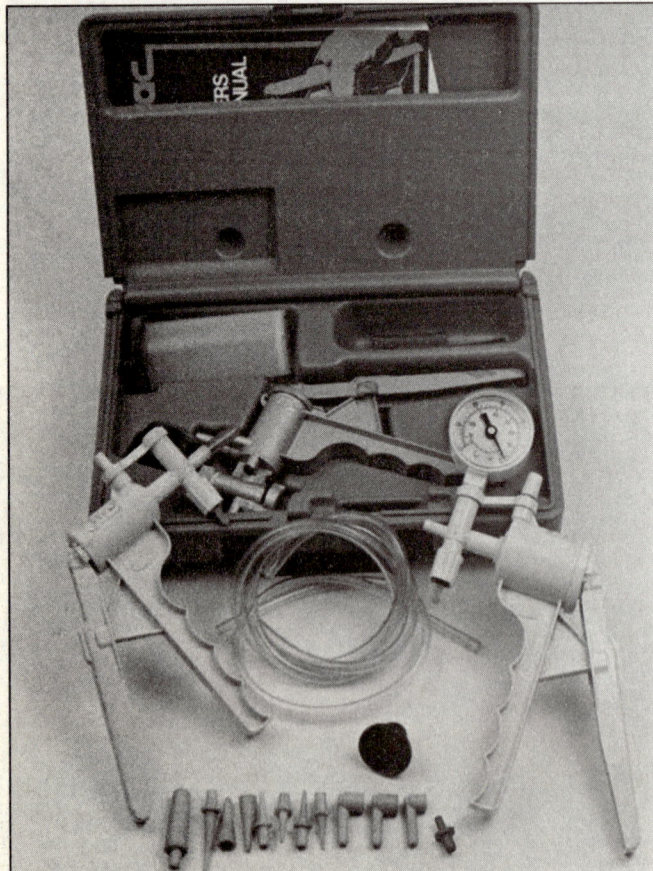
2.15 Vacuum pump kit

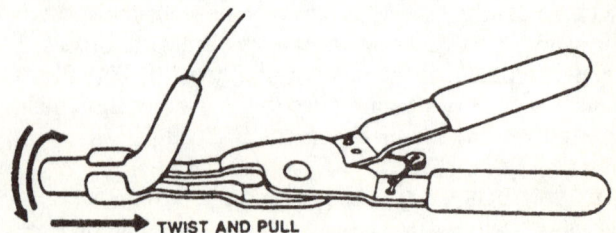
TWIST AND PULL

2.16 HT lead puller

3 Major suppliers of diagnostic equipment

Note: *The details below are correct at the time of writing (Spring 2004).*

Alba Diagnostics Ltd
Bankhead Avenue
Bankhead Industrial Estate
Glenrothes
Fife
Scotland
KY7 6JG   Tel: 01592 774333
www.brakefluidtester.com

ASNU (UK) Ltd
14 King George Avenue
Bushey, Herts
WD23 4NT   Tel: 0208 4204494

ATP Electronic Developments Ltd
Unit 7
Hemlock Way
Cannock, Staffordshire
WS11 2GF   Tel: 01543 467466
www.atpelectronics.co.uk

AutoDiagnos Ltd
St. Christopher House
217 Wellington Road South
Stockport
SK2 6NG   Tel: 0161 2094470
www.autodiagnos.com

Crypton Ltd
Crypton Technology Business Park
Bristol Road
Bridgwater, Somerset
TA6 4BX   Tel: 01278 436200
www.cryptontechnology.com

Fluke (UK) Ltd
52 Hurricane Way
Norwich, Norfolk,
NR6 6JB   Tel: 0207 9420700
www.fluke.co.uk

Gunson Ltd
Bristol Road
Bridgwater, Somerset
TA6 4BX   Tel: 01278 436240
www.gunson.co.uk

Intermotor
Occupation Road
Hucknall, Nottingham
NG15 6DZ   Tel: 0115 9528000
www.intermotor.co.uk

Lucas Aftermarket Operations
Stratford Road
Solihull
Birmingham
B90 4AX   Tel: 0121 5065999

Omitec Instrumentation Ltd
Hopton Industrial Estate
London Road
Devizes, Wiltshire
SN10 2EU   Tel: 0870 2400050
www.omitec.com

Robert Bosch Ltd
PO Box 98
Broadwater Park
Denham, Uxbridge
Middx
UB9 5HJ   Tel: 01895 834466
www.bosch.co.uk

SPX UK Ltd
Genoa House
Everdon Park
Heartlands Business Park
Daventry, Northants
NN11 5YJ   Tel: 01327 303400
www.spx.com

Sykes-Pickavant Ltd
Churchbridge Works,
Walsall Road,
Cannock
Staffs.
WS11 8JR   Tel: 01922 702000
www.sptools.co.uk

4 Training courses

Note: *The details below are correct at the time of writing (Spring 2004).*

There are a number of companies that specialise in training for the motor industry. The same training courses are usually available to the general public. Please contact the various bodies listed below if you wish to learn more about training for the automotive industry.

AA External Training Courses
Contact Centre
Carr Ellison House
William Armstrong Drive
Newcastle-upon-Tyne
NE4 7YA   Tel: 0800 551188

Crypton Ltd
Bristol Road
Bridgwater, Somerset
TA6 4BX   Tel: 01278 436210

Delphi Diesel Aftermarket
Stratford Road
Shirley
West Midlands
B90 4DT   Tel: 0121 7466000

Lucas Test
International Training Centre
Unit 7, Mica Close
Tamworth
Staffs
B77 4QH   Tel: 0827 63503

Automotive Diagnostics Solutions
Preston Technology Management Centre
Marsh Lane, Preston, Lancs.
PR1 8UD   Tel: 01772 201597

Autodiagnos Ltd.
St Christopher House
217 Wellington Road South
Stockport, Ches.
SK2 6NG   Tel: 0870 2406331

Facom UK ltd.
Diagnostic research centre
Lancaster House
Bowerhill Industrial Estate
Melksham, Wilts.
SN12 6TT   Tel: 01225 791883

5   Technical information

Note: *The details below are correct at the time of writing (Spring 2004).* Specific information on the various systems is essential if effective diagnosis and repairs are to be completed. Companies that specialise in automotive technical information are listed below.

Autodata Ltd.
Priors Way Industrial Estate
Maidenhead, Berks.
SL6 2HP   Tel: 01628 634321

Glass's Information Services Ltd
No. 1 Princes Road
Weybridge, Surrey
KT13 9TU
Tel: 01932 823823

Robert Bosch Ltd
PO Box 98, Broadwater Park
North Orbital Road, Denham
UXBRIDGE
MIDDLESEX
UB9 5HJ
Tel: 01895 838352

Sun Diagnostics UK
Horsely's Fields
KINGS LYNN
NORFOLK
PE30 5DD
Tel: 01553 692422

Omitec Instrumentation Ltd
Hopton Industrial Estate
London Road
Devizes, Wiltshire
SN10 2EU
Tel: 0870 2400050

General fault diagnosis

1   Introduction

1 As a general rule, it is usually beneficial to work through the checks listed in "Basic inspection" before connecting the fault code reader. The reason for this is clear - electrical and HT faults may adversely affect electronic control module operation, giving incorrect or spurious results, and causing much confusion. Only after electrical and HT problems have been resolved should the operation of the ECM and its sensors be evaluated.

2 The fault code reader can be used for the following tasks:

 a) *Reading fault codes.*
 b) *Clearing fault codes.*
 c) *Datastream testing (not all systems, for example Ford EEC IV cannot provide Datastream).*
 d) *Actuator and component testing.*
 e) *Service adjustments.*
 f) *ECM coding.*
 g) *Snapshot function.*

Limitations of Self-Diagnosis systems

3 Some may see the fault code reader (FCR) as a panacea for solving all electronic problems in the vehicle, but reading the fault code is only the beginning. To a large degree, the software designed into the vehicle ECM provides the information to be decoded by the FCR. The FCR makes the most of this information, but if certain facilities or data are not designed for output at the diagnostic plug, these facilities will not be available to the FCR.

4 In many instances, the FCR can provide the answer to a puzzling fault very quickly. However, it will not provide all the answers, because some faults (including actual ECM faults) may not even generate a fault code.

5 There are a number of distinct limitations to Self-Diagnosis systems:

 a) *The vehicle manufacturer lays down the basic data that can be extracted from the engine management system by the FCR, and the Self-Diagnosis system and FCR must work within those limitations.*
 b) *A code will not be stored if the ECM is not programmed to recognise that a particular component is faulty.*
 c) *Spurious codes can be triggered by electrical or secondary HT faults.*
 d) *One or more spurious codes can be triggered by a faulty component that may or may not trigger a code by itself.*
 e) *The fault code indicates a faulty circuit, and not necessarily a component. For example, a faulty sensor, wiring fault, or corroded connector may cause a code indicating a coolant temperature sensor (CTS) fault. Always check the wiring and connectors, and apply proper tests to the component before judging it to be faulty.*

f) Limited range or out of range sensors. If the sensor remains within its design parameters, even if the parameters are incorrect for certain operating conditions, a fault code may not be stored. For example, a faulty CTS will generate a fault code if it is open-circuit or shorted to earth. However, if the CTS is stuck at either the hot or cold resistance, a code may not be generated, although the engine will indeed run badly at some temperatures.

g) Some vehicle systems are capable of logging faults that occur intermittently, and others are not.

h) In some instances, a fault code may be lost when the ignition is switched off, and due allowance should be made for this kind of system.

i) Older vehicles with basic electronic fuel injection systems do not support Self-Diagnosis.

Testing Self-Diagnosis systems

6 Is the engine management system warning light (where fitted) illuminated while the engine is running? If so, this is indicative of a system fault. **Note:** *Be aware that some lights do not illuminate for faults that are designated as minor faults.*

7 Connect an FCR to the diagnostic plug, and interrogate the electronic control module for fault codes. Alternatively, initiate flash codes if this is possible (see illustration 3.1). **Note:** *It is particularly important that the FCR instructions are carefully followed in respect of connecting to the system under test and retrieving fault codes. Most operational problems in using FCR equipment are related to a failure to read and follow the instructions.*

8 Once the fault codes have been retrieved, refer to the fault code tables and identify the fault. Refer to Chapter 4 and follow the appropriate component test procedures to check out the relevant circuits. Some systems may aid diagnosis by generating codes that indicate why the signal is deemed faulty.

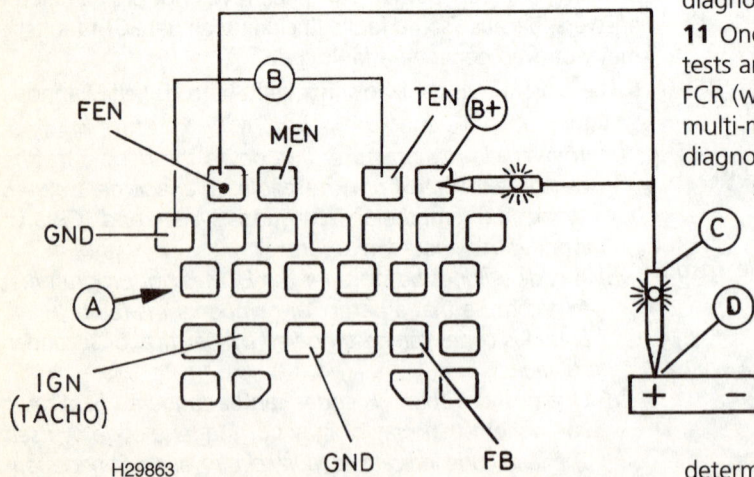

3.1 Initiating flash codes with the aid of an LED and a jumper lead connected to a typical SD connector

A   17-pin SD connector
B   Jumper lead
C   LED test light
D   Battery positive terminal

Examples

a) Open (high) or short (low) sensor circuit: The typical voltage range for a sensor with a 5.0 volt reference supply may be 4.8 to 0.2 volts. If the ECM detects voltage above 4.8 at the higher end or voltage less than 0.2 at the lower end, a fault code will be generated. Reasons for a high voltage are typically a defective component, an open-circuit, an absent 5.0 volt reference voltage or the reference voltage might be shorted to battery positive. Reasons for a low voltage are typically a defective component or a short to earth.

b) If the actuator signal is high, the fault is likely to be an open driver circuit or the ECM is not completing the circuit by "driving" the relevant ECM pin to earth.

c) If the actuator signal is low, the signal is shorted to earth or the component voltage supply is absent.

d) Implausible codes are created with reference to other circuits, and where the ECM has no direct evidence of a fault. If the engine speed is increasing, the throttle position sensor indicates a wide-open throttle yet the airflow sensor (AFS) does not indicate an increase in airflow - the AFS signal is implausible, and a fault code would be generated.

e) Out-of-range faults are stored if the signal voltage or current does not change as expected over a period of time.

f) Adaptive faults usually occur due to external influences. For example, a mixture problem will affect the oxygen sensor adaptive control, while a cooling system fault might cause overheating which in turn may affect adaptive knock control.

9 If fault codes are not stored, use the FCR to view Datastream (live data on system sensors and actuators, not available for all systems).

10 Use a fault code reader to interrogate the ECM via the diagnostic plug.

11 Once the FCR has diagnosed one or more faults, further tests are usually required, and the technician may use the FCR (where possible), or it may be necessary to use a digital multi-meter (DMM) or an oscilloscope to complete the diagnosis. Refer to the component tests in Chapter 4. Test specifications and specific wiring diagrams will be required to carry out these tests correctly. Always refer to the appropriate wiring diagram prior to conducting tests.

12 If more than one code is generated, it is usually best to test and cure each component in the same order in which they are generated.

13 Once the FCR has found a fault, a Datastream enquiry (some systems only) is a quick method of determining where the fault might lie. This data may take various forms, but is essentially electrical data on voltage, frequency, dwell or pulse duration, temperature etc. provided by the various sensors and actuators. Unfortunately, such data is not available in all vehicle systems, and Datastream is not an option if you are working with flash codes. Since the data is in real time, various tests can be made, and the response of the sensor or actuator evaluated.

14 Driving or actuating the system actuators such as the idle control valve, relays and injectors through the ECM is an excellent method of testing effectiveness of the actuator and associated wiring circuit. If the actuator operates when driven in this fashion, you have proved that there is little wrong with the circuit or component.

15 It may also be possible to test the signals from certain sensors (only where provided in the system software). For example, A check could be made of the throttle position sensor signal as the throttle is moved from the closed to the fully-open position and then returned to the closed position. A fault will be registered if the potentiometer track is deemed to be defective. If this test is made on Volvo vehicles, the ECM will generate a code where the test is deemed satisfactory. Lack of a code indicates a fault in the component or circuit.

16 Use an oscilloscope or DMM to check voltages at the faulty component. Compare with the vehicle specifications in the relevant system Chapter.

17 Use an ohmmeter to check the faulty circuit for continuity of the wiring and component resistance. Compare with the vehicle specifications in the relevant system Chapter. **Note:** Refer the vehicle's wiring diagram prior to using an ohmmeter to check the wiring. If the vehicle has multiplexed wiring, refer to the manufacturers instructions.

18 A faulty circuit should be tested and any faults that are discovered must be repaired. The FCR should then be used to clear the errors, and the ECM interrogated once again to see if other fault codes are still present.

19 An important point to bear in mind is that the ECM will only store faults about the electronic circuits. Mechanical faults, ignition secondary faults or fuel problems will still require diagnosis using time-honoured methods.

20 Road test the vehicle and then recheck the SD system for faults. If faults have returned, or are still present, more tests will be required.

Important note: Test procedures may involve routines that could cause one or more additional fault codes to be stored. This fact should be recognised during tests, and all codes must be cleared once testing is complete.

Intermittent faults

21 Wiggle the component wiring, apply heat from a hairdryer, or freeze with a cold spray.

22 Intermittent faults can be extremely difficult to find, and on-road testing is often desirable, with fault codes or Datastream information being generated as the fault occurs. Take the vehicle for a road test with the fault code reader or digital multi-meter attached.

23 If the vehicle ECM and your FCR provide a snapshot (recorder) mode, hook up the FCR and take the vehicle for a road test with an assistant. Ask the assistant to start the snapshot routine to record data when the fault occurs. Return to the workshop and evaluate the data.

Basic inspection

No matter what is the problem, the following checks are an essential pre-requisite to the use of diagnostic equipment. In many instances, the fault will be revealed during these procedures. Make a careful visual inspection of the following items. Not all checks will be appropriate for all engines. This basic inspection can save a great deal of valuable diagnostic time. Worn but electrically-sound components do not always fail tests.

☐ Check the engine oil level and oil condition. Maintenance of the lubrication system is particularly important for good engine operation. In catalyst-equipped vehicles, contaminated oil, a poorly-maintained PCV system or an oil-burning engine will contaminate the catalyst in a very short period of time.

☐ Check the crankcase breather (PCV) system condition. Clean all filters (there will be at least one to the air cleaner), clean away accumulated sludge, and ensure that the hoses are clear.

☐ Check the coolant level and cooling system condition. Maintenance of the cooling system is particularly important for good engine operation. An engine that is overcooled or running too hot will cause an incorrect coolant temperature sensor signal to be passed to the EMS, which may result in incorrect output signals. This will affect timing and fuelling actuation.

☐ Check the automatic transmission fluid level and condition, where applicable.

☐ Check the battery condition.

☐ Check the battery for security.

☐ Check the battery electrolyte level.

☐ Check the battery cables and connections.

☐ Check the drivebelt(s) condition and tension.

☐ Check the operation of the charging system (alternator and associated wiring).

☐ Remove the spark plugs and check the condition. Renew if necessary.

☐ Check that the spark plug electrode gap is correct.

☐ Check that the spark plug type is the correct type for the vehicle.

☐ Check the HT leads very carefully. A defective lead may not be immediately apparent to the naked eye - if the age of the leads is not known, or if a mixture of different leads has been fitted, replace the leads as a set.

☐ If the HT lead condition is satisfactory, check that the leads are routed sensibly in the engine compartment. It is not desirable to have a significant length of lead in contact with a metal component, or one which will become hot. HT leads should be kinked as little as possible - if the lead is bent back on itself, the lead may be fractured or the insulation may break down.

☐ Remove the distributor cap (where fitted) and check the condition, both external and internal. Look for cracks or signs of tracking.

- [ ] Look for oil or water that may have seeped into the cap (where fitted) through a defective seal.
- [ ] Check the rotor arm condition and measure the resistance where appropriate. Take care when trying to remove the rotor arm, as it may be bonded to the distributor shaft.
- [ ] Check the coil tower condition. Look for cracks or signs of tracking.
- [ ] Visually inspect all connections, multi-plugs and terminals. Check for corrosion and loose or displaced terminals.
- [ ] Check for air/vacuum leaks. Check the vacuum hoses, inlet manifold, air trunking, oil dipstick seal and rocker cover seal.
- [ ] Check the air filter condition. Renew if it is even slightly dirty.
- [ ] Check the exhaust system condition.
- [ ] Check the fuel system condition. Check for fuel leaks, and for worn or broken components. If available, the probe from a gas analyser with HC meter can be passed over the fuel and evaporation pipes and hoses. If the HC meter registers a measurement, that component may be leaking fuel or vapour.
- [ ] Check the throttle body for a carbon build-up - usually as a result of fumes from the crankcase breather system. The carbon can cause a sticking or jacked-open throttle, which can cause idle, cruising and other running problems. Carburettor cleaning fluid usually cleans away the carbon nicely.

Digital multi-meter (DMM) tests

2   Introduction

Generally speaking, test results obtained using a voltmeter or oscilloscope (particularly recommended) are more reliable and may reveal more faults than the ohmmeter. Voltage tests are much more dynamic and are obtained with voltage applied to the circuit, which is far more likely to reveal a problem than if the circuit is broken and the component measured for resistance. In some instances, disconnecting a multi-plug may break the actual connection that is at fault, and the circuit test may then reveal "no fault found".

In addition, the oscilloscope may reveal some faults that the voltmeter fails to find. The 'scope is particularly useful for analysing and displaying the complex signals and waveforms from some sensors and actuators. With the proliferation of small, portable handheld oscilloscopes at a cost of less than £2500, the 'scope is not quite in the province of the home mechanic, but every workshop that is serious about fault diagnosis should certainly have one.

For the purposes of this book, we will generally test the majority of components with reference to the voltmeter. Resistance or continuity tests using an ohmmeter will be mentioned where appropriate.

3.2 The art of backprobing for DC voltage - circuit multi-plugs connected and ignition on. Attach the negative probe to an engine earth and push the positive probe past the insulation boot until it makes contact with the terminal connection

Ideally, the connection point for measuring data values from sensors and actuators is at the ECM multi-plug (with the ECM multi-plug connected). The ECM multi-plug is the point through which all incoming and outgoing signals will pass, and dynamically testing at this point is considered to give more accurate results. However, for a variety of reasons, it is not always possible to test at the ECM multi-plug - other points of testing will usually give satisfactory results.

3   Voltage tests

Connecting equipment probes

⊘ *Caution! Don't use the 'backprobing' method on components in a multiplex circuit - refer to the manufacturers information or wiring diagram.*

1 Connect the voltmeter negative probe to an engine earth.
2 Use the positive probe to backprobe for voltage at the actual terminals of the component under test (see illustrations 3.2 and 3.3). Note: This procedure will give acceptable results in most instances, and is one that we would recommend to non-professionals.

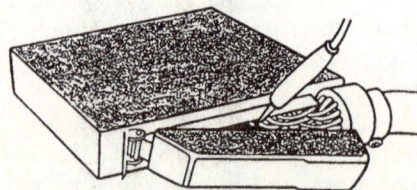

H.21249

3.3 Backprobing at the ECM terminals

3 Alternatively, if possible, peel back the insulated boot to the ECM multi-plug and backprobe the terminals using the equipment probes.

4 If the ECM terminals are not accessible, then ideally connect a break-out box (BOB) between the ECM and its multi-plug. This is the preferred method and will avoid any possibility of damage to the ECM terminals. Otherwise, the ECM multi-plug could be disconnected and the ECM multi-plug terminals probed for voltages. **Note:** *This procedure is mainly used for checking voltage supplies to the ECM and integrity of the earth connections.*

> ⚠ *Warning: Refer to Warning No 3 (in the Reference Section at the end of this book) before disconnecting the ECM multi-plug.*

5 Unless otherwise stated, attach the voltmeter negative test lead to an earth on the engine, and probe or backprobe the component terminal under test with the voltmeter positive test lead.

> ⚠ *Warning: DO NOT push round tester probes into square or oblong terminal connectors. This leads to terminal deformation and poor connections. A split pin is the correct shape for inserting into square or oblong terminals.*

6 In this book, the multi-plug diagram usually shows the terminals of the harness connector. When back-probing the multi-plug (or viewing the sensor connector terminals), the terminal positions will be reversed.

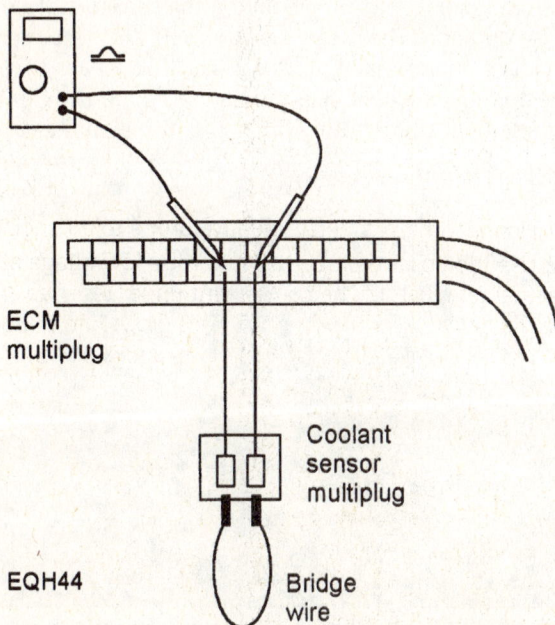

ECM multiplug

EQH44

Coolant sensor multiplug

Bridge wire

3.4 Check continuity of circuit between the ECM and the component multi-plug

Probing for supply or reference voltage

7 With the ignition on, and the component multi-plug connected or disconnected as stated in the appropriate test, probe or backprobe for nominal battery voltage or the reference voltage 5.0 volt supply.

Probing for signal voltage

8 With the ignition on, and the component multi-plug connected, backprobe for nominal battery voltage or the reference voltage 5.0 volt supply.

Earth or return

Method 1

9 With the ignition on, and the component multi-plug connected, backprobe for 0.25 volts max. The voltage at the earth or return connection to the majority of sensors should be less than 0.15 volts.

Method 2

10 This procedure can be carried out with the component multi-plug connected or disconnected. Attach the voltmeter positive test lead to the supply or reference terminal, and the voltmeter negative test lead to the earth or return terminal. The voltmeter should indicate supply voltage if the earth is satisfactory.

4   Resistance tests

1 Ensure that the ignition is off, and that the circuit or component under test is isolated from a voltage supply.

> ⚠ *Warning: DO NOT push round tester probes into square or oblong terminal connectors. This leads to terminal deformation and poor connections. A split pin is the correct shape for inserting into square or oblong terminals.*

2 Circuits that begin and end at the ECM are best tested for resistance (and continuity) at the ECM multi-plug, after it has been disconnected (see illustration 3.4).

> ⚠ *Warning: Refer to Warning No 3 (in the Reference Section at the end of this book) before disconnecting the ECM multi-plug.*

3 The use of a break-out box (BOB) is also recommended for resistance tests, but the BOB must be connected to the ECM multi-plug, and **not** to the ECM itself.

4 If the resistance test for a sensor circuit is made at the ECM multi-plug pins, and the sensor has a common connection to the ECM (either through a 5.0 volt reference supply and/or a sensor earth return), the multi-plug connectors for the remaining components must be disconnected. If this procedure is not followed, the results may be inaccurate.

5 When checking continuity of a circuit or continuity to earth, the maximum resistance should be less than 1.0 ohm.

6 When checking the resistance of a component against specifications, care should be taken in evaluating the condition of that component as the result of a good or bad test result. A component with a resistance outside of its operating parameters may not necessarily be faulty. Conversely, a circuit that measures within its operating parameters may still be faulty. However, an open-circuit or a very high resistance will almost certainly be indicative of a fault. The ohmmeter is more useful for checking circuit continuity than it is for indicating faulty components **(see illustration 3.5)**.

Checking for continuity of circuit

Note: *These tests can be used to quickly check for continuity of a circuit between most components (sensors and actuators) and the ECM.*

7 Disconnect the ECM multi-plug.

> ⚠ *Warning: Refer to Warning No 3 (in the Reference Section at the end of this book) before disconnecting the ECM multi-plug.*

8 Disconnect the component multi-plug, and connect a temporary bridge wire between terminals 1 and 2 at the component multi-plug.

9 Identify the two ECM pins which are connected to the component under test.

10 Connect an ohmmeter between the two pins at the ECM multi-plug. The meter should display continuity of the circuit.

11 If there is no continuity, check for a break in the wiring or a bad connection between the ECM pin and its corresponding terminal at the multi-plug.

12 Move one of the ohmmeter probes and touch to earth. The ohmmeter should display an open-circuit.

13 If the component is connected to the ECM by more than two wires, repeat the test using a combination of two wires at one time.

<hr>

5 Duty cycle tests

Connecting equipment probes

1 Connect the negative dwell meter probe to an engine earth.

2 Use the positive probe to backprobe the signal terminal of the component under test *(see illustration 3.6)*.

3 Make the duty cycle tests at various engine temperatures, with the engine cranking or running and at different engine speeds.

Possible dwell meter problems

Use of dwell meter during primary cranking tests

4 Although meaningful readings can generally be obtained with most modern DMMs, it is true that some may not be totally accurate during a cranking test on the primary ignition. This occurs when the meter's own preset trigger level may not be suitable for capturing the true voltage level of the component being tested.

Use of dwell meter during injector tests

5 Where the injector is either the current controlled type or the peak and hold kind; very few dwell meters may be capable of registering the rapid pulsing to earth or the current holding that occurs during the second stage of the pulse duration. The meter may only register the switch-on circuit of approximately 1.0 or 2.0%. This means that the injector duty cycle reading will be inaccurate and not representative of the total pulse width seen in the circuit.

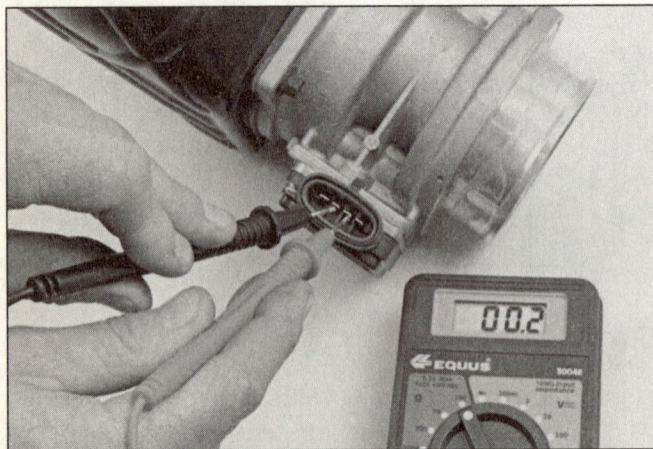

3.5 Measuring resistance: Detach the circuit multi-plug, select the appropriate resistance range and then touch the probes to the two terminals under test

3.6 Connect the dwell meter positive probe to the coil negative terminal 1 and measure the duty cycle at various engine-operating speeds

6 Variable potentiometer

1 It can be very useful to make certain tests on an engine at various operating temperatures. If the engineer has to wait for the engine to cool, reach normal operating temperature or any other important temperature, the task of testing can be irksome and prolonged. Most fuel injection ECMs (and some electronic ignition ECMs) recognise engine temperature by monitoring the voltage signal returned from the coolant temperature sensor (CTS). **Note:** *In a very few instances this signal may be returned from the oil temperature sensor (OTS) in addition or instead of the CTS.*

2 If a variable resistor (potentiometer) is connected between the CTS or OTS terminals *(see illustration 3.7)* the engine temperature may be simulated over the entire engine operating temperature range. Obtain a variable resistor (potentiometer or "pot"); a simple pot can be obtained from an electrical/electronic component store. Although the simple pot type is adequate for most tests, we recommend the use of the best quality pot that you can obtain. A good quality pot will give more "feel" and better control of the engine. The pot range should be from 1 ohm to 100 000 ohms.

Testing procedure

3 The following procedures should be followed when using the pot with either the OTS or CTS:

a) *Disconnect the CTS multi-plug.*
b) *Connect the pot between the two multi-plug terminal.*
c) *Set the pot to the correct resistance for the temperature that you wish to simulate.*
d) *Vary the resistance and make the test procedures as required.*
e) *On some engines you will set fault codes during test procedures, and these codes must be erased after testing is completed.*
f) *Refer to the fault code section in the relevant Chapter for instructions on how to clear fault codes.*

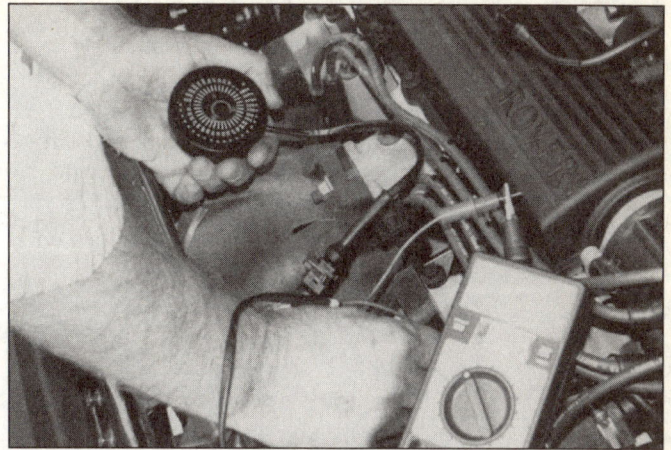

3.7 Using a variable potentiometer to vary the CTS resistance. Voltage change can be measured and the engine can be fooled into thinking it is cold or hot when the reverse is the case. This means that simulated cold running tests can be accomplished with the engine hot and without waiting for it to cool

7 Multiplexing and Networks

As vehicles become more and more complex, the amount, and weight of vehicle wiring harnesses become a significant factor in their design and construction. In order to reduce the amount of wiring, some later models are being equipped with Multiplex wiring.

Using this system, electrical actuators/motors/controllers are connected to a 'ring' loom of two, or three, wires. One wire supplies the electrical power, whist another is the vehicle ground (earth). The remaining wire is the 'signal' wire.

The central control unit sends a signal to the relevant component to operate. The processor within that component recognises the signal, and connects the component to the power and earth wires. On two wire systems, the signal from the control unit is embedded in the electrical power, in the form of a frequency modulation, or pattern.

As the requirements relating to fuel economy, exhaust emissions, driving safety and comfort become ever more stringent, intensive communication between the various vehicle ECUs becomes necessary. To avoid the physical connections between these units becoming unmanageable (some ECUs had 121 connector pins), Bosch developed a system whereby all these components communicate via two wires. These two wires are known as a 'data bus' *(see illustration 3.8)*. Each ECU has an integral transceiver which sends and receives signal 'packets' along these wires. As the packet travels along the data bus, each ECU examines the packet and check whether it needs the data or ignores it. Using this system allows rapid and reliable data transfer between the ECUs/controllers of a network. The first manufacturer to use this system in a production vehicle was

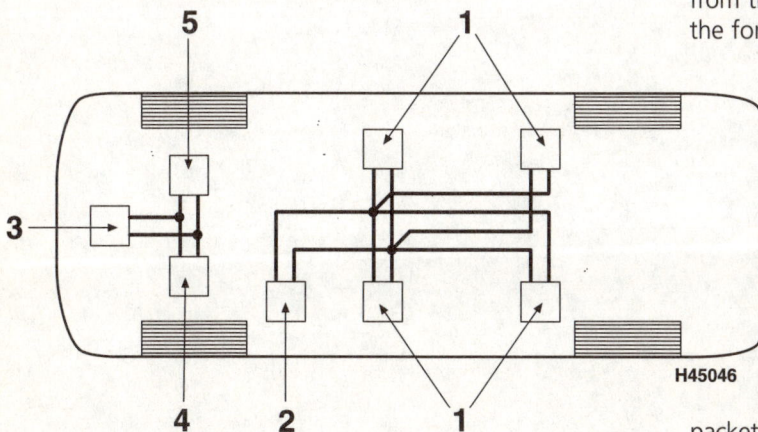

H45046

3.8 Vehicle area networks

1 *Door control units*
2 *Central control unit*
3 *Engine control unit*
4 *Automatic gearbox control unit*
5 *ABS control unit*

VW. They named their system CAN (Controlled Area Network) Data Bus, or subsequently, VAN (Vehicle Area Network).

Obviously from a fault finding perspective, the traditional probing with a multimeter may not reveal the expected results, and may cause damage. Fortunately, vehicles with Multiplex wiring and/or Networks are also equipped with sophisticated self-diagnosis systems, which monitor the integrity of circuits, controllers and components of the vehicle. Fault-finding using an appropriate reader/scanner should be relatively straight-forward and precise. However, as expensive ECUs and components are involved, always interrogate the system for stored faults first, and always examine the relevant wiring diagram before getting the multimeter out and backprobing connectors.

Component test procedures

4

Chapter 4

1   Introduction

Refer to the Haynes companion volume, "Automotive Engine Management and Fuel Injection Systems Manual" (Book No 3344, available from the publishers of this title) for a description of the function of each component.

Prior to commencing tests on any of the EMS components, the following checks should always be made.

a) Inspect the component multi-plug for corrosion and damage.

b) Check that the terminal pins in the multi-plug are fully pushed home and making good contact with the component (see illustration 4.1).

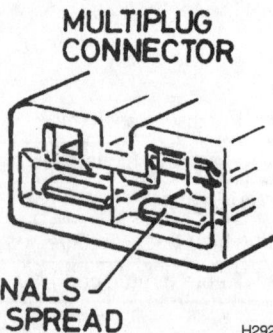

4.1 Check that the terminal pins in the multi-plug connector are pushed home, and are not damaged, to ensure that a good contact is made with the component under test

The test procedures described here are general in nature, and should be used in conjunction with a wiring diagram and specific measurement values for the system under test.

Primary trigger test procedures

2   General information

The primary trigger is the most important sensor in the system. Until the ECM senses a signal from the primary trigger, the fuel pump relay, ignition and injection functions will not be actuated. Test procedures for the main types of trigger are detailed below.

Either the engine will fail to start or will misfire if the primary trigger is defective. Both ignition and fuel injection will cease or be disrupted, depending on the severity of the fault.

Note: *Some later systems may utilise the cylinder identification or camshaft signal if the primary trigger is defective, and the system will engage the limp-home or LOS function.*

Some systems will generate a fault code if the ignition is turned on and the engine is not running (typical examples include Vauxhall and the VW/Audi group). The code is cleared from memory once the engine has successfully started.

3   Inductive crank angle sensor (CAS)

Note: *These tests are also generally applicable to RPM, TDC sensors and distributor-located inductive triggers.*

Remove the CAS from the engine block, and inspect the end surface for corrosion and damage.

Measure the CAS resistance *(see illustration 4.2)* and compare to the specifications for the vehicle being tested. Typical resistance for the CAS is in the range 200 to 1500 ohms. **Note:** *Even if the resistance is within the quoted specifications, this does not prove that the CAS can generate an acceptable signal.*

Check the CAS signal *(see illustration 4.3)*:

a) *Where possible, an oscilloscope should be used to check for a satisfactory signal. A minimum AC peak-to-peak voltage of about 4.0 to 5.0 volts should be obtained. Check for even peaks. One or more peaks much smaller than the others would indicate a missing or damaged CAS lobe.*

b) *Detach the CAS or ECM multi-plug.*

Warning: Refer to Warning No 3 (in the Reference Section at the end of this book) before disconnecting the ECM multi-plug.

c) *Connect an AC voltmeter between the two terminals leading to the CAS. If a third wire is present, it will be a shield wire.*

d) *Crank the engine. A minimum AC RMS voltage of about 0.7 volts should be obtained, although most good sensors will provide an output of more than 1.4 AC RMS voltage.*

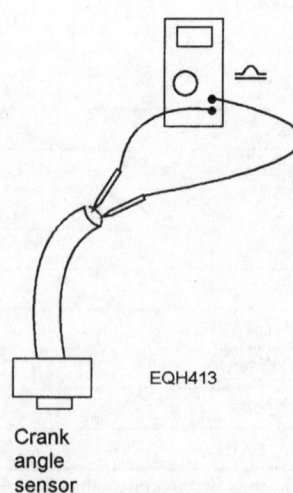

4.2 Measure the CAS resistance

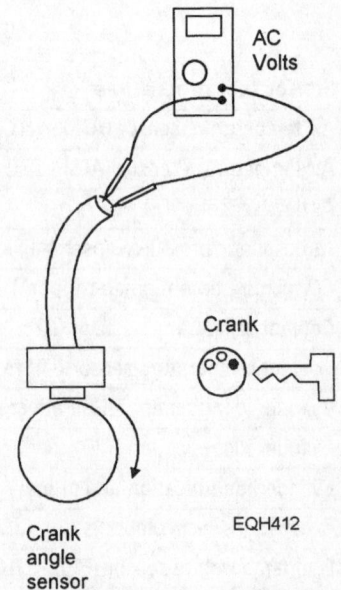

4.3 Check the CAS output with an AC voltmeter

Note: *The AC voltmeter at least proves that a signal is being generated by the CAS. However, the AC voltage is an average voltage, and does not clearly indicate damage to the CAS lobes or that the sine wave is regular in formation.*

4 In some systems, the CAS may be shielded. To test the shielding, proceed as follows:

a) *Locate the wiring multi-plug connector or disconnect the ECM multi-plug (refer to the warning above).*

b) *Attach an ohmmeter probe to one of the sensor terminals.*

c) *Attach the other ohmmeter probe to the shield wire terminal. A reading of infinity should be obtained.*

d) *Move the ohmmeter probe from the shield wire terminal and connect it to earth. A reading of infinity should also be obtained.*

Note: *The shield wire on the CAS in some systems is connected to the CAS earth return wire. In such a case, continuity will be registered on the ohmmeter, and this is normal for that vehicle. Refer to the wiring diagrams for the system under test to determine how the CAS is wired.*

4	Hall-effect sensor (HES)

Quick HES test (non-runner, no spark)

Note: *In most systems the HES is located in the distributor. However, a flywheel-mounted HES is found in some VW/Audi systems.*

1 Remove the HT "king" lead from the distributor cap centre tower, and connect it to the cylinder head via a spark jumper.

2 Detach the HES multi-plug at the distributor *(refer to illustration 4.16).*

3 Identify the supply, signal and earth terminals.

4 Briefly flash a small jumper lead between the (O) and (-) terminals on the HES harness multi-plug *(see illustration 4.4).*

5 If a spark jumps across the spark jumper terminals to the cylinder head, the coil and amplifier are capable of

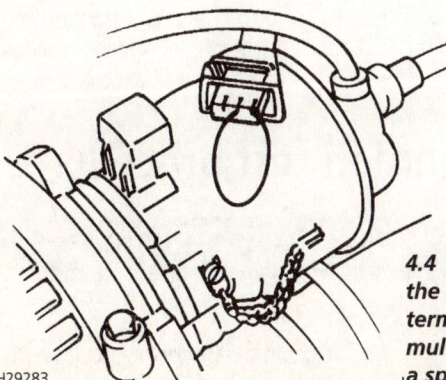

4.4 Very briefly flash the (0) and (-) terminals at the HES multi-plug to check for a spark

H29283

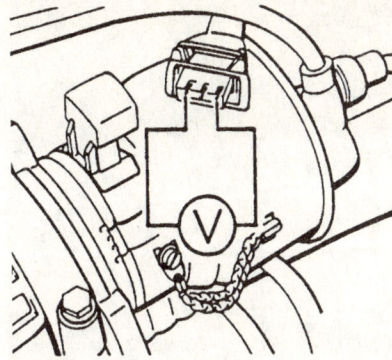

4.5 Connect a voltmeter between the HES (+) and (-) terminals. As the engine is turned, a voltage of between 10 and 12 volts should be obtained

producing a spark, and the Hall switch in the distributor is suspect.

HES test procedures

6 Roll back the rubber protection boot to the HES multi-plug.

7 Connect the voltmeter negative or dwell meter probe to an engine earth.

8 Identify the supply, signal and earth terminals.

9 Connect the voltmeter positive or dwell meter probe to the wire attached to the HES signal terminal.

10 Allow the engine to idle.

11 An average voltage of approximately 7 to 8 volts, or an approximate duty cycle of 35% should be obtained

Signal voltage or duty cycle signal not available

12 Stop the engine, and remove the distributor cap.

13 With the HES multi-plug connected, and the ignition on, connect the voltmeter positive probe to the signal terminal *(see illustration 4.5).*

14 Turn the engine over slowly. As the trigger vane cut-out space moves in and out of the air gap, the voltage should alternate between 10 to 12 volts and zero volts.

Signal voltage not available

15 Disconnect the HES multi-plug at the distributor.

16 Probe output terminal 2 (O) of the harness multi-plug with the voltmeter positive probe. A voltage of between 10 and 12 volts should be obtained.

17 If there is no voltage from the ECM to terminal 2, check for continuity of the signal wiring between the HES and the ECM. Recheck for voltage at the ECM terminal. If no voltage is available at the ECM, check all voltage supplies and earth connections to the ECM. If the voltage supplies and earth connections are satisfactory, the ECM is suspect.

18 Check the voltage supply (10 to 12 volts) at HES terminal number 1 (+). If the supply is unsatisfactory, check for continuity of the wiring between the HES and the ECM.

19 Check the earth connection at HES terminal number 3 (-).

20 If the voltage supply and earth are satisfactory, the HES in the distributor is suspect.

4.6 Optical crank angle sensor. The arrow points to the optical pick-up. Beneath the pick-up is the rotor disc containing two rows of slits. The large rectangular slit indicates the position of number 1 cylinder

5 Optical crank angle sensor (CAS)

1 Recommended test equipment for measuring the optical CAS signal is an oscilloscope. However, a DMM that can measure volts, duty cycle, RPM (tachometer) and frequency could also be used to test for a rudimentary signal. **Note:** *Nissan and other Far Eastern manufacturers typically utilise the optical distributor as the primary trigger.*

2 Remove the distributor cap and visually inspect the rotor plate for damage and eccentricity. If necessary, remove the distributor from the engine and rotate the shaft. The shaft and rotor plate must rotate without deviation or distortion *(see illustration 4.6).*

RPM signal output tests

Note: *The CAS and ECM multi-plug must remain connected during signal output tests. The following tests are typical, and may need modifying for some applications due to variations in wiring.*

Note: *In order to conduct the RPM and TDC tests, it is also possible to remove the distributor from the engine, switch on the ignition and rotate the distributor shaft by hand.*

3 Connect the test equipment between terminals 1 (earth or signal return) and 4 (RPM signal) at the CAS multi-plug or the corresponding multi-plug terminals at the ECM.

4 Crank or run the engine.

5 On an oscilloscope, a high-frequency square waveform switching between zero and 5 volts should be obtained. Check for even peaks. One or more peak that is much smaller than the others could indicate a damaged slit.

6 A digital voltmeter should indicate switching between zero and 5 volts. The duty cycle, RPM and frequency meters should indicate a signal output. The frequency of the RPM signal should be greater than that obtained when testing the TDC sensor signal (see below).

7 If the signal is non-existent, very weak or intermittent, check for a voltage supply to CAS terminal 2 and check the CAS earth at terminal 1. Also check the sensor for damage, dirt or oil, the distributor and rotor plate for damage, and for continuity between the CAS signal terminal and the ECM pin.

8 Run the engine at various engine speeds, and check for a consistent signal that meets the same requirements as the cranking test.

TDC signal output tests

Note: *The CAS and ECM multi-plug must remain connected during signal output tests.*

9 Connect the meter between terminals 1 (earth or signal return) and 3 (TDC signal) at the CAS multi-plug or the corresponding multi-plug terminals at the ECM.

10 Crank or run the engine.

11 On an oscilloscope, a high-frequency square waveform switching between zero and 5 volts should be obtained. Check for even peaks. One or more peak that is much smaller than the others could indicate a damaged slit.

12 A digital voltmeter should indicate switching between zero and 5 volts. The duty cycle, RPM and frequency meters should indicate a signal output. The frequency of the TDC signal should be less than that obtained when testing the RPM sensor signal (see above).

13 If the signal is non-existent, very weak or intermittent, check for a voltage supply to CAS terminal 2 and check the CAS earth at terminal 1. Also check the sensor for damage, dirt or oil, the distributor and rotor plate for damage, and for continuity between the CAS signal terminal and the ECM pin.

14 Run the engine at various engine speeds, and check for a consistent signal that meets the same requirements as the cranking test.

CAS shield connection

15 The CAS signal wires are shielded against RFI. Locate the wiring multi-plug connector or disconnect the ECM multi-plug. Attach an ohmmeter probe to the wire attached to sensor signal terminal 3, and attach the other ohmmeter probe to earth. A reading of infinity should be obtained.

16 Move the first ohmmeter probe to the wire attached to sensor signal terminal 4. A reading of infinity should also be obtained.

Primary ignition test procedures

6 Primary ignition

General

1 Check the coil terminals for good clean connections, and clean away accumulations of dirt and the residue from a maintenance spray. The residue will attract dirt, and this may lead to bleeding of the HT current to earth.

2 Inspect the ignition coil for signs of tracking, particularly around the coil tower area.

Note: *Although the following tests are accomplished with the aid of a basic dwell meter, an oscilloscope is a more suitable instrument for analysing the signals generated by the primary ignition.*

Engine non-runner test procedures

3 Connect the dwell meter negative probe to an engine earth.

4 Connect the dwell meter positive probe to the coil negative (-) terminal (usually marked 1 in Bosch systems).

5 Crank the engine on the starter.

6 A duty cycle reading of approximately 5 to 20% should be obtained. If there is a satisfactory primary signal, the primary ignition (including the primary trigger) are providing an acceptable signal.

Primary signal not available (amplifier inside the ECM)

7 Check the primary trigger for a good signal (refer to CAS or HES test).

8 Switch on the ignition.

9 Check for a voltage supply to the coil positive (+) terminal (15). If there is no voltage, check the wiring back to the supply (usually the ignition switch, but could be one of the relays).

10 Check for voltage to the coil negative (-) terminal (1). If there is no voltage, remove the wire to the coil (-) terminal and recheck. If there is still no voltage, check the coil primary resistance *(see Illustration 4.7)*.

11 If the voltage is at nominal battery level, check for a short to earth between the coil number 1 terminal and the

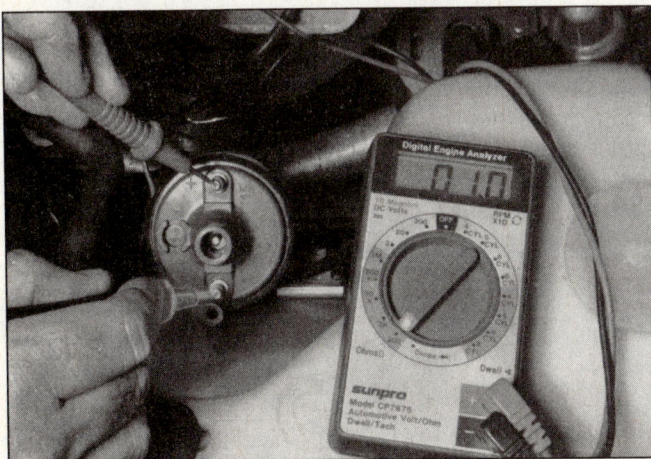

DCV

4.8 Detach the ECM multi-plug and check for battery voltage at the ECM primary ignition terminal

earth

ECM multiplug

EQH417

appropriate ECM pin. If there is still no voltage, the coil is suspect.

12 Detach the ECM multi-plug and check for battery voltage at the appropriate ECM pin *(see Illustration 4.8)*. If there is no voltage, check for continuity between the coil number 1 terminal and the appropriate ECM pin.

> *Warning: Refer to Warning No 3 (in the Reference Section at the end of this book) before disconnecting the ECM multi-plug.*

13 If the wiring is satisfactory, check all ECM voltage supplies and earth connections. If testing reveals no faults, the ECM is suspect. However, a substitute ignition coil should be tried before renewing the ECM.

14 If the ignition system is of distributorless type (DIS), repeat the tests for the second or third coil (where fitted). The ECM connection varies according to system.

Primary signal not available (separate external amplifier)

15 Check the primary trigger for a good signal (Refer to CAS or HES test).

16 Switch the ignition on.

17 Check for a voltage supply to the coil positive (+) terminal (15). If there is no voltage, check the wiring back to the supply (usually the ignition switch or one of the system relays).

18 Check for voltage to the coil negative (-) terminal (1). If there is no voltage, remove the wire to the coil (-) terminal and recheck. If there is still no voltage, check the coil primary resistance, the coil is suspect *(refer to illustration 4.4)*.

19 If the voltage is equal to battery voltage, check for a short to earth between the coil number 1 terminal and the amplifier. If the wiring is satisfactory, the amplifier is suspect.

20 Disconnect the amplifier multi-plug.

4.7 Check the coil primary resistance. Disconnect the low tension wires and connect the ohmmeter between the positive and negative terminals

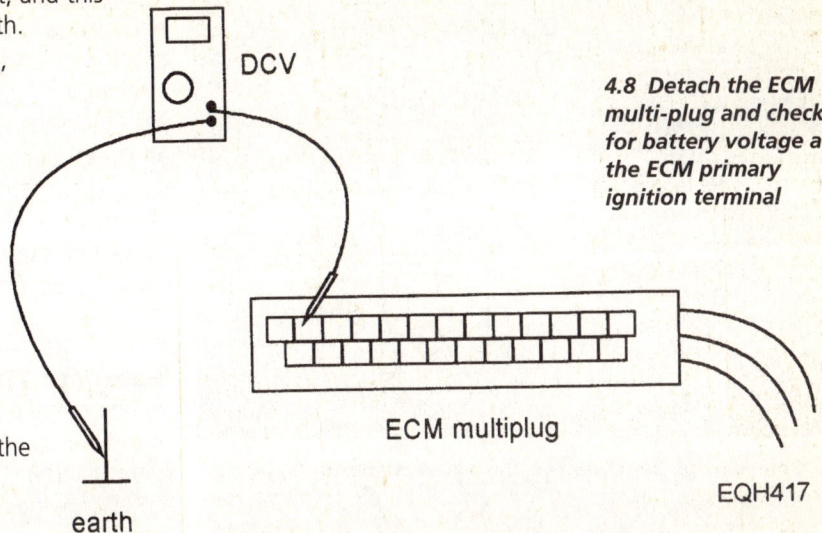

4.9 Checking for voltage at the amplifier terminal (1) that is connected to the ignition coil terminal No. 1. The voltmeter negative probe is connected to the amplifier earth connection (2)

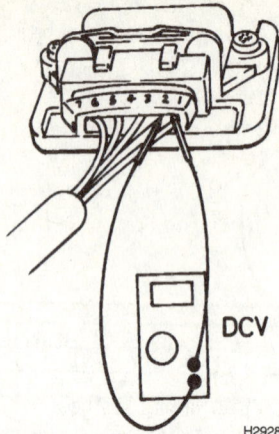

DCV

H29284

⚠ Warning: Refer to Warning No 3 (in the Reference Section at the end of this book) before disconnecting the multi-plug.

21 Check for voltage at the amplifier terminal that is connected to the ignition coil terminal 1 (see illustration 4.9). If there is no voltage, check for continuity of wiring between the amplifier and ignition coil terminal number 1.

22 Check for voltage to the amplifier from the ignition switch.

23 Check the amplifier earth connection.

24 Crank the engine and check for a control signal from the ECM to the amplifier. **Note:** Although it is possible to use a dwell meter to check for a duty cycle signal from the ECM to the amplifier, the integrity of the signal may be difficult to establish. Once again, an oscilloscope is more likely to make sense of this signal.

25 If there is no control signal, check the continuity of the wiring between the amplifier and the ECM terminal.

26 If the control signal is satisfactory, but there is no output from the amplifier, this suggests a faulty amplifier.

27 If the wiring is satisfactory, check all ECM voltage supplies and earth connections. If testing reveals no faults, the ECM is suspect. However, a substitute ignition coil and/or amplifier should be tried before renewing the ECM.

28 If the ignition system is of distributorless type (DIS), repeat the tests for the second coil. The ECM connection varies according to system.

Engine running test procedures

29 Connect the dwell meter negative probe to an engine earth.

30 Connect the dwell meter positive probe to the coil negative (-) terminal (usually marked 1 in Bosch systems).

31 Run the engine at idle and various speeds, and record the duty cycle values. Approximate values are given below:

Idle speed - 5 to 20%
2000 rpm - 15 to 35%
3000 rpm - 25 to 45%

32 It is important that the duty cycle in % increases in value as the engine rpm is raised. If your DMM can measure the duty cycle in ms, the reading should not change much in value as the engine rpm is raised.

33 Check the amplifier earth.

34 Check that devices such as a radio suppresser or anti-theft alarm have not been connected to the coil primary (−) terminal.

35 All other tests and any detailed primary analysis requires the aid of an oscilloscope.

Sensor test procedures

7   Airflow sensor (AFS)

General

1 Inspect the air trunking from the AFS and check for splits, poor fitting or damage. A large vacuum leak at this point will cause the engine to fire but fail to continue running and a small vacuum leak will adversely affect the AFR.

2 The AFS may be one of various types: vane, KE-Jetronic, hot-wire, hot-film or vortex type, depending on system.

Vane type AFS

3 Connect the voltmeter negative probe to an engine earth.

4 Identify the supply, signal and earth terminals.

5 Connect the voltmeter positive probe to the wire attached to the AFS signal terminal (see illustration 4.10).

6 Remove the air trunking.

7 Remove the air filter box so that the AFS flap can be easily opened and closed.

8 Open and close the AFS flap several times and check for smooth operation. Also check that the flap does not stick.

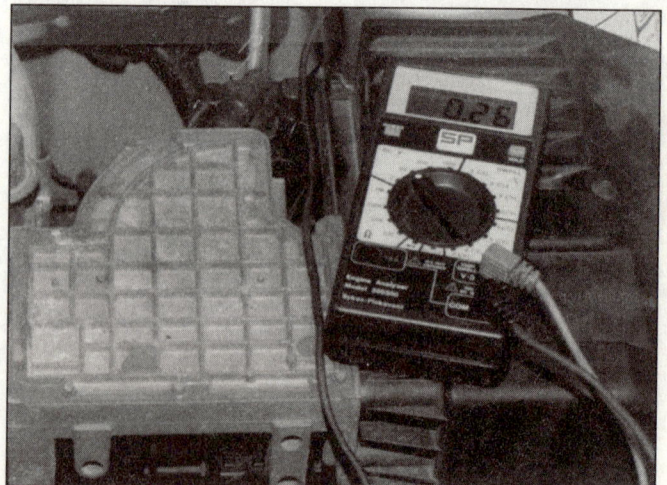

4.10 Backprobing the AFS for voltage

9 Switch on the ignition (engine stopped). A voltage of approximately 0.20 to 0.30 volts should be obtained.

10 Open and close the flap several times, and check for a smooth voltage increase to a maximum of 4.0 to 4.5 volts. **Note:** *If a digital voltmeter is used, then it is useful for it to have a bar graph facility. The smoothness of the voltage increase can then be more easily seen.*

11 Refit the air trunking. Start the engine and allow it to idle. A voltage of approximately 0.5 to 1.5 volts should be obtained.

12 Open the throttle to no more than 3000 rpm. A voltage of approximately 2.0 to 2.5 volts should be obtained.

13 Snap open the throttle. A voltage greater than 3.0 volts should be obtained.

Erratic signal output

14 An erratic output occurs when the voltage output is stepped, drops to zero or becomes open-circuit.

15 When the AFS signal output is erratic, this usually suggests a faulty signal track or a sticking flap. In this instance, a new or reconditioned AFS may be the only cure.

16 Sometimes the wiper arm becomes disengaged from the signal track at certain points during its traverse. This can also give an erratic output.

17 Remove the top cover from the AFS and check that the wiper arm touches the track during its swing from the open to the closed position. Carefully bending the arm so that it touches the signal track, or careful cleaning of the track, can cure an erratic signal output.

Signal voltage not available

18 Check for the 5.0 volt reference voltage supply at the AFS supply terminal.

19 Check the earth return connection at the AFS earth terminal.

20 If the supply and earth are satisfactory, check for continuity of the signal wiring between the AFS and the ECM.

21 If the supply and/or earth are unsatisfactory, check for continuity of the wiring between the AFS and the ECM.

22 If the AFS wiring is satisfactory, check all voltage supplies and earth connections to the ECM. If the voltage supplies and earth connections are satisfactory, the ECM is suspect.

Signal or supply voltage at battery voltage level

23 Check for a short to a wire connected to the battery positive (+) terminal or a switched supply voltage.

Resistance tests

24 Connect an ohmmeter between the AFS signal terminal and supply terminal or the AFS signal terminal and earth terminal.

25 Open and close the AFS flap several times, and check for a smooth resistance change. As the AFS flap is moved slowly from the closed to the fully-open position, the AFS resistance may increase and decrease in a series of steps. This is normal. If the AFS resistance becomes open or short-circuit, a fault is revealed.

26 We are not providing resistance specifications for the AFS described in this book. It is less important that the resistance of the AFS remains within arbitrary values, than the operation is correct.

27 Connect an ohmmeter between the AFS earth terminal and supply terminal. A stable resistance should be obtained.

28 Renew the AFS if the resistance is open-circuit or shorted to earth. Refer to the comments on resistance readings in Chapter 3.

KE-Jetronic type AFS

29 The AFS in KE-Jetronic systems is attached to the metering unit sensor plate. As the sensor plate moves, the signal varies in a similar fashion to the vane AFS fitted in other systems.

30 The general method of testing, and the resistance and voltage values, are similar to the vane type AFS described above.

Hot-wire or Hot-film type AFS

Note: *The voltage measurements are based on the Vauxhall 16-valve engines with Motronic 2.5. The readings from other vehicles should be similar.*

Signal wire

31 Switch on the ignition. A voltage of approximately 1.4 volts should be obtained.

32 Start the engine and allow it to idle. A voltage of approximately 2.0 volts should be obtained.

33 Snap open the throttle several times. The voltage will not increase significantly over the idle value during this off-load test. **Note:** *If a digital voltmeter is used, then it is useful for it to have a bar graph facility. The smoothness of the voltage increase can then be more easily seen.*

34 It is less easy to test the AFS hot-wire signal output because it is impossible to simulate full-load conditions in the workshop without putting the vehicle on a chassis dynamometer (rolling road). However, the following test procedure will usually prove if the signal output is consistent.

35 Disconnect the air trunking so that the hot-wire is exposed.

36 Switch on the ignition.

37 Use a length of plastic tubing to blow air over the hot-wire.

38 It should be possible to plot a voltage curve, although the curve will be much steeper than that obtained with the engine running.

Erratic signal output

39 The signal output is erratic when the voltage does not follow a smooth curve, if the voltage drops to zero, or if it becomes open-circuit.

40 Check the AFS resistance as follows. Connect an ohmmeter between AFS terminals 2 and 3. A resistance of approximately 2.5 to 3.1 ohms should be obtained.

41 When the AFS signal output is erratic, and all supply and earth voltages are satisfactory, this suggests a faulty AFS. In this case, a new or reconditioned AFS may be the only cure.

Signal voltage not available

42 Check for the battery voltage supply to AFS terminal number 5.

43 Check the earth return connection at AFS terminal number 2.

44 Check the earth connection at AFS terminal number 1.

45 If the supply and earths are satisfactory, check for continuity of the signal wiring between the AFS and the ECM.

46 If the supply and/or earths are unsatisfactory, check for continuity of the supply and/or earth wiring between the AFS and the ECM.

47 If the AFS wiring is satisfactory, check all voltage supplies and earth connections to the ECM. If the voltage supplies and earth connections are satisfactory, the ECM is suspect.

Vortex type AFS

48 The vortex type AFS relies on the intake manifold design to create a turbulent airflow. A radio signal is passed through the airflow as it flows through the sensor. Variations in the turbulence cause a change in frequency that the sensor returns to the ECM as a measure of airflow into the engine.

49 Identify the signal terminal. At idle speed, the signal output should be typically 27 to 33 Hz. The frequency will increase as the engine speed is increased.

50 Identify the earth terminals. A voltage of less than 0.2 volts should be obtained.

51 Identify the supply terminal. Battery voltage should be obtained.

52 It is probable that the sensor will also house air temperature and air pressure sensors. These sensors should be tested as described under the test for the appropriate sensor.

8 Air temperature sensor (ATS) - NTC type

1 The majority of ATSs used in motor vehicles are of the NTC type. A negative temperature coefficient (NTC) sensor is a thermistor in which the resistance decreases as the temperature rises. A positive temperature coefficient (PTC) sensor is a thermistor in which the resistance rises as the temperature rises.

2 The ATS may be located in the inlet tract of the airflow sensor or in the inlet manifold. If the ATS is located in the airflow sensor, it shares a common earth return. Both types of ATS are examples of two-wire sensors, and test procedures are similar.

3 Connect the voltmeter negative probe to an engine earth.

4 Identify the signal and earth terminals.

5 Connect the voltmeter positive probe to the wire attached to the ATS signal terminal (see illustration 4.11).

6 Switch the ignition on (engine stopped).

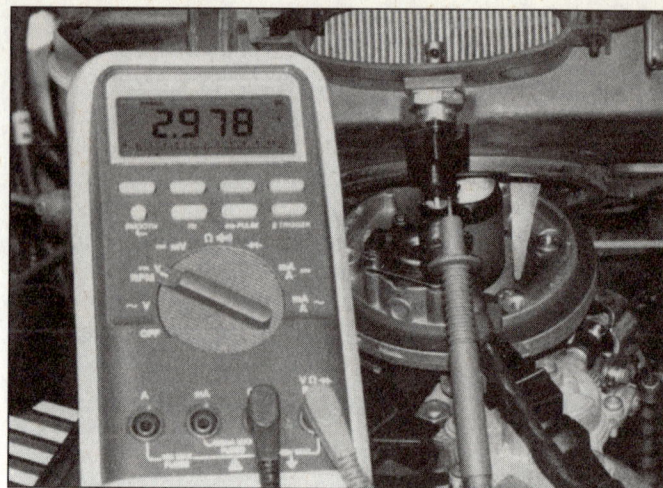

4.11 Backprobing for an ATS signal (ATS located in the air filter box)

7 A voltage of approximately 2 to 3 volts, depending upon air temperature, is likely to be obtained. Refer to the ATS chart for typical voltages at various temperatures.

8 The signal voltage will vary according to the temperature of the air in the AFS inlet tract or inlet manifold. As the engine compartment or inlet manifold air rises in temperature, the voltage signal passed to the ECM will reduce. When the engine is cold, the air temperature will match the ambient temperature. After the engine has started, the temperature of the air in the engine compartment and the inlet manifold will rise. The temperature of the air in the inlet manifold will rise to approximately 70° or 80°C, which is a much higher temperature than that of the air in the engine compartment.

9 When undergoing tests at various temperatures, the ATS can be warmed with a hair-dryer or cooled with a product like "Freezit", which is an ice cold aerosol spray, sold in electronic component shops. As the ATS is heated or cooled, the temperature will change and so too will the resistance and voltage.

ATS voltage and resistance table (typical NTC type)

Temp (°C)	Resistance (ohms)	Volts
0	4800 to 6600	4.00 to 4.50
10	4000	3.75 to 4.00
20	2200 to 2800	3.00 to 3.50
30	1300	3.25
40	1000 to 1200	2.50 to 3.00
50	1000	2.50
60	800	2.00 to 2.50
80	270 to 380	1.00 to 1.30
110		0.50
–	Open-circuit	5.0 ± 0.1
–	Short to earth	Zero

10 Check that the ATS voltage corresponds to the temperature of the ATS. A temperature gauge is required here.

11 Start the engine and allow it to warm up to normal operating temperature. As the engine warms up, the voltage should reduce in accordance with the ATS chart.

12 Proceed with the following tests and checks if the ATS signal voltage is zero (supply is open-circuit or shorted to earth) or at 5.0 volt level (ATS is open-circuit).

Zero volts obtained at the ATS signal terminal

13 Check that the ATS signal terminal is not shorted to earth.

14 Check for continuity of the signal wiring between the ATS and the ECM.

15 If the ATS wiring is satisfactory, yet there is no voltage is output from the ECM, check all voltage supplies and earth connections to the ECM. If the voltage supplies and earth connections are satisfactory, the ECM is suspect.

5.0 volts obtained at the ATS signal terminal

16 This is the open-circuit voltage, and will be obtained in the event of one or more of the following conditions:

a) *The signal terminal in the ATS (or AFS) multi-plug is not making contact with the ATS.*
b) *The ATS is open-circuit.*
c) *The ATS earth connection is open-circuit.*

Signal or supply voltage at battery voltage level

17 Check for a short to a wire connected to the battery positive (+) terminal or a switched supply voltage.

Resistance tests with an ohmmeter

18 A resistance test may be made at various temperatures, and a comparison made with the temperature/resistance chart. Refer to the voltage tests above for a method of heating/cooling the ATS.

19 When the ATS resistance is within the stated parameters for a cold engine (20°C) the coolant temperature should also be within ± 5°C. of that figure.

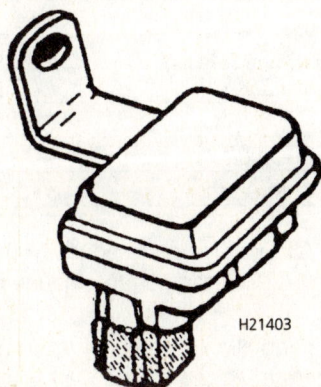

4.12 Atmospheric pressure sensor

9   Air temperature sensor (ATS) - PTC type

1 The PTC type ATS is fitted to a small number of systems (mainly Renault vehicles). A positive temperature coefficient (PTC) sensor is a thermistor in which the resistance rises as the temperature rises.

2 The general method of testing is similar to the NTC type previously described; with reference to the values in the ATS (PTC) resistance and voltage table.

ATS resistance and voltage table (typical PTC type)

Temp (°C)	Resistance (ohms)	Volts
0	254 to 266	0.5
20	283 to 297	0.5 to 1.5
40	315 to 329	1.5
–	open-circuit	5.0 ± 0.1
–	short to earth	zero

10   Atmospheric pressure sensor (APS)

1 The APS detects changes in atmospheric pressure, and returns the information to the ECM in the form of a voltage (*see illustration 4.12*).

2 Connect the negative oscilloscope or voltmeter probe to an engine earth, or to the earth return at terminal 1 of the APS sensor.

3 Connect the positive oscilloscope or voltmeter probe to the wire attached to the APS sensor signal terminal.

4 Switch the ignition on.

5 The voltage generated by atmospheric pressure at sea level may be typically 3.0 volts. The voltage will change slightly to reflect changes in pressure and also when the vehicle operates at different altitudes. The changes in voltage are likely to be relatively small. If the voltage does not fall within the expected parameters, continue with the following tests.

Signal voltage not available

6 Check the reference voltage supply - usually 5.0 volts.

7 Check the earth return. Expect a voltage less than 0.25 volts.

8 If the supply and earth are satisfactory, check for continuity of the signal wiring between the APS sensor and the ECM.

9 If the supply and/or earth are unsatisfactory, check for continuity of the wiring between the APS sensor and the ECM.

10 If the APS sensor wiring is satisfactory, check all voltage supplies and earth connections to the ECM. If the voltage supplies and earth connections are satisfactory, the ECM is suspect.

Signal or supply voltage at battery level

11 Check for a short to a wire connected to the battery positive (+) terminal or a switched supply voltage

11 CO/mixture potentiometer ("pot")

1 The CO pot may be located in the airflow sensor (AFS), or may be a separate sensor located in the engine compartment or may be directly attached to the ECM. If located in the airflow sensor, the CO pot shares a common earth return.

2 The CO pot is an example of a three-wire sensor, and test procedures follow similar paths regardless of the pot's location.

3 The CO pot attached to the ECM cannot be tested separately, and a new ECM is required if the CO pot fails.

4 Roll back the rubber protection boot to the CO pot multi-plug (or airflow sensor multi-plug if located in the AFS).

5 Connect the voltmeter negative probe to an engine earth.

6 Identify the supply, signal and earth terminals.

7 Connect the voltmeter positive probe to the wire attached to the CO pot signal terminal.

8 A voltage of approximately 2.5 volts should be obtained in most systems (see illustration 4.13).

9 Record the exact voltage so that the voltage can be reset to the exact value after tests are complete.

10 Remove the tamperproof cap from the adjustment screw.

11 Turn the adjustment screw one way and then the other. The voltage should vary smoothly.

CO pot voltage does not alter during adjustment

12 Check for the 5.0 volt reference voltage supply to the sensor.

CO POT.

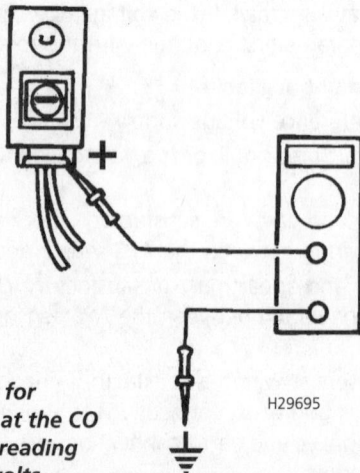

4.13 Checking for signal voltage at the CO pot - a typical reading would be 2.5 volts

H29695

13 Check the earth return connection to the sensor.

14 If the supply and earth are satisfactory, check for continuity of the signal wiring between the CO pot and the ECM.

15 If the supply and/or earth are unsatisfactory, check for continuity of the supply and/or earth wiring between the CO pot or AFS (as appropriate) and the ECM.

16 If the AFS wiring is satisfactory, check all voltage supplies and earth connections to the ECM. If the voltage supplies and earth connections are satisfactory, the ECM is suspect.

12 Coolant temperature sensor (CTS) - NTC type

1 The majority of CTSs used in motor vehicles are of the NTC type. A negative temperature coefficient (NTC) sensor is a thermistor in which the resistance decreases as the temperature rises. A positive temperature coefficient (PTC) sensor is a thermistor in which the resistance rises as the temperature rises.

2 Roll back the rubber protection boot to the CTS multi-plug.

3 Connect the voltmeter negative probe to an engine earth.

4 Identify the signal and earth terminals.

5 Connect the voltmeter positive probe to the wire attached to the CTS signal terminal.

6 With the engine cold and not running, switch on the ignition.

7 A voltage of approximately 2 to 3 volts, depending upon temperature, is likely to be obtained. Refer to the CTS chart below for typical voltages at various temperatures.

CTS voltage and resistance table (typical)

Temp (°C)	Resistance (ohms)	Volts
0	4800 to 6600	4.00 to 4.50
10	4000	3.75 to 4.00
20	2200 to 2800	3.00 to 3.50
30	1300	3.25
40	1000 to 1200	2.50 to 3.00
50	1000	2.50
60	800	2.00 to 2.50
80	270 to 380	1.00 to 1.30
110		0.50
–	Open-circuit	5.0 ± 0.1
–	Short to earth	zero

8 Check that the CTS voltage corresponds to the temperature of the CTS. A temperature gauge is required here.

9 Start the engine and allow it to warm up to normal operating temperature. As the engine warms up, the voltage should reduce in accordance with the CTS chart.

10 A common problem may occur where the CTS varies in

resistance (and voltage) outside of its normal range. If the CTS voltage measurement is normally 2 volts cold/0.5 volts hot, a faulty CTS may give a voltage of 1.5 volts cold/ 1.25 volts hot, resulting in the engine being difficult to start when cold and running richer than normal when hot. This will **not** result in the generation of a fault code (unless the ECM is programmed to recognise voltage changes against time) because the CTS is still operating within its design parameters. Renew the CTS if this fault occurs. **Note:** *The above example is typical, and not meant to represent an actual voltage obtained in a particular system under test.*

11 Proceed with the following tests and checks if the CTS signal voltage is zero (supply is open-circuit or shorted to earth) or at 5.0 volt level (CTS is open-circuit).

Zero volts obtained at the CTS signal terminal

12 Check that the CTS signal terminal is not shorted to earth.

13 Check for continuity of the signal wiring between the CTS and the ECM.

14 If the CTS wiring is satisfactory, yet no voltage is output from the ECM, check all voltage supplies and earth connections to the ECM. If the voltage supplies and earth connections are satisfactory, the ECM is suspect.

5.0 volts obtained at the CTS signal terminal

15 This is the open-circuit voltage, and will be obtained in the event of one or more of the following conditions:

  a) *The signal terminal in the CTS multi-plug is not making contact with the CTS.*
  b) *The CTS is open-circuit.*
  c) *The CTS earth connection is open-circuit.*

Signal or supply voltage at battery voltage level

16 Check for a short to a wire connected to the battery positive (+) terminal or a switched supply voltage.

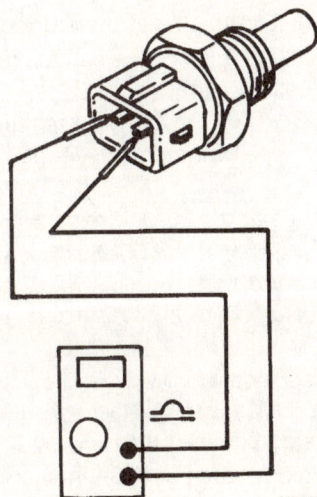

4.14 Checking the CTS resistance

Resistance tests with an ohmmeter

CTS on vehicle

17 A resistance test may be made at various temperatures and a comparison made with the temperature/ resistance chart *(see illustration 4.14)*. When the resistance is within the stated parameters for a cold engine (20°C), the coolant temperature should be within ±5°C of that figure.

18 An allowance should be made for a temperature obtained by probing the outside of the CTS or coolant passage. This is because the actual temperature of the coolant may be hotter than the surface temperature of the CTS.

CTS off vehicle

19 Place the CTS in a suitable container of water, and measure the temperature of the water.

20 Measure the resistance of the CTS, and check the resistance against the temperature chart.

21 Heat the water, periodically measuring the water temperature and the CTS resistance, and comparing the resistance with the temperature chart.

13 Coolant temperature sensor (CTS) - PTC type

1 The PTC type coolant temperature sensor is fitted to a small number of systems (mainly Renault vehicles). A positive temperature coefficient (PTC) sensor is a thermistor in which the resistance rises as the temperature rises.

2 The general method of testing is similar to the NTC type previously described; with reference to the values in the CTS (PTC) resistance and voltage table.

CTS resistance and voltage table (typical PTC type)

Temp (°C)	Resistance (ohms)	Volts
0	254 to 266	0.5
20	283 to 297	0.6 to 0.8
80	383 to 397	1.0 to 1.2
–	Open-circuit	5.0 ± 0.1
–	Short to earth	zero

14 Cylinder identification (CID) - inductive sensor

1 The inductive phase sensor which identifies the cylinders for sequential injection operation may be fitted inside the distributor or mounted upon the camshaft.

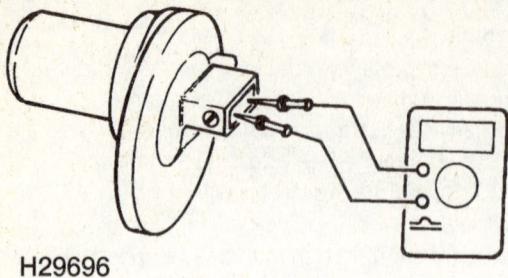

H29696

4.15 An ohmmeter is connected between the two terminals to check the resistance of the inductive phase sensor (CID)

2 Measure the CID resistance *(see illustration 4.15)* and compare to specifications for the vehicle under test. Typical CID resistance is in the range 200 to 900 ohms.

3 Detach the CID or ECM multi-plug.

> **!** *Warning: Refer to Warning No 3 (in the Reference Section at the end of this book) before disconnecting the ECM multi-plug.*

4 Connect an AC voltmeter between the two terminals at the CID or at the corresponding multi-plug terminals at the ECM. **Note:** *Better results are usually obtained by probing the + terminal, although the signal can often be obtained upon the CID earth return.*

5 Crank the engine. A minimum AC RMS voltage of about 0.40 volts should be obtained.

6 Reconnect the CID or ECM multi-plug.

7 Backprobe the CID signal and earth terminals.

8 Start the engine and allow it to idle. A minimum AC RMS voltage of about 0.75 volts should be obtained.

4.16 Hall-effect phase sensor (CID) - multi-plug disconnected

15 Cylinder identification - Hall-effect sensor

1 The Hall-effect phase sensor which identifies the cylinders for sequential injection operation may be fitted inside the distributor or mounted upon the camshaft. The following procedures describe how to test the distributor-located sensor. Testing the camshaft-located type will follow similar lines.

2 Connect the voltmeter negative or dwell meter probe to an engine earth.

3 Identify the supply, signal and earth terminals. The terminals may be marked as follows:

- 0 *Output*
- + *Signal*
- - *Earth*

4 Connect the voltmeter positive or dwell meter probe to the wire attached to the HES signal terminal *(see illustration 4.16)*. **Note:** *The multi-plug must be connected.*

5 Allow the engine to idle. An average voltage of approximately 2.5 volts or an approximate duty cycle of 50% should be obtained

Signal voltage or duty cycle signal not available

6 Stop the engine.

7 Remove the distributor cap.

8 HES multi-plug connected, ignition on.

9 Voltmeter positive probe connected to the signal terminal.

10 Turn the engine over slowly. As the trigger vane cut-out space moves in and out of the air gap, the voltage should alternate between 5.0 volts and zero volts.

Signal voltage not available

11 Disconnect the HES multi-plug at the distributor.

12 Probe output terminal 2 (O) of the harness multi-plug with the voltmeter positive probe.

13 If there is no voltage from the ECM to terminal 2, check for continuity of the signal wiring between the HES and the ECM.

14 Recheck for voltage at the ECM terminal.

15 If no voltage is available at the ECM, check all voltage supplies and earth connections to the ECM. If the voltage supplies and earth connections are satisfactory, the ECM is suspect.

16 Check the voltage supply (5.0 volts) at HES terminal number 1 (+). If the supply is unsatisfactory, check for continuity of the wiring between the HES and the ECM.

17 Check the earth connection at HES terminal number 3 (–).

18 If the voltage supply and earth are satisfactory, the HES in the distributor is suspect.

16 Cylinder identification and primary trigger - phase sensor faults

1 The timing of the phase sensor and the primary trigger is particularly important in sequential fuel injected vehicles. If the phasing is out of synchronisation, at best the engine may sink into LOS mode with loss of power and increased emissions. At worst, the engine may fail to start.

2 Reasons for phasing errors:

  a) *Incorrectly adjusted distributor. Only if the distributor is adjustable.*

  b) *Slack timing belt (very common fault).*

  c) *Misalignment of timing belt.*

17 Exhaust gas recirculation system (EGR)

1 The main components in an EGR system are the EGR valve, control solenoid and lift sensor (some systems) and vacuum hoses (where fitted) *(see illustration 4.17)*. The components could be tested as follows.

2 Check the vacuum hoses for condition.

3 Warm the engine to normal operating temperature (this condition must exist for all tests).

Control solenoid tests

4 Start the engine and allow it to idle.

5 Disconnect the multi-plug from the EGR control solenoid.

6 Attach a temporary jumper wire from the battery positive terminal to the supply terminal on the solenoid valve.

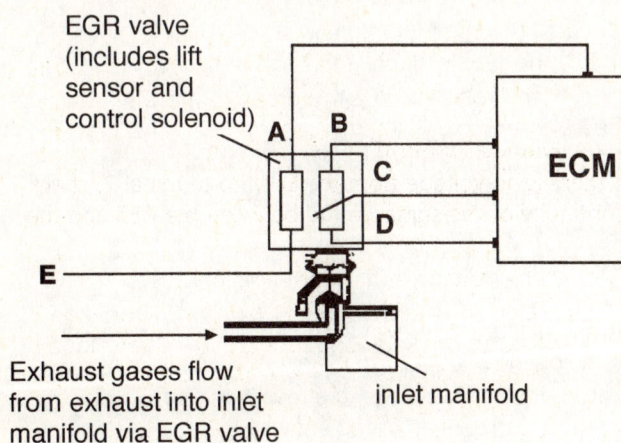

EGR valve (includes lift sensor and control solenoid)

E

ECM

Exhaust gases flow from exhaust into inlet manifold via EGR valve

inlet manifold

4.17 EGR valve including lift sensor

  A   Control solenoid switched earth
  B   Reference voltage supply to lift sensor
  C   Lift sensor signal
  D   Lift sensor earth return through the ECM
  E   Supply from the relay or ignition

7 Attach a temporary jumper wire from the solenoid valve earth terminal to an earth on the engine.

8 The EGR valve should actuate and the idle quality deteriorate. If not, the EGR valve or solenoid are suspect.

9 Check for voltage to the control solenoid supply terminal.

10 Check continuity of the control solenoid and compare to the vehicle specifications.

EGR sensor tests

11 Backprobe the EGR sensor multi-plug (where possible), or connect a break-out box (BOB) between the ECM multi-plug and the ECM.

12 Connect the voltmeter negative probe to an engine earth, or to the earth return of the EGR sensor.

13 Connect the voltmeter positive probe to the wire attached to the EGR sensor signal terminal.

14 Start the engine and allow it to idle; the EGR signal voltage will be typically 1.2 volts.

15 Disconnect the multi-plug from the EGR control solenoid and attach jumper leads to the control solenoid as described above.

16 The EGR solenoid valve should fully actuate, and the sensor signal voltage should increase to over 4.0 volts. **Note:** *It is very difficult to open the EGR valve so that a smooth output can be obtained from the valve. However, checking the sensor voltage at the fully-closed and fully-open position should allow a judgement on whether the sensor is operating correctly.*

17 Remove the temporary jumper wires from the solenoid, and the sensor signal voltage should decrease.

18 If the EGR sensor signal voltage does not behave as described, refer to the relevant fault condition tests below.

Erratic signal output

19 An erratic output occurs when the voltage output is stepped, or drops to zero or becomes open-circuit and this usually suggests a faulty EGR sensor.

20 Check for a 5.0 volt reference voltage and good earth connection on the other two wires.

Signal or supply voltage at battery voltage level

21 Check for a short to a wire connected to the battery positive (+) terminal.

18 Fuel temperature sensor (FTS) - NTC type

1 The FTS measures the fuel temperature in the fuel rail.

2 The majority of FTSs used in motor vehicles are of the NTC type. A negative temperature coefficient (NTC) sensor is a thermistor in which the resistance decreases (negatively) as the temperature (ie fuel temperature) rises.

3 The general method of testing, and the resistance and voltages, are similar to the NTC type coolant temperature sensor previously described.

4.18 Typical knock sensor

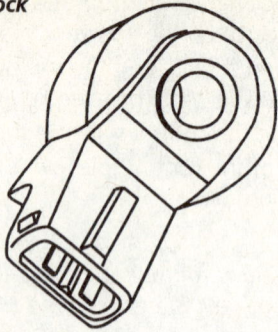

19 Fuel temperature switch (FS) - test procedure

1 The FS operates when the fuel temperature in the fuel rail rises above a pre-determined value.

2 Supply to the FS is usually 12 volts from a switched battery supply.

3 Battery voltage will be available at the earth side of the switch when the temperature is under the switching temperature.

4 Zero voltage will be obtained at the earth side of the switch when the temperature is above the switching temperature.

20 Knock sensor (KS)

1 Attach the probe of an inductive timing light to the HT lead of number 1 cylinder *(see illustration 4.18)*.

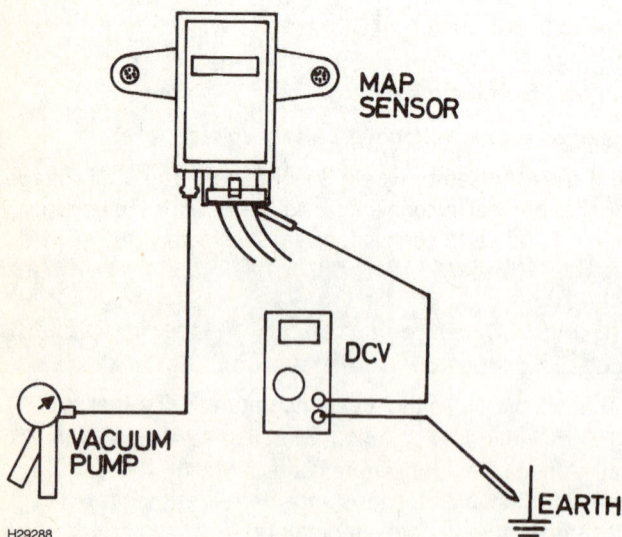

4.19 Using a vacuum pump and a voltmeter to check the MAP sensor signal

2 Connect an AC voltmeter or oscilloscope to the KS terminals

3 Allow the engine to idle.

4 Gently tap the engine block close to number 1 cylinder.

5 The timing should be seen to retard and a small voltage (approximately 1.0 volt) should be displayed upon the voltmeter or oscilloscope.

21 Manifold absolute pressure (MAP) sensor - analogue type

Note: *Where the MAP sensor is located internally in the ECM, voltage tests are not possible.*

1 Use a T-connector to connect a vacuum gauge between the inlet manifold and the MAP sensor.

2 Allow the engine to idle. If the engine vacuum is low (less than 425 to 525 mm Hg), check for the following faults:

   a) A vacuum leak.
   b) A damaged or perished vacuum pipe.
   c) A restricted vacuum connection.
   d) An engine problem, eg. misalignment of the cam belt.
   e) A leaky MAP diaphragm (inside the ECM if the MAP sensor is internal).

3 Disconnect the vacuum gauge and connect a vacuum pump in its place.

4 Use the pump to apply vacuum to the MAP sensor until approximately 560 mmHg is reached.

5 Stop pumping, and the MAP sensor diaphragm should hold pressure for a minimum of 30 seconds at this vacuum setting.

External MAP sensor only

6 Connect the voltmeter negative probe to an engine earth.

7 Identify the supply, signal and earth terminals.

8 Connect the voltmeter positive probe to the wire attached to the MAP sensor signal terminal.

9 Disconnect the vacuum pipe from the MAP sensor.

10 Connect a vacuum pump to the sensor *(see illustration 4.19)*.

11 Switch the ignition on.

12 Compare the ignition on voltage to that specified.

13 Apply vacuum as shown in the table and check for a smooth voltage change.

14 In turbocharged engines, the results will be slightly different to normally aspirated engines.

Erratic signal output

15 An erratic output occurs when the voltage output is stepped, drops to zero or becomes open-circuit. This usually suggests a faulty MAP sensor. In this instance, a new sensor is the only cure.

Voltage table (signal terminal)

16 Checking conditions - engine stopped, vacuum applied with pump.

Vacuum applied	Volts	MAP (bar)
Zero	4.3 to 4.9	1.0 ± 0.1
200 mbar	3.2	0.8
400 mbar	2.2	0.6
500 mbar	1.2 to 2.0	0.5
600 mbar	1.0	0.4

Condition	Volts (app.)	MAP (bar)	Vacuum (bar)
Full-throttle	4.35	1.0 ± 0.1	zero
Ignition on	4.35	1.0 ± 0.1	zero
Idle speed	1.5	0.28 to 0.55	0.72 to 0.45
Deceleration	1.0	0.20 to 0.25	0.80 to 0.75

Turbocharged engines

Condition	Volts (app.)	MAP (bar)	Vacuum (bar)
Full-throttle	2.2	1.0 ± 0.1	zero
Ignition on	2.2	1.0 ± 0.1	zero
Idle speed	0.2 to 0.6	0.28 to 0.55	0.72 to 0.45

Pressure applied	Volts
0.9 bar	4.75

(a test of turbo boost pressure)

Signal voltage not available

17 Check the reference voltage supply (5.0 volts).

18 Check the earth return.

19 If the supply and earth are satisfactory, check for continuity of the signal wiring between the MAP sensor and the ECM.

20 If the supply and/or earth are unsatisfactory, check for continuity of the wiring between the MAP sensor and the ECM.

21 If the MAP sensor wiring is satisfactory, check all voltage supplies and earth connections to the ECM. If the voltage supplies and earth connections are satisfactory, the ECM is suspect.

Signal or supply voltage at battery voltage level

22 Check for a short to a wire connected to the battery positive (+) terminal or a switched supply voltage.

Other checks

23 Check for excessive fuel in the vacuum trap or hose.

24 Check for a faulty vacuum hose or a vacuum leak.

25 Check for mechanical, ignition or a fuel fault resulting in low engine vacuum.

22 Manifold absolute pressure (MAP) sensor - digital type

1 Set the DMM to the volts scale.

2 Switch on the ignition.

3 Identify the supply, signal and earth terminals.

4 Connect the voltmeter positive probe to the wire attached to the MAP sensor signal terminal. An average voltage of approximately 2.5 volts should be obtained. If not, refer to the *"Signal voltage not available"* tests below.

5 Set the meter to the tachometer 4-cylinder scale (all engines).

6 Disconnect the vacuum hose to the MAP sensor.

7 Connect the positive DMM probe to the signal terminal, and connect the negative probe to the earth terminal.

8 An rpm reading of 4500 to 4900 should be obtained.

9 Attach a vacuum pump to the MAP sensor hose connection. During the following tests, the vacuum should hold steady at all of the pressure settings.

Apply 200 mbar - the rpm should drop by 525 ± 120 rpm.
Apply 400 mbar - the rpm should drop by 1008 ± 120 rpm.
Apply 600 mbar - the rpm should drop by 1460 ± 120 rpm.
Apply 800 mbar - the rpm should drop by 1880 ± 120 rpm.

10 Release the pressure, and the measured rpm value should return to the original setting of 4500 to 4900.

11 Renew the MAP sensor if it fails to behave as described.

Signal voltage not available

12 Check the reference voltage supply (5.0 volts).

13 Check the earth return.

14 If the supply and earth are satisfactory, check for continuity of the signal wiring between the MAP sensor and the ECM.

15 If the supply and/or earth are unsatisfactory, check for continuity of the wiring between the MAP sensor and the ECM.

16 If the MAP sensor wiring is satisfactory, check all voltage supplies and earth connections to the ECM. If the voltage supplies and earth connections are satisfactory, the ECM is suspect.

Signal or supply voltage at battery voltage level

17 Check for a short to a wire connected to the battery positive (+) terminal or a switched supply voltage.

Other checks

18 Check for excessive fuel in the vacuum trap or hose.

19 Check for a faulty vacuum hose or a vacuum leak.

20 Check for mechanical, ignition or a fuel fault resulting in low engine vacuum.

4.20 Typical power steering pressure switch (PSPS)

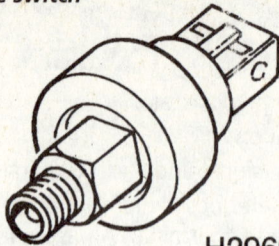

H29697

23 Oil temperature sensor (OTS) - NTC type

1 The majority of OTSs used in motor vehicles are of the NTC type. A negative temperature coefficient (NTC) sensor is a thermistor in which the resistance decreases as the temperature rises.

2 The general method of testing, and the resistance and voltage values, are similar to the NTC type coolant temperature sensor previously described.

24 Power steering pressure switch (PSPS) test procedure

1 The PSPS operates when the steering is turned *(see illustration 4.20)*. The information from the switch is used to increase the engine idle speed, to compensate for the extra load placed on the engine by the power steering pump.

2 Supply to the PSPS is usually made from a switched battery supply or from the ECM.

3 Battery voltage will be available at both the supply and earth side of the switch when the wheels are in the straight-ahead position.

4 Zero voltage will be obtained at the earth side of the switch when the wheels are turned. **Note:** *In some systems, zero voltage will be obtained with the wheels straight-ahead, and battery voltage when the wheels are turned.*

25 Throttle switch (TS)

Note: *The following procedures apply for a typical three-wire throttle switch. However, in some three-wire TS applications, the idle switch alone or the full-load switch alone may be connected. Also in other applications, separate idle and full-load switches may be provided. On some Rover models, the TS is located on the accelerator pedal. Whatever the arrangement, the basic test procedure will be similar for all types.*

Voltage tests

1 The three wires to the TS multi-plug connector are earth, idle signal and full-load signal.

2 Connect the voltmeter negative probe to an engine earth.

3 Identify the idle signal, full-load signal and earth terminals.

4 Switch on the ignition (engine not running).

5 Connect the voltmeter positive probe to the wire attached to the TS idle signal terminal.

6 Zero volts should be obtained. If the meter indicates 5.0 volts, loosen the screws and adjust the TS so that zero volts is obtained. **Note:** *On some vehicles, the throttle switch may not be adjustable.*

Zero volts cannot be obtained (throttle closed)

7 Check the throttle valve position.

8 Check the TS earth connection.

9 Carry out the TS resistance tests (below).

10 If the voltage is satisfactory with the throttle closed, crack open the throttle - the switch should "click" and the voltage should rise to 5.0 volts.

Voltage low or non-existent (throttle open)

11 Check that the TS idle terminal is not shorted to earth.

12 Disconnect the TS multi-plug and check for 5.0 volts at the multi-plug idle terminal. If there is no voltage, proceed with the following checks.

13 Check for continuity of the idle signal wiring between the TS and the ECM.

14 If the TS wiring is satisfactory, check all voltage supplies and earth connections to the ECM. If the voltage supplies and earth connections are satisfactory, the ECM is suspect.

Voltage satisfactory (throttle open)

15 Reconnect the voltmeter probe to the wire attached to the TS full-load signal terminal.

16 With the throttle in either the idle or just open positions, the meter should indicate 5.0 volts.

Voltage low or non-existent (throttle closed or just open)

17 Check the earth connection.

18 Check that the TS full-load terminal is not shorted to earth.

19 Disconnect the TS multi-plug, and check for 5.0 volts at the full-load multi-plug terminal. If there is no voltage, proceed with the following checks

20 Check for continuity of the full-load signal wiring between the TS and the ECM.

21 If the TS wiring is satisfactory, check all voltage supplies and earth connections to the ECM. If the voltage supplies and earth connections are satisfactory, the ECM is suspect.

Voltage satisfactory (throttle closed or just open)

22 Fully open the throttle. As the throttle angle becomes greater than 72°, the voltage should drop to zero volts. If the voltage does not drop, the throttle switch is suspect.

Resistance tests

23 Disconnect the TS multi-plug.

24 Connect an ohmmeter between the TS earth terminal (sometimes marked 18) and terminal 2 (idle contact).

25 With the throttle switch closed, the ohmmeter should indicate very close to zero ohms.

26 Slowly open the throttle. As the TS cracks open, it should "click" - the resistance should become open-circuit and remain so, even as the throttle is opened fully.

27 Reconnect the ohmmeter between the earth terminal (sometimes marked 18) and terminal 3 (full-load contact).

28 With the throttle switch closed, the ohmmeter should indicate an open-circuit.

29 Slowly open the throttle. As the TS cracks open, it should "click" - the resistance should remain open-circuit until the throttle angle becomes greater than 72°, when the resistance should change to continuity of approximately zero ohms.

30 If the TS does not behave as described, and it is not prevented from opening or closing fully by a binding throttle linkage, the TS is suspect.

26 Throttle potentiometer sensor (TPS or "throttle pot")

Voltage tests

1 Connect the voltmeter negative probe to an engine earth.

2 Identify the supply, signal and earth terminals. **Note:** *Although the majority of TPSs are usually three-wire types, some sensors may include additional terminals that function as a throttle switch. If so, test the switch using similar routines to those described for the throttle switch above.*

3 Connect the voltmeter positive probe to the wire attached to the TPS signal terminal *(see illustration 4.21)*.

4 Switch on the ignition (engine stopped). In most systems, a voltage less than 0.7 volts should be obtained.

5 Open and close the throttle several times, and check for a smooth voltage increase to a maximum of 4.0 to 4.5 volts. **Note:** *If a digital voltmeter is used, then it is useful for it to have a bar graph facility. The smoothness of the voltage increase can then be more easily seen.*

Erratic signal output

6 An erratic output occurs when the voltage output is stepped, or drops to zero or becomes open-circuit.

7 When the TPS signal output is erratic, this usually suggests a faulty potentiometer. In this instance, a new or reconditioned TPS is the only cure.

Signal voltage not available

8 Check for the 5.0 volt reference voltage supply at the TPS supply terminal.

9 Check the earth return connection at the TPS earth terminal.

10 If the supply and earth are satisfactory, check for continuity of the signal wiring between the TPS and the ECM.

11 If the supply and/or earth are unsatisfactory, check for continuity of the wiring between the TPS and the ECM.

12 If the TPS wiring is satisfactory, check all voltage supplies and earth connections to the ECM. If the voltage supplies and earth connections are satisfactory, the ECM is suspect.

Signal or supply voltage at battery voltage level

13 Check for a short to a wire connected to the battery positive (+) terminal or a switched supply voltage.

Resistance tests

14 Connect an ohmmeter between the TPS signal terminal and supply terminal or the TPS signal terminal and earth terminal.

15 Open and close the throttle several times, and check for a smooth resistance change. If the TPS resistance becomes open or short-circuit, a fault is revealed.

16 We have not provided resistance specifications for the throttle pots described in this book. For one thing, many vehicle manufacturers do not publish test values. Also, it is less important that the resistance of the TPS remains within

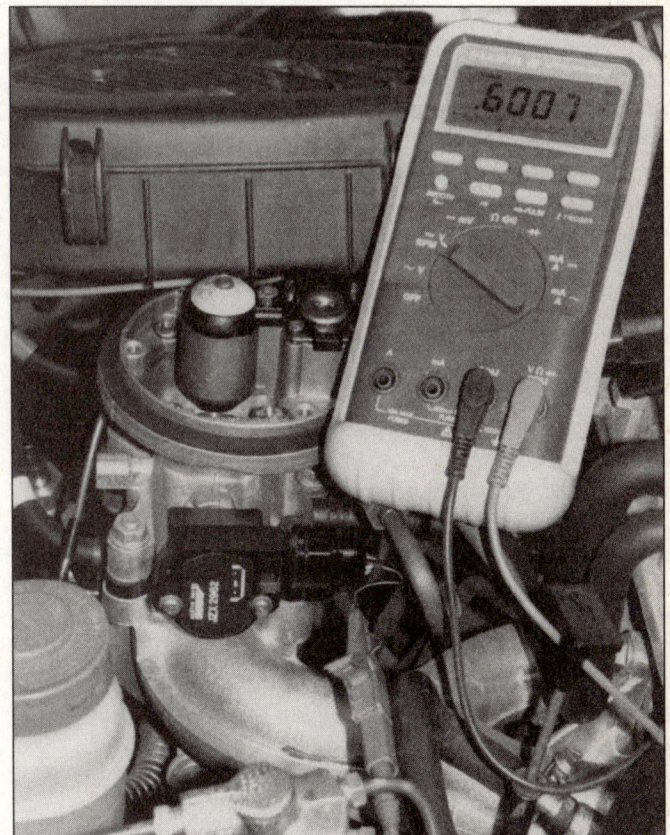

4.21 Throttle pot output being measured with the aid of a voltmeter. Here a paper clip has been inserted into the rear of the sensor to allow voltmeter connection

4.22 Typical vehicle speed sensor wiring

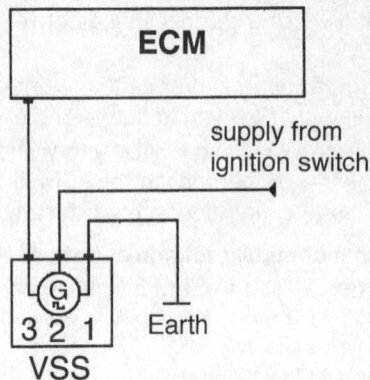

4.23 Vehicle speed sensor (GM type)

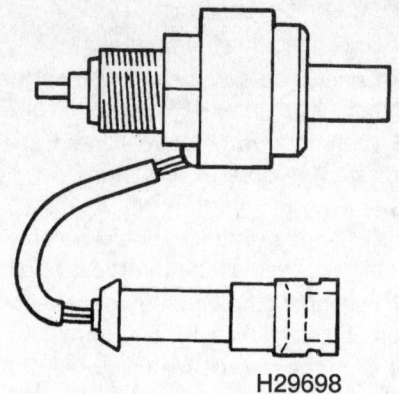

H29698

arbitrary values, than the operation is correct (varies consistently with throttle operation).

17 Connect an ohmmeter between the TPS earth terminal and supply terminal. A stable resistance should be obtained.

18 Renew the TPS if the resistance is open-circuit or shorted to earth.

Mono-Motronic and Mono-Jetronic

19 Dual throttle position sensors are usually provided in these systems. By using two signals, the ECM is able to more accurately calculate the engine load and other factors. Specific vehicle data is required to set and test these sensors, although it is possible to check for a smooth output on both signal wires in a similar fashion to other throttle position sensors described above. Typically, the signal from one TPS will range from 0 to 4.0 volts, and the other TPS from 1.0 to 4.5 volts.

27 Vehicle speed sensor (VSS)

Voltage tests

Note: *These test procedures apply to the most common type of VSS that operates upon the Hall-effect principle.*

1 The VSS may be located on the gearbox, on the speedometer drive behind the instrument panel, or on the rear axle.

2 Connect the voltmeter negative or dwell meter probe to an engine earth.

3 Identify the supply, signal and earth terminals *(see illustrations 4.22 and 4.23)*.

4 Connect a voltmeter positive or dwell meter probe to the wire attached to the VSS signal terminal.

5 The drive wheels must rotate for a signal to be generated. This may be accomplished by using one of the two following methods:

a) Push the vehicle forward.

b) Place the vehicle upon a ramp, or jack up the vehicle so that the drive wheels can freely turn.

6 Rotate the wheels by hand so that a duty cycle or voltage can be obtained.

No signal or an erratic duty cycle or voltage

7 With the VSS multi-plug disconnected, and the ignition on.

8 Check the voltage at the signal terminal. A voltage between 8.5 and 10.0 volts should be obtained.

9 Check the voltage supply at the VSS supply terminal. A voltage slightly less than battery voltage should be obtained.

10 Check the VSS earth connection.

Supply and earth voltages satisfactory

11 The VSS is suspect, or the VSS is not being rotated by the speedometer drive (ie. broken cable or gearbox fault).

No signal voltage

12 Check the voltage at the ECM multi-plug terminal.

13 If voltage is satisfactory at the ECM, check the diode in the wire between the ECM and VSS. Also check the continuity of the signal wiring.

14 If no voltage is available at the ECM, check all voltage supplies and earth connections to the ECM. If the voltage supplies and earth connections are satisfactory, the ECM is suspect.

Other types of VSS

15 Apart from the Hall-effect type of vehicle speed sensor, there is also a reed switch type and an inductive type.

Reed switch type

16 The signal output with the drive wheels rotating is essentially that of a square waveform. Switching is from zero to five volts, or from zero to battery voltage. A duty cycle of 40 to 60% may also be obtained.

Inductive type

17 The signal output with the drive wheels rotating is essentially that of an AC waveform. The signal output will vary according to speed of rotation, in a similar fashion to the crank angle sensor described earlier.

Actuator test procedures

28 Carbon filter solenoid valve (CFSV)

1 Identify the supply and signal terminals.

2 Switch the ignition on.

3 Check for battery voltage at the CFSV supply terminal. If there is no voltage, trace the wiring back to the battery, ignition switch or relay output as appropriate.

4 Check the CFSV resistance. Remove the multi-plug and measure the resistance of the CFSV between the two terminals. The resistance of the CFSV is typically 40 ohms.

5 Disconnect the ECM multi-plug.

> ⊘ *Warning: Refer to Warning No 3 (in the Reference Section at the end of this book) before dis-connecting the ECM multi-plug.*

6 Use a jumper lead to very briefly touch the switching pin in the ECM multi-plug to earth.

7 If the CFSV actuates, check the ECM main voltage supplies and earths. If tests reveal no fault, the ECM is suspect.

8 If the CFSV does not actuate, check for continuity of wiring between the CFSV and the ECM switching pin.

9 On some vehicles, it is possible to obtain a duty cycle reading on the signal terminal. The engine will need to be at normal operating temperature and the engine speed raised above idle speed.

29 Idle speed control

Operation check

1 Allow the engine to idle.

2 Check that the idle speed lies within its operating limits.

3 Load the system by switching on the headlights, heated rear window and heater fan. The idle speed should barely change.

4 If possible, squeeze one of the air hoses. The idle speed should surge and then return too normal *(see illustration 4.24)*.

5 If the idle condition meets the above criteria, it is unlikely to be at fault.

6 Faults in one or more of the items on the following list will adversely affect idle integrity, and could bring about the generation of idle related fault codes. These items should be checked before attempting diagnosis of the idle speed control valve (ISCV) or stepper motor.

a) Engine mechanical fault.
b) Incorrect ignition timing.
c) An induction vacuum leak.
d) Incorrect CO level.

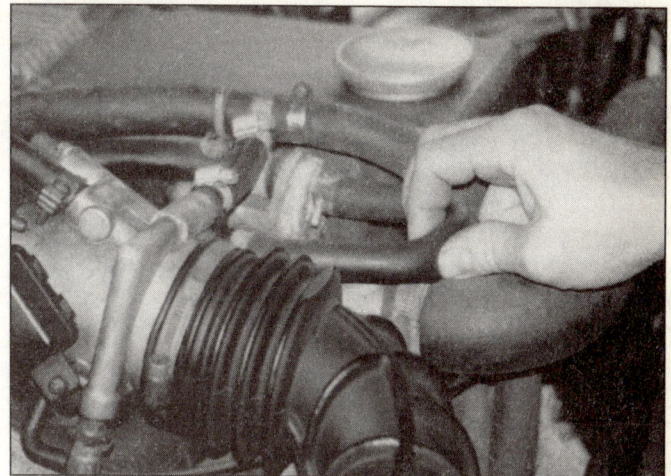

4.24 Squeeze an idle air hose while the engine is running at idle speed to check idle speed control valve (ISCV) response

e) Clogged air filter.
f) An incorrectly-adjusted throttle valve.
g) Carbon-fouled throttle plate.
h) An incorrectly-adjusted throttle switch or throttle pot.

ISCV test procedure (two-wire)

7 A voltmeter and/or dwell meter are suitable instruments for testing the two-wire ISCV in most systems. **Note:** *A dwell meter will not give good results when connected to Ford systems - a voltmeter or oscilloscope is a better choice.*

8 Connect the negative probe to an engine earth.

9 Connect the voltmeter positive or dwell meter probe to the wire attached to the ISCV signal terminal.

10 Start the engine and allow it to idle.

11 With the engine hot, a varying voltage between 7.0 to 9.0 volts, a duty cycle of 40 to 44%, and a frequency of 110 are likely to be obtained *(see illustration 4.25)*.

4.25 Backprobing for a typical dwell at the ISCV, engine at idle speed

12 When the engine is cold or placed under load, the voltage will decrease and the duty cycle will increase. Frequency is likely to remain stable for most idle control valves (the frequency will usually alter in Ford valves). **Note:** *The reading on a digital voltmeter will indicate the average voltage.*

13 Load the engine by switching on the headlights, heated rear window and heater fan. The average voltage will decrease and the duty cycle will increase. The frequency of pulse should remain constant.

14 If an air leak or another fault is present resulting in more air bypassing the throttle, the ISCV duty cycle will be lower than normal as the ECM pulses the ISCV less open.

15 When more load is placed upon the engine, the ECM pulses the ISCV more open (larger duty cycle) to increase the idle speed.

16 In addition, if the engine is mechanically unsound or the throttle valve is dirty, the ECM may pulse the ISCV more open to increase the idle speed. This may result in an uneven idle and a larger than normal duty cycle.

ISCV signal not available

17 Check the ISCV resistance. Typically, a resistance of 8 to 16 ohms should be obtained.

18 With the ignition on, check for battery voltage at the supply terminal. If there is no voltage, trace the wiring back to the main relay or ignition switch as appropriate.

19 Disconnect the ISCV multi-plug.

20 With the ignition on, use a jumper lead to very briefly touch the actuator pin in the ISCV multi-plug to earth.

21 If the ISCV actuates, check the ECM main voltage supplies and earths. If testing reveals no fault, the ECM is suspect.

22 If the ISCV does not actuate, check for continuity of wiring between the ISCV multi-plug and the ECM.

ISCV test procedure (Bosch three-wire)

23 A voltmeter and a dwell meter are suitable instruments for testing the Bosch three-wire ISCV.

24 Connect the voltmeter negative or dwell meter probe to an engine earth.

25 Connect the voltmeter positive or dwell meter probe to the wire attached to one of the two ISCV signal terminals.

26 Start the engine and allow it to idle.

27 When the engine is hot, a varying voltage or a duty cycle of either approximately 31% or 69% will be obtained. The duty cycle obtained will depend upon which terminal the instrument is connected.

28 When the engine is cold or placed under load, the voltage will decrease and the duty cycle will increase. **Note:** *The reading on a digital voltmeter will indicate the average voltage.*

29 Load the engine by switching on the headlights, heated rear window and heater fan. The average voltage will decrease and the duty cycle will increase.

30 If an air leak or another fault is present resulting in more air bypassing the throttle, the ISCV duty cycle will be lower than normal as the ECM pulses the ISCV less open.

31 When more load is placed upon the engine, the ECM pulses the ISCV more open (larger duty cycle) to increase the idle speed.

32 In addition, if the engine is mechanically unsound or the throttle valve is dirty, the ECM may pulse the ISCV more open to increase the idle speed. This may result in an uneven idle and a larger than normal duty cycle.

33 Switch the voltmeter positive or dwell meter probe to the wire attached to the other one of the two ISCV signal terminals.

34 With the engine hot, a varying voltage or a duty cycle of either approximately 31% or 69% will be obtained. The duty cycle obtained will depend upon which terminal the instrument is connected.

ISCV signal not available

35 Check the ISCV resistance (see below).

36 With the ignition on, check for battery voltage at the supply terminal.

37 If there is no voltage, trace the wiring back to the main relay or ignition switch as appropriate.

38 Disconnect the ISCV multi-plug.

39 Switch on the ignition. Use a jumper lead to very briefly touch one of the two actuator pins in the ISCV multi-plug to earth.

40 If the ISCV actuates, check the ECM main voltage supplies and earths. If testing reveals no fault, the ECM is suspect.

41 If the ISCV does not actuate, check for continuity of wiring between the ISCV multi-plug and the ECM.

42 Switch the jumper lead to very briefly touch the other ISCV actuator pin in the ISCV multi-plug to earth. Evaluate the results as in paragraphs 40 and 41 above.

ISCV resistance (three-wire)

43 Remove the ISCV multi-plug.

44 Connect an ohmmeter between the centre terminal and one of the outer terminals. A resistance of 20 ohms should be obtained.

45 Reconnect the ohmmeter between the centre terminal and the other outer ISCV terminal. A resistance of 20 ohms should be obtained.

46 Reconnect the ohmmeter between the two outer ISCV terminals. A resistance of 20 ohms should be obtained.

Stepper motors

47 A number of different types of stepper motor are used in motor vehicles. Specific test procedures for a number of popular types are detailed in the Haynes companion volume *"Automotive Engine Management and Fuel Injection Systems Manual"*.

48 A switch is sometimes incorporated into the stepper motor assembly. Refer to the throttle switch tests for a general description of earth and supply tests. Idle switch operation is particularly important for good idle quality. If the ECM does not recognise the idle condition, idle control cannot be implemented.

49 The typical stepper motor employs two motor windings. The ECM positions the stepper motor by energising the windings in one direction and then the reverse. A voltmeter or oscilloscope could be used to test for a stepper motor signal. However, although a signal can usually be obtained on all of the motor terminals, the signal is fleeting and will only be generated as the motor winding is actuated.

50 Check the resistance of both windings and compare to the vehicle specifications. Values are usually under 100 ohms.

VW/Audi idle control motors

51 The type of control motor fitted to many current VW/Audi vehicles incorporates a reversible stepper motor winding, a Hall sensor that signals the stepper motor position, a TPS, and an idle switch. An 8-terminal multi-plug connects the motor to the wiring loom. The component parts that make up the control motor can be tested by referring to the test procedures described under the headings for individual components.

30 Multi-point injection system (MPi) fuel injectors

1 Check for corrosion in the connection plugs between the relay and the injector, and the ECM and the injector. Corrosion in connection plugs is a common reason for poor injector performance.

2 Connect the dwell meter negative probe to an engine earth.

3 Identify the supply and signal terminals. **Note:** *An injector dwell reading will only be obtained upon the signal terminal which is the wire connecting the injector to the ECM. If you cannot obtain a reading, reconnect the probe to the other terminal and retry.*

4 Connect the dwell meter positive probe to the wire attached to the injector signal terminal.

5 Although the following tests are accomplished with the aid of a basic dwell meter, an oscilloscope is a more suitable instrument for analysing the signals generated by the electronic fuel injector circuits.

6 Initially, the probe can be connected to the signal terminal of any one of the injectors.

Current-controlled or peak-and-hold injection circuits (dwell meter)

7 When the injector is of the current-controlled kind, very few dwell meters may be capable of registering the second stage of the pulse duration. The meter may only register the switch-on circuit of approximately 1.0 or 2.0%. This means that the injector duty cycle reading will be inaccurate and not representative of the total pulse width seen in the circuit. Only a small number of DMMs can actually measure this circuit satisfactorily.

Engine non-runner test procedures

8 Crank the engine.

9 A duty cycle reading (injector duty cycle) of approximately 5 to 10% should be obtained. If the dwell meter can measure the value in milliseconds, this could be even more useful.

Good injector signal

10 Check for an injector pulse on the other injectors.

11 If the injector signal is satisfactory and if the primary ignition signal is also providing an acceptable signal, the fault is unlikely to be related to the ECM.

Poor or no injector signal on one or more injectors

Note: *In some Motronic systems, the frequency of injection increases for several seconds during initial cranking.*

12 Check the fuel pressure and fuel flow.

13 Check the primary trigger (crank angle sensor or Hall-effect sensor) for a good signal.

14 Check the voltage at the signal terminal of the injector multi-plug. Battery voltage should be obtained.

15 If there is no voltage, check the injector resistance and the injector voltage supply.

16 Disconnect the ECM multi-plug.

! *Warning: Refer to Warning No 3 (in the Reference Section at the end of this book) before disconnecting the ECM multi-plug.*

17 Switch on the ignition.

18 Use a jumper lead to very briefly touch each one of the injector actuator pins in the ECM multi-plug to earth *(see illustration 4.26)*.

19 If the injector actuates, check the ECM main voltage supplies and earth's. If tests reveal no fault, the ECM is suspect.

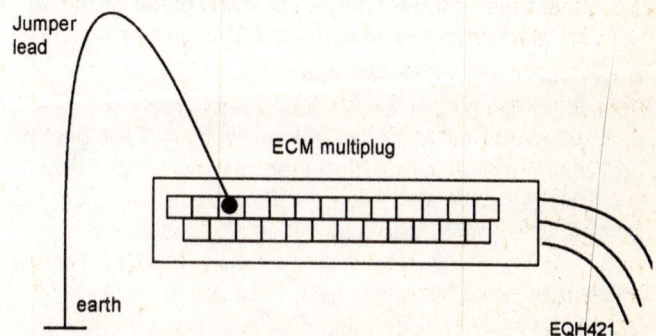

Jumper lead

ECM multiplug

earth

EQH421

4.26 Using a jumper lead to very briefly touch an injector actuator pin in the ECM multi-plug to earth

20 If the injector does not actuate, check for battery voltage at the ECM pin. If voltage is present, the injector is suspect. If there is no voltage, check for continuity of wiring between the injector multi-plugs and the ECM multi-plug.

21 If the injector circuit is banked or sequential, individually check each connection to the ECM.

Duty cycle too long or too short

22 Check the coolant temperature sensor, then check the airflow sensor or MAP sensor. **Note:** *If the ECM has entered LOS due to a fault in one of the sensors, the engine may generally behave quite well whilst the engine is hot, but may be difficult to start when cold.*

Engine running tests

23 Run the engine at various speeds. Record the duty cycle, and compare to the approximate values in the following table. When the engine is cold, the values will slightly increase.

Engine speed	Duty cycle
Idle speed	*3 to 6%*
2000 rpm	*7 to 14%*
3000 rpm	*11 to 16%*
Slow throttle increase	*As above*
Rapid throttle increase	*20% or more*
Deceleration*	*Zero*

*Raise the engine speed to approximately 3000 rpm and release the throttle

24 Evaluate the results obtained as follows:

  a) *The duty cycle in % should increase in value as the engine rpm is raised.*

  b) *Under rapid acceleration, the duty cycle should show a great increase in value.*

  c) *Under deceleration, when the engine is hot, the duty cycle should drop to zero (digital meter) and reappear as the engine speed sinks below approximately 1200 rpm.*

  d) *Where the meter does not drop to zero, check the throttle valve for correct adjustment and the TPS or TS for correct operation.*

  e) *Noise from the injectors should also temporarily disappear as the cut-off operates.*

  f) *Note that a slow-responding digital meter may not show the drop to zero on deceleration.*

Duty cycle too long or too short

25 Check the coolant temperature sensor, then check the airflow sensor or MAP sensor. **Note:** *If the ECM has entered LOS due to a fault in one of the sensors, the engine may generally behave quite well whilst the engine is hot, but may be difficult to start when cold.*

Injector resistance tests

26 Remove each injector multi-plug and measure the resistance of the injector between the two terminals. On current-controlled injectors, the resistance will typically be 4 ohms; on most other systems, typically 16 ohms.

27 When dealing with parallel injector circuits, or banked injectors, one faulty injector can be harder to spot. Assuming that the resistance of one single injector is 16 ohms, the values that are likely to be obtained with various configurations of injector circuit are as follows:

Four injectors in bank

Resistance (ohms)	Condition
4 to 5	*All injectors ok*
5 to 6	*One injector suspect*
8 to 9	*Two injectors suspect*
16 to 17	*Three injectors suspect*

Three injectors in bank

Resistance (ohms)	Condition
5 to 6	*All injectors ok*
8 to 9	*One injector suspect*
16 to 17	*Two injectors suspect*

Two injectors in bank

Resistance (ohms)	Condition
8 to 9	*Both injectors ok*
16 to 17	*One injector suspect*

31 Single-point injection system (SPi) fuel injector

1 Connect the dwell meter negative probe to an engine earth.

2 Identify the supply and signal terminals.

3 Connect the dwell meter positive probe to the wire attached to the Injector signal terminal. **Note:** *The majority of SPi systems utilise current control, and the average dwell meter will not accurately measure this kind of injection signal. An oscilloscope is therefore recommended for signal tests on the majority of SPi systems.*

Engine non-runner test procedures

4 Crank the engine.

5 A duty cycle reading (injector duty cycle) of some description should be obtained. If the dwell meter can measure the full pulse width value in milliseconds, this could be even more useful. If a signal is obtained, this at least indicates that the ECM is capable of switching the injection circuit. However, it does not prove that the signal is totally satisfactory.

Good injector signal

6 If the injector signal is satisfactory and the primary ignition signal is also acceptable, the fault is unlikely to be related to the ECM.

Poor or no injector signal

7 Check the fuel pressure and fuel flow.

8 Check the crank angle sensor, Hall-effect sensor or other primary trigger for a good signal.

9 Check the voltage at the signal terminal of the injector multi-plug. Battery voltage should be obtained. If there is no voltage:

a) *Check the injector resistance.*
b) *Check the ballast resistor resistance (where fitted).*
c) *Check for continuity of wiring between the injector multi-plug and the ECM multi-plug.*
d) *Check the voltage supply to the injector.*

10 Disconnect the ECM multi-plug.

Warning: Refer to Warning No 3 (in the Reference Section at the end of this book) before disconnecting the ECM multi-plug.

11 Switch on the ignition.

12 Use a jumper lead to very briefly touch the injector actuator pin in the ECM multi-plug to earth *(refer to illustration 4.26)*.

13 If the injector actuates, check the ECM main voltage supplies and earths. If testing reveals no fault, the ECM is suspect.

14 If the injector does not actuate, check for battery voltage at the ECM pin. If voltage is present, the injector is suspect. If there is no voltage, check for continuity of wiring between the injector multi-plugs and the ECM multi-plug.

Pulse width too long or too short (if an accurate measurement can be made)

15 Check the coolant temperature sensor and the MAP sensor. **Note:** *If the ECM has entered LOS due to a fault in one of the sensors, the engine may generally behave quite well whilst the engine is hot, but may be difficult to start when cold.*

Engine running tests

16 Please refer to the multi-point fuel injection (MPi) section above which describes test procedures applicable to checking both MPi and SPi operation in a running engine.

Resistance tests

17 Remove the injector multi-plug *(see illustration 4.27)* and measure the resistance of the injector between the two terminals. The resistance value for most single-point injectors is less than 2 ohms, but the specifications for the vehicle under test should be consulted.

18 Where a ballast resistor is fitted: Remove the resistor multi-plug and measure the resistance of the ballast resistor between the two terminals. Refer to the particular specifications for the vehicle under test.

32   Variable induction solenoid (VIS)

General information

1 Better response can be obtained from the engine under various operating conditions by utilising a secondary throttle valve to vary the volume of air flowing through the inlet manifold. The ECM actuates the VIS, which in turn actuates the secondary throttle valve *(see illustration 4.28)*.

Testing

2 Check the vacuum hoses for condition.

3 Disconnect the multi-plug from the VIS.

4 Attach a temporary jumper wire from the battery positive terminal to the supply terminal on the solenoid valve.

5 Attach a temporary jumper wire from the solenoid valve earth terminal to an earth on the engine.

6 The VIS valve and the secondary throttle should actuate. If not, the solenoid and/or throttle mechanism is suspect.

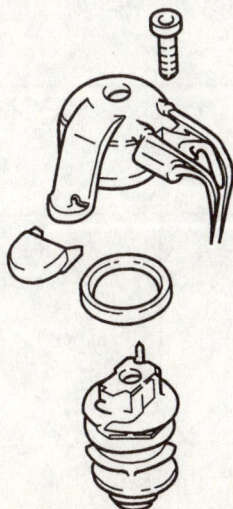

4.27 Single-point injector

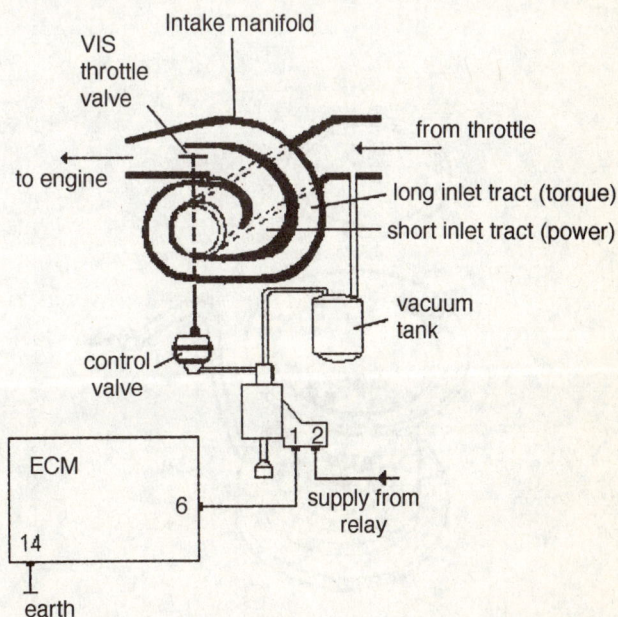

4.28 Typical variable induction system (VIS) wiring and components

7 Check for supply voltage to the control solenoid multi-plug.

8 Check the continuity of the control solenoid.

9 Check the continuity of wiring from the control solenoid to the ECM.

10 If all wiring and components are satisfactory, the ECM is suspect.

33 Throttle body heater and manifold heater

Quick check

1 Start the engine from cold and feel the area around the throttle body or inlet manifold (as appropriate). If the heater is working, this area should become very hot quite quickly. Take care not to burn your fingers!

Throttle body heater and inlet manifold heater tests

2 Allow the engine to idle.

3 Attach the voltmeter negative probe to an earth.

4 Attach the voltmeter positive probe to the heater supply connector *(see illustration 4.29)*; battery voltage should be obtained.

5 If there is no voltage supply, check the throttle body heater supply. Check the continuity of the wiring between the relay and the heater.

6 If there is battery voltage available, but the heater does not operate, check the heater resistance and the heater earth.

4.29 Typical inlet manifold heater

34 Variable valve timing control solenoid (VVTCS)

General information

1 Better response can be obtained from the engine under various operating conditions by utilising a control solenoid to vary the valve timing according to engine efficiency. The ECM actuates the VVTCS, which in turn actuates the valve timing. A number of different methods are used to vary the valve timing, but the control method will be similar to the method described.

Testing

2 Check the vacuum hoses for condition (where used).

3 Disconnect the multi-plug from the VVTCS.

4 Attach a temporary jumper wire from the battery positive terminal to the supply terminal on the solenoid valve.

5 Attach a temporary jumper wire from the solenoid valve earth terminal to an earth on the engine.

6 The solenoid valve should actuate. If not, the solenoid is suspect.

7 Check for supply voltage to the control solenoid multi-plug.

8 Check the continuity of the control solenoid.

9 Check the continuity of wiring from the control solenoid to the ECM.

10 If all wiring and components are satisfactory, the ECM is suspect.

35 Wastegate control solenoid (WCS) - turbocharged engines

1 The two wires to the WCS connector are supply and ECM-actuated earth *(see illustration 4.30)*.

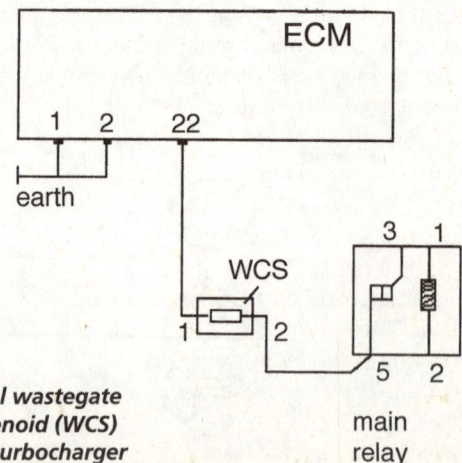

4.30 Typical wastegate control solenoid (WCS) wiring for turbocharger

2 Backprobe the WCS multi-plug.

3 Connect the voltmeter negative probe to an engine earth.

4 Connect the voltmeter positive probe to the wire attached to WCS supply terminal.

5 Switch the ignition on and check for battery voltage.

6 If no voltage is obtained, check for a supply fault.

7 Use an ohmmeter to check the WCS for continuity.

ECM and fuel system test procedures

<table>
<tr><td>36</td><td>ECM faults</td></tr>
</table>

1 When a fault code is generated that suggests an ECM fault, the following procedures should first be followed before the ECM is replaced.

2 Check the ECM earth, voltage supplies and relays as described below.

3 Where possible, try a substitute ECM (known good unit) and check that the fault code does not reappear.

4 If the ECM is replaced, on most modern vehicles, it will need to be re-coded in order for the immobiliser to permit the engine to start. This can only be carried out by a dealer or suitably equipped specialist.

<table>
<tr><td>37</td><td>ECM voltage supplies and earths</td></tr>
</table>

(!) *Warning: Refer to Warning No 3 (in the Reference Section at the end of this book) before disconnecting the ECM multi-plug.*

1 Inspect the ECM multi-plug for corrosion and damage.

2 Check that the terminals in the ECM multi-plug are fully pushed home and making good contact with the ECM pins. **Note:** *Poor contact and corrosion are common reasons for inaccurate signals from the ECM.*

3 Voltage supplies and earths are best measured at the ECM multi-plug. Use one of these test methods:

a) *Peel back the ECM multi-plug insulation (not always possible) and backprobe the ECM multi-plug pins.*

b) *Attach a break-out box (BOB) between the ECM and its multi-plug, and probe the box for voltages.*

c) *Detach the ECM from its multi-plug, and probe for voltages at the multi-plug pins.*

4 Attach the voltmeter negative probe to an engine earth for the ECM connected tests.

5 Identify the various types of connection and the relevant

ECM pins from a wiring diagram for the vehicle in question. **Note:** *Not all of the following connections will be available in any particular system.*

ECM battery supply pin

6 This pin is directly connected to the battery (+) terminal, and a constant voltage should be available at all times, even with the ignition key off.

7 With the ECM multi-plug connected:

a) *Backprobe the relevant ECM pin - nominal battery voltage should be obtained. If voltage is low or non-existent, check the battery condition and supply circuit.*

b) *Start the engine and raise the engine speed to 2500 rpm. Ensure that the voltage rises to between 13.0 and 15.0 volts (refer to vehicle specifications). Check the alternator if the voltage remains low.*

8 With the ECM multi-plug disconnected:

a) *Attach the voltmeter negative probe to an ECM earth pin.*

b) *Attach the voltmeter positive probe to the relevant ECM pin - nominal battery voltage should be obtained. If voltage is low or non-existent, check the battery condition and supply circuit.*

c) *Start the engine and raise the engine speed to 2500 rpm. Ensure that the voltage rises to between 13.0 and 15.0 volts (refer to vehicle specifications). Check the alternator if the voltage remains low.*

ECM cranking supply pin

9 This pin is connected to the ignition switch starter terminal, and a battery voltage will only be available during engine cranking.

10 With the ECM multi-plug connected:

a) *Backprobe the relevant ECM pin.*

b) *Crank the engine on the starter - battery voltage should only be obtained during cranking.*

11 With the ECM multi-plug disconnected:

a) *Attach the voltmeter negative probe to an ECM earth pin.*

b) *Attach the voltmeter positive probe to the relevant ECM pin*

c) *Crank the engine on the starter - battery voltage should only be obtained during cranking.*

12 In either case, if there is no voltage or the voltage is low, check the starter motor or the supply back to the ignition switch starter terminal.

ECM supply from the ignition switch

13 This pin is connected to the ignition switch, and voltage should be available at all times whilst the ignition is switched on or the engine is running.

14 With the ECM multi-plug connected:

a) *Backprobe the relevant ECM pin.*

b) *Switch on the ignition - nominal battery voltage should be obtained. If the voltage is low or non-existent, check the battery condition and supply circuit.*

c) *Start the engine and raise the engine speed to 2500 rpm. Ensure that the voltage rises to between 13.0 and 15.0 volts (refer to vehicle specifications). Check the alternator if the voltage remains low.*

15 With the ECM multi-plug disconnected:

a) *Attach the voltmeter negative probe to an ECM earth pin.*

b) *Attach the voltmeter positive probe to the relevant ECM pin.*

c) *Switch on the ignition - nominal battery voltage should be obtained. If the voltage is low or non-existent, check the battery condition and supply circuit.*

d) *Start the engine and raise the engine speed to 2500 rpm. Ensure that the voltage rises to between 13.0 and 15.0 volts (refer to vehicle specifications). Check the alternator if the voltage remains low.*

ECM supply from the main system relay

16 This pin is connected to the main relay, and voltage should be available at all times whilst the ignition is switched on or the engine is running. This supply may be made to more than one ECM pin.

17 With the ECM multi-plug connected:

a) *Backprobe the relevant ECM pin.*

b) *Switch on the ignition - nominal battery voltage should be obtained. If the voltage is low or non-existent, check the battery condition and supply circuit back to the main system relay. Also check the relay itself.*

c) *Start the engine and raise the engine speed to 2500 rpm. Ensure that the voltage rises to between 13.0 and 15.0 volts (refer to vehicle specifications). Check the alternator if the voltage remains low.*

18 With the ECM multi-plug disconnected:

a) *Attach the voltmeter negative probe to an ECM earth pin.*

b) *Attach the voltmeter positive probe to the relevant ECM pin.*

c) *Switch on the ignition - nominal battery voltage should be obtained. If the voltage is low or non-existent, check the battery condition and supply circuit back to the main system relay. Also check the relay itself.*

d) *Start the engine and raise the engine speed to 2500 rpm. Ensure that the voltage rises to between 13.0 and 15.0 volts (refer to vehicle specifications). Check the alternator if the voltage remains low.*

ECM earth connections

19 With the ECM multi-plug connected:

a) *Switch on the ignition.*

b) *Attach the voltmeter negative probe to an engine earth.*

c) *Attach the voltmeter positive probe to the earth terminal under test - the voltmeter should indicate 0.25 volts maximum.*

20 With the ECM multi-plug disconnected (ignition on or off):

a) *Attach the voltmeter negative probe to the earth terminal under test.*

b) *Attach the voltmeter positive probe to the ECM battery supply or directly to the battery positive terminal - the voltmeter should indicate battery voltage if the earth is satisfactory.*

ECM coding earth pins

Note: *The coding pins are used to code the ECM for certain vehicle configurations (some systems only).*

21 With the ECM multi-plug connected:

a) *Switch on the ignition.*

b) *Attach the voltmeter negative probe to an engine earth*

c) *Attach the voltmeter positive probe to the coding earth pin under test. The voltmeter should indicate 0.25 volts maximum if the coding earth is connected, or 5.0 volts if the coding earth is not connected.*

ECM relay driver pins

22 Depending on system, the ECM may drive the main relay, fuel pump relay or OS relay winding to earth.

23 Unless otherwise stated, the relay(s) and ECM multi-plug should be connected when testing.

Main relay driver

24 Identify the ECM relay driver pins.

25 With the ignition off, backprobe the ECM main relay driver pin with the voltmeter positive probe - battery voltage should be obtained. If there is no voltage, check the relay and the relay wiring.

26 Switch the ignition on - the voltage should drop to near zero. If not, switch the ignition off and disconnect the ECM multi-plug (refer to the Warning at the start of this Section).

27 Connect a temporary jumper lead from the driver pin to earth. If the relay operates, check all voltage supplies and earth connections to the ECM - if the wiring is satisfactory, the ECM is suspect. If the relay does not operate, check the relay and the relay wiring. **Note:** *In some systems, the main relay winding is connected directly to earth.*

Pump relay driver

28 The main relay driver operation (previous test) must be satisfactory before commencing this test, including when the main relay winding is directly connected to earth.

29 With the ignition switched on, backprobe the pump relay driver with the voltmeter positive probe - battery voltage should be obtained. If there is no voltage, check the relay and the relay wiring.

30 Crank or run the engine, and the voltage should drop to near zero. If not, switch off the ignition and disconnect the ECM multi-plug (refer to the Warning at the start of this Section).

31 Connect a temporary jumper lead from pin 3 to earth. If the relay operates, check all voltage supplies and earth connections to the ECM - if the wiring is satisfactory, the ECM is suspect. If the relay does not operate, check the relay and the relay wiring.

32 Essentially, the tests for any additional relay drivers are similar to the pump driver tests.

38   System relay

Quick test

1 If the engine does not run, or a relay-fed component does not function, the following method is a quick way of determining whether the relay is defective.

2 Check for a supply voltage at the component(s) supplied by the relay.

3 If voltage is not available, by-pass the relay (see below) and retest the component for voltage, or attempt to run the engine.

4 If the engine runs or voltage is now available, test the relay (see below) or renew the relay.

5 If voltage is not available, check for supply, earth and output voltages at the relay terminals. Trace supply faults back to the source (*see illustration 4.31*). Check for a blown fuse or fusible link in the supply line.

Common relay terminal connections (standard relays)

Terminal no.	Function
Main relay no. 30	Supply from the battery positive terminal. Constant voltage available.
Main relay no. 86	Supply from the battery positive terminal or the ignition switch. Either constant or switched voltage available.
Main relay no. 85	Relay winding, connected to earth or ECM driver terminal. Voltage almost zero when ignition switched on.
Main relay no. 87	Output terminal supplies voltage to ECM, ISCV, injectors etc. Battery voltage available when ignition switched on.
Pump relay no. 30	Supply from the battery positive terminal. Constant voltage available.
Pump relay no. 86	Supply from the main relay terminal 87 or the ignition switch. Either constant or switched voltage available.
Pump relay no. 85	Relay winding, ECM driver terminal. Voltage less than 1.25 volts when engine cranking or running.
Pump relay no. 87	Output terminal supplies voltage to fuel pump and sometimes OS heater. Battery voltage available when engine cranking or running

Terminal 85a and 85b similar to terminal 85 depending on use. Terminal 87a and 87b similar to terminal 87 depending on use. Dual relays operate in a similar fashion, but may use different numbers.

Some Citroën, Peugeot, Renault and Far Eastern systems (including Japanese manufacturers) may use a numerical system from 1 to 5 or 6, or even up to 15 depending upon the number of pins.

Citroën, Peugeot and Fiat 15-pin relay (typical)

Terminal no.	Function
1	Relay output terminal. Usually connected to fuel pump circuit.
2	Battery supply to relay. Supply from the battery positive terminal. Constant voltage available.
3	Battery supply to relay. Supply from the battery positive terminal. Constant voltage available.
4	Relay output terminal. Components supplied vary depending on system.
5	Relay output terminal. Components supplied vary depending on system.
6	Relay output terminal. Components supplied vary depending on system.
7	Relay earth or driver terminal.
8	Battery supply to relay. Supply from the battery positive terminal. Constant voltage available.
9	Relay output terminal. Usually connected to fuel pump circuit.
10	Relay earth or driver terminal.
11	Battery supply to relay. Supply from the battery positive terminal. Constant voltage available.
12	Unused.
13	Relay output terminal. Components supplied vary depending on system.
14	Supply from the ignition switch. Switched voltage available.
15	Battery supply to relay. Supply from the battery positive terminal. Constant voltage available.

Note: *Although the functions of the above terminal numbers are generally as stated, there are wide differences in how the relay is wired in any particular application.*

Bypassing the relay

6 Remove the relay from the relay multi-plug.

7 Connect a fused (15 amp) jumper lead between the battery supply terminal (usually terminal 30) and the output

4.31 Test the relay by probing for voltages

4.32 Bypass the relay by connecting a jumper lead between terminals 30 and 87, and power will be supplied to the components attached to terminal 87

terminal (usually terminal 87) on the terminal block, where power to the fuel pump or other fuel injection components is required (see illustration 4.32).

8 Do not run the fuel pump continually under this condition, and disconnect the bypass whenever a particular test is completed.

Testing 4-pin relays

9 Remove the relay from the terminal block, and connect an ohmmeter across terminals 30 and 87.

10 Attach a wire between terminal 86 and a 12 volt supply.

11 Attach a wire between terminal 85 and earth.

12 The ohmmeter should indicate continuity.

39 Oxygen sensor (OS)

1 Connect the voltmeter negative probe to an engine earth.

2 Identify the terminals. Depending upon system there could be one, three or four terminals:

    OS heater earth.
    OS heater supply.
    OS signal.
    OS return or earth.

3 Connect the voltmeter positive probe to the wire attached to the OS signal terminal.

4 If an MOT-specification four-gas analyser with Lambda is attached to the exhaust system, the following values should be obtained.

    CO: as vehicle specification.
    HC: less than 50 rpm
    CO_2:   greater than 15.0
    O_2:   less than 2.0
    Lambda: 1.0 ± 0.03

5 Run the engine to operating temperature.

6 Raise the engine speed to 3000 rpm for 30 seconds. This

will raise the temperature of the OS so that switching should occur.

7 Hold the engine speed at a steady 2500 rpm. If the engine is allowed to idle for prolonged periods, the OS will become cool and switching may stop.

8 Check for OS switching. See below for full details and analysis.

OS heater tests

9 Check for battery voltage at the OS heater supply terminal. If there is no voltage, trace the supply wiring back to the relay or ignition switch as appropriate. Also check the OS heater earth connection.

OS signal output

Condition	Voltage
Engine running (hot at 2500 rpm)	200 to 1000 mV
Throttle fully-open	1.0 volt constant
Fuel cut-off	0 volt constant
Switching frequency	1 sec intervals (approximately)

OS switching tests

10 All closed-loop catalyst vehicles monitor the presence of oxygen in the exhaust system, and adjust the injector output to keep the air-fuel ratio (AFR) within Lambda 1.0 ± 0.03. The switching of the OS is fundamental to the proper operation of the injection system. It is vitally important that OS switching occurs correctly.

11 Attach a suitable oscilloscope or voltmeter to the OS switching wire.

12 Increase the engine speed to between 2500 and 3000 rpm for a period of 3 minutes in order to heat the OS and light the catalyst.

13 Allow the engine to fast idle and check for OS switching.

14 The OS voltage should switch high and low from approximately 200 mV to 800 mV at a frequency of 8 to 10 times every 10 seconds (1 Hz) (see illustration 4.33).

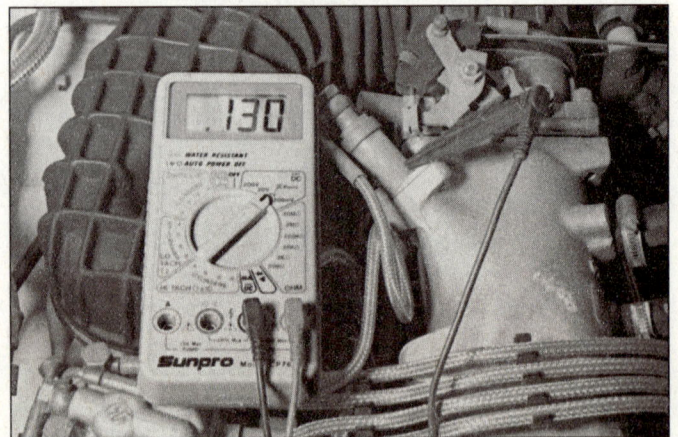

4.33 Oxygen sensor switching voltage low - 0.130 volts is equivalent to 130 millivolts, and indicates a weak mixture

Note: *A digital voltmeter will indicate an average voltage of approximately 450 mV. A sluggish OS may appear to be switching correctly, and may not reveal that the voltage is slightly high. An oscilloscope is the more accurate form of test equipment and will reveal most faults. However, if the voltmeter has a max. and min. function, the range of average switching will be more easily spotted.*

No OS switching

15 Check the Self-Diagnosis system for fault codes. If the OS has failed, the ECM will either go into open-loop, or use a fixed voltage of approximately 0.45 to establish Lambda = 1.0.

16 Check the OS heater circuit (heated OS only, 2, 3 or 4-wire types). Refer to the OS tests in the system specific Chapter.

17 If the OS heater circuit has failed, the OS may never (or only occasionally) reach operating temperature.

18 Snap accelerate the engine - as the AFR goes rich, the OS should give a high voltage.

19 If the exhaust is equipped with an CO inspection port before the cat, measure the CO vol % and HC at the port. If the cat is operating efficiently, the following tests may not be so productive when the CO is measured at the exhaust tailpipe.

20 Increase the engine speed to between 2500 and 3000 rpm for a period of 3 minutes to heat the OS and light the catalyst.

21 Allow the engine to fast idle.

22 Place the system in open-loop by disconnecting the multi-plug to the OS.

Multi-point injection engines

23 Remove the vacuum hose from the fuel pressure regulator, and seal the hose end.

Single-point injection engines

24 Briefly clamp the fuel return line from the pressure regulator back to the fuel tank.

All engines

25 The CO should increase and the OS voltage should switch high.

26 Return the system to closed-loop operation by reconnecting the multi-plug to the OS.

27 The CO should return to normal as the engine responds to the rich mixture. This proves that the OS and ECM can handle a rich mixture.

Multi-point injection engines

28 Refit the vacuum hose to the pressure regulator.

All engines

29 Place the system in open-loop by disconnecting the multi-plug to the OS.

30 Half pull the dipstick or detach a vacuum hose to introduce a vacuum leak.

31 The CO should decrease, and the OS voltage should switch low.

32 Return the system to closed-loop operation by reconnecting the multi-plug to the OS.

33 The CO should return to normal as the engine responds to the lean mixture. This proves that the OS and ECM can handle a weak mixture.

40 Inertia switch

1 The inertia switch is a safety device designed to isolate the fuel pump or cut the engine electrical system during a crash. Heavy deceleration or a thump close to its location can sometimes affect it.

2 Reset the inertia switch by pressing down the reset button.

3 If voltage is still not available at the fuel pump or other protected circuits, continue with the tests.

Checking inertia switch operation

4 Inspect the inertia switch terminal connections for corrosion and damage.

5 Check that the terminal connections are making good contact with the switch.

6 Study a specific wiring diagram to identify the circuit which the inertia switch protects. Typical circuits are:
 a) *Relay output to the fuel pump.*
 b) *Relay supply.*
 c) *Relay driver circuit to the ECM.*

7 Check the supply voltage and earth connections to the inertia switch.

41 Fuel pump and circuit

Fuel pump test procedures

1 Locate the fuel pump. Typically, the fuel pump will either be bolted to the chassis next to the fuel tank, or located inside the fuel tank itself. Access to the in-tank pump is often gained by burrowing under the rear passenger seat or boot floor.

2 Connect the voltmeter negative probe to an earth.

3 Identify the supply and earth terminals.

4 Connect the voltmeter positive probe to the wire attached to the fuel pump supply terminal.

5 Crank the engine or bypass the fuel pump relay - battery voltage should be obtained

Voltage supply not available

 a) *Check the fuel pump fuse (where fitted).*
 b) *Check the fuel pump relay.*
 c) *Check/reset the inertia switch (where fitted).*
 d) *Check continuity of the wiring.*

6 Attach the voltmeter positive probe to the fuel pump earth terminal.

7 Crank the engine or bypass the relay. A voltage of 0.25 volts maximum should be obtained.

Chapter 4

42 Mixture control or adaptive faults

1 A whole variety of different reasons may be responsible for fault codes that indicate mixture control or adaptive problems. Other codes may also be raised that could narrow the field.

Rich mixture or out of limit adaptive function
2 Check for excessive engine blowby, high fuel pressure, coolant temperature sensor, airflow sensor, MAP sensor, evaporative control, EGR system, and for leaking injectors.

Weak mixture or out of limit adaptive function
3 If one cylinder is showing a problem or the engine misfires, check the spark plugs, fuel pressure, idle control, induction system for vacuum leaks, fuel injectors for fouling, exhaust system for leaks, engine compression, valve gear, head gasket and secondary HT system.

Index of vehicles

Index of vehicles

Model	Engine code	Year	System
33, 1.7ie, Sportwagon, 4x4 cat	307.37	1993 to 1995	Bosch Motronic MP3.1
33, Boxer 16V, 4x4 and cat	307.46	1990 to 1995	Bosch Motronic ML4.1
75 3.0i V6 cat	061.20	1987 to 1993	Bosch Motronic ML4.1
145 1.3ie SOHC	AR33501	1994 to 1997	Weber IAW 8F.6B
145 1.6ie SOHC	AR33201	1994 to 1996	Bosch Motronic MP3.1
145 1.6ie SOHC	AR33201	1994 to 1997	GM Multec XM
145 1.7 16V DOHC	AR33401	1994 to 1997	Bosch Motronic M2.10.3
145 2.0 16V DOHC	AR67204	1996 to 1997	Bosch Motronic M2.10.3
146 1.3ie SOHC	AR33501	1994 to 1997	Weber IAW 8F.6B
146 1.6ie SOHC	AR33201	1994 to 1996	GM Multec XM
146 1.7 16V DOHC	AR33401	1994 to 1998	Bosch Motronic M2.10.3
146 2.0 16V DOHC	AR67204	1996 to 2001	Bosch Motronic M2.10.3
155 T-Spark DOHC cat	AR671.03	1992 to 1992	Bosch Motronic 1.7
155 1.8 T-Spark DOHC cat	AR671.02	1992 to 1998	Bosch Motronic 1.7
155 2.0 T-Spark DOHC cat	AR671.02	1992 to 1996	Bosch Motronic 1.7
155 2.5 V6 SOHC cat	AR673.01/03	1992 to 1996	Bosch Motronic 1.7
155 2.0 16V DOHC T-Spark	AR67204	1996 to 1998	Bosch Motronic M2.10.3
164 2.0 T-Spark DOHC	064.20	1990 to 1993	Bosch Motronic ML4.1
164 2.0 T-Spark DOHC cat	064.16	1990 to 1993	Bosch Motronic ML4.1
164 2.0 T-Spark DOHC 16V	AR64.103	1993 to 1998	Bosch Motronic 1.7
164 V6	064.10	1988 to 1993	Bosch Motronic ML4.1
164 V6 and cat	064.12	1988 to 1993	Bosch Motronic ML4.1
164 V6 Cloverleaf cat SOHC	064.301	1990 to 1993	Bosch Motronic ML4.1
164 V6 24V	066.301	1993 to 1995	Bosch Motronic 1.7
164 V6 24V	AR66.302	1995 to 1998	Bosch Motronic 1.7
164 V6 24V Cloverleaf	064.304	1994 to 1998	Bosch Motronic 1.7
164 V6 24V Cloverleaf	AR64.308	1995 to 1998	Bosch Motronic 1.7
GTV 2.0 16V DOHC	AR162.01	1996 to 2001	Bosch Motronic M2.10.3
Spider DOHC cat	015.88	1990 to 1994	Bosch Motronic ML4.1
Spider 2.0 16V DOHC	AR162.01	1996 to 1998	Bosch Motronic M2.10.3

Plus All models equipped with EOBD (approximately January 2001-on)

Chapter 5

Self-Diagnosis

1   Introduction

The engine management systems (EMSs) fitted to Alfa Romeo vehicles are mainly of Bosch origin, and include: Bosch Motronic versions ML4.1, 1.7, 2.10.3/4, MP3.1 and also Multec XM and Weber IAW 8F 6B. All Alfa engine management systems control primary ignition, fuelling and idle functions from within the same control module.

Self-Diagnosis (SD) function

Each electronic control module (ECM) has a self-test capability that continually examines the signals from certain engine sensors and actuators, and compares each signal to a table of programmed values. If the diagnostic software determines that a fault is present, the ECM stores one or more fault codes. Codes will not be stored about components for which a code is not available, or for conditions not covered by the diagnostic software.

Bosch Motronic ML4.1 and 1.7

In these systems, the EMS generates 4-digit flash codes for retrieval by manual methods. When a fault code reader (FCR) is used to retrieve fault codes, the code numbers displayed upon the FCR screen may well be different. Refer to the fault code table at the end of this Chapter, and refer to the columns headed "Flash code" or "FCR code" as appropriate.

All other systems

Alfa-Romeo software does not generate fault code numbers for systems other than Bosch Motronic ML4.1 and 1.7, and the FCR normally displays faults on the FCR screen without reference to a specific code number. Although actual code numbers are not available, faults in one or more of the circuits and component covered by the diagnostic software will cause a fault to be stored.

Limited operating strategy (LOS)

Alfa Romeo systems featured in this Chapter utilise LOS (a function that is commonly called the "limp-home mode"). Once certain faults have been identified (not all faults will initiate LOS), the ECM will implement LOS, and refer to a programmed default value rather than the sensor signal. This enables the vehicle to be safely driven to a workshop/garage for repair or testing. Once the fault has cleared, the ECM will revert to normal operation.

Adaptive or learning capability

Alfa systems also utilise an adaptive function that will modify the basic programmed values for most effective operation during normal running and with due regard to engine wear.

Self-Diagnosis warning light

US models are equipped with a "Check Engine" warning light located within the instrument panel; as demanded by US OBDII regulations. Fault codes indicating failure of emission-related components may be retrieved through the flashing of the light. Only European models equipped with EOBD are equipped with a MIL (Malfunction Warning Light).

2   Self-Diagnosis connector location

Bosch Motronic ML4.1

The two SD connectors are located in the passenger compartment under the facia. The 3-pin multi-plug is provided for dedicated FCR use (see illustration 5.1) and the 4-pin multi-plug is provided for retrieving flash codes.

Bosch Motronic M1.7

The 3-pin SD connector is provided for both dedicated FCR use and for retrieving flash codes, and is normally located under the passenger's side facia close to the ECM.

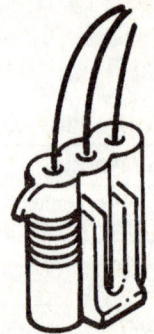

H29338

5.1 Three-pin SD connector for FCR use

Other systems (not EOBD)

The 3-pin SD connector is provided for FCR use alone, and may be located in the engine compartment on the right-hand wing, in the centre console close to the ECM, or under the driver's side or passenger's side facia close to the ECM.

EOBD models

The 16-pin connector is located underneath the steering column - refer to Chapter 38.

3   Retrieving fault codes without a fault code reader (FCR) - flash codes

Note: *During the course of certain test procedures, it is possible for additional fault codes to be generated. Care must be taken that any codes generated during test routines do not mislead diagnosis; all codes must be cleared once testing is complete. Flash code numbers retrieved using manual methods may be different to those code numbers displayed with the aid of an FCR. Refer to the fault code table at the end of this Chapter, in the column headed "Flash code".*

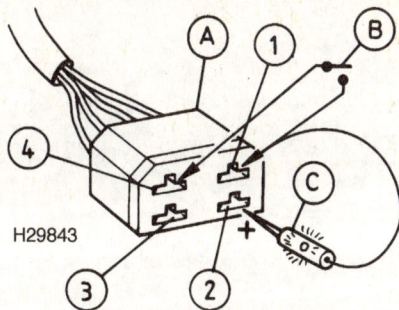

A SD connector
B Accessory switch
C LED diode light

H29843

5.2 Motronic ML4.1 - connect an accessory switch and LED to the 4-pin SD connector in order to retrieve flash codes

Bosch Motronic ML4.1

1 Attach an LED diode light and an accessory switch to the 4-pin SD connector (see illustration 5.2).

2 Switch on the ignition - the LED should illuminate.

3 Close the accessory switch for between 2.5 and 5.0 seconds, and then open the switch. The LED will illuminate for 2.5 seconds and then begin to flash.

4 The 4-digit fault codes are indicated by the flashing of the LED as follows:

  a) The four digits are indicated by four series of flashes.
  b) The first series of flashes indicates the first digit, the second series of flashes indicates the second digit, and so on until all four digits have been flashed.
  c) Each series consists of a number of 1- or 2-second flashes, separated by short pauses. Each integer (whole number) in the range 1 to 9 is represented by a number of 1-second flashes, and each zero is represented by 2-second flashes.
  d) A 2.5-second pause separates each series of flashes.
  e) The code number "1213" is indicated by a 1-second flash, a short pause, two 1-sec-ond flashes, a short pause, one 1-second flash, a short pause and three 1-second flashes. After a 2.5-second pause, the code will be repeated.

5 Count the number of flashes in each series and record the code. Refer to the tables at the end of the Chapter to determine the meaning of the fault code.

6 Each code will be repeated until the accessory switch is once more closed for between 2.5 and 5.0 seconds and then opened. The next code will then be displayed. A maximum of five codes can be stored by ML4.1 at one time.

7 Continue retrieving codes until code 0000 is transmitted. Code 0000 signifies that no more codes are stored.

8 If code 4444 is transmitted, no fault codes are stored.

9 Turn off the ignition and remove the diode light and accessory switch to end fault code retrieval.

Bosch Motronic 1.7

10 Ensure that the throttle potentiometer sensor (TPS) is functional. The following procedures cannot be triggered if the ECM does not receive correct signals from the TPS.

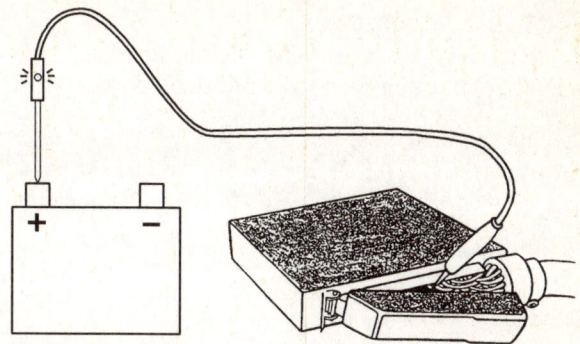

H.21249

5.3 Motronic 1.7 - connect a diode test light between the battery (+) supply and ECM pin number 8 in order to retrieve flash codes

11 Connect a diode test light between the battery (+) supply and ECM pin number 8 as shown (see illustration 5.3).
Note: It will be necessary to detach the back of the ECM multi-plug so that the LED negative probe can backprobe the ECM pin number with the multi-plug connected. Care must be taken that the ECM pins are not damaged by this process, and the LED probe must not short two pins together.

12 Switch on the ignition without starting the engine, and fully depress and release the accelerator pedal five times in succession. This process must be completed with 5.0 seconds of turning on the ignition.

13 The LED will illuminate for 2.5 seconds and then begin to flash.

14 The 4-digit fault codes are indicated by the flashing of the LED as follows:

  a) The four digits are indicated by four series of flashes.
  b) The first series of flashes indicates the first digit, the second series of flashes indicates the second digit and so on until all four digits have been flashed.
  c) Each series consists of a number of 1- or 2-second flashes, separated by short pauses. Each integer (whole number) in the range 1 to 9 is represented by a number of 1-second flashes, and each zero is represented by 2-second flashes.
  d) A 2.5-second pause separates each series of flashes.
  e) The code number "1213" is indicated by a 1-second flash, a short pause, two 1-second flashes, a short pause, one 1-second flash, a short pause and three 1-second flashes. After a 2.5-second pause, the code will be repeated.

15 Count the number of flashes in each series, and record the code. Refer to the tables at the end of the Chapter to determine the meaning of the fault code.

16 Each code will be repeated until the accelerator pedal is fully depressed and released five times in succession within a period of 5.0 seconds. The next code will then be displayed.

17 Continue retrieving codes until code 0000 or 1000 is transmitted. Code 0000 (or 1000) signifies that no more codes are stored.

18 If code 4444 is transmitted, no fault codes are stored.

19 Turn off the ignition and remove the diode light to end fault code retrieval.

All other systems

20 Flash codes are not available. A dedicated fault code reader (FCR) must be used to retrieve fault codes.

4   Clearing fault codes without a fault code reader (FCR)

Bosch Motronic ML4.1

1 Follow the procedure described in Section 3 to retrieve fault codes.
2 When code 0000 is transmitted, close the accessory switch for approximately 10 seconds, and then open the switch. All fault codes are now cleared from the ECM memory.
3 Turn off the ignition and remove the accessory switch.

Bosch Motronic M1.7

4 Follow the procedure described in Section 3 to retrieve fault codes.
5 When code 0000 or 1000 is transmitted, fully depress the accelerator pedal for approximately 10 seconds and then release. All fault codes are now cleared from the ECM memory.
6 Turn off the ignition.

All systems (alternative method)

7 Turn off the ignition and disconnect the battery negative terminal for a period of approximately 5 minutes.
8 Re-connect the battery negative terminal.
Note: *The first drawback to this method is that battery disconnection will initialise all ECM adaptive values. Re-learning the appropriate adaptive values requires starting the engine from cold, and driving at various engine speeds for approximately 20 to 30 minutes. The engine should also be allowed to idle for approximately 10 minutes. The second drawback is that the radio security codes, clock setting and other stored values will be initialised, and these must be re-entered once the battery has been reconnected. Where possible, an FCR should be used for code clearing. On models with EOBD, an FCR must be used for clearing fault codes.*

5   Actuator testing without a fault code reader (FCR)

Bosch Motronic ML4.1 only

1 Attach an LED diode light and an accessory switch to the 4-pin SD connector *(refer to illustration 5.2)*.
2 Close the accessory switch and switch on the ignition.
3 Wait 2.5 to 5.0 seconds and then open the accessory switch. The LED light will flash code number 1411 and the injector circuit will actuate. Audible operation of the injector solenoids should be heard.

> **!** *Warning: The injectors will actuate for as long as the circuit is closed, and there is a real danger of filling the cylinders with petrol. If testing is required for more than 1 second, disconnect the fuel pump supply (or remove the fuel pump fuse) before commencing this test.*

4 Discontinue the injector test by closing the accessory switch once more.
5 Wait 2.5 to 5.0 seconds and then open the accessory switch. The LED will flash code number 1412 and the ISCV circuit will actuate. Audible operation of the idle control solenoid should be heard.
6 Discontinue the ISCV test by closing the accessory switch once more.
7 Wait 2.5 to 5.0 seconds and then open the accessory switch. The LED will flash code number 1414 and the valve timing actuator circuit will actuate (if so equipped). Audible operation of the valve timing control solenoid should be heard.
8 Discontinue the valve timing actuator test by closing the accessory switch once more.
9 Wait 2.5 to 5.0 seconds and then open the accessory switch. The LED will flash code number 1414 and the CFSV circuit will actuate (if so equipped). Audible operation of the carbon filter solenoids should be heard.
10 Discontinue the CFSV circuit test by closing the accessory switch once more.
11 Wait 2.5 to 5.0 seconds and then open the accessory switch. The LED will flash code number 0000 and the actuator tests are completed.
12 Turn off the ignition and remove the diode light and accessory switch to end actuator activation.

All other systems

13 A dedicated fault code reader (FCR) must be used to test the actuators.

6   Self-Diagnosis with a fault code reader (FCR)

Note: *During the course of certain test procedures, it is possible for additional fault codes to be generated. Care must be taken that codes generated during test routines do not mislead diagnosis.*

All Alfa Romeo models

1 Connect an FCR to the SD/diagnostic connector. Use the FCR for the following purposes, in strict compliance with the FCR manufacturer's instructions:
  a) *Retrieving fault codes or displaying faults.*
  b) *Clearing fault codes or faults.*
  c) *Testing actuators.*

2 On Bosch Motronic ML4.1 and 1.7 systems, the code numbers displayed upon the FCR screen may be different to the code numbers retrieved during the manual method described in Section 3. Refer to the fault code table at the end of this Chapter, in the column headed "FCR codes".

3 Codes must always be cleared after component testing, or after repairs involving the removal or replacement of an engine management component.

7   Guide to test procedures

1 Use an FCR to interrogate the ECM for faults or codes (as applicable), or manually gather codes, as described in Section 3 or 6.

Codes stored

2 If one or more fault codes are gathered, refer to the fault code table at the end of this Chapter to determine their meaning.

3 If several codes are gathered, look for a common factor such as a defective earth return or supply.

4 Refer to the component test procedures in Chapter 4, where you will find a means of testing the majority of components and circuits found in the modern EMS.

5 Once the fault has been repaired, clear the codes and run the engine under various conditions to determine if the problem has cleared.

6 Check the ECM for fault codes once more. Repeat the above procedures where codes are still being stored.

7 Refer to Chapter 3 for more information on how to effectively test the engine management system.

No codes stored

8 Where a running problem is experienced, but no codes are stored, the fault is outside of the parameters designed into the SD system. Refer to Chapter 3 for more information on how to effectively test the engine management system.

9 If the problem points to a specific component, refer to the test procedures in Chapter 4, where you will find a means of testing the majority of components and circuits found in the modern EMS.

Fault code table

Bosch Motronic ML4.1 and 1.7

Flash code	FCR code	Description
0000	-	End of fault code output
1000	-	End of fault code output
1211	037	Battery
1212	052	Throttle switch (TS), idle switch
1213	053	Throttle switch (TS), full-load switch
1214	045	Coolant temperature sensor (CTS) or CTS circuit
1215	043	CO adjuster or CO circuit
1216	012	Throttle pot sensor (TPS) or TPS circuit
1221	007	Vane airflow sensor (AFS) or AFS circuit
1222	004	Idle speed control valve (ISCV) or ISCV circuit
1223	010	Oxygen sensor (OS) or OS circuit
1224	028	Oxygen sensor (OS) or OS circuit
1225	044	Air temperature sensor (ATS) or ATS circuit
1226	100	Electronic control module (ECM)
1227	-	Injectors or injector circuit
1228	-	Injectors or injector circuit
1229	-	Air conditioning (A/C) heater control or A/C circuit
1231	031	Vehicle speed signal (VSS) - automatic transmission or VSS circuit
1232	032	Injectors (four-cylinder: 1 & 3, six-cylinder: 1, 2 & 4) or injector circuit
1233	002	Injectors (four-cylinder: 2 & 4, six-cylinder: 3, 5 & 6) or injector circuit
1234	013	Automatic transmission (AT) or AT circuit
1235	085	Air conditioning (A/C) or A/C circuit
1236	021	Air conditioning (A/C) compressor control or A/C circuit
1243	1003	Fuel pump relay or circuit
1244	034	Carbon filter solenoid valve (CFSV) or CFSV circuit

Flash code	FCR code	Description
1245	023	Variable valve timing actuator (Twin Spark models) or circuit
1251	001	Electronic control module (ECM)
1252	009	Crank angle sensor (CAS) or CAS circuit
1254	-	Throttle pot sensor (TPS) or TPS circuit
1255	-	Camshaft position (CMP) sensor or CMP sensor circuit
1265	015	Self-Diagnosis (SD) warning light or SD circuit
2111	-	Knock sensor (KS) 1 or KS circuit
2112	-	Knock sensor (KS) 2 or KS circuit
2113	-	Electronic control module (ECM)
2116	-	Electronic control module (ECM)
4444	-	No faults found in the ECM. Proceed with normal diagnostic methods

All systems except Bosch Motronic ML4.1 and 1.7

Alfa-Romeo software does not usually generate fault codes, and the FCR normally displays faults on the FCR screen without reference to a specific code number. Although actual code numbers are not available, faults in one or more of the circuits and components covered by the diagnostic software will cause a fault to be stored.

For a list of the allocated EOBD codes beginning with P0 (Generic Powertrain), refer to Chapter 1, Section 1.

Notes

Audi

Index of vehicles

Model	Engine code	Year	System
Audi A3 1.6	AEH	1996 to 2002	Simos
Audi A3 1.8	AGN	1996 to 1997	Bosch Motronic 3.2
Audi A3 1.8i	AGN	1997 to 2002	Bosch Motronic 3.8.2
Audi A3 1.8 Turbo	AGU	1996 to 2002	Bosch Motronic 3.2
Audi A4 1.6	ADP	1995 to 2001	Bosch Motronic 3.2
Audi A4 1.8	ADR	1995 to 2001	Bosch Motronic 3.2
Audi A4 1.8 Turbo	AEB	1995 to 2001	Bosch Motronic 3.2
Audi A4 2.6	ABC	1995 to 2001	VAG MPFi
Audi A4 2.8	AAH	1995 to 2001	VAG MPi
Audi A4 2.8	ACK	1996 to 2001	Bosch Motronic MPi
Audi A6 2.0i	ABK	1993 to 1997	VAG Digifant
Audi A6 2.8 30V	ACK	1995 to 2001	Bosch Motronic
Audi A6 S6 2.2 cat	AAN	1991 to 1997	Bosch Motronic M2.3.2
Audi A6 2.6	ABC	1992 to 1997	VAG MPFi
Audi A6 2.8	AAH	1991 to 1997	VAG MPi
Audi A6 S6 4.2	AHK	1996 to 1997	Bosch Motronic
Audi A6 S6 4.2	AEC	1994 to 1997	Bosch Motronic
Audi A8 2.8i V6	AAH	1994 to 2002	VAG MPFi
Audi A8 2.8	ACK	1996 to 2002	Bosch Motronic
Audi A8 3.7	AEW	1995 to 2002	Bosch Motronic
Audi A8 4.2	ABZ	1994 to 2002	Bosch Motronic M2.4
Audi V8 3.6 cat	PT	1989 to 1994	Bosch Motronic M2.4
Audi V8 4.2 cat	ABH	1992 to 1994	Bosch Motronic M2.4
Audi 80 1.6 cat	ABM	1992 to 1995	Bosch Mono-Motronic MA1.2
Audi 80 1.6 cat	ADA	1993 to 1995	VAG MPi
Audi 80 1.8i and 4x4 cat	JN	1986 to 1991	Bosch KE-Jetronic
Audi 80 1.8i and 4x4 cat	PM	1988 to 1989	Bosch Mono-Jetronic A2.2
Audi 80 1.8 and 4x4 cat	PM	1990 to 1991	Bosch Mono-Motronic
Audi 80 2.0i Quattro cat	ABT	1992 to 1995	Bosch Mono-Motronic
Audi 80 Coupe 16V 2.0 cat	6A	1990 to 1995	Bosch KE1.2 Motronic
Audi 80 Coupe 2.0 and 4x4 cat	3A	1988 to 1990	Bosch KE1.1 Motronic
Audi 80 Coupe and 4x4 2.0 cat	AAD	1990 to 1992	Bosch KE1.2 Motronic
Audi 80 2.0 cat	ABK	1992 to 1995	VAG Digifant
Audi 80, 90 Coupe and Cabrio 2.3	NG	1987 to 1995	Bosch KE3-Jetronic
Audi 80 2.3 cat	NG	1992 to 1994	Bosch KE3-Jetronic

Model	Engine code	Year	System
Audi 80 2.6 cat	ABC	1992 to 1995	VAG MPFi
Audi 80, 90 2.0 cat	PS	1987 to 1991	Bosch KE Jetronic
Audi 80, 90 2.8 cat	AAH	1992 to 1994	VAG MPi
Audi 80 S2	ABY	1993 to 1995	Bosch Motronic + Turbo
Audi 90 Coupe 2.0 20V cat	NM	1988 to 1991	VAG MPi
Audi 90 Coupe and 4x4 2.3 cat	7A	1988 to 1991	VAG MPi
Audi 100 1.8i cat	4B	1988 to 1991	Bosch Mono-Jetronic
Audi 100 1.8i cat	PH	1985 to 1991	Bosch KE-Jetronic
Audi 100 2.0 cat	AAE	1991 to 1994	Bosch Mono-Motronic MA1.2
Audi 100 2.0i	ABK	1993 to 1996	VAG Digifant
Audi 100 2.0 cat	AAD	1991 to 1994	Bosch KE-Motronic
Audi 100 4x4 2.0 16V cat	ACE	1992 to 1994	Bosch KE-Motronic
Audi 100 S4 2.2 cat	AAN	1991 to 1997	Bosch Motronic 2.3.2
Audi 100 2.3E cat	NF	1986 to 1991	Bosch KE3-Jetronic
Audi 100 2.3 cat	AAR	1991 to 1994	Bosch KE3-Jetronic
Audi 100 2.6	ABC	1992 to 1997	VAG MPFi
Audi 100 2.8	AAH	1991 to 1997	VAG MPi
Audi 100 S4 4.2	ABH	1993 to 1994	Bosch Motronic
Audi 200 4x4 Turbo cat	3B	1989 to 1991	Bosch Motronic + Turbo
Audi Coupe S2	3B	1990 to 1993	Bosch Motronic + Turbo
Audi Coupe and Cabrio 2.0 cat	ABK	1992 to 1997	VAG Digifant
Audi Coupe and Cabrio 2.6 cat	ABC	1993 to 1997	VAG MPFi
Audi Coupe and Cabrio 2.8	AAH	1991 to 1997	VAG MPi
Audi Coupe S2	ABY	1993 to 1996	Bosch Motronic + Turbo
Audi Quattro 20V cat	RR	1989 to 1991	Bosch Motronic + Turbo
Audi RS2 Avant	ADU	1994 to 1996	Bosch Motronic + Turbo

Plus *All models equipped with EOBD (approximately January 2001-on)*

Self-Diagnosis

1 Introduction

The engine management and fuel injection systems fitted to Audi vehicles are mainly of Bosch origin. Bosch Motronic, Mono-Jetronic, Mono-Motronic 1.1 and 1.2, KE-Motronic 1.1 and 1.2, KE-3 Jetronic, Simos, VAG Digifant, VAG MPi and VAG MPFi may be fitted.

All Audi engine management systems (EMSs) control primary ignition, fuelling and idle functions from within the same control module; the exceptions are Mono-Jetronic and KE-3 Jetronic systems, which control fuelling and idle functions alone.

Self-Diagnosis (SD) function

Each ECM has a self-test capability that continually examines the signals from certain engine sensors and actuators, and compares each signal to a table of programmed values. If the diagnostic software determines that a fault is present, the ECM stores one or more fault codes. Codes will not be stored about components for which a code is not available, or for conditions not covered by the diagnostic software.

Audi systems are capable of generating two kinds of fault codes - 4-digit flash codes and 5-digit fault codes.

Evolution of Audi systems has meant that the codes generated, and their reading procedures, now fall into one of three groups. The changeover point in a particular vehicle range is not always obvious.

a) *Some early systems will only generate 4-digit flash codes which can be retrieved via the warning light (where fitted), an LED light, or a dedicated fault code reader (FCR). These systems include Mono-Jetronic and Mono-Motronic MA1.2.1.*

b) *Later systems can generate both 4-digit flash codes and 5-digit fault codes. The 4-digit flash codes are generated via the warning light (where fitted), or an LED light, whilst a dedicated FCR is required to retrieve the 5-digit codes. These systems include Bosch Motronic versions 2.3, 2.4, and 2.7, KE-3 Jetronic, KE-Motronic and Mono-Motronic (early 45-pin ECM).*

c) *The very latest systems can only generate 5-digit fault codes, and these must be retrieved with the aid of a dedicated FCR. These systems include Bosch Motronic versions 2.9, 3.2, 3.8.2 (and later), Mono-Motronic MA1.2.2 (later 45-pin ECM), Simos, VAG Digifant (68-pin ECM) and VAG MPi and MPFi. All models equipped with EOBD only generate 5-digit fault codes.*

Limited operating strategy (LOS)

Audi systems featured in this Chapter utilise LOS (a function that is commonly called the "limp-home mode"). Once certain faults have been identified (not all faults will initiate LOS), the ECM will implement LOS and refer to a programmed default value rather than the sensor signal. This enables the vehicle to be safely driven to a workshop/garage for repair or testing. Once the fault has cleared, the ECM will revert to normal operation.

Adaptive or learning capability

Audi systems also utilise an adaptive function that will modify the basic programmed values for most effective

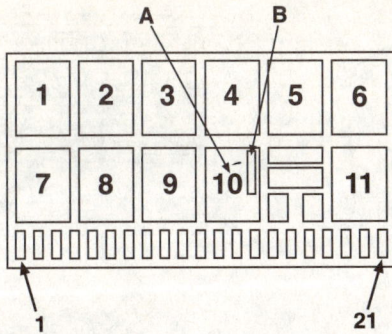

6.1 Use a fuse to bridge the test contacts located in the relay box for Audi 80 and 100 models prior to July 1988
A Fuel pump relay location   B Test contacts

operation during normal running, and with due regard to engine wear.

Self-Diagnosis (SD) warning light
Certain models are equipped with a SD warning light located within the instrument panel.

2   Self-Diagnosis connector location

Mono-Jetronic (Audi 80 and 100 1.8i up to July 1988)
On top of the fuel pump relay *(see illustration 6.1)* for flash code retrieval alone.

Mono-Jetronic (Audi 80 and 100 1.8i from August 1988)
Dual 2-pin SD connectors located in the passenger's side footwell *(see illustration 6.2)* for flash code retrieval and FCR use.

Bosch Mono-Motronic
Dual 2-pin SD connectors located in the passenger's side footwell, under the facia, *(refer to illustration 6.2)* or in the engine compartment left-hand fusebox close to the bulkhead *(see illustration 6.3)* for flash code retrieval and FCR use. The ECM is usually located in the driver's or passenger's side footwell, or in the engine compartment behind the bulkhead.

Bosch KE3-Jetronic and KE-Motronic 1.1
Dual 2-pin SD connectors located underneath a cover above the foot pedals in the driver's side footwell; for flash code retrieval and FCR use.

Bosch KE-Motronic 1.2 and Motronic 2.3
Dual 2-pin SD connectors located underneath a cover above the foot pedals in the driver's side footwell, or triple 2-pin

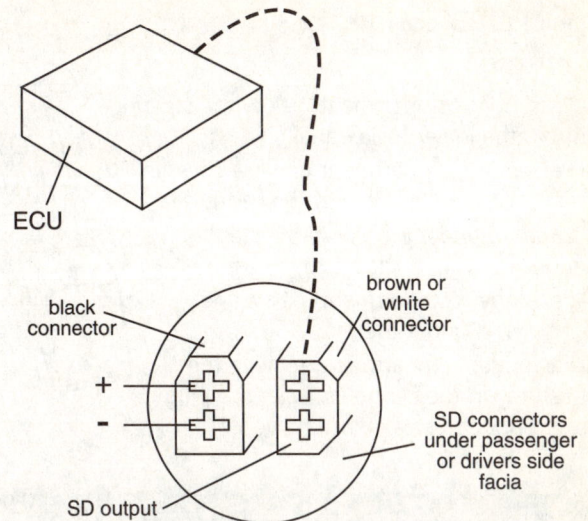

6.2 Location of SD connectors under the facia

connectors located underneath a cover above the foot pedals in the driver's side footwell or in the engine compartment fusebox close to the bulkhead; for flash code retrieval and FCR use.

Bosch Motronic 2.4
Four 2-pin SD connectors located in the passenger's side footwell, under the facia; for flash code retrieval and FCR use.

VAG Digifant
Dual 2-pin connectors located In the passenger's side footwell, under the facia, *(refer to illustration 6.2)* or in the left-hand electrical box close to the bulkhead *(refer to illustration 6.3)* for FCR use alone.

VAG MPi and MPFi
Dual 2-pin SD connectors located above the foot pedals in the driver's side footwell; for FCR use alone.

16-pin OBD connector (A3 models including Bosch Motronic 3.2, 3.8.2 and Simos)
Situated under a cover in the front console.

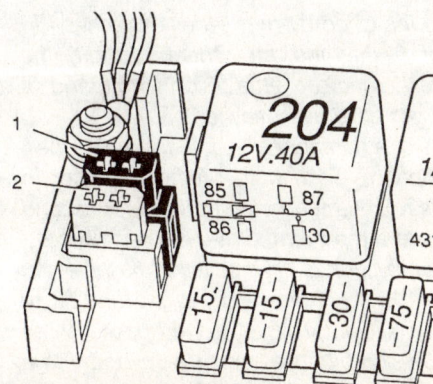

6.3 Location of SD connectors in engine compartment fusebox
1 Power supply
2 Data transfer

6•3

16-pin EOBD connector - *refer to Chapter 38.*

A2 – Passenger compartment, below the steering column in the lower facia panel.

A3 – Passenger compartment under a cover in the centre console, in front of the gearlever.

A4 – Situated under a cover in the rear passenger console, adjacent to the ashtray.

A6 – Passenger compartment, below the steering wheel under the facia.

A8 – Passenger compartment, remove the front ashtray in the centre console -the plug is located under a small plastic cover.

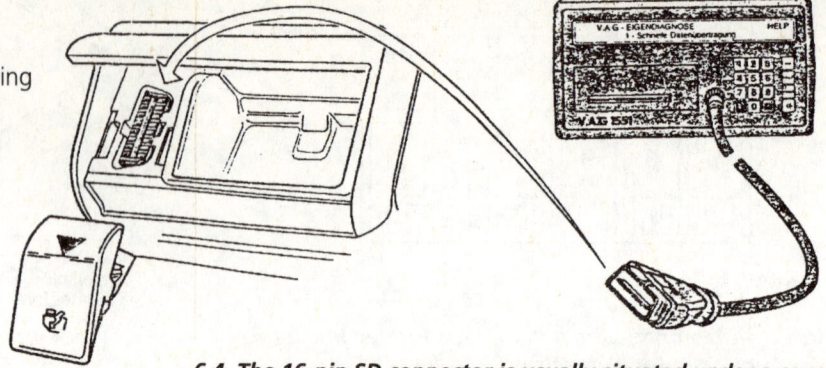

6.4 The 16-pin SD connector is usually situated under a cover in the rear passenger console, adjacent to the ashtray

3 Retrieving fault codes without a fault code reader (FCR) - flash codes

Note: *During the course of certain test procedures, it is possible for additional fault codes to be generated. Care must be taken that any codes generated during test routines do not mislead diagnosis. All codes must be cleared once testing is complete. 4-digit flash codes retrieved manually may be different to those codes displayed with the aid of an FCR. Refer to the fault code table at the end of this Chapter, in the column headed "Flash code".*

Mono-Jetronic (prior to July 1988)

1 Start the engine and allow it to warm up to normal operating temperature. **Note:** *Oxygen sensor (OS) fault codes can only be retrieved after a road test of at least 10 minutes' duration.*

2 Stop the engine and switch on the ignition.

3 If the engine will not start, crank the engine for at least 6.0 seconds and leave the ignition switched on.

4 Use a fuse to short the test contacts on the fuel pump relay for at least 5.0 seconds *(refer to illustration 6.1).*

5 Remove the fuse, and the SD warning light will flash to indicate the 4-digit fault code as follows:

  a) *The four digits are indicated by four series of flashes.*

  b) *The first series of flashes indicates the first digit, the second series of flashes indicates the second digit, and so on until all four digits have been flashed.*

  c) *Each series consists of a number of 1- or 2-second flashes, separated by short pauses. Each integer (whole number) in the range 1 to 9 is represented by a number of 1-second flashes and each zero is represented by 2-second flashes.*

  d) *A 2.5-second pause separates each series of flashes.*

  e) *The code number "1231" is indicated by a 1-second flash, a short pause, two 1-sec-ond flashes, a short pause, three 1-second flashes, a short pause and a 1-second flash. After a 2.5-second pause, the code will be repeated.*

6 Count the number of flashes in each series, and record the code. Refer to the tables at the end of the Chapter to determine the meaning of the fault code.

7 Each code will be repeated until the fuse is re-inserted. Remove the fuse after 6.0 seconds, and the next code will then be displayed.

8 Continue retrieving codes until code 0000 is transmitted. Code 0000 signifies that no more codes are stored, and is displayed when the light flashes off and on at 2.5 second intervals.

9 If code 4444 is transmitted, no fault codes are stored.

10 Turn off the ignition to end fault code retrieval.

Bosch Mono-Jetronic (after July 1988), KE-Jetronic, KE-Motronic 1.1 and 1.2, Motronic 2.3 and 2.4

11 Attach an accessory switch to the dual 2-pin, 3-pin or 4-pin SD connectors *(see illustrations 6.5 to 6.7).* If the vehicle is not equipped with a facia-mounted SD warning light, connect a diode LED light between the battery (+) supply and the SD connector as shown.

12 Start the engine and allow it to warm up to normal operating temperature. Note: Oxygen sensor (OS) fault codes can only be retrieved after a road test of at least 10 minutes' duration.

13 Stop the engine and switch on the ignition.

14 If the engine will not start, crank the engine for at least 6 seconds and leave the ignition switched on.

15 Close the accessory switch for at least 5 seconds. Open the switch, and the warning light or LED light will flash to indicate the 4-digit fault codes as follows:

  a) *The four digits are indicated by four series of flashes.*

  b) *The first series of flashes indicates the first digit, the second series of flashes indicates the second digit, and so on until all four digits have been flashed.*

  c) *Each series consists of a number of 1- or 2-second flashes, separated by short pauses. Each integer (whole number) in the range 1 to 9 is represented by a number of 1-second flashes, and each zero is represented by 2-second flashes.*

  d) *A 2.5-second pause separates each series of flashes.*

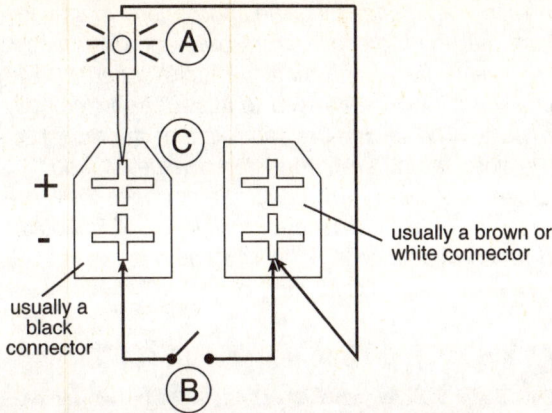

6.5 Initiation of flash codes - dual 2-pin SD connectors
A LED diode light   B Accessory switch   C SD connectors

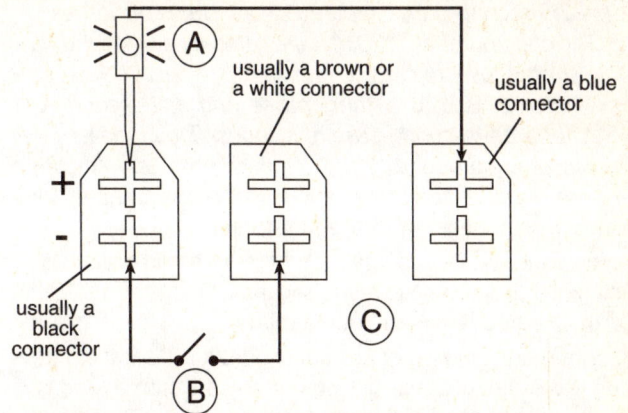

6.6 Initiation of flash codes - triple 2-pin SD connectors
A LED diode light   B Accessory switch   C SD connectors

e) *The code number "1231" is indicated by a 1-second flash, a short pause, two 1-sec-ond flashes, a short pause, three 1-second flashes, a short pause and a 1-second flash. After a 2.5-second pause, the code will be repeated.*

16 Count the number of flashes in each series, and record the code. Refer to the tables at the end of the Chapter to determine the meaning of the fault code.

17 The code will be repeated until the accessory switch is once more closed for at least 5 seconds. Open the switch, and the next code will then be displayed.

18 Continue retrieving codes until code 0000 is transmitted. Code 0000 signifies that no more codes are stored, and is displayed when the light flashes off and on at 2.5-second intervals.

19 If code 4444 is transmitted, no fault codes are stored.

20 Turn off the ignition and remove the accessory switch and diode light to end fault code retrieval.

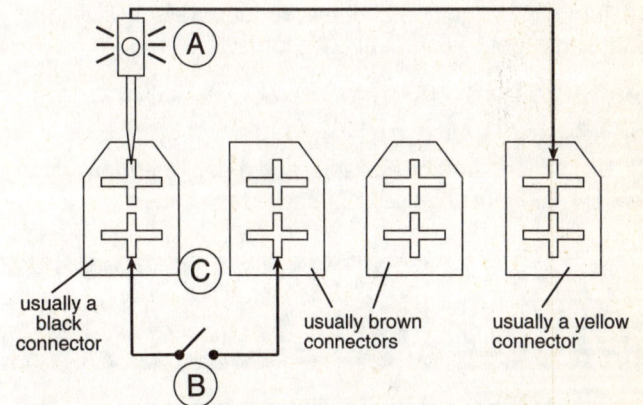

6.7 Initiation of flash codes - four 2-pin SD connectors
A LED diode light   B Accessory switch   C SD connectors

Bosch Mono-Motronic (35-pin version 1.2.1 and 45-pin version 1.2.2)

21 Attach an accessory switch to the dual 2-pin SD connectors. If the vehicle is not equipped with a facia-mounted SD warning light, connect a diode LED light between the battery (+) supply and ECM pin number 33 (35-pin) or ECM pin number 4

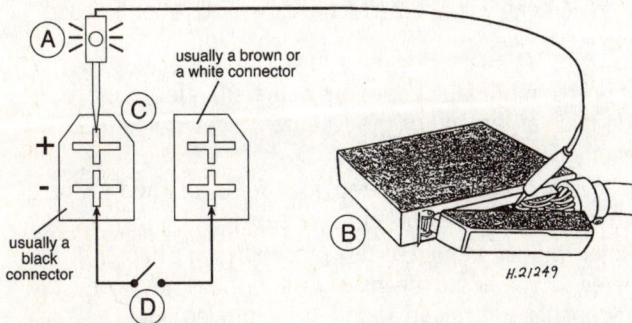

6.8 Initiation of 35-pin and some 45-pin Mono-Motronic flash codes (see text)
A LED diode light   B ECM   C SD connectors   D Accessory switch

(45-pin) as shown *(see illustration 6.8)*. **Note:** *It will be necessary to detach the back of the ECM multi-plugs so that the LED negative probe can backprobe the ECM pin number with the multi-plug connected.*

22 Start the engine and allow it to warm up to normal operating temperature. **Note:** *Oxygen sensor (OS) fault codes can only be retrieved after a road test of at least 10 minutes' duration.*

23 Stop the engine and switch on the ignition.

24 If the engine will not start, crank the engine for at least 6 seconds and leave the ignition switched on.

25 Close the accessory switch for at least 5 seconds. Open the switch, and the warning light or LED light will flash to indicate the 4-digit fault codes as follows:

a) *The four digits are indicated by four series of flashes.*

b) *The first series of flashes indicates the first digit, the second series of flashes indicates the second digit, and so on until all four digits have been flashed.*

c) *Each series consists of a number of 1- or 2-second flashes, separated by short pauses. Each integer (whole number) in the range 1 to 9 is represented by a number of 1-second flashes, and each zero is represented by 2-second flashes.*

d) A 2.5-second pause separates each series of flashes.

e) The code number "1231" is indicated by a 1-second flash, a short pause, two 1-sec-ond flashes, a short pause, three 1-second flashes, a short pause and a 1-second flash. After a 2.5-second pause, the code will be repeated.

26 Count the number of flashes in each series, and record the code. Refer to the tables at the end of the Chapter to determine the meaning of the fault code.

27 The code will be repeated until the accessory switch is once more closed for at least 5 seconds. Open the switch, and the next code will then be displayed.

28 Continue retrieving codes until code 0000 is transmitted. Code 0000 signifies that no more codes are stored, and is displayed when the light flashes off and on at 2.5-second intervals.

29 If code 4444 is transmitted, no fault codes are stored.

30 Turn off the ignition and remove the accessory switch and diode light to end fault code retrieval.

Systems with 16-pin OBD/EOBD connector or 68-pin ECM multi-plug

31 Flash codes are not available, and a dedicated fault code reader (FCR) must be used to retrieve fault codes.

4   Clearing fault codes without a fault code reader (FCR)

Bosch Mono-Jetronic, Mono-Motronic, KE-Jetronic and KE-Motronic

1 Carry out the procedure in Section 3 to retrieve the fault codes.

2 Turn off the ignition.

3 Use a fuse to short the test contacts on the fuel pump relay (Mono-Jetronic to July 1988 only) or close the accessory switch (all other systems).

4 Switch on the ignition.

5 Open the accessory switch after a period of 5 seconds, or remove the fuse. All fault codes should now be cleared.

6 Turn off the ignition.

Cancelling fault codes 2341 or 2343 (OS)

7 Turn off the ignition (take out the key). Remove the ECM multi-plug connector from the ECM for at least 30 seconds.

> **(!)** *Refer to Warning number 3 in the Reference Section at the back of this book.*

All systems (alternative)

8 Turn off the ignition and disconnect the battery negative terminal for a period of approximately 5 minutes.

9 Re-connect the battery negative terminal.

Note: *The first drawback to this method is that battery disconnection will re-initialise all ECM adaptive values (not*

Mono-Jetronic). Re-learning the appropriate adaptive values requires starting the engine from cold, and driving at various engine speeds for approximately 20 to 30 minutes. The engine should also be allowed to idle for approximately 10 minutes. The second drawback is that the radio security codes, clock setting and other stored values will be initialised, and these must be re-entered once the battery has been reconnected. Where possible, an FCR should be used for code clearing. On vehicles equipped with EOBD, an FCR must be used to clear fault codes.

5   Self-Diagnosis with a fault code reader (FCR)

Note: *During the course of certain test procedures, it is possible for additional fault codes to be generated. Care must be taken that any codes generated during test routines do not mislead diagnosis.*

All Audi models

1 Connect an FCR to the SD connector. Use the FCR for the following purposes, in strict compliance with the FCR manufacturer's instructions:

a) Retrieving fault codes or displaying faults.

b) Clearing fault codes.

c) Testing actuators.

d) Making service adjustments.

e) Displaying Datastream.

f) Coding the ECM.

2 The FCR may be able to display both 4-digit flash codes and/or 5-digit fault codes. Refer to the fault code table at the end of this Chapter.

3 Codes must always be cleared after component testing, or after repairs involving the removal or replacement of an EMS component.

6   Guide to test procedures

1 Use an FCR to interrogate the ECM for fault codes, or manually gather codes as described in Sections 3 or 5.

Codes stored

2 If one or more fault codes are gathered, refer to the fault code table at the end of this Chapter to determine their meaning.

3 If several codes are gathered, look for a common factor such as a defective earth return or supply.

4 Refer to the component test procedures in Chapter 4, where you will find a means of testing the majority of components and circuits found in the modern EMS.

5 Once the fault has been repaired, clear the codes and run the engine under various conditions to determine if the problem has cleared.

6 Check the ECM for fault codes once more. Repeat the above procedures where codes are still being stored.

7 Refer to Chapter 3 for more information on how to effectively test the engine management system.

No codes stored

8 Where a running problem is experienced, but no codes are stored, the fault is outside of the parameters designed into the SD system. Refer to Chapter 3 for more information on how to effectively test the engine management system.

9 If the problem points to a specific component, refer to the test procedures in Chapter 4, where you will find a means of testing the majority of components and circuits found in the modern EMS.

Fault code table

Note: *Similar codes are generated by each system, although a small number of codes may suggest alternative meanings depending on which system and what components are fitted. For example, one particular code may indicate an airflow sensor or a MAP sensor, depending on which of those component is fitted. When a code with an alternative meaning is generated, the correct meaning will usually be obvious.*

Flash code	FCR code	Description
4444	00000	No faults found in the ECM. Proceed with normal diagnostic methods
0000	-	End of fault code output
1111	65535	Internal ECM failure
1231	00281	Vehicle speed sensor (VSS) or VSS circuit
1232	00282	Throttle pot sensor (TPS) or TPS circuit
1232	00282	Idle speed stepper motor (ISSM) or ISSM circuit (alternative code).
2111	00513	Engine speed (RPM) sensor or RPM sensor circuit
2112	00514	Top dead centre (TDC) sensor or TDC circuit
2112	00514	Crank angle sensor (CAS)
2113	00515	Hall-effect sensor (HES) or HES circuit

Note: *Fault code number 2113 will always be present when the ignition is turned on and the engine is stopped in systems that utilise a Hall sensor as the primary trigger.*

2114	00535	Distributor
2121	00516	Idle speed stepper motor (ISSM) idle contacts
2121	00516	Ignition control valve circuit fault (alternative code)
2122	-	No engine speed signal
2123	00517	Throttle switch (TS), full load switch
2141	00535	Knock control 1 (ECM)
2142	00524	Knock sensor (KS) or KS circuit
2142	00545	AT signal missing (alternative code)
2143	00536	Knock control 2 (ECM)
2144	00540	Knock sensor (KS) 2 or KS circuit
2212	00518	Throttle pot sensor (TPS) fault or TPS circuit
2214	00543	Maximum engine speed exceeded
2222	00519	Manifold absolute pressure (MAP) sensor or MAP sensor circuit
2223	00528	Atmospheric pressure sensor (APS) or APS circuit
2224	00544	Turbocharger maximum boost pressure exceeded
2231	00533	Idle control
2232	00520	Vane airflow sensor (AFS) or AFS circuit
2232	00520	Mass airflow (MAF) sensor or MAF sensor circuit (alternative code)
2233	00531	Vane airflow sensor (AFS) or AFS circuit
2233	00531	Mass airflow (MAF) sensor or MAF circuit (alternative code)
2234	00532	Supply voltage incorrect
2242	00521	CO pot or CO pot circuit
2312	00522	Coolant temperature sensor (CTS) or CTS circuit
2314	00545	Engine/gearbox electrical connection
2322	00523	Air temperature sensor (ATS) or ATS circuit
2323	00522	Vane airflow sensor (AFS)
2323	00522	Mass airflow (MAF) sensor (alternative code)
2324	00553	Vane airflow sensor (AFS)

Flash code	FCR code	Description
2324	00553	Mass airflow (MAF) sensor (alternative code)
2341	00537	Oxygen sensor (OS) control Inoperative
2342	00525	Oxygen sensor (OS) or OS circuit
2343	00558	Mixture control adjustment, weak
2344	00559	Mixture control adjustment, rich
2413	00561	Mixture control limits
4332	00750	Electronic control module (ECM)
4343	01243	Carbon filter solenoid valve (CFSV) or CFSV circuit
4411	01244	Injector No. 1 or injector circuit
4412	01247	Injector No. 2 or injector circuit
4413	01249	Injector No. 3 or injector circuit
4414	01250	Injector No. 4 or injector circuit
4421	01251	Injector No. 5 or injector circuit
4431	01253	Idle speed control valve (ISCV) or ISCV circuit
4442	01254	Turbocharger boost pressure solenoid valve (BPSV) or BPSV circuit
-	00527	Intake manifold temperature
-	00530	Throttle pot sensor (TPS) or TPS circuit
-	00532	Supply voltage incorrect
-	00543	Maximum engine speed exceeded
-	00549	Consumption signal
-	00545	Engine gearbox electrical connection
-	00554	Oxygen sensor (OS) control 2
-	00555	Oxygen sensor (OS) or OS circuit
-	00560	Exhaust gas recirculation (EGR) valve or EGR circuit
-	00561	Mixture control 1
-	00575	Manifold absolute pressure (MAP) sensor or MAP sensor circuit
-	00577	Knock control cylinder 1 or circuit
-	00578	Knock control cylinder 2 or circuit
-	00579	Knock control cylinder 3 or circuit
-	00580	Knock control cylinder 4 or circuit
-	00581	Knock control cylinder 5 or circuit
-	00582	Knock control cylinder 6 or circuit
-	00585	Exhaust gas recirculation (EGR) temperature sensor or EGR circuit
-	00586	Exhaust gas recirculation (EGR) valve or EGR circuit
-	00609	Amplifier 1 or amplifier circuit
-	00610	Amplifier 2 or amplifier circuit
-	00611	Amplifier 3 or amplifier circuit
-	00624	Air conditioning (A/C)
-	00625	Vehicle speed sensor (VSS) or VSS circuit
-	00635	Oxygen sensor (OS) heater or OS circuit
-	00640	Oxygen sensor (OS) or OS circuit
-	00670	Idle speed stepper motor (ISSM) pot or ISSM circuit
-	00689	Excessive air in inlet manifold
-	00750	Self-Diagnosis warning light
-	01025	Self-Diagnosis warning light
-	01087	Basic setting not completed
-	01088	Mixture control 2
-	01119	Gear recognition signal

Flash code	FCR code	Description
-	01120	Camshaft timing control
-	01165	Throttle pot sensor (TPS) or TPS circuit
-	01182	Altitude adaptation
-	01235	Secondary air valve
-	01242	Electronic control module (ECM) or ECM circuit
-	01247	Carbon filter solenoid valve (CFSV) or CFSV circuit
-	01252	Injector valve No. 4 or injector valve circuit
-	01257	Idle speed control valve (ISCV) or ISCV circuit
-	01259	Fuel pump relay or circuit
-	01262	Turbocharger boost pressure solenoid valve (BPSV) or BPSV circuit
-	01264	Secondary air pump
-	01265	Exhaust gas recirculation (EGR) valve or EGR circuit
-	16486	Mass airflow (MAF) sensor or MAF circuit, signal low
-	16487	Mass airflow (MAF) sensor or MAF circuit, signal high
-	16496	Air temperature sensor (ATS) or ATS circuit, signal low
-	16497	Air temperature sensor (ATS) or ATS circuit, signal high
-	16500	Coolant temperature sensor (CTS) or CTS circuit
-	16501	Coolant temperature sensor (CTS) or CTS circuit, signal low
-	16502	Coolant temperature sensor (CTS) or CTS circuit, signal high
-	16504	Throttle pot sensor (TPS) or TPS circuit
-	16505	Throttle pot sensor (TPS) or TPS circuit, signal implausible
-	16506	Throttle pot sensor (TPS) or TPS circuit, signal low
-	16507	Throttle pot sensor (TPS) or TPS circuit, signal high
-	16514	Oxygen sensor (OS) or OS circuit
-	16515	Oxygen sensor (OS) or OS circuit
-	16516	Oxygen sensor (OS) or OS circuit, signal high
-	16518	Oxygen sensor (OS) or OS circuit
-	16519	Oxygen sensor (OS) or OS circuit
-	16534	Oxygen sensor (OS) or OS circuit
-	16535	Oxygen sensor (OS) or OS circuit
-	16536	Oxygen sensor (OS) or OS circuit, signal high
-	16538	Oxygen sensor (OS) or OS circuit
-	16554	Injector bank 1
-	16555	Injector bank 1, fuel system too lean
-	16556	Injector bank 1, fuel system too rich
-	16557	Injector bank 2
-	16558	Injector bank 2, fuel system too lean
-	16559	Injector bank 2, fuel system too rich
-	16684	Engine misfire
-	16685	Cylinder No. 1 misfire
-	16686	Cylinder No. 2 misfire
-	16687	Cylinder No. 3 misfire
-	16688	Cylinder No. 4 misfire
-	16689	Cylinder No. 5 misfire
-	16690	Cylinder No. 6 misfire
-	16691	Cylinder No. 7 misfire
-	16692	Cylinder No. 8 misfire
-	16705	RPM sensor or circuit
-	16706	RPM sensor or circuit
-	16711	Knock sensor (KS) 1 signal or KS circuit, signal low
-	16716	Knock sensor (KS) 2 signal or KS circuit, signal low
-	16721	Crank angle sensor (CAS) or CAS circuit
-	16785	Exhaust gas
-	16786	Exhaust gas
-	16885	Vehicle speed sensor (VSS) or VSS circuit
-	16989	Electronic control module (ECM)
-	17509	Oxygen sensor (OS) or OS circuit
-	17514	Oxygen sensor (OS) or OS circuit
-	17540	Oxygen sensor (OS) or OS circuit
-	17541	Oxygen sensor (OS) or OS circuit

Flash code	FCR code	Description
-	17609	Injector valve No. 1 or injector circuit
-	17610	Injector valve No. 4 or injector circuit
-	17611	Injector valve No. 3 or injector circuit
-	17612	Injector valve No. 4 or injector circuit
-	17613	Injector valve No. 5 or injector circuit
-	17614	Injector valve No. 6 or injector circuit
-	17615	Injector valve No. 7 or injector circuit
-	17616	Injector valve No. 8 or injector circuit
-	17621	Injector valve No. 1 or injector circuit
-	17622	Injector valve No. 2 or injector circuit
-	17623	Injector valve No. 3 or injector circuit
-	17624	Injector valve No. 4 or injector circuit
-	17625	Injector valve No. 5 or injector circuit
-	17626	Injector valve No. 6 or injector circuit
-	17627	Cylinder No. 7 misfire
-	17628	Cylinder No. 8 misfire
-	17733	Knock sensor (KS) control No. 1 cylinder or KS circuit
-	17734	Knock sensor (KS) control No. 2 cylinder or KS circuit
-	17735	Knock sensor (KS) control No. 3 cylinder or KS circuit
-	17736	Knock sensor (KS) control No. 4 cylinder or KS circuit
-	17737	Knock sensor (KS) control No. 5 cylinder or KS circuit
-	17738	Knock sensor (KS) control No. 6 cylinder or KS circuit
-	17739	Knock sensor (KS) control No. 7 cylinder or KS circuit
-	17740	Knock sensor (KS) control No. 8 cylinder or KS circuit
-	17747	Crank angle sensor (CAS) and vehicle speed sensor (VSS) signal transposed
-	17749	Ignition output 1, short-circuit to earth
-	17751	Ignition output 2, short-circuit to earth
-	17753	Ignition output 3, short-circuit to earth
-	17799	Camshaft sensor (CMP) or CMP circuit
-	17800	Camshaft sensor (CMP) or CMP circuit
-	17801	Ignition output 1
-	17802	Ignition output 2
-	17803	Ignition output 3
-	17808	Exhaust gas recirculation (EGR) valve or EGR circuit
-	17810	Exhaust gas recirculation (EGR) valve or EGR circuit
-	17815	Exhaust gas recirculation (EGR) valve or EGR circuit, signal too small
-	17816	Exhaust gas recirculation (EGR) valve or EGR circuit, signal too large
-	17817	Carbon filter solenoid valve (CFSV) or CFSV circuit
-	17818	Carbon filter solenoid valve (CFSV) or CFSV circuit
-	17908	Fuel pump relay or fuel pump circuit
-	17910	Fuel pump relay or fuel pump circuit
-	17912	Intake system
-	17913	Idling switch, throttle switch (TS) or TS circuit
-	17914	Idling switch, throttle switch (TS) or TS circuit
-	17915	Idle speed control valve (ISCV) or ISCV circuit
-	17916	Idle speed control valve (ISCV) or ISCV circuit
-	17917	Idle speed control valve (ISCV) or ISCV circuit
-	17918	Idle speed control valve (ISCV) or ISCV circuit
-	17919	Inlet manifold changeover valve (IMCV) or IMCV circuit
-	17920	Inlet manifold changeover valve (IMCV) or IMCV circuit
-	17966	Throttle drive
-	17978	Electronic immobiliser
-	18008	Voltage supply
-	18010	Battery
-	18020	Electronic control module (ECM) incorrectly coded

EOBD models

For a list of the allocated EOBD codes beginning with P0 (Generic Powertrain), refer to Chapter 1, Section 1.

7

Index of vehicles

Model	Engine code	Year	System
316i (E30) and cat	M40/B16 164E1	1988 to 1993	Bosch Motronic 1.3
316i (E36) cat	M40/B16 164E1	1990 to 1993	Bosch Motronic 1.7
316i (E36) cat and Compact	M43/B16	1993 to 1999	Bosch Motronic 1.7
318i (E30) Touring and cat	M40/B18 184E11	1988 to 1993	Bosch Motronic 1.3
318i (E30) and Touring	M40/B18	1989 to 1992	Bosch Motronic 1.7
318i (E36) and cat	M40/B18 184E2	1991 to 1993	Bosch Motronic 1.7
318i (E36)	M43/B18	1993 to 1999	Bosch Motronic 1.7
318iS (E30) 16V Touring and cat	M42/B18 184S1	1990 to 1991	Bosch Motronic 1.7
318iS (E36) and Compact	M42/B18 184S1	1992 to 1996	Bosch Motronic 1.7
320i (E30)	M20/B20 206EE	1986 to 1988	Bosch Motronic 1.1
320i (E30) and Touring and cat	M20/B20 206EE	1988 to 1993	Bosch Motronic 1.3
320i (E36) 24V cat	M50/B20 206S1	1991 to 1993	Bosch Motronic 3.1
320i (E36) 24V cat	M50 2.0 Vanos	1993 to 1996	Bosch Motronic 3.1
320i (E36) 24V cat	M50/B20	1993 to 1996	Siemens MS4.0
325i (E30) and 4x4	M20/B25 6K1	1985 to 1987	Bosch Motronic 1.1
325i and Touring (E30)	M20/B25 6K1	1988 to 1993	Bosch Motronic 1.3
325iX (E30-4)	M20/B25 6E2	1985 to 1987	Bosch Motronic 1.1
325ix and Touring	M20/B25 6E2	1988 to 1993	Bosch Motronic 1.3
325i (E36) 24V cat	M50/B25 256S1	1991 to 1993	Bosch Motronic 3.1
325i (E36) 24V	M50 2.5 Vanos	1993 to 1996	Bosch Motronic 3.1
325e (E30) and cat	M20/B27	1986 to 1991	Bosch Motronic 1.1
518i (E34)	M40/B18	1988 to 1993	Bosch Motronic 1.3
518i (E34) cat	M43/B18	1993 to 1996	Bosch Motronic 1.7
520i (E34) and cat	M20/B20M 206KA	1988 to 1991	Bosch Motronic 1.3
520i (E34) 24V and Touring cat	M50/B20 206S1	1990 to 1993	Bosch Motronic 3.1
520i (E34) 24V and Touring cat	M50 2.0 Vanos	1993 to 1996	Bosch Motronic 3.1
520i (E34) 24V cat	M50/B20	1993 to 1996	Siemens MS4.0
525i (E34) and cat	M20/B25M 256K1	1988 to 1991	Bosch Motronic 1.3
525i (E34) 24V cat	M50/B25 256S1	1990 to 1993	Bosch Motronic 3.1
525i (E34) 24V	M50 2.5 Vanos	1993 to 1996	Bosch Motronic 3.1
530i (E34) and cat	M30/B30M 306KA	1988 to 1992	Bosch Motronic 1.3

Model	Engine code	Year	System
540i (E34) V8 4.0 322V DOHC cat	M60	1993 to 1996	Bosch Motronic 3.3
535i (E34) and cat	M30/B35M 346KB	1988 to 1993	Bosch Motronic 1.3
635 CSi (E24)	M30/B34	1986 to 1987	Bosch Motronic 1.1
635 CSi (E24) and cat	M30/B35M 346EC	1988 to 1990	Bosch Motronic 1.3
M635 CSi (E24)	M88/3	1987 to 1989	Bosch Motronic 1.3
730i (E32) and cat	M30/B30M2 306KA	1986 to 1987	Bosch Motronic 1.1
730i (E32) and cat	M30/B30M2 306KA	1988 to 1994	Bosch Motronic 1.3
730i (E32) V8 3.0 cat	M60B330	1992 to 1994	Bosch Motronic 3.3
735i (E32) and cat	M30/B35M2	1986 to 1987	Bosch Motronic 1.1
735i (E32) and cat	M30/B35M2 346EC	1987 to 1992	Bosch Motronic 1.3
740iL (E32) V8 cat	M60/B40	1992 to 1994	Bosch Motronic 3.3
740i (E38) V8 4.0 32V DOHC cat	M60	1994 to 1997	Bosch Motronic 3.3
750i and cat	M70/B50 5012A	1992 to 1994	Bosch Motronic 1.7
750iL	M70/B50 5012A	1992 to 1994	Bosch Motronic 1.7
750i	M70/B54	1994 to 1997	Bosch Motronic 1.2
840i (E31) V8 4.0 32V DOHC cat	M60	1993 to 1997	Bosch Motronic 3.3
850i	M70/B50 5012A	1989 to 1994	Bosch Motronic 1.7
M3 (E36)	S50/B30	1993 to 1997	Bosch Motronic 3.3
M5 (E34)	S38/B38 386S1	1992 to 1996	Bosch Motronic 3.3
Z1	M20/B25	1988 to 1992	Bosch Motronic 1.3

Plus All models equipped with EOBD (approximately January 2001-on)

Self-Diagnosis

1 Introduction

The engine management systems (EMSs) fitted to BMW models are mainly Bosch Motronic or Siemens. All BMW engine management systems control primary ignition, fuelling and idle functions from within the same ECM.

Self-Diagnosis (SD) function

Each ECM has a self-test capability that continually examines the signals from certain engine sensors and actuators, and compares each signal to a table of programmed values. If the diagnostic software determines that a fault is present, the ECM stores one or more fault codes. Codes will not be stored about components for which a code is not available, or for conditions not covered by the diagnostic software. Depending upon system, BMW control modules will generate either 2-digit, 3-digit or 5-digit fault codes, and a dedicated FCR must be used for retrieval. Flash codes that can be retrieved without an FCR are only available in US market models.

Bosch Motronic 1.2

Early BMW V12 engines are equipped with Bosch Motronic M1.2, which has two electronic control modules. Each module is allocated to a bank of 6 cylinders (ECM 1 for the right-hand bank, and ECM 2 for the left-hand bank) and gathers data from its own sensors. Each ECM stores its own fault codes, and should be treated independently.

Limited operating strategy (LOS)

BMW systems featured in this Chapter utilise LOS (a function that is commonly called the "limp-home mode"). Once certain faults have been identified (not all faults will initiate LOS), the ECM will implement LOS and refer to a programmed default value rather than the sensor signal. This enables the vehicle to be safely driven to a workshop/garage for repair or testing. Once the fault has cleared, the ECM will revert to normal operation.

Adaptive or learning capability

BMW systems also utilise an adaptive function that will modify the basic programmed values for most effective operation during normal running, and with due regard to engine wear.

Self-Diagnosis (SD/MIL) warning light

BMW models for the US market are equipped with a facia-mounted "Check Engine" warning light as demanded by US OBDII regulations. Fault codes indicating failure of emission-related components may be retrieved through the flashing of the light. Only European market models equipped with EOBD are equipped with a warning light.

2 Self-Diagnosis connector location

Non-EOBD models

The SD connector is for FCR use alone, and is located in the engine compartment along the left or right-hand wing, either close to the bulkhead or suspension turret (see illustration 7.1).

7.1 BMW 20-pin SD connector. Unscrew the cap and attach the FCR to the exposed connector

EOBD models

The 16-pin connector is located behind a cover above the pedals under the facia - refer to Chapter 38.

3 Retrieving fault codes without a fault code reader (FCR) - flash codes

Bosch Motronic 1.1, 1.2 and 1.3 (US models only)

A limited number of emissions-related flash codes are available via the flashing of the facia-mounted "Check Engine" warning light. Refer to the flash code table at the end of this Chapter to determine the meaning of the flash code.

4 Clearing fault codes without a fault code reader (FCR)

1 Turn off the ignition and disconnect the battery negative terminal for a period of approximately 2 minutes.

2 Re-connect the battery negative terminal.

Note: *The first drawback to this method is that battery disconnection will re-initialise all ECM adaptive values. Re-learning the appropriate adaptive values requires starting the engine from cold, and driving at various engine speeds for approximately 20 to 30 minutes. The engine should also be allowed to idle for approximately 10 minutes. The second drawback is that the radio security codes, clock setting and other stored values will be initialised, and these must be re-entered once the battery has been reconnected. Where possible, an FCR should be used for code clearing. On models equipped with EOBD, an FCR must be used for code clearing.*

5 Self-Diagnosis with a fault code reader (FCR)

Note: *During the course of certain test procedures, it is possible for additional fault codes to be generated. Care must be taken that any codes generated during test routines do not mislead diagnosis*

All BMW models

1 Connect an FCR to the SD connector. Use the FCR for the following purposes, in strict compliance with the FCR manufacturer's instructions:

a) *Retrieving fault codes.*
b) *Clearing fault codes.*
c) *Testing actuators.*
d) *Displaying Datastream.*

2 Codes must always be cleared after component testing, or after repairs involving the removal or replacement of an EMS component. **Note:** *Many of the fault code numbers correspond to the ECM pin number - eg. fault code 04 corresponds to ECM pin number 4 (non-EOBD models).*

6 Guide to test procedures

1 Use an FCR to interrogate the ECM for fault codes, or (where possible) manually gather codes as described in Sections 3 or 5.

Codes stored

2 If one or more fault codes are gathered, refer to the fault code tables at the end of this Chapter to determine their meaning.

3 If several codes are gathered, look for a common factor such as a defective earth return or supply.

4 Refer to the component test procedures in Chapter 4, where you will find a means of testing the majority of components and circuits found in the modern EMS.

5 Once the fault has been repaired, clear the codes and run the engine under various conditions to determine if the problem has cleared.

6 Check the ECM for fault codes once more. Repeat the above procedures where codes are still being stored.

7 Refer to Chapter 3 for more information on how to effectively test the EMS.

No codes stored

8 Where a running problem is experienced, but no codes are stored, the fault is outside of the parameters designed into the SD system. Refer to Chapter 3 for more information on how to effectively test the EMS.

9 If the problem points to a specific component, refer to the test procedures in Chapter 4, where you will find a means of testing the majority of components and circuits found in the modern EMS.

Chapter 7

Fault code tables

Bosch Motronic 1.1, 1.2, 1.3 (flash codes)

Flash code	Description
01	Vane airflow sensor (AFS) or AFS circuit
02	Oxygen sensor (OS) or OS circuit
03	Coolant temperature sensor (CTS) or CTS circuit
04	Throttle switch (TS), full-load switch

Bosch Motronic 1.1, 1.2, 1.3

Flash code	Description
01	Electronic control module (ECM) or ECM circuit
03	Fuel pump relay or fuel pump relay circuit
04	Idle speed control valve (ISCV) or ISCV circuit
05	Carbon filter solenoid valve (CFSV) or CFSV circuit
07	Airflow sensor (AFS) or AFS circuit
10	Oxygen sensor (OS) or OS circuit, exhaust emissions too rich or too lean
15	Warning light (US only) or circuit
16	Injectors (cylinders 1+3) or injector circuit
17	injectors (cylinders 2+4) or injector circuit
23	Oxygen sensor (OS), heater relay or OS circuit
28	Oxygen sensor (OS) or OS circuit
29	Vehicle speed sensor (VSS) or VSS circuit
33	Solenoid valve kickdown prevent or circuit
37	Electronic control module (ECM), supply exceeds 16 volts
43	CO pot (non-cat models) or CO pot circuit
44	Air temperature sensor (ATS) or ATS circuit
45	Coolant temperature sensor (CTS) or CTS circuit
51	Ignition timing intervention (models with EGS only)
52	Throttle switch (TS) or TS circuit
53	Throttle switch (TS) or TS circuit
54	Torque converter clutch (models with EGS only) or circuit
100	Output stage (Bosch Motronic 1.3 only)
101	Engine operation not possible

EOBD models

For a list of the allocated EOBD codes beginning with P0 (Generic Powertrain), refer to Chapter 1, Section 1.

Bosch Motronic 1.7 and 3.1

Flash code	Description
000	No faults found in the ECM. Proceed with normal diagnostic methods
001	Fuel pump relay or fuel pump relay circuit
001	Crank angle sensor (CAS) or CAS circuit (alternative code)
002	Idle speed control valve (ISCV) or ISCV circuit
003	Injector number 1 or injector Group one circuit
004	Injector number 3 or circuit
005	Injector number 2 or circuit
006	Injectors or injector circuit
012	Throttle position switch (TPS) or TPS circuit
016	Crank angle sensor (CAS) or CAS circuit
018	Amplifier to electronic control module (ECM) terminal 18 or amplifier circuit
019	Electronic control module (ECM)
023	Ignition amplifier number 2 cylinder or circuit
024	Ignition amplifier number 3 cylinder or circuit
025	Ignition amplifier number 1 cylinder or circuit
026	Electronic control module (ECM) supply
029	Idle speed control valve (ISCV) or ISCV circuit
031	Injector number 5 or Injector circuit
032	Injector number 6 or injector Group two circuit
033	Injector number 4 or Injector circuit
036	Carbon filter solenoid valve (CFSV) or CFSV circuit
037	Oxygen sensor (OS) or OS circuit
041	Mass airflow (MAF) sensor or MAF circuit
046	Electronic control module (ECM)
048	Air conditioning (AC) compressor or AC circuit
050	Ignition amplifier cylinder number 4 or circuit
051	Ignition amplifier cylinder number 6 or circuit
054	Electronic control module (ECM)
055	Ignition amplifier or circuit
062	Electronic throttle control or circuit
064	Ignition timing (electronic AT)
067	Vehicle speed sensor (VSS) or VSS circuit
067	Crank angle sensor (CAS) or CAS circuit
070	Oxygen sensor (OS) or OS circuit
073	Vehicle speed sensor (VSS) or VSS circuit
076	CO potentiometer (non-cat)
077	Intake air temperature sensor (ATS) or ATS circuit
078	Engine coolant temperature sensor (CTS) or CTS circuit
081	Alarm system or circuit
082	Traction control or circuit
083	Suspension control or circuit
085	Air conditioning (AC) compressor or AC circuit
100	Electronic control module (ECM)
200	Electronic control module (ECM)
201	Oxygen sensor (OS) control or OS circuit
202	Electronic control module (ECM)
203	Ignition primary or circuit
204	Electronic throttle control signal or circuit
300	Engine

Citroën

Index of vehicles

Model	Engine code	Year	System
AX 1.0i cat	TU9M/L.Z (CDY)	1992 to 1997	Bosch Mono-Motronic MA3.0
AX 1.0i cat	TU9M/L.Z (CDZ)	1992 to 1996	Bosch Mono-Motronic MA3.0
AX 1.1i cat	TU1M (HDZ)	1989 to 1992	Bosch Mono-Jetronic A2.2
AX 1.1i cat	TU1M/L.Z (HDY)	1992 to 1997	Magneti-Marelli G6-11
AX 1.1i cat	TU1M/L.Z (HDZ)	1992 to 1997	Magneti-Marelli G6-11
AX GT 1.4 cat	TU3M (KDZ)	1988 to 1990	Bosch Mono-Jetronic A2.2
AX GT and 1.4i cat	TU3FMC/L.Z (KDY)	1990 to 1992	Bosch Mono-Jetronic A2
AX 1.4i cat	TU3FM/.Z (KDX)	1992 to 1996	Bosch Mono-Motronic MA3.0
AX 1.4 GTi	TU3J2/K (K6B)	1991 to 1992	Bosch Motronic MP3.1
AX 1.4 GTi cat	TU3J2/L.Z (KFZ)	1991 to 1996	Bosch Motronic MP3.1
Berlingo 1.1	TU1M (HDZ)	1996 to 2001	Bosch Motronic MA3.1
Berlingo 1.4	TU3JP (KFX)	1996 to 2001	Magneti-Marelli
BX 14i cat	TU3M (KDY)	1991 to 1994	Bosch Mono-Jetronic A2.2
BX 16i cat	XU5M (BDZ)	1990 to 1992	Bosch Mono-Jetronic or MM G5/6
BX 16i cat	XU5M3Z (BDY)	1991 to 1994	Magneti-Marelli G6-10
BX19 GTi and 4X4	XU9J2 (D6D)	1990 to 1992	Bosch Motronic MP3.1
BX19 GTi 16V	XU9J4 (D6C)	1987 to 1991	Bosch Motronic ML4.1
BX19 TZi 8V cat	XU9JAZ (DKZ)	1990 to 1993	Bosch Motronic 1.3
BX19 16V DOHC cat	XU9J4Z (DFW)	1990 to 1992	Bosch Motronic 1.3
BX19 16V DOHC	XU9J4K (D6C)	1991 to 1992	Bosch Motronic 1.3
BX19i 4X4 cat	DDZ(XU9M)	1990 to 1993	Fenix 1B
C15E 1.1i Van cat	TU1M (HDZ)	1990 to 2001	Bosch Mono-Jetronic A2.2
C15E 1.4i Van cat	TU3F.M/Z (KDY)	1990 to 1995	Bosch Mono-Jetronic A2.2
C15E 1.4i Van cat	TU3F.M/W2 (KDY2)	1993 to 1995	Bosch Mono-Jetronic A2.2
Evasion 2.0i cat	XU10J2CZ/L (RFU)	1994 to 2001	Magneti-Marelli 8P22
Evasion 2.0i turbo cat	XU10J2CTEZ/L(RGX)	1994 to 2001	Bosch Motronic MP3.2
Jumper 2.0i cat	XU10J2U (RFW)	1994 to 2001	Magneti-Marelli DCM8P-11
Jumpy 1.6i	220 A2.000	1995 to 2001	Bosch Mono-Motronic MA1.7
Relay 2.0i cat	XU10J2U (RFW)	1994 to 2001	Magneti-Marelli DCM8P-11
Saxo 1.0	TU9M/L3/L	1996 to 2001	Bosch Mono-Motronic MA3.1
Saxo 1.1	TU1M/L3/L	1996 to 2001	Bosch Mono-Motronic MA3.1

Model	Engine code	Year	System
Saxo 1.4	TU3JP/L3	1996 to 2001	Magneti-Marelli
Saxo 1.6	TU5JP/L3 (NFZ)	1996 to 2001	Bosch Motronic MA5.1
Synergie 2.0i cat	XU10J2CZ/L (RFU)	1994 to 2001	Magneti-Marelli 8P22
Synergie 2.0i turbo cat	XU10J2CTEZ/L(RGX)	1994 to 2001	Bosch Motronic MP3.2
Xantia 1.6i cat	XU5JP/Z (BFX)	1993 to 2000	Magneti-Marelli DCM8P13
Xantia 1.8i 16V	XU7JP4/L3 (LFY)	1995 to 1997	Bosch Motronic MP5.1.1
Xantia 1.8i and Break	XU7JP/Z (LFZ)	1993 to 1997	Bosch Motronic MP5.1
Xantia 2.0i and Break	XU10J2C/Z (RFX)	1993 to 1998	Magneti-Marelli DCM8P20
Xantia 2.0i 16V cat	XU10J4D/Z (RFY)	1993 to 1995	Bosch Motronic MP3.2
Xantia 2.0i 16V and Break	XU10J4R/Z/L3(RFV)	1995 to 2001	Bosch Motronic MP5.1.1
Xantia Activa 2.0i	XU10J4D/Z (RFT)	1994 to 1996	Bosch Motronic MP3.2
Xantia Turbo 2.0i CT	XU10J2CTE/L3 (RGX)	1995 to 2001	Bosch Motronic MP3.2
XM 2.0i MPi	XU10J2 (R6A)	1990 to 1992	Magneti-Marelli BA G5
XM 2.0i cat	XU10J2/Z (RFZ)	1990 to 1992	Bosch Motronic MP3.1
XM 2.0i cat	XU10J2/Z (RFZ)	1992 to 1994	Bosch Motronic MP5.1
XM 2.0i 16V cat	XU10J4R/L/Z (RFV)	1994 to 1999	Bosch Motronic MP5.1.1
XM 2.0i turbo cat	XU10J2TE/Z (RGY)	1993 to 1994	Bosch Motronic MP3.2
XM 2.0i CT turbo cat	XU10J2TE/L/Z(RGX)	1994 to 1996	Bosch Motronic MP3.2
XM 3.0 V6 LHD	ZPJ (S6A)	1989 to 1993	Fenix 3B
XM 3.0 V6 cat	ZPJ (SFZ)	1989 to 1994	Fenix 3B
XM 3.0 V6 cat	ZPJ (UFZ)	1994 to 1997	Fenix 3B
XM 3.0 V6 Estate	ZPJ/Z (UFY)	1995 to 1996	Fenix 3B
XM 3.0 V6 24V cat	ZPJ4/Y3 (SKZ)	1990 to 1994	Fenix 4
XM 3.0 V6 24V	ZPJ4/Y3 (UKZ)	1994 to 1997	Fenix 4B
ZX 1.1i cat	TU1M/Z (HDY)	1991 to 1994	Bosch Mono-Jetronic A2.2
ZX 1.1i cat	TU1M/Z (HDZ)	1991 to 1994	Bosch Mono-Jetronic A2.2
ZX 1.1i cat	TU1M/Z (HDY)	1994 to 1997	Bosch Mono-Motronic MA3.0
ZX 1.1i cat	TU1M/Z (HDZ)	1994 to 1998	Bosch Mono-Motronic MA3.0
ZX 1.4i cat	TU3M/Z (KDY)	1991 to 1992	Bosch Mono-Jetronic A2.2
ZX 1.4i and Break cat	TU3M (KDX)	1992 to 1997	Bosch Mono-Motronic MA3.0
ZX 1.4i and Break cat	TU3M (KDX)	1994 to 1996	Magneti-Marelli G6-14
ZX 1.6i	XU5M.2K (B4A)	1991 to 1992	Magneti-Marelli G5 S2
ZX 1.6i	XU5M.3K (B4A)	1991 to 1993	Magneti-Marelli G6.12
ZX 1.6i cat	XU5M.3Z (BDY)	1992 to 1993	Magneti-Marelli G6.10
ZX 1.6i and Break cat	XU5JP/Z (BFZ)	1994 to 1998	Magneti-Marelli 8P-13
ZX 1.6i and Break cat	XU5JP/Z (BFZ)	1995 to 1998	Sagem/Lucas 4GJ
ZX 1.8i and Break cat	XU7JP/Z (LFZ)	1992 to 1998	Bosch Motronic MP5.1
ZX 1.8i and Break cat	XU7JP/Z (LFZ)	1995 to 1998	Magneti-Marelli 8P-10
ZX 1.9 8V	XU9JAZ (DKZ)	1992 to 1994	Bosch Motronic 1.3
ZX 1.9i	XU9JA/K (D6E)	1991 to 1992	Bosch Motronic MP3.1
ZX 2.0i cat	XUJ10J2/C/L/Z(RFX)	1992 to 1996	Magneti-Marelli 8P-20
ZX 2.0i 16V cat	XUJ10J4/D/L/Z(RFY)	1992 to 1995	Bosch Motronic MP3.2
ZX 2.0i 16V	XUJ10J4/D/L/Z(RFT)	1994 to 1997	Bosch Motronic MP3.2

Plus All models equipped with EOBD (approximately January 2001-on)

Self-Diagnosis

1 Introduction

The engine management systems (EMSs) fitted to Citroën vehicles are mainly of Bosch or Magneti-Marelli origin. The majority of Citroën EMSs control primary ignition, fuelling and idle functions from within the same control module. Early versions of Bosch Motronic 4.1 and 1.3 utilised an auxiliary air valve (AAV) that was not ECM-controlled. The Mono-Jetronic system controls fuelling and idle functions alone.

Self-Diagnosis (SD) function

Each electronic control module (ECM) has a self-test capability that continually examines the signals from certain engine sensors and actuators, and compares each signal to a table of programmed values. If the diagnostic software determines that a fault is present, the ECM stores one or more fault codes. Codes will not be stored about components for which a code is not available, or for conditions not covered by the diagnostic software. In Citroën systems, the control module generates 2-digit fault codes for retrieval either by manual means or by fault code reader (FCR). On models equipped with EOBD, 5-digit fault codes are generated, and an FCR must be used for fault code retrieval and clearing.

Limited operating strategy (LOS)

Citroën systems featured in this Chapter utilise LOS (a function that is commonly called the "limp-home mode"). Once certain faults have been identified (not all faults will initiate LOS), the ECM will implement LOS and refer to a programmed default value rather than the sensor signal. This enables the vehicle to be safely driven to a workshop/garage for repair or testing. Once the fault has cleared, the ECM will revert to normal operation.

Adaptive or learning capability

Citroën systems also utilise an adaptive capability that will modify the basic programmed values for most effective operation during normal running, and with due regard to engine wear.

Self-Diagnosis (SD/MIL) warning light

The majority of Citroën models are equipped with a SD/MIL warning light located within the instrument panel. When the ignition is switched on, the light will illuminate. Once the engine has started, the light will extinguish if the diagnostic software determines that a major fault is not present. If the light illuminates at any time during a period of engine running, the ECM has diagnosed presence of a major fault. Please note that failure of certain components designated as "minor" faults will not cause the light to illuminate. The warning light can be triggered to transmit flash codes on non-EOBD models.

2 | Self-Diagnosis connector location

The 2-pin SD connector is coloured green, and is located in the engine compartment. It is commonly mounted along the left- or right-hand wing, either close to the ECM, the battery, or the cooling system expansion bottle. In some vehicles, the SD connector is located inside the relay box on either the left- or right-hand wing. The SD connector is provided for both manual retrieving of flash codes and for dedicated FCR use.

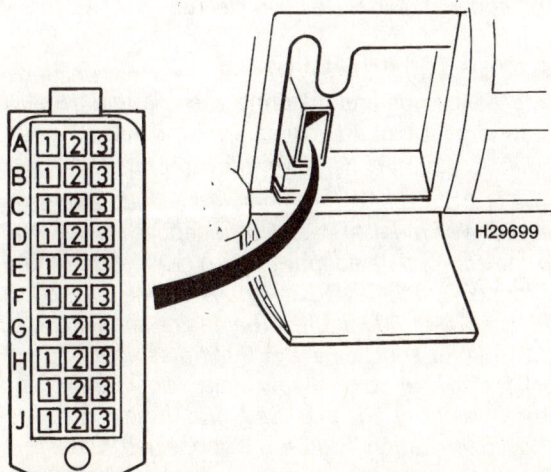

8.1 30-pin SD connector and common location

The 30-pin SD connector fitted to many later models is located in the passenger compartment, either under the facia or behind a cover on the facia *(see illustration 8.1)*. The 30-pin SD connector is provided for FCR use alone

On models equipped with EOBD, the 16-pin connector is located beneath the facia - refer to Chapter 38.

3 | Retrieving fault codes without a fault code reader (FCR) - flash codes

Note: *During the course of certain test procedures, it is possible for additional fault codes to be generated. Care must be taken that any codes generated during test routines do not mislead diagnosis. All codes must be cleared once testing is complete.*

Bosch Motronic ML4.1

1 Attach an on/off accessory switch to the green 2-pin SD connector *(see illustration 8.2)*.

2 Switch on the ignition - the warning light should illuminate.

3 Close the accessory switch - the light will extinguish.

4 Open the switch after 3 seconds. The warning light will begin to flash the 2-digit fault codes as follows:

   a) The two digits are indicated by two series of flashes.
   b) The first series of flashes indicates the multiples of ten, the second series of flashes indicates the single units.

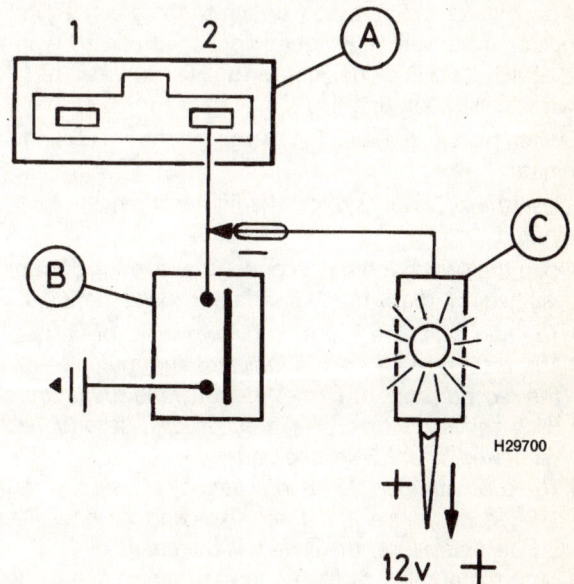

8.2 Retrieve flash codes by connecting an accessory switch and LED (when warning light not fitted) to terminal 2 in the 2-pin SD connector

A SD connector   B Accessory switch   C LED

c) *Each series consists of a number of 1-second flashes, separated by a 1.5-second pause.*

d) *The code number "13" is indicated by a 1-second flash, a 1.5-second pause and three 1-second flashes. After a 2.5-second pause, the code will be repeated.*

5 Count the number of flashes in each series, and record the code. Refer to the tables at the end of the Chapter to determine the meaning of the fault code.

6 The first code to be indicated will be code "12", which indicates initiation of diagnosis.

7 The warning light will extinguish. Wait for 3 seconds before retrieving the next code.

8 Close the accessory switch for 3 seconds.

9 Open the switch. The warning light will begin flashing to indicate the next fault code.

10 The warning light will extinguish. Wait for 3 seconds before continuing.

11 Repeat the same procedure to retrieve further codes.

12 Continue retrieving codes until code "11" is transmitted. Code 11 signifies that no more codes are stored.

13 If the engine is a non-starter, crank the engine on the starter motor for 5 seconds and return the ignition key to the "on" position. Do not switch off the ignition.

14 If code 11 is the first code transmitted after code 12, no faults are stored by the ECM.

15 After code 11 is transmitted, the complete test may be repeated from the start.

16 Turn off the ignition to end fault code retrieval.

All other systems with green 2-pin SD connector

17 Attach an on/off accessory switch to the green 2-pin SD connector. If the vehicle is not equipped with an SD warning light, attach an LED diode light to the SD connector as shown in illustration 8.1.

18 Switch on the ignition. The warning light or LED should illuminate.

19 Close the accessory switch, the light will remain illuminated.

20 Open the switch after 3 seconds. The warning light or LED will begin to flash the 2-digit fault codes as follows.

a) *The two digits are indicated by two series of flashes.*

b) *The first series of flashes indicates the multiples of ten, the second series of flashes indicates the single units.*

c) *Each series consists of a number of 1-second flashes, separated by a 1.5-second pause.*

d) *The code number "13" is indicated by a 1-second flash, a 1.5-second pause and three 1-second flashes. After a 2.5-second pause, the code will be repeated.*

21 Count the number of flashes in each series, and record the code. Refer to the tables at the end of the Chapter to determine the meaning of the fault code.

22 The first code indicated will be code "12", which indicates initiation of diagnosis.

23 Before continuing, wait 3 seconds for the warning light or LED to illuminate.

24 Close the accessory switch for 3 seconds.

25 Open the switch. The warning light will begin flashing to indicate the next fault code.

26 Before continuing, wait 3 seconds for the warning light or LED to illuminate.

27 Repeat the same procedure to retrieve further codes.

28 Continue retrieving codes until code 11 is transmitted. Code 11 signifies that no more codes are stored.

29 If the engine is a non-starter, crank the engine on the starter motor for 5 seconds and return the ignition key to the "on" position. Do not switch off the ignition.

30 If code 11 is the first code transmitted after code 12, no faults are stored by the ECM.

31 After code 11 is transmitted, the complete test may be repeated from the start.

32 Turn off the ignition to end fault code retrieval.

All other systems with 30-pin or 16-pin SD connector

33 AN FCR is required for those systems equipped with the 30-pin or 16-pin SD connector.

4   Clearing fault codes without a fault code reader (FCR)

All systems with 2-pin SD connector

1 Repair all circuits indicated by the fault codes.

2 Switch on the ignition.

3 Perform the above routines to retrieve code 11 - no fault codes.

4 Close the accessory switch for more than 10 seconds, and then open the switch.

5 All fault codes should have been cleared.

All systems (alternative)

6 Turn off the ignition and disconnect the battery negative terminal for a period of approximately 2 minutes.

7 Reconnect the battery negative terminal.

Note: *The first drawback to this method is that battery disconnection will re-initialise all ECM adaptive values. Re-learning the appropriate adaptive values requires starting the engine from cold, and driving at various engine speeds for approximately 20 to 30 minutes. The engine should also be allowed to idle for approximately 10 minutes. The second drawback is that the radio security codes, clock setting and other stored values will be initialised, and these must be re-entered once the battery has been reconnected. Where possible, an FCR should be used for code clearing. On models equipped with EOBD, an FCR must be used for code clearing.*

5 Actuator testing without a fault code reader (FCR)

Bosch Motronic ML4.1
1 Attach an on/off accessory switch to the green 2-pin SD connector *(refer to illustration 8.1)*.
2 Close the accessory switch.
3 Switch on the ignition.
4 Wait 3 seconds and then open the accessory switch. The warning light will flash the appropriate code (see actuator selection code table) and the injector circuit will actuate. Audible operation of the injector solenoids should be heard.

> (!) *Warning: The injectors will actuate for as long as the circuit is closed, and there is a real danger of filling the cylinders with petrol. If testing is required for more than 1 second, disconnect the fuel pump supply (or remove the fuel pump fuse) before commencing this test.*

5 Discontinue the injector test and continue with the next test by closing the accessory switch once more.
6 Wait 3 seconds and then open the accessory switch. The warning light will flash the appropriate code (see actuator selection code table) and the next actuator circuit will function.
7 Repeat the procedure to test each one of the other actuators in turn.
8 Turn off the ignition to end the test.

Systems with 30-pin or 16-pin connector
9 A dedicated FCR must be used to test the actuators for these systems.

6 Self-Diagnosis with a fault code diagnosis (FCR)

Note: *During the course of certain test procedures, it is possible for additional fault codes to be generated. Care must be taken that any codes generated during test routines do not mislead diagnosis.*

All Citroën models
1 Connect an FCR to the SD connector. Use the FCR for the following purposes, in strict compliance with the FCR manufacturer's instructions:
   a) *Retrieving fault codes.*
   b) *Clearing fault codes.*
   c) *Testing actuators.*
   d) *Displaying Datastream.*
   e) *Making adjustments to the ignition timing or mixture (some Magneti-Marelli systems)*
2 Codes must always be cleared after component testing, or after repairs involving the removal or replacement of an EMS component.

7 Guide to test procedures

1 Use an FCR to interrogate the ECM for fault codes, or manually gather codes as described in Sections 3 or 6.

Codes stored
2 If one or more fault codes are gathered, refer to the fault code tables at the end of this Chapter to determine their meaning.
3 If several codes are gathered, look for a common factor such as a defective earth return or supply.
4 Refer to the component test procedures in Chapter 4, where you will find a means of testing the majority of components and circuits found in the modern EMS.
5 Once the fault has been repaired, clear the codes and run the engine under various conditions to determine if the problem has cleared.
6 Check the ECM for fault codes once more. Repeat the above procedures where codes are still being stored.
7 Refer to Chapter 3 for more information on how to effectively test the EMS.

No codes stored
8 Where a running problem is experienced, but no codes are stored, the fault is outside of the parameters designed into the SD system. Refer to Chapter 3 for more information on how to effectively test the EMS.
9 If the problem points to a specific component, refer to the test procedures in Chapter 4, where you will find a means of testing the majority of components and circuits found in the modern EMS.

Chapter 8

Fault code tables

FCR code	Description
11	End of diagnosis
12	Initiation of diagnosis
13x	Air temperature sensor (ATS) or ATS circuit
14x	Coolant temperature sensor (CTS) or CTS circuit
15	Fuel pump relay, supply fault or fuel pump control circuit
18	Turbo coolant pump control
21x	Throttle pot sensor (TPS) or TPS circuit
21x	Throttle switch (TS), idle contact or TS circuit
22	Idle speed control valve (ISCV), supply fault
23	Idle speed control valve (ISCV) or ISCV circuit
25x	Variable induction solenoid valve (VISV) L or circuit
26x	Variable induction solenoid valve (VISV) C or circuit
27x	Vehicle speed sensor (VSS) or VSS circuit
31x	Throttle switch (TS), idle contact or TS circuit
31x	Oxygen sensor (OS), mixture regulation or OS circuit (alternative code)
32	Mixture regulation, exhaust, inlet leak(s) or fuel pressure
33x	Airflow sensor (AFS) or AFS circuit
33x	Manifold absolute pressure (MAP) sensor or MAP sensor circuit (alternate code)
33x	Throttle pot sensor (TPS) or TPS circuit (alternate code, Mono-Jetronic only)
34	Carbon filter solenoid valve (CFSV) or CFSV circuit
35	Throttle switch (TS), full-load contact
36	Oxygen sensor (OS) heater control or OS circuit
41	Crank angle sensor (CAS) or CAS circuit
42	Injectors or injector circuit
43x	Knock sensor (KS), knock regulation
44x	Knock sensor (KS), knock detection
45	Ignition coil control (coil 1)
46	Turbo boost pressure solenoid valve (BPSV) or BPSV circuit
47	Turbo pressure regulation
51x	Oxygen sensor (OS) or OS circuit
52	Mixture control, supply voltage, air or exhaust leak
53x	Battery voltage, charging or battery fault
54	Electronic control module (ECM)
55x	CO pot or CO pot circuit
56	Immobiliser system
57	Ignition coil 2
58	Ignition coil 3

FCR code	Description
59	Ignition coil 4
61	Variable turbo regulation valve or circuit
62x	Knock sensor (KS) 2 or KS circuit
63x	Oxygen sensor (OS) or OS circuit
64	Mixture control B
65x	Cylinder identification (CID) or CID circuit
71	Injector No. 1 control or injector circuit
72	Injector No. 2 control or injector circuit
73	Injector No. 3 control or injector circuit
74	Injector No. 4 control or injector circuit
75	Injector No. 5 control or injector circuit
76	Injector No. 6 control or injector circuit
79x	Manifold absolute pressure (MAP) sensor or MAP sensor circuit

x Faults that typically will cause the ECM to enter LOS and use a default value in place of the sensor.

Some faults are designated as "major" faults, and will illuminate the warning light. However, "major" faults vary from system to system, and it is best to interrogate the ECM for codes if a fault is suspected. Codes designated as "minor" faults will not illuminate the warning light.

EOBD models

For a list of the allocated EOBD codes beginning with P0 (Generic Powertrain), refer to Chapter 1, Section 1.

Actuator selection code

Code	Description
81	Fuel pump relay
82	Injector or injector circuit
83	Idle speed control valve (ISCV) or ISCV circuit
84	Carbon filter solenoid valve (CFSV) or CFSV circuit
85	Air conditioning (A/C) compressor supply relay
91	Fuel pump or fuel pump relay
92	Injector or injector circuit
93	Idle speed control valve (ISCV) or ISCV circuit
94	Carbon filter solenoid valve (CFSV) or CFSV circuit
95	Air conditioning (A/C) compressor supply relay

The above codes are displayed during actuator test mode when the relevant circuit has been actuated. Not all components may be present in any one particular system.

Daewoo

Index of vehicles

Model	Engine code	Year	System
Nexia 1.5 8V SOHC	-	1995 to 1997	GM-Multec
Nexia 1.5 16V DOHC	-	1995 to 1997	GM-Multec
Espero 1.5 16V DOHC	-	1995 to 1997	GM-Multec
Espero 1.8 8V SOHC	-	1995 to 1997	GM-Multec
Espero 2.0 8V SOHC	-	1995 to 1997	GM-Multec

Plus All models equipped with EOBD (approximately January 2001-on)

Self-Diagnosis

1   Introduction

The engine management system (EMS) fitted to Daewoo vehicles is the GM-Multec IEFI-6 and IEFI-S. Daewoo engine management systems control primary ignition, fuelling and idle functions from within the same control module.

Self-Diagnosis (SD) function

Each ECM has a self-test capability that continually examines the signals from certain engine sensors and actuators, and compares each signal to a table of programmed values. If the diagnostic software determines that a fault is present, the ECM stores one or more fault codes. Codes will not be stored about components for which a code is not available, or for conditions not covered by the diagnostic software. In Daewoo systems, the control module generates 2-digit fault codes for retrieval either by manual means or by fault code reader (FCR). Models equipped with EOBD generate 5-digit fault codes, which can only be retrieved or cleared by means of an FCR.

Limited operating strategy (LOS)

Daewoo systems featured in this Chapter utilise LOS (a function that is commonly called the "limp-home mode"). Once certain faults have been identified (not all faults will initiate LOS), the ECM will implement LOS and refer to a programmed default value rather than the sensor signal. This enables the vehicle to be safely driven to a workshop/garage for repair or testing. Once the fault has cleared, the ECM will revert to normal operation.

Adaptive or learning capability

Daewoo systems also utilise an adaptive function that will modify the basic programmed values for most effective operation during normal running, and with due regard to engine wear.

Self-Diagnosis (SD) warning light

Daewoo models are equipped with an SD warning light located within the instrument panel.

| 2 | Self-Diagnosis connector location |

All Daewoo models

The SD connector is located in the driver's footwell, behind the right-hand kick panel close to the ECM (see illustration 9.1). The connector can be used for both manual retrieval of flash codes and for dedicated FCR use.

On models with EOBD, the 16-pin connector is locate under the facia - refer to Chapter 38.

| 3 | Retrieving fault codes without a fault code reader (FCR) - flash codes |

Note: *During the course of certain test procedures, it is possible for additional fault codes to be generated. Care must be taken that any codes generated during test routines do not mislead diagnosis. All codes must be cleared once testing is complete.*

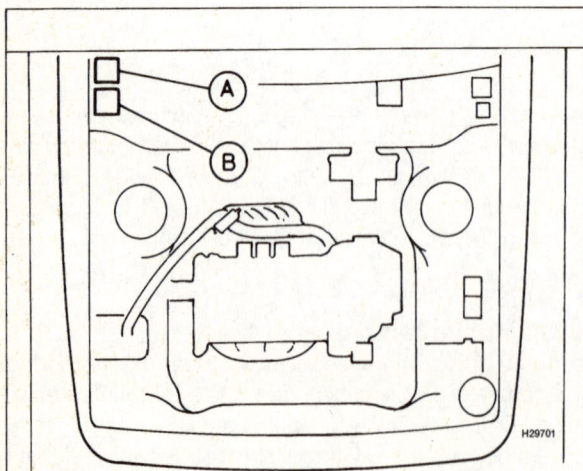

9.1 Location of SD connector and ECM
A ECM   B SD connector

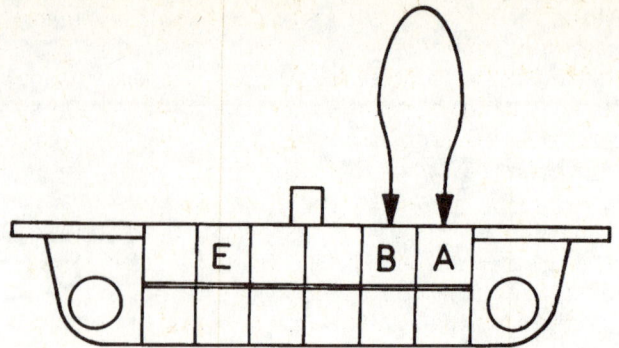

9.2 Retrieve flash codes by connecting a bridge wire between terminals A and B on the SD connector

1 Use a jumper lead to bridge terminals A and B in the SD connector (see illustration 9.2).
2 Switch on the ignition, but do not start the engine.
3 The codes are displayed on the SD warning light in the instrument panel. The flashing of the light indicates the 2-digit fault codes as follows:
a) The two digits are indicated by two series of flashes.
b) The first series of flashes indicates the multiples of ten, the second series of flashes indicates the single units.
c) A 0.4-second flash followed by a 1.2-second interval indicates fault codes in multiples of ten. A 0.4-second flash followed in quick succession by another flash indicates units.
d) A 3.2-second pause separates the transmission of each individual code.
e) Code number "12" is indicated by one short (0.4-second) flash, followed by a 1.2-second pause then two flashes of 0.4 seconds in quick succession.
4 Count the number of flashes in each series, and record each code as it is transmitted. Refer to the table at the end of the Chapter to determine the meaning of the fault code.
5 The first code transmitted will be code "12", which signifies code initiation.
6 Each flash code will be repeated three times followed by the next code in sequence.
7 Continue retrieving codes until all stored codes have been retrieved and recorded.
8 Turn off the ignition and remove the jumper lead to end fault code retrieval.

| 4 | Clearing fault codes without a fault code reader (FCR) |

All systems

1 Turn off the ignition and disconnect the battery negative terminal for a period of approximately 5 minutes.
2 Reconnect the battery negative terminal.

Note: *The first drawback to this method is that battery disconnection will re-initialise all ECM adaptive values. Re-learning the appropriate adaptive values requires starting the engine from cold, and driving at various engine speeds for approximately 20 to 30 minutes. The engine should also be allowed to idle for approximately 10 minutes. The second drawback is that the radio security codes, clock setting and other stored values will be initialised, and these must be re-entered once the battery has been reconnected. Where possible, an FCR should be used for code clearing. On models equipped with EOBD, an FCR must be used to clear codes.*

5 Self-Diagnosis with a fault code reader (FCR)

Note: *During the course of certain test procedures, it is possible for additional fault codes to be generated. Care must be taken that any codes generated during test routines do not mislead diagnosis.*

All Daewoo models

1 Connect an FCR to the SD connector. Use the FCR for the following purposes, in strict compliance with the FCR manufacturer's instructions:

   a) Retrieving fault codes.
   b) Clearing fault codes.
   c) Displaying Datastream.

2 Codes must always be cleared after component testing, or after repairs involving the removal or replacement of an EMS component.

6 Guide to test procedures

1 Use an FCR to interrogate the ECM for fault codes, or manually gather codes as described in Sections 3 or 5.

Codes stored

2 If one or more fault codes are gathered, refer to the fault code table at the end of this Chapter to determine their meaning.

3 If several codes are gathered, look for a common factor such as a defective earth return or supply.

4 Refer to the component test procedures in Chapter 4, where you will find a means of testing the majority of components and circuits found in the modern EMS.

5 Once the fault has been repaired, clear the codes and run the engine under various conditions to determine if the problem has cleared.

6 Check the ECM for fault codes once more. Repeat the above procedures where codes are still being stored.

7 Refer to Chapter 3 for more information on how to effectively test the EMS.

No codes stored

8 Where a running problem is experienced, but no codes are stored, the fault is outside of the parameters designed into the SD system. Refer to Chapter 3 for more information on how to effectively test the EMS.

9 If the problem points to a specific component, refer to the test procedures in Chapter 4, where you will find a means of testing the majority of components and circuits found in the modern EMS.

Fault code table

Flash/ FCR code	Description
12	No faults found in the ECM. Proceed with normal diagnostic methods
13	Oxygen sensor (OS) or OS circuit
14	Coolant temperature sensor (CTS) or CTS circuit
21	Throttle pot sensor (TPS) or TPS circuit
23	Air temperature sensor (ATS) or ATS circuit
24	Vehicle speed sensor (VSS) or VSS circuit
32	Exhaust gas recirculation (EGR) error or EGR circuit
33	Manifold absolute pressure (MAP) sensor or MAP sensor circuit
42	Ignition control circuit error

Flash/ FCR code	Description
44	Oxygen sensor (OS) lean or OS circuit
45	Oxygen sensor (OS) rich or OS circuit
51	Electronic control module (ECM) error
54	CO adjust error

Models with EOBD

For a list of the allocated EOBD codes beginning with P0 (Generic Powertrain), refer to Chapter 1, Section 1.

Notes

Daihatsu

Index of vehicles

Model	Engine code	Year	System
Applause	HD-E	1989 to 1996	Daihatsu EFi
Charade 1.3i cat SOHC 16V	HC-E	1991 to 1993	Daihatsu EFi
Charade 1.3 SOHC 16V	HC-E	1993 to 1999	Daihatsu MPi
Charade 1.5i SOHC 16V	HE-E	1996 to 1999	Daihatsu MPi
Charade 1.6i SOHC 16V	HD-E	1993 to 1996	Daihatsu MPi
Hi-Jet	CB42	1995 to 1999	Daihatsu MPi
Sportrak cat SOHC 16V	HD-E	1990 to 2001	Daihatsu EFi

Plus All models equipped with EOBD (approximately January 2001-on)

Self-Diagnosis

1   Introduction

The engine management system (EMS) fitted to Daihatsu vehicles is the Daihatsu MPi/EFi system, which controls primary ignition, fuel injection, turbocharging pressure (where applicable) and idle functions from within the same ECM.

Self-Diagnosis (SD) function

Each ECM has a self-test capability that continually examines the signals from certain engine sensors and actuators, and compares each signal to a table of programmed values. If the diagnostic software determines that a fault is present, the ECM stores one or more fault codes. Codes will not be stored about components for which a code is not available, or for conditions not covered by the diagnostic software. In Daihatsu systems, the ECM generates 2-digit fault codes for retrieval as flash codes by manual methods alone. On models equipped with EOBD, the ECM generates 5-digit fault codes, which can only be retrieved or clear by means of as FCR.

Limited operating strategy (LOS)

Daihatsu systems featured in this Chapter utilise LOS (a function that is commonly called the "limp-home mode"). Once certain faults have been identified (not all faults will initiate LOS), the ECM will implement LOS and refer to a programmed default value rather than the sensor signal. This enables the vehicle to be safely driven to a workshop/garage for repair or testing. Once the fault has cleared, the ECM will revert to normal operation.

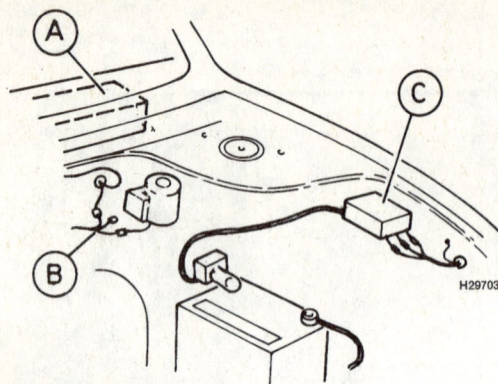

10.1 Location of SD connector, ECM and fuse and relay box for Charade 1987 to 1993

A ECM   B Ignition coil and SD connector   C Fuse and relay box

Adaptive or learning capability

Daihatsu systems also utilise an adaptive function that will modify the basic programmed values for most effective operation during normal running, and with due regard to engine wear.

Self-Diagnosis (SD) warning light

Daihatsu models are equipped with an SD warning light located within the instrument panel.

2   Self-Diagnosis connector location

Charade GT-Ti

The SD connector is located near the ignition coil *(see illustration 10.1)*, and is provided for manual retrieval of flash codes alone.

Applause 1.6i and Sportrak 1.6i

The SD connectors are located near the distributor *(see illustration 10.2)*, and are provided for manual retrieval of flash codes alone.

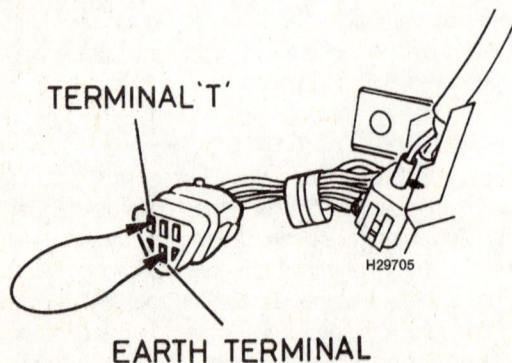

10.3 SD connector terminals for Charade 1987 to 1993

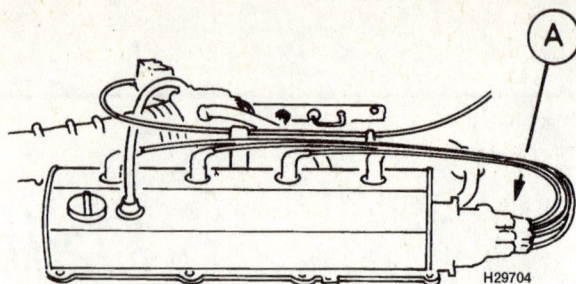

10.2 Location of SD connector for Applause 1989 to 1995 and Sportrak 1991 to 1996

A SD connector located near distributor

All models with EOBD

The diagnostic connector (SD) is located under the facia - refer to Chapter 38.

3   Retrieving fault codes without a fault code reader (FCR) - flash codes

Note: *During the course of certain test procedures, it is possible for additional fault codes to be generated. Care must be taken that any codes generated during test routines do not mislead diagnosis. All codes must be cleared once testing is complete.*

Charade models

1 Use a jumper lead to bridge terminals "T" and earth in the SD connector *(see illustration 10.3)*.

Applause and Sportrak models

2 Use a jumper lead to bridge terminals 5 and 6 in the SD connector *(see illustration 10.4)*.

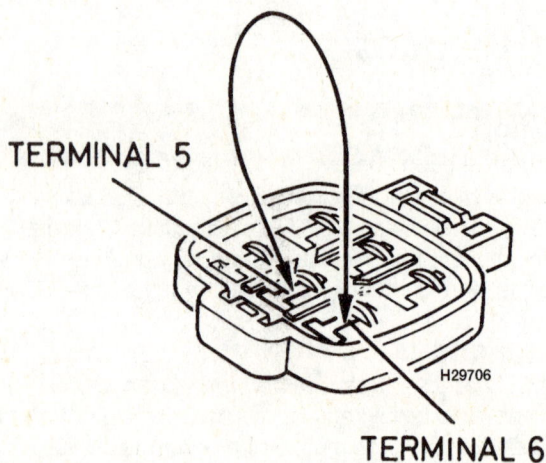

10.4 SD connector terminals for Applause 1989 to 1995 and Sportrak 1991 to 1996

All models (except EOBD)

3 Switch on the ignition, but do not start the engine.

4 The codes are displayed on the SD warning light in the instrument panel. The flashing of the light indicates the 2-digit fault codes as follows:

   a) *A 4.5-second pause signals the beginning of the code transmission sequence.*
   b) *The two digits are indicated by two series of flashes.*
   c) *The first series of flashes indicates the multiples of ten, the second series of flashes indicates the single units.*
   d) *Tens are indicated by a 0.5-second flash, while units are indicated by 0.5-second flashes separated by a 1.2-second pause.*
   e) *A 2.5-second pause separates the tens from the units.*
   f) *A 4.5-second pause separates the transmission of one code from another.*
   g) *Code number "12" is indicated by one short (0.5-second) flash, followed by a 2.5-second pause and then two flashes of 0.5 seconds in quick succession.*

5 Count the number of flashes in each series, and record each code as it is transmitted. Refer to the table at the end of the Chapter to determine the meaning of the fault code.

6 The fault codes are displayed in sequence, and then repeated after a 4.5-second pause.

7 Continue retrieving codes until all stored codes have been transmitted and recorded.

8 If the first transmitted code is "1" (repeated three times), no faults are stored.

9 Turn off the ignition and remove the jumper lead to end fault code retrieval.

4 Clearing fault codes without a fault code reader (FCR)

Method 1

1 Remove the ECM back-up fuse for a minimum of 10 seconds (*see illustration 10.5*).

Method 2

2 Turn off the ignition and disconnect the battery negative terminal for a period of at least 10 seconds.

3 Reconnect the battery negative terminal.

Note: *The first drawback to this method is that battery disconnection will re-initialise all ECM adaptive values. Re-learning the appropriate adaptive values requires starting the engine from cold, and driving at various engine speeds for approximately 20 to 30 minutes. The engine should also be allowed to idle for approximately 10 minutes. The second drawback is that the radio security codes, clock setting and other stored values will be initialised, and these must be re-entered once the battery has been reconnected. On models with EOBD, fault codes can only be cleared by means of an FCR.*

5 Self-Diagnosis with a fault code reader (FCR)

Models equipped with EOBD only

1 Connect an FCR to the SD connector. Use the FCR for the following purposes, in strict compliance with the FCR manufacturer's instructions:

   a) *Retrieving fault codes.*
   b) *Clearing fault codes.*
   c) *Displaying Datastream.*

2 Codes must always be cleared after component testing, or after repairs involving the removal or replacement of an EMS component.

6 Guide to test procedures

1 Manually gather codes or use an FCR as described in Sections 3 or 5.

Codes stored

2 If one or more fault codes are gathered, refer to the fault code table at the end of this Chapter to determine their meaning.

3 If several codes are gathered, look for a common factor such as a defective earth return or supply.

4 Refer to the component test procedures in Chapter 4, where you will find a means of testing the majority of components and circuits found in the modern EMS.

5 Once the fault has been repaired, clear the codes and run the engine under various conditions to determine if the problem has cleared.

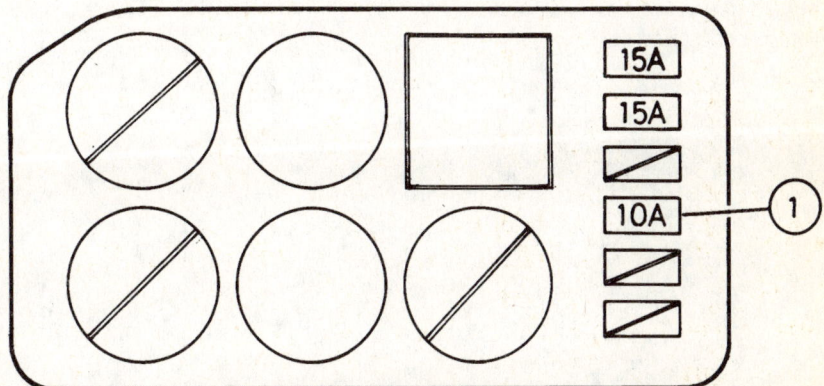

H29707

10.5 Location of ECM back-up fuse (1) in fusebox for Applause 1989 to 1995 and Sportrak 1991 to 1996

6 Check the ECM for fault codes once more. Repeat the above procedures where codes are still being stored.

7 Refer to Chapter 3 for more information on how to effectively test the EMS.

No codes stored

8 Where a running problem is experienced, but no codes are stored, the fault is outside of the parameters designed into the SD system. Refer to Chapter 3 for more information on how to effectively test the EMS.

9 If the problem points to a specific component, refer to the test procedures in Chapter 4, where you will find a means of testing the majority of components and circuits found in the modern EMS.

Fault code table

Daihatsu MPi/EFi

Flash code	Description
01	No faults found in the ECM. Proceed with normal diagnostic methods
02	Manifold absolute pressure (MAP) sensor or MAP sensor circuit
03	Ignition signal
04	Coolant temperature sensor (CTS) or CTS circuit
05	CO adjuster (non-catalyst models)
05	Oxygen sensor (OS) or OS circuit (alternative code)
06	Engine speed sensor (distributor)
07	Throttle position sensor (TPS) incorporating idling switch or TPS circuit
08	Air temperature sensor (ATS) or ATS circuit

Flash code	Description
09	Vehicle speed sensor (VSS) or VSS circuit
10	Starter signal
11	Switch signal idle, auto or A/C.05
12	Exhaust gas regulation (EGR) or EGR circuit
15	Oxygen sensor (OS) or OS circuit, voltage too low
16	Oxygen sensor (OS) or OS circuit, voltage too high

EOBD models

For a list of the allocated EOBD codes beginning with P0 (Generic Powertrain), refer to Chapter 1, Section 1.

Fiat

Index of vehicles

Model	Engine code	Year	System
Brava 1.4 12V	182 AA.1AA	1996 to 1999	Bosch Mono-Motronic SPi
Brava 1.6 16V	182 A4.000	1996 to 1999	Weber Marelli IAW
Bravo 2.0	182 A1.000	1996 to 1999	Bosch Motronic M2.10.4
Cinquecento 899 OHV DIS cat	1170 A1.046	1993 to 1998	Weber-Marelli IAW SPi
Cinquecento 900 OHV DIS cat	170 A1.046	1992 to 1994	Weber-Marelli IAW SPi
Cinquecento Sporting	176 B2000	1995 to 1998	Weber-Marelli IAW SPi
Coupe 16V	836 A3.000	1994 to 1997	Weber-Marelli IAW MPi
Coupe 16V Turbo	175 A1.000	1994 to 1996	Weber-Marelli IAW MPi
Coupe 2.0 20V	-	1997 to 2001	Bosch Motronic M2.10.4
Croma 2000ie	834 B.000	1986 to 1989	Weber-Marelli IAW MPi
Croma 2000ie DOHC 8V	154 C.000	1989 to 1991	Weber-Marelli IAW MPi
Croma 2.0ie DOHC	154 C3.000	1990 to 1992	Weber-Marelli IAW MPi
Croma 2.0ie DOHC DIS cat	154 C3.046	1991 to 1994	Weber-Marelli IAW MPi
Croma 2.0ie 16V cat	154 E1.000	1993 to 1995	Bosch Motronic M1.7
Fiorino 1500 SOHC cat	149 C1.000	1991 to 1995	Bosch Mono-Jetronic A2.4
Panda 1.0ie OHC and 4x4 cat	156 A2.246	1991 to 1996	Bosch Mono-Jetronic A2.4
Panda 1.1ie OHC cat	156 C.046	1991 to 1997	Bosch Mono-Jetronic A2.4
Panda 899	1170A1.046	1992 to 1997	Weber-Marelli IAW SPi
Punto 55	176 A6.000	1994 to 1997	Weber-Marelli IAW SPi
Punto 60	176 A7.000	1994 to 1997	Weber-Marelli IAW SPi
Punto 75	176 A8.000	1994 to 1999	Weber-Marelli IAW MPi
Punto GT	176 A4.000	1994 to 1997	Bosch Motronic M2.7 MPi
Regata 100 Sie & Weekend 1.6 DOHC	149 C3.000	1986 to 1988	GM/Delco SPi
Regata 100 Sie & Weekend 1.6 DOHC	1149 C3.000	1988 to 1990	Weber MIW Centrajet SPi
Tempra 1.4ie SOHC DIS cat	160 A1.046	1992 to 1994	Bosch Mono-Jetronic A2.4
Tempra 1.6ie SOHC DIS cat	159 A3.046	1991 to 1992	Bosch Mono-Jetronic A2.4
Tempra 1.6ie SOHC cat	159 A3.046	1993 to 1994	Bosch Mono-Motronic MA1.7
Tempra 1.8ie DOHC 8V	159 A4.000	1990 to 1992	Weber-Marelli IAW MPi
Tempra 1.8ie DOHC 8V cat	159 A4.046	1992 to 1994	Weber-Marelli IAW MPi
Tempra 1.8 DOHC	835 C2.000	1993 to 1996	Weber-Marelli IAW MPi
Tempra 2.0ie and 4x4 DOHC 8V	159 A6.046	1991 to 1997	Weber-Marelli IAW MPi
Tipo 1.4ie cat	160 A1.046	1991 to 1996	Bosch Mono-Jetronic A2.4
Tipo 1.6ie SOHC DIS cat	159 A3.046	1990 to 1992	Bosch Mono-Jetronic A2.4
Tipo 1.6ie SOHC	835 C1.000	1994 to 1996	Bosch Mono-Motronic MA1.7
Tipo 1.6ie SOHC cat	159 A3.046	1993 to 1995	Bosch Mono-Motronic MA1.7
Tipo 1.8ie DOHC 8V	159 A4.000	1990 to 1992	Weber-Marelli IAW MPi

Model	Engine code	Year	System
Tipo 1.8ie DOHC 8V	159 A4.000	1992 to 1995	Weber-Marelli IAW MPi
Tipo 1.8i DOHC 16V	160 A5.000	1990 to 1991	Weber-Marelli IAW MPi
Tipo 1.8ie DOHC 8V cat	159 A4.046	1992 to 1994	Weber-Marelli 8F
Tipo 2.0ie DOHC 8V cat	159 A5.046	1990 to 1992	Weber-Marelli IAW MPi
Tipo 2.0ie DOHC 8V cat	159 A6.046	1992 to 1995	Weber-Marelli IAW MPi
Tipo 2.0ie DOHC 16V cat	160 A8.046	1991 to 1995	Weber-Marelli IAW MPi
Ulysse 2.0 SOHC 89kW	ZFA220000	1995 to 2002	Weber-Marelli IAW MPi
Ulysse 2.0 Turbo	ZFA220000	1995 to 2002	Bosch Motronic 3.2
Uno 1.0ie SOHC and Van cat	156 A2.246	1992 to 1995	Bosch Mono-Jetronic
Uno 1.1ie SOHC	156 C.046	1989 to 1995	Bosch Mono-Jetronic
Uno 70 1.4 SOHC	146 C1.000	1990 to 1992	Bosch Mono-Jetronic
Uno 1.4 SOHC cat	160 A1.046	1990 to 1995	Bosch Mono-Jetronic
Uno 1.5ie SOHC DIS cat	149 C1.000	1993 to 1994	Bosch Mono-Jetronic
Uno 994	146 C7.000	1994 to 1996	Weber-Marelli IAW SPi

Plus All models equipped with EOBD (approximately January 2001-on)

Self-Diagnosis

1 Introduction

The engine management systems (EMSs) fitted to Fiat vehicles are mainly of Bosch or Weber-Marelli origin. Fiat engine management systems control the primary ignition, fuelling and idle functions from within the same control module. The Mono-Jetronic system controls fuelling and idle speed alone.

Self-Diagnosis (SD) function

Each ECM has a self-test capability that continually examines the signals from certain engine sensors and actuators, and compares each signal to a table of programmed values. If the diagnostic software determines that a fault is present, the ECM stores a fault. Codes will not be stored about components for which a code is not available, or for conditions not covered by the diagnostic software.

GM-Delco SPi

In the GM-Delco SPi system, the EMS generates 2-digit fault codes for retrieval by both manual means and by fault code reader (FCR).

All other Fiat systems

Fiat software does not generate fault code numbers for the majority of Fiat systems. A fault code reader (FCR) normally displays faults on the FCR screen without reference to a specific code number. Although actual code numbers are not available, faults in one or more of the circuits and components covered by the diagnostic software will cause a fault to be stored.

Limited operating strategy (LOS)

Fiat systems featured in this Chapter utilise LOS (a function that is commonly called the "limp-home mode"). Once certain faults have been identified (not all faults will initiate LOS), the ECM will implement LOS and refer to a programmed default value rather than the sensor signal. This enables the vehicle to be safely driven to a workshop/garage for repair or testing. Once the fault has cleared, the ECM will revert to normal operation.

Adaptive or learning capability

Fiat systems also utilise an adaptive function that will modify the basic programmed values for most effective operation during normal running, and with due regard to engine wear.

Self-Diagnosis (SD) warning light

Many Fiat models are equipped with an SD warning light located within the instrument panel. When the ignition is switched on, the light will illuminate. Once the engine has started, the light will extinguish if the diagnostic software determines that a fault is not present. If the light remains illuminated at any time whilst the engine is running, the ECM has diagnosed presence of a system fault.

2 Self-Diagnosis connector location

GM (Delco) SPi

The 3-pin SD connector (see illustration 11.1) is located under the passenger's side glove compartment, close to the ECM. Both manual retrieval of flash codes and dedicated FCR use is possible.

Bosch Mono-Jetronic

The 3-pin SD connector is usually located on the bulkhead in the engine compartment. Alternative locations are close to the ECM under the passenger's side glove compartment, or in the centre console. The SD connector is provided for use by a dedicated FCR alone.

H29338

11.1 3-pin SD connector used for retrieving fault codes from Fiat systems

Bosch Mono-Motronic MA 1.7

The 3-pin SD connector is usually located beside the ECM on the right-hand inner wing in the engine compartment. Alternative locations are close to the ECM under the passenger's side glove compartment, or in the centre console. The SD connector is provided for use by a dedicated FCR alone.

Bosch Motronic 1.7 MPi

The 3-pin SD connector is usually located close to the ECM under the passenger's side glove compartment, and is provided for use by a dedicated FCR alone.

Bosch Motronic 2.7 MPi

The 3-pin SD connector is usually located close to the ECM on the bulkhead in the engine compartment, and is provided for use by a dedicated FCR alone.

Bosch Motronic 2.10.4

The 3-pin SD connector is usually located close to the right-hand side suspension turret in the engine compartment, and is provided for use by a dedicated FCR alone.

Hitachi

The 3-pin SD connector is usually located close to the ECM behind the passenger's side footwell trim, and is provided for use by a dedicated FCR alone.

Weber-Marelli MPi

The 3-pin SD connector is usually located in the engine compartment on the right-hand bulkhead, or in the passenger compartment under the facia, close to the ECM. The SD connector is provided for use by a dedicated FCR alone.

Weber-Marelli SPi

The 3-pin SD connector is usually located in the engine compartment beside the ECM on the left-hand wing (Cinquecento) or beside the ECM on the right-hand wing (other vehicles). The SD connector is provided for use by a dedicated FCR alone.

Models with EOBD

The 16-pin connector is located under the facia - refer to Chapter 38.

3 Retrieving fault codes without a fault code reader (FCR) - flash codes

Note: *During the course of certain test procedures, it is possible for additional fault codes to be generated. Care must be taken that any codes generated during test routines do not mislead diagnosis. All codes must be cleared once testing is complete.*

Fiat GM (Delco) SPi

1 Switch on the ignition - the SD warning light should illuminate.

2 Use a jumper lead to bridge terminals A and B in the 3-pin SD connector (light blue/white and black).

3 The stepper motor will operate once so that the plunger will fully extend and then retract.

4 The codes are displayed on the SD warning light in the instrument panel. The flashing of the light indicates the 2-digit fault codes as follows:

  a) *The two digits are indicated by two series of flashes.*
  b) *The first series of flashes indicates the multiples of ten, while the second series of flashes indicates the single units.*
  c) *A single flash indicates fault codes in tens, while a flash followed in quick succession by a second flash indicates units.*
  d) *A 3.2-second pause separates the transmission of each individual code.*
  e) *Code number "12" is indicated by one single flash, followed by a 1.2-second pause, then two flashes in quick succession.*

5 Count the number of flashes in each series, and record each code as it is transmitted. Refer to the tables at the end of the Chapter to determine the meaning of the fault code.

6 The first code transmitted is code "12", which signifies code initiation. Code 12 is repeated twice more for a total transmission of three times.

7 After transmitting code "12", the warning light will extinguish.

8 After a 3.2-second pause, the warning light will begin transmitting all stored fault codes. Each code is transmitted three times, with a pause for 3.2 seconds between each code.

9 If no fault codes are stored, the warning light will continually flash code "12".

10 Turn off the ignition and remove the jumper lead to end fault code retrieval.

All other systems

11 A fault code reader (FCR) is required to display faults generated in SD systems fitted to other Fiat vehicles.

4 Clearing fault codes without a fault code reader (FCR)

All systems (except EOBD)

1 Turn off the ignition and disconnect the battery negative terminal for a period of approximately 2 minutes.

2 Reconnect the battery negative terminal.

Note: *The first drawback to this method is that battery disconnection will re-initialise all ECM adaptive values. Re-learning the appropriate adaptive values requires starting the engine from cold, and driving at various engine speeds for approximately 20 to 30 minutes. The engine should also be allowed to idle for approximately 10 minutes. The second drawback is that the radio security codes, clock setting and other stored values will be initialised, and these must be re-entered once the battery has been reconnected. Where*

Chapter 11

possible, an FCR should be used for code clearing. On models equipped with EOBD, the codes must be retrieved and cleared by means of an FCR.

5 Self-Diagnosis with a fault code reader (FCR)

Note: *During the course of certain test procedures, it is possible for additional fault codes to be generated. Care must be taken that any codes generated during test routines do not mislead diagnosis.*

All Fiat models

1 Connect an FCR to the SD connector. Use the FCR for the following purposes, in strict compliance with the FCR manufacturer's instructions:

   a) *Displaying fault codes (GM).*
   b) *Displaying system faults (all other systems).*
   c) *Clearing stored fault codes or system faults.*
   d) *Testing actuators.*
   e) *Displaying Datastream.*
   f) *Making adjustments to the ignition timing or mixture (some vehicles).*

2 Codes or stored faults must always be cleared after component testing, or after repairs involving the removal or replacement of an EMS component.

6 Guide to test procedures

1 Use an FCR to interrogate the ECM for fault codes, or (where possible) manually gather codes as described in Sections 3 or 5.

Codes stored

2 If one or more fault codes are gathered, refer to the fault code tables at the end of this Chapter to determine their meaning.

3 If several codes are gathered, look for a common factor such as a defective earth return or supply.

4 Refer to the component test procedures in Chapter 4, where you will find a means of testing the majority of components and circuits found in the modern EMS.

5 Once the fault has been repaired, clear the codes and run the engine under various conditions to determine if the problem has cleared.

6 Check the ECM for fault codes once more. Repeat the above procedures where codes are still being stored.

7 Refer to Chapter 3 for more information on how to effectively test the EMS.

No codes stored

8 Where a running problem is experienced, but no codes are stored, the fault is outside of the parameters designed into the SD system. Refer to Chapter 3 for more information on how to effectively test the EMS.

9 If the problem points to a specific component, refer to the test procedures in Chapter 4, where you will find a means of testing the majority of components and circuits found in the modern EMS.

Fault code tables

GM-Delco SPi

Flash/ FCR code	Description
14	Coolant temperature sensor (CTS) or CTS circuit
15	Coolant temperature sensor (CTS) or CTS circuit
21	Throttle position sensor (TPS) or TPS circuit
22	Throttle position sensor (TPS) or TPS circuit
23	Air temperature sensor (ATS) or ATS circuit
25	Air temperature sensor (ATS) or ATS circuit
33	Manifold absolute pressure (MAP) sensor signal or circuit
34	Manifold absolute pressure (MAP) sensor signal or circuit
42	Ignition circuit
51	Electronic control module (ECM)
52	Electronic control module (ECM)
55	Electronic control module (ECM)

All other systems

Fiat software does not usually generate fault codes. The FCR normally displays faults on the FCR screen without reference to a specific code number. Although actual code numbers are not available, faults in one or more of the following list of circuits and components will cause a fault to be stored.

EOBD models

For a list of the allocated EOBD codes beginning with P0 (Generic Powertrain), refer to Chapter 1, Section 1.

List of circuits checked by Fiat SD system

Adaptive control limits. When the limits are reached, this suggests a serious engine (mechanical) condition.
Air temperature sensor (ATS) or ATS circuit
Battery voltage too low or too high
Crank angle sensor (CAS) or CAS circuit, loss of signal
Carbon filter solenoid valve (CFSV) or CFSV circuit
Coolant temperature sensor (CTS) or CTS circuit
Electronic control module (ECM)
Distributor phase sensor circuit (CID)
Ignition coil(s) control or circuit
Injector control or injector circuit
Knock sensor (KS) or KS circuit
Oxygen sensor (OS) or OS circuit
Manifold absolute pressure (MAP) sensor or MAP sensor circuit
Manifold absolute pressure (MAP) sensor, no correlation between MAP signal and throttle position sensor (TPS) and crank angle sensor (CAS) signals
Mismatch between crank angle sensor (CAS) signal and distributor phase sensor signal or circuit
Oxygen sensor (OS) or OS circuit
Relay control or circuit
Self-Diagnosis (SD) warning light or circuit
Idle speed stepper motor (ISSM) or ISSM circuit
Tachometer
Throttle pot sensor (TPS) or TPS circuit

Ford

Index of vehicles

Model	Engine code	Year	System
Cougar 2.0	EBDA	1998 to 2001	Ford EEC V
Cougar 2.5	LCBA	1998 to 2001	Ford EEC V
Escort 1.3 cat	HCS	1991 to 1992	Ford EEC IV
Escort 1.3 cat	J6A	1991 to 1995	Ford EEC IV
Escort 1.3i and Van	JJA/J4C	1995 to 1999	Ford EEC V
Escort 1.4 CFi cat	F6D	1989 to 1990	Ford EEC IV
Escort 1.4 CFi cat	F6F	1990 to 1995	Ford EEC IV
Escort 1.4 CFi cat	F6G	1990 to 1995	Ford EEC IV
Escort 1.4i	PTE F4	1994 to 1999	Ford EEC V
Escort 1.6i XR3i	LJA	1989 to 1992	Ford EEC IV
Escort 1.6i XR3i cat	LJB	1989 to 1992	Ford EEC IV
Escort 1.6 16V cat	L1E	1992 to 1999	Ford EEC IV
Escort 1.6i	LJA	1989 to 1990	Ford EEC IV
Escort 1.6i and cat	LJE	1990 to 1992	Ford EEC IV
Escort XR3i 1.6 and cat	LJD	1989 to 1992	Ford EEC IV
Escort RS Cosworth DOHC turbo cat	N5F	1992 to 1996	Weber IAW
Escort RS2000 and cat	N7A	1991 to 1995	Ford EEC IV
Escort 1.8i 16V cat	RDA	1992 to 1995	Ford EEC IV
Escort 1.8i 16V cat	RQB	1992 to 1995	Ford EEC IV
Escort 2.0i 7 4x4 cat	N7A	1991 to 1999	Ford EEC IV
Fiesta 1.1 and Van cat	G6A	1989 to 1999	Ford EEC IV
Fiesta 1.25	DHA	1995 to 1999	Ford EEC V
Fiesta 1.3 Van Courier cat	HCS	1991 to 1994	Ford EEC IV
Fiesta 1.3i and Courier cat	J6B	1991 to 1996	Ford EEC IV
Fiesta 1.3 and Courier	JJA	1995 to 1999	Ford EEC V
Fiesta 1.4i and Van cat	F6E	1989 to 1995	Ford EEC IV
Fiesta 1.4	FHA	1995 to 1999	Ford EEC V
Fiesta Classic 1.4	PTE F4A	1995 to 1996	Ford EEC IV
Fiesta XR2i 1.6 cat	LJD	1989 to 1993	Ford EEC IV
Fiesta RS turbo 1.6	LHA	1990 to 1992	Ford EEC IV
Fiesta 1.6i and cat	LUC	1989 to 1992	Ford EEC IV
Fiesta XR2i 1.6	LJC	1989 to 1993	Ford EEC IV
Fiesta 1.6i 16V	L1G	1994 to 1995	Ford EEC IV
Fiesta XR2i 1.8i 16V cat	RDB	1992 to 1995	Ford EEC IV
Fiesta 1.8i 16V cat	RQC	1992 to 1995	Ford EEC IV
Focus 1.4	FXDA/C	1998 to 2002	Ford EEC V

Model	Engine code	Year	System
Focus 1.6	FYDA/C	1998 to 2002	Ford EEC V
Focus 1.8	F/EYDC	1998 to 2002	Ford EEC V
Focus 2.0	EDDC	1998 to 2002	Ford EEC V
Galaxy 2.0	NSD	1995 to 1999	Ford EEC V
Galaxy 2.3	Y5B	1996 to 2000	Ford EEC V
Galaxy 2.8 and 4x4	AAA	1995 to 2000	Ford EEC V
Granada 2.0 EFi	NRA	1985 to 1989	Ford EEC IV
Granada 2.0i and cat	N9B	1989 to 1995	Ford EEC IV
Granada 2.0 EFi 4wd cat	N9D	1989 to 1992	Ford EEC IV
Granada 2.4 V6	ARC	1987 to 1993	Ford EEC IV
Granada 2.4 V6 cat	ARD	1987 to 1991	Ford EEC IV
Granada 2.9 V6 and 4x4	BRC	1987 to 1992	Ford EEC IV
Granada 2.9 V6 cat	BRD	1987 to 1994	Ford EEC IV
Granada 2.9 V6 cat	BRE	1987 to1992	Ford EEC IV
Granada 2.9 V6 cat	BOA	1991 to 1995	Ford EEC IV
Ka 1.3	JJB	1996 to 2002	Ford EEC V
Maverick 2.4i	KA24E	1993 to 1999	Nissan ECCS
Mondeo 1.6 DOHC cat	L1F/J	1993 to 1996	Ford EEC IV
Mondeo 1.6i 16V	L1J	1996 to 2000	Ford EEC V
Mondeo 1.8i 16V	RKB	1996 to 2000	Ford EEC V
Mondeo 1.8i and 4x4 cat	RKA/B	1993 to 1996	Ford EEC IV
Mondeo 2.0i 16V 4x4 cat	NGA	1993 to 1996	Ford EEC IV
Mondeo 2.0i 16V	NGA	1996 to 2000	Ford EEC V
Mondeo 2.5 V6 DOHC cat	SEA	1994 to 1996	Ford EEC IV
Mondeo 2.5i	SEA	1996 to 2000	Ford EEC V
Orion 1.3 cat	HCS	1991 to 1992	Ford EEC IV
Orion 1.3 cat	J6A	1991 to 1995	Ford EEC IV
Orion 1.4 CFi cat	F6D	1989 to 1990	Ford EEC IV
Orion 1.4 CFi cat	F6F	1990 to 1995	Ford EEC IV
Orion 1.4 CFi cat	F6G	1990 to 1995	Ford EEC IV
Orion 1.6i and cat	LJE	1990 to 1993	Ford EEC IV
Orion 1.6i cat	LJF	1990 to 1994	Ford EEC IV
Orion 1.6i	LJA	1989 to 1990	Ford EEC IV
Orion 1.6 DOHC 16V cat	L1E	1992 to 1997	Ford EEC IV
Orion 1.6i	LJA	1989 to 1990	Ford EEC IV
Orion 1.8i 16V DOHC cat	RDA	1992 to 1995	Ford EEC IV
Orion 1.8i 16V DOHC cat	RQB	1992 to 1997	Ford EEC IV
Probe 2.0i DOHC 16V cat	-	1994 to 1997	Mazda EGi
Probe 2.5i 24V cat	V6	1994 to 1997	Mazda EGi
Sapphire 1.6 CVH cat	L6B	1990 to 1993	Ford EEC IV
Sapphire 1.8 CVH cat	R6A	1992 to 1993	Ford EEC IV
Sapphire 2.0 EFi DOHC	N9A	1989 to 1992	Ford EEC IV
Sapphire 2.0 EFi 8V cat	N9C	1989 to 1992	Ford EEC IV
Scorpio 2.0i	NSD	1994 to 1997	Ford EEC IV
Scorpio 2.0 EFi	NRA	1985 to 1989	Ford EEC IV
Scorpio 2.0i 16V	N3A	1994 to 1996	Ford EEC V
Scorpio 2.0i and cat	N9B	1989 to 1995	Ford EEC IV
Scorpio 2.0i	NSD	1994 to 1997	Ford EEC V
Scorpio 2.3i 16V	Y5A	1996 to 1997	Ford EEC V
Scorpio 2.8 4x4	PRE	1985 to 1987	Ford EEC IV
Scorpio 2.9 V6 and 4x4	BRC	1987 to 1992	Ford EEC IV
Scorpio 2.9 V6 cat	BRD	1987 to 1995	Ford EEC IV
Scorpio 2.9 V6 cat	BRE	1987 to 1995	Ford EEC IV
Scorpio 2.9 V6 24V cat	BOA	1991 to 1995	Ford EEC IV
Scorpio 2.9i V6	BRG	1994 to 1997	Ford EEC V
Scorpio 2.9i V6 24V	BOB	1994 to 1999	Ford EEC V
Sierra 1.6 CVH cat	L6B	1990 to 1993	Ford EEC IV
Sierra 1.8 CVH cat	R6A	1992 to 1993	Ford EEC IV
Sierra 2.0 EFi DOHC 8V	N9A	1989 to 1992	Ford EEC IV
Sierra 2.0 EFi 8V cat	N9C	1989 to 1992	Ford EEC IV
Sierra 2.9 XR 4x4 V6	B4A	1989 to 1991	Ford EEC IV
Sierra 2.9 XR 4x4 V6 cat	B4B	1989 to 1993	Ford EEC IV
Transit Van 2.0 CFi cat	N6T	1990 to 1991	Ford EEC IV
Transit Van 2.0 CFi cat	-	1991 to 1992	Ford EEC IV
Transit 2.9 V6 EFi	BRT	1991 to 1994	Ford EEC IV
Transit and Tourneo 2.0i DOHC cat	NSG	1994 to 2000	Ford EEC V
Transit and Tourneo 2.0i	NSF	1994 to 2000	Ford EEC V
Transit 2.9 EFi	B4T	1989 to 1991	Ford EEC IV

Plus All models equipped with EOBD (approximately January 2001-on)

Self-Diagnosis

1   Introduction

The engine management system (EMS) fitted to the majority of Ford vehicles from 1985 to 1996 was Ford EEC IV. In 1996, EEC V began to replace EEC IV on some models; eventually EEC V will replace all vehicles currently equipped with EEC IV. Other engine management systems fitted to European Ford vehicles include Weber IAW (Ford Cosworth), Mazda EGi (Ford Probe) and Nissan ECCS (Ford Maverick).

The various engine management systems fitted to the Ford vehicle range control the primary ignition, fuelling and idle functions from within the same ECM.

Self-Diagnosis (SD) function

Each engine management system has a self-test capability that continually examines the signals from certain engine sensors and actuators, and compares each signal to a table of programmed values. If the diagnostic software determines that a fault is present, the ECM stores one or more fault codes. Codes will not be stored about components for which a code is not available, or for conditions not covered by the diagnostic software. In particular, the Ford EEC IV system has grown in sophistication over the years. When first utilised in 1985, it generated less than ten 2-digit codes. By 1996 the latest version, which has now evolved into EEC V, is capable of generating over a hundred 3-digit codes. All models equipped with EOBD generate 5-digit codes.

Ford EEC V system

Ford EEC V software does not generate fault code numbers, and the fault code reader (FCR) normally displays any faults on the FCR screen without reference to a specific code number. Although code numbers are not available, faults in one or more of the circuits or components covered by the diagnostic software will cause a fault to be stored.

Limited operating strategy (LOS)

In 1988, EEC IV was equipped with keep alive memory (KAM) which utilises LOS, otherwise known as the "limp-home mode". Prior to the fitting of KAM, EEC IV systems did not utilise LOS. Once certain codes have been generated (not all codes will initiate LOS), the ECM will implement LOS and refer to a programmed default value rather than the sensor signal. This enables the vehicle to be safely driven to a workshop/garage for repair or testing. Once the fault has cleared, the ECM will revert to normal operation. Other Ford vehicles that utilise LOS include those equipped with Ford EEC V, Ford Probe (Mazda EGi) and Ford Maverick (Nissan ECCS). Ford Cosworth vehicles equipped with Weber IAW do not utilise LOS.

Adaptive or learning capability

All Ford vehicles equipped with EEC IV (with KAM), EEC V, Mazda EGi and Nissan ECCS systems also utilise an adaptive function that will modify the basic programmed values for most effective operation during normal running, and with due regard to engine wear. However, Ford Cosworth (Weber IAW) does not utilise adaptive control.

Self-Diagnosis (SD) warning light

The Ford Maverick alone is equipped with a facia-mounted SD warning light. In addition, an LED is located upon the ECM casing. When the ignition is switched on, the SD warning light and the LED will illuminate. Once the engine has started, the light and LED will extinguish unless the diagnostic software determines that a system fault is present. If the light or LED illuminates at any time during a period of engine running, the ECM has diagnosed presence of a system fault. The warning light and LED can also be triggered to transmit flash codes.

All models equipped with EOBD have a MIL (Malfunction Indicator Light) on the facia to alert the driver to the presence of one or more fault codes.

2   Self-Diagnosis connector location

Ford EEC IV: 2.0 SOHC, 2.0 DOHC, 2.4, 2.8 and 2.9 V6

The 3-pin or 5-pin SD connector is located in the engine compartment, close to the battery (see illustration 12.1).

Ford EEC IV: CFi, EFi and Zetec (Escort and Fiesta)

The 3-pin SD connector is located in the engine compartment, behind the left-hand headlamp or left-hand wing (see illustration 12.2 overleaf).

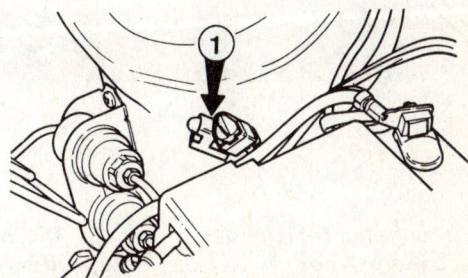

12.1 The EEC IV (2.0 litre/V6) SD connector is located close to the battery

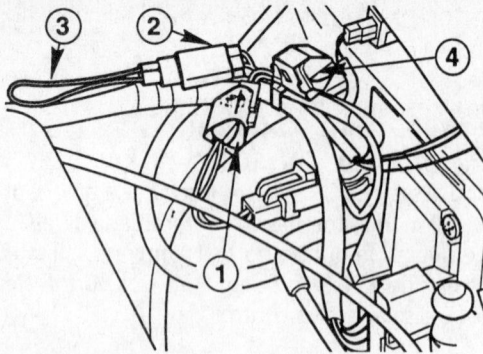

12.2 The EEC IV (Escort/Fiesta) SD connector is located behind the left-hand headlight or on the left-hand wing

1 FDS2000 diagnostic connector
2 Octane connector
3 Octane loop wire
4 SD connector

Ford EEC IV: Zetec (Mondeo)

The 3-pin SD connector is located on a plate on the engine compartment bulkhead along with the octane plug and the FDS2000 connector (see illustration 12.3).

Ford EEC IV and V (16-pin)

The 16-pin OBD connector (see illustration 12.4) is usually located in the passenger compartment, under the steering column, or in the passenger footwell behind the trim, or behind the ashtray in the centre console (Ford Galaxy) - EOBD vehicles refer to Chapter 38.

Ford Probe (Mazda EGi)

The SD connector is located in the engine compartment, close to the battery (see illustration 12.5).

Ford Cosworth (Weber IAW)

The SD connector is located behind the glove compartment, next to the ECM (see illustration 12.6).

Ford Maverick (Nissan ECCS)

The SD connector is located in the passenger compartment, underneath the instrument panel in the facia (see illustration 12.7).

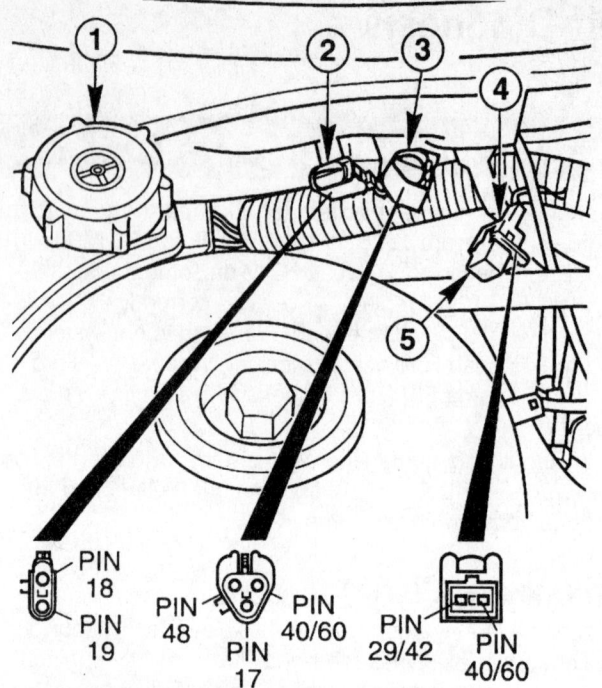

12.3 The EEC IV (Mondeo) SD connector is located on a plate along with the octane plug and the FDS2000

1 Power steering reservoir
2 FDS2000 diagnostic connector
3 SD connector
4 Octane connector
5 Octane plug

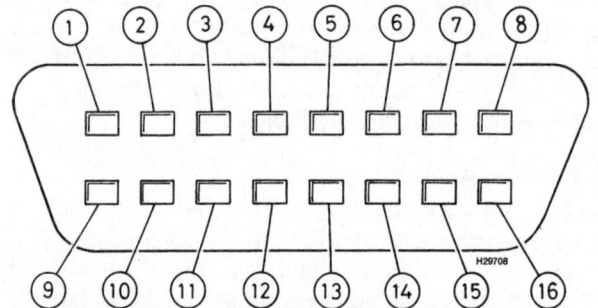

12.4 The 16-pin OBD connector (Ford EEC IV and V)

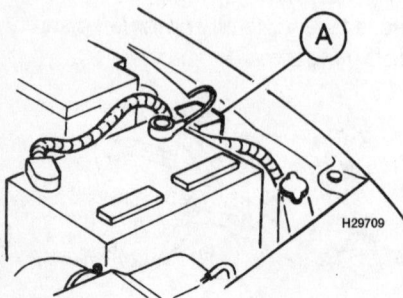

12.5 The SD connector (A) is located close to the battery (Probe)

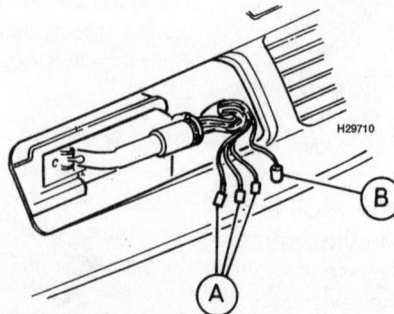

12.6 The Weber IAW SD connector is located behind the glove compartment, next to the ECM (Cosworth)

A Timing adjustment connections
B SD connector

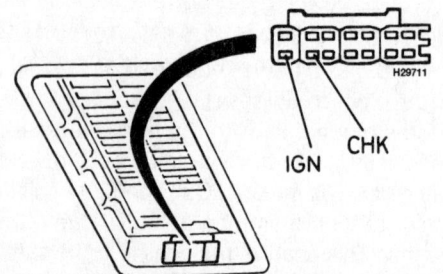

12.7 The SD connector is located underneath the instrument panel in the facia (Maverick)

3 Ford EEC IV enhanced 2-digit fault code retrieval - general

1 The notes in this section should be read in conjunction with the sections about retrieving codes with and without an FCR.

2 Models prior to 1988 do not include keep-alive memory (KAM). Where reference is made to KAM in this section and in the test routines, the reference should be ignored for those systems not so equipped.

3 "Hard" fault codes are codes generated by faults that are present at the exact moment of the test. "Soft" fault codes are codes generated by faults that that have occurred at some point during the past 10 or 40 driving cycles (depending on vehicle) but are not present at the moment of testing. Soft codes are stored in KAM. **Note:** *An engine drive cycle is defined as a period when the vehicle was started with a coolant temperature below 49°C, and continued running until the coolant temperature exceeded 65°C.*

4 Ford EEC IV enhanced (2-digit) has three modes of fault diagnosis, and a service-set mode. The three fault diagnosis modes are:

> **Mode 1:** *Ignition on, engine stopped: A static test of the engine sensors, and retrieval of hard fault codes and soft (KAM) codes.*
>
> **Mode 2:** *Continuous running: A test of the engine sensors during normal engine operation, at idle or during a road test.*
>
> **Mode 3:** *Engine running and service-set mode: A dynamic test of the engine sensors. In the service-set mode, the ignition timing and idle speed can be set. It is not possible to make these adjustments outside of service-set mode.*

5 Although the tests are independent of one another and may be accomplished individually, the following sequence is recommended for more accurate testing.

6 Execute the Mode 1 procedure (see Section 5). Record any codes stored in KAM, but do not attempt to repair faults indicated by KAM at this stage. All hard faults must be rectified (in the order of transmission), and this test must conclude with code 11 (no hard faults found) before continuing with the Mode 2 test. Continue to ignore KAM codes for the moment.

7 Execute the Mode 2 test, which may be performed with the vehicle stationary or during a road test. Rectify all faults before continuing with the Mode 3 test. **Note:** *The Mode 2 test is provided for European vehicles only (not USA); with the exception of 2.4 and 2.9 V6 catalyst-equipped European vehicles.*

8 Execute the Mode 3 test, rectify any faults indicated, and then make adjustments under the service-set mode (if required). **Note:** *An engine running test for 1988 and later vehicles cannot be performed if a hard code is present before the test begins.*

9 Fault codes that were retrieved from KAM can now be investigated and rectified as necessary. Rectifying the hard faults generated during the three test procedures may solve the reason for the generation of soft codes without further testing.

10 It is good practice to turn the ignition off and wait 10 seconds between each test, to avoid an erroneous self-diagnosis test.

11 Before commencing an SD test, ensure that the following conditions are met:

> a) *The engine has attained normal operating temperature.*
> b) *Automatic transmission is in neutral or Park.*
> c) *The handbrake is firmly applied.*
> d) *The air conditioning is switched off.*
> e) *Where applicable, the octane and idle adjust (service-set) wires have been disconnected.*

4 Ford EEC IV enhanced 3-digit fault code retrieval - general

1 The notes in this section should be read in conjunction with the sections about retrieving codes with an FCR.

2 "Hard" fault codes are codes generated by faults that are present at the exact moment of the test. "Soft" fault codes are codes generated by faults that that have occurred at some point during the past 40 driving cycles (most vehicles) or 80 driving cycles (24-valve V6), but are not present at the moment of testing. Soft codes are stored in keep-alive memory (KAM). **Note:** *An engine drive cycle is defined as a period when the vehicle was started with a coolant temperature below 49°C, and continued running until the coolant temperature exceeded 65°C.*

3 Ford EEC IV enhanced (3-digit) has two modes of fault diagnosis and a service-set mode. The two fault diagnosis modes are:

Mode 1

4 Ignition on, engine stopped:

> i) *A static test of the engine sensors and retrieval of hard fault codes and soft (KAM) codes.*
> ii) *A static "wiggle test" of sensors and connections.*
> iii) *A switch monitor test of selected actuators.*

Mode 2

5 Engine running and service-set mode:

> i) *A dynamic test of the engine sensors.*
> ii) *A service-set mode where the idle speed and cylinder balance can be checked.*
> iii) *A dynamic "wiggle test" of sensors and connections.*

6 Although the tests are independent of one another and may be accomplished individually, the following sequence is recommended for more accurate testing.

7 Execute the Mode 1 procedure (see Section 6). Record any codes stored in KAM, but do not attempt to repair faults indicated by KAM at this stage. All hard faults must be rectified (in the order of transmission) and this test must conclude with code 111 (no hard faults found) before continuing with the Mode 2 test. Continue to ignore KAM codes for the moment.

8 Execute the Mode 2 test, rectify any faults indicated, and then make adjustments under the service-set mode (if required). **Note:** *An engine running test for 1988 and later vehicles cannot be performed if a hard code is present before the test begins.*

9 Fault codes that were retrieved from KAM can now be investigated and rectified as necessary. Rectifying the hard faults generated during the two test procedures may solve the reason for the generation of soft codes without further testing.

10 It is good practice to turn the ignition off and wait 10 seconds between each test, to avoid an erroneous self-diagnosis test.

11 Before commencing an SD test, ensure that the following conditions are met:

   a) *The engine has attained normal operating temperature.*
   b) *Automatic transmission is in neutral or Park.*
   c) *The handbrake is firmly applied.*
   d) *The air conditioning is switched off.*
   e) *Where applicable, the octane and idle adjust (service-set) wires have been disconnected.*

5 Retrieving fault codes without a fault code reader (FCR) - flash codes

Note: *During the course of certain test procedures, it is possible for additional fault codes to be generated. Care must be taken that any codes generated during test routines do not mislead diagnosis. All codes must be cleared once testing is complete.*

Ford EEC IV (basic)

1 Ensure that the engine has attained normal operating temperature before commencing tests.

2 Attach an LED diode light between terminal 3 at the SD connector (negative lead) and the battery positive terminal (*see illustration 12.8*). **Note:** *It is also possible to retrieve flash codes by connecting an analogue voltmeter in a similar fashion, and counting the needle sweeps.*

3 Use a jumper lead to bridge terminals 1 and 2 in the SD connector.

4 Start the engine and allow it to idle. **Note:** *If the engine is a non-starter, crank the engine on the starter motor.* After approximately 45 seconds, the LED test light will begin to flash the 2-digit fault codes as follows:

   a) *The two digits are indicated by two series of flashes.*

   b) *The first series of flashes indicates the multiples of ten, the second series of flashes indicates the single units.*
   c) *Both tens and units are indicated by 1-second flashes separated by 1-second pauses.*
   d) *A 4-second pause separates the tens from the units, and a 6-second pause separates the transmission of each individual code.*
   e) *Code number "12" is indicated by one flash of 1-second duration, followed by a 4-second pause then two flashes of 1-second duration separated by a 1-second pause.*

5 Count the number of flashes in each series, and record each code as it is transmitted. Refer to the tables at the end of the Chapter to determine the meaning of the fault code. **Note:** *The engine idle speed will fluctuate during code retrieval. If the idle speed does not fluctuate, this suggests a faulty ISCV or ISCV circuit.*

6 Fault codes generated by the basic EEC IV system are only available whilst the fault is present and when the ignition is switched on. If the fault is permanent (present all the time), then an appropriate code will be stored each time the ignition is switched on. However, if the fault is intermittent and the ignition is switched off, the fault code will be lost until the fault recurs.

7 Continue retrieving codes until all stored codes have been retrieved and recorded.

8 If code 11 is transmitted, no fault codes are stored.

9 Switch off the ignition and remove the jumper lead and LED test light to end fault code retrieval.

Ford EEC IV enhanced (retrieving 2-digit codes)

10 Read the notes in the Section 3 before performing tests in this section. **Note:** *Because of the complexity of retrieving fault codes from Ford vehicles with EEC IV enhanced, and the unreliability of manual methods, the use of an FCR is strongly recommended so that errors may be avoided.*

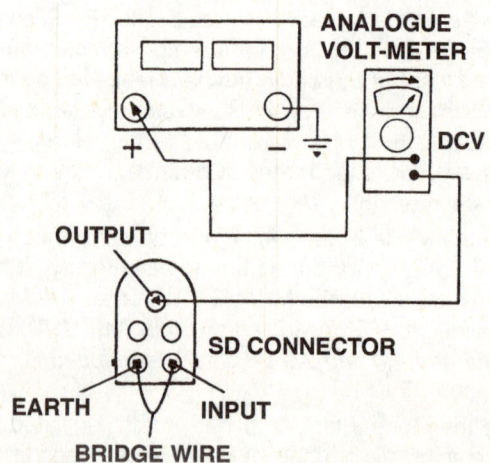

12.8 Retrieving codes from 5-pin Ford EEC IV and Weber IAW systems

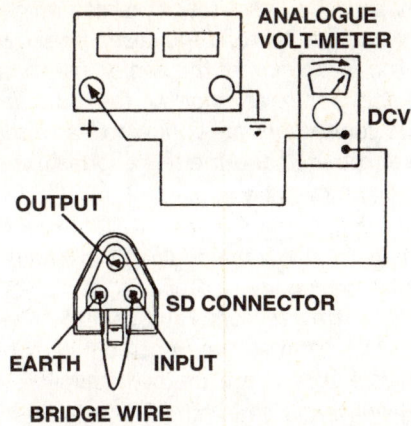

ANALOGUE VOLT-METER

DCV

OUTPUT

SD CONNECTOR

EARTH   INPUT

BRIDGE WIRE

12.9 Retrieving codes from 3-pin Ford EEC IV and Weber IAW systems

11 Attach an LED diode light between terminal 3 at the SD connector (negative lead) and the battery positive terminal *(see illustration 12.9)*.

12 Use a jumper lead to bridge terminals 1 and 2 in the SD connector.

Mode 1 test

13 Switch on the ignition (do not crank the engine if the engine is a non-starter). After approximately 45 seconds, the LED will begin to flash the 2-digit fault codes as follows:

a) *The two digits are indicated by two series of flashes.*

b) *The first series of flashes indicates the multiples of ten, the second series of flashes indicates the single units.*

c) *Code digit pulses are 0.5-second on and 0.5-second off.*

d) *A 2-second pause separates the digits of each code, and a 4-second pulse separates the transmission of each individual code. EEC IV with KAM: After all codes have been transmitted, a pause of 6 to 9 seconds is followed by single flash (separator code). A second pause of 6 to 9 seconds is followed by another single flash, and then any intermittent ("soft") fault codes stored in KAM are transmitted.*

e) *Code number "12" is indicated by one flash of 0.5 seconds duration, followed by a 2-second pause then two flashes of 0.5 seconds' duration separated by a 0.5 second pause.*

f) *After the last hard code is transmitted, a pause of 6 to 9 seconds is followed by a single flash (separator code), another 6 to 9 second pause, and then the soft (KAM) codes are transmitted.*

14 Count the number of flashes in each series, and record each code as it is transmitted. Refer to the tables at the end of the Chapter to determine the meaning of the fault code.

15 Command codes will be transmitted at certain points during the procedure. On retrieving a command code, the engineer is required to take certain actions. If these actions are not taken, a fault will be stored and the "ignition on" code retrieval routine must be repeated.

16 If code 10 appears (some automatic transmission vehicles from 1991), depress fully and release the accelerator pedal and the brake pedal (kickdown must be activated). If the appropriate action is not completed within 10 seconds of code 10 appearing, the ECM will store a fault code. If procedural codes are retrieved, switch off the ignition, wait 10 seconds, and then restart the Mode 1 test.

17 Fault codes generated by the enhanced system (without KAM) are only available whilst the fault is present and when the ignition is switched on. If the fault is permanent (present all the time), then an appropriate code will be stored each time the ignition is switched on. However, if the fault is intermittent and the ignition is switched off, the fault code will be lost until the fault recurs.

18 All fault codes transmitted during this stage indicate the presence of hard faults.

19 If code 11 is transmitted, no fault codes are stored.

20 After all codes have been transmitted, they will be repeated once. The next action will depend upon the vehicle.

21 Models without keep-alive memory (KAM):

a) *Code 10 will be displayed, which indicates that the ECM has commenced "wiggle test" mode.*

b) *Proceed to paragraph 23 and follow the "wiggle test" procedure.*

22 Models with keep-alive memory (KAM):

a) *A separator code will be displayed (code 10, 2.4/2.9 V6 catalyst, or code 20, all others) and then all KAM codes will be transmitted. **Note:** If code 11 is transmitted, no fault codes are stored in KAM.*

b) *After any KAM codes have been transmitted, they will be repeated once. The codes in KAM will then be cleared and code 10 will be displayed, which indicates that the ECM has commenced "wiggle test" mode.*

c) *Proceed to paragraph 23 and follow the "wiggle test" procedure.*

Wiggle test

23 All suspect components, wires and connections should now be gently tapped or wiggled. If the ECM detects a fault during this process, it will be stored in KAM (where KAM is fitted). Repeat the Mode 1 test to retrieve codes detected during the wiggle test and stored in KAM. Record all codes for vehicles without KAM, because they will not be retained in ECM memory.

24 Rectify all faults in the exact order of transmission. Repeat the Mode 1 test until hard fault codes are no longer generated, and then move on to the Mode 2 test. **Note:** *In order to avoid an erroneous self-diagnosis test, it is good practice to switch off the ignition and wait 10 seconds before initiating another Mode 1 test, or before commencing a Mode 2 test.*

25 Switch off the ignition and remove the jumper lead and LED test light to end fault code retrieval.

Mode 2 test

26 Attach an LED diode light between terminal 3 at the SD connector (negative lead) and the battery positive terminal *(refer to illustrations 12.8 and 12.9)*. **Note:** *The Mode 2 test* *is not available for 2.4 and 2.9 V6 catalyst-equipped European vehicles.*

27 Start the engine. Wait four seconds, then use a jumper lead to bridge terminals 1 and 2 in the SD connector.

28 After a few seconds, the LED will begin to flash the 2-digit fault codes. Refer to the description in the Mode 1 test for details of what the flashes represent.

29 Count the number of flashes in each series, and record each code as it is transmitted. Refer to the tables at the end of the Chapter to determine the meaning of the fault code.

30 Fault codes will be continuously displayed while the engine is running. Code 11 indicates "no fault found".

31 All suspect components, wires and connections should now be gently tapped or wiggled, and/or the vehicle could be road-tested.

32 Rectify all faults in the exact order of transmission. Repeat the Mode 1 and Mode 2 tests until both tests are successfully concluded, with no hard fault codes being generated. Only then move onto the Mode 3 test. **Note:** *In order to avoid an erroneous self-diagnosis test, it is good practice to switch off the ignition and wait 10 seconds before initiating another Mode 1 or Mode 2 test, or before commencing a Mode 3 test.*

33 Switch off the ignition and remove the jumper lead and LED test light to end fault code retrieval. **Note:** *The jumper lead and LED test light may remain connected if another Mode 1 or Mode 2 test is to follow on.*

Mode 3 test (and service-set mode)

Note: *The EEC IV version fitted to most 1988 and later engines will not perform an engine running test if any hard codes are present before the test begins.*

34 Turn the ignition off.

35 Attach an LED diode light between terminal 3 at the SD connector (negative lead) and the battery positive terminal *(refer to illustrations 12.8 and 12.9).*

36 Use a jumper lead to bridge terminals 1 and 2 in the SD connector.

37 Switch on the ignition, wait three seconds, start the engine and allow it to idle.

38 Run the engine at 2000 rpm until it has attained normal operating temperature.

39 Once the self-test procedure commences, code 50 (identification of European ECM) will be transmitted. If this code is transmitted alone, or along with one or more coolant temperature sensor (CTS) fault codes, the engine temperature is either too low or the CTS is signalling a too-low temperature. The latter reason could be due to an engine cooling system fault, or an out-of-range sensor that is still within the CTS parameters and will not therefore generate a fault code. The Mode 3 test will not commence until the ECM has verified that operating temperature has been attained.

40 Once the ECM has verified the temperature, the test proper will commence. The engine speed will rise to a fast

idle as EEC IV runs through a set of pre-determined tests of sensors and actuators. **Note:** *If the speed does not rise within 60 seconds, check that the engine is at operating temperature and then re-attempt the test. Also, if any one of the service-set connections are connected, an appropriate code will be transmitted and the test aborted.*

41 When code 10 is displayed, blip the throttle so that the engine speed momentarily rises above 3000 rpm (4000 rpm on catalyst models). Allow the engine to idle again. The "blip" test loads the airflow sensor or MAP sensor, throttle pot and other dynamic sensors. Fault codes will be stored if signal(s) do not conform to the expected parameters, or if the signal is absent or not executed correctly.

42 Fault codes detected during the Mode 3 test will now be transmitted. If fault codes are present, these must be rectified before it is possible to enter service-set mode.

43 If no faults are detected, code 11 will be transmitted, followed by code 60 which signifies the start of service-set mode. **Note:** *Ford 2.4 and 2.9 V6 engines with catalyst will not transmit code 60. Once code 11 has been transmitted, the system has effectively commenced service-set mode.*

Service-set mode

44 When the ECM enters service-set mode, the ignition timing and idle speed are de-regulated, and adjustments can be made to the base ignition timing (models with distributor alone) and the base idle speed (where possible). Where it is not possible to adjust the base ignition timing (DIS models) or base idle speed, the values can still be checked and compared with published specifications. If the measured values are incorrect, this suggests a system or ECM fault.

45 After 2 minutes (catalyst models) or 10 minutes (European non-catalyst models), code 70 will be displayed. This signifies the end of service-set mode, and that the ECM has regained control of the ignition timing and idle speed. If adjustments have not been completed, re-enter code 60 by repeating the Mode 3 and service-set routines.

46 Switch off the ignition and remove the jumper lead and LED test light to end fault code retrieval.

47 Remember to re-connect the octane and idle adjust (service-set) wires, where these were disconnected prior to commencing the self-test procedures.

Ford EEC IV (3-digit) and EEC V

48 An FCR is required to display fault codes generated by Ford EEC IV (3-digit) and EEC V.

Weber IAW (Ford Cosworth)

49 Ensure that the engine has attained normal operating temperature before commencing tests.

50 Attach an LED diode test light between terminal 3 at the SD connector (negative lead) and the battery positive terminal *(refer to illustration 12.8).*

51 Use a jumper lead to bridge terminals 1 and 2 in the SD connector.

52 Switch on the ignition or start the engine and allow it to idle. **Note:** *If the engine is a non-starter, crank the engine on the starter motor. After approximately 45 seconds, the LED will begin to flash the 2-digit fault codes as follows:*

a) *The two digits are indicated by two series of flashes.*
b) *The first series of flashes indicates the multiples of ten, the second series of flashes indicates the single units.*
c) *Both tens and units are indicated by 1-second flashes separated by 1-second pauses.*
d) *A 4-second pause separates the tens from the units, and a 6-second pulse separates the transmission of each individual code.*
e) *Code number "12" is indicated by one flash of 1-second duration, followed by a 4-second pause, then two flashes of 1-second duration separated by a 1-second pause.*

53 Count the number of flashes in each series, and record each code as it is transmitted. Refer to the tables at the end of the Chapter to determine the meaning of the fault code.

54 Fault codes generated by the Weber IAW system are only available whilst the fault is present and the ignition is switched on. If the fault is permanent (present all the time), then an appropriate code will be stored each time the ignition is switched on. However, if the fault is intermittent and the ignition is switched off, the fault code will be lost.

55 Continue retrieving codes until all stored codes have been retrieved and recorded.

56 Switch off the ignition and remove the jumper lead and LED test light to end fault code retrieval.

Mazda EGi (Ford Probe)

57 Mazda EGi has three modes of fault diagnosis. The three modes are as follows:

i) *Mode 1 - ignition on, engine off: A static test of the engine sensors. All faults must be repaired (in the order of transmission) before continuing with the engine running test.*
ii) *Mode 2 - engine running: A dynamic test of the engine sensors.*
iii) *Mode 3 - switch monitor test: A test of various ECM switched inputs.*

Note: *The sequence of testing must observe the above order for accurate diagnosis.*

Mode 1 - retrieving codes

58 Attach an analogue voltmeter between terminal FEN at the SD connector (voltmeter negative lead) and the battery positive terminal (voltmeter positive lead) *(see illustration 12.10)*.

59 Bridge terminals TEN and GND in the SD connector with the aid of a jumper lead.

60 Switch on the ignition. If the ECM has stored one or more fault codes, the voltmeter needle will begin to sweep between 12 and 9 volts. If no codes are stored, the needle will remain on 12 volts.

a) *The first series of sweeps indicates the multiples of ten, the second series of sweeps indicates the single units.*

b) *Tens are indicated by sweeps of 1.2 seconds "on" (9 volts) and less than one second "off" (12 volts). A 1.6-second pause (12 volts) separates the digits of each code.*
c) *Single units are indicated by sweeps of 0.4 seconds "on" (9 volts) and less than one second "off" (12 volts).*
d) *A 4-second pause (12 volts) separates the transmission of one code from another.*

61 Count the number of sweeps in each series and record each code as it is transmitted. Refer to the tables at the end of the Chapter to determine the meaning of the fault code.

62 Continue retrieving codes until all stored codes have been retrieved and recorded.

63 Switch off the ignition and remove the jumper lead and analogue voltmeter to end fault code retrieval.

Mode 2 - retrieving codes

64 Start the engine, run it to normal operating temperature and then stop the engine.

65 Attach an analogue voltmeter between terminal FEN at the SD connector (voltmeter negative lead) and the battery positive terminal (voltmeter positive lead) *(refer to illustration 12.5)*.

66 Bridge terminals TEN and GND in the SD connector with the aid of a jumper lead.

67 Start the engine and allow it to idle. If the ECM has stored one or more fault codes, the voltmeter needle will begin to sweep between 12 and 9 volts. If no codes are stored, the needle will remain on 12 volts:

a) *The first series of sweeps indicates the multiples of ten, the second series of sweeps indicates the single units.*
b) *Tens are indicated by sweeps of 1.2 seconds "on" (9 volts) and less than 1 second "off" (12 volts). A 1.6-second pause (12 volts) separates the digits of each code.*
c) *Single units are indicated by sweeps of 0.4 seconds "on" (9 volts) and less than 1 second "off" (12 volts).*
d) *A 4-second pause (12 volts) separates the transmission of one code from another.*

68 Count the number of sweeps in each series, and record each code as it is transmitted. Refer to the tables at the end of the Chapter to determine the meaning of the fault code.

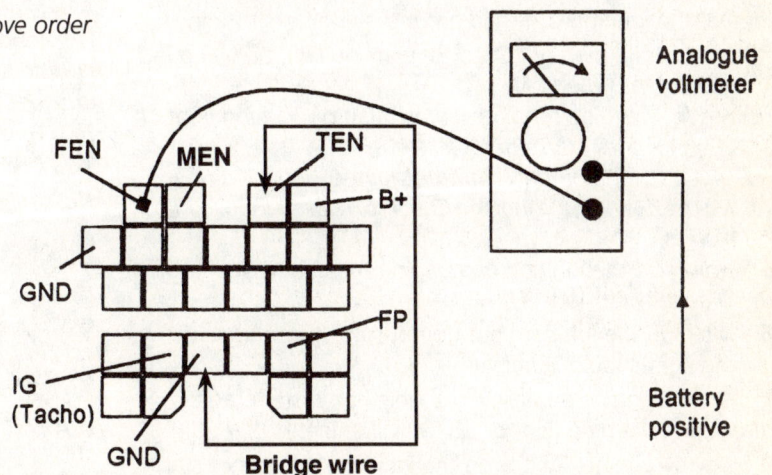

12.10 Retrieving codes from Ford Probe models

69 Continue retrieving codes until all stored codes have been retrieved and recorded.

70 Switch off the ignition and remove the jumper lead and analogue voltmeter to end fault code retrieval.

Mode 3 - switch monitor test

71 Attach an analogue voltmeter *(see illustration 12.11)* between terminal MEN at the SD connector (voltmeter negative lead) and the battery positive terminal (voltmeter positive lead).

72 Bridge terminals TEN and GND in the SD connector with the aid of a jumper lead.

73 The voltmeter needle will remain on 12 volts. When one of the switches on the following list is turned on, the voltmeter needle will fall to 9 volts. If the voltmeter fails to respond as a particular switch is actuated, the switch and its wiring should be tested for faulty operation.

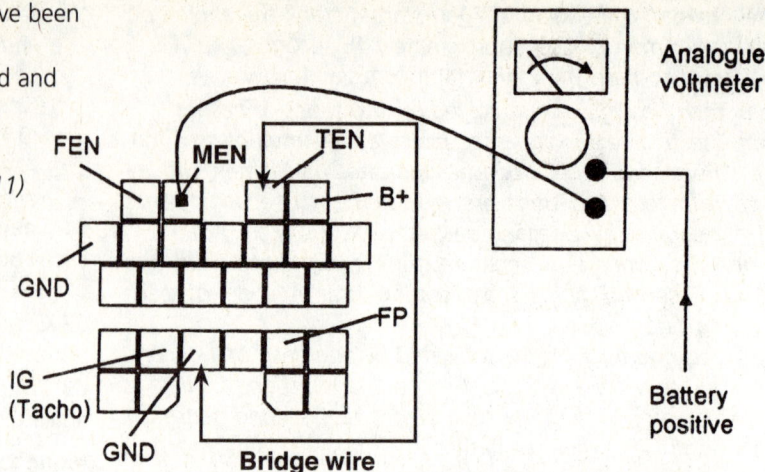

12.11 Using a voltmeter to monitor switch action in Ford Probe models

Switch	Circuit
Turn on the A/C switch	*Air conditioning (A/C)*
Turn on the A/C blower switch	*Air conditioning (A/C)*
Turn on the blower switch on to high position	*Blower motor*
Depress the throttle pedal	*Idle switch*
Fully depress the throttle pedal	*Cooling fan relay (high speed)*
Turn on the headlights	*Headlights*
Select D (automatic transmission)	*Park/neutral circuit*
Depress the clutch (manual transmission)	*Clutch pedal switch and circuitry*
Fully depress the brake pedal	*Brake on/off switch and circuitry*
Turn on the heated rear window	*Heated rear window*

Nissan ECCS (Ford Maverick)

74 There are two modes to retrieving codes and associated information. Output from each mode differs according to whether the ignition is turned on or the engine is running.

  a) *Mode 1, ignition on: Check of warning light bulb and red LED set into the ECM.*
  b) *Mode 1, engine running: Illumination of warning light or LED indicates a system fault.*
  c) *Mode 2, ignition on: Output of fault codes.*
  d) *Mode 2, engine running: Check of closed-loop control system.*

75 Turning off the ignition or stopping the engine will return the SD system to Mode 1.

76 Switch on the ignition, but do not start the engine. The warning light should illuminate.

77 Start the engine and allow it to idle. If a system fault is present, the warning light or LED will illuminate.

78 Stop the engine. Switch on the ignition, but do not start the engine.

79 Bridge terminals IGN and CHK in the SD connector with the aid of a jumper lead *(see illustration 12.12)*.

80 Remove the bridge after two seconds. The SD warning light or LED will begin to flash the 2-digit fault codes as follows:

  a) *The two digits are indicated by two series of flashes.*
  b) *The first series of flashes indicates the multiples of ten, the second series of flashes indicates the single units.*
  c) *Tens are indicated by 0.6-second flashes separated by 0.6-second pauses. Units are indicated by 0.3-second flashes separated by 0.3-second pauses.*
  d) *A 0.9-second pause separates the tens from the units, and a 2.1-second pulse separates the transmission of each individual code.*
  e) *Code 42 is indicated by four 0.6-second flashes, a 0.9-second pause followed by two 0.3-second flashes.*
  f) *Once all fault codes have been transmitted in numerical order of smallest code first and greatest code last, the light will pause for 2.1 seconds and then repeat the sequence. This will continue until the test connector connections are bridged once more.*

81 If code 55 is transmitted, no fault codes are stored.

82 Bridge terminals IGN and CHK in the SD connector with the aid of a jumper lead. Remove the bridge after 2 seconds. The ECM will revert to Mode 1.

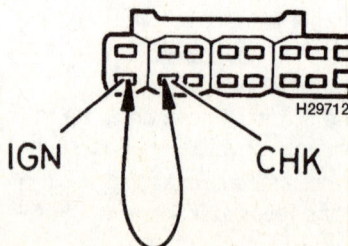

12.12 Retrieving codes from Ford Maverick models. Use a jumper wire to bridge the IGN and CHK terminals

Check the closed-loop mixture control (catalyst models only)

83 Stop the engine and switch on the ignition.

84 Bridge terminals IGN and CHK in the SD connector with the aid of a jumper lead. Remove the bridge after 2 seconds. The SD warning light or LED will begin to flash the 2-digit fault codes as described in paragraph 80.

85 Start the engine and run it to normal operating temperature.

86 Raise the engine speed to 2000 rpm for a period of 2 minutes.

87 Observe the warning light or LED display:

Light or LED switches off and on at a frequency of 5 times in 10 seconds: Engine is in closed-loop control.
Light or LED remains off or on: Engine is in open-loop control.
When the light or LED is on, the fuelling is lean.
When the light or LED is off, the fuelling is rich.

88 The light or LED will reflect the current condition of lean or rich by staying on or off immediately before switching to open-loop control.

6 Clearing fault codes without a fault code reader (FCR)

Ford EEC IV (basic and enhanced without KAM), Weber IAW

1 Early variations of EEC IV and Weber IAW do not retain fault codes after the ignition is switched off.

Ford EEC IV enhanced (with KAM)

2 Fault codes stored in KAM ("soft" codes) are automatically cleared once retrieval is completed and the ECM moves into "wiggle test" mode. "Hard" fault codes are not retained after the ignition is switched off.

Ford EEC V

3 The only manual method of clearing fault codes generated by Ford EEC V is to disconnect the battery - see paragraphs 9 and 10.

Mazda EGi (Ford Probe)

4 Ensure that the ignition switch is switched off.

5 Disconnect the battery negative terminal.

6 Fully depress the brake pedal for between 5 and 10 seconds.

7 Reconnect the battery negative terminal. Refer to the note after paragraph 10 below.

Nissan ECCS (Ford Maverick)

8 The codes will remain stored until one of the following actions are performed:

a) *The codes are displayed (Mode 2) and then the SD function is switched back to Mode 1.*

b) *The vehicle battery is disconnected for 24 hours - refer to the note after paragraph 10 below.*

c) *The fault is automatically cleared once the starter motor has been used for a total of 50 times after the fault has been fixed. If the fault recurs before 50 starts have been made, the counter will be reset to zero, and another 50 starts must occur before the fault is automatically cleared. This procedure occurs on an individual fault code basis, and each code will only be cleared after 50 starts have taken place without recurrence of the fault on that particular circuit.*

Alternative method - Ford EEC IV and EEC V

9 Switch off the ignition and disconnect the battery negative terminal for a period of approximately 2 minutes.

10 Reconnect the battery negative terminal.

Note: *The first drawback to disconnecting the battery is that it will re-initialise all ECM adaptive values. Re-learning the appropriate adaptive values requires starting the engine and allowing it to idle for approximately 3 minutes. The engine should then be warmed-up to normal operating temperature and the engine speed raised to 1200 rpm for approximately 2 minutes. Re-learning can be completed by driving at various engine speeds for approximately 20 to 30 minutes in various driving conditions. The second drawback is that the radio security codes, clock settings and other stored values will be initialised, and these must be re-entered once the battery has been reconnected. Where possible, an FCR should be used for code clearing on Ford vehicles.* **Note:** *On models equipped with EOBD, an FCR must be used to retrieve and clear any fault codes.*

7 Self-Diagnosis with a fault code reader (FCR)

Note: *During the course of certain test procedures, it is possible for additional fault codes to be generated. Care must be taken that any codes generated during test routines do not mislead diagnosis. A failure to retrieve codes satisfactorily from Ford EEC IV is usually caused by incorrect operation of the FCR, or a failure to observe the correct test procedures.*

Ford EEC IV (basic system) and Weber IAW

1 Connect an FCR to the SD connector, and use the FCR to retrieve fault codes in strict compliance with the FCR manufacturer's instructions.

2 Both EEC IV (basic) and Weber IAW are only capable of generating a small number of fault codes, and do not employ any of the more sophisticated features of later systems.

3 On the EEC IV (basic) system, the idle speed will fluctuate during code retrieval. If the idle speed does not fluctuate, this suggests a faulty ISCV or ISCV circuit.

Chapter 12

Ford EEC IV (retrieving 2-digit codes)

4 Connect an FCR to the SD connector, and use the FCR for the following purposes in strict compliance with the FCR manufacturer's instructions:

i) **Mode 1** - ignition on, engine stopped: A static test of the engine sensors, and retrieval of hard fault codes and soft (KAM) codes.

ii) **Mode 2** - continuous running: A test of the engine sensors during normal engine operation, at idle or during a road test (not 2.4/2.9 cat).

iii) **Mode 3** - engine running and service-set mode: A dynamic test of the engine sensors. In the service-set mode, the ignition timing and idle speed can be set. It is not possible to make these adjustments outside of service-set mode.

5 Read the notes in Section 3 before performing tests in this section.

Mode 1 test

6 Turn on the FCR and then switch on the ignition. After approximately 45 seconds, the FCR will display the 2-digit fault codes.

7 Record each code as it is transmitted. Refer to the tables at the end of the Chapter to determine the meaning of the fault code.

8 Command codes will be transmitted at certain points during the procedure. On retrieving a command code, the engineer is required to take certain actions. If these actions are not taken, a fault will be stored, and the Mode 1 code retrieval routine must be repeated.

9 If code 10 appears (some automatic transmission vehicles from 1991), depress fully and release the accelerator pedal and the brake pedal (kickdown must be activated). If the appropriate action is not completed within 10 seconds of code 10 appearing, the ECM will store a fault code. If procedural codes are retrieved, switch off the ignition, wait 10 seconds, and then restart the Mode 1 test.

10 Fault codes generated by the enhanced system (without KAM) are only available whilst the fault is present and when the ignition is switched on. If the fault is permanent (present all the time), then an appropriate code will be stored each time the ignition is switched on. However, if the fault is intermittent and the ignition is switched off, the fault code will be lost until the fault recurs.

11 All fault codes transmitted during this stage indicate the presence of hard faults. If code 11 is transmitted, no fault codes are stored.

12 After all codes have been transmitted they will be repeated once. The next action will depend upon the vehicle.

13 Models without keep-alive memory (KAM):

a) Code 10 will be displayed, which indicates that the ECM has commenced "wiggle test" mode.

b) Proceed to paragraph 15 and follow the "wiggle test" procedure.

14 Models with keep-alive memory (KAM):

a) A separator code will be displayed (code 10, 2.4/2.9 V6 catalyst, or code 20, all others) and then all KAM codes

will be transmitted. **Note:** If code 11 is transmitted, no fault codes are stored in KAM.

b) After any KAM codes have been transmitted, they will be repeated once. The codes in KAM will then be cleared and code 10 will be displayed, which indicates that the ECM has commenced "wiggle test" mode.

c) Proceed to paragraph 15 and follow the "wiggle test" procedure.

Wiggle test

15 All suspect components, wires and connections should now be gently tapped or wiggled. If the ECM detects a fault during this process, it will be stored in keep-alive memory (where KAM is fitted). **Note:** Some FCRs will beep or an LED will flash to indicate the occurrence of a fault or a bad connection during this procedure. Repeat the mode 1 test to retrieve codes detected during the wiggle test and stored in KAM. Record all codes for vehicles without KAM, because they will not be retained in ECM memory.

16 Rectify all faults in the exact order of transmission. Repeat the Mode 1 test until hard fault codes are no longer generated, and then move on to the Mode 2 test. **Note:** In order to avoid an erroneous self-diagnosis test, it is good practice to switch off the ignition and wait 10 seconds before initiating another Mode 1 test, or before commencing a Mode 2 test.

17 Switch off the ignition to end fault code retrieval.

Mode 2 test

Note: The Mode 2 test is not available for 2.4 and 2.9 V6 catalyst-equipped European vehicles.

18 Start the engine. Wait 4 seconds, then turn on the FCR to initiate codes.

19 After a few seconds, the FCR will begin to display the 2-digit fault codes.

20 Record each code as it is transmitted. Refer to the tables at the end of the Chapter to determine the meaning of the fault code.

21 Fault codes will be continuously displayed while the engine is running. Code 11 indicates "no fault found".

22 All suspect components, wires and connections should now be gently tapped or wiggled, and/or the vehicle could be road-tested.

23 Rectify all faults in the exact order of transmission. Repeat the Mode 1 and Mode 2 tests until both tests are successfully concluded with no hard fault codes being generated. Only then move onto the Mode 3 test. **Note:** In order to avoid an erroneous self-diagnosis test, it is good practice to switch off the ignition and wait 10 seconds before initiating another Mode 1 or Mode 2 test, or before commencing a Mode 3 test.

24 Switch off the FCR to end fault code retrieval.

Mode 3 test (and service-set mode)

Note: The EEC IV version fitted to most 1988 and later engines will not perform a Mode 3 test if any hard codes are present before the test begins.

25 Turn the ignition off, then turn on the FCR to initiate codes.

26 Switch on the ignition, wait 3 seconds, then start the engine and allow it to idle.

27 Run the engine at 2000 rpm until it has attained normal operating temperature.

28 Once the self-test procedure commences, code 50 (identification of European ECM) will be transmitted. If this code is transmitted alone, or along with one or more coolant temperature sensor (CTS) fault codes, the engine temperature is either too low or the CTS is signalling a too-low temperature. The latter reason could be due to an engine cooling system fault, or an out-of-range sensor that is still within the CTS parameters and will not therefore generate a fault code. The Mode 3 test will not commence until the ECM has verified that operating temperature has been attained.

29 Once the ECM has verified the temperature, the test proper will commence. The engine speed will rise to a fast idle as EEC IV runs through a set of pre-determined tests of sensors and actuators. **Note:** *If the speed does not rise within 60 seconds, check that the engine is at operating temperature and then re-attempt the test. Also, If any one of the service-set connections are connected, an appropriate code will be transmitted and the test aborted.*

30 When code 10 is displayed, blip the throttle so that the engine speed momentarily rises above 3000 rpm (4000 rpm on catalyst models). Allow the engine to idle again. The "blip" test loads the airflow sensor or MAP sensor, throttle pot and other dynamic sensors. Fault codes will be stored if signal(s) do not conform to the expected parameters, or if the signal is absent or not executed correctly.

31 Fault codes detected during the Mode 3 test will now be transmitted. If fault codes are present, these must be rectified before it is possible to enter service-set mode.

32 If no faults are detected, code 11 will be transmitted, followed by code 60 which signifies the start of service-set mode. **Note:** *Ford 2.4 and 2.9 V6 engines with catalyst will not transmit code 60. Once code 11 has been transmitted, the system has effectively commenced service-set mode.*

Service-set mode

33 When the ECM enters service-set mode, the ignition timing and idle speed are de-regulated, and adjustments can be made to the base ignition timing (models with distributor alone) and the base idle speed (where possible). Where it is not possible to adjust the base ignition timing (DIS models) or base idle speed, the values can still be checked and compared with published measurement values. If the measured values are incorrect, this suggests a system or ECM fault.

34 On Transit 2.9 models with catalyst, the throttle plate can be checked for correct setting and adjusted and reset as necessary.

35 After 2 minutes (catalyst models) or 10 minutes (European non-catalyst models), code 70 will be displayed.

This signifies the end of service-set mode, and that the ECM has regained control of the ignition timing and idle speed. If adjustments have not been completed, re-enter code 60 by repeating the Mode 3 test and service-set routines.

36 Switch off the ignition and remove the FCR to end fault code retrieval.

37 Remember to re-connect the octane and idle adjust (service-set) wires, where these were disconnected prior to commencing the self-test procedures.

Ford EEC IV (retrieving 3-digit codes)

38 Connect an FCR to the SD connector, and use the FCR for the following purposes, in strict compliance with the FCR manufacturer's instructions.

39 Mode 1 - Ignition on, engine stopped:

   i) A static test of the engine sensors and retrieval of hard fault codes and soft (KAM) codes.

   ii) A static "wiggle test" of sensors and connections.

   iii) A switch monitor test of selected actuators.

40 Mode 2 - Engine running and service-set mode:

   i) A dynamic test of the engine sensors.

   ii) A service-set mode where the idle speed and cylinder balance can be checked.

   iii) A dynamic "wiggle test" of sensors and connections.

41 Read the notes in Section 4 before performing the tests in this section.

Mode 1 test

42 Switch on the FCR, and then switch on the ignition. After a few seconds, the FCR will display the 3-digit fault codes.

43 Record each code as it is transmitted. Refer to the tables at the end of the Chapter to determine the meaning of the fault code.

44 Command codes will be transmitted at certain points during the procedure. On retrieving a command code, the engineer is required to take certain actions. If these actions are not taken, a fault will be stored, and the Mode 1 code retrieval routine must be repeated.

45 When code 010 appears, depress fully and release the accelerator pedal (automatic transmission kickdown must be activated). If the appropriate action is not completed within 10 seconds of code 010 appearing, the ECM will store a fault code. If procedural codes are retrieved, switch off the ignition, wait 10 seconds, and then restart the Mode 1 test.

46 All fault codes transmitted during this stage indicate the presence of hard faults. If code 111 is transmitted, no fault codes are stored.

47 After all hard codes have been transmitted, they will be repeated once.

48 A separator code (code 010) will be displayed, and then all the "soft" codes logged by KAM will be transmitted. **Note:** *If code 111 is transmitted, no fault codes are stored in KAM.*

49 After all KAM codes have been transmitted, they will be repeated once.

Actuator test mode

50 Code 111 will be displayed which indicates that the ECM has commenced actuator test mode. The switching of the circuits to the following list of actuators (where fitted) can now be tested.

> *Carbon filter solenoid valve (CFSV).*
> *Electronic vacuum regulator (EVR).*
> *Idle speed control valve (ISCV).*
> *Wide-open throttle (WOT) position (air conditioning cut-off).*
> *Torque converter lock-up clutch solenoid.*
> *Self-diagnosis (SD) connector.*

51 Connect a voltmeter in turn to each of the actuator signal terminals (backprobe the circuit, or connect a break-out box between the ECM multi-plug and the ECM). The voltmeter will indicate nominal battery voltage if the supply circuit is satisfactory.

52 Fully depress and release the accelerator pedal. The ECM will energise all of the actuators, and the voltmeter will indicate near zero volts for the one actuator that is being measured. Some actuators will click as they are actuated.

53 Fully depress and release the accelerator pedal. The ECM will de-energise all of the actuators and the voltmeter will again indicate nominal battery voltage for the actuator that is being measuring. Some actuators will click as they are switched off.

54 Each time the accelerator pedal is depressed, all of the actuators will be switched on and off, and a black dot will appear and disappear in sympathy on the FCR display. Move the voltmeter to each of the components in turn, and test the switching of the component by depressing the accelerator pedal.

55 If the component does not actuate or the voltmeter does not indicate the voltage as indicated, refer to the test procedures appropriate to each component in Chapter 4.

56 How next to proceed depends on the specific instructions for the FCR being used. However, pressing a button twice on the FCR control panel is the method normally used.

Wiggle test mode

57 The system is now in "wiggle test" mode. All suspect components, wires and connections should now be gently tapped or wiggled. If the ECM detects a fault during this process, it will be stored in keep-alive memory (KAM). **Note:** *Some FCRs will beep or an LED will flash to indicate the occurrence of a fault or a bad connection during this procedure.* Repeat the Mode 1 test to retrieve codes detected during the wiggle test and stored in KAM.

58 Switch off the FCR, and then switch off the ignition to end fault code retrieval.

59 Codes are cleared by repeating the Mode 1 test up the point of code transmission. Pressing a button on the FCR control panel is the usual method of clearing the codes in KAM.

60 Rectify all faults in the exact order of transmission. Repeat the Mode 1 test until hard fault codes are no longer generated, and then move onto the Mode 2 test. Note: In order to avoid an erroneous self-diagnosis test, it is good practice to switch off the ignition and wait 10 seconds before initiating another Mode 1 test, or before commencing a Mode 2 test.

Mode 2 test

Note: *The EEC IV version fitted to most 1988 and later engines will not perform a Mode 2 test if any hard codes are present before the test begins.*

61 Turn the ignition off, then switch on the FCR to initiate codes.

62 Switch on the ignition, wait three seconds, start the engine and allow it to idle.

63 Run the engine at 2000 rpm until it has attained normal operating temperature.

64 If this code is transmitted alone, or along with one or more coolant temperature sensor (CTS) fault codes, the engine temperature is either too low or the CTS is signalling a too-low temperature. The latter reason could be due to an engine cooling system fault, or an out-of-range sensor that is still within the CTS parameters and will not therefore generate a fault code. The Mode 2 test will not commence until the ECM has verified that operating temperature has been attained.

65 Once the ECM has verified the temperature, the test proper will commence. The engine speed will rise to a fast idle as EEC IV runs through a set of pre-determined tests of sensors and actuators. **Note:** *If the speed does not rise within 60 seconds, check that the engine is at operating temperature and then re-attempt the test. Also, if the air conditioning is switched on, or an automatic transmission vehicle is in "D", an appropriate code will be transmitted and the test aborted.*

66 Once the self-test procedure commences, code 020 (command code for Zetec engines) or code 030 (command code for V6 engines) will be transmitted.

67 The following test functions must be completed within 10 seconds of the command code appearance:

> a) *Fully depress and release the brake pedal, otherwise fault code 536 will be stored.*
> b) *Fully turn the steering wheel to full lock in one direction and then straighten the wheels. This actuates the power steering pressure switch (PSPS). If the PSPS is faulty, fault code 519 will be stored. If the PSPS is not actuated, fault code 521 will be stored. If the vehicle is not equipped with power steering, the code will still appear, and in this instance it should be ignored.*
> c) *Automatic transmission vehicles only: Switch on and off the overdrive cancel switch (if fitted), then switch on and off the performance/cancel switch (if fitted).*

68 After approximately 20 seconds, code 010 will be displayed. The following test function must be completed within 10 seconds of the command code appearance:

> a) *Blip the throttle so that the engine speed momentarily rises above 3000 rpm. The "blip" test loads the airflow sensor or MAP sensor, throttle pot and other dynamic sensors. Fault codes will be stored if signal(s) do not conform to the expected parameters, or if the signal is absent or not executed correctly.*

69 Allow the engine to idle once again. Fault codes detected during the Mode 2 test will now be transmitted. During transmission of the codes, the black dot will flash in synchronisation on the FCR display.

70 Code 998 may be transmitted, followed by a code relating to one of the sensors listed below. If this happens, proceed as described in paragraph 71. If not, proceed to paragraph 72.

  a) *Airflow sensor.*
  b) *Air temperature sensor.*
  c) *Coolant temperature sensor.*
  d) *Throttle pot.*
  e) *Delta pressure feedback electronic system sensor (EGR system).*
  f) *Electronic pressure transducer.*

71 If code 998 is transmitted, followed by a code relating to one of the sensors listed in paragraph 70, proceed as follows:

  a) *Exit the Mode 2 test.*
  b) *Stop the engine.*
  c) *Test the component as detailed in the relevant component test procedure (Chapter 4) and rectify all faults.*
  d) *Restart the Mode 2 test.*

72 If fault codes are present, these must be rectified before it is possible to enter service-set mode.

73 If code 536 or code 521 are transmitted, incorrect practices were adopted during the routines. Repeat the Mode 2 test procedure.

74 Code 111 will be transmitted if no faults are detected. When the black dot ceases flashing, this signifies the start of service-set mode. The last transmitted code will remain displayed on the FCR screen, which should ordinarily be code 111.

Service-set mode

75 When the ECM enters service-set mode, the idle speed is de-regulated and set at the base idle value (usually slightly higher than normal idle). No adjustments are possible, although the idle speed can be checked against specifications. If the measured values are incorrect, this suggests a system or ECM fault.

76 On engines with sequential injection, fully depressing the accelerator pedal during the 2 minutes service-set mode will set the ECM into cylinder balance test mode. Each injector is switched off in turn for a predetermined moment. The ECU checks for a calibrated fall in rpm, and will set a fault code if there appears to be a problem. After 2 minutes, the engine rpm will rise briefly and then settle at normal idle speed. This signifies the end of the service-set mode.

Wiggle test mode

77 The ECM will now enter "wiggle test" mode.

78 All suspect components, wires and connections should now be gently tapped or wiggled. If the ECM detects a fault during this process, it will be stored in keep-alive memory (KAM). **Note:** *Some FCRs will beep or an LED will flash to indicate the occurrence of a fault or a bad connection during*

this procedure. Repeat the Mode 1 test to retrieve fault codes stored in KAM after being detected during the wiggle test.

79 Rectify all faults in the exact order of transmission. Repeat the Mode 1 test until hard fault codes are no longer generated. **Note:** *In order to avoid an erroneous self-diagnosis test, it is good practice to switch off the ignition and wait 10 seconds before initiating another Mode 1 test, or before commencing a Mode 2 test.*

80 Switch off the FCR and switch off the ignition to end fault code retrieval. Remove the FCR from the vehicle SD connector.

Ford EEC V

81 Connect an FCR to the SD connector, and use the FCR for the following purposes, in strict compliance with the FCR manufacturer's instructions:

  a) *Displaying system faults.*
  b) *Clearing system faults.*
  c) *Testing actuators.*
  d) *Displaying Datastream.*

82 Faults must always be cleared after component testing, or after repairs involving the removal or replacement of an EMS component.

Ford Probe and Maverick

83 Connect an FCR to the SD connector, and use the FCR for the following purposes, in strict compliance with the FCR manufacturer's instructions:

  a) *Retrieving fault codes.*
  b) *Clearing fault codes.*
  c) *Testing switch inputs to ECM.*

84 Codes must always be cleared after component testing, or after repairs involving the removal or replacement of an EMS component.

8 Guide to test procedures

1 Use an FCR to interrogate the ECM for fault codes, or manually gather codes as described in Sections 5 or 7.

Codes stored

2 If one or more fault codes are gathered, refer to the fault code tables at the end of this Chapter to determine their meaning.

3 If several codes are gathered, look for a common factor such as a defective earth return or supply.

4 Refer to the component test procedures in Chapter 4, where you will find a means of testing the majority of components and circuits found in the modern EMS.

5 Once the fault has been repaired, clear the codes and run the engine under various conditions to determine if the problem has cleared.

6 Check the ECM for fault codes once more. Repeat the above procedures where codes are still being stored.

7 Refer to Chapter 3 for more information on how to effectively test the EMS.

No codes stored

8 Where a running problem is experienced, but no codes are stored, the fault is outside of the parameters designed into the SD system. Refer to Chapter 3 for more information on how to effectively test the EMS.

9 If the problem points to a specific component, refer to the test procedures in Chapter 4, where you will find a means of testing the majority of components and circuits found in the modern EMS.

Fault code tables

EEC IV "basic" (2.0 SOHC and 2.8 V6 engines)

Code	Description
11	No faults found in the ECM. Proceed with normal diagnostic methods
12	Airflow sensor (AFS) or AFS circuit number one
13	Coolant temperature sensor (CTS) or CTS circuit
14	Air temperature sensor (ATS) or ATS circuit (in AFS)
15	Throttle pot sensor (TPS) or TPS circuit
22	Airflow sensor (AFS) number two or AFS circuit
23	Airflow sensor (AFS) or AFS circuit number one and number two
31	Wiring/module fault
32	Wiring/module fault

EEC IV "enhanced", two-digit codes (except 2.4/2.9 V6 catalyst and 1.8 CFi)

Code	Description
10	Command code. Operator action required as follows: Ignition on, engine off: wiggle test Engine running: load engine by "blipping" the throttle. The engine speed must exceed 2500rpm
11	No faults found in the ECM. Proceed with normal diagnostic methods
13	Coolant temperature sensor (CTS) or CTS circuit
14	Air temperature sensor (ATS) or ATS circuit
15	Throttle pot sensor (TPS) or TPS circuit
16	Airflow sensor (AFS) or AFS circuit number two
17	Manifold absolute pressure (MAP) sensor or MAP sensor circuit
18	Low battery voltage
19	Keep-alive memory (KAM) or KAM circuit, end and restart SD test. If code repeats, make ECM circuit tests
20	Separator code. Separates "soft" (KAM) codes from "hard" codes (codes of a permanent nature)
21	Ignition, irregular signal
22	Airflow sensor (AFS) or AFS circuit number one, voltage too high
23	Coolant temperature sensor (CTS) or CTS circuit, voltage too high
24	Air temperature sensor (ATS) or ATS circuit
25	Throttle pot sensor (TPS) or TPS circuit, voltage too high
26	Airflow sensor (AFS) number two, voltage too high
27	Manifold absolute pressure (MAP) sensor or MAP sensor circuit, value too high
28	Oxygen sensor (OS) or OS circuit
28	Oxygen sensor (OS) 1 or OS circuit (2.0 DOHC 16V only), rich mixture or failed sensor
29	Oxygen sensor (OS) 2 or OS circuit (2.0 DOHC 16V only), rich mixture or failed sensor
30	Marker code, identifies ECM for 6-cylinder engines
31	Electronic control module (ECM) or ECM circuit ROM/RAM failure
32	Airflow sensor (AFS) or AFS circuit number two, voltage too low
33	Coolant temperature sensor (CTS) or CTS circuit, voltage too low
34	Air temperature sensor (ATS) or ATS circuit
35	Throttle pot sensor (TPS) or TPS circuit, voltage too low

Code	Description
36	Airflow sensor (AFS) or AFS circuit number two, voltage too low
37	Manifold absolute pressure (MAP) sensor or MAP sensor circuit, value too low
38	Oxygen sensor (OS) 1 or OS circuit (2.0 DOHC 16V only), lean mixture or failed sensor
39	Oxygen sensor (OS) 2 (2.0 DOHC 16V only), lean mixture or failed sensor
42	Manifold absolute pressure (MAP) sensor or MAP sensor circuit
43	Throttle pot sensor (TPS) or TPS circuit
44	"Blip" test not performed or late response to message
45	Vehicle speed sensor (VSS) or VSS circuit
46	Idle speed control valve (ISCV) or ISCV circuit failure, max rpm not achieved
47	Idle speed control valve (ISCV) or ISCV circuit failure, min rpm not achieved
48	Idle speed control valve (ISCV) or ISCV circuit
50	European electronic control module (ECM) fitted
51	Air conditioning (AC) "on", turn A/C off and repeat SD test
52	Automatic transmission: Vehicle in "D" during SD test - select "N" or "P" and repeat SD test
53	Octane adjust (OA) wire number one earthed. Disconnect service adjust wire and repeat SD test
54	Octane adjust (OA) wire number two earthed. Disconnect service adjust wires and repeat SD test
55	Idle speed adjust wire earthed. Disconnect service adjust wire and repeat SD test
57	Throttle moved during self-diagnosis (SD) test (prior to code 10), repeat SD test
58	Phasing of profile ignition pick-up. (PIP) and spark advance word (SAW)
59	CO pot or CO pot circuit, outside test limits
60	Start of service-set mode
61	Loss of power - cylinder 1
62	Loss of power - cylinder 2
63	Loss of power - cylinder 3
64	Loss of power - cylinder 4
65	Brake on/off switch
66	Kickdown switch or circuit
67	Fuel temperature switch (FTS) or FTS circuit
68	Turbo boost pressure solenoid valve (BPSV) or BPSV circuit
69	Turbo boost pressure solenoid valve (BPSV) or BPSV circuit
70	End of service-set mode
72	Wastegate control solenoid (WCS) (1.6 CVH Turbo only) or WCS circuit
73	Carbon filter solenoid valve (CFSV) or CFSV circuit
74	3/4 shift solenoid
75	Clutch converter lock-up solenoid
76	Brake "on" indicated
77	Kickdown indicated
78	Power steering pressure switch (PSPS), PSPS not activated during SD procedure. Check if PSPS fitted, if so repeat SD procedure
91	Oxygen sensor (OS) or OS circuit, connections interchanged (2.0 16V DOHC engine)

EEC IV "enhanced", two-digit codes (2.4/2.9 V6 catalyst and 1.8 CFi)

Code	Description
10	Command code/separator code for KAM
10	Operator action required as follows:
	Engine running: Load engine by "blipping" the throttle. The engine speed must exceed 2500 rpm
11	No faults found in the ECM. Proceed with normal diagnostic methods (system pass)
12	Idle speed control valve (ISCV) or ISCV circuit
12	Idle speed stepper motor (ISSM) or ISSM circuit, idle contacts (1.8 CFi)
13	Idle speed control valve (ISCV) or ISCV circuit
	Idle speed stepper motor (ISSM) or ISSM circuit, idle contacts (1.8 CFi)
14	Erratic profile ignition pick-up (PIP) signal or circuit
15	Keep-alive memory (KAM)/read only memory (ROM) (module failure) or KAM/ROM circuit
16	Engine test speed too low
17	Idle speed stepper motor (ISSM) or ISSM circuit, idle contacts (1.8 CFi)
18	Ignition module operation (IDM) or IDM circuit
19	Voltage supply to module
20	4-cylinder identification mode (1.8 CFi)
21	Coolant temperature sensor (CTS) or CTS circuit
22	Manifold absolute pressure (MAP) sensor or MAP sensor circuit
23	Throttle pot sensor (TPS) or TPS circuit
24	Air temperature sensor (ATS) or ATS circuit
25	Knock sensor (KS) or KS circuit
27	Cruise control delayed
28	Cruise control - speed too advanced
29	Vehicle speed sensor (VSS) or VSS circuit
30	Marker code - identifies ECM for 6-cylinder engines
31	Electronic pressure transducer (EPT) or EPT circuit, voltage too low
32	Electronic pressure transducer (EPT) or EPT circuit, outside specification
33	No exhaust gas recirculation (EGR)
34	Electronic pressure transducer (EPT) or EPT circuit, outside specification
35	Electronic pressure transducer (EPT) or EPT circuit, voltage too high
36	No increase in engine test speed
37	Decrease in engine test speed
38	Idle speed stepper motor (ISSM) or ISSM circuit, idle contacts (1.8 CFi)
39	Torque converter lock-up clutch
40	Unused
41	Heated exhaust gas oxygen (HEGO) sensor 1 (cylinders 1,2,3) or HEGO sensor circuit, lean mixture
42	Heated exhaust gas oxygen (HEGO) sensor 1 (cylinders 1,2,3) or HEGO sensor circuit, rich mixture
43	Idle speed stepper motor (ISSM) or ISSM circuit, idle contacts
45	Idle speed stepper motor (ISSM) or ISSM circuit, idle contacts (1.8 CFi)
46	Unused
47	Cruise control switch operation or circuit
48	Cruise control switch sticking or circuit
49	Cruise control signal or circuit
50	Unused
51	Coolant temperature sensor (CTS) or CTS circuit, voltage too high
52	Power steering pressure switch (PSPS) or PSPS circuit
53	Throttle pot sensor (TPS) or TPS circuit, voltage too high
54	Air temperature sensor (ATS) or ATS circuit
55	Unused
56	Unused
57	Octane adjust (OA) - service loom connector
58	Injection delayed through service adjust facility
59	Idle adjust - service loom connector
60	Unused
61	Coolant temperature sensor (CTS) or CTS circuit, voltage too low
62	Automatic transmission (AT) shift solenoid 4/3, closed
63	Throttle pot sensor (TPS) or TPS circuit, voltage too low
64	Air temperature sensor (ATS) or ATS circuit, voltage too low
65	Unused
66	Unused
67	Air conditioning (A/C) switched on, or automatic transmission in "D"
68	Idle speed stepper motor (ISSM) or ISSM circuit, idle contacts (1.8 CFi)
69	Shift valve for 3/2 gear open
70	Unused
71	Idle speed stepper motor (ISSM) or ISSM circuit, idle contacts (1.8 CFi)
72	Manifold absolute pressure (MAP) sensor or MAP sensor circuit
73	Throttle pot sensor (TPS), no reaction to test
74	Brake light switch circuit open
75	Brake light switch short-circuit
76	Unused
77	Late response to "blip throttle" command code
78	Unused
79	Unused
80	Unused
81	Manifold absolute pressure (MAP) sensor or MAP sensor circuit (Transit V6)
82	Secondary air feed valve or circuit (secondary combustion)
83	Heavy duty fan switch
84	Electronic vacuum regulator (EVR) system or EVR circuit
84	Exhaust gas recirculation (EGR) valve or EGR circuit (1.8 CFi)
85	Carbon filter solenoid valve (CFSV) or CFSV circuit
86	Unused
87	Electric fuel pump
88	Electric fan - if fitted
89	Solenoid torque converter lock-up clutch
90	Unused
91	Heated exhaust gas oxygen (HEGO) sensor 2 (cylinders 4,5,6) or HEGO sensor circuit, lean mixture
92	Heated exhaust gas oxygen (HEGO) sensor 2 (cylinders 4,5,6) or HEGO sensor, rich mixture
93	Idle speed stepper motor (ISSM) or ISSM circuit, idle contacts (1.8 CFi)
96	Throttle pot sensor (TPS) or TPS circuit
98	Air charge temperature (ACT) sensor or ACT sensor circuit
98	Engine coolant temperature (ECT) sensor or ECT sensor circuit
98	Manifold absolute pressure (MAP) sensor or MAP sensor circuit
98	Throttle pot sensor (TPS) or TPS circuit
99	Throttle pot sensor (TPS) or TPS circuit

EEC IV "enhanced", three-digit codes

Code	Description
010	Separator/command code. Momentarily press accelerator fully
020	Command code. Momentarily press brake pedal fully
10	Cylinder 1 low
20	Cylinder 2 low
30	Cylinder 3 low
40	Cylinder 4 low
50	Cylinder 5 low
60	Cylinder 6 low
70	Cylinder 7 low
80	Cylinder 8 low
90	Pass cylinder balance test
111	All systems ok (system pass)
112	Air temperature sensor (ATS) or ATS circuit
113	Air temperature sensor (ATS) or ATS circuit
114	Air temperature sensor (ATS) or ATS circuit
116	Coolant temperature sensor (CTS) or CTS circuit, normal operating temperature not reached
117	Coolant temperature sensor (CTS) or CTS circuit, normal operating temperature not reached
118	Coolant temperature sensor (CTS) or CTS circuit, normal operating temperature not reached
121	Throttle pot sensor (TPS) or TPS circuit
122	Throttle pot sensor (TPS) or TPS circuit
123	Throttle pot sensor (TPS) or TPS circuit
124	Throttle pot sensor (TPS) or TPS circuit
125	Throttle pot sensor (TPS) or TPS circuit
129	Mass airflow (MAF) sensor or MAF sensor circuit. No change in MAF sensor signal. Repeat SD procedure whilst depressing throttle during SD test
136	Oxygen sensor (OS) or OS circuit
137	Oxygen sensor (OS) or OS circuit
139	Oxygen sensor (OS) or OS circuit
144	Oxygen sensor (OS) or OS circuit
157	Mass airflow (MAF) sensor or MAF circuit
158	Mass airflow (MAF) sensor or MAF circuit
159	Mass airflow (MAF) sensor or MAF circuit
167	Throttle pot sensor (TPS) or TPS circuit, no change in TPS whilst depressing throttle during SD test. Repeat SD procedure
171	Oxygen sensor (OS) or OS circuit
172	Oxygen sensor (OS) or OS circuit, mixture too lean
173	Oxygen sensor (OS) or OS circuit, mixture too rich
174	Oxygen sensor (OS) or OS circuit
175	Oxygen sensor (OS) or OS circuit
176	Oxygen sensor (OS) or OS circuit
177	Oxygen sensor (OS) or OS circuit
178	Oxygen sensor (OS) or OS circuit
179	Fuel system or fuel system circuit, mixture too lean
181	Fuel system or fuel system circuit, mixture too rich
182	Idle mixture too lean
183	Idle mixture too rich
184	Mass airflow (MAF) sensor or MAF sensor circuit
185	Mass airflow (MAF) sensor or MAF sensor circuit
186	injector or injector circuit, opening time (pulse width too long)
187	injector or injector circuit, opening time (pulse width too short)
188	Oxygen sensor (OS) or OS circuit, voltage too low
189	Oxygen sensor (OS), voltage too high
191	Idle mixture too lean
192	Idle mixture too lean
194	Oxygen sensor (OS) or OS circuit
195	Oxygen sensor (OS) or OS circuit
211	Profile ignition pick-up (PIP) signal or circuit
212	Tachometer circuit
213	Spark advance word (SAW) signal or SAW circuit
214	Cylinder identification (CID) sensor or CID sensor circuit

Code	Description
215	Electronic distributorless ignition system (EDIS) ignition coil or circuit
216	Electronic distributorless ignition system (EDIS) ignition coil or circuit
217	Electronic distributorless ignition system (EDIS) ignition coil or circuit
218	Tachometer circuit
222	Tachometer circuit
226	Electronic distributorless ignition system (EDIS) module or circuit
227	Crank angle sensor (CAS) or CAS circuit
227	Engine speed sensor or circuit (EEC V)
228	Electronic distributorless ignition system (EDIS) ignition coil winding 1 or circuit
229	Electronic distributorless ignition system (EDIS) ignition coil winding 2 or circuit
231	Electronic distributorless ignition system (EDIS) ignition coil winding 3 or circuit
232	Primary circuit of ignition coil
233	Electronic distributorless ignition system (EDIS) module or circuit
234	Ignition coil or circuit
235	Ignition coil or circuit
236	Ignition coil or circuit
237	Ignition coil or circuit
238	Electronic distributorless ignition system (EDIS) module or circuit
239	Profile ignition pick-up (PIP) or PIP circuit, PIP signal present under cranking
241	Electronic control module (ECM), incorrect SD data, repeat SD procedure
243	Coil failure
311	Pulse air system or circuit faulty
312	Pulse air system or circuit faulty
313	Pulse air system or circuit faulty
314	Pulse air system or circuit faulty
315	Pulse air system or circuit faulty
316	Pulse air system or circuit faulty
326	Electronic pressure transducer (EPT) or delta pressure feedback electronic (DPFE) system or circuits
327	Electronic pressure transducer (EPT) or delta pressure feedback electronic (DPFE) system or circuits
328	Electronic vacuum regulator (EVR) or EVR circuit
332	Exhaust gas recirculation (EGR) or EGR circuit
334	Electronic vacuum regulator (EVR) or EVR circuit
335	Electronic pressure transducer (EPT) or EPT circuit
335	Delta pressure feedback electronic (DPFE) system or DPFE circuit (alternative code)
336	Exhaust pressure to high
337	Electronic pressure transducer (EPT), delta pressure feedback electronic (DPFE) system, or electronic vacuum regulator (EVR) system or circuits
338	Coolant temperature sensor (CTS) or CTS circuit
339	Coolant temperature sensor (CTS) or CTS circuit
341	Octane adjuster (OA) or OA circuit
411	Self-diagnosis test. Engine speed during test too low. Check that no induction leaks are present, then repeat SD procedure
412	Self-diagnosis test. Engine speed during test too high
413	Idle speed control valve (ISCV) or ISCV circuit
414	idle speed control valve (ISCV) or ISCV circuit
415	idle speed control valve (ISCV) or ISCV circuit
416	idle speed control valve (ISCV) or ISCV circuit
452	Vehicle speed sensor (VSS) or VSS circuit
511	Read only memory (ROM) fault or ROM circuit
512	Keep-alive memory (KAM) fault or KAM circuit
513	ECM reference voltage
519	Power steering pressure switch (PSPS) or PSPS circuit. PSPS not activated during SD test. Check if PSPS fitted, if so try SD test again, then test PSPS circuit
521	Power steering pressure switch (PSPS) or PSPS circuit. PSPS not activated during SD test. Check if PSPS fitted, if so try SD test again, then test PSPS circuit
522	Drive/neutral switch or circuit

Code	Description
523	Drive/neutral switch or circuit
528	Clutch switch error or circuit
536	Brake on/off switch or circuit, switch not activated during SD test. Repeat SD procedure
538	Operator error during self-diagnosis test. Repeat SD procedure
539	Air conditioning (A/C) on during SD test. Repeat SD procedure
542	Fuel pump or fuel pump circuit
543	Fuel pump or fuel pump circuit
551	idle speed control valve (ISCV) or ISCV circuit
552	Pulse air circuit
556	Fuel pump or fuel pump circuit
558	Electronic vacuum regulator (EVR) or EVR circuit
563	High speed electronic drive fan or circuit
564	Electronic drive fan relay/circuit
565	Carbon filter solenoid valve (CFSV) or CFSV circuit
566	3rd/4th gear solenoid automatic transmission
573	Electronic drive fan relay/circuit
574	High speed electronic drive fan or circuit
575	Fuel pump or fuel pump circuit, or inertia switch or circuit
576	Kickdown switch or circuit. Carry out system test
577	Kickdown switch or circuit not activated during SD test. Repeat SD procedure
612	4/3 switch failed - automatic transmission
613	4/3 switch failed - automatic transmission
614	3/2 switch failed - automatic transmission
615	3/2 switch failed - automatic transmission
621	Shift solenoid 1 or circuit failure
622	Shift solenoid 2 or circuit failure
624	EPC solenoid or circuit
625	EPC solenoid or circuit
628	MLUS (lock-up solenoid, automatic transmission) or circuit
629	Torque converter lock-up clutch solenoid
634	Drive/neutral switch or circuit
635	Transmission temperature switch or circuit
636	Transmission temperature switch or circuit
637	Transmission temperature switch or circuit
638	Transmission temperature switch or circuit
639	TSS or TSS circuit
645	1st gear failure
645	2nd gear failure
645	3rd gear failure
645	4th gear failure
649	ETV or circuit (automatic transmission)
651	ETV or circuit (automatic transmission)
652	MLUS (lock-up solenoid - automatic transmission)
653	Transmission control switch not activated during SD test. Repeat SD procedure
658	Automatic transmission performance/economy switch not activated during SD test
998	Rectify codes following 998 (see Section 7, paragraph 70). Coolant temperature sensor (CTS), Air temperature sensor (ATS), airflow sensor (AFS) or throttle position sensor (TPS). Repeat SD procedure

Ford EEC V

Ford EEC V software does not generate fault codes. Any faults in the system are displayed on the FCR screen without reference to a specific code number. Faults in one or more of the system circuits or components will cause a fault to be stored. Broadly speaking, the circuits and components checked by EEC V are very similar to those checked by EEC IV.

Ford Weber IAW

Code	Description
11	TDC sensor or TDC sensor circuit
12	Distributor phase sensor or circuit
13	Phasing speed/TDC to distributor sensor or circuit
21	Air temperature sensor (ATS) or ATS circuit
22	Air temperature sensor (ATS) or ATS circuit
22	Knock sensor (KS) or KS circuit (alternative code)
23	Coolant temperature sensor (CTS) or CTS circuit
31	Coolant temperature sensor (CTS) or CTS circuit
31	Heated exhaust gas oxygen (HEGO) sensor or HEGO sensor circuit (alternative code)
32	Manifold absolute pressure (MAP) sensor or MAP sensor circuit
33	Manifold absolute pressure (MAP) sensor or MAP sensor circuit
33	Throttle pot sensor (TPS) or TPS circuit (alternative code)

Ford Probe (Mazda EGi)

Code	Description
02	Crank angle sensor (CAS) or CAS circuit
03	Cylinder identification sensor (CID) or CID circuit
04	Crank angle sensor (CAS) or CAS circuit
05	Knock sensor (KS) or KS circuit
08	Airflow sensor (AFS) or AFS circuit
09	Coolant temperature sensor (CTS) or CTS circuit
10	Air temperature sensor (ATS) or ATS circuit
12	Throttle pot sensor (TPS) or TPS circuit
14	Barometric pressure sensor (BPS) or BPS circuit
15	Heated exhaust gas oxygen (HEGO) sensor or HEGO sensor circuit
16	Exhaust gas recirculation (EGR) Valve or EGR circuit
17	Heated exhaust gas oxygen (HEGO) sensor or HEGO sensor circuit
23	Heated exhaust gas oxygen (HEGO) sensor or HEGO sensor circuit
24	Heated exhaust gas oxygen (HEGO) sensor or HEGO sensor circuit
25	Fuel pressure regulator control (FPRC) solenoid or FPRC circuit
26	Carbon filter solenoid valve (CFSV) or CFSV circuit
28	Exhaust gas recirculation (EGR) valve or EGR circuit
29	Exhaust gas recirculation (EGR) valve or EGR circuit
34	Idle speed control valve (ISCV) or ISCV circuit
41	Variable resonance induction system (VRIS) or VRIS circuit
46	Variable resonance induction system (VRIS) or VRIS circuit
67	Low cooling fan relay or circuit

Ford Maverick (Nissan ECCS)

Code	Description
11	RPM sensor
12	Mass airflow (MAF) sensor circuit
13	Coolant temperature sensor (CTS) or CTS circuit
21	Ignition signal or circuit
34	Knock sensor (KS) or KS circuit
41	Air temperature sensor (ATS) or ATS circuit
42	Fuel temperature sensor (FTS) or FTS circuit
43	Throttle pot sensor (TPS) or TPS circuit
54	Automatic transmission (AT), signal lost
55	No faults found

Models with EOBD

For a list of the allocated EOBD codes beginning with P0 (Generic Powertrain), refer to Chapter 1, Section 1.

Notes

Honda

13

Index of vehicles

Index of vehicles

Model	Engine code	Year	System
Accord 1.8i	F18A3	1995 to 1999	Honda PGM-Fi
Accord EFi A4 SOHC	A2	1985 to 1989	Honda PGM-Fi
Accord 2.0i-16 A2 DOHC 16V	B20	1987 to 1989	Honda PGM-Fi
Accord 2.0i SOHC 16V & cat	F20A4	1989 to 1992	Honda PGM-Fi
Accord 2.0i F20A8 SOHC & cat	F20A5	1992 to 1996	Honda PGM-Fi
Accord 2.0i Coupe SOHC cat	F20A7	1992 to 1996	Honda PGM-Fi
Accord 2.2i SOHC 16V cat	F22A3/A7/A8	1989 to 1996	Honda PGM-Fi
Accord 2.2i	F22Z2	1996 to 1998	Honda PGM-Fi
Accord 2.3i DOHC 16V cat	H23A2	1993 to 1996	Honda PGM-Fi
Aerodeck EFi A4 SOHC	A20	1985 to 1989	Honda PGM-Fi
Aerodeck 2.2i SOHC 16V cat	F22A3/A7/A8	1989 to 1996	Honda PGM-Fi
Ballade EXi SOHC 3W	EW3	1986 to 1989	Honda PGM-Fi
Civic CRX	EW3	1984 to 1987	Honda PGM-Fi
Civic GT	EW3	1984 to 1987	Honda PGM-Fi
Civic 1.4i 5-door	D14A2	1995 to 2000	Honda PGM-Fi
Civic 1.4i 3-door	D14A4	1996 to 2000	Honda PGM-Fi
Civic 1.5 VEi SOHC 16V VTEC cat	D15Z1	1991 to 1995	Honda PGM-Fi
Civic 1.5 LSi SOHC 16V	D15B2	1991 to 1995	Honda PGM-Fi
Civic Coupe SOHC 16V cat	D15B2	1991 to 1995	Honda PGM-Fi
Civic 1.5i VTEC-E SOHC 16V	D15Z3	1995 to 1997	Honda PGM-Fi
Civic 1.5i 3- & 4-door	D15Z6	1996 to 2000	Honda PGM-Fi
Civic 1.6i-16 DOHC 16V	D16A9	1987 to 1992	Honda PGM-Fi
CRX 1.6i-16 DOHC 16V	D16A9	1987 to 1992	Honda PGM-Fi
Civic 1.6 VT DOHC 16V VTEC cat	B16A1	1990 to 1991	Honda PGM-Fi
CRX 1.6 VT DOHC 16V VTEC cat	B16A1	1990 to 1991	Honda PGM-Fi
Civic 1.6 ESi SOHC 16V VTEC cat	D16Z6	1991 to 1998	Honda PGM-Fi
CRX 1.6 ESi SOHC 16V VTEC cat	D16Z6	1991 to 1996	Honda PGM-Fi
Civic 1.6 VTi DOHC 16V VTEC cat	B16A2	1991 to 1995	Honda PGM-Fi
CRX 1.6 VTi DOHC 16V VTEC cat	B16A2	1991 to 1995	Honda PGM-Fi
Civic 1.6i SOHC 16V	D16Y3	1995 to 2000	Honda PGM-Fi
Civic 1.6i VTEC SOHC 16V	D16Y2	1995 to 1997	Honda PGM-Fi

Model	Engine code	Year	System
Civic 1.6i Coupe	D16Y7	1996 to 2000	Honda PGM-Fi
Civic 1.6i VTEC Coupe	D16Y8	1996 to 1998	Honda PGM-Fi
Concerto 1.5i SOHC 16V cat	D15B2	1991 to 1995	Honda PGM-Fi
Concerto 1.6 DOHC 16V	D16A9	1989 to 1991	Honda PGM-Fi
Concerto 1.6 DOHC 16V auto	D16Z4	1989 to 1991	Honda PGM-Fi
Concerto 1.6i SOHC 16V cat	D16Z2	1992 to 1995	Honda PGM-Fi
Concerto 1.6i DOHC 16V cat	D16A8	1992 to 1995	Honda PGM-Fi
Integra EX 16 A2 DOHC 16V	D16	1986 to 1990	Honda PGM-Fi
Legend	C25A2	1986 to 1988	Honda PGM-Fi
Legend 2.7 and Coupe SOHC	C27A2	1988 to 1991	Honda PGM-Fi
Legend 2.7 SOHC cat	C27A1	1990 to 1991	Honda PGM-Fi
Legend 3.2 SOHC 24V cat	C32A2	1992 to 1997	Honda PGM-Fi
NSX DOHC 24V VTEC cat	C30A	1991 to 1999	Honda PGM-Fi
Prelude Fi	B20A1	1985 to 1987	Honda PGM-Fi
Prelude 4WS 2.0i-16 DOHC 16V	B20A7	1987 to 1992	Honda PGM-Fi
Prelude 4WS 2.0i-16 DOHC cat	B20A9	1987 to 1992	Honda PGM-Fi
Prelude 2.0i 16V SOHC cat	F20A4	1992 to 2001	Honda PGM-Fi
Prelude 2.2i VTEC DOHC 16V	H22A2	1994 to 1997	Honda PGM-Fi
Prelude 2.3i 16V DOHC 16V cat	H23A2	1992 to 1997	Honda PGM-Fi
Shuttle 1.6i 4WD SOHC 16V	D16A7	1988 to 1990	Honda PGM-Fi
Shuttle 2.2i	F22B8	1995 to 1998	Honda PGM-Fi

Plus All models equipped with EOBD (approximately January 2001-on)

Self-Diagnosis

1   Introduction

The engine management system fitted to Honda vehicles is Honda PGM-Fi, which controls the primary ignition, fuel injection and idle functions from within the same control module.

Self-Diagnosis (SD) function

The ECM has a self-test capability that continually examines the signals from certain engine sensors and actuators, and then compares each signal to a table of programmed values. If the diagnostic software determines that a fault is present, the ECM stores one or more fault codes. Codes will not be stored about components for which a code is not available, or for conditions not covered by the diagnostic software. In models manufactured before 1992, the control module generates 2-digit fault codes for display on an LED set into the ECM casing. In models manufactured after 1992, the control module generates 2-digit fault codes for display on an SD warning light on the facia panel. On models equipped with EOBD, the ECM generates 5-digit fault codes. Fault code retrieval by FCR is only possible on vehicles equipped EOBD.

Limited operating strategy (LOS)

Honda systems featured in this Chapter utilise LOS (a function that is commonly called the "limp-home mode"). Once certain faults have been identified (not all faults will initiate LOS), the ECM will implement LOS and refer to a programmed default value rather than the sensor signal. This enables the vehicle to be safely driven to a workshop/garage for repair or testing. Once the fault has cleared, the ECM will revert to normal operation.

Adaptive or learning capability

Honda systems also utilise an adaptive function that will modify the basic programmed values for most effective operation during normal running, and with due regard to engine wear.

Self-Diagnosis (SD) warning light

Generally, the majority of Honda models before 1992 were equipped with an SD warning light located within the instrument panel and a red LED mounted on the ECM (see illustration 13.1). The Legend 2.5i and 2.7i were fitted with both a red and a yellow LED, the yellow LED being for rpm adjustment only (these models were not fitted with a SD connector). Once the ignition has been switched on, the SD light illuminates as a bulb check, and after a few seconds

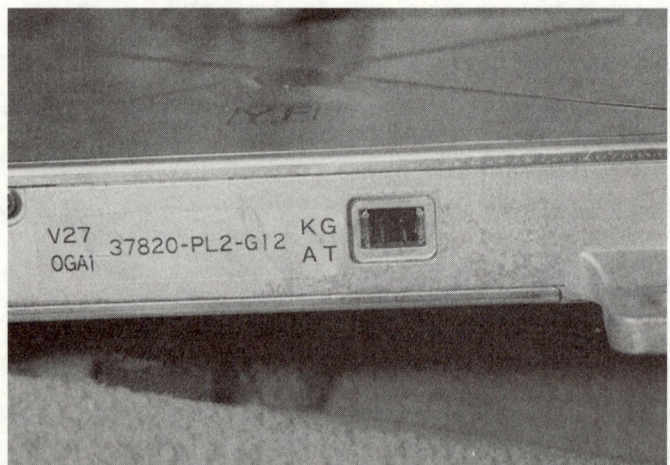

13.1 Location of LED set into the ECM (either just a red, or a red and a yellow)

extinguishes. If the SD warning light comes on at any time when the engine is running, this indicates that a fault in the system has been identified. The LED mounted in the ECM will flash to display a fault code, while the SD warning light will remain illuminated without flashing. When the ignition is switched off, both the SD warning light and LED will extinguish. When the ignition is switched on again, the SD warning light will only illuminate if the fault is still present and the LED will resume flashing the fault code. This code will be stored in memory until cleared by following the procedure described later.

From approximately 1992 onwards, the majority of Honda vehicles are equipped with an SD connector and SD warning light, while the LED(s) mounted on the ECM are no longer fitted. Once the ignition has been turned on, the SD light illuminates as a bulb check, and after a few seconds extinguishes. If the SD warning light comes on at any time when the engine is running, this indicates that a fault in the system has been identified. If a fault is indicated, bridging the terminals in the SD connector triggers the SD procedure as described later.

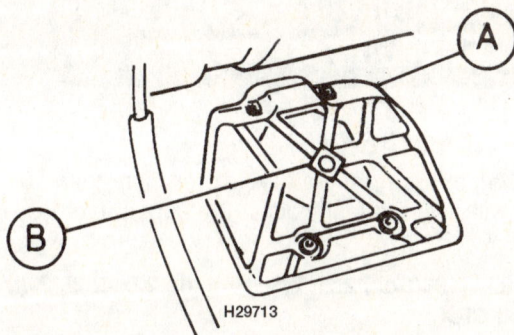

13.2 ECM located under the passenger's side carpet, under a metal cover
A Metal cover   B Hole to view LED

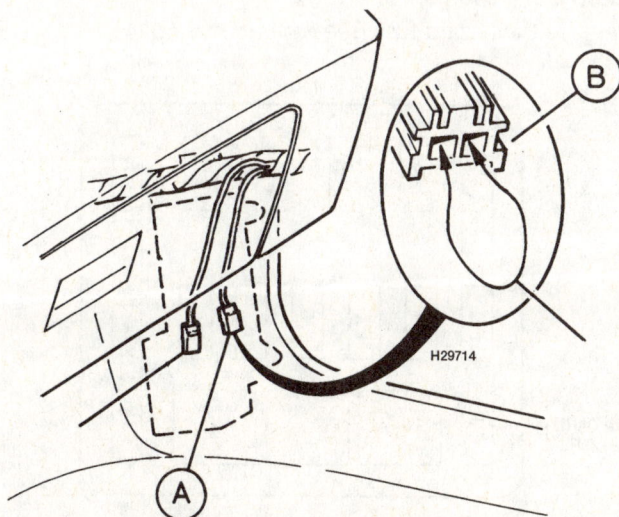

13.3 Honda SD connector (1992 onwards)
A Location of SD connector   B Terminals in SD connector bridged

On models equipped with EOBD, the MIL (Malfunction Indicator Light) in the instrument cluster alerts the driver to the presence of one or more stored faults. Code retrieval and clearing is only possible by means of an FCR.

2   Self-Diagnosis connector location

Note: *It is not always possible to pinpoint the changeover date from LED to SD connector in the Honda range. However, if the ECM is equipped with an LED and a SD connector is not fitted, the vehicle belongs to the first group. The vehicle belongs to the second group if the vehicle is equipped with a SD connector and an LED is not fitted to the ECM.*

Models up to 1992
The ECM is either located under the driver's seat or fitted to the passenger's side footwell, under the carpet and under a metal cover *(see illustration 13.2)*. Self-diagnosis is conducted by observing the behaviour of an LED, which is mounted in the ECM. An SD connector is not fitted to these vehicles.

Models after 1992
The SD connector is located under the facia on the passenger's side *(see illustration 13.3)*. An LED is not fitted to the ECM on these vehicles.

Models equipped with EOBD
The 16-pin diagnostic connector is located under the facia - refer to Chapter 38.

3   Retrieving fault codes without a fault code reader (FCR) - flash codes

Note: *During the course of certain test procedures, it is possible for additional fault codes to be generated. Care must be taken that any codes generated during test routines do not mislead diagnosis. All codes must be cleared once testing is complete.*

Honda models before 1992 (LED on ECM)
Note: *Record the fault codes from the red LED only. The yellow LED, where fitted, is for rpm adjustment checks only.*
1 Switch on the ignition.
2 Observe the red LED mounted in the ECM casing *(refer to illustration 13.1)*:
   a) *The flashes are transmitted as a straight count - eg. 15 flashes indicates code 15.*
   b) *The LED will pause for two seconds between codes before transmitting the next code.*
   c) *When all codes have been transmitted, the LED will pause for two seconds and then repeat the sequence.*

3 Count the number of flashes, and record each code as it is transmitted. Refer to the table at the end of the Chapter to determine the meaning of the fault code.

4 If the number of flashes indicates a number for which there is no code, the ECM is suspect. Recheck several times, and then check the earth and supply voltages to the ECM before fitting a replacement.

5 When the ignition is switched off, the LED will extinguish. However, the LED will resume flashing once the ignition has been switched on again.

6 If the fault(s) have been corrected, the LED will continue to flash until the ECM memory is cleared. The method is detailed below.

Honda models after 1992 (SD connector)

7 Switch on the ignition.

8 Use a jumper lead to bridge the two terminals in the SD connector.

> ⊘ *Warning: A 3-pin "service check" connector is positioned adjacent to the SD connector in some models. This connector must not be bridged in an attempt to retrieve fault codes.*

9 The codes are displayed on the SD warning light in the instrument panel. The flashing of the light indicates the 2-digit fault codes as follows:

 a) *The two digits are indicated by two series of flashes.*
 b) *The first series of flashes indicates the multiples of ten, the second series of flashes indicates the single units.*
 c) *2-second flashes separated by short intervals indicates fault codes in tens, 1-second flashes separated by short intervals indicates fault codes in units.*
 d) *A short pause separates the transmission of each individual code.*
 e) *Code number "12" is indicated by one 2-second flash followed by a short pause, then two flashes of 1 second separated by short pauses.*
 f) *Code number "8" is indicated by eight 1-second flashes.*

10 Count the number of flashes, and record each code as it is transmitted. Refer to the table at the end of the Chapter to determine the meaning of the fault code.

11 If the number of flashes indicates a number for which there is no code, the ECM is suspect. Recheck the code output several times, and then check the earth and supply voltages before fitting a replacement ECM.

12 After the first code is transmitted, the warning light will pause and then transmit the next code.

13 When all codes have been transmitted, the warning light will pause and then repeat the sequence.

14 Turn off the ignition and remove the jumper lead to end fault code retrieval.

4 Clearing fault codes without a fault code reader (FCR)

Preferred method

1 Removing a fuse from the fusebox for more than 10 seconds will clear the fault codes. The appropriate fuse is given below.

Accord 2.0i (1990-on) 2.2i, 2.3i, Prelude 2.0i, 2.2i, 2.3i, Civic and CRX

2 Remove the (ECM) back-up fuse (7.5 amp) *(see illustration 13.4)*.

Civic DX, Bali, Ballade, Integra, Concerto, Accord 2.0i (1986-89)

3 Remove the hazard fuse *(see illustration 13.5)*.

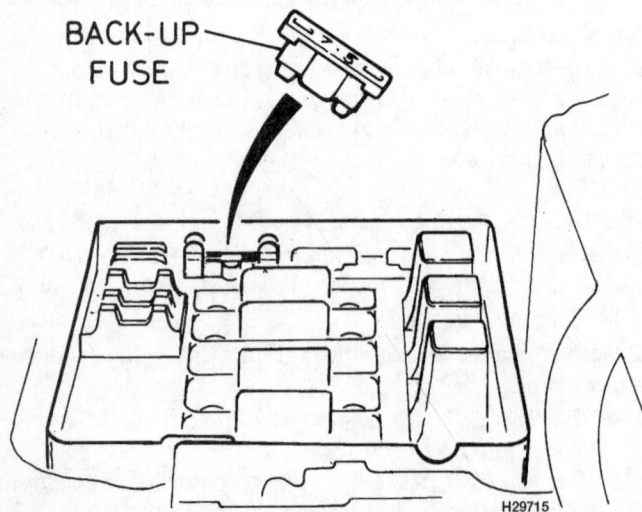

13.4 Fusebox located in the engine compartment
Location of back-up fuse

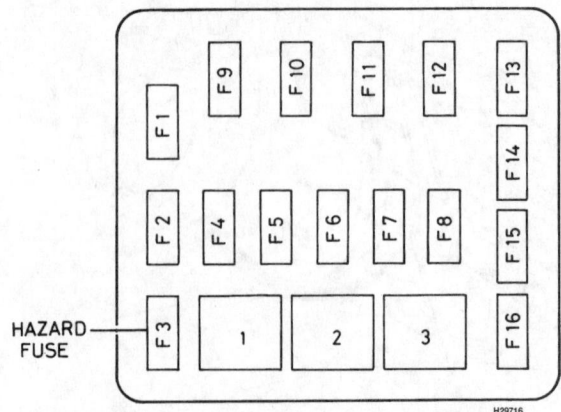

13.5 Fusebox located in the engine compartment
Location of hazard fuse

ALTERNATOR FUSE

F 26	F 25	F 24	F 23	F 22	F 21	F 20	F 29
							F 28
1		2	3	4			F 27
F 40	F 39	F 38	F 37	F 36	F 35	F 34	F 33	F 32	F 31	F 30

H29717

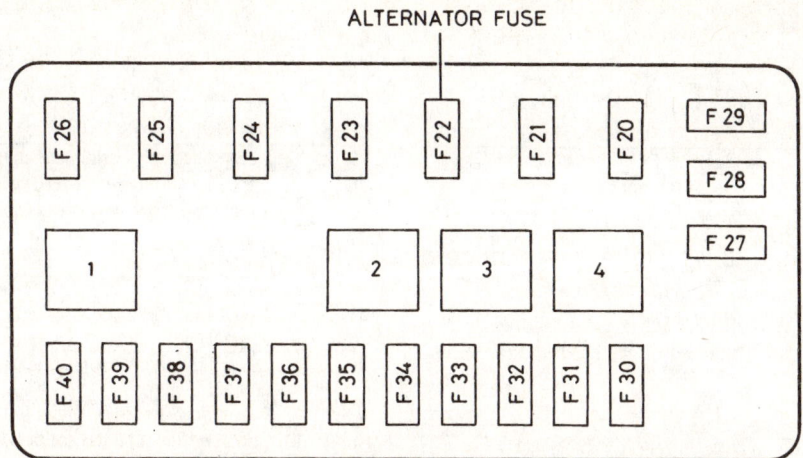

13.6 Fusebox located in the engine compartment
Location of alternator fuse

Legend 2.5i and 2.7i

4 Remove the alternator fuse **(see illustration 13.6)**.

Alternative method

5 Turn off the ignition and disconnect the battery negative terminal for a period of approximately 2 minutes.
6 Re-connect the battery negative terminal.
Note: *The first drawback to this method is that battery disconnection will re-initialise all ECM adaptive values. Re-learning the appropriate adaptive values requires starting the engine from cold, and driving at various engine speeds for approximately 20 to 30 minutes. The engine should also be allowed to idle for approximately 10 minutes. The second drawback is that the radio security codes, clock setting and other stored values will be initialised, and these must be re-entered once the battery has been reconnected. Where possible, codes should be cleared by removing the correct fuse.*

5 Self-Diagnosis with a fault code reader (FCR)

Note: *During the course of certain test procedures, it is possible for additional fault codes to be generated. Care must be taken that any codes generated during test routines do not mislead diagnosis.*

EOBD models only

1 Connect an FCR to the 16-pin diagnostic connector. Use the FCR for the following purposes, in strict compliance with the FCR manufacturer's instructions:

a) *Displaying fault codes.*
b) *Clearing stored fault codes or system faults.*
c) *Testing actuators.*
d) *Displaying Datastream.*

2 Codes or stored faults must always be cleared after component testing, or after repairs involving the removal or replacement of an EMS component.

6 Guide to test procedures

1 Manually gather codes or use an FCR as described in Sections 3 or 5.

Codes stored

2 If one or more fault codes are gathered, refer to the fault code table at the end of this Chapter to determine their meaning.
3 If several codes are gathered, look for a common factor such as a defective earth return or supply.
4 Refer to the component test procedures in Chapter 4, where you will find a means of testing the majority of components and circuits found in the modern EMS.
5 Once the fault has been repaired, clear the codes and run the engine under various conditions to determine if the problem has cleared.
6 Check the ECM for fault codes once more. Repeat the above procedures where codes are still being stored.
7 Refer to Chapter 3 for more information on how to effectively test the EMS.

No codes stored

8 Where a running problem is experienced, but no codes are stored, the fault is outside of the parameters designed into the SD system. Refer to Chapter 3 for more information on how to effectively test the engine management system.
9 If the problem points to a specific component, refer to the test procedures in Chapter 4, where you will find a means of testing the majority of components and circuits found in the modern EMS.

Chapter 13

Fault code table

Honda PGM-Fi

Code	Description
0	Electronic control module (ECM) or ECM circuit
1	Oxygen sensor (OS) or OS circuit (except D16A9 engine)
3	Manifold absolute pressure (MAP) sensor or MAP sensor circuit
5	Manifold absolute pressure (MAP) sensor or MAP sensor circuit
4	Crank angle sensor (CAS) or CAS circuit
6	Coolant temperature sensor (CTS) or CTS circuit
7	Throttle pot sensor (TPS) or TPS circuit
8	Top dead centre (TDC) position sensor or TDC sensor circuit
9	No. 1 cylinder position (CID sensor)
10	Air temperature sensor (ATS) or ATS circuit
11	CO pot or CO pot circuit
12	Exhaust gas recirculation (EGR) system or EGR circuit
13	Atmospheric pressure sensor (APS) or APS circuit
14	Idle speed control valve (ISCV) or ISCV circuit
15	Ignition output signal
16	Fuel injector or fuel injector circuit (D15B2 engine)
17	Vehicle speed sensor (VSS) or VSS circuit
18	Ignition timing

Code	Description
19	Automatic transmission lock-up control solenoid valve A/B
20	Electronic load detector (ELD) or ELD circuit
21	Spool solenoid valve or spool solenoid circuit
22	Valve timing oil pressure switch
30	Automatic transmission fuel injection signal A
31	Automatic transmission fuel injection signal B
41	Oxygen sensor (OS) heater or OS circuit (D16Z6, D16Z7, B16A2 engine)
41	Linear firflow (LAF) sensor heater or LAF sensor circuit (D15Z1 engine)
43	Fuel supply system or circuit (D16Z6, D16Z7, B16Z2 engine)
48	Linear airflow (LAF) sensor or LAF sensor circuit (D15Z1 engine)

Models with EOBD

For a list of the allocated EOBD codes beginning with P0 (Generic Powertrain), refer to Chapter 1, Section 1.

Hyundai

Index of vehicles

Index of vehicles

Model	Engine code	Year	System
Accent 1.3i SOHC	-	1995 to 2000	Hyundai MPi
Accent 1.5i SOHC	-	1995 to 2000	Hyundai MPi
Coupe 1.6 DOHC 16V	G4GR	1996 to 2001	Hyundai MPi
Coupe 1.8 DOHC 16V	G4GM	1996 to 2001	Hyundai MPi
Coupe 2.0 DOHC 16V	G4GF	1996 to 2001	Hyundai MPi
Lantra 1.5i SOHC cat	4G15/G4J	1993 to 1995	Hyundai MPi
Lantra 1.6i DOHC cat	4G61	1991 to 1995	Hyundai MPi
Lantra 1.6 DOHC 16V	G4GR	1996 to 1998	Hyundai MPi
Lantra 1.8i DOHC cat	4G67	1992 to 1995	Hyundai MPi
Lantra 1.8 DOHC 16V	G4GM	1996 to 1999	Hyundai MPi
Pony X2 1.5i SOHC cat	4G15/G4J	1990 to 1994	Hyundai MPi
S Coupe 1.5i SOHC cat	4G15/G4J	1990 to 1992	Hyundai MPi
S Coupe 1.5i SOHC	Alpha	1992 to 1996	Bosch Motronic M2.10.1
S Coupe 1.5i turbo SOHC	Alpha	1992 to 1996	Bosch Motronic M2.7
Sonata 1.8 SOHC	4G62	1989 to 1992	Hyundai MPi
Sonata 2.0 SOHC	4G63	1989 to 1992	Hyundai MPi
Sonata 2.0 16V DOHC	-	1992 to 1997	Hyundai MPi
Sonata 2.4 SOHC	4G64	1989 to 1992	Hyundai MPi
Sonata 3.0i SOHC	V6	1994 to 1998	Hyundai MPi

Plus All models equipped with EOBD (approximately January 2001-on)

Chapter 14

Self-Diagnosis

1 Introduction

The engine management systems fitted to Hyundai vehicles include Bosch Motronic versions 2.7, 2.10.1 and Hyundai MPi. All Hyundai engine management systems control primary ignition, fuel injection and idle functions from within the same ECM.

Self-Diagnosis (SD) function

Each ECM has a self-test capability that continually examines the signals from certain engine sensors and actuators, and compares each signal to a table of programmed values. If the diagnostic software determines that a fault is present, the ECM stores one or more fault codes. Codes will not be stored about components for which a code is not available, or for conditions not covered by the diagnostic software.

In Hyundai MPi, the ECM generates 2-digit fault codes for retrieval both by FCR and by manual means as flash codes. In Bosch Motronic M2.7 and M2.10.1, 4-digit flash codes are generated for retrieval by manual means, and 2 or 3-digit codes are generated for retrieval by an FCR. Refer to the fault code tables at the end of this Chapter. On models equipped with EOBD, an FCR must be used to retrieve and clear any stored codes.

Limited operating strategy (LOS)

Hyundai systems featured in this Chapter utilise LOS (a function that is commonly called the "limp-home mode"). Once certain faults have been identified (not all faults will initiate LOS), the ECM will implement LOS and refer to a programmed default value rather than the sensor signal. This enables the vehicle to be safely driven to a workshop/garage for repair or testing. Once the fault has cleared, the ECM will revert to normal operation.

Adaptive or learning capability

Hyundai systems also utilise an adaptive function that will modify the basic programmed values for most effective operation during normal running, and with due regard to engine wear.

Self-Diagnosis (SD) warning light

Many Hyundai vehicles are equipped with a facia-mounted SD warning light located within the instrument panel. If the light illuminates at any time during a period of engine running, the ECM has diagnosed presence of a system fault. The warning light can also be triggered (some systems) to transmit flash codes.

2 Self-Diagnosis connector location

All Hyundai models

The Hyundai SD connector is in the fusebox on the driver's left or right-hand (driver's) side and under the facia (see illustrations 14.1 and 14.2). The SD connector is provided for both flash code and FCR retrieval purposes.

The 16-pin EOBD diagnostic connector is located under the facia.

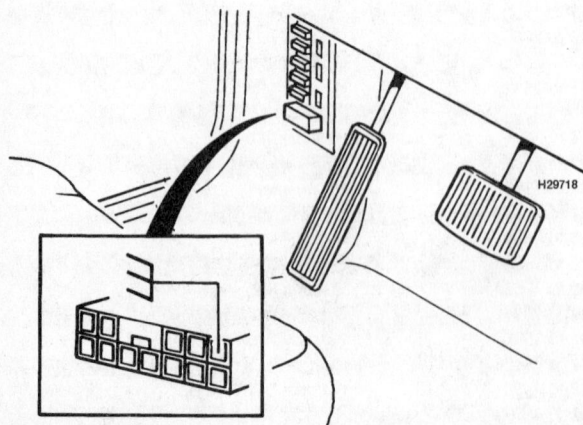

14.1 Location of SD connector in fusebox

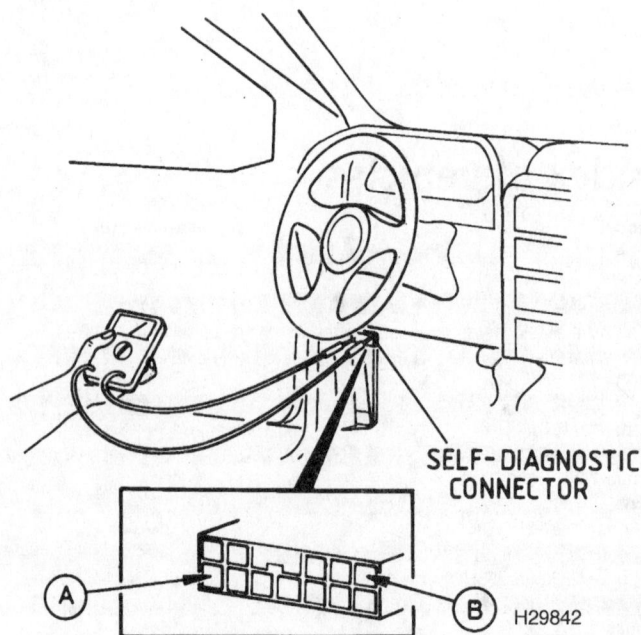

14.2 Analogue voltmeter attached to SD connector terminals A and B

3   Retrieving codes without a fault code reader (FCR) - flash codes

Note: *During the course of certain test procedures, it is possible for additional fault codes to be generated. Care must be taken that any codes generated during test routines do not mislead diagnosis. All codes must be cleared once testing is complete.*

Hyundai MPi without SD warning light (voltmeter method)

1 Attach an analogue voltmeter between the A and B terminals in the SD connector *(see illustration 14.2).*
2 Switch on the ignition.
3 If the ECM has stored one or more fault codes, the voltmeter needle will begin to sweep between a higher and lower level. If no codes are stored, the needle will remain level. The voltmeter sweeps may be interpreted as follows:
  a) *The first series of swings indicates the multiples of ten, the second series of swings indicates the single units.*
  b) *The voltmeter needle will move for a longer period of deflection when transmitting codes in tens, and a shorter spell of deflection for units. If no faults are found, the meter will indicate regular on/off pulses.*
4 Count the number of sweeps in each series, and record each code as it is transmitted. Refer to the tables at the end of the Chapter to determine the meaning of the fault code.
5 Turn off the ignition and remove the voltmeter to end fault code retrieval.

Hyundai MPi without SD warning light (LED test light method)

6 Attach an LED diode test light between the A and B terminals in the SD connector *(see illustration 14.3).*
7 Switch on the ignition
8 After approximately 3 seconds, the codes are displayed as 2-digit flash codes on the LED as follows:
  a) *The two digits are indicated by two series of flashes.*
  b) *The first series of flashes indicates the multiples of ten, the second series of flashes indicates the single units.*
  c) *Tens are indicated by 1.5-second flashes separated by 0.5-second pauses. Units are indicated by 0.5-second flashes separated by 0.5-second pauses.*
  d) *A 2-second pause separates the tens from the units.*
  e) *Code "42" is indicated by four 1.5-second flashes, a 2-second pause, followed by two 0.5-second flashes.*
9 Count the number of flashes in each series, and record each code as it is transmitted. Refer to the tables at the end of the Chapter to determine the meaning of the fault code.
10 The codes will be displayed sequentially, and repeated after a 3-second pause.

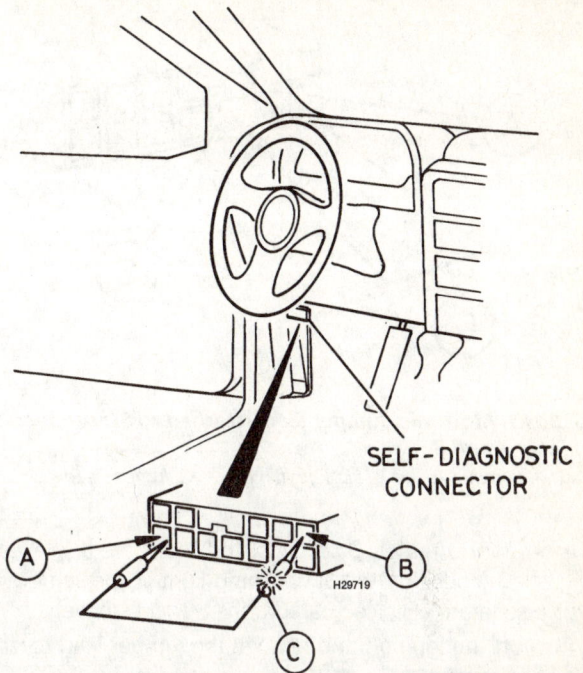

SELF-DIAGNOSTIC CONNECTOR

14.3 LED diode light attached to SD connector terminals A and B
A Earth - terminal A   B SD Terminal B   C LED

11 Transmission of eight on/off pulses of 0.5 seconds, repeated after a pause of 3 seconds, indicates that no faults are stored.
12 Turn off the ignition and remove the test light to end fault code retrieval.

Hyundai MPi with SD warning light
13 Switch on the ignition.
14 Use a jumper lead to bridge the A and B terminals in the SD connector *(see illustration 14.4).*

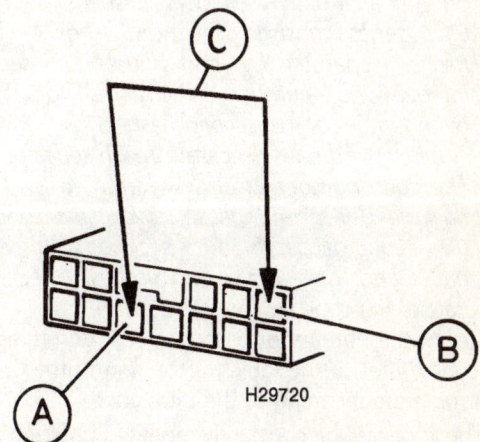

14.4 Hyundai MPi: Jumper lead attached to SD connector terminals A and B
A Earth - terminal A   B SD Terminal B   C Jumper lead

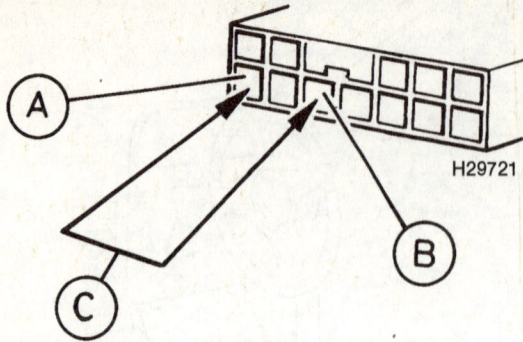

14.5 Bosch Motronic: Jumper lead attached to SD connector terminals A and B

A Earth - terminal A   B SD Terminal B   C Jumper lead

15 After approximately 3 seconds, the codes are displayed as 2-digit flash codes on the SD warning light in the same way as for a separate LED (see paragraphs 8 to 11 above).

16 Turn off the ignition and remove the jumper lead to end fault code retrieval.

Bosch Motronic M2.7 and 2.10.1

Note: *4-digit flash codes retrieved manually may be different to those codes displayed with the aid of an FCR. Refer to the fault code tables at the end of this Chapter, in the column headed "Flash code".*

17 Switch on the ignition.

18 Use a jumper lead to bridge the A and B terminals in the SD connector **(see illustration 14.5)**.

19 Remove the jumper lead after approximately 2 to 3 seconds.

20 The warning light will begin to flash the 4-digit fault codes as follows:

a) *The four digits are indicated by four series of flashes.*

b) *The first series of flashes indicates the first digit, the second series of flashes indicates the second digit, and so on until all 4 digits have been flashed.*

c) *Each series consists of a number of 1- or 2-second flashes, separated by short pauses (0.5 seconds). Each integer (whole number) in the range 1 to 9 is represented by a number of 1.5-second flashes.*

d) *A 2.5-second pause separates each series of flashes.*

e) *The code number "1233" is indicated by a 1.5-second flash, a 0.5-second pause, two 1.5-second flashes, a 0.5-second pause, three 1.5-second flashes, a 0.5-second pause and three 1.5-second flashes. After a 2.5-second pause, the code will be repeated.*

21 Count the number of flashes in each series, and record the code. Refer to the tables at the end of the Chapter to determine the meaning of the fault code.

22 The code will be constantly repeated until the jumper lead is used to bridge the A and B terminals in the SD connector once more. Remove the jumper lead after approximately 2 to 3 seconds, and the next fault code will be displayed.

23 Continue this procedure until all stored codes have been displayed. End of code transmission will be indicated on the SD warning light by code "3333".

24 Turn off the ignition and remove the jumper lead to end fault code retrieval.

4   Clearing fault codes without a fault code reader (FCR)

Hyundai MPi

1 Turn off the ignition and disconnect the battery negative terminal for a period of approximately 15 seconds.

2 Reconnect the battery negative terminal.

Note: *The first drawback to this method is that battery disconnection will re-initialise all ECM adaptive values. Re-learning the appropriate adaptive values requires starting the engine from cold, and driving at various engine speeds for approximately 20 to 30 minutes. The engine should also be allowed to idle for approximately 10 minutes. The second drawback is that the radio security codes, clock setting and other stored values will be initialised, and these must be re-entered once the battery has been reconnected. Where possible, an FCR should be used for code clearing.*

Bosch Motronic 2.10.1 and M2.7

3 Retrieve codes from the ECM by the methods described above until code "3333" is transmitted.

4 Use the jumper lead to bridge the A and B terminals in the SD connector for 10 seconds, and the codes will be cleared.

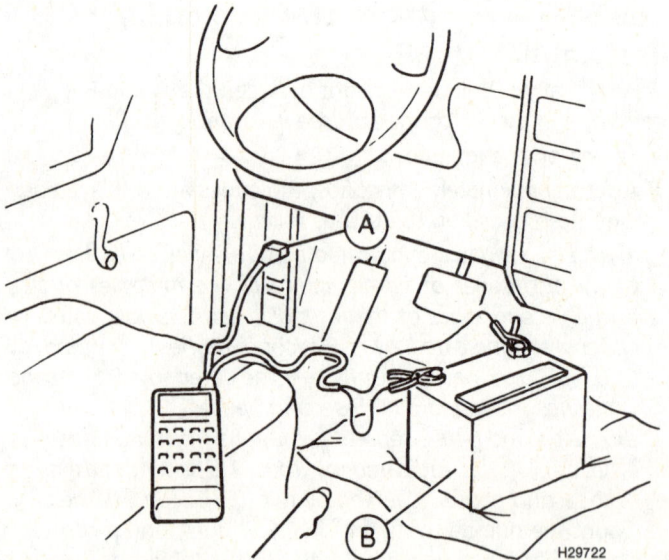

14.6 FCR attached to SD connector

A SD connector

B The slave battery provides supply voltage for the FCR

5 Self-Diagnosis with a fault code reader (FCR)

Note: *During the course of certain test procedures, it is possible for additional fault codes to be generated. Care must be taken that any codes generated during test routines do not mislead diagnosis.*

All Hyundai models

1 Connect an FCR to the SD connector, and use the FCR for the following purposes, in strict compliance with the FCR manufacturer's instructions *(see illustration 14.6)*:

    a) *Retrieving fault codes.*
    b) *Clearing fault codes.*

2 The FCR may be able to display 4-digit flash codes, 2-digit fault codes or 5-digit EOBD codes. Refer to the fault code tables at the end of this Chapter, in the column headed *"Flash code"* or *"FCR code"* as appropriate.

3 Codes must always be cleared after component testing, or after repairs involving the removal or replacement of an EMS component.

6 Guide to test procedures

1 Use an FCR to interrogate the ECM for fault codes, or manually gather codes as described in Sections 3 or 5.

Codes stored

2 If one or more fault codes are gathered, refer to the fault code tables at the end of this Chapter to determine their meaning.

3 If several codes are gathered, look for a common factor such as a defective earth return or supply.

4 Refer to the component test procedures in Chapter 4, where you will find a means of testing the majority of components and circuits found in the modern EMS.

5 Once the fault has been repaired, clear the codes and run the engine under various conditions to determine if the problem has cleared.

6 Check the ECM for fault codes once more. Repeat the above procedures where codes are still being stored.

7 Refer to Chapter 3 for more information on how to effectively test the EMS.

No codes stored

8 Where a running problem is experienced, but no codes are stored, the fault is outside of the parameters designed into the SD system. Refer to Chapter 3 for more information on how to effectively test the engine management system.

9 If the problem points to a specific component, refer to the test procedures in Chapter 4, where you will find a means of testing the majority of components and circuits found in the modern EMS.

Fault code tables

Hyundai MPi

Flash/ FCR code	Description
11	Oxygen sensor (OS) or OS circuit
12	Airflow sensor (AFS) or circuit
13	Air temperature sensor (ATS) or ATS circuit
14	Throttle position sensor (TPS) or circuit
15	Motor position sensor
21	Coolant temperature sensor (CTS) or CTS circuit
22	Crank angle sensor (CAS) or circuit
23	Cylinder number one top dead centre (TDC) sensor or TDC sensor circuit

Flash/ FCR code	Description
24	Vehicle speed sensor (VSS) or VSS circuit
25	Atmospheric pressure sensor (APS) or APS circuit
41	Injector or circuit
42	Fuel pump or circuit
43	No faults found in the ECM. Proceed with normal diagnostic methods
44	Ignition coil
59	Rear oxygen sensor (OS) or OS circuit

Chapter 14

Bosch Motronic 2.7 and 2.10.1

Flash code	FCR code	Description
1121	36	Electronic control module (ECM) or ECM circuit (Motronic 2.7)
1122	-	Electronic control module (ECM)
1233	-	Electronic control module (ECM), read only memory (ROM) failure
1234	-	Electronic control module (ECM), random access memory (RAM) failure
2121	-	Manifold absolute pressure (MAP) sensor or MAP sensor circuit
2121	21	Turbo wastegate solenoid valve or circuit (Motronic 2.7)
2222	-	Start of fault code output
3112	17	Injector Number 1 or injector circuit
3114	04	Idle speed control valve (ISCV) or ISCV circuit
3116	16	Injector Number 3 or injector circuit
3117	07	Vane airflow sensor (AFS) or AFS circuit
3121	49	Manifold absolute pressure (MAP) sensor or MAP sensor circuit (Motronic 2.7)
3122	22	Idle speed control valve (ISCV) or ISCV circuit
3128	28	Oxygen sensor (OS) or OS circuit
3135	05	Carbon filter solenoid valve (CFSV) or CFSV circuit
3137	37	Battery voltage supply to electronic control module (ECM) or circuit
3145	45	Coolant temperature sensor (CTS) or CTS circuit
3149	40	Air conditioning (A/C)
3152	226	Boost pressure signal or circuit (Motronic 2.7)
3152	-	Manifold absolute pressure (MAP) sensor or MAP sensor circuit
3153	53	Throttle pot sensor (TPS) or TPS circuit
3159	09	Crank angle sensor (CAS) or CAS circuit
3211	11	Knock sensor (KS) or KS circuit
3222	08	Camshaft position sensor (CMP) or CMP circuit
3224	222	Knock sensor (KS) or KS circuit (Motronic 2.10.1)

Flash code	FCR code	Description
3224	-	Electronic control module (ECM) (Motronic 2.7)
3232	-	Camshaft position sensor (CMP) or CMP circuit
3232	229	Cylinder identification (CID) sensor or CID sensor circuit
3233	-	Electronic control module (ECM) (Motronic 2.7)
3233	-	Knock sensor (KS) or KS circuit
3234	34	Injector Number 2 or injector circuit
3235	35	Injector Number 4 or injector circuit
3241	141	Electronic control module (ECM) or ECM circuit (Motronic 2.10.1)
3242	142	Electronic control module (ECM) or ECM circuit (Motronic 2.10.1)
3243	143	Electronic control module (ECM) or ECM circuit (Motronic 2.10.1)
3333	-	End of fault code output
4133	133	Fuel pump or fuel pump circuit (Motronic 2.10.1)
4151	101	Oxygen sensor (OS) or OS circuit (Motronic 2.10.1)
4151	-	Air/fuel control fault (Motronic 2.7)
4152	103	Oxygen sensor (OS) or OS circuit
4153	102	Oxygen sensor (OS) or OS circuit
4154	104	Oxygen sensor (OS) or OS circuit
4155	-	Electronic control module (ECM)
4156	-	Manifold absolute pressure (MAP) sensor or MAP sensor circuit
4156	227	Boost pressure signal or circuit (Motronic 2.7)
4444	-	No faults found in the ECM. Proceed with normal diagnostic methods

Models with EOBD

For a list of the allocated EOBD codes beginning with P0 (Generic Powertrain), refer to Chapter 1, Section 1.

Isuzu

15

Index of vehicles

Index of vehicles

Model	Engine code	Year	System
Piazza Turbo	4Z C1T	1986 to 1990	Isuzu I-Tec + Turbo
Trooper 2.6	4ZE1	1988 to 1992	Isuzu I-Tec
Trooper 3.2i	6VD1	1993 to 1998	Isuzu I-Tec

Plus All models equipped with EOBD (approximately January 2001-on)

Self-Diagnosis

1   Introduction

Isuzu vehicles are equipped with the Isuzu I-Tec engine management system that controls primary ignition, fuel injection and idle functions from within the same control module.

Self-Diagnosis (SD) function

The ECM has a self-test capability that continually examines the signals from certain engine sensors and actuators, and compares each signal to a table of programmed values. If the diagnostic software determines that a fault is present, the ECM stores one or more fault codes. Codes will not be stored about components for which a code is not available, or for conditions not covered by the diagnostic software. The Isuzu I-Tec system generates 2-digit fault codes for retrieval either by manual means or by fault

code reader (FCR). On models equipped with EOBD, any stored fault codes can only be retrieved or cleared by means of an FCR.

Limited operating strategy (LOS)

Isuzu systems featured in this Chapter utilise LOS (a function that is commonly called the "limp-home mode"). Once certain codes have been generated (not all codes will initiate LOS), the ECM will implement LOS and refer to a programmed default value rather than the sensor signal. This enables the vehicle to be safely driven to a workshop/garage for repair or testing. Once the fault has cleared, the ECM will revert to normal operation.

Self-Diagnosis (SD) warning light

Isuzu vehicles are equipped with an SD warning light located within the instrument panel.

2 Self-Diagnosis connector locations

Piazza Turbo

The SD connectors are located above the foot pedals and under the facia (see illustrations 15.1 and 15.2). The Piazza Turbo is provided with two 1-pin connectors (male and female) and one 3-pin connector. The 3-pin multi-plug is provided for dedicated FCR use, and the two 1-pin multi-plugs are provided for retrieving flash codes.

Trooper

The SD connectors are located above the foot pedals and under the facia (see illustration 15.1). The Trooper is provided with one 3-pin connector (see illustration 15.3). The 3-pin multi-plug is provided for both dedicated FCR use and for retrieving flash codes.

EOBD models

The 16-pin diagnostic connector is located under the facia.

3 Retrieving codes without a fault code reader (FCR) - flash codes

Note: During the course of certain test procedures, it is possible for additional fault codes to be generated. Care must be taken that any codes generated during test routines do not mislead diagnosis. All codes must be cleared once testing is complete.

1 Locate the SD connector.
2 On Piazza Turbo models, connect the 1-pin male and female SD connector plugs together (refer to illustration 15.2).
3 On Trooper models, use a jumper lead to bridge terminals 1 and 3 in the 3-pin SD connector (refer to illustration 15.3).
4 Switch on the ignition, but do not start the engine.
5 The codes are displayed on the SD warning light in the instrument panel. The flashing of the light indicates the 2-digit fault codes as follows:
   a) The two digits are indicated by two series of flashes.
   b) The first series of flashes indicates the multiples of ten, the second series of flashes indicates the single units.
   c) Tens and units are indicated by 0.4-second flashes, separated by a short pause.
   d) A pause of 1.2 seconds separates tens and units.
   e) A 3.2-second pause separates the transmission of each individual code.
   f) Code number "12" is indicated by one 0.4-second flash, followed by a 1.2-second pause, then two flashes of 0.4 seconds in quick succession.

6 Count the number of flashes in each series, and record each code as it is transmitted. Refer to the table at the end of the Chapter to determine the meaning of the fault code.
7 Fault codes are displayed in sequence, and repeated three times before the next code is transmitted.
8 On Piazza Turbo models, when code number "12" is transmitted, this indicates the start of the test procedure. If "12" is repeated constantly, no faults are stored.
9 On Trooper models, when code number "12" is transmitted, this indicates that the engine has not been started and faults have not been stored.
10 Continue processing until all stored codes have been retrieved and recorded.
11 Turning off the ignition and disconnecting the connectors or jumper lead will end fault code retrieval.

4 Clearing fault codes without a fault code reader (FCR)

Piazza Turbo models

1 Turn off the ignition and remove fuse 4 located in the fuse junction box.
Note: The drawback to this method is that the radio security codes, clock setting and other stored values will be initialised, and these must be re-entered once the fuse is refitted. Where possible, an FCR should be used for code clearing.

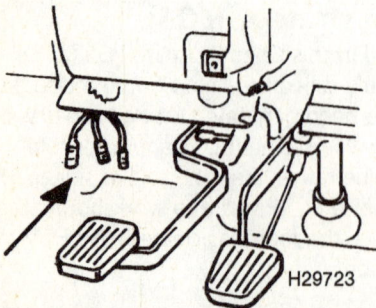

15.1 Location of SD connectors for Piazza models

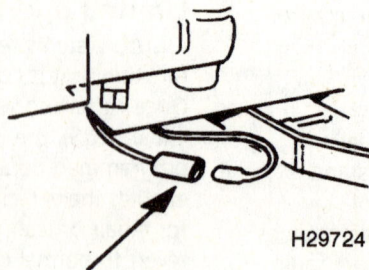

15.2 Initiate the self-test by connecting the 1-pin male and female terminals together

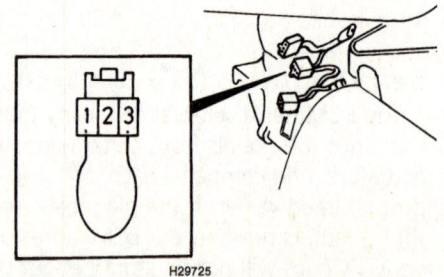

15.3 Location of SD connector for Trooper models. Initiate the self-test by bridging the terminals

Trooper models

2 Turn off the ignition and remove fuse 13 from the fusebox. Fuse 4 may be removed instead, but removing fuse 13 obviates the need to reset the radio and clock.

5   Self-Diagnosis with a fault code reader (FCR)

Note: *During the course of certain test procedures, it is possible for additional fault codes to be generated. Care must be taken that any codes generated during test routines do not mislead diagnosis.*

All Isuzu models

1 Connect an FCR to the SD connector. Use the FCR for the following purposes, in strict compliance with the FCR manufacturer's instructions:

  a) *Retrieving fault codes.*
  b) *Clearing fault codes.*
  c) *Datastream (EOBD models only).*

2 Codes must always be cleared after component testing, or after repairs involving the removal of an EMS component.

6   Guide to test procedures

1 Use and FCR to interrogate the ECM for fault codes, or manually gather codes as described in Sections 3 or 5.

Codes stored

2 If one or more fault codes are gathered, refer to the fault code table at the end of this Chapter to determine their meaning.

3 If several codes are gathered, look for a common factor such as a defective earth return or supply.

4 Refer to the component test procedures in Chapter 4, where you will find a means of testing the majority of components and circuits found in the modern EMS.

5 Once the fault has been repaired, clear the codes and run the engine under various conditions to determine if the problem has cleared.

6 Check the ECM for fault codes once more. Repeat the above procedures where codes are still being stored.

7 Refer to Chapter 3 for more information on how to effectively test the EMS.

No codes stored

8 Where a running problem is experienced, but no codes are stored, the fault is outside of the parameters designed into the SD system. Refer to Chapter 3 for more information on how to effectively test the engine management system.

9 If the problem points to a specific component, refer to the test procedures in Chapter 4, where you will find a means of testing the majority of components and circuits found in the modern EMS.

Fault code table

Isuzu I-Tec

Flash/FCR code	Description
12	Engine is not started (Trooper)
12	Start of fault code output (Piazza)
13	Oxygen sensor (OS) or OS circuit
14	Coolant temperature sensor (CTS) or CTS circuit
15	Coolant temperature sensor (CTS) or CTS circuit
21	Throttle switch (TS), idle and full-load contacts both closed
22	Starter signal circuit
23	Power transistor for ignition or circuit
25	Vacuum switching valve system for pressure regulator or circuit
26	Carbon filter solenoid valve (CFSV) or CFSV circuit, high voltage
27	Carbon filter solenoid valve (CFSV) or CFSV circuit, low voltage
33	Fuel injector system or fuel injector circuit
35	Power transistor for ignition or circuit
41	Crank angle sensor (CAS) or CAS circuit
43	Throttle switch (TS), full-load switch
44	Oxygen sensor (OS) or OS circuit
45	Oxygen sensor (OS) or OS circuit
51	Electronic control module (ECM) or ECM circuit
52	Electronic control module (ECM) or ECM circuit
53	Vacuum switching valve system for pressure regulator or circuit
54	Ignition control
61	Airflow sensor (AFS) or AFS circuit
62	Airflow sensor (AFS) or AFS circuit
63	Vehicle speed sensor (VSS) or VSS circuit
64	Fuel injector system or fuel injector circuit
65	Throttle switch (TS), full-load switch
66	Knock sensor
72	Exhaust gas regulation (EGR) or EGR circuit
73	Exhaust gas regulation (EGR) or EGR circuit

Models with EOBD

For a list of the allocated EOBD codes beginning with P0 (Generic Powertrain), refer to Chapter 1, Section 1.

Notes

Index of vehicles

Index of vehicles

Model	Engine code	Year	System
This Chapter			
XJ6/Sovereign 3.2 DOHC cat	AJ-6	1990 to 1994	Lucas LH-15CU
XJ6/Sovereign 3.6 24V	AJ-6	1986 to 1989	Lucas LH-9CU
XJ6/Sovereign 4.0	AJ-6	1991 to 1998	Lucas LH-15CU
XJ-S 4.0	AJ-6	1991 to 1997	Lucas LH-15CU
Plus All models equipped with EOBD (approximately January 2001-on)			
Other Jaguar vehicles/systems not covered by this book			
Double 6 6.0 SOHC cat	V12	1993 to 1994	Lucas LH-36CU
V12 6.0 SOHC cat	V12	1993 to 1994	Lucas LH-36CU
XJ6 3.2 DOHC 24V	AJ16	1994 to 1997	Lucas GEMS
XJ6 4.0 Sport	AJ16	1994 to 1997	Lucas GEMS
XJR 4.0 Supercharged	AJ16	1994 to 1997	Lucas GEMS
XJ-S V12 6.0	V12	1993 to 1996	Lucas LH-36CU
XJ-S V12 6.0 R-cat	V12	1993 to 1997	Lucas LH-36CU
XJ12 6.0 V12 SOHC	V12	1994 to 1997	Lucas LH-36CU
XJ-S & XJSC V12 OHC	V12	1990 to 1993	Lucas LH-26CU
XJ-S & XJSC V12 R-cat	V12	1990 to 1993	Lucas LH-26CU

Chapter 16

Self-Diagnosis

1   Introduction

The engine management systems (EMSs) fitted to Jaguar vehicles are mainly of Lucas origin, and include LH-9CU, LH-15CU, LH-26CU and LH-36CU. All Jaguar engine management systems control primary ignition, fuelling and idle functions from within the same control module. Lucas LH-9CU and LH-15CU alone are covered by this book. Fault code tables and methods of retrieving data for other models were not available at the time of going to press. However, it is certain that a dedicated fault code reader (FCR) is required to retrieve codes and other data from the majority of Jaguar models.

Self-Diagnosis (SD) function

Each ECM has a self-test capability that continually examines the signals from certain engine sensors and actuators, which then compares each signal to a table of programmed values. If the diagnostic software determines that a fault is present, the ECM stores one or more fault codes. Codes will not be stored about components for which a code is not available, or for conditions not covered by the diagnostic software.

Lucas LH-9CU and LH-15CU systems generate 2-digit fault codes for retrieval and display on the facia-mounted vehicle condition monitor, and for retrieval by a dedicated FCR.

Limited operating strategy (LOS)

Jaguar systems featured in this Chapter utilise LOS (a function that is commonly called the "limp-home mode"). Once certain codes have been identified (not all codes will initiate LOS), the ECM will implement LOS and refer to a programmed default value rather than the sensor signal. This enables the vehicle to be safely driven to a workshop/garage for repair or testing. Once the fault has cleared, the ECM will revert to normal operation.

Adaptive or learning capability

Jaguar systems also utilise an adaptive function that will modify the basic programmed values for most effective operation during normal running, and with due regard to engine wear.

Self-Diagnosis (SD) display (vehicle condition monitor)

Jaguar models are equipped with a facia-mounted SD display panel called the vehicle condition monitor.

2   Self-Diagnosis connector location

The SD connector provided for FCR use is located in front of the battery in the engine compartment. The connector is usually coloured brown, round and is of 6-pin design. In

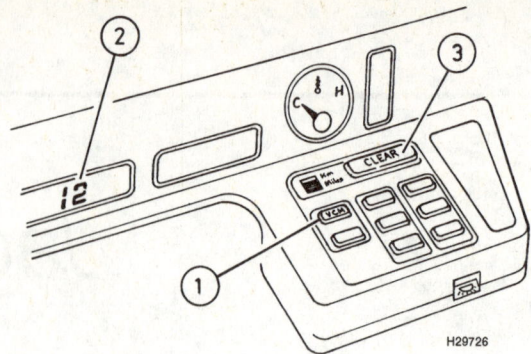

16.1 Vehicle condition monitor
1 Button   2 Code display   3 VCM display clear button

addition, the vehicle is equipped with a vehicle condition monitor (VCM) for fault code retrieval. The VCM is mounted below the instrument panel *(see illustration 16.1).*

Models with EOBD are equipped with a 16-pin diagnostic connector, mounted under the facia.

3   Retrieving fault codes without a fault code reader (FCR)

Note: *During the course of certain test procedures, it is possible for additional fault codes to be generated. Care must be taken that any codes generated during test routines do not mislead diagnosis. Codes must be cleared once testing is complete.*

1 Fault codes can be retrieved from Jaguar vehicles via the vehicle condition monitor (VCM).

2 If the engine is running, stop the engine by turning off the ignition and wait for a minimum period of 5 seconds before proceeding.

3 Switch on the ignition.

4 Press the VCM button on the facia and codes will be displayed. If an asterisk appears on the VCM display, multiple faults have been detected.

5 Turning off the ignition ends fault code retrieval.

4   Clearing fault codes without a fault code reader (FCR)

1 Turn off the ignition and disconnect the battery negative terminal for a period of at least 30 seconds.

2 Reconnect the battery negative terminal.

Note: *The first drawback to this method is that battery disconnection will re-initialise all ECM adaptive values. Re-learning the appropriate adaptive values requires starting the engine from cold, and driving at various engine speeds for approximately 20 to 30 minutes. The engine should also be allowed to idle for approximately 10 minutes. The second drawback is that the radio security codes, clock setting and* other stored values will be initialised, and these must be re-entered once the battery has been reconnected. Where possible, an FCR should be used for code clearing on these vehicles.

On models with EOBD, any stored fault codes can only be retrieved or cleared using an FCR.

5 Self-Diagnosis with a fault code reader (FCR)

Note 1: *During the course of certain test procedures, it is possible for additional fault codes to be generated. Care must be taken that any codes generated during test routines do not mislead diagnosis.*

Note 2: *Fault code tables and methods of retrieving data for systems other than Lucas LH-9CU and LH-15CU were not available at the time of going to press. However, it is certain that a dedicated FCR is required to retrieve codes and other data from the majority of Jaguar models.*

All Jaguar models

1 Connect an FCR to the SD connector. Use the FCR for the following purposes, in strict compliance with the FCR manufacturer's instructions:

a) Retrieving fault codes.
b) Clearing fault codes.
c) Datastream (EOBD models only).

2 Codes must always be cleared after component testing, or after repairs involving the removal of an EMS component.

6 Guide to test procedures

1 Use an FCR to interrogate the ECM for fault codes, or display the codes on the VCM, as described in Sections 3 or 5.

Codes stored

2 If one or more fault codes are gathered, refer to the fault code tables at the end of this Chapter to determine their meaning.

3 If several codes are gathered, look for a common factor such as a defective earth return or supply.

4 Refer to the component test procedures in Chapter 4, where you will find a means of testing the majority of components and circuits found in the modern EMS.

5 Once the fault has been repaired, clear the codes and run the engine under various conditions to determine if the problem has cleared.

6 Check the ECM for fault codes once more. Repeat the above procedures where codes are still being stored.

7 Refer to Chapter 3 for more information on how to effectively test the EMS.

No codes stored

8 Where a running problem is experienced, but no codes are stored, the fault is outside of the parameters designed into the SD system. Refer to Chapter 3 for more information on how to effectively test the engine management system.

9 If the problem points to a specific component, refer to the test procedures in Chapter 4, where you will find a means of testing the majority of components and circuits found in the modern EMS.

Fault code tables

Lucas LH-9CU

Fault code	Description
01	Throttle pot sensor (TPS) or TPS circuit
02	Airflow sensor (AFS) or AFS circuit
03	Coolant temperature sensor (CTS) or CTS circuit
04	Throttle pot sensor (TPS) or TPS circuit
05	TPS or circuit/AFS or circuit
06	TPS or circuit/AFS or circuit
07	Vehicle speed sensor (VSS) or VSS circuit

Lucas LH-15CU

FCR code	Description
11	Throttle pot sensor (TPS) or TPS circuit
12	Airflow sensor (AFS) or AFS circuit
14	Coolant temperature sensor (CTS) or CTS circuit
16	Air temperature sensor (ATS) or ATS circuit
17	Throttle pot sensor (TPS) or TPS circuit
18	Throttle pot sensor (TPS) or TPS circuit, signal resistance low at idle
18	Airflow sensor (AFS) or AFS circuit, signal resistance low at idle (alternative code)
19	Throttle pot sensor (TPS) or TPS circuit, signal resistance high at idle
19	Airflow sensor (AFS) or AFS circuit, signal resistance high at idle (alternative code)
22	Heated oxygen sensor (OS) or OS circuit
22	Fuel pump or fuel pump circuit
23	Fuel supply or circuit, rich exhaust indicated
24	Ignition amplifier supply or circuit
26	Oxygen sensor (OS) or OS circuit, lean exhaust/vacuum leak
29	Electronic control module (ECM), self check
33	Fuel injector or fuel injector circuit
34	Fuel injector or fuel injector circuit
37	Exhaust gas recirculation (EGR) solenoid circuit
39	Exhaust gas recirculation (EGR) circuit
44	Oxygen sensor (OS) or OS circuit, rich or lean condition
46	Idle speed control valve (ISCV) coil 1 or ISCV circuit
47	Idle speed control valve (ISCV) coil 2 or ISCV circuit
48	Idle speed control valve (ISCV) or ISCV circuit
68	Vehicle speed sensor (VSS) or VSS circuit, incorrect signal voltage
69*	Neutral safety switch circuit, engine cranks in drive.
89	Carbon filter solenoid valve (CFSV) or CFSV circuit

***Note:** 1990 and 1991 models: Code 69 may be set erroneously if voltage drops sufficiently during cranking. Check battery and then rotary switch adjustment to remedy.*

Models with EOBD

For a list of the allocated EOBD codes beginning with P0 (Generic Powertrain), refer to Chapter 1, Section 1.

Notes

Kia

17

Index of vehicles

Model	Engine code	Year	System
Mentor 1.6i SOHC 8V	-	1995 to 1999	Kia EGi
Sportage 2.0i SOHC 8V	FE	1995 to 1998	Bosch Motronic M2.10.1
Sportage 2.0i DOHC 16V	FE	1995 to 1999	Bosch Motronic M2.10.1

Plus All models equipped with EOBD (approximately January 2001-on)

Self-Diagnosis

1   Introduction

Kia vehicles are equipped with the Kia EGi and Bosch Motronic engine management systems that control primary ignition, fuel injection and idle functions from within the same control module.

Self-Diagnosis (SD) function
The electronic control module (ECM) has a self-test capability that continually examines the signals from certain engine sensors and actuators, and then compares each signal to a table of programmed values. If the diagnostic software determines that a fault is present, the ECM stores one or more fault codes in the ECM memory. Codes will not be stored about components for which a code is not available, or for conditions not covered by the diagnostic software. Kia systems generate 2-digit fault codes (Kia EGi) or 3-digit fault codes (Bosch Motronic 2.10.1) for retrieval by manual means or by a dedicated fault code reader (FCR). Models equipped with EOBD generate 5-digit fault codes, which can only be retrieved or cleared using an FCR.

Limited operating strategy (LOS)
Kia systems featured in this Chapter utilise LOS (a function that is commonly called the "limp-home mode"). Once certain faults have been identified (not all faults will initiate LOS), the ECM will implement LOS and refer to a programmed default value rather than the sensor signal. This enables the vehicle to be safely driven to a workshop/garage for repair or testing. Once the fault has cleared, the ECM will revert to normal operation.

Adaptive or learning capability
Kia systems also utilise an adaptive function that will modify the basic programmed values for most effective operation during normal running, and with due regard to engine wear.

2 Self-Diagnosis connector location

Note: *On models without EOBD, the Kia SD connector is provided both for retrieving flash codes and for dedicated FCR use.*

Mentor 1.6i (EGi)

The SD connector is attached to the engine compartment bulkhead *(see illustration 17.1).*

Sportage 2.0i (Bosch Motronic)

The SD connector is located behind the airflow sensor, adjacent to the left-hand inner wing *(see illustration 17.2).*

EOBD models

The 16-pin connector is located under the facia - refer to Chapter 38.

3 Retrieving fault codes without a fault code reader (FCR) - flash codes

Note: *During the course of certain test procedures, it is possible for additional fault codes to be generated. Care must be taken that any codes generated during test routines do not mislead diagnosis. All codes must be cleared once testing is complete.*

1 Attach an LED positive probe to terminal A and the negative probe to terminal B in the SD connector *(see illustration 17.3)* **Note:** *If the LED does not behave as described, reverse the connections to the SD connector.*

2 Connect a jumper lead between terminals C and D in the SD connector *(refer to illustration 17.3).*

3 Switch on the ignition. The light on the LED will illuminate for 3 seconds and then extinguish.

4 If the ECM has stored one or more fault codes, the LED will then flash the 2-digit codes as follows:

a) *The two digits are indicated by two series of flashes.*

b) *The first series of flashes indicates the multiples of ten, the second series of flashes indicates the single units.*

c) *Tens are indicated by a 1.2-second flash. Units are indicated by 0.5-second flashes, separated by 0.5-second pauses.*

d) *A 1.6-second pause separates the tens from the units, and a 4-second pause separates the transmission of one code from another.*

e) *Code "34 is indicated by three 1.2-second flashes, followed by a 1.6-second pause, then four 0.5-second flashes.*

5 Count the number of flashes in each series, and record the code. Refer to the tables at the end of the Chapter to determine the meaning of the fault code.

6 If the LED remains extinguished, the ECM has stored no faults.

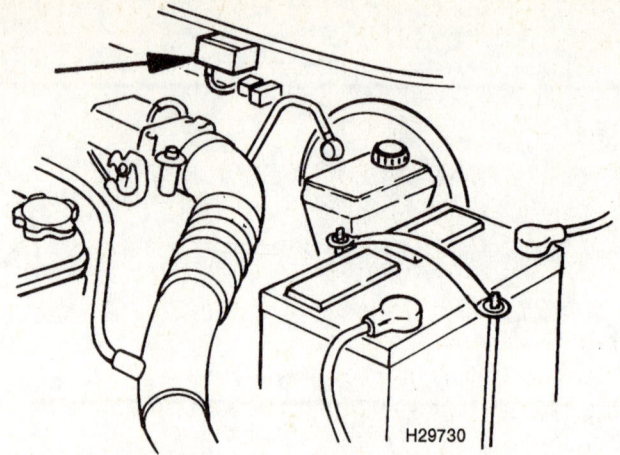

17.1 The SD connector attached to the bulkhead in the engine compartment (arrowed)

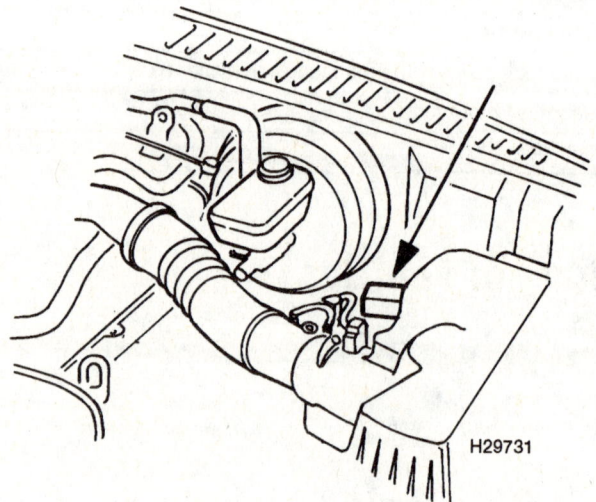

17.2 The SD connector located behind the airflow sensor in the engine compartment (arrowed)

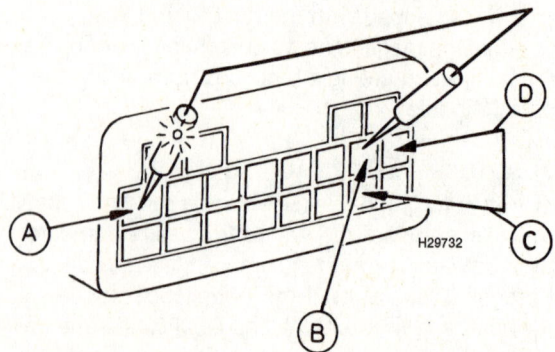

17.3 SD connector terminals for fault code retrieval

A Tester positive terminal

B Tester negative terminal

C Terminal for jumper lead bridge

D Terminal for jumper lead bridge

7 Continue retrieving codes until all stored codes have been retrieved and recorded.

8 Turn off the ignition and remove the LED and jumper lead to end fault code retrieval.

4 Clearing fault codes without a fault code reader (FCR)

1 Disconnect the negative battery terminal, and press the brake pedal for at least 5 seconds.

2 Reconnect the battery negative terminal.

Note: *The first drawback to this method is that battery disconnection will re-initialise all ECM adaptive values. Re-learning the appropriate adaptive values requires starting the engine from cold, and driving at various engine speeds for approximately 20 to 30 minutes. The engine should also be allowed to idle for approximately 10 minutes. The second drawback is that the radio security codes, clock setting and other stored values will be initialised, and these must be re-entered once the battery has been reconnected. Where possible, an FCR should be used for code clearing. On models equipped with EOBD, an FCR must be used to retrieve and clear fault codes.*

5 Self-Diagnosis with a fault code reader (FCR)

Note: *During the course of certain test procedures, it is possible for additional fault codes to be generated. Care must be taken that any codes generated during test routines do not mislead diagnosis.*

All Kia models

1 Connect an FCR to the SD connector. Use the FCR for the following purposes, in strict compliance with the FCR manufacturer's instructions:

a) *Retrieving fault codes.*
b) *Clearing fault codes.*
c) *Datastream (models with EOBD only).*

2 Codes must always be cleared after component testing, or after repairs involving the removal or replacement of an engine management system component.

6 Guide to test procedures

1 Use an FCR to interrogate the ECM for fault codes, or gather codes manually, as described in Sections 3 or 5.

Codes stored

2 If one or more fault codes are gathered, refer to the fault code tables at the end of this Chapter to determine their meaning.

3 If several codes are gathered, look for a common factor such as a defective earth return or supply.

4 Refer to the component test procedures in Chapter 4, where you will find a means of testing the majority of components and circuits found in the modern EMS.

5 Once the fault has been repaired, clear the codes and run the engine under various conditions to determine if the problem has cleared.

6 Check the ECM for fault codes once more. Repeat the above procedures where codes are still being stored.

7 Refer to Chapter 3 for more information on how to effectively test the EMS.

No codes stored

8 Where a running problem is experienced, but no codes are stored, the fault is outside of the parameters designed into the SD system. Refer to Chapter 3 for more information on how to effectively test the engine management system.

9 If the problem points to a specific component, refer to the test procedures in Chapter 4, where you will find a means of testing the majority of components and circuits found in the modern EMS.

Fault code tables

Kia EGi

Flash/ FCR code	Description	Flash/ FCR code	Description
02	Engine speed sensor	14	Atmospheric pressure sensor (APS) or APS circuit
03	Cylinder identification (CID) sensor or CID sensor circuit	15	Oxygen sensor (OS) or OS circuit
08	Airflow sensor (AFS) or AFS circuit	17	Oxygen sensor (OS) or OS circuit
09	Coolant temperature sensor (CTS) or CTS circuit	25	Fuel pressure regulator solenoid valve
10	Air temperature sensor (ATS) or ATS circuit	26	Carbon filter solenoid valve (CFSV) or CFSV circuit
12	Throttle pot sensor (TPS) or TPS circuit	34	Idle speed control valve (ISCV) or ISCV circuit

Chapter 17

Bosch Motronic M2.10.1

Flash code	FCR code	Description
02	047	Crank angle sensor (CAS) or CAS circuit
03	008	Cylinder identification (CID) sensor or CID sensor circuit
07	229	Cylinder identification (CID) sensor or CID sensor circuit
08	007	Airflow sensor (AFS) or AFS circuit
09	045	Coolant temperature sensor (CTS) or CTS circuit
11	169	Electronic control module (ECM)
12	053	Throttle pot sensor (TPS) or TPS circuit
15	028	Oxygen sensor (OS) or OS circuit
17	065	Oxygen sensor (OS) or OS circuit
18	017	Injector valve No. 1 or Injector valve circuit
19	016	Injector valve No. 2 or Injector valve circuit
20	035	Injector valve No. 3 or Injector valve circuit
21	034	Injector valve No. 4 or Injector valve circuit
24	003	Fuel pump or circuit
26	005	Carbon filter solenoid valve (CFSV) or CFSV circuit
28	121	Exhaust gas recirculation (EGR) valve or EGR circuit
34	004	Idle speed control valve (ISCV) or ISCV circuit
35	103	Oxygen sensor (OS) or OS circuit

Flash code	FCR code	Description
36	102	Oxygen sensor (OS) or OS circuit
37	104	Oxygen sensor (OS) or OS circuit
46	136	Air conditioning (A/C)
48	141	Electronic control module (ECM)
48	142	Electronic control module (ECM)
49	143	Electronic control module (ECM)
56	22	Idle speed control valve (ISCV) or ISCV circuit
57	040	Air conditioning (A/C)
73	009	Crank angle sensor (CAS) or CAS circuit
88	154	Electronic control module (ECM)
99	153	Electronic control module (ECM)
99	037	Battery voltage supply to ECM, voltage low

Models with EOBD

For a list of the allocated EOBD codes beginning with P0 (Generic Powertrain), refer to Chapter 1, Section 1.

Lancia

18

Index of vehicles

Index of vehicles

Model	Engine code	Year	System
Y10 LXie and 4wd 1108 SOHC FIRE	156 C.000	1989 to 1993	Bosch Mono-Jetronic A2.2
Y10 1108ie and 4x4 SOHC cat	156 C.046	1990 to 1992	Bosch Mono-Jetronic A2.2
Y10 1108ie and 4x4 SOHC cat	156 C.046	1992 to 1994	Bosch Mono-Motronic MA1.7
Dedra 1.6ie SOHC	835 A1.000	1990 to 1994	Weber MIW Centrajet 2
Dedra 1600ie SOHC cat	835 A1.046	1990 to 1994	Bosch Mono-Jetronic A2.2
Dedra 1.8ie DOHC	835 A2.000	1990 to 1993	Weber-Marelli IAW MPi
Dedra 1.8ie DOHC cat	835 A2.046	1990 to 1994	Weber-Marelli IAW MPi
Dedra 2.0ie DOHC	835 A5.000	1990 to 1992	Weber-Marelli IAW MPi
Dedra 2.0ie DOHC cat	835 A5.045	1990 to 1994	Weber-Marelli IAW MPi
Dedra 2.0ie DOHC cat	835 A5.046	1990 to 1994	Weber-Marelli IAW MPi
Dedra 2.0ie DOHC Turbo and cat	835 A8.000	1991 to 1996	Weber-Marelli IAW MPi
Dedra 2.0ie Integrale Turbo and cat	835 A7.000	1991 to 1996	Weber-Marelli IAW MPi
Delta 2.0 16V Turbo	836.A2.000	1993 to 1997	Weber-Marelli IAW MPi
Delta 1600ie DOHC	831 B7.000	1986 to 1989	Weber-Marelli IAW MPi
Delta 1600ie DOHC	831 B7.000	1989 to 1990	Weber-Marelli IAW MPi
Delta 1600ie DOHC static	831 B7.000	1991 to 1992	Weber-Marelli IAW MPi
Delta HF Turbo and Martini 1600 DOHC	831 B3.000	1986 to 1992	Weber-Marelli IAW MPi
Delta HF Turbo DOHC cat	831 B7.046	1991 to 1993	Weber-Marelli IAW MPi
Delta HF Integrale Turbo DOHC	831 B5.000	1988 to 1989	Weber-Marelli IAW MPi
Delta HF Integrale Turbo DOHC	831 C5.000	1988 to 1989	Weber-Marelli IAW MPi
Delta HF Integrale Turbo 16V DOHC	831 D5.000	1989 to 1992	Weber-Marelli IAW MPi
Delta HF Integrale Turbo 16V and cat	831 E5.000	1991 to 1994	Weber-Marelli IAW MPi
Prisma 1600ie DOHC	831 B7.000	1986 to 1989	Weber-Marelli IAW MPi
Prisma 1600ie DOHC	831 B7.000	1989 to 1990	Weber-Marelli IAW MPi
Prisma 1600ie DOHC static	831 B7.000	1991 to 1992	Weber-Marelli IAW MPi
Scudo 1.6i	220 A2.000	1996 to 1997	Bosch Motronic 1.7
Thema FL 2000ie 16V DOHC cat	834 F1.000	1992 to 1994	Bosch Motronic M1.7
Thema FL 2000ie Turbo 16V DOHC cat	834 F2.000	1992 to 1994	Bosch Motronic M2.7
Thema FL 3000 V6 SOHC cat	834 F.000	1992 to 1994	Bosch Motronic M1.7

Plus All models equipped with EOBD (approximately January 2001-on)

Chapter 18

Self-Diagnosis

1   Introduction

The engine management systems (EMSs) fitted to Lancia vehicles are mainly of Bosch or Weber-Marelli origin. Apart from Mono-Jetronic, Lancia engine management systems control the primary ignition, fuelling and idle functions from within the same control module. The Mono-Jetronic system controls fuelling and idle speed alone.

Self-Diagnosis (SD) function

Each ECM has a self-test capability that continually examines the signals from certain engine sensors and actuators, and compares each signal to a table of programmed values. If the diagnostic software determines that a fault is present, the ECM stores a fault. Codes will not be stored about components for which a code is not available, or for conditions not covered by the diagnostic software.

Lancia software does not generate fault code numbers (except EOBD models) - a fault code reader (FCR) normally displays any faults on the FCR screen without reference to a specific code number. Although actual code numbers are not available, faults in one or more of the circuits and components covered by the diagnostic software will cause a fault to be stored. Flash codes are not available - a dedicated FCR is required for code retrieval.

Limited operating strategy (LOS)

Lancia systems featured in this Chapter utilise LOS (a function that is commonly called the "limp-home mode"). Once certain faults have been identified (not all faults will initiate LOS), the ECM will implement LOS and refer to a programmed default value rather than the sensor signal. This enables the vehicle to be safely driven to a workshop/garage for repair or testing. Once the fault has cleared, the ECM will revert to normal operation.

Adaptive or learning capability

Lancia systems also utilise an adaptive function that will modify the basic programmed values for most effective operation during normal running, and with due regard to engine wear.

Self-Diagnosis (SD) warning light

Many Lancia models are equipped with an SD warning light located within the instrument panel. When the ignition is switched on, the light will illuminate. Once the engine has started, the light will extinguish if the diagnostic software determines that a system fault is not present. If the light illuminates at any time during a period of engine running, the ECM has diagnosed presence of a system fault. All EOBD models, are equipped with a MIL (Malfunction Indicator Light) in the instrument cluster, to alert the driver to the presence of a stored fault.

2   Self-Diagnosis connector location

Note: *Flash codes are not available in Lancia systems, and the SD connector is provided for connection to a dedicated FCR alone.*

Bosch Motronic 1.7

The 3-pin SD connector **(see illustration 18.1)** is usually located close to the ECM under the passenger's side glove compartment.

Bosch Mono-Jetronic A2.2

The 3-pin SD connector is usually located on the bulkhead, or may be situated close to the ECM under the passenger's side glove compartment, or in the centre console.

Bosch Mono-Motronic MA 1.7

The 3-pin SD connector is usually located beside the ECM on the right-hand wing in the engine compartment. Alternative locations are close to the ECM under the passenger's side glove compartment, or in the centre console.

Weber-Marelli MPi

The 3-pin SD connector is usually located in the engine compartment on the right-hand bulkhead or under the passenger's side facia, close to the ECM.

Weber Centrajet

The 3-pin SD connector is usually located beside the ECM on the front right-hand wing in the engine compartment.

Models with EOBD

The 16-pin diagnostic connector is located under the facia.

3   Retrieving faults without a fault code reader (FCR)

A fault code reader (FCR) is required to display faults generated in SD systems fitted to Lancia vehicles - although an SD warning light is fitted to many Lancia models, it cannot be used to display flash codes.

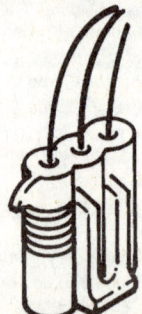

18.1 3-pin SD connector used for retrieving fault codes from Lancia systems

H29338

4   Clearing faults without a fault code reader (FCR)

All systems (except EOBD)

1 Turn off the ignition and disconnect the battery negative terminal for a period of approximately 2 minutes.

2 Reconnect the battery negative terminal.

Note: *The first drawback to this method is that battery disconnection will re-initialise all ECM adaptive values. Re-learning the appropriate adaptive values requires starting the engine from cold, and driving at various engine speeds for approximately 20 to 30 minutes. The engine should also be allowed to idle for approximately 10 minutes. The second drawback is that the radio security codes, clock setting and other stored values will be initialised, and these must be re-entered once the battery has been reconnected. Where possible, an FCR should be used for code clearing. On models equipped with EOBD, an FCR must be used to retrieve and clear any fault codes.*

5   Self-Diagnosis with a fault code reader (FCR)

Note: *During the course of certain test procedures, it is possible for additional fault codes to be generated. Care must be taken that any codes generated during test routines do not mislead diagnosis.*

All Lancia models

1 Connect an FCR to the SD connector. Use the FCR for the following purposes, in strict compliance with the FCR manufacturer's instructions:

   a) Displaying system faults.
   b) Clearing stored system faults.
   c) Testing actuators.
   d) Displaying Datastream.
   e) Making adjustments to the ignition timing or mixture (some vehicles).

2 Stored faults must always be cleared after component testing, or after repairs involving the removal of an EMS component.

6   Guide to test procedures

1 Use an FCR to interrogate the ECM for faults.

Faults stored

2 If several faults are gathered, look for a common factor such as a defective earth return or supply.

3 Refer to the component test procedures in Chapter 4, where you will find a means of testing the majority of components and circuits found in the modern EMS.

4 Once the fault has been repaired, clear the faults and run the engine under various conditions to determine if the problem has cleared.

5 Check the ECM for faults once more. Repeat the above procedures where faults are still being stored.

6 Refer to Chapter 3 for more information on how to effectively test the EMS.

No faults stored

7 Where a running problem is experienced, but no faults are stored, the fault is outside of the parameters designed into the SD system. Refer to Chapter 3 for more information on how to effectively test the engine management system.

8 If the problem points to a specific component, refer to the test procedures in Chapter 4, where you will find a means of testing the majority of components and circuits found in the modern EMS.

Fault table

All Lancia models

Lancia software does not usually generate fault codes. The FCR normally displays faults on the FCR screen without reference to a specific code number. Although actual code numbers are not available, faults in one or more of the following list of circuits and components will cause a fault to be stored.

Circuits checked by Lancia SD system

Adaptive control limits. When the limits are reached, this suggests a serious engine (mechanical) condition.
Air temperature sensor (ATS) or ATS circuit
Battery voltage too low or too high
Crank angle sensor (CAS) or CAS circuit loss of signal
Carbon filter solenoid valve (CFSV) or CFSV circuit
Coolant temperature sensor (CTS) or CTS circuit
Electronic control module (ECM)
Distributor phase sensor circuit (CID)
Ignition coils control
Injector control or injector circuit
Knock sensor (KS) or KS circuit
Oxygen sensor (OS) or OS circuit
Manifold absolute pressure (MAP) sensor or MAP sensor circuit
Manifold absolute pressure (MAP) sensor - no correlation between MAP signal and throttle position sensor (TPS) and crank angle sensor (CAS) signals
Mismatch between crank angle sensor (CAS) signal and distributor phase sensor signal or circuit
Oxygen sensor (OS) or OS circuit
Relay control or circuit
Self-diagnosis (SD) warning light or circuit
Idle speed stepper motor (ISSM) or ISSM circuit
Tachometer or circuit
Throttle pot sensor (TPS) or TPS circuit

Models with EOBD

For a list of the allocated EOBD codes beginning with P0 (Generic Powertrain), refer to Chapter 1, Section 1.

Notes

Land Rover 19

Index of vehicles

Index of vehicles

Model	Engine code	Year	System
Discovery MPi 2.0 20HD DOHC 16V	M16i	1993 to 1995	Rover MEMS MPi
Discovery 2.0 MPi DOHC 16V	20T4	1995 to 1997	Rover MEMS MPi
Discovery 3.5 V8i	V8	1990 to 1992	Lucas 14CUX
Discovery 3.5 V8i cat	V8	1990 to 1995	Lucas 14CUX
Discovery 3.9i V8	V8	1995 to 1998	Lucas 14CUX
Range Rover 3.9 EFi V8	3.9L	1989 to 1996	Lucas 14CUX
Range Rover 4.0i	4.0L	1994 to 2001	Lucas 14CUX
Range Rover 4.2i cat	4.2L	1992 to 1994	Lucas 14CUX

Plus All models equipped with EOBD (approximately January 2001-on)

Self-Diagnosis

1 Introduction

The engine management systems (EMSs) fitted to Land Rover vehicles are of Bosch, Lucas or Rover origin. Bosch & Rover MEMS controls primary ignition, fuelling and idle functions from within the same control module. Lucas 14CUX controls fuel injection and idle functions alone.

Self-Diagnosis (SD) function

Each electronic control module (ECM) has a self-test capability that continually examines the signals from certain engine sensors and actuators, and then compares each signal to a table of programmed values. If the diagnostic software determines that a fault is present, the ECM stores one or more fault codes in the ECM memory. Codes are not stored about components for which a code is not available or for conditions not covered by the diagnostic software.

Lucas 14CUX generates 2-digit fault codes for retrieval by a dedicated fault code reader (FCR).

Rover MEMS software does not generate fault code numbers - a fault code reader normally displays faults on the FCR screen without reference to a specific code number. Although actual code numbers are not available, faults in one or more of the circuits and components covered by the diagnostic software will cause a fault to be stored.

It is not possible to retrieve flash codes from the Lucas 14CUX system, Bosch systems, or from Rover MEMS.

Chapter 19

Limited operating strategy (LOS)

Land Rover systems featured in this Chapter utilise LOS (a function that is commonly called the "limp-home mode"). Once certain faults have been identified (not all faults will initiate LOS), the ECM will implement LOS and refer to a programmed default value rather than the sensor signal. This enables the vehicle to be safely driven to a workshop/garage for repair or testing. Once the fault has cleared, the ECM will revert to normal operation.

Adaptive or learning capability

Land Rover systems also utilise an adaptive function that will modify the basic programmed values for most effective operation during normal running, and with due regard to engine wear.

2 Self-Diagnosis connector location

Lucas 14CUX

The SD connector is located either under the driver's seat (early models) or behind the driver's footwell kick-panel trim (later models) (see illustrations 19.1 and 19.2) and is provided for use by a dedicated FCR alone.

Rover MEMS

The SD connector is located in the engine compartment close to the ECM on the right-hand wing (see illustration 19.3), and is provided for use by a dedicated FCR alone.

Models with EOBD

The 16-pin diagnostic connector is located under the facia on Discovery and Freelander models, between the front seats on Defender models, and to the right side of the facia on Range Rover models - refer to Chapter 38.

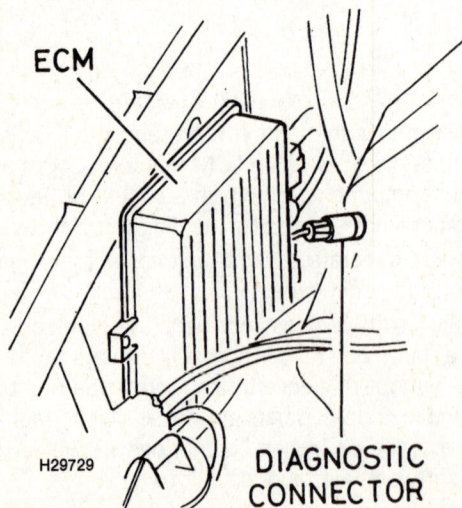

19.1 Location of SD connector and ECM - Lucas 14CUX, early models

A SD connector   B ECM

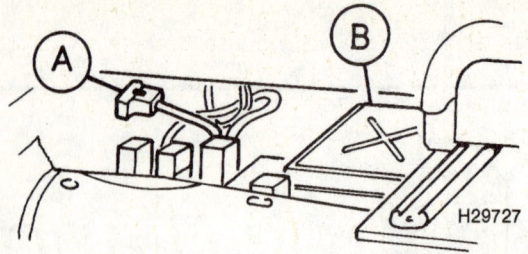

19.2 Location of SD connector and ECM - Lucas 14CUX, later models

A SD connector   B ECM

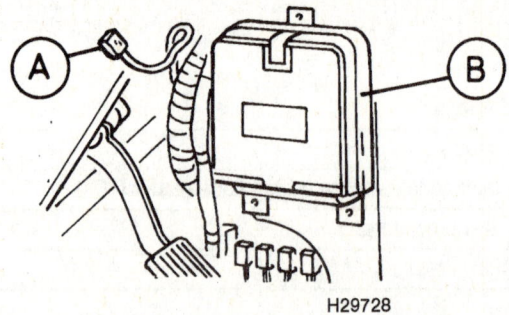

19.3 Location of SD connector and ECM - Rover MEMS

3 Retrieving fault codes without a fault code reader (FCR)

The only method of retrieving fault codes from the systems fitted to Land Rovers is by use of a dedicated FCR.

4 Clearing fault codes without a fault code reader (FCR)

The only method of clearing fault codes from systems fitted to Land Rovers is by use of a dedicated FCR.

5 Self-Diagnosis with a fault code reader (FCR)

Note: During the course of certain test procedures, it is possible for additional fault codes to be generated. Care must be taken that any codes generated during test routines do not mislead diagnosis.

All Land Rover models

1 Connect an FCR to the SD connector. Use the FCR for the following purposes, in strict compliance with the FCR manufacturer's instructions:

a) *Displaying fault codes and system faults.*

b) *Clearing fault codes and system faults.*

c) *Testing actuators.*

d) *Displaying Datastream.*

e) *Making adjustments to the mixture (some non-cat vehicles).*

2 Stored faults must always be cleared after component testing, or after repairs involving the removal or replacement of an EMS component.

6   Guide to test procedures

1 Use an FCR to interrogate the ECM for fault codes.

Codes stored

2 If one or more fault codes are gathered, refer to the fault code tables at the end of this Chapter to determine their meaning.

3 If several codes are gathered, look for a common factor such as a defective earth return or supply.

4 Refer to the component test procedures in Chapter 4, where you will find a means of testing the majority of components and circuits found in the modern EMS.

5 Once the fault has been repaired, clear the codes and run the engine under various conditions to determine if the problem has cleared.

6 Check the ECM for fault codes once more. Repeat the above procedures where codes are still being stored.

7 Refer to Chapter 3 for more information on how to effectively test the EMS.

No codes stored

8 Where a running problem is experienced, but no codes are stored, the fault is outside of the parameters designed into the SD system. Refer to Chapter 3 for more information on how to effectively test the engine management system.

9 If the problem points to a specific component, refer to the test procedures in Chapter 4, where you will find a means of testing the majority of components and circuits found in the modern EMS.

Fault code tables

Lucas 14CUX

FCR code	Description
12	Mass airflow (MAF) sensor or MAF sensor circuit
14	Coolant temperature sensor (CTS) or CTS circuit
15	Fuel temperature sensor (FTS) or FTS circuit
17	Throttle pot sensor (TPS) or TPS circuit
18	Throttle pot sensor (TPS) or TPS circuit
19	Throttle pot sensor (TPS) or TPS circuit
21	Electronic control module (ECM) or ECM circuit
25	Ignition misfire
28	Air leak
29	Electronic control module (ECM) memory check
34	Injector, bank A or injector circuit
36	Injector, bank B or injector circuit
40	Misfire, bank A or circuit
44	Oxygen sensor (OS) A or OS circuit
45	Oxygen sensor (OS) B or OS circuit
48	Idle air control valve (IACV) or IACV circuit
50	Misfire, bank B or circuit
59	Group fault - air leak or fuel supply
68	Vehicle speed sensor (VSS) or VSS circuit
69	Gear selector switch or circuit
88	Carbon filter solenoid valve (CFSV) or CFSV circuit

Rover MEMS

Rover MEMS software does not usually generate fault codes. The FCR normally displays faults on the FCR screen without reference to a specific code number. Although actual code numbers are not available, faults in one or more of the following list of circuits and components will cause a fault to be stored.

All models with EOBD

For a list of the allocated EOBD codes beginning with P0 (Generic Powertrain), refer to Chapter 1, Section 1.

Circuits checked by Rover MEMS system

Airflow sensor

Carbon filter solenoid valve

CO resistor

Coolant temperature sensor (CTS) or CTS circuit

Fuel pressure regulator

Fuel pump relay

Fuel temperature sensor

Idle speed stepper motor

Injector valves

Oxygen sensor (OS) or OS circuit

Throttle pot sensor (TPS) or TPS circuit

Vehicle speed sensor

Notes

Index of vehicles

Model	Engine code	Year	System
Lexus GS300	2JZ-GE	1993 on	Toyota TCCS
Lexus LS400	1UZ-FE	1990 to 1993	Toyota TCCS

Plus All models equipped with EOBD (approximately January 2001-on)

Self-Diagnosis

1   Introduction

The engine management system (EMS) fitted to Lexus vehicles is the Toyota TCCS which controls the primary ignition, fuel injection and the idle functions from within the same control module.

Self-Diagnosis (SD) function

The electronic control module (ECM) has a self-test capability that continually examines the signals from certain engine sensors and actuators, and then compares each signal to a table of programmed values. If the diagnostic software determines that a fault is present, the ECM stores one or more fault codes in the ECM memory. Codes will not be stored about components for which a code is not available, or for conditions not covered by the diagnostic software.

Limited operating strategy (LOS)

Lexus models with Toyota TCCS featured in this Chapter utilise LOS (a function that is commonly called the "limp-home mode"). Once certain faults have been identified (not all faults will initiate LOS), the ECM will implement LOS and refer to a programmed default value rather than the sensor signal. This enables the vehicle to be safely driven to a workshop/garage for repair or testing. Once the fault has cleared, the ECM will revert to normal operation.

Adaptive or learning capability

Lexus with Toyota TCCS also utilises an adaptive function that will modify the basic programmed values for most effective operation during normal running, and with due regard to engine wear.

Chapter 20

Self-Diagnosis (SD) warning light

Lexus vehicles are equipped with an SD/MIL warning light located within the instrument panel.

2 Self-Diagnosis connector location

The SD connector (Toyota data communication link, or TDCL) is located under the facia, on the driver's side (see illustration 20.1).

On models equipped with EOBD, the 16-pin diagnostic connector is located under the facia - refer to Chapter 38.

3 Retrieving fault codes without a fault code reader (FCR) - flash codes

Note: During the course of certain test procedures, it is possible for additional fault codes to be generated. Care must be taken that any codes generated during testing do not mislead diagnosis. All codes must be cleared once testing is complete.

Note: On models equipped with EOBD, an FCR must be used to retrieve and clear fault codes.

1 Ensure that the engine is at normal operating temperature, and that all switches and auxiliary equipment are turned off.

2 The throttle switch must be functioning correctly, and the transmission in neutral before implementing the diagnostic procedure.

3 Switch on the ignition, but do not start the engine.

4 Use a jumper lead to bridge the terminals TE1 and E1 in the SD connector (see illustration 20.2).

5 The codes are output on the SD warning light. The flashing of the light indicates the 2-digit fault codes as follows:

  a) The two digits are indicated by two series of flashes.
  b) The first series of flashes indicates the multiples of ten, the second series of flashes indicates the single units.
  c) Both tens and units are indicated by 0.5-second flashes, separated by 0.5-second pauses.
  d) A 1.5-second pause separates the tens from the units. A 2.5-second pause separates the transmission of each individual code.
  e) Code "34" is indicated by three 0.5-second flashes, followed by a 1.5-second pause, followed by four 0.5-second flashes.

6 Count the number of flashes in each series, and record each code as it is transmitted. Refer to the table at the end of the Chapter to determine the meaning of the fault code.

7 Fault codes will be transmitted in sequential order, and repeated after the highest recorded code has been displayed.

8 When all codes have been transmitted, the warning light will pause and then repeat the sequence.

20.1 The TDCL connector is located under the driver's side facia

9 If no faults have been detected, the warning light will flash on and off every 0.5 seconds for eight flashes. After a 3-second pause, the sequence will be repeated.

10 Turn off the ignition and remove the jumper lead to end fault code retrieval.

Models with the 2JZ-GE engine

Note: Ensure that the preparatory conditions, which were set for the fault code retrieval mode, are still applicable (see paragraphs 1 and 2). The jumper lead between terminals TE1 and E1 should be disconnected.

11 Use a jumper lead to bridge terminals TE2 and E1 in the SD connector (refer to illustration 20.2).

12 Switch on the ignition. **Note:** If the jumper lead is connected after the ignition is switched on, the test mode will fail to start.

13 The SD warning light will flash regularly to indicate that the system has initiated test mode.

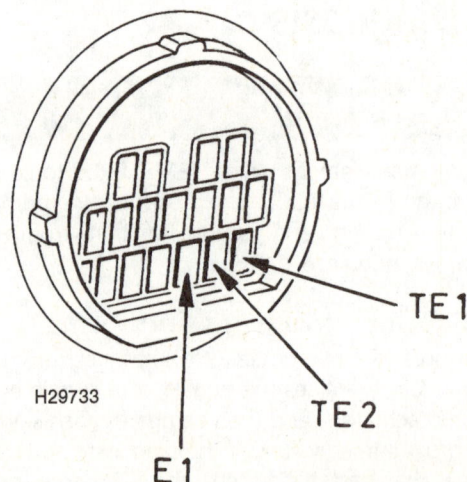

H29733

20.2 Bridge terminals TE1 and E1 in the SD connector. This causes the system to flash the fault codes on the SD warning light

14 Start the engine and road test the vehicle. Drive at a speed of more than 6 mph (10 km/h), and attempt to reproduce the conditions during which the fault might occur.

15 Bring the vehicle to a halt with the ignition still on.

16 Remove the jumper lead from terminals TE2 and E1, and place the lead between terminals TE1 and E1.

17 The codes recorded during the road test will now be output on the SD warning light. The flashing of the light indicates the 2-digit fault codes, in the same way as described previously (see paragraphs 5 to 9).

18 Turn off the ignition and remove the jumper lead to end fault code retrieval.

4   Clearing fault codes without a fault code reader (FCR)

Method 1

1 Remove the 20-amp EFi fuse from the fusebox for a minimum of 30 seconds (see illustration 20.3).

2 Replace the EFi fuse, and the fault codes should be cleared from the ECM memory.

Method 2

3 Turn off the ignition and disconnect the battery negative terminal for a period of approximately fifteen seconds.

4 Reconnect the battery negative terminal. **Note:** *The first drawback to this method is that battery disconnection will re-initialise all ECM adaptive values. Re-learning the appropriate adaptive values requires starting the engine from cold, and driving at various engine speeds for approximately 20 minutes. The second drawback is that radio security codes and other programmed values will be re-initialised, and these will require re-entering once the battery has been reconnected. Where possible, use the first method described above (or use an FCR) for code clearing. On models equipped with EOBD, an FCR must be used to retrieve and clear fault codes.*

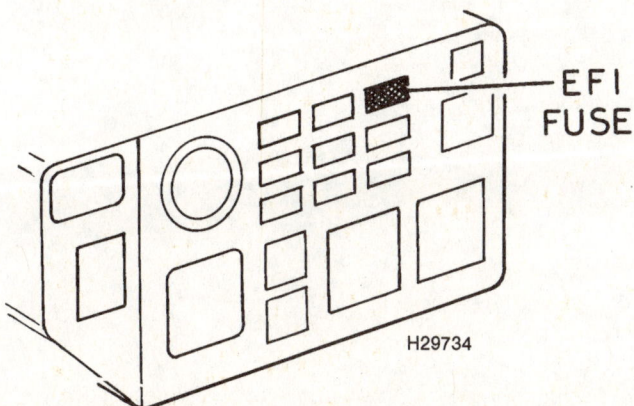

20.3 Position of the EFi fuse in the fusebox

5   Self-Diagnosis with a fault code reader (FCR)

Note: *During the course of certain test procedures, it is possible for additional fault codes to be generated. Care must be taken that any codes generated during test routines do not mislead diagnosis.*

All Lexus models

1 Prior to fault code retrieval, ensure that the engine is at normal operating temperature, and that the throttle switch is functioning correctly (indicating the idle condition).

2 Connect an FCR to the SD connector. Use the FCR for the following purposes, in strict compliance with the FCR manufacturer's instructions:

    a) *Retrieving fault codes.*
    b) *Clearing fault codes.*
    c) *Making adjustments.*
    d) *Displaying Datastream.*

3 Codes must always be cleared after component testing, or after repairs involving the removal or replacement of an EMS component.

6   Guide to test procedures

1 Use an FCR to interrogate the ECM for fault codes, or gather fault codes manually, as described in Sections 3 or 5.

Codes stored

2 If one or more fault codes are gathered, refer to the fault code table at the end of this Chapter to determine their meaning.

3 If several codes are gathered, look for a common factor such as a defective earth return or supply.

4 Refer to the component test procedures in Chapter 4, where you will find a means of testing the majority of components and circuits found in the modern EMS.

5 Once the fault has been repaired, clear the codes and run the engine under various conditions to determine if the problem has cleared.

6 Check the ECM for fault codes once more. Repeat the above procedures where codes are still being stored.

7 Refer to Chapter 3 for more information on how to effectively test the EMS.

No codes stored

8 Where a running problem is experienced, but no codes are stored, the fault is outside of the parameters designed into the SD system. Refer to Chapter 3 for more information on how to effectively test the engine management system.

9 If the problem points to a specific component, refer to the test procedures in Chapter 4, where you will find a means of testing the majority of components and circuits found in the modern EMS.

Chapter 20

Fault code tables

All Lexus models (except EOBD)

Flash/ FCR code	Description
12	No RPM signal to electronic control module (ECM) while cranking
13	RPM signal or circuit
14	Missing ignition No. 1 signal from amplifier
15	Missing ignition No. 2 signal from amplifier
16	Transmission control signal or circuit
17	No. 1 camshaft position sensor (CMP) signal or circuit
18	No. 2 camshaft position sensor (CMP) signal or circuit
21	Oxygen sensor (OS) or OS circuit
22	Coolant temperature sensor (CTS) or CTS circuit
24	Air temperature sensor (ATS) or ATS circuit
25	Lean exhaust
26	Rich exhaust
27	Oxygen sensor (OS) or OS circuit
28	Oxygen sensor (OS) or OS circuit
29	Oxygen sensor (OS) or OS circuit
31	Mass airflow (MAF) sensor or MAF sensor circuit
35	Altitude compensation circuit

Flash/ FCR code	Description
41	Throttle pot sensor (TPS) or TPS circuit
43	Starter signal circuit open
47	Sub-throttle pot sensor (TPS) or TPS circuit
51	Neutral switch off (transmission not in neutral) or air conditioning switched on during test
52	Knock sensor (KS) or KS circuit
53	Knock control computer problem
55	No. 2 knock sensor (KS) or KS circuit
71	Exhaust gas recirculation (EGR) sensor or circuit
99	Continuous flash, no codes present

All models with EOBD

For a list of the allocated EOBD codes beginning with P0 (Generic Powertrain), refer to Chapter 1, Section 1.

Mazda

Index of vehicles

Model	Engine code	Year	System
121 1.3 SOHC 16V cat	B3	1991 to 1995	Mazda EGi-S SPi
323 1.3i SOHC 16V cat	B3	1991 to 1995	Mazda EGi MPi
323 1.3i SOHC 16V	B3	1995 to 1998	Mazda EGi MPi
323 1.5i DOHC 16V	Z5	1994 to 1998	Mazda EGi MPi
323 1600i	B6	1985 to 1987	Mazda EGi MPi
323 1.6i Turbo 4x4 DOHC	B6	1986 to 1989	Mazda EGi MPi
323 1.6i SOHC 16V cat	B6	1991 to 1994	Mazda EGi MPi
323 1.6i Estate SOHC cat	B6E	1991 to 1994	Mazda EGi MPi
323 1.8i DOHC 16V cat	BP	1991 to 1994	Mazda EGi MPi
323 2.0i DOHC V6 24V	KF	1996 to 1998	Mazda EGi MPi
626 1.8i cat DOHC 16V	FP	1992 to 1998	Mazda EGi MPi
626 2000i fwd	FE	1985 to 1987	Mazda EGi MPi
626 2.0i GT DOHC 16V	FE	1987 to 1990	Mazda EGi MPi
626 2.0i DOHC 16V	FE	1990 to 1993	Mazda EGi MPi
626 2.0i DOHC 16V cat	FE	1990 to 1995	Mazda EGi MPi
626 2.0i DOHC 16V cat	FS	1992 to 1998	Mazda EGi MPi
626 2.2i 4x4 SOHC cat	F2	1990 to 1993	Mazda EGi MPi
626 2.5i DOHC V6 cat	KL	1992 to 1998	Mazda EGi MPi
E2000	FE	1994 to 2001	Mazda EGi MPi
MX-3 1.6i SOHC 16V	B6	1991 to 1998	Mazda EGi MPi
MX-3 1.8i DOHC V6	K8	1991 to 1998	Mazda EGi MPi
MX-5 1.8i DOHC 16V	BP	1995 to 2001	Mazda EGi MPi
MX-6 2.5i V6 DOHC cat	KL	1992 to 1998	Mazda EGi MPi
Xedos 6 1.6i DOHC 16V	B6	1994 to 1998	Mazda EGi MPi
Xedos 6 2.0i DOHC 24V	KF	1992 to 2000	Mazda EGi MPi
Xedos 9 2.0i DOHC 24V	KF	1994 to 1995	Mazda EGi MPi
Xedos 9 2.5i DOHC 24V	KL	1994 to 1998	Mazda EGi MPi
RX7	RE13B	1986 to 1990	Mazda EGi MPi

Plus All models equipped with EOBD (approximately January 2001-on)

Self-Diagnosis

1 Introduction

The engine management system (EMS) fitted to Mazda vehicles is Mazda EGi, which exists in both MPi and SPi forms. Mazda EGi controls the primary ignition, fuel injection and idle functions from within the same control module.

Self-Diagnosis (SD) function

Each ECM has a self-test capability that continually examines the signals from certain engine sensors and actuators, and compares each signal to a table of programmed values. If the diagnostic software determines that a fault is present, the ECM stores one or more fault codes. Codes will not be stored about components for which a code is not available, or for conditions not covered by the diagnostic software.

Mazda EGi generates fault codes for retrieval by manual means (flash codes) or by a dedicated fault code reader (FCR). Until 1995, the fault code structure was 2-digit. After 1995, in some Mazda models the fault code structure was changed to 4-digit. The code tables at the end of the Chapter indicate the meaning for both 2- and 4 digit codes. All models equipped with EOBD generate 5-digit fault codes, for which an FCR must be used to retrieve or clear.

Limited operating strategy (LOS)

Mazda systems featured in this Chapter utilise LOS (a function that is commonly called the "limp-home mode"). Once certain faults have been identified (not all faults will initiate LOS), the ECM will implement LOS and refer to a programmed default value rather than the sensor signal. This enables the vehicle to be safely driven to a workshop/garage for repair or testing. Once the fault has cleared, the ECM will revert to normal operation.

Adaptive or learning capability

Mazda systems also utilise an adaptive function that will modify the basic programmed values for most effective operation during normal running, and with due regard to engine wear.

Self-Diagnosis (SD) warning light

The majority of Mazda models are equipped with a SD warning light located within the instrument panel. All models equipped with EOBD have a MIL (Malfunction Warning Light) in the instrument cluster.

2 Self-Diagnosis connector location

In some early 323 models (engine code B6, 1985) and many 626 models from 1987 to 1993 (engine codes FE, F2 and F3), a green 6-pin SD connector in conjunction with a single-pin connector are provided, and these are usually located close together. Mazda 121, 323 from 1987 and all other 626 models utilise a 17-pin SD connector.

6-pin SD connector

In the engine compartment, close to the wiper motor, behind the left-hand front strut mounting, or to the rear of the left-side inner wing (see illustrations 21.1 and 21.2). The SD connectors on 1985 323 models are located under the passenger's side facia close to the ECM.

17-pin SD connector

In the engine compartment, next to the battery (see illustration 21.3) or close to the airflow sensor.

Models equipped with EOBD

The 16-pin diagnostic connector is located under the facia - refer to Chapter 38.

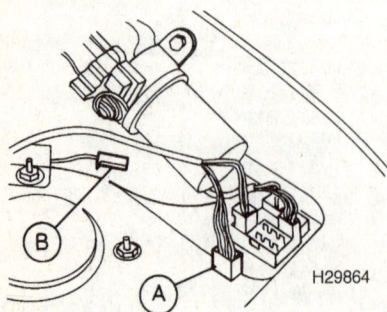

21.1 Green 6-pin and 1-pin SD connectors located near to the wiper motor
A Green six-pin connector
B 1-pin connector

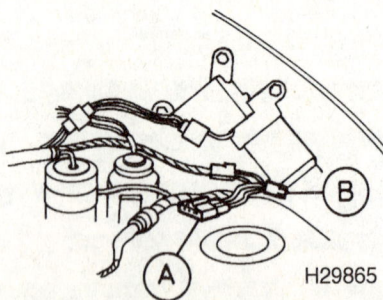

21.2 Green 6-pin and 1-pin SD connectors close together on the loom
A Green six-pin connector
B 1-pin connector

21.3 17-pin SD connector located next to the battery

3 Retrieving fault codes without a fault code reader (FCR) - flash codes

Note: *During the course of certain test procedures, it is possible for additional fault codes to be generated. Care must be taken that any codes generated during test routines do not mislead diagnosis. All codes must be cleared once testing is complete.*

6-pin SD connector

1 Locate the green 6-pin connector and then attach an LED diode light between the B+ terminal and the signal terminal in the 6 pin connector (see illustration 21.4).

2 Locate the green single-pin terminal, and use a jumper wire to connect it to earth.

3 Switch on the ignition, do not start the engine. The light will remain illuminated for 3 seconds, and then flash to indicate the fault code. If the light extinguishes, no fault codes are stored.

4 Fault codes are displayed on the LED Light as 2-digit flash codes. Codes 1 to 9 are displayed as a series of short pulses 0.4 seconds in duration, with a 0.4-second pause between each pulse; thus, 8 flashes indicates code number 8.

5 The numbers from 10 to 69 are displayed by two series of flashes:

a) *The first series of flashes indicates the multiples of ten, the second series of flashes indicates the single units.*

b) *Tens are indicated by 1.2-second flashes, separated by a short pause.*

c) *A pause of 1.6 seconds separates tens and units (the light remains extinguished during pauses).*

d) *Units are indicated by 0.4-second flashes, separated by a short pause.*

e) *Four long flashes and one short flash, for example, displays code 41.*

f) *A pause of 4 seconds separates the transmission of each individual code.*

g) *The code is repeated with a 4-second pause between each code that is displayed.*

6 Count the number of flashes in each series, and record each code as it is transmitted. Refer to the tables at the end of the Chapter to determine the meaning of the fault code.

7 Continue retrieving codes until all stored codes have been retrieved and recorded.

8 Turn off the ignition and remove the diode light to end fault code retrieval.

17-pin SD connector

9 Use a jumper lead to bridge terminals TEN and GND in the 17-pin SD connector (see illustration 21.5). On models without a warning light, connect an LED diode light (see illustration 21.6)

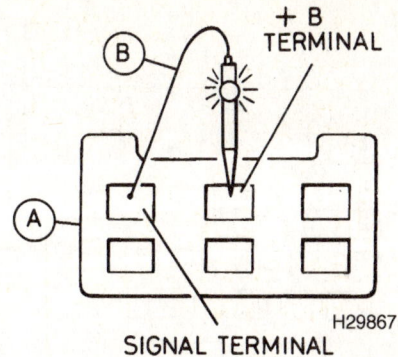

21.4 Connect an LED test light between pins A and B in order to retrieve flash codes from vehicles with the 6-pin connector
A Green 6-pin connector
B LED attached between signal terminal and B+ terminal

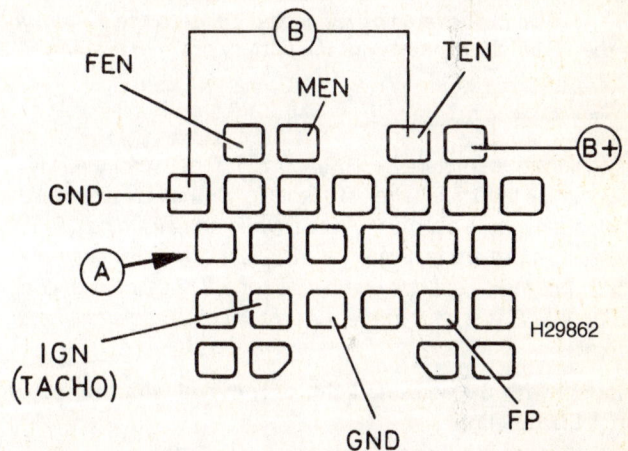

21.5 Connect a jumper lead between pins TEN and GND in order to retrieve flash codes with the aid of the SD warning light
A 17-pin SD connector   B Jumper lead

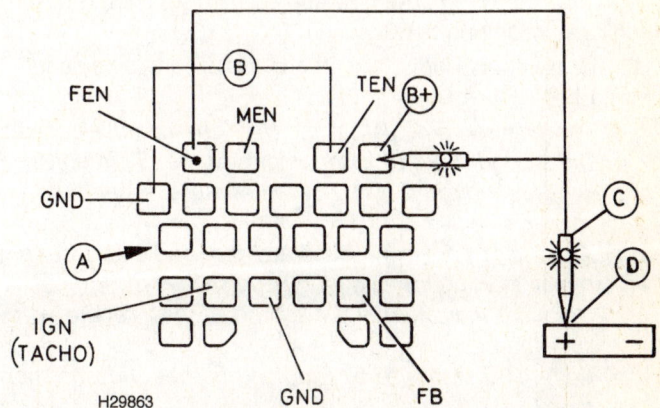

21.6 Connect an LED test light and a jumper lead to the correct pins in the SD connector in order to retrieve flash codes. The positive probe must be connected either to the B+ terminal in the 17-pin SD connector or the battery positive terminal
A 17-pin SD connector   C LED test light
B Jumper lead   D Battery positive terminal

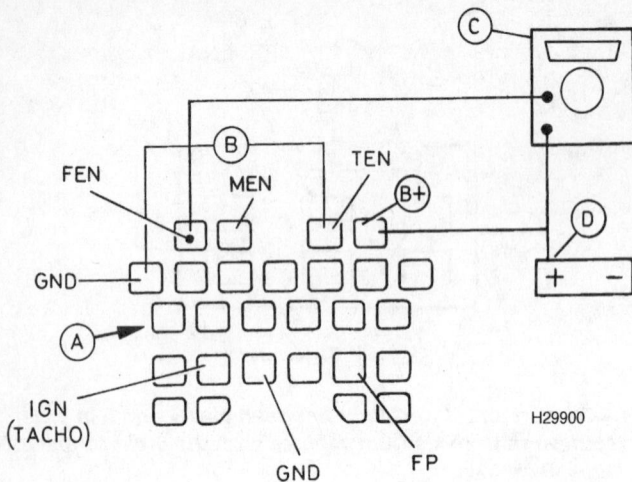

21.7 Connect an analogue voltmeter and a jumper lead to the correct pins in the SD connector in order to retrieve flash codes. The positive probe must be connected either to the B+ terminal in the 17-pin SD connector or the battery positive terminal

A   17-pin SD connector
B   Jumper lead

C   Analogue voltmeter
D   Battery positive terminal

or analogue voltmeter (see illustration 21.7) between the FEN and the B+ terminal in the SD connector or the FEN terminal and the battery positive terminal. **Note:** *Up to and including 1987, the fault codes are generated as a straight count. For example, 15 flashes indicates code number 15, or 5 flashes indicate code number 5. Please refer to the correct fault code table for these models.*

Models with SD warning light, or retrieval with the aid of an LED test light

10 Switch on the ignition, but do not start the engine.

11 Fault codes are displayed on the LED light or the SD warning light as 2-digit flash codes. Codes 1 to 9 are displayed as a series of short pulses 0.4 seconds in duration, with a 0.4-second pause between each pulse; thus, 8 flashes indicates code number 8.

12 The numbers from 10 to 69 are displayed by two series of flashes:

a) *The first series of flashes indicates the multiples of ten, the second series of flashes indicates the single units.*
b) *Tens are indicated by 1.2-second flashes, separated by a short pause.*
c) *A pause of 1.6 seconds separates tens and units (the light remains extinguished during pauses).*
d) *Units are indicated by 0.4-second flashes, separated by short pauses.*
e) *Code 41 is displayed by four long flashes and one short flash.*
f) *After a 4-second pause, the code is repeated.*
g) *A pause of 4 seconds separates the transmission of each individual code.*

13 Count the number of flashes in each series, and record each code as it is transmitted. Refer to the tables at the end of the Chapter to determine the meaning of the fault code.

14 Continue retrieving codes until all stored codes have been retrieved and recorded.

15 Turn off the ignition and remove the jumper lead and test light (where used) to end fault code retrieval.

Retrieval with the aid of an analogue voltmeter

16 Switch on the ignition, but do not start the engine.

17 Fault codes are displayed on the analogue voltmeter as needle sweeps; the number of needle sweeps indicates the fault code.

18 Count the number of sweeps in each series, and record each code as it is transmitted. Refer to the tables at the end of the Chapter to determine the meaning of the fault code.

19 Continue retrieving codes until all stored codes have been retrieved and recorded.

20 Turn off the ignition and remove the jumper lead and voltmeter to end fault code retrieval.

4-digit fault codes

21 Some Mazda models from 1995 onwards have a 4-digit fault code structure. The code tables at the end of the Chapter indicate the meaning for both 2- and 4-digit codes, but at the time of going to press, we do not have information on whether 4-digit codes can be retrieved by manual means.

Models with EOBD

On all models with EOBD, an FCR must be used to retrieve and clear fault codes.

4   Clearing codes without a fault code reader (FCR)

Preferred method

1 Turn the ignition key to the "ACC" position.

2 Remove the 60-amp BTN fuse and the 30-amp EGi fuse. The fusebox is located in the engine compartment.

3 Wait for 20 seconds and then refit the fuses. All stored fault codes should now be cleared.

Alternative method

4 Disconnect the battery negative terminal for at least 20 seconds.

5 Fully depress the brake pedal for at least 5 seconds and then release it.

6 Reconnect the battery negative terminal.

Note: *The first drawback to this method is that battery disconnection will re-initialise all ECM adaptive values. Re-learning the appropriate adaptive values requires starting the engine from cold, and driving at various engine speeds for approximately 20 minutes. The second drawback is that the radio security codes, clock setting and other stored values will be initialised, and these must be re-entered once the battery has been reconnected. Where possible, use the preferred method described above, or clear the codes using a fault code reader. On all models with EOBD, an FCR must be used to retrieve and clear fault codes.*

5 Self-Diagnosis with a fault code reader (FCR)

Note: *During the course of certain test procedures, it is possible for additional fault codes to be generated. Care must be taken that any codes generated during test routines do not mislead diagnosis.*

All Mazda models

1 Connect an FCR to the SD connector. Use the FCR for the following purposes, in strict compliance with the FCR manufacturer's instructions:

a) *Retrieving fault codes.*
b) *Clearing fault codes.*
c) *Checking switches.*
d) *Making adjustments to timing and idle speed.*
e) *Datastream (EOBD models only).*

2 Codes must always be cleared after component testing, or after repairs involving the removal of an EMS component.

6 Guide to test procedures

1 Use an FCR to interrogate the ECM for fault codes, or (where possible) gather codes manually, as described in Sections 3 or 5.

Codes stored

2 If one or more fault codes are gathered, refer to the fault code tables at the end of this Chapter to determine their meaning.

3 If several codes are gathered, look for a common factor such as a defective earth return or supply.

4 Refer to the component test procedures in Chapter 4, where you will find a means of testing the majority of components and circuits found in the modern EMS.

5 Once the fault has been repaired, clear the codes and run the engine under various conditions to determine if the problem has cleared.

6 Check the ECM for fault codes once more. Repeat the above procedures where codes are still being stored.

7 Refer to Chapter 3 for more information on how to effectively test the EMS.

No codes stored

8 Where a running problem is experienced, but no codes are stored, the fault is outside of the parameters designed into the SD system. Refer to Chapter 3 for more information on how to effectively test the engine management system.

9 If the problem points to a specific component, refer to the test procedures in Chapter 4, where you will find a means of testing the majority of components and circuits found in the modern EMS.

Fault code tables overleaf

Chapter 21

Fault code tables

Mazda EGi (straight count, models up to and including 1987)

Flash/ FCR code	Description
01	No ignition reference signal
02	Airflow sensor (AFS) or AFS circuit
03	Coolant temperature sensor (CTS) or CTS circuit
04	Air temperature sensor (ATS) or ATS circuit
06	Throttle pot sensor (TPS) or TPS circuit
09	Atmospheric pressure sensor (APS) or APS circuit
15	Air temperature sensor (ATS) or ATS circuit

Mazda EGi (1988-on models)

Flash/ FCR code	4-digit code	Description
1	-	Ignition pulse
2	0335	RPM sensor or circuit, NE signal
3	1345	RPM sensor or circuit, G signal
4	-	RPM sensor or circuit, NE signal
5	0325	Knock sensor (KS) or KS circuit
6	-	Vehicle speed sensor (VSS) or VSS circuit
8	0100	Vane or mass airflow sensor (AFS or MAF) or circuit
9	0115	Coolant temperature sensor (CTS) or CTS circuit
10	0110	Air temperature sensor (ATS) or ATS circuit
12	0120	Throttle pot sensor (TPS) or TPS circuit
14	-	Electronic control module (ECM) or ECM circuit
14	-	Atmospheric pressure sensor (APS) or APS circuit (alternative code)
15	0134	Oxygen sensor (OS) or OS circuit
16	1402	Exhaust gas recirculation (EGR) Valve or EGR circuit
17	1170	Oxygen sensor (OS) or OS circuit
17	1170	FBC system or circuit (alternative code)
23	0154	Oxygen sensor (OS) or OS circuit
24	1173	Oxygen sensor (OS) or OS circuit
25	-	Fuel pressure regulator solenoid valve
26	0443	Carbon filter solenoid valve (CFSV) or CFSV circuit
28	1485	Solenoid valve, exhaust gas recirculation (EGR) vacuum, or circuit
29	1486	Solenoid valve, exhaust gas recirculation (EGR) vent, or circuit
31	-	Idle speed control valve (ISCV) or ISCV circuit

Flash/ FCR code	4-digit code	Description
34	0505	Idle speed control valve (ISCV) A or ISCV circuit
35	-	Idle speed control valve (ISCV) B or ISCV circuit
35	-	Solenoid valve, variable induction system 1
46	-	Solenoid valve, variable induction system 2
55	0715	Vehicle Speed sensor (VSS) or VSS circuit
56	0710	Temperature sensor - automatic transmission (AT) or circuit
60	0750	Solenoid valve - 1-2 shift, automatic transmission (AT) or circuit
61	0755	Solenoid valve - 2-3 shift, automatic transmission (AT) or circuit
62	0760	Solenoid valve - 3-4 shift, automatic transmission (AT) or circuit
63	1743	Solenoid valve - lock-up, automatic transmission (AT) or circuit
64	1765	Solenoid valve - 3-2 shift, automatic transmission (AT) or circuit
64	1765	Cooling fan relay (alternative code)
65	1744	Lock-up solenoid, automatic transmission (AT)
66	0745	Line pressure solenoid, automatic transmission (AT)
67	-	Cooling fan relay, low temperature
68	-	Cooling fan relay, high temperature
69	-	Cooling fan thermistor
71	1602	Immobiliser unit, PCM communication error
72	1603	ID number unregistered (immobiliser)
73	1621	Code words do not match (immobiliser)
74	1622	ID numbers do not match (immobiliser)
75	1623	Code word/ID number writing and reading error (immobiliser)
76	1604	Code word unregistered (immobiliser)
	1605	Electronic control module (ECM) or ECM circuit
	1606	Code words do not match (immobiliser)
	1607	ID numbers do not match (immobiliser)
	1608	PCM internal circuit malfunction

All models with EOBD

For a list of the allocated EOBD codes beginning with P0 (Generic Powertrain), refer to Chapter 1, Section 1.

Mercedes

22

Index of vehicles

Model	Engine code	Year	System
C180	111.920	1993 to 2000	PMS (Siemens)
190E cat	102.962	1988 to 1993	Bosch KE3.5-Jetronic
190E 2.3 cat	102.985	1989 to 1993	Bosch KE3.5-Jetronic
190E 2.5-16 & cat	102.990	1988 to 1993	Bosch KE3.1-Jetronic
190E 2.5-16 Evolution	102.991	1989 to 1992	Bosch KE3.1-Jetronic
190E 2.6	103.942	1989 to 1993	Bosch KE3.5-Jetronic
190E 2.6 cat	103.942	1987 to 1993	Bosch KE3.5-Jetronic
C200	111.941	1994 to 2000	PMS (Siemens)
E200	111.941	1992 to 1996	PMS/Motronic 6.0/6.1
200E & TE cat	102.963	1988 to 1993	Bosch KE3.5-Jetronic
C220	111.961	1993 to 1997	HFM
E220	111.960	1992 to 1997	HFM
C230 & Kompressor	-	1995 to 2000	HFM
230E, TE & CE cat	102.982	1988 to 1993	Bosch KE3.5-Jetronic
230GE	102.980	1989 to 1991	Bosch KE3.5-Jetronic
260E & cat	103.940	1989 to 1993	Bosch KE3.5-Jetronic
260E 4-Matic & cat	103.943	1988 to 1992	Bosch KE3.5-Jetronic
260SE & cat	103.941	1988 to 1992	Bosch KE3.5-Jetronic
C280	104.941	1993 to 1997	HFM
E280 cat	104.942	1992 to 1996	HFM
S280	104.944	1993 to 1998	HFM
SL280	104.943	1993 to 1998	HFM
E300	103.985	1992 to 1995	Bosch KE3.5-Jetronic
300SE, SEL & cat	103.981	1986 to 1992	Bosch KE3.5-Jetronic
300E, TE, CE & cat	103.983	1987 to 1993	Bosch KE3.5-Jetronic
300E & cat	103.985	1988 to 1993	Bosch KE3.5-Jetronic
300E-24, TE-24 & CE-24 cat	104.980	1989 to 1993	Bosch KE5.2-Jetronic/EZ-L ignition

Chapter 22

Model	Engine code	Year	System
300TE 4-Matic & cat	103.985	1988 to 1993	Bosch KE3.5-Jetronic
300SL & cat	103.984	1989 to 1995	Bosch KE5.2-Jetronic/EZ-L ignition
300SL-24 & cat	104.981	1989 to 1995	Bosch KE5.2-Jetronic/EZ-L ignition
E320	104.992	1992 to 1997	HFM
S320	104.994	1993 to 1997	HFM
SL320	104.991	1993 to 1998	HFM
400S, SE & SEL	119.971	1991 on	Bosch LH4.1-Jetronic/EZ-L ignition
E420	119.975	1992 to 1995	Bosch LH4.1-Jetronic/EZ-L ignition
S420	119.971	1993 to 1999	Bosch LH4.1-Jetronic/EZ-L ignition
500E	119.974	1992 on	Bosch LH4.1-Jetronic/EZ-L ignition
500SL	119.972	1992 on	Bosch LH4.1-Jetronic/EZ-L ignition
500SE & SEL	119.970	1991 on	Bosch LH4.1-Jetronic/EZ-L ignition
500SEC	119.970	1992 on	Bosch LH4.1-Jetronic/EZ-L ignition
500SL cat	119.960	1989 to 1994	Bosch KE5.2-Jetronic/EZ-L ignition
E500	119.974	1992 to 1995	Bosch LH4.1-Jetronic/EZ-L ignition
S500	119.970	1993 to 1998	Bosch LH4.1-Jetronic/EZ-L ignition
SL500	119.972	1993 to 1998	Bosch LH4.1-Jetronic/EZ-L ignition
600SEL	120.980	1991 to 1996	Bosch LH-Jetronic/EZ-L ignition
S600 cat	120.980	1991 to 1996	Bosch LH4.1-Jetronic/EZ-L ignition
S600	120.980	1996 to 2001	Bosch LH4.1-Jetronic/EZ-L ignition
SL600	120.981	1993 to 2001	Bosch LH4.1-Jetronic/EZ-L ignition

Plus All models equipped with EOBD (approximately January 2001-on)

Self-Diagnosis

1 Introduction

Some Mercedes vehicles are equipped with an engine management system (EMS) that controls primary ignition, fuelling and idle functions from within the same ECM. Other Mercedes vehicles are equipped with a separate electronic ignition module that controls primary ignition, and an electronic injection module that controls fuelling and idle functions. All of these engine management, ignition and fuel systems are equipped with a self-diagnosis system capable of generating fault codes.

Engine management systems covered by this Chapter are of Bosch or Siemens origin. The electronic ignition module with self-diagnosis is Bosch EZ-L.

Where the vehicle is equipped with Bosch EZ-L ignition and either the LH-Jetronic or KE-Jetronic fuel system, fault codes will be generated separately by the ignition and fuel systems. In some vehicles, one 16-pin or 38-pin SD connector is provided for both ignition and fuel code retrieval. In other vehicles, ignition and fuel system codes are retrieved via separate SD connectors. Whatever; ignition and fuel codes must be retrieved separately on systems other than Motronic, HFM and PMS.

Mercedes KE and LH-Jetronic systems are capable of generating two very different kinds of fault codes. These are 2-digit fault codes and 2-digit duty cycle codes. Fault codes are similar to those generated by most other systems. Duty cycle codes provide data on the Lambda control system and faults that have occurred very recently (within the last four engine starts).

Bosch EZ-L ignition, Bosch Motronic, HFM and PMS systems generate fault codes only.

Fault codes retrieved in conjunction with an LED light are listed in the code tables at the end of the Chapter as 2-digit flash codes. In addition, when an FCR is used to retrieve codes, the codes displayed on the FCR may be 2-digit or 3-digit; both kinds are indicated where appropriate.

All models equipped with EOBD require an FCR to retrieve or clear fault codes.

Duty cycle % codes

If a fault occurs on any of the monitored circuits during a period of engine running (only a small number of circuits will generate duty cycle % codes), the ECM will increment a counter, but will not store a fault at this stage. If the fault is present at the next two engine starts, the ECM will again increment the counter each time. If the fault is still present after four consecutive engine starts, the fault is recorded in non-volatile memory. If the fault disappears before four consecutive occurrences, the counter is reset to zero. If the fault recurs, the counter will begin incrementing from the zero point. The duty cycle % routine will display this code, along with any faults that are present but have not yet been stored into memory (if the fault has occurred in less than four consecutive engine starts).

Self-Diagnosis (SD) function

Each ECM has a self-test capability that continually examines the signals from certain engine sensors and actuators, and compares each signal to a table of programmed values. If the diagnostic software determines that a fault is present, the ECM stores one or more fault codes. Codes will not be stored about components for which a code is not available, or for conditions not covered by the diagnostic software.

Limited operating strategy (LOS)

Mercedes systems featured in this Chapter utilise LOS (a function that is commonly called the "limp-home mode"). Once certain faults have been identified (not all faults will initiate LOS), the ECM will implement LOS and refer to a programmed default value rather than the sensor signal. This enables the vehicle to be safely driven to a workshop/garage for repair or testing. Once the fault has cleared, the ECM will revert to normal operation.

Adaptive or learning capability

Mercedes systems also utilise an adaptive function that will modify the basic programmed values for most effective operation during normal running, and with due regard to engine wear.

Self-Diagnosis warning light

Some Mercedes models are equipped with an SD warning light located within the instrument panel, which may be used to display flash codes. All models equipped with EOBD have a MIL (Malfunction Indicator Light) within the instrument panel.

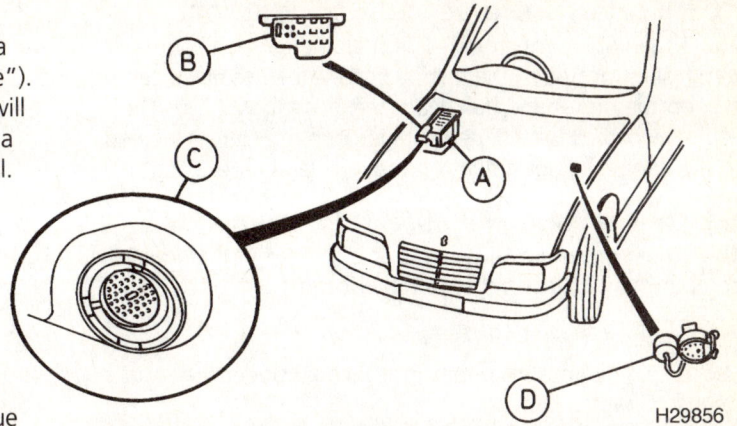

22.1 SD connector locations in Mercedes models

A SD connector location
B 16-pin SD connector (when fitted)
C 38-pin SD connector (when fitted)
D 9-pin SD connector (when fitted)

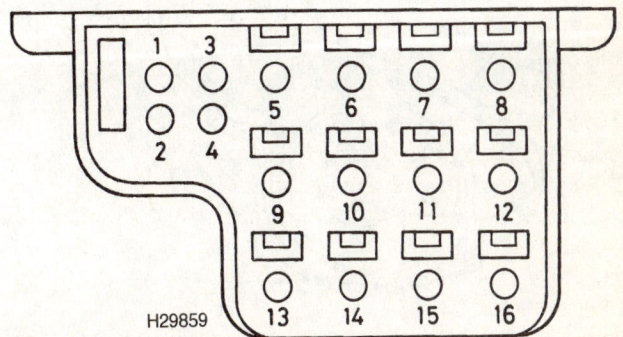

22.2 9-pin SD connector

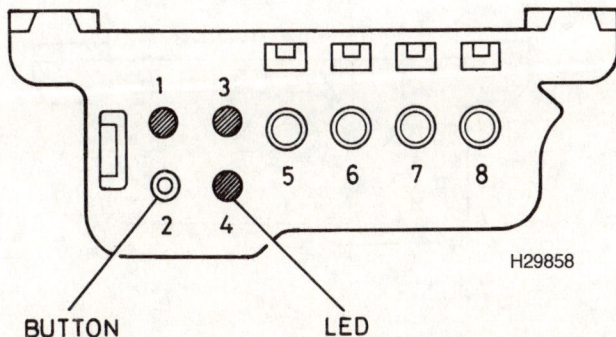

22.3 8-pin SD connector

2 Self-Diagnosis connector location

Note: *All Mercedes SD connectors are provided both for retrieving flash codes and for dedicated FCR use.*

Bosch KE3.1-Jetronic
The 9-pin SD connector is located in the engine compartment on the left-hand inner wing, close to the ignition module (see illustrations 22.1 and 22.2).

Bosch KE3.5-Jetronic
The 8-pin SD connector is located in the engine compartment on the right-hand bulkhead (see illustration 22.3).

Bosch KE5.2-Jetronic and EZ-L ignition
The 16-pin SD connector (2-digit fuel and ignition code retrieval) is located in the engine compartment on the right-hand bulkhead (see illustration 22.4). The 9-pin SD connector (OS percentage code retrieval) is located in the engine compartment on the left-hand inner wing.

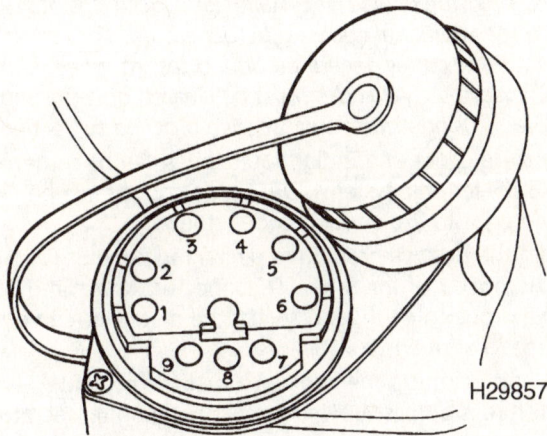

22.4 16-pin SD connector

Chapter 22

Bosch LH4.1-Jetronic and EZ-L ignition

The 38-pin SD connector (2-digit fuel and ignition code retrieval) is located in the engine compartment's electrical box on the right-hand bulkhead *(see illustration 22.5)*. The 9-pin SD connector (OS percentage code retrieval) is located in the engine compartment on the left-hand inner wing.

Bosch Motronic MP6.0/6.1, HFM and PMS

The 16-pin or 38-pin SD connector is located in the engine compartment on the right-hand bulkhead.

All models with EOBD

The 16-pin diagnostic connector is located under the facia - refer to Chapter 38.

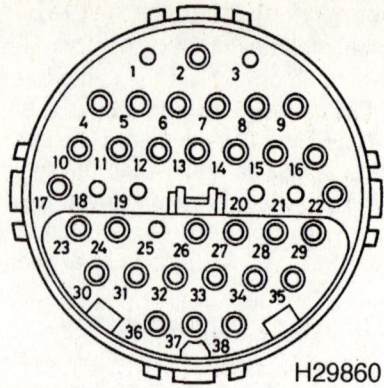

22.5 38-pin SD connector

---

3 Bosch KE3.1-Jetronic duty cycle code retrieval

Note: *During the course of certain test procedures, it is possible for additional codes to be generated. Care must be taken that any codes generated during test routines do not mislead diagnosis. All codes must be cleared once testing is complete.*

1 Duty cycle codes alone can be retrieved from KE3.1-Jetronic.

2 Attach the positive probe of a digital multi-meter (DMM) to pin number 3 of the 9-pin SD connector. Attach the DMM negative probe to earth, and switch the meter to read duty cycle *(see illustration 22.6)*.

3 Switch on the ignition.

4 The meter should display the 2-digit duty cycle codes as a percentage.

5 Record the duty cycle percentage, and compare the value with the duty cycle % code chart at the end of this Chapter.

6 Turning off the ignition ends duty cycle code retrieval. Remove the DMM probes from the SD connector.

---

4 Bosch KE3.5-Jetronic duty cycle and flash code retrieval

Note: *During the course of certain test procedures, it is possible for additional codes to be generated. Care must be taken that any codes generated during test routines do not mislead diagnosis. All codes must be cleared once testing is complete. If using a fault code reader, proceed to Section 9.*

1 Duty cycle codes and 2-digit fault codes can be retrieved from KE3.5-Jetronic systems. Duty cycle codes must be retrieved prior to 2-digit fault code retrieval.

2 Attach the positive probe of a digital multi-meter (DMM) to pin number 3 of the 8-pin SD connector. Attach the DMM negative probe to earth, and switch the meter to read duty cycle *(see illustration 22.7)*.

3 Start and warm-up the engine so that the coolant temperature is at least 80°C (normal operating temperature).

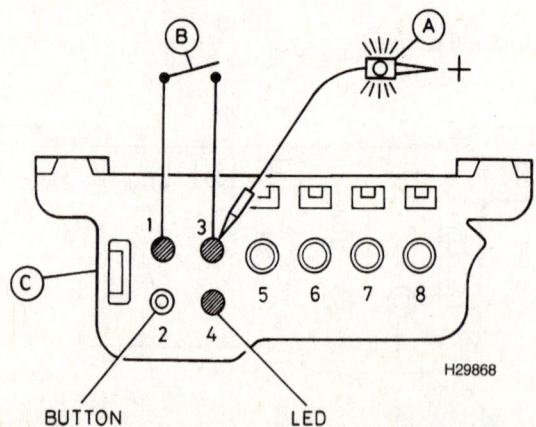

22.6 Connect a digital multi-meter (A) to the 9-pin SD connector (B) in order to retrieve percentage codes

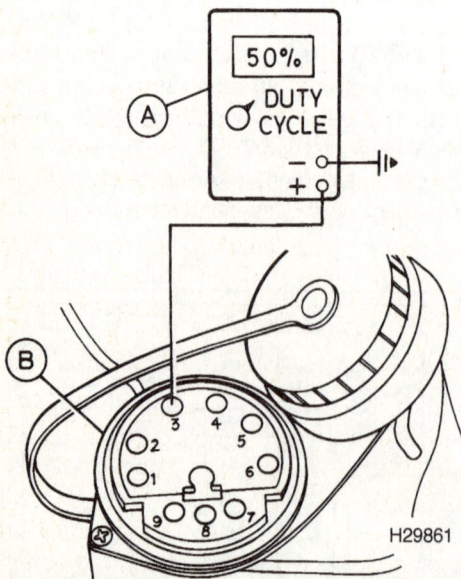

22.7 Connect a diode light (A) and accessory switch (B) to the 8-pin SD connector (C) in order to retrieve flash codes

4 Stop the engine and switch on the ignition.

5 The meter should display the 2-digit duty cycle codes as a percentage.

6 Record the duty cycle and compare the value with the duty cycle % code chart.

7 Turning off the ignition ends duty cycle code retrieval. Remove the DMM probes from the SD connector.

8 The method of retrieving 2-digit fault codes differs according to the type of 8-pin SD connector fitted. Some 8-pin SD connectors have an LED and button, others do not.

9 If the SD connector does not contain an LED and button, attach an accessory switch between pins 3 and 1 in the SD connector. Connect an LED diode test light between the battery (+) supply and SD pin 3 as shown (refer to illustration 22.7).

10 Switch on the ignition.

11 Close the accessory switch or depress the button for at least 5 seconds, and then open the switch or release the button. After approximately 2 seconds, the LED will begin to flash.

12 The LED displays the 2-digit fault codes as a straight count. One flash is equal to one code number, so five flashes denotes fault code number 5, twenty-two flashes denotes fault code number 22, and so on. Each flash lasts for 0.5 seconds, and there is a 1-second pause between each digit.

13 Count the number of flashes, and record the code. Refer to the tables at the end of the Chapter to determine the meaning of the flash code.

14 If code number 1 is transmitted, no faults codes are stored.

15 Retrieve subsequent codes by once more closing the accessory switch or depressing the button for at least 5 seconds. Open the switch or release the button, and after approximately 2 seconds the LED will begin to flash.

16 Repeat code retrieval by turning off the ignition and repeating the whole procedure from the beginning.

17 Turning off the ignition ends fault code retrieval. Remove the accessory switch and diode light from the SD connector where these components were used.

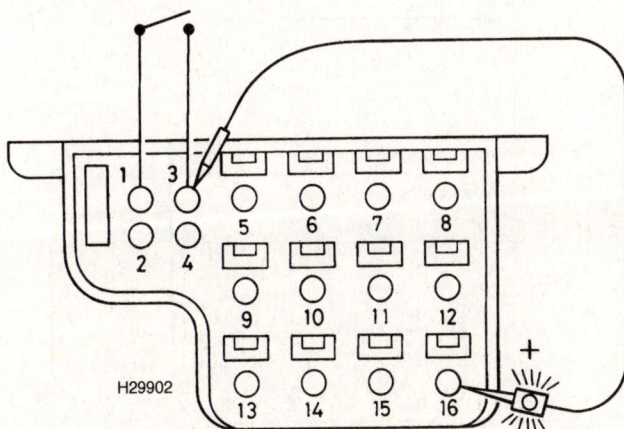

22.8 Connect a diode light and accessory switch to the 16-pin SD connector in order to retrieve flash codes

5 Bosch KE5.2-Jetronic and EZ-L ignition module duty cycle and flash code retrieval (16-pin)

Note: *During the course of certain test procedures, it is possible for additional codes to be generated. Care must be taken that any codes generated during test routines do not mislead diagnosis. All codes must be cleared once testing is complete. If using a fault code reader, proceed to Section 9.*

1 Duty cycle codes and 2-digit fault codes can be retrieved from KE5.2-Jetronic systems. Duty cycle codes are available either with the engine stopped (ignition on) or with the engine running at idle speed, and must be retrieved prior to 2-digit fault code retrieval. In addition, EZ-L ignition codes can be retrieved from the 16-pin SD connector.

2 Attach the positive probe of a digital multi-meter (DMM) to pin number 3 of the 9-pin SD connector. Attach the DMM negative probe to earth, and switch the meter to read duty cycle (refer to illustration 22.6).

3 Start and warm-up the engine so that the coolant temperature is at least 80°C (normal operating temperature).

4 Stop the engine. Ensure that the air conditioning is turned off, and the automatic transmission selector (where applicable) is in "P". Switch on the ignition.

5 The meter should display the 2-digit duty cycle codes as a percentage.

6 Record the duty cycle. The displayed value will be 50% if all sensor inputs are within the pre-determined operating parameters. If the display indicates another value, refer to the duty cycle % code chart at the end of this Chapter to determine the reason.

7 Start the engine and allow it to idle. The duty cycle should fluctuate if the system is operating correctly. If the duty cycle value remains fixed at one particular figure, refer to the duty cycle % code chart to determine the reason.

8 Turning off the ignition ends duty cycle code retrieval. Remove the DMM probes from the 9-pin SD connector. All of the following fault code retrieval routines must be performed after duty cycle code retrieval.

9 Attach an accessory switch between pins 3 and 1 in the 16-pin SD connector. Connect an LED diode test light between SD pin 16 (+) and SD pin 3 (–) as shown (see illustration 22.8).

10 Switch on the ignition.

11 Close the accessory switch for 2 to 4 seconds, and then open the switch. After approximately 2 seconds, the LED light will begin to flash.

12 The LED light displays the 2-digit fault codes as a straight count. One flash is equal to one code number, so five flashes denotes fault code number 5, twenty-two flashes denotes fault code number 22, and so on. Each flash lasts for 0.5 seconds, and there is a 1-second pause between each digit.

13 Count the number of flashes, and record the code. Refer to the tables at the end of the Chapter to determine the meaning of the flash code.

14 If code number 1 is transmitted, no faults codes are stored.

15 Retrieve subsequent codes by closing the accessory switch once more for 2 to 4 seconds. Open the switch, and after approximately 2 seconds the LED light will begin to flash. After all stored codes have been displayed, the codes will be repeated.

16 Turning off the ignition ends KE5.2 fault code retrieval. Remove the accessory switch and diode light from the SD connector.

Engine systems control module flash code retrieval (16-pin)

17 Fault codes from the engine systems control module can be retrieved by following the next set of routines.

18 Attach an accessory switch between pins 14 and 1 in the 16-pin SD connector. Connect an LED diode test light between SD pin 16 (+) and SD pin 14 (–) as shown (see illustration 22.9).

19 Switch on the ignition. The method for code retrieval is identical to that described above (paragraphs 11 to 16).

20 Retrieve ignition fault codes by following the routines described below (Bosch EZ-L).

Bosch EZ-L ignition module flash code retrieval (16-pin)

21 Only 2-digit fault codes can be retrieved from Bosch EZ-L ignition.

22 Attach the wires of an accessory switch between pins 8 and 1 in the 16-pin SD connector. Connect a diode test light between SD pin 16 (+) and SD pin 8 (–) as shown (see illustration 22.10).

23 Start the engine and warm it to normal operating temperature.

24 Allow the engine to idle.

25 Raise the engine speed to between 3100 and 3600 rpm for approximately 8 seconds, and then allow the engine to idle once more.

26 Detach the vacuum hose from the connection on the EZ-L ignition module.

27 Move the automatic transmission selector lever from the "P" position to "D", and then back to "P".

28 Raise the engine speed to 5000 rpm for a minimum of 2 seconds, and then allow the engine to idle once more.

29 Reconnect the vacuum hose to the connection on the EZ-L ignition module.

30 Raise the engine speed to 2300 rpm, and then briefly snap the throttle fully open so that the throttle switch full-load contacts become closed. Allow the engine to idle once more. **Note:** *If the ignition is turned off at any point, the whole procedure must be restarted from the beginning of the EZ-L ignition codes retrieval routine.*

31 Close the accessory switch for between 2 and 4 seconds, and then open the switch. After approximately 2 seconds, the LED light will begin to flash.

32 The LED light displays the 2-digit fault codes as a straight count. One flash is equal to one code number, so five flashes denotes fault code number 5, twenty-two flashes denotes fault code number 22, and so on. Each flash lasts for 0.5 seconds, and there is a 1-second pause between each digit.

33 Count the number of flashes, and record the code. Refer to the tables at the end of the Chapter to determine the meaning of the flash code.

34 If code number 1 is transmitted, no faults codes are stored.

35 Retrieve subsequent codes by once more closing the accessory switch for between 2 and 4 seconds. Open the switch, and after approximately 2 seconds the LED light will begin to flash.

36 Turning off the ignition ends ignition module fault code retrieval, and also clears all fault codes from memory. Fault codes are not retained in memory after the ignition has been turned off.

37 Remove the accessory switch and diode light from the SD connector.

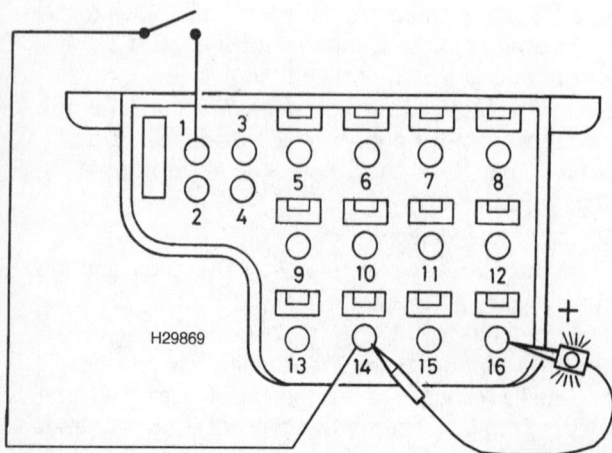

22.9 Connect a diode light and accessory switch to the 16-pin SD connector in order to retrieve control module flash codes

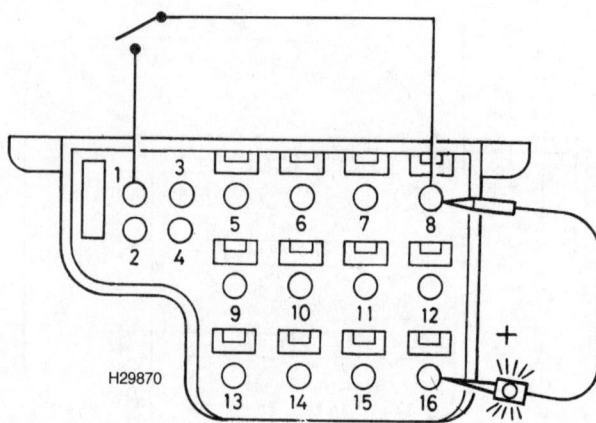

22.10 Connect a diode light and accessory switch to the 16-pin SD connector in order to retrieve ignition flash codes

6 Bosch LH4.1-Jetronic and EZ-L ignition module duty cycle and flash code retrieval (38-pin)

Note: *During the course of certain test procedures, it is possible for additional codes to be generated. Care must be taken that any codes generated during test routines do not mislead diagnosis. All codes must be cleared once testing is complete. If using a fault code reader, proceed to Section 9.*

1 Duty cycle codes and 2-digit fault codes can be retrieved from LH4.1-Jetronic systems. Duty cycle codes are available either with the engine stopped (ignition on) or with the engine running at idle speed, and must be retrieved prior to 2-digit fault code retrieval. In addition, EZ-L ignition codes can also be retrieved from the 38-pin SD connector.

2 Attach the positive probe of a digital multi-meter (DMM) to pin number 3 of the 9-pin SD connector. Attach the DMM negative probe to earth, and switch the meter to read duty cycle *(refer to illustration 22.6)*.

3 Start and warm-up the engine so that the coolant temperature is at least 80°C (normal operating temperature).

4 Stop the engine. Ensure that the air conditioning is turned off, and the automatic transmission selector is in "P" (where applicable). Switch on the ignition.

5 The meter should display the 2-digit duty cycle codes as a percentage.

6 Record the duty cycle. The displayed value will be 50% if all sensor inputs are within the pre-determined operating parameters. If the display indicates another value, refer to the duty cycle % code chart to determine the reason.

7 Start the engine and allow it to idle. The duty cycle should fluctuate if the system is operating correctly. If the duty cycle value remains fixed at one particular figure, refer to the duty cycle % code chart to determine the reason.

8 Turning off the ignition ends duty cycle code retrieval.

Remove the DMM probes from the SD connector. All of the following fault code retrieval routines must be performed immediately after duty cycle code retrieval.

9 Attach the wires of an accessory switch between pins 1 and 4 in the 38-pin SD connector. Connect an LED diode test light between SD pin 3 (+) and SD pin 4 (–) as shown *(see illustration 22.11)*.

10 Switch on the ignition.

11 Close the accessory switch for between 2 and 4 seconds, and then open the switch. After approximately 2-seconds the LED light will begin to flash.

12 The LED light displays the 2-digit fault codes as a straight count. One flash is equal to one code number, so five flashes denotes fault code number 5, twenty-two flashes denotes fault code number 22, and so on. Each flash lasts for 0.5 seconds, and there is a 1-second pause between each digit.

13 Count the number of flashes, and record the code. Refer to the tables at the end of the Chapter to determine the meaning of the flash code.

14 If code number 1 is transmitted, no faults codes are stored.

15 Retrieve subsequent codes by once more closing the accessory switch for at least 5 seconds. Open the switch, and after approximately 2 seconds the LED light will begin to flash. After all stored codes have been displayed, the codes will be repeated.

16 Turning off the ignition ends LH4.1 fault code retrieval. Remove the accessory switch and diode light from the SD connector.

Bosch EZ-L ignition module flash code retrieval (38-pin)

17 Attach the wires of an accessory switch between pins 1 and 17 in the 38-pin SD connector. Connect a diode test light between SD pin 3 (+) and SD pin 17 (–) as shown *(see illustration 22.12)*.

18 Switch on the ignition.

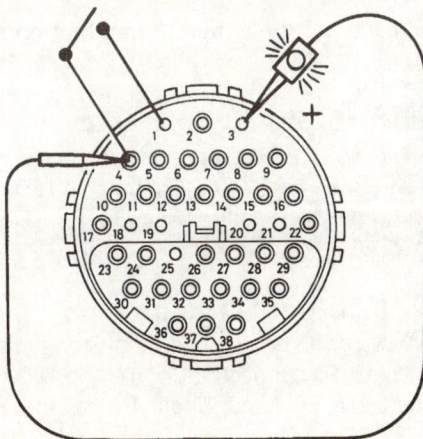

H29871

22.11 Connect a diode light and accessory switch to the 38-pin SD connector in order to retrieve flash codes

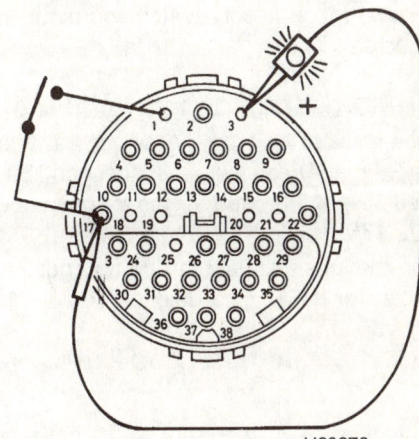

H29872

22.12 Connect a diode light and accessory switch to the 38-pin SD connector in order to retrieve ignition flash codes

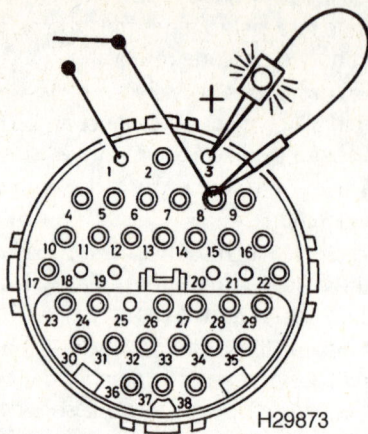

22.13 Connect a diode light and accessory switch to the 38-pin SD connector in order to retrieve base module flash codes

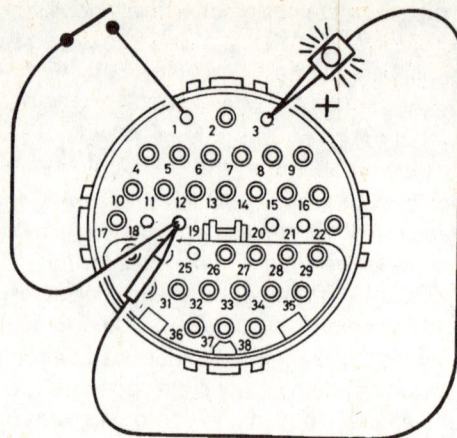

22.14 Connect a diode light and accessory switch to the 38-pin SD connector in order to retrieve diagnostic module flash codes

19 Close the accessory switch for between 2 and 4 seconds, and then open the switch. After approximately 2 seconds the LED will begin to flash.

20 The flashing of the LED light displays the 2-digit fault codes as a straight count. One flash is equal to one code number, so five flashes denotes fault code number 5, twenty-two flashes denotes fault code number 22, and so on. Each flash lasts for 0.5 seconds, and there is a 1-second pause between each digit.

21 Count the number of flashes, and record the code. Refer to the tables at the end of the Chapter to determine the meaning of the flash code.

22 If code number 1 is transmitted, no faults codes are stored.

23 Retrieve subsequent codes by once more closing the accessory switch for between 2 and 4 seconds. Open the switch, and after approximately 2 seconds the LED will begin to flash. After all stored codes have been displayed, the codes will be repeated.

24 Turning off the ignition ends ignition module fault code retrieval. Remove the accessory switch and diode light from the SD connector.

Base module flash code retrieval (38-pin)

25 Attach the wires of an accessory switch between pins 1 and 8 in the 38-pin SD connector. Connect an LED diode test light between SD pin 3 (+) and SD pin 8 (–) as shown (see illustration 22.13).

26 Switch on the ignition. The method for code retrieval is identical to that for the EZ-L module (paragraphs 19 to 24).

Diagnostic module flash code retrieval (38-pin)

27 Attach the wires of an accessory switch between pins 1 and 19 in the 38-pin SD connector. Connect an LED diode test light between SD pin 3 (+) and SD pin 19 (–) as shown (see illustration 22.14).

28 Switch on the ignition. The method for code retrieval is identical to that for the EZ-L module (paragraphs 19 to 24).

7 Bosch Motronic MP6.0/6.1 and HFM/PMS flash code retrieval

Note 1: *During the course of certain test procedures, it is possible for additional codes to be generated. Care must be taken that any codes generated during test routines do not mislead diagnosis. All codes must be cleared once testing is complete. If using a fault code reader, proceed to Section 9.*

Note 2: *Flash codes retrieved using this method may be different to codes retrieved with the aid of an FCR. Refer to the fault code tables at the end of this Chapter - if following the procedures in this Section, use the column headed "Flash code".*

1 Only 2-digit codes can be retrieved from Motronic MP6.0/6.1.

Models with 16-pin SD connector

2 Attach the wires of an accessory switch between pins 1 and 3 in the 16-pin SD connector. Connect an LED diode test light between SD pin 16 (+) and SD pin 3 (–) as shown (refer to illustration 22.8).

Models with 38-pin SD connector

3 Attach the wires of an accessory switch between pins 1 and 4 in the 38-pin SD connector. Connect an LED diode test light between SD pin 3 (+) and SD pin 4 (–) as shown (refer to illustration 22.11).

All models

4 Switch on the ignition.

5 Close the accessory switch for between 2 and 4 seconds, and then open the switch. After approximately 2 seconds, the LED light will begin to flash.

6 The LED displays the 2-digit fault codes as a straight count. One flash is equal to one code number, so five flashes denotes fault code number 5, twenty-two flashes denotes fault code number 22, and so on. Each flash lasts for 0.5 seconds, and there is a 1-second pause between each digit.

7 Count the number of flashes, and record the code. Refer to the tables at the end of the Chapter to determine the meaning of the flash code.

8 If code number 1 is transmitted, no faults codes are stored.

9 Retrieve subsequent codes by once more closing the accessory switch for at least 5 seconds. Open the switch, and after approximately 2 seconds the LED light will begin to flash.

10 Repeat code retrieval by turning off the ignition and repeating the whole procedure from the beginning.

11 Turning off the ignition ends fault code retrieval. Remove the accessory switch and diode light from the SD connector.

8   Clearing fault codes without a fault code reader (FCR)

Note: *It is not possible to clear fault codes by disconnection of the battery terminals. Fault code memory in Mercedes vehicles is non-volatile, and battery power is not required to retain codes. On models with EOBD, an FCR must be used to retrieve and clear fault codes.*

16-pin Bosch EZ-L

1 Turning off the ignition ends fault code retrieval, and also clears all fault codes from memory. Fault codes are not retained in memory after the ignition has been turned off.

All systems except 16-pin Bosch EZ-L

2 Each fault code must be individually cleared as described in the following routines.

3 Carry out the procedure to retrieve the first fault code.

4 Clear the first code by depressing the accessory switch for a period of between 6 and 8 seconds.

5 Continue the process by retrieving and clearing each code in turn until all codes have been cleared.

6 In some systems, several different modules are connected to the SD connector. Each code in each module must be retrieved and then cleared one after the other until all are clear.

7 Turn off the ignition and remove the accessory switch and diode light from the SD connector.

9   Self-Diagnosis with a fault code reader (FCR)

Note: *During the course of certain test procedures, it is possible for additional fault codes to be generated. Care must be taken that any codes generated during test routines do not mislead diagnosis.*

All Mercedes models

1 Connect an FCR to the SD connector. Use the FCR for the following purposes, in strict compliance with the FCR manufacturer's instructions:

a) *Retrieving fault codes.*
b) *Clearing fault codes.*
c) *Testing actuators.*
d) *Making service adjustments.*
e) *Displaying Datastream.*

Note: *Not all of the above functions are available in all vehicles. Fault codes that are retrieved by FCR may be 2-digit or 3-digit. Refer to the tables at the end of this Chapter. Codes retrieved with the aid of an FCR may be different to flash codes retrieved manually.*

2 Codes must always be cleared after component testing, or after repairs involving the removal of an EMS component.

10   Guide to test procedures

1 Use an FCR to interrogate the ECM for fault codes, or gather flash codes manually.

Codes stored

2 If one or more fault codes are gathered, refer to the fault code tables at the end of this Chapter to determine their meaning.

3 If several codes are gathered, look for a common factor such as a defective earth return or supply.

4 Refer to the component test procedures in Chapter 4, where you will find a means of testing the majority of components and circuits found in the modern EMS.

5 Once the fault has been repaired, clear the codes and run the engine under various conditions to determine if the problem has cleared.

6 Check the ECM for fault codes once more. Repeat the above procedures where codes are still being stored.

7 Refer to Chapter 3 for more information on how to effectively test the EMS.

No codes stored

8 Where a running problem is experienced, but no codes are stored, the fault is outside of the parameters designed into the SD system. Refer to Chapter 3 for more information on how to effectively test the engine management system.

9 If the problem points to a specific component, refer to the test procedures in Chapter 4, where you will find a means of testing the majority of components and circuits found in the modern EMS.

Chapter 22

Fault code tables

Bosch LH-Jetronic, LH4.1-Jetronic, KE3.5-Jetronic, KE5.2-Jetronic

Flash/ FCR code	Description
1	No faults found in the ECM. Proceed with normal diagnostic methods
2	Coolant temperature sensor (CTS) 1 or CTS circuit
2	Throttle pot sensor (TPS) or TPS circuit, full-load (KE5.2)
3	Coolant temperature sensor (CTS) 2 or CTS circuit
4	Mass airflow (MAF) sensor or MAF sensor circuit
5	Oxygen sensor (OS) or OS circuit (KE5.2)
6	CO pot or CO pot circuit
7	TN (engine speed) signal incorrect
7	Vehicle speed sensor (VSS) or VSS circuit (LH4.1, KE5.2)
8	Camshaft position sensor (CMP) or CMP circuit
8	Cylinder identification (CID) sensor or CID sensor circuit (LH4.1)
8	Ignition system or circuit (KE5.2)
8	Barometric pressure sensor (BPS) or BPS circuit (KE3.5)
9	Starter signal
9	Pressure actuator (KE5.2, KE3.5)
10	Idle speed control valve (ISCV) or ISCV circuit
10	Throttle pot sensor (TPS) or TPS circuit (LH4.1, KE5.2, KE3.5)
11	Secondary air pump system
12	Mass airflow (MAF) sensor burn-off or MAF sensor circuit
12	Pressure signal from ignition system or circuit (KE5.2)
13	Air temperature sensor (ATS) or ATS circuit
14	Vehicle speed sensor (VSS) or VSS circuit (KE5.2)
15	Catalytic converter control unit (Japan only)
15	Exhaust gas recirculation (EGR) valve (LH4.1)
16	Exhaust gas recirculation (EGR) or EGR circuit
17	Throttle switch (TS), full-load switch
17	Idle speed control valve (ISCV) or ISCV circuit
17	CAN signal (LH4.1) - communication between system computers
17	Oxygen sensor (OS) or OS circuit (KE5.2)
18	Data transfer from ignition system
18	CAN signal (LH4.1) - communication between system computers
18	Idle speed control valve (ISCV) or ISCV circuit (KE5.2)
20	Electronic control module (ECM)
20	CAN signal (LH4.1) - communication between system computers
21	Oxygen sensor (OS) or OS circuit
22	Oxygen sensor (OS) heater or OS circuit
23	Regeneration valve or circuit
23	Carbon filter solenoid valve (CFSV) or CFSV circuit (LH4.1, KE5.2)
24	Left camshaft control actuator or circuit (119 engine)
25	Right camshaft control actuator or circuit (119 engine)
25	Camshaft control actuator or circuit (104 engine)
25	Cold start valve (CSV) or CSV circuit (KE5.2)
26	Automatic transmission (AT) shift point relay or circuit
27	Injectors or injector circuit
27	Data exchange between KE and EZ control units (KE5.2)
28	Electronic control module (ECM)
28	Coolant temperature sensor (CTS) or CTS circuit (KE5.2)
29	1st gear relay (LH4.1)
29	Coolant temperature sensor (CTS) or CTS circuit (KE5.2)
30	Immobiliser system fault (LH4.1)
31	Air temperature sensor (ATS) or ATS circuit (KE5.2)
32	MKV resistor (engine coding plug, KE5.2)
34	Coolant temperature sensor (CTS) or CTS circuit (KE5.2)

Bosch LH4.1 base module

Flash/ FCR code	Description
1	No faults found in the ECM. Proceed with normal diagnostic methods
5	Maximum permissible temperature in module box exceeded
6	Electromagnetic air conditioning compressor clutch blocked
7	Poly-V-belt slipping
9	Voltage supply for electronic control module (ECM) (N3/1) interrupted
10	Voltage supply for electronic control module (ECM) (N3/1) interrupted
10	Voltage supply for fuel injectors interrupted (alternative code)
11	Voltage supply for accessory equipment control modules interrupted
12	Voltage supply for ABS (anti-lock brakes) control module (N30) or ABS/ASR (anti-lock brakes/traction control) control module (N30/1)
12	Automatic locking differential (ASD) control module (N30/2) interrupted (alternative code)
15	Voltage supply for automatic transmission kickdown valve (Y3) interrupted
16	Voltage supply for electromagnetic air conditioning compressor clutch (A9K1) interrupted
17	Voltage supply for module box blower motor (M2/2) interrupted

Bosch LH4.1 diagnostic module

Flash/ FCR code	Description
1	No faults found in the ECM. Proceed with normal diagnostic methods.
2	Oxygen sensor (OS) or OS circuit, inoperative
3	Oxygen sensor (OS) or OS circuit, inoperative
4	Secondary air injection, inoperative
5	Exhaust gas recirculation (EGR) valve or EGR circuit, inoperative
6	Idle speed control valve (ISCV) or ISCV circuit, inoperative
7	Ignition system defective
8	Coolant temperature sensor (CTS) or CTS circuit, open/short-circuit
9	Air temperature sensor (ATS) or ATS circuit, open/short-circuit
10	Mass airflow (MAF) sensor or MAF sensor circuit, voltage too high/low
11	TN (engine speed) signal defective
12	Oxygen sensor (OS) or OS circuit, open/short-circuit
13	Camshaft position sensor (CMP) or CMP circuit, signal defective
14	Variable induction solenoid valve (VISV) or VISV circuit, pressure too low
15	Wide-open throttle, information defective
16	Closed throttle, information defective
17	Data exchange malfunction between individual control modules
18	Adjustable camshaft timing solenoid, open/short-circuit
19	Fuel injectors open/short-circuit or emission control system adaption at limit
20	Speed signal missing
21	Purge switchover valve, open/short-circuit
22	Camshaft position sensor (CMP) or CMP circuit, signal defective
23	Variable induction solenoid valve (VISV) or VISV circuit, pressure with engine running too low
24	Starter ring gear segments defective
25	Knock sensor (KS) or KS circuit
26	Upshift delay switchover valve, open short-circuit
27	Coolant temperature sensor (CTS) or CTS circuit
28	Coolant temperature sensor (CTS) or CTS circuit

Bosch KE5.2 control module

Flash/ FCR code	Description
1	No faults found in the ECM. Proceed with normal diagnostic methods
2	Fuel pump relay or circuit
3	TN (engine speed) signal interrupted
4	Oxygen sensor (OS) or OS circuit
5	Output for secondary air injection pump control defective
6	Output for kickdown switch control defective
9	Oxygen sensor (OS) heater or OS circuit, open
11	Air conditioning (AC) compressor engagement signal missing
12	Output for air conditioning (AC) compressor control defective
13	Excessive air conditioning compressor belt slippage
14	Speed signal implausible
15	Short-circuit detected in fuel pump circuit

Bosch EZ-L ignition

Flash/ FCR code	Description
01	No faults found in the ECM. Proceed with normal diagnostic methods
02	Knock sensor (KS) or KS circuit
03	Coolant temperature sensor (CTS) or CTS circuit
04	Manifold absolute pressure (MAP) sensor or MAP sensor circuit
05	Knock sensor (KS) or KS circuit
06	Camshaft position sensor (CMP) or CMP circuit
07	Knock sensor (KS) or KS circuit
08	Automatic transmission
09	Automatic transmission
10	Data exchange between KE and EZ control units
11	Ignition control
12	Vehicle speed sensor (VSS) or VSS circuit
13	Throttle pot sensor (TPS) or TPS circuit
14	Throttle pot sensor (TPS) or TPS circuit
15	Ignition end stage fault
16	Ignition end stage fault
17	Vehicle speed sensor (VSS) or VSS circuit
18	Crank angle sensor (CAS) or CAS circuit
20	Electronic control module (ECM) or ECM circuit
21	Manifold absolute pressure (MAP) sensor or MAP sensor circuit
26	Data exchange between LH and EZ control units
27	Data exchange between LH and EZ control units
34	Ignition fault No.1 cylinder
35	Ignition fault No.5 cylinder
36	Ignition fault No.4 cylinder
37	Ignition fault No.8 cylinder
38	Ignition fault No.6 cylinder
39	Ignition fault No.3 cylinder
40	Ignition fault No.7 cylinder
41	Ignition fault No.2 cylinder

Bosch Motronic 6.0/6.1

Flash/ FCR code	Description
1	No faults found in the ECM. Proceed with normal diagnostic methods
2	Coolant temperature sensor (CTS) or CTS circuit
3	Air temperature sensor (ATS) or ATS circuit
4	Manifold absolute pressure (MAP) sensor or MAP sensor circuit
5	Throttle switch (TS) or TS circuit
6	Throttle pot sensor (TPS) or TPS circuit
7	Throttle pot sensor (TPS) or TPS circuit
8	Idle speed control valve (ISCV) or ISCV circuit
9	Oxygen sensor (OS) or OS circuit
11	Oxygen sensor (OS) or OS circuit
13	Oxygen sensor (OS) or OS circuit
14	Injectors 4 cylinder Nos. 1 and 4
15	Injectors 4 cylinder Nos. 2 and 3
20	Oxygen sensor (OS) or OS circuit
21	Ignition primary circuit, cylinders 1 and 4
22	Ignition primary circuit, cylinders 2 and 3
24	Engine speed signal or circuit
26	Octane encoding or circuit
27	Engine speed signal or circuit
28	Vehicle speed sensor (VSS) or VSS circuit
29	Variable induction solenoid valve (VISV) or VISV circuit, preheating relay or circuit
30	Fuel pump circuit
31	CO adjuster or CO circuit
36	Carbon filter solenoid valve (CFSV) or CFSV circuit
37	Automatic transmission (AT)
49	Electronic control module (ECM)

Chapter 22

HFM

Flash code	FCR code	Description
1	-	No faults found in the ECM. Proceed with normal diagnostic methods
2	002	Coolant temperature sensor (CTS) or CTS circuit, short-circuit
2	003	Coolant temperature sensor (CTS) or CTS circuit, open-circuit
2	004	Coolant temperature sensor (CTS) or CTS circuit, implausible signal
2	005	Coolant temperature sensor (CTS) or CTS circuit, loose contact
3	006	Air temperature sensor (ATS) or ATS circuit, short-circuit
3	007	Air temperature sensor (ATS) or ATS circuit, open-circuit
3	008	Air temperature sensor (ATS) or ATS circuit, loose contact
4	009	Mass airflow (MAF) sensor or MAF sensor circuit, implausibly high signal
4	010	Mass airflow (MAF) sensor or MAF sensor circuit, open-circuit
5	011	Throttle switch (TS)
5	012	Throttle switch (TS), closed
5	013	Throttle switch (TS), loose contact
6	014	Throttle pot sensor (TPS) or TPS circuit, implausibly high signal
6	015	Throttle pot sensor (TPS) or TPS circuit, implausibly low signal
6	016	Throttle pot sensor (TPS) or TPS circuit, loose contact
7	017	Throttle pot sensor (TPS) or TPS circuit, implausibly high signal
7	018	Throttle pot sensor (TPS) or TPS circuit, implausibly low signal
7	019	Throttle pot sensor (TPS) or TPS circuit, loose contact
8	020	Idle speed control valve (ISCV) or ISCV circuit, bottom control stop
8	021	Idle speed control valve (ISCV) or ISCV circuit, top control stop
9	023	Oxygen sensor (OS) or OS circuit, voltage high
9	024	Oxygen sensor (OS) or OS circuit, cold or open-circuit
9	025	Oxygen sensor (OS) or OS circuit, sensor voltage implausible
11	029	Oxygen sensor (OS) or OS circuit, heater current low
11	030	Oxygen sensor (OS) or OS circuit, heater current high
11	031	Oxygen sensor (OS) or OS circuit, heater short-circuit
13	035	Oxygen sensor (OS) or OS circuit, mixture lean
13	036	Oxygen sensor (OS) or OS circuit, mixture rich
14	037	Injector No. 1, short-circuit
14	038	Injector No. 1, open/short-circuit
15	039	Injector No. 2, short-circuit to positive
15	040	Injector No. 2, open/short-circuit to earth
16	041	Injector No. 3, short-circuit to positive
16	042	Injector No. 3, open/short-circuit to positive
17	043	Injector No. 4, short-circuit to positive
17	044	Injector No. 4, open/short-circuit to positive
20	049	Oxygen sensor (OS) or OS circuit
20	050	Oxygen sensor (OS) or OS circuit
20	051	Oxygen sensor (OS) or OS circuit
20	052	Oxygen sensor (OS) or OS circuit
20	053	Oxygen sensor (OS) or OS circuit
20	054	Oxygen sensor (OS) or OS circuit
22	055	Ignition coil, No. 1 cylinder misfire or circuit
22	056	Ignition coil, No. 4 cylinder misfire or circuit
22	057	Ignition coil or circuit, current not reached
23	058	Ignition coil, No. 2 cylinder misfire or circuit

Flash code	FCR code	Description
23	059	Ignition coil, No. 3 cylinder misfire or circuit
23	060	Ignition coil or circuit, current not reached
24	064	Crank angle sensor (CAS) or CAS circuit
24	065	Crank angle sensor (CAS) or CAS circuit
24	066	Crank angle sensor (CAS) or CAS circuit
25	067	Camshaft position (CMP) sensor or CMP sensor circuit
26	068	Electronic control module (ECM)
26	069	Electronic control module (ECM)
27	070	RPM sensor or circuit
27	071	RPM sensor or circuit
28	072	Vehicle speed sensor (VSS) or VSS circuit, signal not recognised
28	073	Vehicle speed sensor (VSS) or VSS circuit, signal implausibly high
29	074	Variable induction solenoid valve (VISV) or VISV circuit, heater relay or circuit
29	075	Variable induction solenoid valve (VISV) or VISV circuit, heater relay or circuit
30	076	Fuel pump relay or circuit
32	079	Knock sensor (KS) 1 or circuit
32	080	Knock sensor (KS) 2 or circuit
33	081	Ignition timing, maximum retardation at No. 1 cylinder
33	082	Ignition timing, variation in cylinder firing point greater than 6°
34	083	Knock sensor (KS) control circuit in ECM
34	084	Oxygen sensor (OS) or OS circuit
36	086	Carbon filter solenoid valve (CFSV) or CFSV circuit
36	087	Carbon filter solenoid valve (CFSV) or CFSV circuit
37	088	Automatic transmission (AT) or AT circuit
38	089	Camshaft timing actuator, short-circuit to positive
38	090	Camshaft timing actuator, open/short-circuit to earth
43	101	No starter signal, terminal 50
-	107	Dwell angle control at ignition output stage
49	110	Electronic control module (ECM), supply voltage implausible
49	111	Electronic control module (ECM), supply voltage low
50	112	Electronic control module (ECM)
-	113	Electronic control module (ECM)
-	114	Incorrect electronic control module (ECM) coding, from 01/94
-	115	Incorrect electronic control module (ECM) coding, from 01/94
-	116	Infra-red control unit signal from 12/94
-	117	Attempt to start when infra-red locking system locked, from 12/94

PMS (Siemens)

Flash code	FCR code	Description
01	-	No faults found in the ECM. Proceed with normal diagnostic methods
02	02	Coolant temperature sensor (CTS) or CTS circuit
02	00	Coolant temperature sensor (CTS) or CTS circuit
02	01	Coolant temperature sensor (CTS) or CTS circuit
03	03	Air temperature sensor (ATS) or ATS circuit
03	04	Air temperature sensor (ATS) or ATS circuit
04	06	Manifold absolute pressure (MAP) sensor or MAP sensor circuit
04	05	Manifold absolute pressure (MAP) sensor or MAP sensor circuit
05	07	Throttle pot sensor (TPS) or TPS circuit
06	13	Throttle pot sensor (TPS) or TPS circuit
06	14	Throttle pot sensor (TPS) or TPS circuit
07	15	Idle speed control valve (ISCV) or ISCV circuit
07	16	Idle speed control valve (ISCV) or ISCV circuit
08	17	Idle speed control valve (ISCV) or ISCV circuit
08	20	Idle speed control valve (ISCV) or ISCV circuit
08	21	Idle speed control valve (ISCV) or ISCV circuit
09	22	Oxygen sensor (OS) or OS circuit
09	23	Oxygen sensor (OS) or OS circuit
11	30	Oxygen sensor (OS) or OS circuit
11	32	Oxygen sensor (OS) or OS circuit
11	31	Oxygen sensor (OS) or OS circuit
13	37	Oxygen sensor (OS) or OS circuit
13	36	Oxygen sensor (OS) or OS circuit
14	42	Injectors (4-cylinder) numbers 2 and 3
14	40	Injectors (4-cylinder) numbers 1 and 4
14	41	Injectors (4-cylinder) numbers 1 and 3
15	43	Injectors (4-cylinder) numbers 2 and 4
20	54	Oxygen sensor (OS) or OS circuit
20	55	Oxygen sensor (OS) or OS circuit
20	57	Oxygen sensor (OS) or OS circuit
20	56	Oxygen sensor (OS) or OS circuit
21	64	Ignition primary circuit - cylinders 1 and 4
21	62	Ignition primary circuit - cylinders 1 and 4
21	63	Ignition primary circuit - cylinders 1 and 4
22	65	Ignition primary circuit - cylinders 2 and 3
22	67	Ignition primary circuit - cylinders 2 and 3
22	66	Ignition primary circuit - cylinders 2 and 3
24	73	Engine speed sensor or circuit
24	75	Engine speed sensor or circuit
26	77	MKV (engine coding plug)
26	80	MKV (engine coding plug)
27	81	Tachometer circuit
27	82	Tachometer circuit
28	83	Vehicle speed sensor (VSS) or VSS circuit
28	84	Vehicle speed sensor (VSS) or VSS circuit
29	86	Variable induction solenoid valve (VISV) or VISV circuit, preheating relay
29	85	Variable induction solenoid valve (VISV) or VISV circuit, preheating relay
30	00	Fuel pump circuit
30	87	Fuel pump circuit
36	A4	Carbon filter solenoid valve (CFSV) or CFSV circuit
36	A3	Carbon filter solenoid valve (CFSV) or CFSV circuit
37	A5	Automatic transmission (AT)
49	E6	Electronic control module (ECM)

Bosch KE3.1-Jetronic, KE3.5-Jetronic, KE5.2-Jetronic, LH4.1-Jetronic

Duty cycle %	Description
0%	Oxygen sensor (OS) or OS circuit
0%	Self-Diagnosis connector (non-cat vehicles)
10%	Throttle pot sensor (TPS) or TPS circuit
20%	Throttle pot sensor (TPS) or TPS circuit
20%	Injectors or injectors circuit (LH4.1)
30%	Coolant temperature sensor (CTS) or CTS circuit
40%	Airflow sensor (AFS) or AFS circuit
50%	Oxygen sensor signal (cat vehicles)
50%	Input signals ok
60%	Vehicle speed sensor (VSS) or VSS circuit
60%	Camshaft position sensor (CMP) or CMP circuit
70%	Engine speed signal
80%	Air temperature sensor (ATS) or ATS circuit
80%	Barometric pressure sensor (BPS) or BPS circuit (KE3.5)
80%	Drive engaged (KE5.2)
80%	CAN signal (LH4.1) - communication between system computers
90%	Pressure actuator (KE5.2)
90%	Safety fuel cut-off active (LH4.1)
100%	Oxygen sensor (OS) or OS circuit
100%	Electronic control module (ECM) (non-cat vehicles)

All models with EOBD

For a list of the allocated EOBD codes beginning with P0 (Generic Powertrain), refer to Chapter 1, Section 1.

Notes

Mitsubishi

Index of vehicles

Model	Engine code	Year	System
3000 GT 24V	6G72	1992 to 1999	Mitsubishi ECI-Multi- MPi
Carisma 1.6 SOHC 16V	4G92	1996 to 1999	Mitsubishi ECI-Multi- MPi
Carisma 1.8 SOHC 16V	4G93	1996 to 1997	Mitsubishi ECI-Multi- MPi
Carisma 1.8 DOHC 16V	4G93	1996 to 1997	Mitsubishi ECI-Multi- MPi
Colt 1.3i SOHC 12V cat	4G13	1992 to 1996	Mitsubishi ECI-Multi- MPi
Colt 1.3 SOHC 12V	4G13	1996 to 2001	Mitsubishi ECI-Multi- MPi
Colt 1600 GTi DOHC	4G61	1988 to 1990	Mitsubishi ECI-Multi- MPi
Colt 1.6i SOHC 16V	4G92	1992 to 1996	Mitsubishi ECI-Multi- MPi
Colt 1.6i 4x4 SOHC 16V cat	4G92	1992 to 1996	Mitsubishi ECI-Multi- MPi
Colt 1.6 SOHC 16V	4G92	1996 to 2001	Mitsubishi ECI-Multi- SEFi
Colt 1800 GTi-16V DOHC 16V	4G67	1990 to 1993	Mitsubishi ECI-Multi- MPi
Colt 1.8 GTi DOHC 16V cat	4G93	1992 to 1995	Mitsubishi ECI-Multi- MPi
Cordia 1800 Turbo	4G62T	1985 to 1989	Mitsubishi ECI-Multi- MPi
Galant 1800 SOHC 16V cat	4G93	1993 to 1997	Mitsubishi ECI-Multi- MPi
Galant Turbo	4G63T	1985 to 1988	Mitsubishi ECI-Multi- Turbo
Galant 2000 GLSi SOHC	4G63	1988 to 1993	Mitsubishi ECI-Multi- MPi
Galant 2000 GTi 16V DOHC	4G63	1988 to 1993	Mitsubishi ECI-Multi- MPi
Galant 2000 4WD DOHC	4G63	1989 to 1994	Mitsubishi ECI-Multi- MPi
Galant 2000 4WS cat DOHC	4G63	1989 to 1994	Mitsubishi ECI-Multi- MPi
Galant 2.0i SOHC 16V cat	-	1993 to 1997	Mitsubishi ECI-Multi- MPi
Galant 2.0i V6 DOHC 24V	6A12	1993 to 1997	Mitsubishi ECI-Multi- MPi
Galant Sapporo 2400	4G64	1987 to 1989	Mitsubishi ECI-Multi- MPi
Galant 2.5i V6 DOHC 24V	6G73	1993 to 1995	Mitsubishi ECI-Multi- MPi
L300 SOHC 16V	4G63	1994 to 2001	Mitsubishi ECI-Multi- MPi
Lancer 1600 GTi 16V DOHC	4G61	1988 to 1990	Mitsubishi ECI-Multi- MPi
Lancer 1.6i SOHC 16V	4G92	1992 to 1996	Mitsubishi ECI-Multi- MPi
Lancer 1.6i 4x4 SOHC 16V cat	4G92	1992 to 1996	Mitsubishi ECI-Multi- MPi
Lancer 1800 GTi DOHC 16V	4G67	1990 to 1993	Mitsubishi ECI-Multi- MPi
Lancer 1.8 GTi DOHC 16V cat	4G93	1992 to 1995	Mitsubishi ECI-Multi- MPi
Lancer 1800 4WD cat	4G37-8	1989 to 1993	Mitsubishi ECI-Multi- MPi
Shogun 3.5i V6 DOHC 24V	6G74	1994 to 1997	Mitsubishi ECI-Multi- MPi
Sigma Estate 12V	6G72	1993 to 1996	Mitsubishi ECI-Multi- MPi
Sigma Wagon 12V cat	6G72	1993 to 1996	Mitsubishi ECI-Multi- MPi
Sigma 3.0i 24V cat	6G72	1991 to 1996	Mitsubishi ECI-Multi- MPi
Space Wagon 1.8i SOHC 16V	4G93	1991 to 1999	Mitsubishi ECI-Multi- MPi
Space Wagon 2.0i DOHC 16V	4G63	1992 to 1998	Mitsubishi ECI-Multi- MPi
Starion Turbo	4G63T	1986 to 1989	Mitsubishi ECI-Multi- + Turbo
Starion 2.6 Turbo cat	G54B1	1989 to 1991	Mitsubishi ECI-Multi- + Turbo

Plus All models equipped with EOBD (approximately January 2001-on)

Chapter 23

Self-Diagnosis

1   Introduction

Mitsubishi vehicles are equipped with the Mitsubishi ECI-Multi engine management system that controls primary ignition, fuel injection and idle functions from within the same control module.

Self-Diagnosis (SD) function

The ECM (Electronic control module) has a self-test capability that continually examines the signals from certain engine sensors and actuators, and then compares each signal to a table of programmed values. If the diagnostic software determines that a fault is present, the ECM stores one or more fault codes in the ECM memory. Codes will not be stored about components for which a code is not available, or for conditions not covered by the diagnostic software. Mitsubishi systems generate 2-digit fault codes for retrieval by manual means or by a dedicated FCR. On models equipped with EOBD, the 5-digit codes can only be retrieved or cleared by means of an FCR.

Limited operating strategy (LOS)

Mitsubishi systems featured in this Chapter utilise LOS (a function that is commonly called the "limp-home mode"). Once certain faults have been identified (not all faults will initiate LOS), the ECM will implement LOS and refer to a programmed default value rather than the sensor signal. This enables the vehicle to be safely driven to a workshop/garage for repair or testing. Once the fault has cleared, the ECM will revert to normal operation.

Adaptive or learning capability

Mitsubishi systems also utilise an adaptive function that will modify the basic programmed values for most effective operation during normal running, and with due regard to engine wear.

Self-Diagnosis (SD) warning light

Mitsubishi models are equipped with a Self-Diagnosis warning light located within the instrument panel (see illustration 23.1).

2   Self-Diagnosis connector location

Note: The Mitsubishi SD connector is provided both for retrieving flash codes and for dedicated FCR use.

Early Shogun models

The SD connector is located in the console, below the radio (see illustration 23.2).

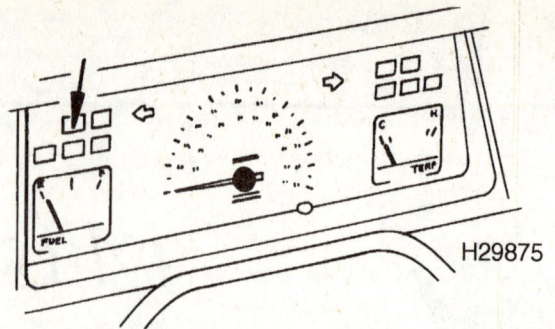

23.1 SD warning light in instrument panel (arrowed)

23.2 SD connector located below radio in centre console (arrowed)

Galant 2.0 and Sapporo 2.4, Colt/Lancer, Sigma, Shogun 3.0V6

The SD connector is located below the facia, next to the fusebox (see illustration 23.3).

Models with EOBD

The 16-pin diagnostic connector is located under the facia - refer to Chapter 38.

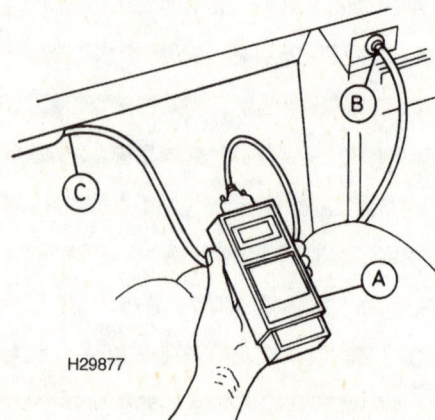

23.3 FCR attached for fault code reading

A   FCR
B   Cigarette lighter used for electrical power source
C   SD connector

3 Retrieving codes without a fault code reader (FCR)

Note: *During the course of certain test procedures, it is possible for additional fault codes to be generated. Care must be taken that any codes generated during test routines do not mislead diagnosis. All codes must be cleared once testing is complete.*

Note: *On models equipped with EOBD, an FCR must be used to retrieve and clear fault codes.*

Analogue voltmeter method

1 Attach an analogue voltmeter to terminals A and B in the SD connector *(see illustration 23.4)*.

2 Switch on the ignition. If the ECM has stored one or more fault codes, the voltmeter needle will begin to sweep between a higher and lower level. If no codes are stored, the needle will remain level. **Note:** *If the voltmeter does not behave as described, reverse the connections to the SD connector.*

a) *The first series of sweeps indicates the multiples of ten, the second series of sweeps indicates the single units.*

b) *The voltmeter needle will move for a longer period of deflection when transmitting codes in tens, and a shorter spell of deflection for units.*

c) *If no faults are found, the meter will indicate regular on/off pulses.*

3 Count the number of sweeps in each series, and record each code as it is transmitted. Refer to the table at the end of the Chapter to determine the meaning of the fault code.

4 Continue retrieving codes until all stored codes have been retrieved and recorded.

5 Turn off the ignition and remove the voltmeter to end fault code retrieval.

LED diode light method

6 Connect an LED diode test light between terminals A and B in the SD connector *(see illustration 23.5)*.

7 Switch on the ignition. If the ECM has stored one or more faults, the LED light will flash to indicate the fault code. **Note:** *If the LED does not illuminate as described, reverse the LED connections to the SD connector.*

a) *The first series of flashes indicates the multiples of ten, the second series indicates the number of single units.*

b) *Tens are indicated by 1.5-second flashes, separated by a short pause of 0.5 seconds.*

c) *A pause of 2 seconds separates tens and units (the light remains extinguished during pauses).*

d) *Units are indicated by 0.5-second flashes, separated by short pauses of 0.5 seconds.*

e) *Four long flashes and one short flash, for example, displays code 41.*

f) *If no faults are found, the LED light will flash on and off eight times at 0.5-second intervals.*

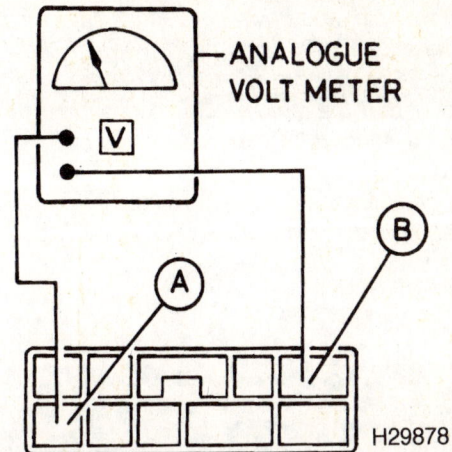

23.4 Terminals A and B of the SD connector bridged by an analogue voltmeter
A Earth terminal   B SD terminal

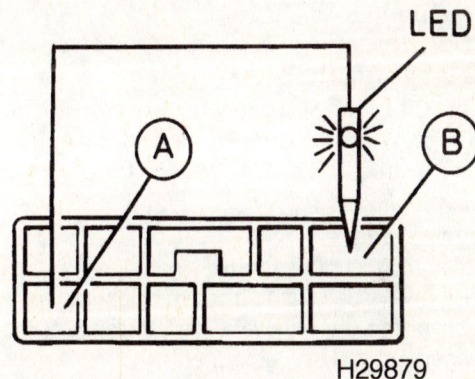

23.5 Terminals A and B of the SD connector bridged by an LED diode light
A Earth terminal   B SD terminal

8 Count the number of flashes in each series, and record each code as it is transmitted. Refer to the table at the end of the Chapter to determine the meaning of the fault code.

9 Continue retrieving codes until all stored codes have been retrieved and recorded.

10 Turn off the ignition and remove the diode light to end fault code retrieval.

4 Clearing fault codes without a fault code reader (FCR)

1 Disconnect the battery negative terminal for at least 30 seconds.

2 Reconnect the battery negative terminal.

Note: *The first drawback to this method is that battery disconnection will re-initialise all ECM adaptive values. Re-*

learning the appropriate adaptive values requires starting the engine from cold, and driving at various engine speeds for approximately 20 to 30 minutes. The engine should also be allowed to idle for approximately 10 minutes. The second drawback is that the radio security codes, clock setting and other stored values will be initialised, and these must be re-entered once the battery has been reconnected. Where possible, an FCR should be used for code clearing. On models equipped with EOBD, an FCR must be used to retrieve and clear fault codes.

5 Self-Diagnosis with a fault code reader (FCR)

Note: *During the course of certain test procedures, it is possible for additional fault codes to be generated. Care must be taken that any codes generated during test routines do not mislead diagnosis.*

All Mitsubishi models

1 Connect an FCR to the SD connector. Use the FCR for the following purposes, in strict compliance with the FCR manufacturer's instructions:

   a) Retrieving fault codes.
   b) Clearing fault codes.
   c) Datastream (EOBD models only).

2 Codes must always be cleared after component testing, or after repairs involving the removal or replacement of an engine management system component.

6 Guide to test procedures

1 Use an FCR to interrogate the ECM for fault codes, or manually gather codes as described in Sections 3 or 5.

Codes stored

2 If one or more fault codes are gathered, refer to the fault code table at the end of this Chapter to determine their meaning.

3 If several codes are gathered, look for a common factor such as a defective earth return or supply.

4 Refer to the component test procedures in Chapter 4, where you will find a means of testing the majority of components and circuits found in the modern EMS.

5 Once the fault has been repaired, clear the codes and run the engine under various conditions to determine if the problem has cleared.

6 Check the ECM for fault codes once more. Repeat the above procedures where codes are still being stored.

7 Refer to Chapter 3 for more information on how to effectively test the EMS.

No codes stored

8 Where a running problem is experienced, but no codes are stored, the fault is outside of the parameters designed into the SD system. Refer to Chapter 3 for more information on how to effectively test the engine management system.

9 If the problem points to a specific component, refer to the test procedures in Chapter 4, where you will find a means of testing the majority of components and circuits found in the modern EMS.

Fault code table

Mitsubishi ECI-Multi

Flash/ FCR code	Description
0	No faults found in the ECM. Proceed with normal diagnostic methods
11	Oxygen sensor (OS) or OS circuit
12	Mass airflow (MAF) sensor or MAF sensor circuit
12	Manifold absolute pressure (MAP) sensor or MAP sensor circuit (alternative code)
13	Air temperature sensor (ATS) or ATS circuit
14	Throttle position sensor (TPS) or TPS circuit
15	Idle speed control valve (ISCV) or ISCV circuit
21	Coolant temperature sensor (CTS) or CTS circuit
22	Crank angle sensor (CAS) or CAS circuit
23	Crank angle sensor (CAS) or CAS circuit (alternative code)
24	Vehicle speed sensor (VSS) or VSS circuit
25	Atmospheric pressure sensor (APS) or APS circuit
31	Knock sensor (KS) or KS circuit
32	Manifold absolute pressure (MAP) sensor or MAP sensor circuit
36	Ignition timing adjuster earthed

Flash/ FCR code	Description
39	Oxygen sensor (OS) or OS circuit
41	Injector or injector circuit
42	Fuel pump or fuel pump circuit
44	Ignition coil (1 and 4 cylinders) or circuit
52	Ignition coil (2 and 5 cylinders) or circuit
53	Ignition coil (3 and 6 cylinders) or circuit
55	Idle speed control valve (ISCV) or ISCV circuit
61	Automatic transmission (AT) electronic control module (ECM) cable
62	Induction control valve sensor or circuit
71	Vacuum solenoid - ETC or circuit
72	Ventilation solenoid - ETC or circuit

All models with EOBD

For a list of the allocated EOBD codes beginning with P0 (Generic Powertrain), refer to Chapter 1, Section 1.

Nissan

24

Index of vehicles

Model	Engine code	Year	System
4x4 Pick-up 2.4i	KA24E	1992 to 1997	Nissan ECCS MPi
4WD Pick-up 2.4i cat	Z24i	1990 to 1994	Nissan ECCS SPi
4WD Wagon 3.0i cat	VG30E	1990 to 1994	Nissan ECCS MPi
100NX 2.0 SOHC 16V cat	SR20DE	1991 to 1994	Nissan ECCS MPi
200 SX 16V Turbo cat	CA18DET	1989 to 1994	Nissan ECCS MPi
200 SX DOHC 16V Turbo	SR20DET	1994 to 2001	Nissan ECCS MPi
300 C	VG30E	1984 to 1991	Nissan ECCS MPi
300 ZX	VG30E	1984 to 1990	Nissan ECCS MPi
300 ZX Turbo	VG30ET	1984 to 1990	Nissan ECCS MPi + Turbo
300 ZX Twin-Turbo cat	VG30DETT	1990 to 1995	Nissan ECCS MPi + Turbo
Almera 1.4 DOHC 16V	GA14DE	1996 to 1999	Nissan ECCS MPi
Almera 1.6 DOHC 16V	GA16DE	1996 to 1999	Nissan ECCS MPi
Almera 2.0 GTi	SR20DE	1996 to 1999	Nissan ECCS MPi
Bluebird ZX Turbo SOHC	CA18T	1986 to 1990	Nissan ECCS MPi + Turbo
Bluebird 2.0i SOHC	CA20E	1988 to 1990	Nissan ECCS MPi
Micra 1.0i DOHC 16V cat	CG10DE	1993 to 2001	Nissan ECCS MPi
Micra 1.3i DOHC 16V cat	CG13DE	1993 to 2001	Nissan ECCS MPi
Maxima & cat	VG30E	1989 to 1994	Nissan ECCS MPi
Patrol 4.2i OHV 128kW	TB42E	1992 to 1997	Nissan ECCS MPi
Prairie 2.0i SOHC cat	CA20E	1989 to 1991	Nissan ECCS MPi
Primera 1.6i	GA16DE	1994 to 1997	Nissan ECCS SPi
Primera 1.6i DOHC 16V	GA16DE	1996 to 1997	Nissan ECCS MPi
Primera 2.0 DOHC cat	SR20Di	1990 to 1995	Nissan ECCS SPi with Hot-wire
Primera Estate 2.0 DOHC 16V cat	SR20Di	1990 to 1996	Nissan ECCS SPi with Hot-wire
Primera 2.0e ZX DOHC 16V	SR20DE	1991 to 1995	Nissan ECCS MPi with Hot-wire
Primera 2.0e GT	SR20DE	1991 to 1995	Nissan ECCS MPi with Hot-wire
Primera 2.0e cat	SR20DE	1991 to 1995	Nissan ECCS MPi with Hot-wire
Primera 2.0i DOHC 16V	SR20DE	1994 to 1997	Nissan ECCS SPi
Primera 2.0i GT DOHC 16V	SR20DE	1994 to 1996	Nissan ECCS SPi
Primera 2.0i DOHC 16V	SR20DE	1996 to 1997	Nissan ECCS MPi
Primera 2.0i GT DOHC 16V	SR20DE	1996 to 1997	Nissan ECCS MPi
QX 2.0 DOHC 24V V6	VQ20DE	1994 to 2001	Nissan ECCS MPi
QX 3.0 DOHC 24V V6	VQ30DE	1994 to 2001	Nissan ECCS MPi
Serena 1.6i DOHC 16V	GA16DE	1993 to 2001	Nissan ECCS MPi
Serena 2.0i DOHC 16V	SR20DE	1993 to 2001	Nissan ECCS MPi
Silvia Turbo ZX	CA18ET	1984 to 1990	Nissan ECCS MPi + Turbo

Model	Engine code	Year	System
Sunny 1.6i SOHC 12V cat	GA16i	1989 to 1991	Nissan ECCS SPi
Sunny ZX Coupe DOHC 16V	CA16DE	1987 to 1989	Nissan ECCS MPi
Sunny 1.8 ZX DOHC 16V cat	CA18DE	1989 to 1991	Nissan ECCS MPi
Sunny GTi-R DOHC 16V	SR20DET	1991 to 1994	Nissan ECCS MPi
Sunny 2.0 GTi DOHC 16V cat	SR20DE	1991 to 1994	Nissan ECCS MPi
Terrano II 2.4	KA24EBF	1993 to 1998	Nissan ECCS MPi
Urvan 2.4i cat	Z24i	1989 to 1994	Nissan ECCS SPi
Vanette 2.4i OHV cat	Z24i	1987 to 1994	Nissan ECCS SPi

Plus All models equipped with EOBD (approximately January 2001-on)

Self-Diagnosis

1   Introduction

The engine management system (EMS) fitted to Nissan vehicles is Nissan ECCS, which exists in both single-point and multi-point injection (SPi and MPi) forms. Nissan ECCS controls the primary ignition, fuel injection and idle functions from within the same control module.

Self-Diagnosis (SD) function

Each ECM (electronic control module) has a self-test capability that continually examines the signals from certain engine sensors and actuators, and then compares each signal to a table of programmed values. If the diagnostic software determines that a fault is present, the ECM stores one or more fault codes in the ECM memory. Codes will not be stored about components for which a code is not available, or for conditions not covered by the diagnostic software. Nissan ECCS generates 2-digit fault codes for retrieval by manual means or by a dedicated FCR.

On models equipped with EOBD, the 5-digit fault codes must be retrieved and cleared using an FCR.

Limited operating strategy (LOS)

Nissan systems featured in this Chapter utilise LOS (a function that is commonly called the "limp-home mode"). Once certain faults have been identified (not all faults will initiate LOS), the ECM will implement LOS and refer to a programmed default value rather than the sensor signal. This enables the vehicle to be safely driven to a workshop/garage for repair or testing. Once the fault has cleared, the ECM will revert to normal operation.

Adaptive or learning capability

Nissan systems also utilise an adaptive function that will modify the basic programmed values for most effective operation during normal running, and with due regard to engine wear.

Self-Diagnosis (SD) warning light

All Nissan models are equipped with either a single red LED, or a red and a green LED, set in the casing of the ECM. In addition, a Self-Diagnosis warning light is located within the instrument panel, and can also be used to display fault codes. The warning light will flash in unison with the LED on the ECM, or will remain illuminated while a fault is stored.

All models equipped with EOBD have a MIL (Malfunction Warning Light) within the instrument panel to alert the driver to the presence of stored faults.

2   Self-Diagnosis connector and ECM locations

Note: *The Nissan SD connector is provided for connecting to a dedicated FCR. Flash codes are retrieved via the SD connector, or by turning a mode selector on the ECM.*

SD connector location

Under a panel on the centre console, under the facia, or behind the fusebox cover (see illustration 24.1).

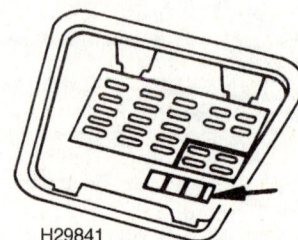

24.1 The SD connector is located behind the fusebox cover

ECM location

Under the facia on the driver's side, under the driver's seat, or behind a cover on the right-hand side of the centre console (see illustration 24.2).

EOBD models

The 16-pin diagnostic connector is located under the facia - refer to Chapter 38.

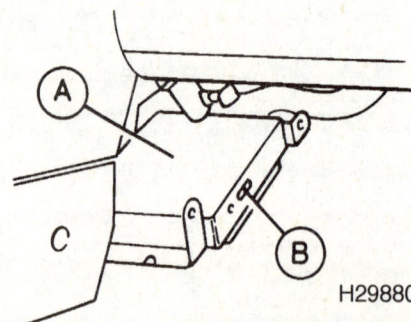

24.2 The ECM (A) and integral LED/LEDs (B) are located under a panel on the centre console under the facia
The single red LED, or the red and green LED(s), will be set into the ECM casing beside the mode selector (as applicable)

3 Retrieving fault codes without a fault code reader (FCR) - flash codes

Note: *During the course of certain test procedures, it is possible for additional fault codes to be generated. Care must be taken that any codes generated during test routines do not mislead diagnosis. All codes must be cleared once testing is complete.*

1 In the Nissan ECCS system, a number of diagnostic modes may be used to retrieve codes and associated information, depending on model and on the number of LEDs present on the electronic control module (ECM).

Single red LED on the ECM

2 There are two self-diagnosis modes available on these models. **Note:** *Where fitted, the SD warning light will flash in unison with the LED on the ECM, or will remain illuminated while fault codes are present.*

Mode I

3 Switch the ignition on.

4 Check that the LED on the ECM casing is illuminated. If not, check the bulb.

5 Start the engine. The LED should extinguish and remain extinguished to indicate that no fault codes have been recorded. If the LED becomes illuminated while the engine is running, a system fault is indicated.

6 Stop the engine and turn off the ignition.

Mode II - fault code retrieval

7 Switch the ignition on.

8 Use a jumper lead to bridge the IGN and CHK terminals in the SD connector *(see illustration 24.3)*. Remove the bridge after 2 seconds, and any fault codes will be displayed on the LED as 2-digit flash codes:

  a) *The first series of flashes indicates the multiples of ten, the second series of flashes indicates the single units.*

  b) *Tens are indicated by 0.6-second flashes, separated by a short pause.*

  c) *A pause of 0.9 seconds separates tens and units (the light remains extinguished during pauses).*

  d) *Units are indicated by 0.3-second flashes, separated by short pauses.*

  e) *Four long flashes and one short flash, for example, displays code 41.*

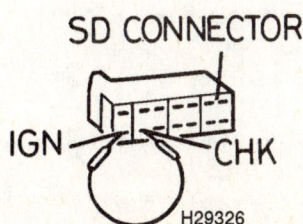

  f) *A pause of 2.1 seconds separates the transmission of each individual code.*

  g) *The code is repeated with a 4-second pause between each code that is displayed.*

9 Count the number of flashes in each series, and record each code as it is transmitted. Refer to the table at the end of the Chapter to determine the meaning of the fault code.

10 Continue retrieving codes until all stored codes have been retrieved and recorded.

11 If the system is free of faults, continue with mode II, engine running (see paragraph 12 onwards). All system faults must be repaired before the closed-loop control system will function correctly.

Mode II - sensor diagnosis, engine running (check of closed-loop control system)

12 Start the engine and run it to normal operating temperature.

13 Raise the engine speed to 2000 rpm for a period of 2 minutes.

14 Observe the warning light or LED display. If the LED switches off and on at a frequency of 5 times in 10 seconds, this indicates that the engine is in closed-loop control. If the LED remains constantly off or on, this indicates that the engine is in open-loop control:

  a) *When the LED is on, the fuelling is lean.*

  b) *When the LED is off, the fuelling is rich.*

15 The SD light or LED will reflect the current condition of lean or rich by staying on or off immediately before switching to open-loop control.

Red and green LEDs on ECM (300ZX 1984-1990 and Silvia Turbo)

16 There are two self-diagnosis modes available on these models. A mode selector is provided on the ECM casing to select the correct SD mode *(see illustration 24.4)*. Carefully use a screwdriver to turn the mode selector as required during the following procedures. Be warned that harsh treatment can damage the mode selector.

Mode I

17 Turn the mode selector fully anti-clockwise.

18 Switch on the ignition.

19 Check that the red and green LEDs on the ECM casing are illuminated. If not, check the bulb(s).

Mode II

20 Turn the mode selector fully clockwise.

SD CONNECTOR

IGN   CHK

H29326

24.3 Use a jumper lead to bridge the IGN and CHK terminals in the SD connector

24.4 A mode selector is provided on the ECM. Carefully use a screwdriver to turn the mode selector as required

21 The ECM red and green LEDs will now display fault codes:

  a) *The red LED indicates the multiples of ten, and the green LED the single units.*

  b) *Two red flashes followed by two green flashes indicates code 22.*

22 During fault code transmission, the following codes will be displayed, even if the components are not faulty:

  a) *23*   b) *24 (VG30ET)*   c) *31*

23 Record all displayed codes and continue. The next part of the routine will determine whether faults do indeed exist in the components represented by code numbers 23, 24 (VG30ET) and 31.

24 Depress the accelerator pedal fully and then release it.

25 The LEDs should flash code numbers 24 (VG30ET) and 31. If code 23 is repeated, this indicates that a fault has been found in that circuit. Record any other codes displayed and continue.

26 On models with the VG30ET engine only, move the transmission selector from neutral to one of the other positions. The LED should flash code 31 to signify that no fault has been recorded. If code 24 is repeated, this indicates that a fault has been found in that circuit. Record any other codes displayed and continue.

27 Start the engine and allow it to idle.

28 The LEDs should flash code number code 14 (VG30ET) and 31. Record any other codes displayed and continue.

29 On models with the VG30ET engine only, drive the vehicle at more than 10km/h. Stop the vehicle, but leave the engine running. If code 14 is repeated, this indicates that a fault has been found in that circuit. Record any other codes displayed and continue

30 Turn the air conditioner switch on and off (where fitted). The LEDs should flash code number 44, indicating that there are no faults in the system. If air conditioning is not fitted to the vehicle, code 31 will be transmitted in place of code 44.

31 Record any other codes displayed, and repair the indicated circuits. Repeat the whole process if necessary.

32 Turn the mode selector fully anti-clockwise.

33 Turn off the ignition and stop the engine.

Red and green LEDs on the ECM (except 300ZX 1984-1990 and Silvia Turbo)

34 There are five self-diagnosis modes available on these models. A mode selector is provided on the ECM casing to select the correct SD mode. Carefully use a screwdriver to turn the mode selector as required during the following procedures. Be warned that harsh treatment can damage the mode selector.

35 Switch on the ignition.

36 Turn the mode selector fully clockwise.

37 Both red and green LEDs will begin to flash, and will cycle through five modes signified by one, two, three, four and five flashes.

38 A mode is selected by turning the mode selector fully anti-clockwise immediately after it has flashed the mode required. To select mode III, turn the mode selector fully anti-clockwise immediately after it has flashed three times.

39 Once the ignition is turned off, the ECM will return to mode I.

40 After self-diagnosis is completed, ensure that the mode selector is returned to the normal running position by turning it fully anti-clockwise. **Note:** *Modes I and II are only available in catalyst-equipped engines. The engine must be at normal operating temperature and functioning in closed-loop control.*

Mode I (oxygen sensor monitor)

41 After the green LED has flashed once, turn the mode selector fully anti-clockwise.

42 Check that the red and green LEDs on the ECM casing are illuminated. If not, check the bulb(s).

43 Start the engine, and the fuel control system will initially enter the open-loop condition:

  a) *The green LED will either remain illuminated or extinguished.*

  b) *The red LED will remain extinguished unless a fault has been detected by the ECM.*

44 After the fuel control system has reached the closed-loop condition, the green LED will begin to flash. If the green LED does not flash, a fault has been detected in the fuel system:

  a) *The green LED will illuminate during lean running conditions and extinguish during rich running conditions.*

  b) *The red LED will remain extinguished unless a fault has been detected by the ECM.*

Mode II (mixture ratio feedback control monitor)

45 After the green LED has flashed twice, turn the mode selector fully anti-clockwise.

46 Check that the green LED on the ECM casing is illuminated, and the red LED is extinguished. If not, check the bulb(s).

47 Start the engine, and the fuel control system will initially enter the open-loop condition. The green and red LEDs will remain synchronised in either the illuminated or extinguished condition.

48 After the fuel control system has reached the closed-loop condition, the green LED will begin to flash. If the green LED does not flash, a fault has been detected in the fuel system.

49 The red light will illuminate during lean running conditions (more than 5% leaner) and extinguish during rich running conditions (more than 5% richer). During the time that the mixture ratio is controlled within 5% of its operating parameters, the red LED will flash in synchronisation with the green LED.

Mode III (fault code output)

Note: *Codes will be stored in the ECM memory until the starter has been operated fifty times, after which it will be cleared or replaced by a new code.*

50 After the green LED has flashed three times, turn the mode selector fully anti-clockwise.

51 The red and green LEDs on the ECM will now display fault codes:

  a) *The red LED indicates the multiples of ten, and the green LED indicates the single units.*

  b) *Two red flashes followed by two green flashes indicates code number 22.*

52 Record all codes that are transmitted. If code 55 is transmitted, no fault is stored.

53 It is now possible to enter the clear codes routine. Refer to Section 4.

54 Turn off the ignition.

Mode IV (switch-on/switch-off monitor)

55 After the green LED has flashed four times, turn the mode selector fully anti-clockwise.

56 The red LED should remain extinguished.

57 Start the engine. The red LED must illuminate during the time that the starter motor is in operation. If the LED remains off, check the starter signal circuit to the ECM.

58 Depress the accelerator pedal. The red LED must illuminate during the time that the accelerator pedal is depressed. If the LED remains off, check the idle switch. The LED can be toggled on and off with every depression of the accelerator pedal.

59 Lift the drive wheels so that the wheels can turn. Observe all safety principles.

60 Engage a gear and drive the wheels so that 12 mph is exceeded. The green LED will illuminate at speeds over 12 mph, and extinguish at speeds below 12 mph. If the green LED does not behave as described, check the VSS circuit.

61 Turn the ignition off.

Mode V (dynamic test of components)

62 Switch on the ignition and start the engine.

63 Turn the mode selector fully clockwise.

64 After the green LED has flashed five times, turn the mode selector fully anti-clockwise.

65 Run the engine under various operating conditions, and observe the LEDs.

66 If the LEDs begin to flash, count the flashes to determine the fault. The fault code is flashed once, and is not stored in memory:

  a) *One red flash - fault detected in the crank angle sensor circuit.*
  b) *Two green flashes - fault detected in the airflow sensor circuit.*
  c) *Three red flashes - fault detected in the fuel pump circuit.*
  d) *Four green flashes - fault detected in the Ignition system circuit.*

67 Stop the engine.

4 Clearing fault codes without a fault code reader (FCR)

1 A number of methods may be used to clear codes from the ECM, depending on model. All methods are described below.

Single red LED on the ECM

2 Turn the ignition.

3 Place the system into mode II and retrieve the fault codes as described in Section 3.

4 After diagnostic mode two has been completed:

  a) *Bridge the SD terminals IGN and CHK.*
  b) *Wait for at least 2 seconds.*
  c) *Disconnect the bridging wire*
  d) *Turn off the ignition.*

Red and green LEDs on the ECM (300ZX 1984-1990 and Silvia Turbo)

5 Use the following method to clear the codes from these models:

  a) *Switch on the ignition.*
  b) *Turn the mode selector fully clockwise for a period exceeding two seconds.*
  c) *Turn the mode selector fully anti clockwise for a period exceeding two seconds.*
  d) *Turn off the ignition.*

Red and green LEDs on the ECM (except 300ZX 1984-1990 and Silvia Turbo)

6 Place the system in to mode III and retrieve the fault codes as described in Section 3. **Note:** *Record all codes before completing the following routines to clear the codes. When selecting mode IV after mode III, the codes will be cleared from the ECM memory.*

  a) *Turn the mode selector fully clockwise.*
  b) *After the LED has flashed four times, turn the mode selector fully anti-clockwise, which selects mode IV.*
  c) *Turn the ignition off.*

All models (alternative method)

7 Disconnect the battery for a period of twenty-four hours. **Note**: *The first drawback to this method is that battery disconnection will re-initialise all ECM adaptive values. Re-learning the appropriate adaptive values requires starting the engine from cold, and driving at various engine speeds for approximately 20 to 30 minutes. The engine should also be allowed to idle for approximately 10 minutes. The second drawback is that the radio security codes, clock setting and other stored values will be initialised, and these must be re-entered once the battery has been reconnected. Where possible, an FCR should be used for code clearing. On models equipped with EOBD, and FCR must be used to retrieve and clear fault codes.*

8 A fault is automatically cleared once the engine starter has been used for a total of fifty times after the fault has cleared. If the fault recurs before 50 starts have been made, the counter will be reset to zero, and another 50 starts must occur before the fault is automatically cleared. This procedure occurs on an individual fault code basis; each code will only be cleared after 50 starts with no recurrence of that particular fault.

5 Self-Diagnosis with a fault code reader (FCR)

Note: *During the course of certain test procedures, it is possible for additional fault codes to be generated. Care must be taken that any codes generated during test routines do not mislead diagnosis.*

All Nissan models

1 Connect an FCR to the SD connector. Use the FCR for the following purposes, in strict compliance with the FCR manufacturer's instructions:

a) *Retrieving fault codes.*
b) *Clearing fault codes.*
c) *Displaying Datastream.*
d) *Checking the closed-loop mixture control.*
e) *Testing actuators.*
f) *Returning adaptive function to original default values.*
g) *Making adjustments:*
  Setting TPS position.
  Setting ignition timing advance.
  Adjusting CO/mixture value (non-catalyst models).
  Setting base idle speed.
h) *Changing the following parameters (engine running):*
  ISCV duty cycle.
  Fuel injection pulse rate.
  Ignition timing retard.
  Coolant temperature sensor (changing temperature).

2 Codes must always be cleared after component testing, or after repairs involving the removal or replacement of an engine management system component.

6 Guide to test procedures

1 Use an FCR to interrogate the ECM for fault codes, or gather codes manually, as described in Sections 3 or 5 .

Codes stored

2 If one or more fault codes are gathered, refer to the fault code table at the end of this Chapter to determine their meaning.

3 If several codes are gathered, look for a common factor such as a defective earth return or supply.

4 Refer to the component test procedures in Chapter 4, where you will find a means of testing the majority of components and circuits found in the modern EMS.

5 Once the fault has been repaired, clear the codes and run the engine under various conditions to determine if the problem has cleared.

6 Check the ECM for fault codes once more. Repeat the above procedures where codes are still being stored.

7 Refer to Chapter 3 for more information on how to effectively test the EMS.

No codes stored

8 Where a running problem is experienced, but no codes are stored, the fault is outside of the parameters designed into the SD system. Refer to Chapter 3 for more information on how to effectively test the engine management system.

9 If the problem points to a specific component, refer to the test procedures in Chapter 4, where you will find a means of testing the majority of components and circuits found in the modern EMS.

Fault code table

Nissan ECCS

Flash/ FCR code	Description
11	Crank angle sensor (CAS) in distributor or CAS circuit
11	RPM or RPM circuit (alternative code)
12	Mass airflow (MAF) sensor or MAF circuit
13	Coolant temperature sensor (CTS) or CTS circuit
14	Vehicle speed sensor (VSS) or VSS circuit
21*	Ignition signal circuit
22	Fuel pump or fuel pump circuit
23	Throttle pot sensor (TPS) - idle or TPS circuit
24	Throttle pot sensor (TPS) or TPS circuit
24	Neutral/park switch (alternative code)
25	Auxiliary air valve (AAV) or AAV circuit
26	Turbo, boost pressure sensor (BPS) or BPS circuit
31	Air conditioning (A/C models)
31	No faults found (non-A/C models) - alternative code
31	Electronic control module (ECM) - alternative code for GA16i, CA18DE engines
32	Starter signal
33	Oxygen sensor (OS) or OS circuit
34	Knock sensor (KS) or KS circuit

Flash/ FCR code	Description
34	Throttle pot sensor (TPS) or TPS circuit (alternative code)
41	Air temperature sensor (ATS) or ATS circuit
42	Fuel temperature sensor (FTS) or FTS circuit
43	Throttle pot sensor (TPS) or TPS circuit
44	No faults found in the ECM. Proceed with normal diagnostic methods
51	Injectors or injector circuit
54	Automatic transmission (AT) signal lost
55	No faults found in the ECM. Proceed with normal diagnostic methods

*Note: *If code 11 and code 21 are both displayed in the same incident, check the CAS circuit before checking other circuits.*

All models with EOBD

For a list of the allocated EOBD codes beginning with P0 (Generic Powertrain), refer to Chapter 1, Section 1.

Index of vehicles

Index of vehicles

Model	Engine code	Year	System
106 1.0 cat	TU9ML/Z (CDY, CDZ)	1993 to 1996	Bosch Mono-Motronic MA3.0
106 1.1	TU1M/L3/L (HDY, HDZ)	1996 to 2001	Bosch Mono-Motronic MA3.1
106 1.1i cat	TU1ML/Z (HDY, HDZ)	1991 to 1992	Bosch Mono-Jetronic A2.2
106 1.1i cat	TU1ML/Z (HDY, HDZ)	1993 to 1996	Magneti-Marelli FDG6
106 1.4	TU3JP/L3	1996 to 2001	Magneti-Marelli 1 AP
106 1.4i 8V SOHC Rallye cat	TU2J2L/Z (MFZ)	1993 to 1996	Magneti-Marelli 8P
106 1.4i	TU3J2K (K6B)	1991 to 1992	Bosch Motronic MP3.1
106 1.4i cat	TU3J2L/Z (KFZ)	1991 to 1996	Bosch Motronic MP3.1
106 1.4i cat	TU3MCL/Z (KDX)	1993 to 1996	Bosch Mono-Motronic MA3.0
106 1.6	TU5JPL/Z (NFZ)	1994 to 1996	Bosch Motronic MP5.1
106 1.6	TU5JP/L3	1996 to 1998	Bosch Motronic 5.2
106 1.6 MPi	TU5J2L/Z/K (NFY)	1994 to 1996	Magneti-Marelli 8P
205 1.1i cat	TU1ML/Z (HDZ)	1989 to 1992	Bosch Mono-Jetronic A2.2
205 1.1i cat	TU1ML/Z (HDZ)	1992 to 1996	Magneti-Marelli FDG6
205 1.4i LC cat	TU3MZ (KDZ)	1988 to 1991	Bosch Mono-Jetronic A2.2
205 1.4i HC cat	TU3ML/Z (KDY)	1991 to 1994	Bosch Mono-Jetronic A2.2
205 1.4i	TU3FM/L (KDY2)	1994 to 1996	Bosch Mono-Motronic MA3.0
205 1.6i cat	XU5M2L/Z (BDY)	1990 to 1991	Magneti-Marelli BAG5
205 1.6i and AT cat	XU5M3L/Z (BDY)	1992 to 1997	Magneti-Marelli FDG6
205 GTi 1.9 8V cat	XU9JAZ (DKZ)	1989 to 1993	Bosch Motronic 1.3
306 1.1i	TU1ML/Z (HDY, HDZ)	1993 to 1997	Magneti-Marelli FDG6
306 1.1i	TU1ML/Z (HDY, HDZ)	1993 to 1996	Bosch Mono-Motronic MA3.0
306 1.4i cat	TU3MCL/Z (KDX)	1993 to 1995	Bosch Mono-Motronic MA3.0
306 1.4i cat	TU3MCL/Z (KDX)	1994 to 1997	Magneti-Marelli FDG6
306 1.6i cat	TU5JPL/Z (NFZ)	1993 to 2001	Bosch Motronic MP5.1
306 1.8i Cabrio and cat	XU7JPL/Z (LFZ)	1993 to 2001	Magneti-Marelli 8P
306 2.0i Cabrio and cat	XU10J2CL/Z (RFX)	1994 to 1997	Magneti-Marelli 8P
306 2.0i 16V cat	XU10J4L/Z (RFY)	1994 to 1996	Bosch Motronic MP3.2
306 2.0i GT-6	XU10J4RS	1996 to 2001	Magneti-Marelli AP 10
309 1.1i cat	TU1ML/Z (HDZ)	1991 to 1994	Bosch Mono-Jetronic A2.2
309 1.4i cat	TU3MZ (KDZ)	1988 to 1991	Bosch Mono-Jetronic A2.2

Model	Engine code	Year	System
309 1.4i cat	TU3ML/Z (KDY)	1991 to 1994	Bosch Mono-Jetronic A2.2
309 1.6i cat	XU5MZ (BDZ)	1989 to 1991	Magneti-Marelli BAG5
309 1.6i cat	XU5M2L/Z (BDY)	1991 to 1992	Magneti-Marelli G5
309 1.6i cat	XU5M3L/Z (BDY)	1992 to 1994	Magneti-Marelli FDG6
309 1.9 8V	XU9JA/Z (DKZ)	1988 to 1992	Bosch Motronic 1.3
309 1.9 16V DOHC	XU9J4K (D6C)	1990 to 1991	Bosch Motronic 4.1
309 1.9 16V DOHC	XU9J4K (D6C)	1991 to 1992	Bosch Motronic 1.3
309 1.9 16V cat	XU9J4L/Z (DFW)	1990 to 1992	Bosch Motronic 1.3
309 1.9 SPi cat	XU9M/Z (DDZ)	1988 to 1993	Fenix 1B
405 1.4i cat	TU3MCL/Z (KDX)	1992 to 1994	Mono Motronic MA3.0
405 1.6i cat	XU5MZ (BDZ)	1989 to 1991	Magneti-Marelli BAG5
405 1.6i cat	XU5M2L/Z (BDY)	1989 to 1991	Magneti-Marelli FDG5
405 1.6i cat	XU5M3Z (BDY)	1991 to 1992	Magneti-Marelli FDG6
405 1.6i cat	XU5M3L/Z (BDY)	1992 to 1993	Magneti-Marelli FDG6
405 1.6i cat	XU5JPL/Z (BFZ)	1989 to 1992	Bosch Motronic 1.3
405 1.6i cat	XU5JPL/Z (BFZ)	1993 to 1995	Magneti-Marelli DCM8P13
405 1.8i cat	XU7JPL/Z (LFZ)	1992 to 1997	Bosch Motronic MP5.1
405 1.9 8V cat	XU9JA/Z (DKZ)	1989 to 1992	Bosch Motronic 1.3
405 1.9 Mi16 and 4x4 16V	XU9J4K (D6C)	1988 to 1991	Bosch Motronic ML4.1
405 1.9 Mi16 and 4x4 16V	XU9J4K (D6C)	1990 to 1992	Bosch Motronic 1.3
405 1.9 Mi16 cat	XU9J4/Z (DFW)	1990 to 1992	Bosch Motronic 1.3
405 1.9i W/distributor	XU9J2K (D6D)	1990 to 1991	Bosch Motronic MP3.1
405 1.9i DIS	XU9J2K (D6D)	1991 to 1992	Bosch Motronic MP3.1
405 1.9 SPi cat	XU9M/Z (DDZ)	1989 to 1992	Fenix 1B
405 2.0i and 4x4 8V cat	XU10J2CL/Z (RFX)	1992 to 1997	Magneti-Marelli 8P
405 2.0i 16V cat	XU10J4/Z (RFY)	1992 to 1995	Bosch Motronic MP3.2
405 2.0i 16V turbo cat	XU10J4TEL/Z (RGZ)	1993 to 1995	Magneti-Marelli AP MPi
406 1.6i cat	XU5JPL3(BFZ)	1996 to 2001	Magneti-Marelli 8P
406 1.8i cat	XU7JPK(L6A)	1996 to 1999	Magneti-Marelli 8P
406 1.8 16V	XU7JP4L	1995 to 2001	Bosch Motronic MP5.1.1
406 2.0 16V	XU10J4RL	1995 to 1999	Bosch Motronic MP5.1.1
406 2.0 Turbo	XU10J2TE/L3	1996 to 1999	Bosch Motronic MP5.1.1
605 2.0i cat	XU10ML/Z (RDZ)	1989 to 1994	Magneti-Marelli G5
605 2.0i cat	XU10J2L/Z (RFZ)	1990 to 1995	Bosch Motronic MP3.1
605 2.0i 16V	XU10J4RL/Z/L3 (RFV)	1995 to 1999	Bosch Motronic MP5.1.1
605 2.0i turbo cat	XU10J2TEL/Z (RGY)	1993 to 1994	Bosch Motronic MP3.2
605 2.0i turbo	XU10J2CTEL/Z (RGX)	1995 to 1999	Bosch Motronic MP3.2
605 3.0i cat	ZPJL/Z (SFZ)	1990 to 1995	Fenix 3B
605 3.0i 24V DOHC cat	ZPJ4L/Z (SKZ)	1990 to 1994	Fenix 4
605 3.0i 24V V6	ZPJ4L/Z (UKZ)	1995 to 1997	Fenix 4
806 2.0	XU10J2CL/Z (RFU)	1995 to 1999	Magneti-Marelli 8P-22
806 2.0 Turbo	XU10J2CTEL/Z (RGX)	1995 to 1997	Bosch Motronic MP3.2
Boxer 2.0	XU10J2U (RFW)	1994 to 2001	Magneti-Marelli 8P11

Plus All models equipped with EOBD (approximately January 2001-on)

Self-Diagnosis

1 Introduction

The engine management systems (EMSs) fitted to Peugeot vehicles are mainly of Bosch origin, and include Bosch Motronic versions 1.3, 3.1, 3.2, 4.1, 5.1. Other systems include Bosch Mono-Jetronic A2.2 and Bosch Mono-Motronic MA3.0, Fenix 1B, 3B and 4, and Magneti-Marelli G5, G6, and 8P.

The majority of Peugeot engine management systems control primary ignition, fuelling and idle functions from within the same control module. Early versions of Motronic 4.1 and 1.3 utilised an auxiliary air valve (AAV) that was not ECM-controlled. Bosch Mono-Jetronic fuel management systems control fuelling and idle functions alone

Self-Diagnosis (SD) function

Each ECM has a self-test capability that continually examines the signals from certain engine sensors and actuators, and compares each signal to a table of programmed values. If the diagnostic software determines that a fault is present, the ECM stores one or more fault codes. Codes will not be stored about components for which a code is not available, or for conditions not covered by the diagnostic software. In Peugeot systems, the control module generates 2-digit fault codes for retrieval either by manual means or by fault code reader (FCR). On models with EOBD, an FCR is required to retrieve and clear fault codes.

Limited operating strategy (LOS)

Peugeot systems featured in this Chapter utilise LOS (a function that is commonly called the "limp-home mode"). Once certain faults have been identified (not all faults will initiate LOS), the ECM will implement LOS and refer to a programmed default value rather than the sensor signal. This enables the vehicle to be safely driven to a workshop/garage for repair or testing. Once the fault has cleared, the ECM will revert to normal operation.

Adaptive or learning capability

Peugeot systems also utilise an adaptive function that will modify the basic programmed values for most effective operation during normal running, and with due regard to engine wear.

Self-Diagnosis warning light

The majority of Peugeot models are equipped with a facia-mounted SD warning light located within the instrument panel. When the ignition is switched on, the light will illuminate. Once the engine has started, the light will extinguish if the diagnostic software determines that a major fault is not present. If the light illuminates at any time during a period of engine running, the ECM has diagnosed presence of a major fault. Please note that failure of certain components designated as "minor" faults will not cause the light to illuminate. The warning light can also be triggered to transmit flash codes (see Section 3).

All models with EOBD are equipped with a MIL (Malfunction Warning Light) within the dashboard to alert the driver to the presence of a fault.

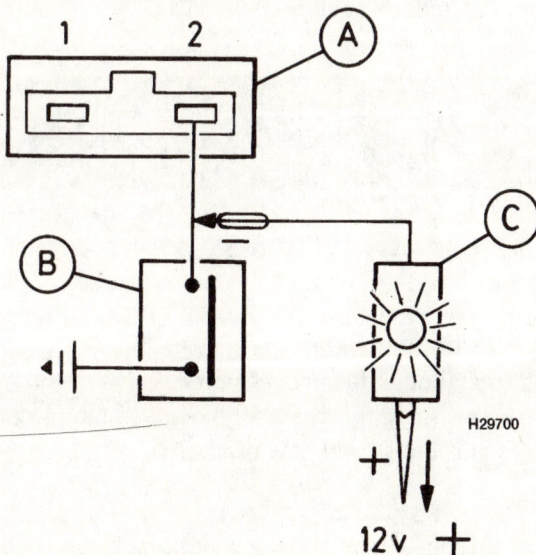

25.1 30-pin SD connector and typical location

2   Self-Diagnosis connector location

The 2-pin SD connector is coloured green, and is located in the engine compartment. It is commonly mounted along the left- or right-hand inner wing, either close to the ECM, the battery, or the cooling system expansion bottle. In some vehicles, the SD connector is located inside the relay box on either the left- or right-hand wing. The SD connector is provided for both manual retrieval of flash codes and for dedicated FCR use.

The 30-pin SD connector fitted to many later models is located in the passenger compartment, either under the facia or behind a cover on the facia (see illustration 25.1) and is for dedicated FCR use alone.

On models with EOBD, the 16-pin diagnostic connector is located under the facia - refer to Chapter 38.

3   Retrieving fault codes without a fault code reader (FCR) - flash codes

Note: During the course of certain test procedures, it is possible for additional fault codes to be generated. Care must be taken that any codes generated during test routines do not mislead diagnosis. All codes must be cleared once testing is complete.

Bosch Motronic ML4.1

1 Attach an on/off accessory switch to the green 2-pin SD connector (see illustration 25.2).

2 Switch on the ignition. The warning light should illuminate.

3 Close the accessory switch. The light will extinguish.

25.2 Retrieve flash codes by connecting an accessory switch and LED light (when a warning light is not fitted) to terminal 2 in the 2-pin SD connector

A SD connector   B Accessory switch   C LED light

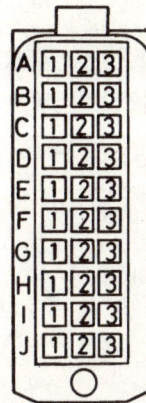

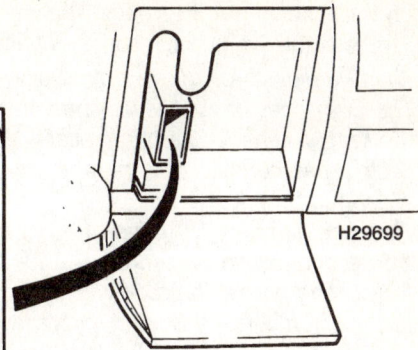

4 Open the switch after 3 seconds. The warning light will begin to flash the 2-digit fault codes as follows:

a) *The two digits are indicated by two series of flashes.*
b) *The first series of flashes indicates the multiples of ten, the second series of flashes indicates the single units.*
c) *Each series consists of a number of 1-second flashes, separated by a 1.5-second pause.*
d) *The code number "13" is indicated by a 1-second flash, a 1.5-second pause and three 1-second flashes. After a 2.5-second pause, the code will be repeated.*

5 Count the number of flashes in each series, and record each code as it is transmitted. Refer to the tables at the end of the Chapter to determine the meaning of the fault code.

6 The first code to be displayed will be code "12", which indicates initiation of diagnosis.

7 The warning light will extinguish; wait for 3 seconds before continuing.

8 Close the accessory switch for 3 seconds.

9 Open the switch. The warning light will begin flashing to indicate a code.

10 The warning light will extinguish; wait for 3 seconds before continuing.

11 Repeat the test to retrieve further codes.

12 Continue retrieving codes until code 11 is transmitted. Code 11 signifies that no more codes are stored.

13 If the engine is a non-starter, crank the engine on the starter motor for 5 seconds, and return the ignition key to the "on" position. Do not switch off the ignition.

14 If code 11 is the first code transmitted after code 12, no faults are stored by the ECM.

15 After code 11 is transmitted, the complete test may be repeated from the start.

16 Switching off the ignition ends fault code retrieval.

All other systems with green 2-pin SD connector

17 Attach an on/off accessory switch to the green 2-pin SD connector *(refer to illustration 25.2)*. If the vehicle is not equipped with an SD warning light, attach an LED diode light to the SD connector as shown in the illustration.

18 Switch on the ignition. The warning light or LED should illuminate.

19 Close the accessory switch; the light will remain illuminated.

20 Open the switch after 3 seconds. The warning light or LED will begin to flash the 2-digit fault codes as follows:

a) *The two digits are indicated by two series of flashes.*
b) *The first series of flashes indicates the multiples of ten, the second series of flashes indicates the single units.*
c) *Each series consists of a number of 1-second flashes, separated by a 1.5-second pause.*
d) *The code number "13" is indicated by a 1-second flash, a 1.5-second pause and three 1-second flashes. After a 2.5-second pause, the code will be repeated.*

21 Count the number of flashes in each series, and record the code. Refer to the tables at the end of the Chapter to determine the meaning of the fault code.

22 The first code indicated will be code "12", which indicates initiation of diagnosis.

23 Before continuing, wait 3 seconds for the warning light or LED to illuminate.

24 Close the accessory switch for 3 seconds; the light or LED will remain illuminated.

25 Open the switch. The warning light or LED will begin flashing to indicate a code.

26 Before continuing, wait 3 seconds for the warning light or LED to illuminate.

27 Repeat the test to retrieve further codes.

28 Continue retrieving codes until code 11 is transmitted. Code 11 signifies that no more codes are stored.

29 If the engine is a non-starter, crank the engine on the starter motor for 5 seconds, and return the ignition key to the "on" position. Do not switch off the ignition.

30 If code 11 is the first code transmitted after code 12, no faults are stored by the ECM.

31 After code 11 is transmitted, the complete test may be repeated from the start.

32 Turning off the ignition ends fault code retrieval.

30-pin SD connector

33 A fault code reader (FCR) is required for those systems equipped with the 30-pin SD connector - flash codes are not available.

Models with EOBD

34 A fault code reader is required for code retrieval and clearing on models equipped with EOBD.

4 Clearing fault codes without a fault code reader (FCR)

All systems with 2-pin SD connector

1 Repair all circuits indicated by the fault codes.

2 Switch on the ignition.

3 Perform the routines described above to retrieve code 11, signifying no other fault codes stored.

4 Close the accessory switch for more than ten seconds.

5 All fault codes should now be cleared.

All systems (alternative)

6 Turn off the ignition and disconnect the battery negative terminal for a period of approximately 2 minutes.

7 Reconnect the battery negative terminal.

Note: *The first drawback to this method is that battery disconnection will re-initialise all ECM adaptive values. Re-*

learning the appropriate adaptive values requires starting the engine from cold, and driving at various engine speeds for approximately 20 to 30 minutes. The engine should also be allowed to idle for approximately 10 minutes. The second drawback is that the radio security codes, clock setting and other stored values will be initialised, and these must be re-entered once the battery has been reconnected. For preference, where possible clear the fault codes manually (2-pin SD connector) or use an FCR for code clearing. A fault code reader is required for code retrieval and clearing on models equipped with EOBD.

5 Actuator testing without a fault code reader (FCR)

Bosch Motronic ML4.1

1 Attach an on/off accessory switch to the green 2-pin SD connector (refer to illustration 25.2).
2 Close the accessory switch.
3 Switch on the ignition.
4 Wait 3 seconds and then open the accessory switch. The warning light will flash the appropriate code (refer to the actuator selection code table at the end of this Chapter) and the injector circuit will actuate. Audible clicking of the injector solenoids should be heard.

> **⚠ Warning:** The injectors will actuate for as long as the circuit is closed, and there is a real danger of filling the cylinders with petrol. If testing is required for more than 1 second, disconnect the fuel pump supply (or remove the fuel pump fuse) before commencing this test.

5 Discontinue the injector test and continue with the next test by closing the accessory switch once more.
6 Wait 3 seconds and then open the accessory switch. The warning light will flash the appropriate code and the next actuator circuit will function.
7 Repeat the procedure to test each of the other actuators in turn
8 Turn off the ignition to end the test.

Systems with 30-pin SD connector

9 A dedicated FCR must be used to test the actuators for these systems.

6 Self-Diagnosis with a fault code reader (FCR)

Note: During the course of certain test procedures, it is possible for additional fault codes to be generated. Care must be taken that any codes generated during test routines do not mislead diagnosis.

All Peugeot models

1 Connect an FCR to the SD connector. Use the FCR for the following purposes, in strict compliance with the FCR manufacturer's instructions:
    a) Retrieving fault codes.
    b) Clearing fault codes.
    c) Testing actuators.
    d) Displaying Datastream.
    e) Making adjustments to the ignition timing or mixture (some Magneti-Marelli systems).
2 Codes must always be cleared after component testing, or after repairs involving the removal or replacement of an EMS component.

7 Guide to test procedures

1 Use an FCR to interrogate the ECM for fault codes, or (where possible) manually gather codes as described in Sections 3 or 6.

Codes stored

2 If one or more fault codes are gathered, refer to the fault code tables at the end of this Chapter to determine their meaning.
3 If several codes are gathered, look for a common factor such as a defective earth return or supply.
4 Refer to the component test procedures in Chapter 4, where you will find a means of testing the majority of components and circuits found in the modern EMS.
5 Once the fault has been repaired, clear the codes and run the engine under various conditions to determine if the problem has cleared.
6 Check the ECM for fault codes once more. Repeat the above procedures where codes are still being stored.
7 Refer to Chapter 3 for more information on how to effectively test the EMS.

No codes stored

8 Where a running problem is experienced, but no codes are stored, the fault is outside of the parameters designed into the SD system. Refer to Chapter 3 for more information on how to effectively test the engine management system.
9 If the problem points to a specific component, refer to the test procedures in Chapter 4, where you will find a means of testing the majority of components and circuits found in the modern EMS.

Fault code tables

Fault codes - all Peugeot models (except EOBD)

Flash/FCR code	Description
11	End of diagnosis
12	Initiation of diagnosis
13x	Air temperature sensor (ATS) or ATS circuit
14x	Coolant temperature sensor (CTS) or CTS circuit
15	Fuel pump relay, supply fault or fuel pump control circuit
18	Turbo coolant pump control
21x	Throttle pot sensor (TPS) or TPS circuit
21x	Throttle switch (TS), idle contact or TS circuit
22	Idle speed control valve (ISCV), supply fault
23	Idle speed control valve (ISCV) or ISCV circuit
25x	Variable acoustic characteristic induction (ACAV) solenoid L or circuit
26x	Vehicle speed sensor (VSS) or VSS circuit
31x	Throttle switch (TS), idle contact or TS circuit
31x	Oxygen sensor (OS), mixture regulation or OS circuit (alternative code)
32	Mixture regulation, exhaust, inlet leak(s) or fuel pressure
33x	Airflow sensor (AFS) or AFS circuit
33x	Manifold absolute pressure (MAP) sensor or MAP sensor circuit (alternative code)
33x	Throttle pot sensor (TPS) or TPS circuit (alternative code, Bosch Mono-Jetronic only)
34	Carbon filter solenoid valve (CFSV) or CFSV circuit
35	Throttle switch (TS), full-load contact
36	Crank angle sensor (CAS) or CAS circuit
42	Injectors or injector circuit
43x	Knock sensor (KS), knock regulation
44x	Knock sensor (KS) (knock detection)
45	Ignition coil control (coil one)
46	Turbo boost pressure solenoid valve (BPSV) or BPSV circuit
47	Turbo pressure regulation
51x	Oxygen sensor (OS) or OS circuit
52	Mixture control, supply voltage, air or exhaust leak
53x	Battery voltage, charging or battery fault
54	Electronic control module (ECM)
55x	CO pot or CO pot circuit
56	Immobiliser system
57	Ignition coil (coil two)
58	Ignition coil (coil three)
59	Ignition coil (coil four)
61	Variable turbo regulation valve or circuit

Flash/FCR code	Description
62x	Knock sensor (KS) 2 or KS circuit
63x	Oxygen sensor (OS) or OS circuit
64	Mixture control B
65x	Cylinder identification (CID) or CID circuit
71	Injector No. 1 control or injector circuit
72	Injector No. 2 control or injector circuit
73	Injector No. 3 control or injector circuit
74	Injector No. 4 control or injector circuit
75	Injector No. 5 control or injector circuit
76	Injector No. 6 control or injector circuit
79x	Manifold absolute pressure (MAP) sensor or MAP sensor circuit

x   Faults that typically will cause the ECM to enter LOS and use a default value in place of the sensor

Some faults are designated as "major" faults and will illuminate the warning light. However, major faults that will illuminate the warning light vary from system to system, and it is best to interrogate the ECM for codes if a fault is suspected. Codes designated as "minor" faults will not illuminate the warning light.

All models with EOBD

For a list of the allocated EOBD codes beginning with P0 (Generic Powertrain), refer to Chapter 1, Section 1.

Actuator selection code

Flash/FCR code	Description
81	Fuel pump relay
82	Injector or injector circuit
83	Idle speed control valve (ISCV) or ISCV circuit
84	Carbon filter solenoid valve (CFSV) or CFSV circuit
85	Air conditioning (A/C) compressor supply relay
91	Fuel pump or fuel pump relay
92	Injector or injector circuit
93	Idle speed control valve (ISCV) or ISCV circuit
94	Carbon filter solenoid valve (CFSV) or CFSV circuit
95	Air conditioning (A/C) compressor supply relay

The above codes are displayed during actuator test mode when the relevant circuit has been actuated. Not all components are present in any one particular system.

Proton

Index of vehicles

Model	Engine code	Year	System
1.3 MPi 12V SOHC cat	4G13-2	1992 to 1997	ECI-Multi- MPi
1.5 MPi 12V SOHC cat	4G15-2	1992 to 1997	ECI-Multi- MPi
Persona 1.3 Compact SOHC 12V	4G13-2	1995 to 2000	ECI-Multi- SEFi
Persona 1.5 SOHC 12V	4G15	1993 to 2000	ECI-Multi- SEFi
Persona 1.5 Compact SOHC 12V	4G15	1993 to 2000	ECI-Multi- SEFi
Persona 1.6 SOHC 16V	4G92	1993 to 2000	ECI-Multi- SEFi
Persona 1.6 Compact SOHC 16V	4G92	1993 to 2000	ECI-Multi- SEFi
Persona 1.8 12V SOHC	4G93	1996 to 2000	ECI-Multi- SEFi
Persona 1.8 16V DOHC	4G93	1996 to 2000	ECI-Multi- SEFi

Plus All models equipped with EOBD (approximately January 2001-on)

Self-Diagnosis

1   Introduction

Proton vehicles are equipped with the ECI-Multi engine management system, which controls primary ignition, fuel injection and idle functions from within the same control module.

Self-Diagnosis (SD) function

The ECM has a self-test capability that continually examines the signals from certain engine sensors and actuators, and then compares each signal to a table of programmed values. If the diagnostic software determines that a fault is present, the ECM stores one or more fault codes in the ECM memory. Codes will not be stored about components for which a code is not available, or for conditions not covered by the diagnostic software. In Proton systems, the control module generates 2-digit fault codes, for retrieval either by manual methods or by using a fault code reader (FCR).

On models equipped with EOBD, the 5-digit fault codes can only be retrieved or cleared using an FCR.

Chapter 26

Limited operating strategy (LOS)

Proton systems featured in this Chapter utilise LOS (a function that is commonly called the "limp-home mode"). Once certain faults have been identified (not all faults will initiate LOS), the ECM will implement LOS and refer to a programmed default value rather than the sensor signal. This enables the vehicle to be safely driven to a workshop/garage for repair or testing. Once the fault has cleared, the ECM will revert to normal operation.

Self-Diagnosis (SD) warning light

Proton models are equipped with a self-diagnosis warning light located within the instrument panel. All models equipped with EOBD, have a MIL (Malfunction Indicator Light) within the instrument cluster, to alert the driver to a fault.

2 Self-Diagnosis connector location

The SD connector is located where the facia and the centre console meet, on the right-hand (driver's) side (see illustration 26.1). **Note:** The Proton SD connector is provided both for retrieving codes via an analogue voltmeter and for dedicated FCR use.

On EOBD models, the 16-pin diagnostic connector is located under the facia - refer to Chapter 38.

3 Retrieving fault codes without a fault code reader (FCR)

Note: During the course of certain test procedures, it is possible for additional fault codes to be generated. Care

must be taken that any codes generated during test routines do not mislead diagnosis. All codes must be cleared once testing is complete.

1 Attach an analogue voltmeter to the A and B terminals in the SD connector (see illustration 26.2).

2 Switch on the ignition. If the ECM has stored one or more fault codes, the voltmeter needle will begin to sweep between a higher and lower level. If no codes are stored, the needle will remain level.

   a) The first series of sweeps indicates the multiples of ten, the second series of sweeps indicates the single units.
   b) The voltmeter needle will move for a longer period of deflection when transmitting codes in tens, and a shorter spell of deflection for units.
   c) If faults are not found, the meter will indicate regular on/off pulses.

3 Count the number of sweeps in each series, and record each code as it is transmitted. Refer to the table at the end of the Chapter to determine the meaning of the fault code.

4 Continue retrieving codes until all stored codes have been retrieved and recorded.

5 Turn off the ignition and remove the voltmeter to end fault code retrieval.

4 Clearing fault codes without a fault code reader (FCR)

1 Turn off the ignition and disconnect the battery negative terminal for a period of at least 30 seconds.

2 Reconnect the battery negative terminal.

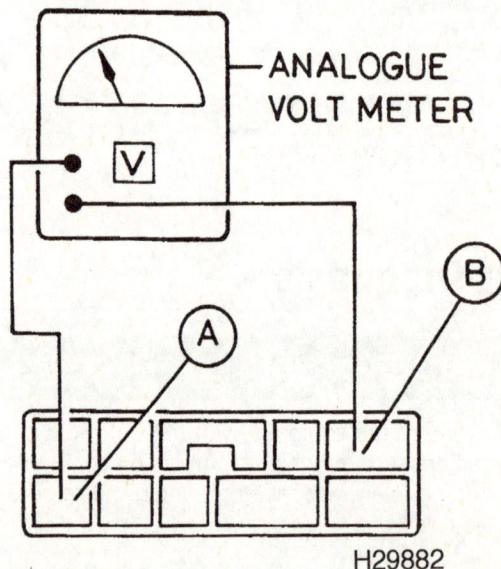

H29881

26.1 FCR attached to read fault codes

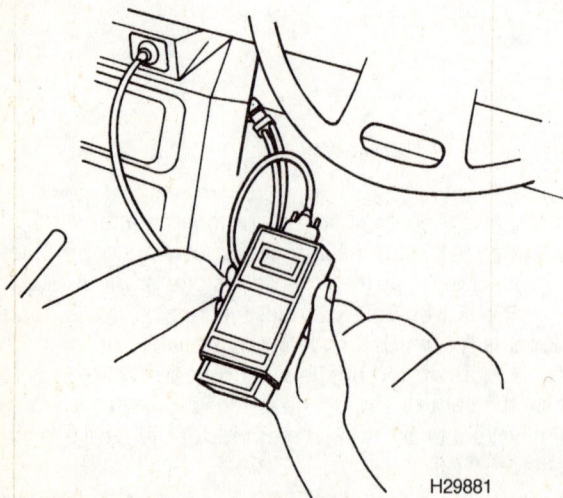

H29882

26.2 Terminals A and B of the SD connector bridged by an analogue voltmeter
A Earth terminal   B SD terminal

Note: *The first drawback to this method is that battery disconnection will re-initialise any ECM adaptive values (where applicable). Re-learning the appropriate adaptive values requires starting the engine from cold, and driving at various engine speeds for approximately 20 to 30 minutes. The engine should also be allowed to idle for approximately 10 minutes. The second drawback is that the radio security codes, clock setting and other stored values will be initialised, and these must be re-entered once the battery has been reconnected. Where possible, an FCR should be used for code clearing. On models with EOBD, an FCR must be used to retrieve and clear fault codes.*

5 Self-Diagnosis with a fault code reader (FCR)

Note: *During the course of certain test procedures, it is possible for additional fault codes to be generated. Care must be taken that any codes generated during test routines do not mislead diagnosis.*

All Proton models

1 Connect an FCR to the SD connector. Use the FCR for the following purposes, in strict compliance with the FCR manufacturer's instructions:

   a) *Retrieving fault codes.*
   b) *Clearing fault codes.*
   c) *Datastream (EOBD only)*

2 Codes must always be cleared after component testing, or after repairs involving the removal or replacement of an EMS component.

6 Guide to test procedures

1 Use an FCR to interrogate the ECM for fault codes, or gather codes using an analogue voltmeter, as described in Sections 3 or 5.

Codes stored

2 If one or more fault codes are gathered, refer to the fault code table at the end of this Chapter to determine their meaning.

3 If several codes are gathered, look for a common factor such as a defective earth return or supply.

4 Refer to the component test procedures in Chapter 4, where you will find a means of testing the majority of components and circuits found in the modern EMS.

5 Once the fault has been repaired, clear the codes and run the engine under various conditions to determine if the problem has cleared.

6 Check the ECM for fault codes once more. Repeat the above procedures where codes are still being stored.

7 Refer to Chapter 3 for more information on how to effectively test the EMS.

No codes stored

8 Where a running problem is experienced, but no codes are stored, the fault is outside of the parameters designed into the SD system. Refer to Chapter 3 for more information on how to effectively test the engine management system.

9 If the problem points to a specific component, refer to the test procedures in Chapter 4, where you will find a means of testing the majority of components and circuits found in the modern EMS.

Fault code table

ECI-Multi

Voltmeter/ FCR code	Description
7	Fuel pump or fuel pump circuit
8	Carbon filter solenoid valve (CFSV) or CFSV circuit
11	Oxygen sensor (OS) or OS circuit
13	Air temperature sensor (ATS) or ATS circuit
14	Throttle pot sensor (TPS) or TPS circuit
16	Power supply
18	Ignition switch or circuit
21	Coolant temperature sensor (CTS) or CTS circuit
22	Crank angle sensor (CAS) or CAS circuit
26	Idle position switch or circuit
27	Power steering pressure switch (PSPS) or PSPS circuit

Voltmeter/ FCR code	Description
28	Air conditioning (A/C) or A/C circuit
29	Inhibitor switch or circuit
32	Vacuum sensor or circuit
41	Injectors or injector circuit
44	Ignition advance
49	Air conditioning or A/C circuit

All models with EOBD

For a list of the allocated EOBD codes beginning with P0 (Generic Powertrain), refer to Chapter 1, Section 1.

Notes

Renault

Index of vehicles

Index of vehicles

Model	Engine code	Year	System
5 1.4 cat	C3J700 (B/C/F407)	1986 to 1990	Renix SPi
5 1.4 cat	C3J760 (B/C/F407)	1990 to 1997	Renix SPi
5 1.7i cat	F3NG716 (B/C408)	1987 to 1991	Renix SPi
5 1.7i cat	F3NG717 (B/C409)	1987 to 1991	Renix SPi
5 1.7 cat	F3N702 (C409)	1989 to 1992	Renix MPi
9 1721 cat	F3N718(L42F/BC37F)	1986 to 1989	Renix SPi
9 1.7 cat	F3N708(L42E/C37E)	1986 to 1989	Renix MPi
11 1721 cat	F3N718(L42F/BC37F)	1986 to 1989	Renix SPi
11 1.7 cat	F3N708 L42E/C37E)	1986 to 1989	Renix MPi
19 1.4i cat	C3J710 (B/C/L532)	1990 to 1992	Renix SPi
19 1.4i cat	C3J700	1991 to 1992	Renix SPi
19 1.4 cat	E7J700 (B/C/L53A)	1991 to 1995	Bosch SPi
19 1.7i cat	F3N740 (B/C/L53B	1990 to 1992	Renix SPi
19 1.7i cat auto	F3N741 (B/C/L53B)	1990 to 1992	Renix SPi
19 1.7 DOHC 16V	F7P700(B/C/L/D53D)	1991 to 1993	Renix MPi
19 1.7 DOHC 16V cat	F7P704(B/C/L/D53D)	1991 to 1995	Renix MPi
19 1.7 DOHC 16V cat	F7P704 (X53D)	1991 to 1995	Renix MPi
19 1.7i cat	F3N746 (B/C/L53F)	1992 to 1993	Renix MPi
19 1.7i cat	F3N742(B/C/L/X53C)	1990 to 1992	Renix MPi
19 1.7i auto cat	F3N743 (X53C)	1990 to 1992	Renix MPi
19 1.8i cat and Cabrio	F3P704 (X53Y)	1992 to 1996	Bosch SPi
19 1.8i cat and Cabrio	F3P705 (X53Y)	1992 to 1995	Bosch SPi
19 1.8i cat and Cabrio	F3P706 (X53Y)	1992 to 1995	Bosch SPi
19 1.8i cat and Cabrio	F3P707 (X53Y)	1992 to 1995	Bosch SPi
19 1.8 cat	F3P700 (X538)	1992 to 1996	Renix MPi
21 1.7i cat	F3N723 (X48F)	1991 to 1995	Renix SPi
21 1.7i cat	F3N722(B/K/L/48E)	1991 to 1995	Renix MPi
21 1721 cat	F3N 726(L42F/BC37F)	1986 to 1989	Renix SPi
21 2.0 12V and 4x4 cat	J7R740 (B/L/X48R)	1991 to 1995	Renix MPi
21 2.0 cat	J7R746 (B/K/L48C)	1991 to 1995	Renix MPi
21 2.0 auto cat	J7R747 (B/K/L48C)	1991 to 1995	Renix MPi

Model	Engine code	Year	System
21 2.0 and 4x4	J7R750 (B/L/K483)	1986 to 1993	Renix MPi
21 2.0 and 4x4 auto	J7R751 (K483)	1986 to 1993	Renix MPi
21 2.0 TXi 12V	J7RG754(X48Q/Y/R)	1989 to 1994	Renix MPi
21 2.0 turbo and 4x4 cat	J7R756 (L48L)	1991 to 1994	Renix MPi
21 2.0 turbo	J7R752 (L485)	1988 to 1992	Renix MPi
21 2.0 turbo 4x4	J7R752 (L485)	1991 to 1992	Renix MPi
21 2.2 cat	J7T754 (B/K/L48K)	1992 to 1995	Renix MPi
21 2.2 auto cat	J7T755 (B/K/L48K)	1992 to 1995	Renix MPi
25 2.0	J7R722 (B29H)	1986 to 1992	Renix MPi
25 2.0 auto	J7R723 (B29H)	1986 to 1992	Renix MPi
25 2.0 TXi 12V	J7RG720 (B292)	1989 to 1992	Renix MPi
25 2.0 TXi 12V auto	J7RG721 (B292)	1989 to 1993	Renix MPi
25 2.0 TXi 12V cat	J7R726 (B294)	1991 to 1993	Renix MPi
25 2.2	J7TE706 (B29E)	1984 to 1987	Renix MPi
25 2.2 auto	J7TG707 (B29E)	1984 to 1987	Renix MPi
25 2.2	J7TJ730 (B29E)	1987 to 1990	Renix MPi
25 2.2 auto	J7TK731 (B29E)	1987 to 1990	Renix MPi
25 2.2 cat	J7T732 (B29B)	1990 to 1991	Renix MPi
25 2.2 auto cat	J7T733 (B29B)	1990 to 1991	Renix MPi
25 2.5 V6 turbo	Z7UA702 (B295	1985 to 1990	Renix MPi
25 2.5 V6 turbo cat	Z7U700 (B29G)	1991 to 1993	Renix MPi
25 V6 2.9i	Z7WA700 (B293)	1989 to 1993	Renix MPi
25 V6 2.9i auto	Z7W701 (B293)	1989 to 1992	Renix MPi
25 V6 2.9i auto	Z7W709 (B293)	1992 to 1993	Renix MPi
25 V6 2.9i cat	Z7W706 (B29F)	1991 to 1992	Renix MPi
25 V6 2.9i cat auto	Z7W707 (B29F)	1991 to 1992	Renix MPi
Alpine 2.5 GTA V6 turbo	Z7UC730 (D501)	1986 to 1992	Renix MPi
Alpine 2.5 GTA V6 turbo cat	Z7U734 (D502)	1990 to 1992	Renix MPi
Alpine 2.5 V6 turbo cat	Z7X744 (D503)	1992 to 1995	Renix MPi
Chamade 1.4i cat	(B/C/L532)C31710	1990 to 1992	Renix SPi
Chamade 1.4i cat	C3J700	1991 to 1992	Renix SPi
Chamade 1.4 cat	E7J700(B/C/L53A)	1991 to 1996	Bosch SPi
Chamade 1.7i cat	F3N742 (X53C)	1990 to 1992	Renix MPi
Chamade 1.7i auto cat	F3N743 (X53C)	1990 to 1992	Renix MPi
Chamade 19 1.7i cat	F3N740	1990 to 1992	Renix SPi
Chamade 19 1.7i auto cat	F3N741 (B/C/L53B)	1990 to 1992	Renix SPi
Chamade 1.8 cat	F3P700	1992 to 1994	Renix MPi
Clio 1.2 cat	E7F700 (B/C/S57A/R)	1991 to 1997	Bosch SPi
Clio 1.2 cat	E7F706 (B/C/S57A/R)	1991 to 1995	Bosch SPi
Clio 1.2i	C3G720 (B/C/S577)	1995 to 1997	Magneti-Marelli SPi
Clio 1.4 cat	E7J718 (B/C/S57T)	1991 to 1998	Bosch SPi
Clio 1.4 auto cat	E7J719 (B/C/S57T)	1991 to 1996	Bosch SPi
Clio 1.4 cat	E7J710 (B/C/S57B/57T)	1991 to 1995	Bosch SPi
Clio 1.4 auto cat	E7J711(B/C/S57B/57T)	1991 to 1995	Bosch SPi
Clio 16V/16S	F7P-7-22 (US87)	1991 to 1997	Siemens Bendix MPi
Clio 1.8 cat	F3P710 (B/C57C)	1991 to 1997	Bosch SPi
Clio 1.8 cat	F3P714 (B/C57U)	1991 to 1994	Bosch SPi
Clio 1.8 cat	F3P712 (C579)	1993 to 1996	Renix MPi
Clio 1.8i auto	F3P755	1995 to 1998	Siemens Bendix MPi
Clio 1.8i	F3P758	1995 to 1998	Siemens Bendix MPi
Clio 1.8 16V DOHC	F7P720 (C575)	1991 to 1992	Renix MPi
Clio 1.8 16V DOHC cat	F7P722 (C57D)	1991 to 1996	Renix MPi
Clio Williams 2.0 cat	F7P	1993 to 1995	Renix MPi
Espace 2.0i TXE and 4x4	J7RE760 (J116)	1988 to 1991	Renix MPi
Espace 2.0i cat	J7R768 (J636)	1991 to 1996	Renix MPi
Espace 2.2i TXE and 4x4 cat	J7T770 (J117)	1991 to 1992	Renix MPi
Espace 2.2i and 4x4 cat	J7T772 (J/S637)	1991 to 1997	Renix MPi
Espace 2.9i V6 and 4X4 cat	Z7W712 (J638)	1991 to 1997	Renix MPi
Espace 2.9i V6 and 4X4 cat	Z7W713 (J638)	1991 to 1997	Renix MPi
Extra 1.2	C3G710	1995 to 1998	Magneti-Marelli SPi
Extra 1.4 cat	C3J760 (B/C/F407)	1990 to 1995	Renix SPi
Extra 1.4 cat	C3J762 (F407)	1992 to 1995	Renix SPi
Extra 1.4 cat	E7J720 (F40V)	1992 to 1995	Bosch SPi
Extra 1.4 cat	E7J724 (F40U)	1992 to 1998	Bosch SPi
Express 1.2	C3G710	1995 to 1998	Magneti-Marelli SPi
Express 1.4 cat	C3J762 (F407)	1992 to 1995	Renix SPi
Express 1.4 cat	E7J720 (F40V)	1992 to 1995	Bosch SPi
Express 1.4 cat	E7J724 (F40U)	1992 to 1998	Bosch SPi

Model	Engine code	Year	System
Laguna 1.8i	F3P720 (B56B)	1994 to 1997	Bosch SPi
Laguna 2.0i	N7Q 700/704	1996 to 2001	Siemens Bendix SEFi
Laguna 2.0i	F3R723/722	1994 to 2001	Siemens Bendix MPi
Laguna 2.0i	F3R722	1994 to 1995	Renix MPi
Laguna 3.0i V6	Z7X760 (B56E)	1994 to 2001	Siemens MPi
Master 2.2i cat	J7T782 (RxxA)	1991 to 1993	Renix MPi
Megane 1.4	E7J764 (BAOE)	1996 to 1999	Fenix 3
Megane 1.6	K7M 702/720	1996 to 1999	Fenix 5
Megane 1.6 Coupe	K7M 702/720	1996 to 1999	Fenix 5
Megane 2.0	F3R750	1996 to 1999	Fenix 5
Safrane 2.0i cat	J7R732 (B540)	1993 to 1997	Renix MPi
Safrane 2.0i auto cat	J7R733 (B540)	1993 to 1995	Renix MPi
Safrane 2.0i 12V cat	J7R734 (B542)	1993 to 1994	Renix MPi
Safrane 2.0i 12V cat	J7R735 (B542)	1993 to 1994	Renix MPi
Safrane 2.2i 12V cat	J7T760 (B543)	1993 to 1997	Renix MPi
Safrane 2.2i 12V auto cat	J7T761 (B543)	1993 to 1995	Renix MPi
Safrane 3.0i V6 cat	Z7X722 (B544)	1993 to 1997	Renix MPi
Safrane 3.0i V6 auto cat	Z7X723 (B544)	1993 to 1995	Renix MPi
Safrane Quadra 3.0i V6 cat	Z7X722 (B544)	1992 to 1994	Renix MPi
Savanna 1.7i cat	F3N722 (X48E)	1991 to 1995	Renix MPi
Savanna 1.7i cat	F3N723 (X48F)	1991 to 1995	Renix SPi
Savanna 2.0 and 4x4	J7R750 (K483)	1986 to 1993	Renix MPi
Savanna 2.0 and 4x4 auto	J7R751 (K483)	1986 to 1993	Renix MPi
Trafic 2.2i and 4x4 cat	J7T 780 (T/VxxA)	1991 to 1993	Renix MPi
Twingo 1.3	C3G (C063)	1994 to 1998	Magneti-Marelli SPi

Plus All models equipped with EOBD (approximately January 2001-on)

Self-Diagnosis

1   Introduction

The engine management systems fitted to Renault vehicles include Bendix, Fenix, Renix, Siemens and Magneti-Marelli, in both multi-point and single-point fuel injection (MPi and SPi) forms. All of the systems are basically similar, and components supplied by Bosch, Bendix, Fenix, Renix Siemens and Magneti-Marelli will be found on almost a "mix-and-match" basis. Renault engine management systems control the primary ignition, fuelling and idle functions from within the same control module.

Self-Diagnosis (SD) function

Each ECM has a self-test capability that continually examines the signals from certain engine sensors and actuators, and compares each signal to a table of programmed values. If the diagnostic software determines that a fault is present, the ECM stores a fault. Codes will not be stored about components for which a code is not available, or for conditions not covered by the diagnostic software. Renault software does not usually generate fault codes and the FCR normally displays faults on the FCR screen without reference to a specific code number.

Renault software does not generate fault code numbers (except on EOBD models), and the FCR normally displays faults on the FCR screen without reference to a specific code number. Although actual code numbers are not available, faults in one or more of the circuits and components covered by the diagnostic software will cause a fault to be stored.

On models equipped with EOBD, the 5-digit fault codes can only be retrieved and clearing using an FCR).

Limited operating strategy (LOS)

Renault systems featured in this Chapter utilise LOS (a function that is commonly called the "limp-home mode"). Once certain faults have been identified (not all faults will initiate LOS), the ECM will implement LOS and refer to a programmed default value rather than the sensor signal. This enables the vehicle to be safely driven to a workshop/garage for repair or testing. Once the fault has cleared, the ECM will revert to normal operation.

Adaptive or learning capability

Renault systems also utilise an adaptive function that will modify the basic programmed values for most effective operation during normal running, and with due regard to engine wear.

Self-Diagnosis warning light

Many Renault models are equipped with an SD warning light located within the instrument panel. When the ignition is switched on, the light will illuminate. Once the engine has started, the light will extinguish if the diagnostic software determines that a fault is not present. If the light remains illuminated at any time whilst the engine is running, the ECM has diagnosed presence of a system fault.

2 Self-Diagnosis connector location

The 12-pin SD connector *(see illustration 27.1)* is for FCR use alone, and usually located in the driver's side fuse/relay box, or close to the MAP sensor or ignition coil/amplifier unit within the engine compartment. Renault engine management systems do not generate flash codes.

On models equipped with EOBD, the 16-pin diagnostic connector is located under the facia - refer to Chapter 38.

3 Retrieving fault codes without a fault code reader (FCR)

Flash codes are not generated in SD systems fitted to Renault vehicles, and an FCR is essential for code retrieval.

4 Clearing fault codes without a fault code reader (FCR)

1 Turn off the ignition and disconnect the battery negative terminal for a period of approximately 2 minutes.
2 Reconnect the battery negative terminal.

Note: *The first drawback to this method is that battery disconnection will re-initialise all ECM adaptive values. Re-learning the appropriate adaptive values requires starting the engine from cold, and driving at various engine speeds for approximately 20 to 30 minutes. The engine should also be allowed to idle for approximately 10 minutes. The second drawback is that the radio security codes, clock setting and other stored values will be initialised, and these must be re-entered once the battery has been reconnected. Where possible, an FCR should be used for code clearing. On models with EOBD, an FCR is essential for retrieving and clearing fault codes.*

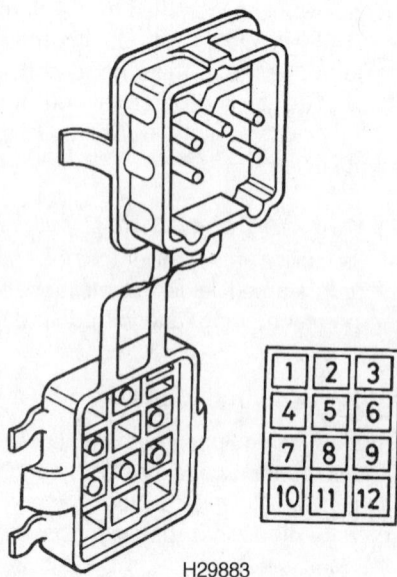

H29883

27.1 Renault SD connector

5 Self-Diagnosis with a fault code reader (FCR)

Note: *During the course of certain test procedures, it is possible for additional faults to be generated. Care must be taken that any faults generated during test routines do not mislead diagnosis.*

All Renault models

1 Connect an FCR to the SD connector. Use the FCR for the following purposes, in strict compliance with the FCR manufacturer's instructions:
  a) *Displaying system faults.*
  b) *Clearing stored system faults.*
  c) *Testing actuators.*
  d) *Viewing Datastream.*
  e) *Making adjustments to the ignition timing or mixture (some vehicles).*
  f) *Changing system parameters (some selected components).*
2 Faults must always be cleared after component testing, or after repairs involving the removal or replacement of an EMS component.

6 Guide to test procedures

1 Use an FCR to interrogate the ECM for faults, as described in Section 5.

Faults stored

2 If one or more faults are gathered, refer to the fault table at the end of this Chapter to determine their meaning.
3 If several faults are gathered, look for a common factor such as a defective earth return or supply.
4 Refer to the component test procedures in Chapter 4, where you will find a means of testing the majority of components and circuits found in the modern EMS.
5 Once the fault has been repaired, clear the codes and run the engine under various conditions to determine if the problem has cleared.
6 Check the ECM for faults once more. Repeat the above procedures where faults are still being stored.
7 Refer to Chapter 3 for more information on how to effectively test the EMS.

No faults stored

8 Where a running problem is experienced, but no faults are stored, the fault is outside of the parameters designed into the SD system. Refer to Chapter 3 for more information on how to effectively test the engine management system.

9 If the problem points to a specific component, refer to the test procedures in Chapter 4, where you will find a means of testing the majority of components and circuits found in the modern EMS.

Fault table

All Renault models (except EOBD)

Renault software does not usually generate fault codes. A fault code reader normally displays faults on the FCR screen without reference to a specific code number. Although actual code numbers are not available, faults in one or more of the following list of circuits and components will cause a fault to be stored.

All models with EOBD

For a list of the allocated EOBD codes beginning with P0 (Generic Powertrain), refer to Chapter 1, Section 1.

List of circuits checked by Renault SD system

Air conditioning (A/C) or A/C circuit
Air temperature sensor (ATS) or ATS circuit
Battery supply to electronic control module (ECM)
Crank angle sensor (CAS) or CAS circuit
CO pot or CO pot circuit (where used - non-cat models only)
Coolant temperature sensor (CTS) or CTS circuit
Fuel pump control (relay driver circuit)
Heated windscreen (if so equipped)
Ignition signal or circuit
Injector or injector circuit
Idle speed control valve (ISCV) or ISCV circuit
Knock sensor (KS) or KS circuit
Manifold absolute pressure (MAP) sensor or MAP sensor circuit
Oxygen sensor (OS) or OS circuit
Power assisted steering or circuit (if so equipped)
Main relay or circuit
Serial (SD) communication
Throttle pot sensor (TPS) or circuit
Throttle switch (TS) or circuit
Vehicle speed sensor (VSS) or VSS circuit (if so equipped)
Note: *Not all components are fitted to all vehicles.*

Notes

Rover/MG

Index of vehicles

Model	Engine code	Year	System
111 1.1 SOHC	K8	1995 to 1999	Rover MEMS SPi
114 1.4 SOHC	K8	1995 to 1999	Rover MEMS SPi
200 Vi DOHC 16V	18K16	1995 to 2000	Rover MEMS MPi
214 1.4 DOHC 16V	K16	1989 to 1992	Rover MEMS SPi
214 1.4 DOHC 16V cat	K16	1990 to 1993	Rover MEMS SPi
214 1.4 DOHC 16V cat	K16	1992 to 1996	Rover MEMS MPi
214 SOHC 8V	14K8	1995 to 1999	Rover MEMS MPi
214 DOHC 16V	14K16	1995 to 1999	Rover MEMS MPi
216 SOHC 16V	D16A7	1989 to 1996	Honda PGM-Fi
216 SOHC 16V cat	D16A6	1989 to 1996	Honda PGM-Fi
216 SOHC 16V auto cat	D16Z2	1989 to 1996	Honda PGM-Fi
216 DOHC 16V	D16A9	1990 to 1994	Honda PGM-Fi
216 DOHC 16V auto	D16Z4	1990 to 1994	Honda PGM-Fi
216 DOHC 16V cat	D16A8	1990 to 1994	Honda PGM-Fi
216 DOHC 16V	16K16	1995 to 1999	Rover MEMS MPi
220 2.0 DOHC 16V cat	20M4 M16	1991 to 1994	Rover MEMS MPi
220 2.0 DOHC 16V turbo cat	20T4 T16	1992 to 1996	Rover MEMS MPi
220 2.0 DOHC 16V cat	20T4 T16	1992 to 1996	Rover MEMS MPi
414 1.4 DOHC 16V	K16	1990 to 1993	Rover MEMS SPi
414 1.4 DOHC 16V cat	K16	1990 to 1993	Rover MEMS SPi
414 1.4 DOHC 16V cat	K16	1992 to 1999	Rover MEMS MPi
414 1.4 DOHC 16V	K16	1995 to 1999	Rover MEMS MPi
416 SOHC 16V	D16A7	1989 to 1996	Honda PGM-Fi
416 SOHC 16V cat	D16A6	1989 to 1996	Honda PGM-Fi
416 SOHC 16V auto cat	D16Z2	1989 to 1996	Honda PGM-Fi
416 DOHC 16V	D16A9	1990 to 1994	Honda PGM-Fi
416 DOHC 16V auto	D16Z4	1990 to 1994	Honda PGM-Fi
416 DOHC 16V cat	D16A8	1990 to 1994	Honda PGM-Fi
416i 1.6 SOHC 16V auto	D16	1995 to 1996	Honda PGM-Fi
416 1.6 DOHC 16V	K16	1995 to 1996	Rover MEMS MPi
420 2.0 DOHC 16V cat	20M4 M16	1991 to 1994	Rover MEMS MPi
420 2.0 DOHC 16V turbo cat	20T4 T16	1992 to 2000	Rover MEMS MPi
420 2.0 DOHC 16V cat	20T4 T16	1992 to 1997	Rover MEMS MPi
618 SOHC 16V	F18A3	1995 to 2000	Honda PGM-Fi
620i SOHC 16V	F20Z2	1993 to 1999	Honda PGM-Fi
620i S SOHC 16V	F20Z1	1993 to 2000	Honda PGM-Fi

Model	Engine code	Year	System
620 2.0 DOHC 16V turbo	20T4 T16	1994 to 1999	Rover MEMS MPi
623i DOHC 16V	H23A3	1993 to 2000	Honda PGM-Fi
820E SPi DOHC	20HD/M16e	1986 to 1990	Rover SPi 10CU
820SE SPi DOHC	20HD/M16e	1986 to 1990	Rover SPi 10CU
820i/Si DOHC cat	20HD-M16	1988 to 1990	Lucas MPi 11CU
820i 2.0 DOHC 16V cat	20T4	1991 to 1996	Rover MEMS MPi
820 2.0 DOHC 16V turbo cat	20T4	1992 to 1999	Rover MEMS MPi
820 DOHC 16V	20T4	1996 to 1999	Rover MEMS MPi
825 Sterling V6	KV6	1996 to 1999	Rover MEMS MPi
825i V6 SOHC 24V	V6 2.5	1986 to 1989	Honda PGM-Fi
827i V6 SOHC 24V	V6 2.7	1988 to 1991	Honda PGM-Fi
827i V6 SOHC 24V cat	V6 2.7	1988 to 1991	Honda PGM-Fi
827i V6 SOHC 24V cat	V6 2.7	1991 to 1996	Honda PGM-Fi
Coupe 1.6	16K16	1996 to 1999	Rover MEMS MPi
Coupe 1.8 16V VVC	18K16	1996 to 1999	Rover MEMS MPi
Cabrio 1.6	16K16	1996 to 1999	Rover MEMS MPi
Cabrio 1.8 16V VVC	18K16	1996 to 1999	Rover MEMS MPi
Tourer 1.6	16K16	1996 to 1999	Rover MEMS MPi
Tourer 1.8 16V VVC	18K16	1996 to 1999	Rover MEMS MPi
Metro 1.1i SOHC cat	K8	1991 to 1994	Rover MEMS SPi
Metro 1.4i SOHC	K8	1991 to 1992	Rover MEMS SPi
Metro 1.4i SOHC cat	K8	1991 to 1994	Rover MEMS SPi
Metro 1.4i GTa DOHC 16V cat	K16	1991 to 1992	Rover MEMS SPi
Metro 1.4 GTi DOHC 16V	K16	1990 to 1992	Rover MEMS SPi
Metro 1.4 GTi DOHC 16V cat	K16	1990 to 1993	Rover MEMS SPi
Metro 1.4 GTi DOHC 16V cat	K16	1991 to 1994	Rover MEMS MPi
MGF 1.8 DOHC 16V	K16	1995 to 2001	Rover MEMS 1.9 MPi
MGF 1.8 VVC DOHC 16V	K16	1995 to 2001	Rover MEMS 2J SFi
MG RV8 OHC 16V	V8 4.0	1993 to 1996	Lucas 14CUX MPi
Mini Cooper 1.3i	12A2DF75	1991 to 1996	Rover MEMS SPi
Mini Cooper 1.3i auto	12A2DF76	1991 to 1996	Rover MEMS SPi
Mini Cooper 1.3i Cabriolet	12A2EF77	1993 to 1994	Rover MEMS SPi
Mini 1.3i	12A2EK71	1996 to 1997	Rover MEMS SPi
Mini 1.3 MPi	12A2LK70	1996 to 2000	Rover MEMS MPi
Montego 2.0 EFi cat	20HF51	1990 to 1992	Lucas MPi 11CU
Montego 2.0 EFi auto cat	20HF52	1990 to 1992	Lucas MPi 11CU
Montego 2.0 EFi	20HE36	1989 to 1992	Rover MEMS MPi
Montego 2.0 EFi auto	20HE37	1989 to 1992	Rover MEMS MPi
Sterling V6 SOHC 24V	V6 2.5	1986 to 1988	Honda PGM-Fi

Plus All models equipped with EOBD (approximately January 2001-on)

Self-Diagnosis

1 Introduction

The engine management systems fitted to Rover vehicles are of Honda and Rover origin. Honda PGM-Fi, MEMS and Rover SPi systems control the primary ignition, fuel injection and idling functions from within the same control module. The Lucas MPi system (Lucas LH-Jetronic) controls the fuel injection and idle functions alone.

Self-Diagnosis (SD) function

Each ECM (electronic control module) has a self-test capability that continually examines the signals from certain engine sensors and actuators, and then compares each signal to a table of programmed values. If the diagnostic software determines that a fault is present, the ECM stores one or more fault codes in the ECM memory. Codes will not be stored about components for which a code is not available, or for conditions not covered by the diagnostic software.

Honda PGM-Fi

The Honda PGM-Fi system generates 2-digit fault codes. Code retrieval in models manufactured before 1992 (approximately) is by ECM-mounted LED, and after 1992 (approximately) by SD warning light. Fault code retrieval by FCR is not possible on vehicles equipped with Honda PGM-Fi.

All other Rover systems (except EOBD)

The majority of Rover systems do not generate fault code numbers. A fault code reader normally displays faults on the FCR screen without reference to a specific code number. Although actual code numbers are not available, faults in one or more of the circuits and components covered by the diagnostic software will cause a fault to be stored.

All EOBD models

The 5-digit fault codes can only be retrieved or cleared using an FCR.

Limited operating strategy (LOS)

The Rover systems featured in this Chapter utilise LOS (a function that is commonly called the "limp-home mode"). Once certain faults have been identified (not all faults will initiate LOS), the ECM will implement LOS and refer to a programmed default value rather than the sensor signal. This enables the vehicle to be safely driven to a workshop/garage for repair or testing. Once the fault has cleared, the ECM will revert to normal operation.

Adaptive or learning capability

Rover systems also utilise an adaptive function that will modify the basic programmed values for most effective operation during normal running, and with due regard to engine wear.

Self-Diagnosis (SD) warning light

The majority of Rover models with PGM-Fi that were manufactured before 1992 are equipped with an SD warning light located within the instrument panel, and a red LED mounted on the ECM.

The 825 2.5i and 2.7i have a red and a yellow LED; the yellow LED is used for rpm adjustment only, while the red LED is used for fault code retrieval. These models are not fitted with an SD connector.

Once the ignition has been switched on, the SD light illuminates as a bulb check, and after a few seconds extinguishes. If the SD warning light comes on at any time when the engine is running, this indicates that a fault in the system has been identified. The LED mounted in the ECM will flash to display a fault code, while the SD warning light will remain illuminated without flashing. When the ignition is switched off, both the SD warning light and LED will extinguish. When the ignition is switched on again, the SD warning light will only illuminate if the fault is still present, and the LED will resume flashing the fault code. This code will be stored in memory until cleared by following the procedures described later.

From approximately 1992 onwards, the majority of Rover vehicles with PGM-Fi are equipped with an SD connector and SD warning light; the LED(s) mounted on the ECM are no longer fitted. Once the ignition has been switched on, the SD light illuminates as a bulb check, and after a few seconds extinguishes. If the SD warning light comes on at any time when the engine is running, this indicates that a fault in the system has been identified. If a fault is indicated, bridging the terminals in the SD connector triggers the SD procedure, as described later. The control module generates 2-digit fault codes for display on the SD warning light.

Vehicles fitted with MEMS, Lucas MPi and Rover SPi are not equipped with either an LED or an SD warning light.

Models equipped with EOBD have a MIL (Malfunction Indicator Light) within the instrument cluster to alert the driver to the presence of a fault.

2 Self-Diagnosis connector location

PGM-Fi systems

The ECM is either located under the driver's seat, or under a metal cover fitted to the passenger's side footwell, under the carpet. The SD connector (where fitted) is located under the kick panel or the facia on the left-hand side (see illustration 28.1). **Note:** *The SD connector is provided for retrieving flash codes alone. Prior to 1992, flash codes can be observed on the LED on the ECM.*

MEMS and Lucas SPi systems

On the majority of vehicles equipped with MEMS and Rover SPi, the SD connector is located adjacent to the ECM. The ECM is located either close to the battery, or mounted centrally on the bulkhead (see illustration 28.2). **Note:** *The SD connector is provided for dedicated FCR use. Flash codes cannot be retrieved from these vehicles.*

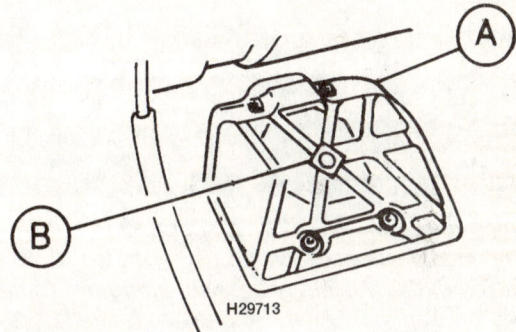

28.1 ECM location - PGM-Fi

A   Under metal cover plate in the front passenger footwell
B   The LED is visible through a cut-out

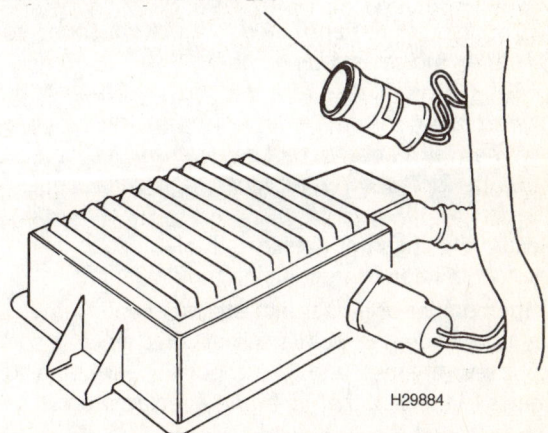

DIAGNOSTIC CONNECTOR PLUG

28.2 Rover MEMS - SD connector located close to the ECM, disconnected from wiring loom

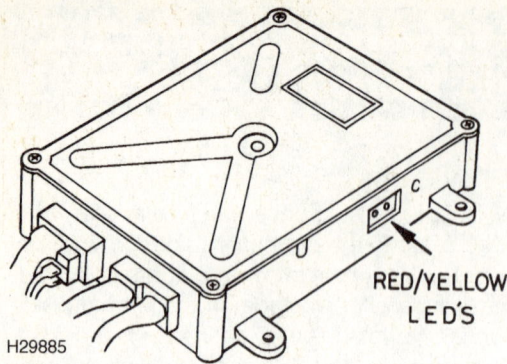

28.3 PGM-Fi ECM with LEDs set into the casing

Lucas MPi systems

On vehicles equipped with Lucas MPi, the SD connector is located close to the injection ECM, either under the driver's or the front passenger's seat.

Models with EOBD

On models equipped with EOBD, the 16-pin diagnostic connector is located under the facia - refer to Chapter 38.

3   Retrieving fault codes without a fault code reader (FCR) - flash codes

Note: *During the course of certain test procedures, it is possible for additional fault codes to be generated. Care must be taken that any codes generated during test routines do not mislead diagnosis. All codes must be cleared once testing is complete.*

Rover 216 and 416 with PGM-Fi (up to 1992)

1 Switch on the ignition.

2 Observe the red LED mounted in the centre of the ECM *(see illustration 28.3)*.

   a) *The flashes are transmitted as a straight count, so fifteen flashes indicates code number 15.*
   b) *The LED will pause for 2 seconds and then transmit the next code.*
   c) *When all codes have been transmitted, the LED will pause for 2 seconds and then repeat the sequence.*

3 Record the codes, and refer to the fault code table at the end of the Chapter to determine their meaning.

4 If the number of flashes indicates a number for which there is no code, the ECM is suspect. Recheck the code output several times, and then check the earth and supply voltages to the ECM before fitting a replacement.

5 When the ignition is switched off, the LED will extinguish. However, the LED will resume flashing once the ignition has been switched on again.

6 If the fault(s) are corrected, the LED will continue to flash until the ECM memory is cleared. The method is detailed in Section 4.

Rover 216, 416, 620 and 623 with PGM-Fi (1992 onwards)

7 Use a jumper lead to bridge the two terminals in the SD connector.

8 Switch on the ignition.

9 Observe the SD warning light on the facia. If the warning light remains on and does not flash, the ECM is in back-up mode. In this instance, the ECM should be removed and checked by one of the specialist ECM testing companies.

10 The flashes are transmitted as a series of long and short flashes:

   a) *Short flashes indicate single units - four short flashes indicates code number 4.*
   b) *Long flashes indicate multiples of ten - four long flashes and one short flash indicates code 41.*

11 After the first code is transmitted, the warning light will pause and then transmit the next code.

12 Count the number of flashes transmitted by the warning light, record the codes and refer to the fault code table at the end of the Chapter to determine their meaning.

13 When all codes have been transmitted, the warning light will pause and then repeat the sequence.

14 If the number of flashes indicates a number for which there is no code, the ECM is suspect. Recheck the code output several times, and then check the earth and supply voltages before fitting a replacement ECM.

Rover 825 2.5i and 827 2.7i with PGM-Fi

15 Switch on the ignition.

16 View the red LED mounted in the centre of the ECM (the yellow LED is used for rpm adjustment).

17 The flashes are transmitted as a straight count:

   a) *Fifteen flashes indicates code number 15.*
   b) *The LED will then pause for 2 seconds and then transmit the next code.*

18 Record the codes. When all codes have been transmitted, the LED will pause for 2 seconds and then repeat the sequence.

19 If the number of flashes indicate a number for which there is no code, the ECM is suspect. Recheck several times and then check the earth and supply voltages to the ECM before fitting a replacement.

20 When the ignition is switched off, the LED will extinguish. However, the LED will resume flashing once the ignition has been switched on again.

21 If the fault(s) are corrected, the LED will continue to flash until the ECM memory is cleared. The method is detailed in Section 4.

All other models

22 A fault code reader (FCR) is required to display faults generated in Rover SD systems other than PGM-Fi.

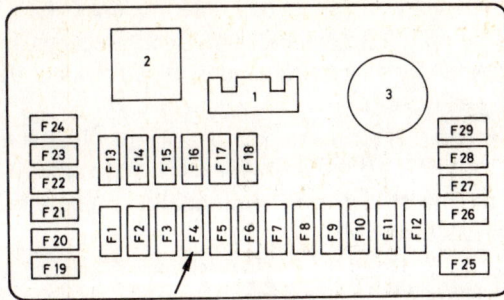

28.4 Location of 10-amp No 4 fuse

4   Clearing fault codes without a fault code reader (FCR)

Rover 216 and 416 with PGM-Fi (before 1992)

1 Clear the fault codes by removing the 10-amp No 4 fuse in the fusebox for a period of 10 seconds *(see illustration 28.4)*.

Rover 216, 416, 620 and 623 with PGM-Fi (after 1992)

2 Clear the fault codes by removing the 7.5-amp No 7 back-up fuse in the fusebox for a period of 30 seconds *(see illustration 28.5)*.

Rover 825 2.5i and 827 2.7i with PGM-Fi

3 Clear the fault codes by removing the 10-amp No 19 alternator fuse in the main fusebox for at least 10 seconds *(see illustration 28.6)*.

Rover 820 and Montego with Lucas MPi

4 Lucas MPi utilises volatile memory, and disconnecting the battery will clear any faults. **Note:** *The first drawback to this method is that battery disconnection will re-initialise all ECM adaptive values. Re-learning the appropriate adaptive values requires starting the engine from cold, and driving at various engine speeds for approximately 20 to 30 minutes. The engine should also be allowed to idle for approximately 10 minutes. The second drawback is that the radio security codes, clock setting and other stored values will be initialised, and these must be re-entered once the battery has been reconnected. Where possible, an FCR should be used for fault clearing.*

Rover 820 with Rover SPi

5 Rover SPi utilises volatile memory, and disconnecting the battery will clear faults. Refer to the note in paragraph 4 above. When disconnecting the battery, the ECM will clear the programmed CO mixture setting and return to a default value, which usually results in a rich mixture. The remedy is to reset the CO mixture with the aid of an FCR. Where possible, an FCR should be used for fault clearing.

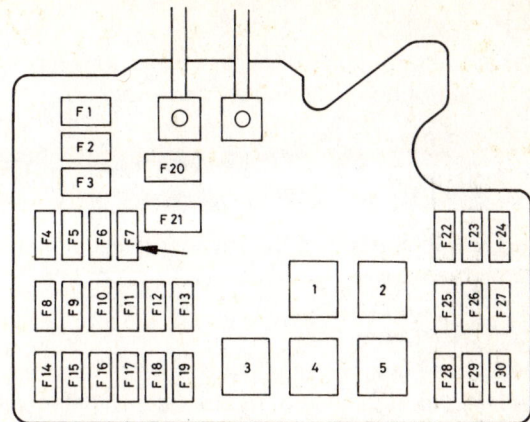

28.5 Location of back-up fuse

Rover MEMS

6 Vehicles fitted with MEMS are equipped with non-volatile memory, and faults cannot be cleared by disconnecting the battery. An FCR must be used for fault clearing in this instance.

EOBD models

7 On models equipped with EOBD, an FCR is essential for retrieving and clearing fault codes.

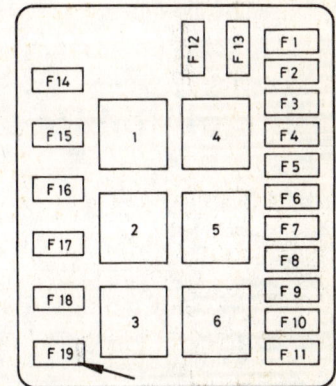

28.6 Location of alternator fuse

5   Self-Diagnosis with a fault code reader (FCR)

Note: *During the course of certain test procedures, it is possible for additional fault codes to be generated. Care must be taken that any codes generated during test routines do not mislead diagnosis.*

All Rover systems except PGM-Fi

1 Connect an FCR to the SD connector. Use the FCR for the following purposes, in strict compliance with the FCR manufacturer's instructions:

    a) Displaying faults.
    b) Clearing fault codes or faults.
    c) Testing actuators.
    d) Displaying Datastream (Rover MEMS and EOBD only).
    e) Making adjustments.

2 Codes must always be cleared after component testing, or after repairs involving the removal or replacement of an engine management component.

PGM-Fi systems

3 Fault code retrieval by FCR is not possible on vehicles equipped with Honda PGM-Fi. Refer to Section 3.

<hr>

6   Guide to test procedures

1 Use an FCR to interrogate the ECM for faults, or gather fault codes manually, as applicable (see Section 3 or 5).

Faults/codes stored

2 If one or more faults or codes are gathered, refer to the fault code tables at the end of this Chapter to determine their meaning.

3 If several faults or codes are gathered, look for a common factor such as a defective earth return or supply.

4 Refer to the component test procedures in Chapter 4, where you will find a means of testing the majority of

components and circuits found in the modern EMS.

5 Once the fault has been repaired, clear the codes and run the engine under various conditions to determine if the problem has cleared.

6 Check the ECM for faults or codes once more. Repeat the above procedures where faults are still being stored.

7 Refer to Chapter 3 for more information on how to effectively test the EMS.

No faults/codes stored

8 Where a running problem is experienced, but no faults are stored, the fault is outside of the parameters designed into the SD system. Refer to Chapter 3 for more information on how to effectively test the engine management system.

9 If the problem points to a specific component, refer to the test procedures in Chapter 4, where you will find a means of testing the majority of components and circuits found in the modern EMS.

Fault code tables

Honda PGM-Fi

Flash/ FCR code	Description
0	Electronic control module (ECM)
1	Oxygen sensor (OS) or OS circuit (except D16A9 engine)
3	Manifold absolute pressure (MAP) sensor or MAP sensor circuit
5	Manifold absolute pressure (MAP) sensor or MAP sensor circuit
4	Crank angle sensor (CAS) or CAS circuit
6	Coolant temperature sensor (CTS) or CTS circuit
7	Throttle pot sensor (TPS) or TPS circuit
8	Top dead centre (TDC) position sensor or TDC circuit
9	No. 1 cylinder position (CID sensor)
10	Air temperature sensor (ATS) or ATS circuit
11	CO pot or CO pot circuit
12	Exhaust gas recirculation (EGR) system or EGR circuit
13	Atmospheric pressure sensor (APS) or APS circuit
14	Idle speed control valve (ISCV) or ISCV circuit
15	Ignition output signal
16	Fuel injector or fuel injector circuit (D15B2 engine)
17	Vehicle speed sensor (VSS) or VSS circuit
18	Ignition timing
19	Automatic transmission lock-up control solenoid valve A/B
20	Electronic load detector (ELD) or ELD circuit
21	Spool solenoid valve (variable valve timing) or spool solenoid circuit
22	Valve timing oil pressure switch
30	Automatic transmission (AT), signal A
31	Automatic transmission (AT), signal B
41	Oxygen sensor (OS) heater or OS circuit (D16Z6, D16Z7, B16A2 engine)
41	Linear airflow (LAF, oxygen sensor) heater or LAF sensor circuit (D15Z1 engine)
43	Fuel supply system or circuit (D16Z6, D16Z7, B16Z2 engine)
48	Linear airflow (LAF, oxygen sensor) sensor or LAF sensor circuit (D15Z1 engine)

Rover MEMS, Lucas MPi and Lucas SPi

Rover software generates only limited fault codes, and the FCR normally displays faults on the FCR screen without reference to a specific code number. Faults in one or more of the following list of circuits and components will cause a fault to be stored. Please note that not all circuits are available on all systems.

All models with EOBD

For a list of the allocated EOBD codes beginning with P0 (Generic Powertrain), refer to Chapter 1, Section 1.

Typical circuits checked by Rover MEMS, Lucas SPi and Lucas MPi

Airflow sensor (AFS) or AFS circuit
Air conditioning
Air temperature sensor (ATS) or ATS circuit
Alternator
Battery supply to ECM
Camshaft position sensor (CMP) or CMP circuit
Coolant temperature sensor (CTS) or CTS circuit
Crank angle sensor (CAS) or CAS circuit
Fuel temperature sensor/switch (FTS) or FTS circuit
Heated rear window
Injectors
Knock sensor (KS) or KS sensor
Manifold absolute pressure (MAP) sensor or MAP circuit
Oxygen sensor (OS) or OS circuit (cat only)
Relay circuit
Stepper motor
Starter motor
Throttle pot sensor (TPS) or TPS circuit
Turbo boost valve
Vehicle speed sensor (VSS) or VSS circuit

29

Index of vehicles

Model	Engine code	Year	System
900i 16V DOHC	B202i	1989 to 1990	Lucas 14CU LH-Jetronic
900 Turbo 16V DOHC	B202 2S	1988 to 1990	Lucas 14CU LH-Jetronic
900 2.0 16V DOHC cat	B202 2L	1989 to 1993	Lucas 14CU LH1-Jetronic
900i 16V DOHC cat	B202i	1990 to 1993	Lucas 14CU LH-Jetronic
900S Turbo cat	B202i	1990 to 1993	Lucas 14CU LH-Jetronic
900 2.0i 16V DOHC	B202i	1993 to 1998	Bosch Motronic 2.10.2
900 Turbo 16V DOHC	B202i	1994 to 1997	Saab Trionic
900i 16V DOHC	B206i	1994 to 1998	Bosch Motronic 2.10.2
900i 16V DOHC	B204L	1994 to 1998	Bosch Motronic 2.10.2
900 2.3i 16V DOHC	B234i	1993 to 1998	Bosch Motronic 2.10.2
900 2.5i 24V DOHC	B258i	1993 to 1997	Bosch Motronic 2.8.1
9000i 16V cat	B202i	1988 to 1993	Bosch LH2.4-Jetronic
9000 and CD16	B202	1991 to 1993	Bosch LH2.4.2-Jetronic
9000 16V cat	B202	1988 to 1993	Bosch LH2.4-Jetronic
9000 Turbo 16	B202	1991 to 1993	Bosch LH2.4.2-Jetronic
9000 Turbo 16 cat	B202	1989 to 1993	Bosch LH2.4-Jetronic
9000 2.0i cat	B204i	1994 to 1998	Saab Trionic
9000 2.0 Turbo cat	B204S	1994 to 1998	Saab Trionic
9000 2.0 Ecopower	B202S	1992 to 1993	Bosch LH2.4-Jetronic
9000 2.0 Turbo Intercooler	B204L	1994 to 1997	Saab Trionic
9000i 2.3 cat	B234i	1990 to 1991	Bosch LH2.4.1-Jetronic
9000i 2.3 cat	B234i	1991 to 1993	Bosch LH2.4.2-Jetronic
9000 2.3i cat	B234i	1994 to 1997	Saab Trionic
9000 2.3 Turbo cat	B234L	1994 to 1998	Saab Trionic
9000 2.3 Turbo cat	B234R	1994 to 1998	Saab Trionic
9000 2.3 Turbo cat	B234R	1993	Saab Trionic
9000 2.3 Turbo cat	B234L	1991 to 1993	Bosch LH2.4-Jetronic/ Saab Direct Ignition
9000 2.3 Ecopower L/P Turbo	B234E	1994 to 1998	Saab Trionic
9000 3.0 24V DOHC	B308i	1995 to 1997	Bosch Motronic 2.8.1

Plus All models equipped with EOBD (approximately January 2001-on)

Chapter 29

Self-Diagnosis

1   Introduction

The engine management systems fitted to Saab vehicles are mainly of Lucas, Bosch, Saab or General Motors origin. Bosch Motronic controls fuel injection, ignition and idle functions from within the same control module. Saab Trionic controls the ignition, fuel injection, idle and turbo boost pressure. Saab Direct Ignition controls ignition and Turbo boost alone. Lucas 14CU and Bosch LH fuel injection systems control fuel injection and idle functions alone.

Self-Diagnosis (SD) function

Each ECM (electronic control module) has a self-test capability that continually examines the signals from certain engine sensors and actuators, and then compares each signal to a table of programmed values. If the diagnostic software determines that a fault is present, the ECM stores one or more fault codes in the ECM memory. Codes will not be stored about components for which a code is not available, or for conditions not covered by the diagnostic software. Saab models generate either 2- or 5-digit fault codes, which may be retrieved either by fault code reader (all systems) or by manual means as flash codes (all except Saab Trionic and Saab Direct Ignition).

All models equipped with EOBD generate 5-digit fault codes which can only be retrieved or cleared using an FCR (Fault Code Reader).

Limited operating strategy (LOS)

Saab systems featured in this Chapter utilise LOS (a function that is commonly called the "limp-home mode"). Once certain faults have been identified (not all faults will initiate LOS), the ECM will implement LOS and refer to a programmed default value rather than the sensor signal. This enables the vehicle to be safely driven to a workshop/garage for repair or testing. Once the fault has cleared, the ECM will revert to normal operation.

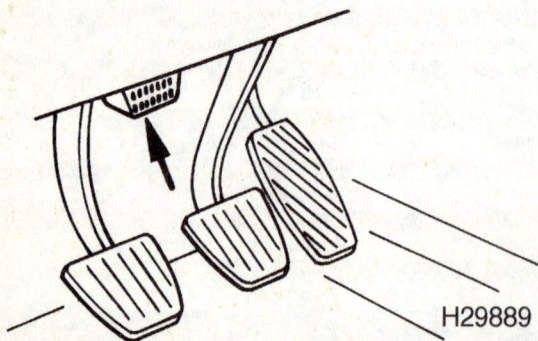

H29889

29.1 Location of 16-pin SD connector (arrowed) under facia and above pedals

Adaptive or learning capability

Saab systems also utilise an adaptive function that will modify the basic programmed values for most effective operation during normal running, and with due regard to engine wear.

Self-Diagnosis (SD) warning light

Saab models are equipped with an SD (Check Engine)/MIL (Malfunction Indicator Light) warning light located within the instrument panel. Some fault conditions will illuminate the light during normal engine operation, and the ECM will need to be interrogated to determine if fault codes are indeed stored in ECM fault memory.

2   Self-Diagnosis connector location

Bosch Motronic and Saab Trionic

The 16-pin SD connector for FCR use and manual code retrieval is located either under the facia on the driver's side above the foot pedals *(see illustration 29.1)* or under the passenger's seat.

Lucas 14CU

The 3-pin SD connector is for FCR use and manual code retrieval, and is located in the engine compartment, adjacent to the heater air intake.

Bosch LH 2.4, 2.4.1, 2.4.2

The SD connector for FCR use and manual code retrieval is situated in one of the following locations: under the rear seat, in the engine compartment, or in front of the gear selector.

Saab Trionic and Saab Direct Ignition

The SD connector is black, and is located close to the ECM under the right-hand front seat.

All models with EOBD

On these models, the 16-pin diagnostic connector is located under the facia - refer to Chapter 38.

3   Retrieving fault codes without a fault code reader (FCR) - flash codes

Note: *During the course of certain test procedures, it is possible for additional fault codes to be generated. Care must be taken that any codes generated during test routines do not mislead diagnosis. All codes must be cleared once testing is complete.*

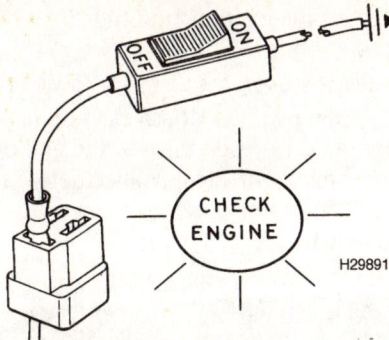

29.2 Initiation of flash codes with the aid of an accessory switch connected to the SD connector - Lucas 14CU and Bosch LH

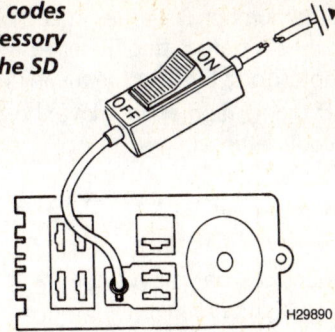

29.3 Initiation of flash codes with the aid of an accessory switch connected to the SD connector - Bosch LH

Lucas 14CU

1 Attach an accessory switch between the SD connector and earth (see illustration 29.2).

2 Switch on the ignition and the SD warning light will illuminate.

3 Immediately close the accessory switch. The SD warning light will extinguish and then illuminate for one short flash.

4 Immediately open the accessory switch.

5 The SD warning light will display the 5-digit fault codes as follows:

    a) The five digits are indicated by five series of flashes.

    b) The first series of flashes indicates the first digit, the second series of flashes indicates the second digit, and so on until all five digits have been flashed.

    c) Each series consists of a number of flashes separated by short pauses. Each integer (whole number) in the range 1 to 9 is represented by a number of short flashes, and each zero is represented by a longer flash.

    d) A pause separates each series of flashes.

    e) The code number "12232" is indicated by a flash, a short pause, two flashes, a short pause, two flashes, a short pause, three flashes, a short pause and two flashes. A long flash is displayed at the beginning and end of each code.

6 Count the number of flashes in each series, and record each code as it is transmitted. Refer to the tables at the end of the Chapter to determine the meaning of the fault code.

7 To retrieve the next code, close the accessory switch and wait for the SD warning light to flash once.

8 Immediately open the accessory switch, and the SD warning light will display the next 5-digit fault code.

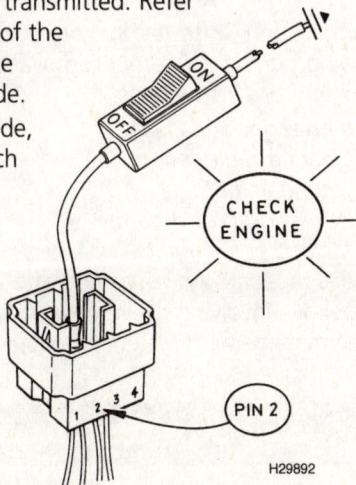

29.4 Initiation of flash codes with the aid of an accessory switch connected to the SD connector - Bosch LH

9 Repeat the procedure until all fault codes have been retrieved.

10 If a return to the first code is required, close the accessory switch and wait for the SD warning light to flash twice, then immediately open the accessory switch. The first code will be transmitted again.

11 Five long flashes indicates that all the fault codes have been retrieved, or that no codes are stored.

12 Turn off the ignition and remove the accessory switch to end fault code retrieval.

Bosch LH 2.4, 2.4.1, 2.4.2

13 Attach an accessory switch between the SD connector and earth (see illustrations 29.2 to 29.4).

14 Switch on the ignition, and the SD warning light will illuminate and then extinguish.

15 Close the accessory switch. The SD warning light will illuminate for one short flash.

16 Immediately open the accessory switch.

17 The SD warning light will display the 5-digit fault codes in the same way as described for the Lucas 14CU system (see paragraphs 5 to 12).

Bosch Motronic 2.8.1 and 2.10.2

18 Attach an accessory switch between pin 6 of the 16-pin SD connector and earth.

19 Switch on the ignition.

20 Close the accessory switch for between 1 and 4 seconds.

21 Open the switch, the SD warning light will now illuminate for 2.5 seconds, extinguish and then flash to indicate the 2-digit fault codes as follows:

    a) The two digits are indicated by two series of flashes.

    b) The first series of flashes indicates the multiples of ten, the second series of flashes indicates the single units.

    c) A 1-second flash followed by a 0.5-second interval indicates fault codes in tens. After a 1.5-second pause, a 1-second flash followed by a 0.5-second interval indicates units.

    d) Code number "12" is indicated by one 1-second flash, followed by a 1.5-second pause, then two 1-second flashes with a 0.5-second pause.

    e) A 2-second pause separates the transmission of each individual code.

22 Count the number of flashes in each series, and record each code as it is transmitted. Refer to the tables at the end of the Chapter to determine the meaning of the fault code.
23 Turn off the ignition and remove the accessory switch to end fault code retrieval.

Saab Trionic, Saab Direct Ignition and all models with EOBD
24 Fault codes can only be retrieved with the aid of a dedicated fault code reader.

4 Clearing fault codes without a fault code reader (FCR)

Bosch LH 2.4, 2.4.1, 2.4.2
1 Retrieve codes from the ECM by the methods described in Section 3. **Note:** *The ECM memory can be cleared only after all codes have been transmitted and the five long flashes have been displayed.*
2 Close the accessory switch, and wait for the warning light to flash three times. Open the accessory switch. The memory has now been cleared of all fault codes.

All other systems (except EOBD)
3 Disconnect the battery negative terminal for five minutes.
4 Reconnect the battery negative terminal.
Note: *The first drawback to this method is that battery disconnection will re-initialise all ECM adaptive values. Re-learning the appropriate adaptive values requires starting the engine from cold, and driving at various engine speeds for approximately 20 to 30 minutes. The engine should also be allowed to idle for approximately 10 minutes. The second drawback is that the radio security codes, clock setting and other stored values will be initialised, and these must be re-entered once the battery has been reconnected. Where possible, an FCR should be used for code clearing.*

Models with EOBD
5 An FCR is essential for retrieving and clearing fault codes.

5 Actuator testing without a fault code reader (FCR) - Bosch LH2.4 only

Bosch LH 2.4 only (1989 Saab 900 T16 automatic)
1 Attach an accessory switch between the SD connector and earth *(refer to illustrations 29.2 to 29.4)*.
2 Close the accessory switch.

3 Switch on the ignition, and the SD warning light will briefly flash once.
4 Immediately open the accessory switch.
5 The warning light will flash the appropriate code (see the actuator selection code table at the end of this Chapter) and the first component circuit will actuate. Audible operation (typically, clicking or buzzing) of the actuator solenoid or component should be heard.

> *Warning: When testing the injectors, there is a real danger of filling the cylinders with petrol. If testing is required for more than 1 second, disconnect the fuel pump supply (or remove the fuel pump fuse) before commencing this test.*

6 Discontinue the first test, and continue with the next component by closing the accessory switch once more.
7 Wait until the SD warning light briefly flashes once, and then immediately open the accessory switch.
8 The warning light will flash the appropriate code, and the next actuator circuit will function.
9 Repeat the procedure to test each of the other actuators in turn.
10 Turn off the ignition to end the test.

6 Self-Diagnosis with a fault code reader (FCR)

Note: *During the course of certain test procedures, it is possible for additional fault codes to be generated. Care must be taken that any codes generated during test routines do not mislead diagnosis.*

All Saab models
1 Connect an FCR to the SD connector. Use the FCR for the following purposes, in strict compliance with the FCR manufacturer's instructions:
   a) *Retrieving fault codes.*
   b) *Clearing fault codes.*
   c) *Testing actuators.*
   d) *Displaying Datastream.*
   e) *Making adjustments.*
2 Codes must always be cleared after component testing, or after repairs involving the removal or replacement of an engine management system component.

7 Guide to test procedures

1 Use an FCR to interrogate the ECM for fault codes, or (where possible) gather codes manually, as described in Sections 3 or 6.

Codes stored

2 If one or more fault codes are gathered, refer to the fault code tables at the end of this Chapter to determine their meaning.

3 If several codes are gathered, look for a common factor such as a defective earth return or supply.

4 Refer to the component test procedures in Chapter 4, where you will find a means of testing the majority of components and circuits found in the modern EMS.

5 Once the fault has been repaired, clear the codes and run the engine under various conditions to determine if the problem has cleared.

6 Check the ECM for fault codes once more. Repeat the above procedures where codes are still being stored.

7 Refer to Chapter 3 for more information on how to effectively test the EMS.

No codes stored

8 Where a running problem is experienced, but no codes are stored, the fault is outside of the parameters designed into the SD system. Refer to Chapter 3 for more information on how to effectively test the engine management system.

9 If the problem points to a specific component, refer to the test procedures in Chapter 4, where you will find a means of testing the majority of components and circuits found in the modern EMS.

Fault code tables

Lucas 14CU

Flash/ FCR code	Description
13212	Throttle pot sensor (TPS) or TPS circuit
13213	Throttle pot sensor (TPS) or TPS circuit
13214	Coolant temperature sensor (CTS) or CTS circuit
13215	Throttle pot sensor (TPS) or TPS circuit
13221	Airflow sensor (AFS) or AFS circuit
13222	Idle air control
13223	Weak mixture
13224	Rich mixture
13225	Oxygen sensor (OS) or OS circuit
13231	Ignition signal
13233	Electronic control module (ECM) fault
13234	Vehicle speed sensor (VSS) or VSS circuit
13235	No "Drive" signal - automatic transmission or circuit

Motronic 2.10.2, 2.8.1

Flash/ FCR code	Description
11	Secondary injection or circuit
12	No faults found in the ECM. Proceed with normal diagnostic methods
21	Airflow sensor (AFS) or AFS circuit
31	Air temperature sensor (ATS) or ATS circuit
41	Coolant temperature sensor (CTS) or CTS circuit
51	Throttle pot sensor (TPS) or TPS circuit
61	Oxygen sensor (OS) cylinder 1, 3, 5 or OS circuit
62	Oxygen sensor (OS) cylinder 2, 4, 6 or OS circuit
71	Oxygen sensor (OS) cylinder 1, 3, 5, rich or lean
72	Oxygen sensor (OS) cylinder 2, 4, 6, rich or lean
73	Oxygen sensor (OS) rich or lean
81	Evaporative emission canister purge valve or circuit
91	Electronic control module (ECM)
92	Electronic control module (ECM)

Saab Trionic

Flash/ FCR code	Description
P0105	Manifold absolute pressure (MAP) sensor or MAP sensor circuit
P0106	Manifold absolute pressure (MAP) sensor or MAP sensor circuit, signal low
P0107	Manifold absolute pressure (MAP) sensor or MAP sensor circuit, signal high
P0108	Manifold absolute pressure (MAP) sensor or MAP sensor circuit
P0110	Air temperature sensor (ATS) or ATS circuit
P0112	Air temperature sensor (ATS) or ATS circuit, signal low
P0113	Air temperature sensor (ATS) or ATS circuit, signal high
P0115	Coolant temperature sensor (CTS) or CTS circuit
P0117	Coolant temperature sensor (CTS) or CTS circuit, signal low
P0118	Coolant temperature sensor (CTS) or CTS circuit, signal high
P0120	Throttle pot sensor (TPS) or TPS circuit
P0121	Throttle pot sensor (TPS) or TPS circuit
P0122	Throttle pot sensor (TPS) or TPS circuit, signal low
P0123	Throttle pot sensor (TPS) or TPS circuit, signal high
P0130	Oxygen sensor (OS) or OS circuit
P0135	Oxygen sensor (OS) or OS circuit
P1130	Oxygen sensor (OS) or OS circuit, current high
P1135	Oxygen sensor (OS) or OS circuit, current low
P0170	Fuel/air mixture or circuit
P0171	Weak mixture
P0172	Rich mixture
P1322	Engine speed (RPM) sensor or circuit
P0325	Knock sensor (KS) or KS circuit
P0335	Engine speed (RPM) sensor or circuit
P0335	Crank angle sensor (CAS) or CAS circuit
P0443	Carbon filter solenoid valve (CFSV) or CFSV circuit
P1443	Carbon filter solenoid valve (CFSV) or CFSV circuit
P1444	Carbon filter solenoid valve (CFSV) or CFSV circuit, current high
P1445	Carbon filter solenoid valve (CFSV) or CFSV circuit, current low
P0500	Vehicle speed sensor (VSS) or VSS circuit
P0501	Vehicle speed sensor (VSS) or VSS circuit
P0502	Vehicle speed sensor (VSS) or VSS circuit, signal low
P0505	Idle speed control valve (ISCV) or ISCV circuit
P1500	Battery voltage
P0605	Electronic control module (ECM)
P1651	Electronic control module (ECM)
P1652	Electronic control module (ECM)

Bosch LH 2.4/2.4.1/2.4.2 (flash codes)

Flash code	Description
12111	Oxygen sensor (OS) fault (fuel air mixture on idling)
12112	Oxygen sensor (OS) fault (fuel air mixture engine at cruising speed)
12113	Idle speed control valve (ISCV) adaption fault, pulse ratio too low
12114	Idle speed control valve (ISCV) adaption fault, pulse ratio to high
12211	Battery voltage, less than 10 volts or greater than 16 volts
12212	Throttle switch (TS), idle contacts
12213	Throttle switch (TS), full-load contacts
12214	Temperature sensor signal faulty (below 90°C or above 160°C)
12221	No air mass meter signal
12222	Air conditioning system faulty
12223	Fuel air mixture lean, OS sensor shorting to earth
12224	Fuel air mixture rich, OS sensor shorting to battery voltage
12225	Oxygen sensor (OS) or OS heater fault
12232	Voltage supply to ECM pin 4 is less than 1 volt
12233	Fault in electronic control module (ECM) - read only memory (ROM)
12241	Mixture lean
12242	Hot-wire burn-off function faulty
12243	No signal from vehicle speed sensor
12244	No "Drive" signal (automatic transmission)
12245	Exhaust gas recirculation (EGR) function faulty
00000	No faults detected, or all fault codes have been transmitted

Bosch LH 2.4 actuator selection code table

Note: *The actuators will actuate in the following sequence. Listen for an audible sound, or touch the component to determine whether it has been activated*

Code	Description
No display	Fuel pump circuit
12411	Injector circuit
12412	Idle speed control valve (ISCV) circuit
12413	Carbon filter solenoid valve (CFSV) circuit
12421	Automatic transmission (auto) drive signal. The SD light ceases flashing when the gear lever is moved from "D" to "N"
12424	Throttle switch (TS), idle contacts. Slightly open the throttle. The SD light ceases flashing once the throttle moves away from the idle position
12431	Throttle switch (TS), full-load contacts. Fully open the throttle. The SD light ceases flashing as the throttle approaches the fully-open position

Bosch LH 2.4/2.4.2 and Saab Direct Ignition (FCR codes)

FCR code (permanent)	FCR code (intermittent)	Description
11111	-	Reply code for OK
42241	22241	High voltage (1991-on)
42251	22251	Electronic control module (ECM) pin 4, signal low
42252	22252	Signal low, less than 10 volts
42291	22291	Battery voltage, less than 10 volts/greater than 16 volts
42440	22440	Oxygen sensor (OS) or OS circuit, rich mixture
42441	22441	Rich mixture, idling (1991-on)
42442	22442	Rich mixture, driving (1991-on)
42450	22450	Oxygen sensor (OS) or OS circuit, weak mixture
42451	22451	Weak mixture, idling (1991-on)
42452	22452	Weak mixture, driving (1991-on)
42460	22460	Oxygen sensor (OS) or OS circuit
42491	22491	Idling mixture incorrect
42492	22492	Driving mixture incorrect
44221	24221	Engine RPM signal absent (1991-on)
44261	24261	Vehicle speed sensor (VSS) or VSS circuit (1991-on)
44360	24360	Crank angle sensor (CAS) or CAS circuit
44460	24460	Engine load signal faulty
44660	24660	Pre-ignition fault (knocking or pinking)
44661	24461	Knock sensor (KS) or KS circuit
44662	24462	Combustion, synchronising fault
44671	24671	Pre-ignition signal over 20 seconds
45641	25641	Mass airflow (MAF) sensor or MAF sensor circuit, signal high
45651	25651	Mass airflow (MAF) sensor or MAF sensor circuit, signal low
45691	25691	Mass Airflow (MAF) sensor or MAF sensor circuit
45723	25723	"Drive" signal (automatic transmission)
45771	25771	Throttle pot sensor (TPS) signal or TPS circuit
45772	25772	Throttle pot sensor (TPS) signal or TPS circuit
46221	26221	Coolant temperature sensor (CTS) or CTS circuit, signal low
46271	26271	Coolant temperature sensor (CTS) or CTS circuit, signal high
46391	26391	Exhaust gas recirculation (EGR) system or EGR circuit
58121	38121	Mass airflow (MAF) sensor or MAF sensor circuit, burn-off absent
58321	38321	Air conditioning valve function or circuit
58322	38322	Evaporative loss control device (ELCD) valve function or circuit
58371	38371	Injector or injector circuit
58372	38372	Evaporative loss control device (ELCD) valve or circuit
58382	38382	Evaporative loss control device (ELCD) valve short-circuit (1991-on)
60000	-	Internal monitoring
60001	-	Read only memory (ROM) fault
60002	-	Random access memory (RAM) fault
67192	-	Electronic control module (ECM), read only memory (ROM)

All models with EOBD

For a list of the allocated EOBD codes beginning with P0 (Generic Powertrain), refer to Chapter 1, Section 1.

SEAT

30

Index of vehicles

Model	Engine code	Year	System
Alhambra 2.0	ADY	1996 to 2001	Simos
Cordoba 1.4i SOHC 8V	ABD	1994 to 1997	Bosch Mono-Motronic
Cordoba 1.6i SOHC 8V	ABU	1993 to 1997	Bosch Mono-Motronic
Cordoba 1.8i SOHC 8V	ABS	1993 to 1995	Bosch Mono-Motronic
Cordoba 1.8i 16V	ADL	1994 to 1998	VAG Digifant
Cordoba 2.0i SOHC 8V	2E	1993 to 1997	VAG Digifant
Ibiza 1.05i SOHC 8V	AAU	1993 to 1997	Bosch Mono-Motronic
Ibiza 1.3i US83	AAV	1993 to 1994	Bosch Mono-Motronic
Ibiza 1.4i SOHC 8V	ABD	1994 to 1997	Bosch Mono-Motronic
Ibiza 1.6i SOHC 8V	ABU	1993 to 1997	Bosch Mono-Motronic
Ibiza 1.8i SOHC 8V	ABS	1993 to 1995	Bosch Mono-Motronic
Ibiza 1.8i 16V	ADL	1994 to 1998	VAG Digifant
Ibiza 2.0i SOHC 8V	2E	1993 to 1997	VAG Digifant
Inca 1.4i	AEX/APQ	1995 to 2000	Bosch Motronic MP 9.0
Inca 1.6i	1F	1995 to 1998	Bosch Mono-Motronic
Toledo 1.6i cat SOHC	1F	1991 to 1998	Bosch Mono-Jetronic
Toledo 1.6i SOHC	1F	1994 to 1997	Bosch Mono-Motronic
Toledo 1.8i SOHC	RP	1991 to 1995	Bosch Mono-Jetronic
Toledo 1.8i cat SOHC	RP	1991 to 1995	Bosch Mono-Jetronic
Toledo 1.8i cat SOHC	RP	1991 to 1996	Bosch Mono-Motronic
Toledo 1.8i SOHC 8V	ABS	1994 to 1997	Bosch Mono-Motronic
Toledo 2.0i	2E	1991 to 1999	VAG Digifant

Plus All models equipped with EOBD (approximately January 2001-on)

Self-Diagnosis

1   Introduction

The engine management systems (EMSs) fitted to SEAT models are of Bosch, VAG, Siemens or Magneti-Marelli origin. Bosch Motronic MP9.0, Mono-Motronic, VAG Digifant and Simos systems control the primary ignition, fuel injection and idling functions from within the same control module. Mono-Jetronic controls the fuel injection and idle functions alone.

Self-Diagnosis (SD) function

Each electronic control module (ECM) has a self-test capability that continually examines the signals from certain engine sensors and actuators, and compares each signal to a table of programmed values. If the diagnostic software

30•1

determines that a fault is present, the ECM stores one or more fault codes. Codes will not be stored about components for which a code is not available, or for conditions not covered by the diagnostic software.

SEAT systems are capable of generating two kinds of fault codes. These are 4-digit flash codes and 5-digit fault codes:

a) *Mono-Jetronic systems can only generate 4-digit flash codes. These can be retrieved via the warning light (where fitted), or by using a separate LED. Alternatively, fault codes can be displayed on a dedicated fault code reader (FCR).*

b) *Later systems can generate both 4-digit and 5-digit fault codes, and retrieval requires a dedicated FCR. These systems include early versions of Bosch Mono-Motronic and some VAG Digifant (45-pin).*

c) *The very latest systems can only generate 5-digit fault codes, and these must be retrieved with the aid of a dedicated FCR. These systems include Bosch Mono-Motronic MA1.2.2 (later 45-pin), Simos and VAG Digifant (68-pin).*

d) *On models equipped with EOBD, the 5-digit fault codes can only be retrieved or cleared using an FCR.*

Limited operating strategy (LOS)

All SEAT models featured in this Chapter except those with Bosch Mono-Jetronic utilise LOS (a function that is commonly called the "limp-home mode"). Once certain faults have been identified (not all faults will initiate LOS), the ECM will implement LOS and refer to a programmed default value rather than the sensor signal. This enables the vehicle to be safely driven to a workshop/garage for repair or testing. Once the fault has cleared, the ECM will revert to normal operation. Bosch Mono-Jetronic does not have LOS.

Adaptive or learning capability

SEAT systems also utilise an adaptive function that will modify the basic programmed values for most effective operation during normal running and with due regard to engine wear.

Self-Diagnosis (SD) warning light

Bosch Mono-Jetronic equipped vehicles are also fitted with an SD warning light located within the instrument panel. SEAT models equipped with engine management systems other than Bosch Mono-Jetronic are not fitted with a SD warning light.

All models equipped with EOBD are fitted with a MIL (Malfunction Indicator Light) within the instrument cluster, to alert the driver to the presence of a fault.

2   Self-Diagnosis connector location

Bosch Mono-Jetronic and Mono-Motronic with dual 2-pin connectors

The two SD connectors are located in the passenger compartment under the facia, or in the switch hole next to the light switch on the instrument panel *(see illustration 30.1)* and is provided for retrieving flash codes (Mono-Jetronic only) and for use with a dedicated fault code reader (FCR).

Alhambra

The 16-pin SD connector is located under the ashtray in the centre console *(see illustration 30.2),* and is provided for use with a dedicated FCR only.

Other systems

The 16-pin SD connector may be located in the passenger compartment to the right of the steering column, or under the facia in the fusebox above the foot pedals - refer to Chapter 38. The SD connector is provided for use with a dedicated FCR only.

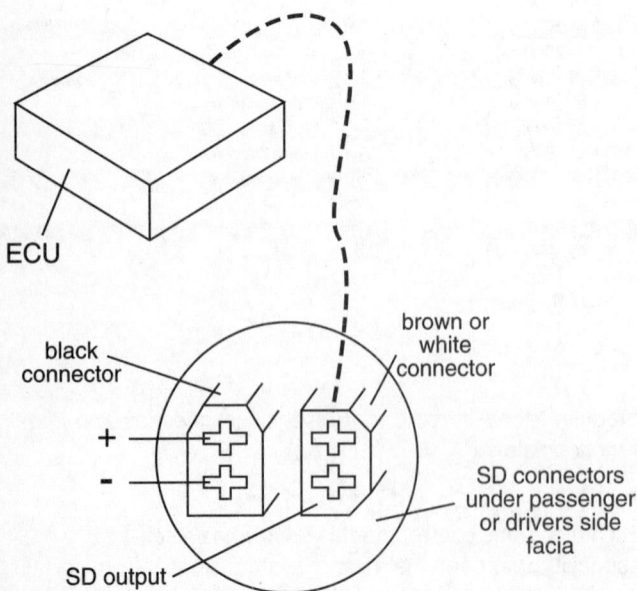

30.1 Location of SD connectors under facia

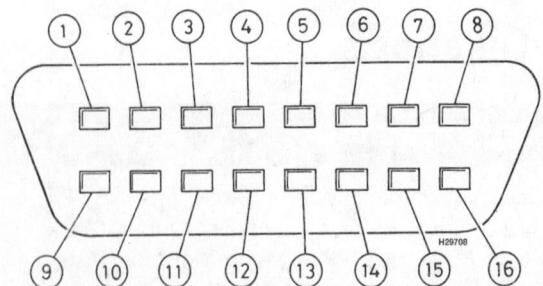

30.2 The 16-pin OBD connector

3 Retrieving fault codes without a fault code reader (FCR) - flash codes

Note: *During the course of certain test procedures, it is possible for additional fault codes to be generated. Care must be taken that any codes generated during test routines do not mislead diagnosis. All codes must be cleared once testing is complete.*

Mono-Jetronic

1 Attach an accessory switch to the dual 2-pin SD connectors *(refer to illustration 30.1)*. If the vehicle is not equipped with a facia-mounted SD warning light, connect an LED diode light between the battery (+) supply and the SD connector as shown *(see illustration 30.3)*.

2 Start the engine and allow it to warm up to normal operating temperature. **Note:** *Oxygen sensor (OS) fault codes can only be retrieved after a road test of at least 10 minutes' duration.*

3 Stop the engine and switch on the ignition.

4 If the engine will not start, crank the engine for at least 6 seconds, and leave the ignition switched on.

5 Close the accessory switch for at least 5 seconds. Open the switch, and the warning light or LED light will flash to indicate the 4-digit fault codes as follows:

 a) *The four digits are indicated by four series of flashes.*
 b) *The first series of flashes indicates the first digit, the second series of flashes indicates the second digit, and so on until all four digits have been flashed.*
 c) *Each series consists of a number of 1- or 2-second flashes, separated by short pauses. Each integer (whole number) in the range 1 to 9 is represented by a number of 1-second flashes, and each zero is represented by 2-second flashes.*
 d) *The code number "1231" is indicated by a 1-second flash, a short pause, two 1-sec-ond flashes, a short pause, three 1-second flashes, a short pause and a 1-second flash.*
 e) *A 2.5-second pause separates each series of flashes. After this pause, the code will be repeated.*

6 Count the number of flashes in each series, and record the code. Refer to the table at the end of the Chapter to determine the meaning of the fault code.

7 The code will be repeated until the accessory switch is once more closed for at least 5 seconds. Open the switch and the next code will then be displayed.

8 Continue retrieving codes until code 0000 is transmitted. Code 0000 signifies that no more codes are stored, and is displayed when the light flashes off and on at 2.5-second intervals.

9 If code 4444 is transmitted, no fault codes are stored.

10 Turning off the ignition ends fault code retrieval.

All other systems

11 Flash codes are not available, and a dedicated FCR must be used to retrieve fault codes.

4 Clearing fault codes without a fault code reader (FCR)

Bosch Mono-Jetronic

1 Carry out the procedure in Section 3 to retrieve all fault codes (wait until code 0000 or code 4444 is displayed).

2 Turn off the ignition, and close the accessory switch.

3 Switch the ignition on.

4 After 5 seconds, open the accessory switch. All fault codes should now be cleared. Turn off the ignition on completion.

All systems (alternative method)

5 Turn off the ignition and disconnect the battery negative terminal for a period of approximately 5 minutes.

6 Reconnect the battery negative terminal.

Note: *The first drawback to this method is that battery disconnection will initialise all ECM adaptive values (not Mono-Jetronic). Re-learning the appropriate adaptive values requires starting the engine from cold, and driving at various engine speeds for approximately 20 to 30 minutes. The engine should also be allowed to idle for approximately 10 minutes. The second drawback is that the radio security codes, clock setting and other stored values will be initialised, and these must be re-entered once the battery has been reconnected. Where possible, an FCR should be used for code clearing. On models with EOBD, an FCR must be used to retrieve and clear fault codes.*

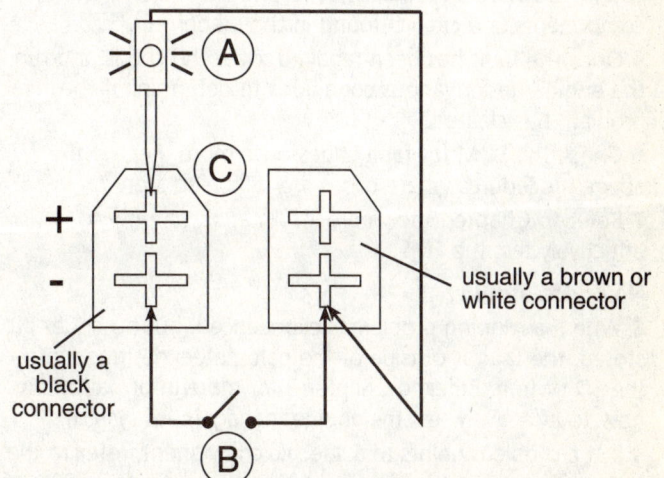

30.3 Initiation of Mono-Jetronic flash codes
A LED diode light   B Accessory switch   C SD connectors

5 Self-Diagnosis with a fault code reader (FCR)

Note: *During the course of certain test procedures, it is possible for additional fault codes to be generated. Care must be taken that any codes generated during test routines do not mislead diagnosis.*

All SEAT models

1 Connect an FCR to the SD connector. Use the FCR for the following purposes, in strict compliance with the FCR manufacturer's instructions:

  a) *Retrieving fault codes.*
  b) *Clearing fault codes.*
  c) *Testing actuators.*
  d) *Displaying Datastream.*
  e) *Making adjustments to the ignition timing or mixture (some systems).*

2 Codes must always be cleared after component testing, or after repairs involving the removal or replacement of an EMS component.

6 Guide to test procedures

Engine management fault codes

1 Use an FCR to interrogate the ECM for fault codes, or manually gather codes (where possible) as described in Section 3 or 5.

Codes stored by ECM

2 If one or more fault codes are gathered, refer to the fault code table at the end of this Chapter to determine their meaning.

3 If several codes are gathered, look for a common factor such as a defective earth return or supply.

4 Refer to the component test procedures in Chapter 4, where you will find a means of testing the majority of components and circuits found in the modern EMS.

5 Once the fault has been repaired, clear the codes and run the engine under various conditions to determine if the problem has cleared.

6 Check the ECM for fault codes once more. Repeat the above procedures where codes are still being stored.

7 Refer to Chapter 3 for more information on how to effectively test the EMS.

No codes stored

8 Where a running problem is experienced, but no codes are stored, the fault is outside of the parameters designed into the SD system. Refer to Chapter 3 for more information on how to effectively test the engine management system.

9 If the problem points to a specific component, refer to the test procedures in Chapter 4, where you will find a means of testing the majority of components and circuits found in the modern EMS.

Non-engine management fault codes

10 A number of codes that could be stored by the ECM and retrieved during the code gathering operation may refer to the air conditioning system, fan control and automatic transmission. This manual specifically covers engine management components, and diagnosis of codes pointing to faults in ancillary components is not covered.

Fault code table

All SEAT models (except EOBD)

Flash code	FCR code	Description
0000	-	End of fault code output
4444	00000	No faults found in the ECM. Proceed with normal diagnostic methods
1111	65535	Electronic control module (ECM)
1231	00281	Vehicle speed sensor (VSS) or VSS circuit
1232	00282	Throttle pot sensor (TPS) or TPS circuit, implausible signal
2111	00513	RPM sensor or circuit
2113	00515	Hall-effect sensor (HES) or HES circuit
2121	00516	Throttle pot sensor (TPS) or TPS circuit
2121	00516	Idle speed switch or circuit (alternative code)
2122	-	No engine speed signal
2142	00545	Automatic transmission signal missing
2212	00518	Throttle pot sensor (TPS) or TPS circuit
2222	00519	Manifold absolute pressure (MAP) sensor or MAP sensor circuit
2231	00533	Idle speed control valve (ISCV) or ISCV circuit
2232	00520	Mass airflow (MAF) sensor or MAF sensor circuit
2234	00532	Voltage supply or circuit
2312	00522	Coolant temperature sensor (CTS) or CTS circuit
2322	00523	Air temperature sensor (ATS) or ATS circuit
2342	00525	Oxygen sensor (OS) or OS circuit
2323	00552	Mass airflow (MAF) sensor or MAF sensor circuit
2341	00537	Oxygen sensor (OS) or OS circuit
2413	00561	Mixture control 1
4343	01243	Changeover valve inlet manifold
4412	01247	Carbon filter solenoid valve (CFSV) or CFSV circuit
4413	01249	Injector valve No.1 or injector circuit
4414	01250	Injector valve No.2 or injector circuit
4421	01251	Injector valve No.3 or injector circuit
4431	-	Idle speed control valve (ISCV) or ISCV circuit
-	00530	Throttle pot sensor (TPS) or TPS circuit
-	00543	Maximum engine speed exceeded
-	00546	Defective data cable
-	00624	Air conditioning (A/C) or A/C circuit
-	00625	Vehicle speed sensor (VSS) or VSS circuit
-	00635	Oxygen sensor (OS) or OS circuit
-	00638	Transmission electrical connector No. 2
-	00670	Throttle pot sensor (TPS) or TPS circuit
-	01087	Basic setting not completed
-	01252	Injector valve No.4 or injector circuit
-	01259	Fuel pump relay or circuit
-	01265	Exhaust gas recirculation (EGR) valve or EGR circuit
-	17978	Electronic control module (ECM)
-	65535	Electronic control module (ECM)

All models with EOBD

For a list of the allocated EOBD codes beginning with P0 (Generic Powertrain), refer to Chapter 1, Section 1.

Index of vehicles

Model	Engine code	Year	System
Favorit 1.3i cat	135B	1992 to 1996	Bosch Mono-Motronic MA1.2.2
Favorit 1.3i cat	136B	1994 to 1996	Bosch Mono-Motronic MA1.2.3
Foreman 1.3i cat	135B	1992 to 1996	Bosch Mono-Motronic MA1.2.2
Foreman 1.3i cat	136B	1994 to 1996	Bosch Mono-Motronic MA1.2.3
Felicia 1.3i	135B	1995 to 2001	Bosch Mono-Motronic MA1.2.2
Felicia 1.3i	136B	1995 to 2001	Bosch Mono-Motronic MA1.2.3
Freeway 1.3i	135B	1992 to 2001	Bosch Mono-Motronic MA1.2.2
Freeway 1.3i	136B	1995 to 2001	Bosch Mono-Motronic MA1.2.3

Plus All models equipped with EOBD (approximately January 2001-on)

Self-Diagnosis

1 Introduction

The engine management systems (EMSs) fitted to recent Skoda vehicles are of Bosch or VAG origin. Skoda engine management systems control primary ignition, fuelling and idle functions from within the same control module.

Self-Diagnosis (SD) function

Each ECM has a self-test capability that continually examines the signals from certain engine sensors and actuators, and compares each signal to a table of programmed values. If the diagnostic software determines that a fault is present,

the ECM stores one or more fault codes. Codes will not be stored about components for which a code is not available, or for conditions not covered by the diagnostic software. In Skoda systems, the control module generates 4-digit fault codes for retrieval either by manual means or by fault code reader (FCR). On models with EOBD, the 5-digit fault codes can only be retrieved and cleared using an FCR.

Limited operating strategy (LOS)

Skoda systems featured in this Chapter utilise LOS (a function that is commonly called the "limp-home mode"). Once certain faults have been identified (not all faults will initiate LOS), the ECM will implement LOS and refer to a programmed default value rather than the sensor signal. This enables the vehicle to be safely driven to a workshop/garage for repair or testing. Once the fault has cleared, the ECM will revert to normal operation.

Adaptive or learning capability

Skoda systems also utilise an adaptive function that will modify the basic programmed values for most effective operation during normal running, and with due regard to engine wear.

2 Self-Diagnosis connector location

Note: *Vehicles fitted with a 135B engine are provided with an SD connector for retrieving flash codes manually and also for dedicated FCR use. Skoda models fitted with the 136B or AAE engines are equipped with an SD connector which can only display fault codes on a dedicated FCR.*

The 5-pin SD connector is located towards the rear of the engine compartment, adjacent to the carbon filter canister and ECM (see illustration 31.1).

On models equipped with EOBD, the 16-pin diagnostic connector is located under the facia - refer to Chapter 38.

3 Retrieving fault codes without a fault code reader (FCR) - flash codes

Note: *During the course of certain test procedures, it is possible for additional fault codes to be generated. Care must be taken that codes generated during test routines do not mislead diagnosis. All codes must be cleared once testing is complete.*

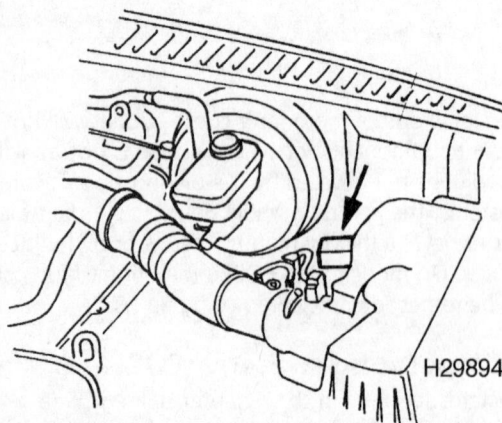

31.1 The SD connector (arrowed) is attached to the engine compartment bulkhead

Bosch Mono-Motronic MA1.2.2

1 Attach an on/off accessory switch between terminals A and D of the SD connector (see illustration 31.2).

2 Connect the positive probe of an LED to terminal E and the negative probe of the LED to terminal C in the SD connector.

3 Switch on the ignition.

4 Close the accessory switch for 4 seconds and then release.

5 The LED light will flash the 4-digit fault codes as follows:

a) *The four digits are indicated by four series of flashes.*

b) *The first series of flashes indicates the first digit, the second series of flashes indicates the second digit, and so on until all four digits have been flashed.*

c) *Each series consists of a number of 1- or 2-second flashes, separated by short pauses. Each integer (whole number) in the range 1 to 9 is represented by a number of 1-second flashes, and each zero is represented by a 2-second flash.*

d) *A pause separates each series of flashes.*

e) *The code number "1231" is indicated by a 1-second flash, a short pause, two 1-sec-ond flashes, a short pause, three 1-second flashes, a short pause and a 1-second flash.*

Note: *If the LED does not behave as described, reverse the connections to the SD connector.*

6 Count the number of flashes in each series, and record each code as it is transmitted. Refer to the tables at the end of the Chapter to determine the meaning of the fault code.

7 Retrieve the next fault code by closing the accessory switch for 3 seconds. The next fault code will then be displayed.

8 Repeat the procedure to retrieve further codes until "0000" is transmitted. Code 0000 signifies that no more codes are stored.

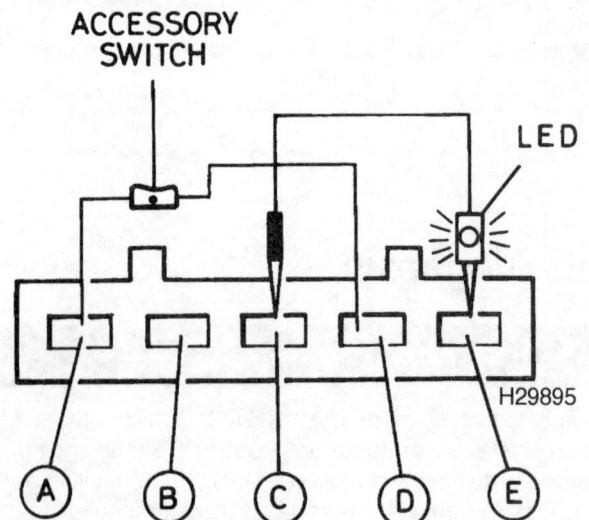

31.2 SD connector terminals for fault code retrieval

A Terminal for jumper lead bridge
B Terminal not used for Code retrieval or actuator test procedures
C Terminal for negative LED probe
D Terminal for jumper lead bridge
E Terminal for positive LED probe

9 Turn off the ignition and remove the jumper lead and LED to end fault code retrieval.

All other systems

10 Flash codes are not available on any other Skoda system, and a fault code reader is required to gather fault codes.

4 Actuator testing without a fault code reader (FCR)

Bosch Mono-Motronic MA1.2.2

1 Attach an on/off accessory switch between terminals A and D of the SD connector (refer to illustration 31.2).
2 Connect the positive probe of an LED to terminal E and the negative probe of the LED to terminal C in the SD connector.
3 Close the accessory switch and then switch on the ignition.
4 Wait 4 seconds and then open the accessory switch.
5 The LED light will flash code "1232", and the idle speed control valve should be heard to move as it extends and retracts.
6 Wait 3 seconds and then close the accessory switch. Wait 4 seconds and then open the accessory switch to implement the next actuator procedure.
7 The LED light will flash code "4342", which can be ignored because it is not relevant to the test procedure for these vehicles.
8 Wait 3 seconds and then close the accessory switch. Wait 4 seconds and then open the accessory switch to Implement the next actuator procedure.
9 The LED light will flash code "4343", and the carbon filter solenoid valve should be heard to operate (a clicking sound).
10 End the actuator test as follows. Wait 3 seconds and then close the accessory switch. Wait 4 seconds and then open the accessory switch. The LED should display a continual sequence of on/off flashes, indicating that the actuator test has been completed, and that fault codes have been cleared from ECM memory.

All other systems

11 Actuator testing without an FCR is not available on any other Skoda system.

5 Clearing fault codes without a fault code reader (FCR)

Bosch Mono-Motronic MA1.2.2

1 Perform the flash code retrieval procedure described in Section 3, and rectify faults as required.
2 Perform the actuator test procedures described in Section 4, and all fault codes will be automatically cleared on completion.

All systems (alternative method)

3 Turn off the ignition and disconnect the battery negative terminal for a period of approximately 5 minutes.
4 Reconnect the battery negative terminal. **Note**: *The first drawback to this method is that battery disconnection will initialise all ECM adaptive values. Re-learning the appropriate adaptive values requires starting the engine from cold, and driving at various engine speeds for approximately 20 to 30 minutes. The engine should also be allowed to idle for approximately 10 minutes. The second drawback is that the radio security codes, clock setting and other stored values will be initialised, and these must be re-entered once the battery has been reconnected. Where possible, an FCR should be used for code clearing. On models with EOBD, an FCR must be used to retrieve and clear fault codes.*

6 Self-Diagnosis with a fault code reader (FCR)

Note: *During the course of certain test procedures, it is possible for additional fault codes to be generated. Care must be taken that any codes generated during test routines do not mislead diagnosis.*

All Skoda models

1 Connect an FCR to the SD connector. Use the FCR for the following purposes, in strict compliance with the FCR manufacturer's instructions:
  a) *Retrieving fault codes.*
  b) *Clearing fault codes.*
  c) *Testing actuators.*
  d) *Datastream*
2 Codes must always be cleared after component testing, or after repairs involving the removal or replacement of an EMS component.

7 Guide to test procedures

1 Use an FCR to interrogate the ECM for fault codes, or (where possible) manually gather codes as described in Section 3 or 5.

Codes stored

2 If one or more fault codes are gathered, refer to the fault code tables at the end of this Chapter to determine their meaning.
3 If several codes are gathered, look for a common factor such as a defective earth return or supply.
4 Refer to the component test procedures in Chapter 4, where you will find a means of testing the majority of components and circuits found in the modern EMS.
5 Once the fault has been repaired, clear the codes and run

the engine under various conditions to determine if the problem has cleared.

6 Check the ECM for fault codes once more. Repeat the above procedures where codes are still being stored.

7 Refer to Chapter 3 for more information on how to effectively test the EMS.

No codes stored

8 Where a running problem is experienced, but no codes are stored, the fault is outside of the parameters designed into the SD system. Refer to Chapter 3 for more information on how to effectively test the engine management system.

9 If the problem points to a specific component, refer to the test procedures in Chapter 4, where you will find a means of testing the majority of components and circuits found in the modern EMS.

Fault code tables

Bosch Mono-Motronic

Flash code	FCR code	Description
1111	65535	Electronic control module (ECM)
2113	00515	Effect sensor (HES) or HES circuit
2121	00156	Throttle pot sensor (TPS) or TPS circuit
2212	00518	Throttle pot sensor (TPS) or TPS circuit
2312	00522	Coolant temperature sensor (CTS) or CTS circuit
2322	00523	Air temperature sensor (ATS) or ATS circuit
2341	00537	Oxygen sensor (OS) or OS circuit
2342	00525	Oxygen sensor (OS) or OS circuit
2343	00558	Oxygen sensor (OS) or OS circuit
2413	00561	Oxygen sensor (OS) or OS circuit
4431	01253	Idle speed control valve (ISCV) or ISCV circuit

Actuator selection code for Bosch Mono-Motronic MA1.2.2

The above codes are displayed during actuator test mode when the relevant circuit has been actuated.

Flash/ FCR code	Description
1232	Idle speed control valve (ISCV) or ISCV circuit
4342	(Not applicable)
4343	Carbon filter canister purge valve

All models with EOBD

For a list of the allocated EOBD codes beginning with P0 (Generic Powertrain), refer to Chapter 1, Section 1.

Index of vehicles

Model	Engine code	Year	System
1.8 Turbo Coupe 4x4	EA82	1986 to 1989	Subaru MPFi + Turbo
Impreza 1.6i SOHC 16V	-	1993 to 1997	Subaru MPFi
Impreza 1.8i SOHC 16V	-	1993 to 1997	Subaru MPFi
Impreza 2.0 Turbo DOHC 16V	-	1994 to 1997	Subaru MPFi
Impreza 2.0i 16V	-	1996 to 1997	Subaru MPFi
Justy (J12) 1.2i cat	-	1992 to 1997	Subaru MPFi
Legacy 1.8i SOHC 16V	AY/EJ18	1991 to 1993	Subaru SPFi
Legacy 2.0 SOHC 16V cat	AY/EJ20EN	1991 to 1996	Subaru MPFi
Legacy 2.0 4 Cam Turbo DOHC 16V	AY/EJ20-GN	1991 to 1994	Subaru MPFi
Legacy 2.2 & cat	EJ22	1989 to 1997	Subaru MPFi
L-Series Coupe 1.8	EA82	1988 to 1990	Subaru MPFi
L-Series Turbo 4x4	EA82	1985 to 1989	Subaru MPFi + Turbo
SVX DOHC 24V	-	1992 to 1997	Subaru MPFi
Vivio SOHC 8V	-	1992 to 1996	Subaru MPFi
XT Turbo Coupe	EA82	1985 to 1989	Subaru MPFi + Turbo
XT Turbo Coupe	EA82	1989 to 1991	Subaru MPFi + Turbo

Plus All models equipped with EOBD (approximately January 2001-on)

Self-Diagnosis

1   Introduction

The engine management system (EMS) fitted to Subaru vehicles is the Subaru MPFi or SPFi system that controls primary ignition, fuel injection and idle functions from within the same control module. The MPFi system offers multi-point fuel injection, while the SPFi is a single-point fuel injection design.

Self-Diagnosis (SD) function

The Subaru electronic control module (ECM) has a self-test capability that continually examines the signals from certain engine sensors and actuators, and then compares each signal to a table of programmed values. If the diagnostic software determines that a fault is present, the ECM stores one or more fault codes in ECM memory. Codes will not be stored about components for which a code is not available, or for conditions not covered by the diagnostic software. In Subaru systems, the control module generates 2-digit fault codes, for retrieval either by manual means or by use of a fault code reader (FCR).

On models equipped with EOBD, an FCR must be used to retrieve or clear the 5-digit fault codes.

Limited operating strategy (LOS)

Subaru systems featured in this Chapter utilise LOS (a function that is commonly called the "limp-home mode"). Once certain faults have been identified (not all faults will initiate LOS), the ECM will implement LOS and refer to a programmed default value rather than the sensor signal. This enables the vehicle to be safely driven to a workshop/garage for repair or testing. Once the fault has cleared, the ECM will revert to normal operation.

Self-Diagnosis (SD) warning light

Subaru models are equipped with an SD warning light located within the instrument panel. In addition on some models, an LED set into the casing of the ECM can also display fault codes.

2   Self-Diagnosis connector location

1 Two types of non-EOBD SD connector are provided in Subaru vehicles.
2 Twin SD connectors are located alongside the ECM, under the steering column, inside the lower trim panel *(see illustration 32.1)*. The test connector is green, and the read-memory connector is black. The twin connectors are provided for flash code retrieval purposes.
3 A single 9-pin SD connector is located under the driver's

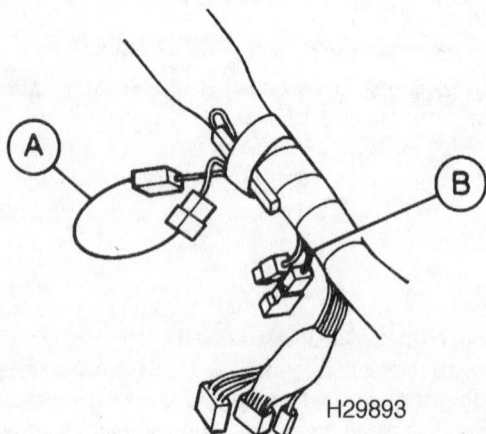

32.1 The green test connectors and the black read-memory connectors are located under the steering column, alongside the ECM

A Green connector   B Black connector

side facia, close to the ECM. The 9-pin SD connector is provided for connection to an FCR.
4 On models with EOBD, the 16-pin diagnostic connector is located under the facia - refer to Chapter 38.

3   Retrieving fault codes without a fault code reader (FCR) - flash codes

Note: *During the course of certain test procedures, it is possible for additional fault codes to be generated. Care must be taken that any codes generated during test routines do not mislead diagnosis. All codes must be cleared once testing is complete.*

1 Fault codes are displayed by both the SD warning light on the instrument panel and by the LED set into the casing of the ECM. Subaru MPFi employs four diagnostic modes, which utilise combinations of the facia-mounted warning light and the LED to display various fault conditions. Each mode can be triggered with either the ignition switched on, engine stopped or with the engine running.

U-check (start-up and drive components)

2 Switch on the ignition. If the ECM is fault free, the SD light will illuminate without flashing, and the LED will display the vehicle specification code (differentiation of catalyst or non-catalyst models).
3 If fault codes have been stored, the warning light remains illuminated while the LED displays the codes. A limited number of 2-digit codes that affect start-up and drive will be displayed in this mode:

    a) *The two digits are indicated by two series of flashes.*
    b) *The first series of flashes indicates the multiples of ten, the second series of flashes indicates the single units.*
    c) *Tens are indicated by 1.2-second flashes separated by 0.3-second pauses. Units are indicated by 0.2-second flashes separated by 0.3-second pauses.*
    d) *Code number "12" is indicated by a flash of 1.2 seconds, followed by a 1.8-second pause, then two flashes of 0.2 seconds.*
    e) *A 1.8-second pause separates the transmission of each individual code.*
    f) *If two or more faults have been stored, the warning light and the LED will display the codes sequentially, lowest numbers first*

4 Count the number of flashes in each series, and record the code. Refer to the table at the end of the Chapter to determine the meaning of the fault code.
5 Start up the engine and allow it to idle. If the system is operating under closed-loop control, the SD warning light should extinguish, and the LED will flash to indicate the switching of the oxygen sensor. If a fault is present, the SD light will remain illuminated.

Read-memory check (minor and intermittent faults)

6 Connect the black read-memory connectors (male and female).

7 Switch on the ignition.

8 If no faults have been stored, the LED will display the vehicle specification code (for catalyst or non-catalyst model), and the SD light should blink regularly.

9 If fault codes are stored, both the SD warning light and the LED will flash to display the fault code. Refer to the information on the U-check (paragraph 3) for a description of what the flashes represent.

10 Count the number of flashes in each series, and record the code. Refer to the table at the end of the Chapter to determine the meaning of the fault code.

11 Start up the engine and allow it to idle. If no faults have been stored, the SD warning light will blink, and the LED will display the vehicle specification code.

12 If fault codes have been stored, both the SD warning light and the LED will flash to display the fault code. Refer to the information on the U-check (paragraph 3) for a description of what the flashes represent.

13 Count the number of flashes in each series, and record the code. Refer to the table at the end of the Chapter to determine the meaning of the fault code.

14 Turn off the ignition and disconnect the black read-memory connectors (male and female) to end fault code retrieval.

D-check (major faults and system test)

15 Start the engine and warm it to normal operating temperature. Stop the engine.

16 Ensure that the two black read-memory connectors are disconnected. Connect the two green multi-plug test connectors (male and female) located alongside the ECM.

17 Switch on the ignition.

18 The LED will display the vehicle specification code (differing for catalyst or non-catalyst models), and the SD light should remain illuminated.

19 Fully depress the accelerator pedal. Allow the pedal to return to the half-throttle position, and hold it there for two seconds. Release the pedal so that it returns to the closed (idle) position.

20 Turn the economy switch on and then off.

21 Start the engine. If fault codes have been stored, both the SD warning light and the LED will flash to display the fault code.

22 If fault codes have been stored, both the SD warning light and the LED will flash to display the fault code. Refer to the information on the U-check (paragraph 3) for a description of what the flashes represent.

23 Count the number of flashes in each series, and record the code. Refer to the table at the end of the Chapter to determine the meaning of the fault code.

24 Drive the vehicle at a speed greater than 7 mph for at least one minute, engaging all forward gears (manual transmission models) during this time. Stop the vehicle and select neutral, leaving the engine running.

25 Raise the engine speed above 2000 rpm for more than 40 seconds. If fault codes have been stored, both the SD warning light and the LED will flash to display the fault code. The SD warning light will flash regularly if no faults have been detected.

26 If fault codes have been stored, both the SD warning light and the LED will flash to display the fault code. Refer to the information on the U-check (paragraph 3) for a description of what the flashes represent.

27 Count the number of flashes in each series, and record the code. Refer to the table at the end of the Chapter to determine the meaning of the fault code.

28 Turn off the ignition and disconnect the two green multi-plug test connectors (male and female) to end fault code retrieval.

4 Clearing fault codes without a fault code reader (FCR)

Clear-memory mode

1 Start the engine and warm it to normal operating temperature. Stop the engine.

2 Connect both the green test connectors and black read-memory connectors (male and female).

3 Switch on the ignition.

4 The LED set into the ECM case will display the vehicle specification code (differing for the catalyst or non-catalyst models) and the SD light should remain illuminated.

5 Fully depress the accelerator pedal. Allow the pedal to return to the half-throttle position, and hold it there for two seconds. Release the pedal so that it returns to the closed (idle) position.

6 Turn the economy switch on and then off.

7 Start the engine. If fault codes have been stored, both the SD warning light and the LED will flash to display the fault code.

8 Drive the vehicle at a speed greater than 7 mph for at least one minute, engaging all forward gears (manual transmission models) during this time. Stop the vehicle and select neutral, leaving the engine running.

9 Raise the engine speed above 2000 rpm for more than 40 seconds. If fault codes have been stored, both the SD warning light and the LED will flash to display the fault code. The SD warning light will flash regularly if no faults have been detected, and all codes will now be cleared from memory.

10 Stop the engine and switch off the ignition. Disconnect the test and read-memory connectors to end fault code clearing.

Chapter 32

5 Self-Diagnosis with a fault code reader (FCR)

Note: *During the course of certain test procedures, it is possible for additional fault codes to be generated. Care must be taken that any codes generated during test routines do not mislead diagnosis.*

All Subaru models

1 Connect an FCR to the SD connector. Use the FCR for the following purposes, in strict compliance with the FCR manufacturer's instructions:

 a) *Retrieving fault codes.*
 b) *Clearing fault codes.*
 c) *Datastream (EOBD models only).*

2 Codes must always be cleared after component testing, or after repairs involving the removal or replacement of an EMS component.

6 Guide to test procedures

1 Use an FCR to interrogate the ECM for fault codes, or gather codes manually, as described in Section 3 or 5.

Codes stored

2 If one or more fault codes are gathered, refer to the fault code table at the end of this Chapter to determine their meaning.

3 If several codes are gathered, look for a common factor such as a defective earth return or supply.

4 Refer to the component test procedures in Chapter 4, where you will find a means of testing the majority of components and circuits found in the modern EMS.

5 Once the fault has been repaired, clear the codes and run the engine under various conditions to determine if the problem has cleared.

6 Check the ECM for fault codes once more. Repeat the above procedures where codes are still being stored.

7 Refer to Chapter 3 for more information on how to effectively test the EMS.

No codes stored

8 Where a running problem is experienced, but no codes are stored, the fault is outside of the parameters designed into the SD system. Refer to Chapter 3 for more information on how to effectively test the engine management system.

9 If the problem points to a specific component, refer to the test procedures in Chapter 4, where you will find a means of testing the majority of components and circuits found in the modern EMS.

Fault code table

Subaru MPFi

Flash/ FCR code	Description
11	Crank angle sensor (CAS) or CAS circuit
12	Starter switch
13	Camshaft position sensor (CMP) or circuit
14	Injector valve No. 1 or injector circuit
15	Injector valve No. 2 or injector circuit
16	Injector valve No. 3 or injector circuit
17	Injector valve No. 4 or injector circuit
18	Injector valve No. 5 or injector circuit
19	Injector valve No. 6 or injector circuit
21	Coolant temperature sensor (CTS) or CTS circuit
22	Knock sensor (KS) 1 or KS circuit
23	Mass airflow (MAF) sensor or MAF sensor circuit
23	Manifold absolute pressure (MAP) sensor or MAP sensor circuit
24	Idle speed control valve (ISCV) or ISCV circuit
26	Air temperature sensor (ATS) or ATS circuit
28	Knock sensor (KS) 2 or KS circuit
29	Crank angle sensor (CAS) or CAS circuit
31	Throttle pot sensor (TPS) or TPS circuit
32	Oxygen sensor (OS) 1 or OS circuit
33	Vehicle speed sensor (VSS) or VSS circuit

Flash/ FCR code	Description
35	Carbon filter solenoid valve (CFSV) or CFSV circuit
37	Oxygen sensor (OS) 2 or OS circuit
38	Engine torque control or circuit
41	Oxygen sensor (OS) learning control
42	Idle switch or circuit
43	Power switch or circuit
44	Turbo wastegate solenoid valve or circuit
45	Turbo pressure sensor solenoid valve or circuit
47	Economy switch or circuit
49	Airflow sensor (AFS) or AFS circuit
51	Inhibitor switch or circuit
52	Parking switch or circuit
62	Electrical load
63	Blower fan switch or circuit

All models with EOBD

For a list of the allocated EOBD codes beginning with P0 (Generic Powertrain), refer to Chapter 1, Section 1.

Suzuki

33

Index of vehicles

Model	Engine code	Year	System
Alto 1.0	G10B	1997 to 2001	Suzuki EPi-MPi
Baleno 1.3	G13BB	1995 to 2001	Suzuki EPi-MPi
Baleno 1.6	G16B	1995 to 2001	Suzuki EPi-MPi
Baleno 1.8	J18A	1996 to 2001	Suzuki EPi-MPi
Cappuccino DOHC 12V	F6A	1993 to 1996	Suzuki EPi-MPi
Swift 1.0i cat SOHC 6V	G10A	1991 to 2001	Suzuki EPi-SPi
Swift GTi DOHC 16V	-	1986 to 1989	Suzuki EPi-MPi
Swift SF 413 GTi DOHC	G13B	1988 to 1992	Suzuki EPi-MPi
Swift SF 413 DOHC cat	G13B	1988 to 1992	Suzuki EPi-MPi
Swift 1.3i DOHC 16V	G13B	1992 to 1995	Suzuki EPi-MPi
Swift Cabrio DOHC cat	G13B	1992 to 1995	Suzuki EPi-MPi
Swift 1.3i cat SOHC 8V	G13BA	1992 to 2001	Suzuki EPi-SPi
Swift SF 416i SOHC 16V	G16B	1989 to 1992	Suzuki EPi-SPi
Swift SF 416i 4x4 SOHC	G16B	1989 to 1992	Suzuki EPi-SPi
Swift SF 416i 4x4 cat	G16B	1989 to 1992	Suzuki EPi-SPi
Vitara EFi SOHC 16V	-	1991 to 2000	Suzuki EPi-MPi
Vitara Sport SPi SOHC	-	1994 to 2000	Suzuki EPi-SPi
Vitara 2.0 V6	-	1995 to 1998	Suzuki EPi-MPi
X-90 1.6	G16B	1996 to 1998	Suzuki EPi-MPi

Plus All models equipped with EOBD (approximately January 2001-on)

Chapter 33

Self-Diagnosis

1 Introduction

Suzuki models are equipped with the Suzuki EPi-MPi or EPi-SPi engine management systems that control primary ignition, fuel injection and idle functions from within the same control module.

Self-Diagnosis (SD) function

Each ECM (electronic control module) has a self-test capability that continually examines the signals from certain engine sensors and actuators, and then compares each signal to a table of programmed values. If the diagnostic software determines that a fault is present, the ECM stores one or more fault codes in the ECM memory. Codes will not be stored about components for which a code is not available, or for conditions not covered by the diagnostic software. In Suzuki systems, the ECM generates 2-digit fault codes for retrieval both manual means as flash codes, or using a dedicated fault code reader (FCR). On models with EOBD, the 5-digit fault codes can only be retrieved or cleared using an FCR.

Limited operating strategy (LOS)

Suzuki systems featured in this Chapter utilise LOS (a function that is commonly called the "limp-home mode"). Once certain faults have been identified (not all faults will initiate LOS), the ECM will implement LOS and refer to a programmed default value rather than the sensor signal. This enables the vehicle to be safely driven to a workshop/garage for repair or testing. Once the fault has cleared, the ECM will revert to normal operation.

Self-Diagnosis (SD) warning light

Suzuki models without EOBD are equipped with an SD warning light located within the instrument panel, on which flash codes may be displayed. On EOBD models, a MIL (Malfunction Indicator Light) is fitted within the instrument panel, to alert the driver to the presence of a fault.

2 Self-Diagnosis connector location

Swift 1.3

The SD connector is located either in the fusebox on the left-hand (passenger) side under the facia (see illustration 33.1), or attached to the monitor coupler next to the battery in the engine compartment (see illustration 33.2). The connector is provided for manual retrieval of flash codes, and for dedicated FCR use.

Swift GTi 1986 to 1989 and Vitara 1.6i

The SD connector is attached to the monitor coupler, which is located next to the battery in the engine compartment (refer to illustration 33.2). The connector is provided for manual retrieval of flash codes, and for dedicated FCR use.

EOBD models

The 16-pin diagnostic connector is located under the facia - refer to Chapter 38.

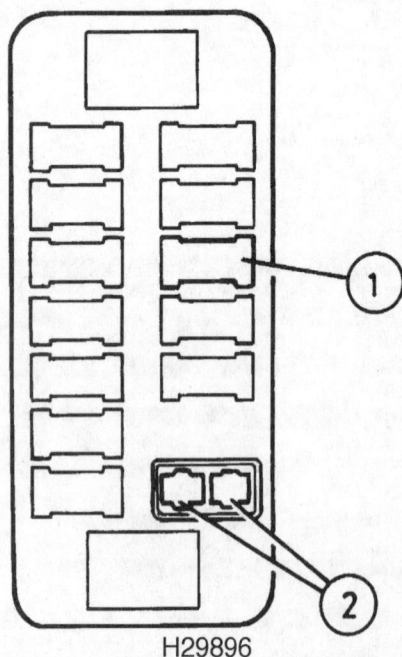

H29896

33.1 The SD connector is located under the passenger's side of the facia, in the fusebox
1 Fusebox   2 SD connector

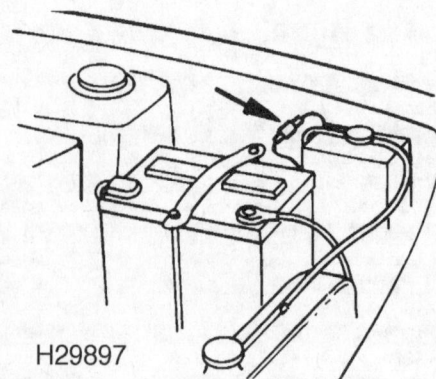

H29897

33.2 The SD connector is located in the engine compartment, next to the battery

3 Retrieving fault codes without a fault code reader (FCR) - flash codes

Note: *During the course of certain test procedures, it is possible for additional fault codes to be generated. Care must be taken that any codes generated during test routines do not mislead diagnosis. All codes must be cleared once testing is complete. On EOBD models, the fault codes can only be retrieved or cleared using an FCR.*

Swift GTi 1986 to 1991

1 Switch on the ignition (do not start the engine).

2 Disconnect the two halves of the SD connector plug, then depress the accelerator pedal fully, releasing it within 10 seconds. If the engine is a non-starter, crank it for 3 to 5 seconds; leave the ignition switched on to avoid losing the codes.

3 The codes are displayed on the SD warning light in the instrument panel. The flashing of the light indicates the 2-digit fault codes as follows:

a) *The two digits are indicated by two series of flashes.*

b) *The first series of flashes indicates the multiples of ten, the second series of flashes indicates the single units.*

c) *Tens are indicated by 0.3-second flashes, separated by short pauses. Units are indicated by 0.3-second flashes, separated by short pauses.*

d) *A 1-second pause separates the tens from the units.*

e) *Code "42" is indicated by four 0.3-second flashes, a 1-second pause, followed by two 0.3-second flashes.*

f) *A 3-second pause separates the transmission of each individual code.*

4 Count the number of flashes in each series, and record each code as it is transmitted. Refer to the table at the end of the Chapter to determine the meaning of the fault code.

5 Each flash code will be repeated three times, followed by the next code in sequence.

6 Code number "12" will be transmitted if no faults are stored.

7 Turn off the ignition and reconnect the two halves of the SD connector to end fault code retrieval.

Swift 1.0i and 1.3i

8 Switch on the ignition (do not start the engine).

9 Connect a spare fuse to the SD connector located in the fusebox *(refer to illustration 33.1)*. If the engine is a non-starter, crank it for 3 to 5 seconds; leave the ignition switched on to avoid losing codes.

10 The codes are displayed on the SD warning light in the instrument panel. The flashing of the light indicates the 2-digit fault codes as follows:

a) *The two digits are indicated by two series of flashes.*

b) *The first series of flashes indicates the multiples of ten, the second series of flashes indicates the single units.*

c) *Tens are indicated by 0.3-second flashes, separated by short pauses. Units are indicated by 0.3-second flashes, separated by short pauses.*

d) *A 1-second pause separates the tens from the units.*

e) *Code "42" is indicated by four 0.3-second flashes, a 1-second pause, followed by two 0.3-second flashes.*

f) *A 3-second pause separates the transmission of each individual code.*

11 Count the number of flashes in each series, and record each code as it is transmitted. Refer to the table at the end of the Chapter to determine the meaning of the fault code.

12 Each flash code will be repeated three times, followed by the next code in sequence.

13 Code number "12" will be transmitted if no faults are stored.

14 Turn off the ignition and remove the fuse from the SD connector to end fault code retrieval.

Vitara 1.6i

15 Switch on the ignition (do not start the engine).

16 Connect a jumper wire between terminals A and B of the SD connector *(see illustration 33.3)*. If the engine is a non-starter, crank it for 3 to 5 seconds; leave the ignition switched on to avoid losing codes

17 The codes are displayed on the SD warning light in the instrument panel. The flashing of the light indicates the 2-digit fault codes as follows:

a) *The two digits are indicated by two series of flashes.*

b) *The first series of flashes indicates the multiples of ten, the second series of flashes indicates the single units.*

c) *Tens are indicated by 0.3-second flashes, separated by short pauses. Units are indicated by 0.3-second flashes, separated by short pauses.*

d) *A 0.6-second pause separates the tens from the units.*

e) *Code "42" is indicated by four 0.3-second flashes, a 0.6-second pause, followed by two 0.3-second flashes.*

f) *A 3-second pause separates the transmission of each individual codes.*

18 Count the number of flashes in each series, and record each code as it is transmitted. Refer to the table at the end of the Chapter to determine the meaning of the fault code.

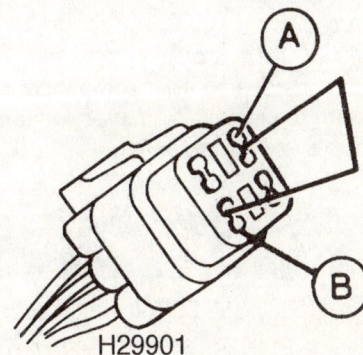

33.3 Use a jumper wire to bridge terminals A and B in the SD connector

19 Each flash code will be repeated three times, followed by the next code in sequence.

20 Code number "12" will be transmitted if no faults are stored.

21 Turn off the ignition and remove the jumper wire to end fault code retrieval.

4 Clearing fault codes without a fault code reader (FCR)

1 Disconnect the battery earth lead for an interval of at least 30 seconds.

2 Reconnect the battery earth lead.

Note: *The first drawback to this method is that battery disconnection will re-initialise all ECM adaptive values. Re-learning the appropriate adaptive values requires starting the engine from cold, and driving at various engine speeds for approximately 20 to 30 minutes. The engine should also be allowed to idle for approximately 10 minutes. The second drawback is that the radio security codes, clock setting and other stored values will be initialised, and these must be re-entered once the battery has been reconnected. Where possible, an FCR should be used for code clearing. On models with EOBD, an FCR must be used to clear fault codes.*

5 Self-Diagnosis with a fault code reader (FCR)

Note: *During the course of certain test procedures, it is possible for additional fault codes to be generated. Care must be taken that any codes generated during test routines do not mislead diagnosis.*

All Suzuki models

1 Connect an FCR to the SD connector. Use the FCR for the following purposes, in strict compliance with the FCR manufacturer's instructions:

a) *Retrieving fault codes.*
b) *Clearing fault codes.*
c) *Datastream (EOBD models only).*

2 Codes must always be cleared after component testing, or after repairs involving the removal or replacement of an engine management system component.

6 Guide to test procedures

1 Use an FCR to interrogate the ECM for fault codes, or gather codes manually, as described in Section 3 or 5.

Codes stored

2 If one or more fault codes are gathered, refer to the fault code table at the end of this Chapter to determine their meaning.

3 If several codes are gathered, look for a common factor such as a defective earth return or supply.

4 Refer to the component test procedures in Chapter 4, where you will find a means of testing the majority of components and circuits found in the modern EMS.

5 Once the fault has been repaired, clear the codes and run the engine under various conditions to determine if the problem has cleared.

6 Check the ECM for fault codes once more. Repeat the above procedures where codes are still being stored.

7 Refer to Chapter 3 for more information on how to effectively test the EMS.

No codes stored

8 Where a running problem is experienced, but no codes are stored, the fault is outside of the parameters designed into the SD system. Refer to Chapter 3 for more information on how to effectively test the engine management system.

9 If the problem points to a specific component, refer to the test procedures in Chapter 4, where you will find a means of testing the majority of components and circuits found in the modern EMS.

Fault code table

Suzuki EPi-MPi and EPi-SPi

Flash/ FCR code	Description
12	No faults found in the ECM. Proceed with normal diagnostic methods
13	Oxygen sensor (OS) or OS circuit
14	Coolant temperature sensor (CTS) or CTS circuit
15	Coolant temperature sensor (CTS) or CTS circuit
21	Throttle pot sensor (TPS) or TPS circuit
22	Throttle pot sensor (TPS) or TPS circuit
23	Air temperature sensor (ATS) or ATS circuit
24	Vehicle speed sensor (VSS) or VSS circuit
25	Air temperature sensor (ATS) or ATS circuit
31	Manifold absolute pressure (MAP) sensor or MAP sensor circuit
32	Manifold absolute pressure (MAP) sensor or MAP sensor circuit
33	Airflow sensor (AFS) or AFS circuit
34	Airflow sensor (AFS) or AFS circuit
41	Ignition signal or circuit
42	Crank angle sensor (CAS) or CAS circuit
44	Idle switch or circuit
45	Idle switch or circuit

All models with EOBD

For a list of the allocated EOBD codes beginning with P0 (Generic Powertrain), refer to Chapter 1, Section 1.

Toyota

34

Index of vehicles

Index of vehicles

Model	Engine code	Year	System
Camry 2.0i OHC	3S-FE	1987 to 1991	Toyota TCCS/MAP or AFS
Camry 2.0i OHC 4WD	3S-FE	1988 to 1989	Toyota TCCS/MAP or AFS
Camry 2.2i 16V DOHC cat	5S-FE	1991 to 1996	Toyota TCCS/AFS, TDCL
Camry 2.2 16V DOHC	5S-FE	1997	Toyota TCCS
Camry 2.5i V6 OHC cat	2VZ-FE	1989 to 1991	Toyota TCCS/AFS
Camry 3.0i V6 24V DOHC cat	3VZ-FE	1991 to 1996	Toyota TCCS/AFS, TDCL
Camry 3.0 V6 DOHC	1MZ-FE	1997	Toyota TCCS
Carina E 1.6i 16V DOHC	4A-FE	1992 to 1998	Toyota TCCS/MAP
Carina E 1.6i 16V DOHC cat	4A-FE	1992 to 1996	Toyota TCCS/MAP, TDCL
Carina E 1.8 16V DOHC	7A-FE	1995 to 1998	Toyota TCCS MPi
Carina II 1.8i OHC	1S-E	1986 to 1988	Toyota TCCS
Carina II 2.0i OHC & cat	3S-FE	1988 to 1992	Toyota TCCS/AFS, TDCL
Carina E 2.0i DOHC cat	3S-FE	1992 to 1998	Toyota TCCS/MAP, TDCL
Carina E 2.0i DOHC cat	3S-GE	1992 to 1995	Toyota TCCS/MAP, TDCL
Celica 1.8i 16V DOHC	7A-FE	1995 to 1999	Toyota TCCS
Celica 2.0 16V DOHC & cat	3S-GE	1990 to 1994	Toyota TCCS/MAP, TDCL
Celica 2.0i 16V DOHC	3S-GE	1994 to 1999	Toyota TCCS
Celica 2.0 16V DOHC	3S-GEL	1985 to 1990	Toyota TCCS/AFS
Celica 2.0 GT-4 turbo 16V cat	3S-GTE	1988 to 1990	Toyota TCCS/AFS
Celica 2.0 GT-4 turbo 16V cat	3S-GTE	1990 to 1993	Toyota TCCS/AFS, TDCL
Celica 2.2i 16V DOHC cat	5S-FE	1991 to 1994	Toyota TCCS/MAP
Celica Supra 2.8i DOHC cat	5M-GE	1984 to 1986	Toyota TCCS
Corolla 1.3i OHC cat	2E-E	1990 to 1992	Toyota TCCS/MAP
Corolla 1.3i 16V DOHC cat	4E-FE	1992 to 1997	Toyota TCCS/MAP, TDCL
Corolla 1.6 GT OHC	4A-GEL	1985 to 1987	Toyota TCCS/MAP
Corolla 1.6 GT coupe OHC	4A-GE	1984 to 1987	Toyota TCCS/MAP
Corolla 1.6 GTi OHC & cat	4A-GE	1987 to 1989	Toyota TCCS/MAP or AFS
Corolla 1.6 GTi OHC	4A-GE	1989 to 1992	Toyota TCCS/AFS, TDCL
Corolla 1.6 GTi OHC cat	4A-GE	1989 to 1992	Toyota TCCS/MAP or AFS, TDCL
Corolla 1.6i and 4x4 OHC cat	4A-FE	1989 to 1992	Toyota TCCS/MAP or AFS, TDCL
Corolla 1.6i 16V DOHC cat	4A-FE	1992 to 1997	Toyota TCCS/MAP, TDCL

Model	Engine code	Year	System
Corolla 1.8i 16V DOHC cat	7A-FE	1993 to 1995	Toyota TCCS/MAP
Hi-Ace 2.4i OHC	2RZ-E	1989 to 1994	Toyota TCCS/MAP
Hi-Ace 2.4i 4x4 OHC	2RZ-E	1989 to 1996	Toyota TCCS/MAP
Land Cruiser Colorado	5VZ-FE	1996 to 2001	Toyota TCCS
Land Cruiser 4.5	1FZ-FE	1995 to 1998	Toyota TCCS
MR2 1.6 OHC	4A-GEL	1984 to 1990	Toyota TCCS/MAP
MR2 2.0 16V DOHC GT cat	3S-GE	1990 to 1999	Toyota TCCS/MAP, TDCL
MR2 2.0 16V DOHC cat	3S-FE	1990 to 1994	Toyota TCCS/AFS, TDCL
Paseo 1.5	5E-FE	1996 to 1998	Toyota TCCS
Picnic 2.0 16V DOHC	3S-FE	1997 to 2001	Toyota TCCS
Previa 2.4i 16V DOHC cat	2TZ-FE	1990 to 2000	Toyota TCCS/AFS, TDCL
RAV 4 2.0i 16V DOHC	3S-FE	1994 to 2000	Toyota TCCS
Starlet 1.3i 12V SOHC	2E-E	1993 to 1996	Toyota TCCS
Starlet 1.3 16V DOHC	4E-FE	1996 to 2000	Toyota TCCS
Supra 3.0i 24V DOHC	7M-GE	1986 to 1993	Toyota TCCS, TDCL
Supra 3.0i 24V DOHC cat	7M-GE	1986 to 1993	Toyota TCCS/AFS, TDCL
Supra 3.0i Turbo DOHC DIS cat	7M-GTE	1989 to 1993	Toyota DIS/MAP
Supra 3.0i Turbo DOHC DIS cat	2JZ-GTE	1993 to 1994	Toyota DIS/MAP
Tarago 2.4i 16V DOHC cat	2TZ-FE	1990 to 1997	Toyota TCCS/AFS
4-Runner 3.0i 4wd V6 SOHC 12V cat	3VZ-E	1991 to 1995	Toyota TCCS/AFS, TDCL

Plus All models equipped with EOBD (approximately January 2001-on)

Note: *In this vehicle list we have identified, where possible, which vehicles are equipped with either an airflow sensor (AFS) or a manifold absolute pressure (MAP) sensor, and where a TDCL self-diagnosis connector is fitted.*

Self-Diagnosis

1 Introduction

The original engine management system (EMS) fitted to Toyota vehicles was Toyota EFi, an analogue system that controlled fuel injection alone.

The first Toyota computer-controlled system (TCCS) was introduced in 1983, and by 1990 had replaced all of the early EFi systems. Toyota TCCS controls the primary ignition, fuel injection and the idle functions from within the same control module. Toyota sometimes refers to early TCCS as EFi, which can cause some confusion when attempting to identify the two systems. However, the original EFi system did not employ a self-diagnosis function.

The first versions of TCCS utilised a 2-pin SD connector, which was later replaced by a multi-pin SD connector. From about 1989, in addition to the multi-pin SD connector, Toyota vehicles were equipped with a Toyota data communication link (TDCL), which enabled full serial analysis by fault code reader. From 1983 to 1987, 4A-GE and 3S-FE engine models equipped with a MAP sensor transmitted fault codes as a straight count from 1 to 11. From about 1988, the 4A-GE or 3S-FE engines could be equipped with either an airflow sensor (AFS) or a MAP sensor, and fault codes were then transmitted as 2-digit codes for both types. All other vehicles equipped with TCCS generate 2-digit codes regardless of whether an AFS or MAP sensor is fitted. Models equipped with EOBD are fitted with a generate 5-digit fault codes, which can only be retrieved or cleared using an FCR (Fault Code Reader).

Self-Diagnosis (SD) function

The electronic control module (ECM) has a self-test capability that continually examines the signals from certain engine sensors and actuators, and then compares each signal to a table of programmed values. If the diagnostic software determines that a fault is present, the ECM stores one or more fault codes in the ECM memory. Codes will not be stored about components for which a code is not available, or for conditions not covered by the diagnostic software.

Limited operating strategy (LOS)

Toyota TCCS systems featured in this Chapter utilise LOS (a function that is commonly called the "limp-home mode"). Once certain faults have been identified (not all faults will initiate LOS), the ECM will implement LOS and refer to a programmed default value rather than the sensor signal. This enables the vehicle to be safely driven to a workshop/garage for repair or testing. Once the fault has cleared, the ECM will revert to normal operation.

Adaptive or learning capability

Toyota systems also utilise an adaptive function that will modify the basic programmed values for most effective operation during normal running, and with due regard to engine wear.

Self-Diagnosis (SD) warning light

All Toyota TCCS systems are equipped with an SD warning light located within the instrument panel. Once the ignition has been switched on, the SD light illuminates as a bulb check; after the engine has started, the warning light should extinguish. If the SD warning light comes on at any time when the engine is running, this indicates that a fault in the system has been identified. If a fault is indicated, bridging the terminals in the SD connector triggers the SD procedure as described later. The SD warning light does not illuminate for some codes.

All models equipped with EOBD, are fitted with a MIL (Malfunction Indicator Light) within the instrument cluster, which illuminates to alert the driver to the presence of a fault.

2 Self-Diagnosis connector location

5M-GE and 6M-GE engines
The very first Toyota models equipped with TCCS were fitted with a 2-pin and a single-pin SD connector positioned together in the loom (see illustration 34.1). The 2-pin and 1-pin connectors are located either close to the wiper motor, or near the distributor.

4A-GE engines (1983 to 1987) and 3S-FE engines (1986 to 1988)
4A-GE and 3S-FE models (with MAP sensor) are equipped with either a 2-pin and single SD connector positioned together in the loom (refer to illustration 34.1) or a multi-pin SD connector (see illustration 34.2). The 2-pin and 1-pin connectors are located either close to the wiper motor, or near the distributor. The multi-pin connector is usually located next to the battery. All models with the multi-pin SD connector also have a MAP sensor.

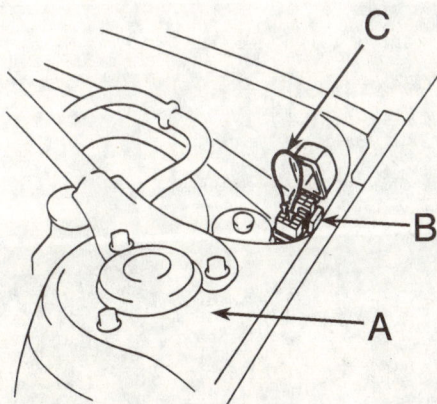

H29898

34.1 The 2-pin SD connector and single-pin connector lie close together on the wiring loom
A 2-pin SD connector (jumper lead is shown bridging the two pins in the connector)
B Single-pin connector

All Toyota engines from 1988
Later Toyota models were fitted with a multi-pin SD connector (refer to illustration 34.2). For most models, this has remained in use until the present day. The multi-pin SD connector is usually located next to the battery. On Previa models, however, the multi-pin SD connector is located at the side of the passenger's seat.

Recent Toyota TCCS with TDCL
Toyota models after 1989/90 were fitted with a TDCL in addition to the multi-pin SD connector. The TDCL connector is located under the facia, either on the passenger's or on the driver's side (see illustration 34.3). **Note:** *The TDCL connector is provided for transmission of fault codes and other data to a dedicated fault code reader. It is also possible to retrieve flash codes from vehicles equipped with the TDCL connector.*

All models with EOBD
On these vehicles, a 16-pin diagnostic connector is located under the facia - refer to Chapter 38.

34.2 Typical location of the multi-pin SD connector
A Left-hand suspension turret
B Multi-pin SD connector
C Jumper lead

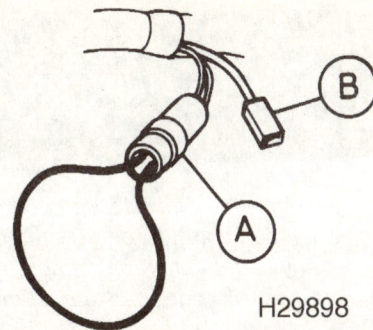

34.3 TDCL connector located under the driver's side facia

3 Retrieving fault codes without a fault code reader (FCR) - flash codes

Note 1: *During the course of certain test procedures, it is possible for additional fault codes to be generated. Care must be taken that any codes generated during test routines do not mislead diagnosis. All codes must be cleared once testing is complete.*

Note 2: *Prior to fault code retrieval, ensure that the engine is at normal operating temperature and the throttle switch is functioning correctly (indicating the idle condition).*

5M-GE and 6M-GE engines

1 Attach a voltmeter between the single-pin connector and a good vehicle earth.

2 Switch on the ignition, but do not start the engine.

3 Use a jumper lead to bridge the terminals of the two-pin connector *(refer to illustration 34.1)*.

4 The voltmeter needle should register 5 volts for two seconds, and then swing down to register 2.5 volts. Codes are output as needle sweeps between 2.5 volts and 5 volts, or between 2.5 volts and zero volts, as follows:

a) *The two digits are indicated by two series of sweeps.*
b) *The first series of sweeps indicate the multiples of ten, the second series of sweeps indicate the single units.*
c) *Tens are indicated by the voltmeter needle sweeping from 2.5 volts to 5 volts. Each sweep lasts for 0.6 seconds.*
d) *Single units are indicated by the voltmeter needle sweeping from 2.5 volts to zero volts. Each sweep lasts for 0.6 seconds.*
e) *A pause of 1 second separates the units from the tens.*
f) *Code number "32" is indicated by three sweeps of the needle from 2.5 volts to 5 volts, followed by a pause of 1 second, and then two sweeps of the needle from 2.5 volts to zero volts.*
g) *The needle will register 2.5 volts, pause for 2 seconds, then transmit the next code.*

5 Count the number of sweeps in each series, and record each code as it is transmitted. Refer to the tables at the end of the Chapter to determine the meaning of the fault code.

6 Fault codes will be transmitted in sequential order, and repeated after the highest recorded code has been displayed.

7 If no fault codes are recorded, the needle will constantly fluctuate between 2.5 volts and 5.0 volts.

8 Turn off the ignition and remove the jumper lead and voltmeter to end fault code retrieval.

4A-GE engines (1983 to 1987) and 3S-FE engines (1986 to 1988) - 2-pin connector

9 Switch on the ignition, but do not start the engine.

10 Use a jumper lead to bridge the terminals of the 2-pin connector *(refer to illustration 34.1)*.

11 The codes are displayed on the SD warning light in the instrument panel. The flashes are output as a straight count.

a) *If a fault code has been stored, the SD warning light will flash at 0.5-second intervals.*
b) *A pause of 1.5 seconds separates each flash.*
c) *A 2.5-second pause separates the transmission of each individual code.*
d) *Code number "4" is indicated by four 0.5-second flashes, with a pause of 1.5 seconds between each flash.*
e) *The codes will be transmitted in sequence. After the highest code is transmitted (in the range 1 to 11), there will be a 4.5-second pause before the sequence is repeated.*

12 Count the number of flashes, and record each code as it is transmitted. Refer to the tables at the end of the Chapter to determine the meaning of the fault code.

13 Fault codes will be transmitted in sequential order, and repeated after the highest recorded code has been displayed.

14 The SD warning light will flash on and off at regular 0.3-second intervals if no faults have been stored.

15 Turn off the ignition and remove the jumper lead to end fault code retrieval.

All Toyota models with a multi-pin connector, except TDCL

16 Switch on the ignition, but do not start the engine.

17 Use a jumper lead to bridge the terminals TE1 and E1 of the multi-pin SD connector *(see illustrations 34.4 and 34.5)*.

Note: *Terminal TE1 is sometimes identified as terminal T or T1.*

4A-GE engines (1983 to 1987) and 3S-FE engines (1986 to 1988) - with MAP sensor

18 The codes are displayed on the SD warning light in the instrument panel. The flashes are output as a straight count.

a) *If a fault code has been stored, the SD warning light will flash at 0.5-second intervals.*
b) *A pause of 1.5 seconds separates each flash.*

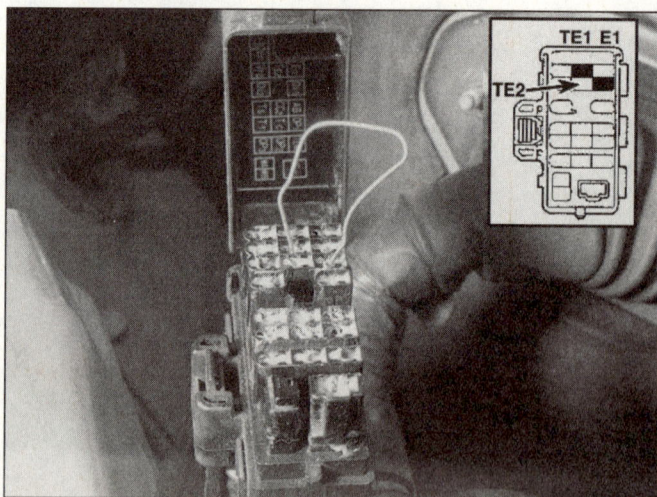

34.4 Bridge terminals TE1 (or T1) and E1 in the SD connector. This causes TCCS to flash fault codes on the SD warning light

c) *A 2.5-second pause separates the transmission of each individual code.*

d) *Code number "4" is indicated by four 0.5-second flashes, with a pause of 1.5 seconds between each flash.*

e) *The codes will be transmitted in sequence. After the highest code is transmitted (in the range 1 to 11) there will be a 4.5-second pause before the sequence is repeated.*

19 Count the number of flashes, and record each code as it is transmitted. Refer to the tables at the end of the Chapter to determine the meaning of the fault code.

20 Fault codes will be transmitted in sequential order, and repeated after the highest recorded code has been displayed.

21 The SD warning light will flash on and off at regular 0.3-second intervals if no faults have been stored.

22 Turn off the ignition and remove the jumper lead to end fault code retrieval.

All other models

23 The codes are output on the SD warning light. The flashing of the light indicates the 2-digit fault codes as follows.

a) *The two digits are indicated by two series of flashes.*

b) *The first series of flashes indicates the multiples of ten, the second series of flashes indicates the single units.*

c) *Tens are indicated by 0.5-second flashes, separated by 0.5-second pauses. Units are indicated by 0.5-second flashes, separated by 0.5-second pauses.*

d) *A 1.5-second pause separates the tens from the units. A 2.5-second pause separates the transmission of each individual code.*

e) *Code "34" is indicated by three 0.5-second flashes, followed by a 1.5-second pause, followed by four 0.5-second flashes.*

24 Count the number of flashes in each series, and record each code as it is transmitted. Refer to the tables at the end of the Chapter to determine the meaning of the fault code.

25 Fault codes will be transmitted in sequential order, and repeated after the highest recorded code has been displayed.

26 When all codes have been transmitted, the warning light will pause and then repeat the sequence.

27 If no faults have been detected, the warning light will flash on and off every 0.5 seconds for eight flashes. After a 3-second pause, the sequence will be repeated.

28 Turn off the ignition and remove the jumper lead to end fault code retrieval.

Toyota models with Toyota TCCS and TDCL

Note: *When a TDCL is provided for fault code retrieval either the multi-pin SD connector or the TDCL connector may be used for fault code retrieval. If TDCL is used, follow the routines described above, using the terminals TE1 and E1 in the TDCL instead of the multi-pin SD connector.*

Additional test mode

29 Ensure that the preparatory conditions described in Note 2 at the start of this Section are met, and that the jumper lead between terminals TE1 and E1 is disconnected (*refer to illustrations 34.4 and 34.5*).

30 Use a jumper lead to bridge terminals TE2 and E1 in the SD connector (*see illustration 34.6*).

31 Switch on the ignition. **Note:** *If the jumper lead is connected after the ignition is switched on, the test mode will fail to start.*

32 The SD warning light will flash regularly to indicate that the system has initiated test mode.

33 Start the engine and road test the vehicle. Run the vehicle at a speed of more than 6 mph (10 km/h) and attempt to reproduce the conditions during which the fault might occur.

34 Bring the vehicle to a halt with the ignition still on.

35 Remove the jumper lead from terminals TE2 and E1, and connect the lead between terminals TE1 and E1.

36 The codes recorded during the road test are output on the SD warning light. The flashing of the light indicates the 2-digit fault codes as follows:

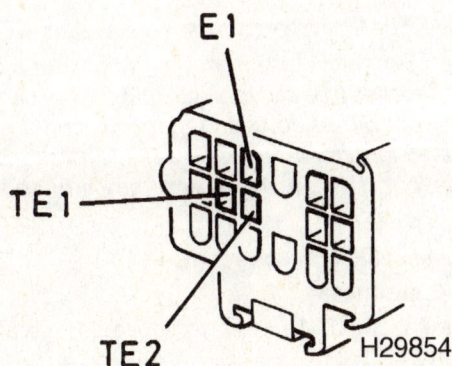

34.5 Alternative (early) SD connector - bridge terminals TE1 (or T1) and E1

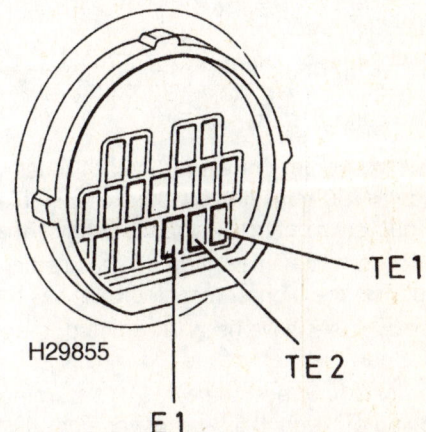

34.6 Layout of the TDCL connector intended for FCR use
TDCL pin numbers are similar to those used in the multi-pin SD connector, and this connector can also be used to retrieve flash codes

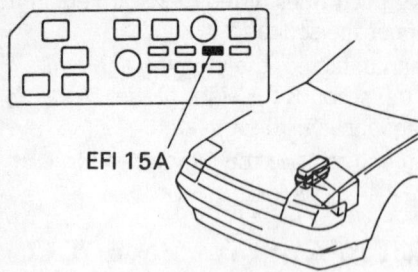

34.7 EFI fuse in the fusebox located behind the left-hand headlight

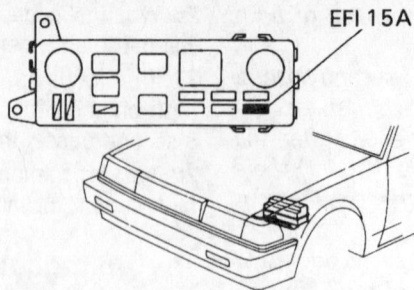

34.8 EFI fuse in the fusebox located behind the left-hand headlight (5M-GE/6M-GE)

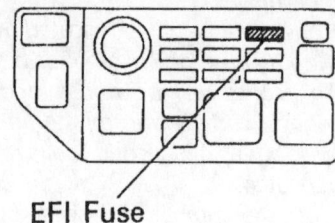

34.9 EFI fuse in the fusebox

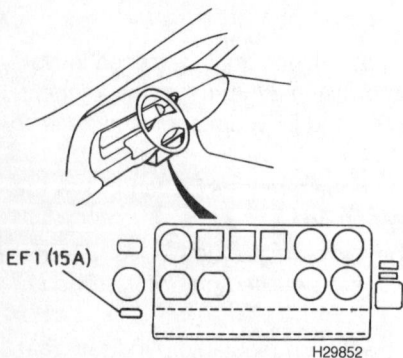

34.10 EFI fuse in the fusebox located under the facia on the driver's side

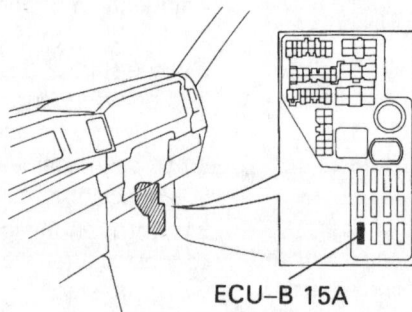

34.11 ECU-B fuse in the fusebox located on the driver's side kick panel under the facia

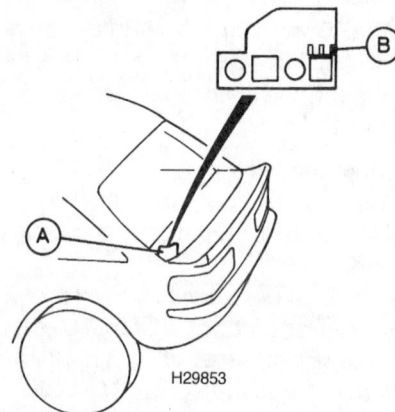

34.12 AM2 fuse (B) in the fusebox (A) located in the left-hand luggage compartment (MR2)

a) The two digits are indicated by two series of flashes.

b) The first series of flashes indicates the multiples of ten, the second series of flashes indicates the single units.

c) Tens are indicated by 0.5-second flashes, separated by 0.5-second pauses. Units are indicated by 0.5-second flashes, separated by 0.5-second pauses.

d) A 1.5-second pause separates the tens from the units. A 2.5-second pause separates the transmission of each individual code.

e) Code "34" is indicated by three 0.5-second flashes, followed by a 1.5-second pause, followed by four 0.5-second flashes.

37 Count the number of flashes in each series, and record each code as it is transmitted. Refer to the tables at the end of the Chapter to determine the meaning of the fault code.

38 Fault codes will be transmitted in sequential order, and repeated after the highest recorded code has been displayed.

39 When all codes have been transmitted, the warning light will pause and then repeat the sequence.

40 If no faults have been detected, the warning light will flash on and off every 0.5 seconds for eight flashes. After a 3-second pause, the sequence will be repeated.

41 Turn off the ignition and remove the jumper lead to end fault code retrieval.

Models with EOBD

42 Fault codes cannot be retrieved or cleared without the use of an FCR.

4 Clearing fault codes without a fault code reader (FCR)

Method 1 - all Toyota models (except EOBD)

1 Remove the 15-amp EFI fuse from the fusebox for a period of at least 30 seconds (see illustrations 34.7 to 34.10). **Note:** The fusebox layout differs according to model, and the fuses are often located in different positions. The illustrations are not exhaustive, but do show the most common fusebox locations and layouts.

Additional fuses which can be removed
2S-E and 1S-E engines

2 Remove the 7.5-amp ECU-B fuse for at least 10 seconds (see illustration 34.11).

4A-GE engines

3 Remove the 7.5 amp AM2 fuse for at least 10 seconds (see illustration 34.12). The fusebox is located either in the

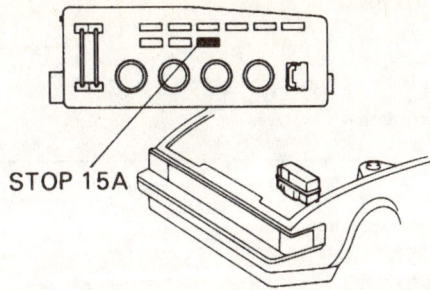

34.13 STOP fuse in the fusebox located behind the left-hand headlight (5M-GE/6M-GE)

engine compartment on the left-hand side between the left-hand suspension turret and the left-hand side headlight, or under the facia on the driver's side, or in the boot on the left-hand side.

5M-GE/6M-GE engines

4 Remove the STOP fuse for at least 10 seconds (see illustration 34.13).

Method 2

5 Turn off the ignition and disconnect the battery negative terminal for a period of approximately 15 seconds.

6 Reconnect the battery negative terminal.

Note: The first drawback to this method is that battery disconnection will re-initialise all ECM adaptive values. Re-learning the appropriate adaptive values requires starting the engine from cold, and driving at various engine speeds for approximately 20 to 30 minutes. The engine should also be allowed to idle for approximately 10 minutes. The second drawback is that the radio security codes, clock setting and other stored values will be initialised, and these must be re-entered once the battery has been reconnected. Where possible, an FCR should be used for code clearing. On models with EOBD, an FCR must be used to retrieve and clear fault codes.

5 Self-Diagnosis with a fault code reader (FCR)

Note 1: During the course of certain test procedures, it is possible for additional fault codes to be generated. Care must be taken that any codes generated during test routines do not mislead diagnosis.

Note 2: Prior to fault code retrieval, ensure that the engine is at normal operating temperature and the throttle switch is functioning correctly (indicating the idle condition).

All Toyota models

1 Connect an FCR to the SD connector. Use the FCR for the following purposes, in strict compliance with the FCR manufacturer's instructions:

  a) Retrieving fault codes.
  b) Clearing fault codes.
  c) Making adjustments.
  d) Displaying Datastream.

2 Codes must always be cleared after component testing, or after repairs involving the removal or replacement of an EMS component.

6 Guide to test procedures

1 Use an FCR to interrogate the ECM for fault codes, or gather codes manually, as described in Section 3 or 5.

Codes stored

2 If one or more fault codes are gathered, refer to the fault code tables at the end of this Chapter to determine their meaning.

3 If several codes are gathered, look for a common factor such as a defective earth return or supply.

4 Refer to the component test procedures in Chapter 4, where you will find a means of testing the majority of components and circuits found in the modern EMS.

5 Once the fault has been repaired, clear the codes and run the engine under various conditions to determine if the problem has cleared.

6 Check the ECM for fault codes once more. Repeat the above procedures where codes are still being stored.

7 Refer to Chapter 3 for more information on how to effectively test the EMS.

No codes stored

8 Where a running problem is experienced, but no codes are stored, the fault is outside of the parameters designed into the SD system. Refer to Chapter 3 for more information on how to effectively test the engine management system.

9 If the problem points to a specific component, refer to the test procedures in Chapter 4, where you will find a means of testing the majority of components and circuits found in the modern EMS.

Chapter 34

Fault code tables

Toyota TCCS fault codes (MAP sensor system, straight count)

Flash/ FCR code	Description
1	System OK
2	Manifold absolute pressure (MAP) sensor or MAP sensor circuit
3	Ignition signal from amplifier
4	Coolant temperature sensor (CTS) or CTS circuit
6	RPM signal or circuit, no RPM, TDC signal
7	Throttle pot sensor (TPS) or TPS circuit
8	Air temperature sensor (ATS) or ATS circuit
9	Vehicle speed sensor (VSS) or VSS circuit
10	Cranking signal or circuit
11	Air conditioning (A/C) switch signal or circuit

Toyota TCCS fault codes (2-digit)

Flash/ FCR code	Description
12	RPM signal or circuit
13	RPM signal or circuit
14	Ignition signal from amplifier
16	ECT control signal or circuit
21	Oxygen sensor (OS) or OS circuit, OS signal decreases
22	Coolant temperature sensor (CTS) or CTS circuit
24	Air temperature sensor (ATS) or ATS circuit
25	Oxygen sensor (OS) lean signal or OS circuit
26	Oxygen sensor (OS) rich signal or OS circuit
27	Oxygen sensor (OS) or OS circuit
28	Oxygen sensor (OS) or OS circuit
31	Airflow sensor (AFS) (when fitted) or AFS circuit
31	Manifold absolute pressure (MAP) sensor (when fitted) or MAP sensor circuit (alternative code)
32	Vane airflow sensor (AFS) or AFS circuit
34	Turbo pressure signal or circuit
35	Turbo pressure signal or circuit
41	Throttle pot sensor (TPS) or TPS circuit
42	Vehicle speed sensor (VSS) or VSS circuit
43	Cranking signal or circuit
47	Throttle pot sensor (TPS) or TPS circuit
51	Air conditioning (A/C) Switch signal or circuit
52	Knock sensor (KS) or KS circuit
53	Knock control (ECM) or circuit
54	Turbo intercooler signal or circuit
55	Knock sensor (KS) (V6) or KS circuit

Note: *Codes 16, 42, 43 and 51 are not retained by the ECM, and are only available whilst the ignition is on. Once the ignition is switched off, these codes will be cleared.*

All models with EOBD

For a list of the allocated EOBD codes beginning with P0 (Generic Powertrain), refer to Chapter 1, Section 1.

Vauxhall/Opel 35

Index of vehicles

Model	Engine code	Year	System
Astra-F 1.4i cat	C14NZ	1990 to 1996	GM-Multec CFi-he
Astra-F 1.4i cat	C14SE	1991 to 1997	GM-Multec MPi
Astra-F 1.4i cat	C14SE	1993 to 1994	GM-Multec MPi-DIS
Astra 1.4i cat	C14NZ	1990 to 1993	GM-Multec ZE CFi
Astra-F 1.4i	X14NZ	1997 to 1998	GM-Multec CFi
Astra-F 1.4i 16V	X14XE	1996 to 1998	GM-Multec-S MPi
Astra-F 1.6 cat	C16NZ	1990 to 1995	GM-Multec CFi
Astra Van 1.6i cat	C16NZ	1991 to 1994	GM-Multec CFi
Astra-F 1.6i cat	C16SE	1992 to 1997	GM-Multec MPi
Astra-F 1.6i	X16SZ	1993 to 1996	GM-Multec CFi
Astra-F 1.6i cat	C16SE	1992 to 1994	GM-Multec MPi
Astra 1.6 cat	C16NZ	1987 to 1993	GM-Multec ZE CFi
Astra-F 1.6i cat	C16NZ	1991 to 1995	GM-Multec ZE CFi
Astra-F 1.6i	X16SZR	1996 to 1998	GM-Multec CFi
Astra-F 1.6i 16V	X16XEL	1995 to 1998	GM-Multec-S
Astra-F 1.8i cat	C18NZ	1991 to 1994	GM-Multec CFi
Astra-F 1.8i 16V	C18XE	1995 on	Simtec 56.1
Astra-F 1.8i 16V	C18XEL	1995 to 1996	Simtec 56.1
Astra-F 1.8i 16V	C18XE	1993 to 1995	Simtec 56
Astra-F 2.0i 16V	X20XEV	1995 to 1996	Simtec 56.1
Astra-F 2.0i cat	C20NE	1991 to 1995	Bosch Motronic 1.5.2
Astra-F 2.0i cat	C20XE	1991 to 1993	Bosch Motronic 2.5
Astra-F 2.0i cat	C20XE	1993 to 1998	Bosch Motronic 2.8
Astra 1.8i	18SE	1987 to 1991	Bosch EZ61 ignition
Astra 1.8i	18E	1984 to 1987	GM-Multec ZE CFi
Astra-F 1.8i 16V	X18XE	1996 to 1998	Simtec 56.5
Astra GTE 2.0	20NE	1987 to 1990	Bosch Motronic ML4.1
Astra GTE 2.0	20SEH	1987 to 1990	Bosch Motronic ML4.1
Astra 2.0i	20SEH	1990 to 1993	Bosch Motronic 1.5
Astra 2.0i cat	C20NE	1991 to 1995	Bosch Motronic 1.5
Astra 2.0i 16V DOHC	20XEJ	1988 to 1991	Bosch Motronic 2.5

Model	Engine code	Year	System
Astra 2.0i 16V DOHC cat	C20XE	1990 to 1995	Bosch Motronic 2.5
Astra-F 2.0i 16V DOHC	-	1993 on	Bosch Motronic 2.5
Belmont 1.4i cat	C14NZ	1990 to 1993	GM-Multec CFi
Belmont 1.6 cat	C16NZ	1987 to 1993	GM-Multec ZE CFi
Belmont 1.8i	18E	1984 to 1987	GM-Multec ZE CFi
Belmont 1.8i	18SE	1987 to 1991	Bosch EZ61 ignition
Belmont 1.8i cat	C18NZ	1990 to 1992	GM-Multec CFi
Calibra 2.0i 16V	X20XEV	1995 to 1996	Simtec 56.1
Calibra 2.0i 16V	X20XEV	1997	Simtec 56.5
Calibra 2.0i SOHC and 4x4 cat	C20NE	1990 to 1996	Bosch Motronic 1.5
Calibra 2.0i 16V 4x4 DOHC cat	C20XE	1990 to 1993	Bosch Motronic 2.5
Calibra 2.0i 16V 4x4 DOHC cat	C20XE	1993 on	Bosch Motronic 2.8
Calibra 2.5i 24V	C25XE	1993 to 1996	Bosch Motronic 2.8
Calibra 2.5i	X25XE	1997	Bosch Motronic 2.8
Carlton 2.0i	20SE	1987 to 1990	Bosch Motronic ML4.1
Carlton 2.0i SOHC	20SE	1990 to 1994	Bosch Motronic 1.5
Carlton 2.0i SOHC cat	C20NEJ	1990 to 1993	Bosch Motronic 1.5
Carlton 2.4i CIH cat	C24NE	1990 to 1993	Bosch Motronic 1.5
Carlton 2.6i CIH cat	C26NE	1990 to 1994	Bosch Motronic 1.5
Carlton 3.0i CIH cat	C30NE	1990 to 1994	Bosch Motronic 1.5
Carlton 24V DOHC 24V cat	C30SE	1989 to 1994	Bosch Motronic 1.5
Carlton 24V Estate DOHC 24V cat	C30SEJ	1990 to 1994	Bosch Motronic 1.5
Cavalier 1.6i cat	C16NZ	1990 to 1993	GM-Multec CFi
Cavalier 1.6i cat	C16NZ2	1993 to 1994	GM-Multec CFi
Cavalier 1.6i 7 cat	E16NZ	1988 to 1995	GM-Multec ZE CFi
Cavalier 1.6i E-Drive	X16XZ	1993 to 1995	GM-Multec ZE CFi
Cavalier 1.6i	C16NZ	1995 on	GM-Multec CFi
Cavalier 1.6i	C16NZ2	1995 on	GM-Multec CFi
Cavalier 1.8i cat	C18NZ	1990 to 1995	GM-Multec CFi
Cavalier 2.0	20NE	1987 to 1988	Bosch Motronic ML4.1
Cavalier SRi 130	20SEH	1987 to 1988	Bosch Motronic ML4.1
Cavalier 2.0 SRi	20SEH	1988 to 1990	Bosch Motronic ML4.1
Cavalier 2.0i SOHC	20NE	1990 to 1993	Bosch Motronic 1.5
Cavalier 2.0i SRi SOHC	20SEH	1990 to 1993	Bosch Motronic 1.5
Cavalier 2.0i 4x4 SOHC	20SEH	1990 to 1993	Bosch Motronic 1.5
Cavalier 2.0i cat SOHC	C20NE	1990 to 1993	Bosch Motronic 1.5
Cavalier 2.0i 16V DOHC	20XEJ	1989 to 1991	Bosch Motronic 2.5
Cavalier 2.0 16V	C20XE	1989 to 1995	Bosch Motronic 2.5
Cavalier 2.0i 16V	X20XEV	1995	Simtec 56.1
Cavalier Turbo cat	C20LET	1993 to 1995	Bosch Motronic 2.7
Cavalier 2.5i 24V	C25XE	1993 to 1995	Bosch Motronic 2.8
Corsa 1.2i cat	X12SZ	1993 to 1996	GM-Multec CFi
Corsa 1.2i cat	C12NZ	1990 to 1994	GM-Multec CFi
Corsa-B and Combo 1.2i	C12NZ	1993 to 1998	GM-Multec CFi
Corsa-B 1.2i E-Drive	X12SZ	1993 to 1999	Multec ZE CFi
Corsa 1.4i cat	C14NZ	1990 to 1993	GM-Multec CFi
Corsa-B 1.4i and Van	C14NZ	1993 to 1998	GM-Multec ZE CFi
Corsa 1.4i cat	C14SE	1993 to 1994	GM-Multec MPi
Corsa-B 1.4i and Van	C14NZ	1993 to 1996	GM-Multec CFi
Corsa-B 1.4i 16V	X14XE	1995 to 2000	GM-Multec XS
Corsa-B and Combo 1.4i	X14SZ	1996 to 2000	GM-Multec CFi
Corsa 1.4i cat	C14SE	1992 to 1993	GM-Multec MPi
Corsa 1.6i cat	C16NZ	1990 to 1992	GM-Multec CFi
Corsa 1.6i cat	C16SE	1992 to 1993	GM-Multec MPi
Corsa 1.6i cat	C16SE	1993 to 1994	GM-Multec MPi
Corsa-A 1.6i SPi cat	C16NZ	1988 to 1991	GM-Multec ZE CFi
Corsa-B 1.6 GSi	C16XE	1993 to 1995	GM-Multec MPi
Corsa 1.6 MPi cat	C16SEI	1990 to 1992	Bosch Motronic 1.5
Corsa-B 1.6i	X16XE	1995 to 2000	GM-Multec XS
Frontera 2.0i cat SOHC	C20NE	1991 to 1995	Bosch Motronic 1.5
Frontera 2.0i	X20SE	1995 to 1998	Bosch Motronic 1.5.4
Frontera 2.2i	X22XE	1995 to 1998	Bosch Motronic 1.5.4
Frontera 2.4i cat CIH	C24NE	1991 to 1995	Bosch Motronic 1.5
Kadett-E 1.4i cat	C14NZ	1990 to 1993	GM-Multec CFi
Kadett-E 1.6 cat	C16NZ	1990 to 1993	GM-Multec CFi
Kadett-E 1.8i cat	C18NZ	1990 to 1991	GM-Multec CFi
Kadett 2.0i	20NE	1987 to 1990	Bosch Motronic ML4.1
Kadett 2.0i	20SEH	1987 to 1990	Bosch Motronic ML4.1

Model	Engine code	Year	System
Kadett GSi 8V 2.0i SOHC	20SEH	1990 to 1993	Bosch Motronic 1.5
Kadett 2.0i cat SOHC	C20NE	1990 to 1993	Bosch Motronic 1.5
Kadett 2.0i 16V DOHC	C20XEJ	1990 to 1991	Bosch Motronic 2.5
Kadett 2.0i 16V DOHC cat	C20XE	1990 to 1992	Bosch Motronic 2.5
Kadett 1.6 cat	C16NZ	1987 to 1993	Multec ZE CFi
Nova 1.2i cat	C12NZ	1990 to 1994	GM-Multec CFi
Nova 1.4i cat	C14NZ	1990 to 1993	GM-Multec CFi
Nova 1.4i cat	C14SE	1992 to 1993	GM-Multec MPi
Nova 1.6i cat	C16NZ	1990 to 1992	GM-Multec CFi
Nova 1.6i cat	C16SE	1992 to 1993	GM-Multec MPi
Nova 1.6i cat	C16SE	1993 to 1994	GM-Multec MPi
Nova 1.6 MPi cat	C16SEI	1990 to 1992	Bosch Motronic 1.5
Omega-B 2.0l	X20SE	1994 to 1997	Bosch Motronic 1.5.4
Omega 2.0i	20SE	1987 to 1990	Bosch Motronic ML4.1
Omega 2.0i SOHC	20SE	1990 to 1993	Bosch Motronic 1.5
Omega 2.0i SOHC cat	C20NE	1990 to 1993	Bosch Motronic 1.5
Omega 2.0i SOHC cat	C20NEJ	1990 to 1993	Bosch Motronic 1.5
Omega-B 2.0i 16V	X20XEV	1994 to 1996	Simtec 56.1
Omega-B 2.0i 16V	X20XEV	1997 to 2001	Simtec 56.5
Omega 2.4i CIH cat	C24NE	1990 to 1993	Bosch Motronic 1.5
Omega 2.5i	X25XE	1994 to 1997	Bosch Motronic 2.8.1
Omega 2.6i CIH cat	C26NE	1990 to 1993	Bosch Motronic 1.5
Omega 3.0i	X30XE	1994 to 1997	Bosch Motronic 2.8.1
Omega 3.0i CIH cat	C30NE	1990 to 1994	Bosch Motronic 1.5
Omega 24V DOHC cat	C30SE	1989 to 1994	Bosch Motronic 1.5
Omega 24V DOHC Estate cat	C30SEJ	1990 to 1994	Bosch Motronic 1.5
Senator 2.6i CIH cat	C26NE	1990 to 1993	Bosch Motronic 1.5
Senator 3.0i CIH cat	C30NE	1990 to 1994	Bosch Motronic 1.5
Senator 24V DOHC cat	C30SE	1989 to 1994	Bosch Motronic 1.5
Senator 24V DOHC Estate cat	C30SEJ	1990 to 1992	Bosch Motronic 1.5
Tigra 1.4i 16V	X14XE	1994 to 2001	GM-Multec MPi
Tigra 1.6i	X16XE	1994 to 2001	GM-Multec MPi
Vectra 1.6i cat	C16NZ	1990 to 1993	GM-Multec CFi
Vectra 1.6i cat	C16NZ2	1993 to 1994	GM-Multec CFi
Vectra 1.6i & cat	E16NZ	1988 to 1995	GM-Multec ZE CFi
Vectra-A 1.6i E-Drive	X16XZ	1993 to 1995	GM-Multec ZE CFi
Vectra-B 1.6i	X16SZR	1995 to 2001	GM-Multec SPi
Vectra-B 1.6i 16V	X16XEL	1995 to 2001	GM-Multec-S SEFi
Vectra 1.8i cat	C18NZ	1990 to 1994	GM-Multec CFi
Vectra-B 1.8i 16V	X18XE	1995 to 1999	Simtec 56.5
Vectra-B 2.0i 16V	X20XEV	1995 to 1999	Simtec 56.5
Vectra 2.0i	20SEH	1987 to 1990	Bosch Motronic ML4.1
Vectra 2.0i cat	C20NE	1991 to 1992	Bosch Motronic 1.5
Vectra 2.0 SOHC	20NE	1990 to 1993	Bosch Motronic 1.5
Vectra 2.0i and 4x4 SOHC	20SEH	1990 to 1993	Bosch Motronic 1.5
Vectra 2.0i SOHC cat	-	1990 to 1993	Bosch Motronic 1.5
Vectra GSi 200016V DOHC	-	1989 to 1991	Bosch Motronic 2.5
Vectra 2.0 16V 4x4 DOHC cat	C20XE	1989 to 1992	Bosch Motronic 2.5
Vectra-A 2.0i 16V	X20XEV	1995	Simtec 56.1
Vectra-A Turbo cat	C20LET	1993 to 1995	Bosch Motronic 2.7
Vectra-A 2.5i 24V	C25XE	1993 to 1995	Bosch Motronic 2.8
Vectra-B 2.5i V6	X25XE	1995 to 2001	Bosch Motronic 2.8.3

Plus All models equipped with EOBD (approximately January 2001-on)

Self-Diagnosis

1   Introduction

The engine management systems fitted to Vauxhall vehicles are mainly of Bosch or GM-Multec origin, and include Bosch Motronic and GM Multec MPi and SPi. Other systems include Simtec and Bosch EZ-Plus.

Bosch Motronic, GM-Multec and Simtec are full engine management systems that control primary ignition, fuelling and idle functions from within the same control module. EZ-Plus controls the ignition function alone.

Self-Diagnosis (SD) function

Each electronic control module (ECM) has a self-test capability that continually examines the signals from certain engine sensors and actuators, and compares each signal to a table of programmed values. If the diagnostic software determines that one or more faults are present, the ECM stores one or more appropriate fault code. Codes will not be stored about components for which a code is not available, or for conditions not covered by the diagnostic software. The fault codes are 2- or 3-digits in length, and may be retrieved either by FCR or by manual means as flash codes. Models equipped with EOBD generated 5-digit fault codes, which can only be retrieved or cleared by means of an FCR.

Limited operating strategy (LOS)

Bosch Motronic, GM-Multec and Simtec systems featured in this Chapter utilise LOS (a function that is commonly called the "limp-home mode"). Once certain faults have been identified (not all faults will initiate LOS), the ECM will implement LOS and refer to a programmed default value rather than the sensor signal. This enables the vehicle to be safely driven to a workshop/garage for repair or testing. Once the fault has cleared, the ECM will revert to normal operation. EZ-Plus systems do not utilise LOS.

Adaptive or learning capability

Vauxhall systems also utilise an adaptive function that will modify the basic programmed values for most effective operation during normal running, and with due regard to engine wear. EZ-Plus systems do not utilise adaptive control.

Self-Diagnosis (SD) warning light

Vauxhall vehicles with engine management are normally fitted with a SD warning light located within the instrument panel.

2 Self-Diagnosis connector location

10-pin SD connector

The SD connector (GM term ALDL - assembly line diagnostic link) is either located under the facia in the passenger compartment fusebox, or in the engine compartment close to the right or left-hand bulkhead (see illustrations 35.1 and 35.2). In Frontera models, the SD connector is located behind the right-hand headlight. **Note:** *The GM 10-pin SD connector is provided for transmission of fault codes to a dedicated FCR. Retrieval of flash codes by manual means is also possible.*

16-pin OBD connector

From 1995 onwards, a 16-pin OBD SD connector, located in a central position under the facia, is provided in some models for transmission of fault codes to a dedicated

35.1 SD connector (ALDl) located under the facia in the passenger compartment fusebox

FCR. In some early models it is also possible to retrieve flash codes from vehicles equipped with the 16-pin OBD connector. A fault code reader must be used to retrieve the 5-digit P-codes generated by later vehicles. For EOBD diagnostic plug locations, refer to Chapter 38.

3 Retrieving fault codes without a fault code reader (FCR) - flash codes

Note: *During the course of certain test procedures, it is possible for additional fault codes to be generated. Care must be taken that any codes generated during test routines do not mislead diagnosis. All codes must be cleared once testing is complete.*

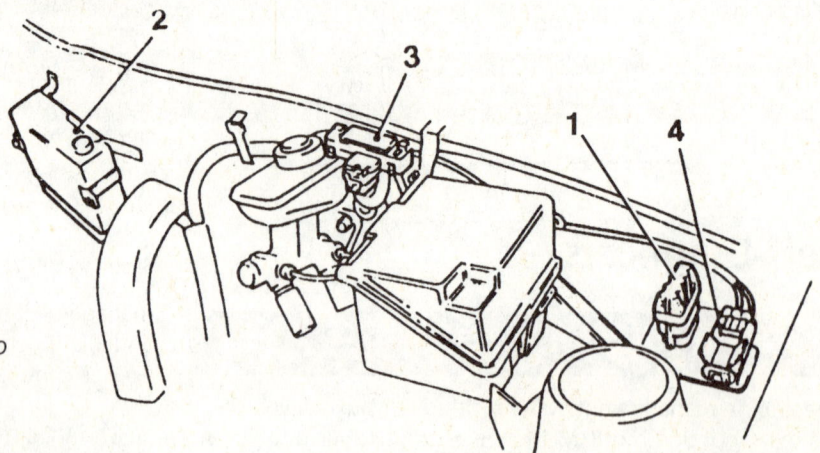

35.2 SD connector (ALDL) located on the bulkhead (Bosch EZ-Plus)

1 SD connector   2 ECM   3 MAP sensor   4 Octane plug

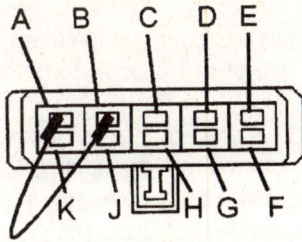

35.3 10-pin SD connector - initiate flash code retrieval by bridging terminals A and B in the SD connector. Observe code output on the SD warning light

10-pin SD connector

1 Use a jumper lead to bridge terminals A and B in the SD connector *(see illustration 35.3)*.

2 The codes are output on the SD warning light. The flashing of the light indicates the fault codes as follows:

a) *The two digits are indicated by two series of flashes.*

b) *The first series of flashes indicates the multiples of ten, the second series of flashes indicates the single units.*

c) *Tens are indicated by 1-second flashes, separated by short pauses. Units are indicated by 1-second flashes, separated by short pauses.*

d) *A short pause separates the tens from the units. A slightly longer pause separates the transmission of each individual code.*

e) *Code "42" is indicated by four 1-second flashes, followed by a pause, followed by two further 1-second flashes.*

3 Count the number of flashes in each series, and record each code as it is transmitted. Refer to the tables at the end of the Chapter to determine the meaning of the fault code.

4 The first code that is retrieved will be code number "12", which indicates the start of code output. Ignore this code.

5 Each flash code will be repeated three times, followed by the next code in sequence.

6 Turn off the ignition and remove the jumper lead to end fault code retrieval.

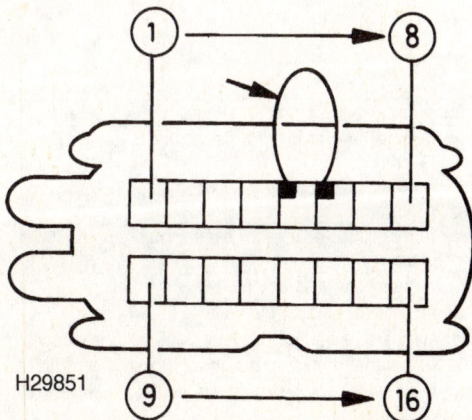

35.4 16-pin SD connector - initiate flash code retrieval by bridging terminals 5 and 6 in the SD connector. Observe code output on the SD warning light

16-pin connector

7 Use a jumper lead to bridge terminals 5 and 6 in the SD connector *(see illustration 35.4)*. **Note:** *2-digit flash code can only be retrieved from some early models equipped with the 16-pin OBD connector. A fault code reader is required 5-digit P-codes.*

8 The codes are output on the SD warning light. The flashing of the light indicates the fault codes in the same way as described for 10-pin SD connector systems in paragraph 2.

9 Count the number of flashes in each series, and record each code as it is transmitted. Refer to the tables at the end of the Chapter to determine the meaning of the fault code.

10 The first code that is retrieved will be code number "12", which indicates the start of code output. Ignore this code.

11 Each flash code will be repeated three times, followed by the next code in sequence.

12 Turn off the ignition and remove the jumper lead to end fault code retrieval.

Oxygen sensor (OS) switching

13 Bridge terminals A and B in the SD connector and run the engine.

C14NZ engine up to February 1991

14 If the OS has not reached operating temperature and is not switching, the warning light will remain illuminated.

C12NZ and C14NZ engines after February 1991

15 If the OS has not reached operating temperature and is not switching, the warning light will flash at a frequency of 2.5 times per second (2.5 Hz).

4 Clearing fault codes without a fault code reader (FCR)

All models (except EOBD)

1 Turn off the ignition and disconnect the battery negative terminal for a period of approximately 5 minutes.

2 Reconnect the battery negative terminal.

Note: *The first drawback to this method is that battery disconnection will re-initialise all ECM adaptive values. Re-learning the appropriate adaptive values requires starting the engine from cold, and driving at various engine speeds for approximately 20 to 30 minutes. The engine should also be allowed to idle for approximately 10 minutes. The second drawback is that the radio security codes, clock setting and other stored values will be initialised, and these must be re-entered once the battery has been reconnected. Where possible, an FCR should be used for code clearing. On models equipped with EOBD, an FCR is essential for retrieving and clearing fault codes.*

5 Self-Diagnosis with a fault code reader (FCR)

Note: *During the course of certain test procedures, it is possible for additional fault codes to be generated. Care must be taken that any codes generated during test routines do not mislead diagnosis.*

All Vauxhall/Opel models

1 Connect an FCR to the SD connector. Use the FCR for the following purposes, in strict compliance with the FCR manufacturer's instructions:

    a) Retrieving fault codes.
    b) Clearing fault codes.
    c) Testing actuators.
    d) Displaying Datastream.

2 Codes must always be cleared after component testing, or after repairs involving the removal or replacement of an EMS component.

6 Guide to test procedures

1 Use an FCR to interrogate the ECM for fault codes, or manually gather codes as described above.

Codes stored

2 If one or more fault codes are gathered, refer to the fault code tables at the end of this Chapter to determine their meaning.

3 If several codes are gathered, look for a common factor such as a defective earth return or supply.

4 Refer to the component test procedures in Chapter 4, where you will find a means of testing the majority of components and circuits found in the modern EMS.

5 Once the fault has been repaired, clear the codes and run the engine under various conditions to determine if the problem has cleared.

6 Check the ECM for fault codes once more. Repeat the above procedures where codes are still being stored.

7 Refer to Chapter 3 for more information on how to effectively test the EMS.

No codes stored

8 Where a running problem is experienced, but no codes are stored, the fault is outside of the parameters designed into the SD system. Refer to Chapter 3 for more information on how to effectively test the engine management system.

9 If the problem points to a specific component, refer to the test procedures in Chapter 4, where you will find a means of testing the majority of components and circuits found in the modern EMS.

Fault code tables

Bosch Motronic, GM Multec and Simtec

Flash/ FCR code	Description
12	Initiation of diagnosis
13	Oxygen sensor (OS) or OS circuit, no change in voltage/open-circuit
14	Coolant temperature sensor (CTS) or CTS circuit, low voltage
15	Coolant temperature sensor (CTS) or CTS circuit, high voltage
16	Knock sensor (KS) or KS circuit, no change in voltage (Bosch Motronic, Simtec)
17	Knock sensor (KS) two or KS circuit, no change in voltage (Bosch Motronic, GM Multec)
18	Knock control unit or circuit, no signal: ECM fault (Bosch Motronic. GM Multec)
19	RPM signal or RPM circuit, interrupted signal
21	Throttle pot sensor (TPS) or TPS circuit, high voltage
22	Throttle pot sensor (TPS) or TPS circuit, low voltage
23	Knock control module or circuit (Bosch Motronic, Simtec)
24	Vehicle speed sensor (VSS) or VSS circuit

Flash/ FCR code	Description
25	Injector number one or injector circuit, high voltage
26	Injector number two or injector circuit, high voltage (Bosch Motronic, Simtec)
27	Injector number three or injector circuit, high voltage (Bosch Motronic, Simtec)
28	Injector number four or injector circuit, high voltage (Bosch Motronic, Simtec)
28	Fuel pump relay contacts or circuit (GM Multec)
29	Fuel pump relay or circuit, low voltage (GM Multec)
29	Injector number five or Injector circuit, high voltage (Bosch Motronic)
31	Engine RPM signal or circuit, no signal (Bosch Motronic)
32	Injector number six or Injector circuit, voltage high (Bosch Motronic)
32	Fuel pump relay or fuel pump circuit, high voltage (GM Multec)
33	Manifold absolute pressure (MAP) sensor or MAP sensor circuit, voltage too high (GM Multec, Bosch Motronic)

Flash/ FCR code	Description
33	Exhaust gas recirculation (EGR) valve - wiring or EGR circuit (Simtec)
34	Exhaust gas recirculation (EGR) valve - wiring or EGR circuit, voltage high (Simtec, Bosch Motronic)
34	Manifold absolute pressure (MAP) sensor or MAP sensor circuit, low voltage (GM Multec)
35	Idle speed control valve (ISCV) or ISCV circuit; poor or no idle speed control (GM Multec, Bosch Motronic)
37	Engine self-diagnosis, low voltage (Bosch Motronic, Simtec)
38	Oxygen sensor (OS) or OS circuit, voltage low (model year 1990 on) (Bosch Motronic, Simtec)
39	Oxygen sensor (OS) or OS circuit, voltage high (model year 1990 on) (Bosch Motronic, Simtec)
41	Vehicle speed sensor (VSS) or VSS circuit, low voltage (Bosch Motronic)
41	Amplifier control signal, cylinders. 2 and 3 (DIS) or circuit, high voltage (GM Multec)
41	Amplifier control signal, cylinders. 1 and 4 (DIS) or circuit, high voltage (GM Multec)
42	Primary ignition w/distributor or circuit, high voltage (GM Multec)
42	Vehicle speed sensor (VSS) or VSS circuit, high voltage (Bosch Motronic)
44	Oxygen sensor (OS) or OS circuit, air/fuel mixture too lean
45	Oxygen sensor (OS) or OS circuit, air/fuel mixture too rich
46	Amplifier (DIS) control signal (A+B) or circuit, high voltage (GM Multec)
46	Air pump relay or circuit (Simtec)
47	Air pump relay or circuit, low voltage (Bosch Motronic, Simtec)
48	Battery voltage, low voltage (Bosch Motronic, Simtec)
49	Battery voltage, high voltage
51	Programmable memory (PROM) error or circuit (Bosch Motronic)
51	Electronic control module (ECM) defective (disconnect and reconnect ECM and then recheck for fault codes) (GM Multec)
52	Engine check light: final stage, high voltage (Bosch Motronic, Simtec)
53	Fuel pump relay or circuit, low voltage (Bosch Motronic, Simtec)
54	Fuel pump relay or circuit, high voltage (Bosch Motronic, Simtec)
55	Electronic control module (ECM) fault
56	Idle speed control valve (ISCV) or ISCV circuit, short to earth (Bosch Motronic, Simtec)
57	Idle speed control valve (ISCV) or ISCV circuit, interruption (Bosch Motronic, Simtec)
59	Inlet manifold valve or circuit, low voltage (Bosch Motronic)
61	Fuel tank vent valve (FTVV) or FTVV circuit, low voltage (Bosch Motronic, Simtec)
62	Fuel tank vent valve (FTVV) or FTVV circuit, high voltage (Bosch Motronic, Simtec)
63	Inlet manifold valve or circuit, high voltage (Bosch Motronic)
63	Amplifier control signal, cylinders 2 and 3 (DIS) low voltage (GM Multec)
64	Amplifier control signal, cylinders 1 and 4 (DIS) low voltage (GM Multec)
64	Primary ignition (w/distributor) or circuit, low voltage (GM Multec)
65	CO pot or CO pot circuit, low voltage (Bosch Motronic)
66	CO pot or CO pot circuit, high voltage (Bosch Motronic)
67	Throttle switch (TS), idle contact (Bosch Motronic)
67	Mass airflow sensor (AFS) or AFS circuit (GM Multec)
69	Air temperature sensor (ATS) or ATS circuit, low voltage (Bosch Motronic, Simtec)
69	Mass airflow sensor (AFS) or AFS circuit (GM Multec)
71	Air temperature sensor (ATS) or ATS circuit, high voltage
72	Throttle switch (TS), full-load contact (Bosch Motronic)
72	Amplifier (DIS) control signal (A+B) or circuit (GM Multec)
73	Airflow sensor (AFS) or AFS circuit, low voltage (Bosch Motronic, Simtec)
74	Airflow sensor (AFS) or AFS circuit, high voltage (Bosch Motronic, Simtec)

Flash/ FCR code	Description
75	Transmission switch, low voltage
76	Automatic transmission torque control or circuit
79	Traction control unit (Bosch Motronic)
81	Injector number one or Injector circuit, low voltage
82	Injector number two or Injector circuit, low voltage (Bosch Motronic, Simtec)
83	Injector number three or Injector circuit, low voltage (Bosch Motronic, Simtec)
84	Injector number four or Injector circuit, low voltage (Bosch Motronic, Simtec)
85	Injector number five or Injector circuit, low voltage (Bosch Motronic)
86	Injector number six or Injector circuit, low voltage (Bosch Motronic)
87	Air conditioning (A/C) cut-off relay or A/C circuit, low voltage (Bosch Motronic, Simtec)
88	Air conditioning (A/C) cut-off relay or A/C circuit, high voltage (Bosch Motronic, Simtec)
89	Oxygen sensor (OS) or OS circuit, low voltage (Bosch Motronic)
91	Oxygen sensor (OS) or OS circuit, high voltage (Bosch Motronic, Simtec)
92	Camshaft position (CMP) sensor or CMP sensor circuit (Simtec)
93	Hall-effect sensor (HES) or HES circuit, low voltage (Bosch Motronic)
93*	Quad drive module (in ECM) (GM Multec)
94	Hall-effect sensor (HES) or HES circuit, high voltage (Bosch Motronic)
95	Hot start valve or circuit, low voltage (Bosch Motronic)
96	Hot start valve or circuit, high voltage (Bosch Motronic)
97	Traction control unit or circuit, incorrect signal (Bosch Motronic)
98	Oxygen sensor (OS) or OS circuit wiring break (Bosch Motronic, Simtec)
99	Code unknown
113	Turbo boost pressure solenoid valve (BPSV) or BPSV circuit (Bosch Motronic)
114	Idle boost pressure, above upper limit (Bosch Motronic)
115	Full boost pressure, below lower limit (Bosch Motronic)
116	Boost pressure, above upper limit (Bosch Motronic)
117	Wastegate valve or circuit, low voltage (Bosch Motronic)
118	Wastegate valve or circuit, high voltage (Bosch Motronic)
121	Oxygen sensor (OS) 2 or OS circuit, lean exhaust (Bosch Motronic)
122	Oxygen sensor (OS) 2 or OS circuit, rich exhaust (Bosch Motronic)
123	Inlet manifold valve 1 (Bosch Motronic)
124	Inlet manifold valve 2 (Bosch Motronic)
132	Exhaust gas recirculation (EGR) valve or EGR circuit (Bosch Motronic)
133	Inlet manifold valve 2 or circuit, high voltage (Bosch Motronic)
133	Inlet manifold valve 2 or circuit, low voltage (Bosch Motronic)
134	Exhaust gas recirculation (EGR) valve 2 or EGR circuit, low voltage (Bosch Motronic)
134	Inlet manifold valve 2 or circuit, high voltage (Bosch Motronic)
135	Check engine light, low voltage (Bosch Motronic)
136	Electronic control module (ECM) (Bosch Motronic)
137	Electronic control module (ECM) box, high temperature (Bosch Motronic)

*Note: If code 93, "quad driver" is present, the fault may be in one of three circuits. The circuits are:

a) Warning light circuit
b) Air conditioning circuit.
c) Engine speed signal to automatic transmission ECM.

If the quad driver is actuated, the FCR will test the circuits and report on which is the faulty one.

Bosch EZ-Plus

Flash/ FCR code	Description
31	No engine RPM output signal
33	Manifold absolute pressure (MAP) sensor or MAP sensor circuit, voltage too high
34	Manifold absolute pressure (MAP) sensor or MAP sensor circuit, voltage too low
36	RON coding circuit
42	No electronic spark timing signal
46	Engine oil temperature, voltage too low
47	Engine oil temperature, voltage too high
48	Battery voltage too low
49	Battery voltage too high
55	Replace electronic control module (ECM)
56	Idle speed control valve (ISCV) or ISCV circuit, voltage too high
57	Idle speed control valve (ISCV) or ISCV circuit, voltage too low

Flash/ FCR code	Description
67	Idle position switch or circuit, voltage too low
68	Idle position switch or circuit, voltage too high
72	Full-load position switch, voltage too low
75	Torque control, voltage too low
76	Continuous torque control or circuit
95	Engine load signal Input, voltage too low
98	Positive temperature co-efficient (PTC) output, voltage too low
99	Positive temperature co-efficient (PTC) output, voltage too high

All models with EOBD

For a list of the allocated EOBD codes beginning with P0 (Generic Powertrain), refer to Chapter 1, Section 1.

Volkswagen

Index of vehicles

Model	Engine code	Year	System
Caddy Pick-up	AEE	1997 to 2001	Magneti-Marelli 1AV
Caravelle 2.0i and cat	AAC	1991 to 2001	VAG Digifant
Caravelle 2.0i cat	AAC	1994 to 1995	VAG Digifant
Caravelle 2.5i	ACU	1994 to 1997	VAG Digifant
Caravelle 2.8	AES	1996 to 1998	Bosch Motronic
Corrado 1.8i (G60 supercharger) cat	PG	1992 to 1993	VAG
Corrado 2.0 16V	9A	1992 to 1996	Bosch KE-Motronic 1.2
Corrado 2.0 8V	ADY	1994 to 1996	Simos
Corrado VR6	ABV	1992 to 1996	Bosch Motronic 2.9
Corrado 2.0i cat	2E	1993 to 1994	VAG Digifant
Golf 1.3i cat	AAV	1991 to 1992	Bosch Mono-Motronic 1.2.1
Golf 1.4i cat	ABD	1991 to 1995	Bosch Mono-Motronic 1.2.3R
Golf 1.4i	AEX	1995 to 1998	Bosch Motronic MP9.0
Golf 1.6i cat	ABU	1993 to 1995	Bosch Mono-Motronic 1.2.3
Golf 1.6i cat	AEA	1994 to 1995	Bosch Mono-Motronic 1.3
Golf 1.6i	AEK	1994 to 1995	Bosch Motronic
Golf 1.6i 8V	AEE	1995 to 1998	Magneti-Marelli 1AV
Golf 1.6 8V	AFT	1996 to 1998	Simos 4S2
Golf 1.8i	GX	1984 to 1992	Bosch KE-Jetronic
Golf 1.8i cat	GX	1984 to 1992	Bosch KE-Jetronic
Golf 16V cat	PL	1986 to 1992	Bosch KE-Jetronic
Golf Syncro 2.9	ABV	1994 to 1998	Bosch Motronic 2.9 MPi
Golf 1.8i cat	AAM	1992 to 1998	Bosch Mono-Motronic 1.2.3
Golf 1.8i cat	ABS	1992 to 1994	Bosch Mono-Motronic 1.2.2
Golf 1.8i and 4x4	ADZ	1994 to 1998	Bosch Mono-Motronic
Golf 1.8i cat	RP	1987 to 1992	Bosch Mono-Jetronic A2.2
Golf 2.0i cat	2E	1991 to 1995	VAG Digifant
Golf 2.0i 16V cat	ABF	1992 to 1998	VAG Digifant

Model	Engine code	Year	System
Golf 2.0i	ADY	1994 to 1997	Simos
Golf 2.0	AGG	1996 to 1998	Simos 4S MPi
Golf VR6	AAA	1992 to 1996	Bosch Motronic 2.7
Jetta 16V cat	PL	1986 to 1992	Bosch KE-Jetronic
Jetta 1.8i cat	RP	1987 to 1992	Bosch Mono-Jetronic A2.2
Jetta 1.8i	GX	1986 to 1992	Bosch KE-Jetronic
Jetta 1.8i cat	GX	1986 to 1992	Bosch KE-Jetronic
LT 2.3	AGL	1997 to 2001	Bosch Motronic
Passat 1.6i cat	1F	1988 to 1990	Bosch Mono-Jetronic
Passat 16V cat	9A	1988 to 1993	Bosch KE1.2-Motronic
Passat 1.6i	AEK	1994 to 1996	Bosch M2.9 Motronic
Passat 1.8 cat	JN	1984 to 1988	Bosch KE-Jetronic
Passat 1.8i and cat	RP	1988 to 1991	Bosch Mono-Jetronic A2.2
Passat 1.8i	RP	1990 to 1991	Bosch Mono-Motronic 1.2.1
Passat 1.8i and cat	RP	1990 to 1991	Bosch Mono-Motronic 1.2.1
Passat 1.8i cat	AAM	1990 to 1992	Bosch Mono-Motronic 1.2.1
Passat 1.8i cat	AAM	1992 to 1994	Bosch Mono-Motronic 1.2.3
Passat 1.8i cat	AAM	1993 to 1994	Bosch Mono-Motronic 1.2.3
Passat 1.8i cat	AAM	1994 to 1995	Bosch Mono-Motronic 1.3
Passat 1.8i	ABS	1991 to 1993	Bosch Mono-Motronic 1.2.1
Passat 1.8i	AAM	1993 to 1996	Bosch Mono-Motronic 1.2.1
Passat 1.8i	ABS	1991 to 1992	Bosch Mono-Motronic 1.2.1
Passat 1.8i	ABS	1992 to 1994	Bosch Mono-Motronic 1.2.3
Passat 1.8i cat	ABS	1992 to 1994	Bosch Mono-Motronic 1.2.3
Passat 1.8i cat	ADZ	1994 to 1997	Bosch Mono-Motronic 1.2.3
Passat 2.0 and Syncro	ADY	1994 to 1996	Simos
Passat 2.0i	AGG	1995 to 1997	Simos
Passat VR6	AAA	1991 to 1993	Bosch Motronic M2.7/2.9
Passat 2.0i and 4 x 4 cat	2E	1992 to 1994	VAG Digifant
Passat 2.0i cat	ABF	1994 to 1995	VAG Digifant
Passat 2.8 VR6	AAA	1993 to 1996	Bosch Motronic M2.7/2.9
Passat 2.9 Syncro	ABV	1994 to 1996	Bosch Motronic M2.9
Polo 1.05i cat	AAK	1989 to 1990	Bosch Mono-Jetronic A2.2
Polo 1.0i cat	AEV	1994 to 1997	Bosch Mono-Motronic 1.2.3
Polo 1.05i cat	AAU	1990 to 1993	Bosch Mono-Motronic 1.2.1
Polo 1.05i cat	AAU	1993 to 1994	Bosch Mono-Motronic 1.2.3
Polo 1.3i cat	AAV	1991 to 1994	Bosch Mono-Motronic 1.2.3
Polo 1.3i cat	ADX	1994 to 1995	Bosch Mono-Motronic 1.3
Polo Classic/Caddy 1.4	AEX	1996 to 1997	Bosch Motronic MP9.0 MPi
Polo Classic/Caddy 1.6	1F	1996 to 1997	Bosch Mono-Motronic
Polo 1.4 8V 44kW	AEX	1995 to 2001	Bosch Motronic MP9.0
Polo 1.4 16V	AFH	1996 to 2001	Magneti-Marelli 1AV
Polo 1.6i 8V	AEE	1995 to 1998	Magneti-Marelli 1AV
Polo Classic 1.6 8V	AFT	1996 to 1998	Simos MPi
Polo 1.6i cat	AEA	1994 to 1996	Bosch Mono-Motronic 1.3
Santana 1.8 cat	JN	1984 to 1988	Bosch KE-Jetronic
Sharan 2.0	ADY	1995 to 2001	Simos
Sharan 2.8	AAA	1995 to 2001	Bosch Motronic 3.8.1
Transporter 2.0i and cat	AAC	1991 to 2001	VAG Digifant
Transporter 2.5i cat	AAF	1991 to 1995	VAG Digifant
Transporter 2.5i cat	ACU	1994 to 1997	VAG Digifant
Transporter 2.8	AES	1996 to 1998	Bosch Motronic
Vento 1.4i cat	ABD	1992 to 1995	Bosch Mono-Motronic 1.2.3R
Vento 1.4i	AEX	1995 to 1998	Bosch Motronic MP9.0
Vento 1.6i 8V	AEE	1995 to 1998	Magneti-Marelli 1AV
Vento 1.6i cat	ABU	1993 to 1994	Bosch Mono-Motronic 1.2.3
Vento 1.6i cat	AEA	1994 to 1995	Bosch Mono-Motronic 1.3
Vento 1.6i	AEK	1994 to 1995	Bosch Motronic
Vento 1.8i cat	AAM	1992 to 1998	Bosch Mono-Motronic 1.2.3
Vento 1.8i cat	ABS	1992 to 1994	Bosch Mono-Motronic 1.2.2
Vento 1.8i and 4x4	ADZ	1994 to 1998	Bosch Mono-Motronic
Vento 2.0i	ADY	1994 to 1997	Simos
Vento VR6	AAA	1992 to 1998	Bosch Motronic 2.7/2.9
Vento 2.0i cat	2E	1992 to 1994	VAG Digifant

Plus *All models equipped with EOBD (approximately January 2001-on)*

Self-Diagnosis

1　Introduction

The engine management systems (EMSs) fitted to VW vehicles are mainly of Bosch, VAG or Magneti-Marelli origin. VW engine management systems that control primary ignition, fuelling and idle functions from within the same control module include Bosch Motronic 2.7, 2.9, Mono-Motronic, KE-Motronic, Simos, VAG Digifant and VAG MPi. VW fuel management systems that control fuelling and idle functions alone include Mono-Jetronic and KE-Jetronic.

VW systems are capable of generating two kinds of fault codes. These are 4-digit flash codes and 5-digit fault codes. Evolution of VW systems divides the code reading procedures into one of three possibilities. The changeover point for each system is not always obvious.

a) *Some early systems will only generate 4-digit flash codes, which can be retrieved via the warning light (where fitted), an LED light or a dedicated FCR. These systems include Mono-Jetronic, Mono-Motronic 1.2.1 (35-pin), VAG Digifant (38-pin).*

b) *Later systems can generate both 4-digit flash codes and 5-digit fault codes. The 4-digit flash codes are generated via the warning light (where fitted), or an LED light, whilst a dedicated FCR is required to retrieve the 5-digit codes. These systems include Bosch Motronic versions 2.7, KE-Jetronic, KE-Motronic, Mono-Motronic (early 45-pin) and some VAG Digifant (45-pin).*

c) *The very latest systems can only generate 5-digit fault codes, which must be retrieved with the aid of a dedicated FCR. These systems include Bosch Motronic versions 2.9, Mono-Motronic MA1.2.2 (later 45-pin), Simos, VAG Digifant (68-pin) and VAG MPi (68-pin), and any model equipped with EOBD.*

Self-Diagnosis (SD) function

Each ECM has a self-test capability that continually examines the signals from certain engine sensors and actuators, and compares each signal to a table of programmed values. If the diagnostic software determines that a fault is present, the ECM stores one or more fault codes. Codes will not be stored about components for which a code is not available, or for conditions not covered by the diagnostic software.

Limited operating strategy (LOS)

VW systems featured in this Chapter utilise LOS (a function that is commonly called the "limp-home mode"). Once certain faults have been identified (not all faults will initiate LOS), the ECM will implement LOS and refer to a programmed default value rather than the sensor signal. This enables the vehicle to be safely driven to a workshop/garage for repair or testing. Once the fault has cleared, the ECM will revert to normal operation.

Adaptive or learning capability

VW systems also utilise an adaptive function that will modify the basic programmed values for most effective operation during normal running, and with due regard to engine wear. The exception to this is the Mono-Jetronic system, which does not have an adaptive or learning capability.

Self-Diagnosis (SD) warning light

Certain models are equipped with an SD warning light located within the instrument panel.

2　Self-Diagnosis connector location

Note: *The VAG SD connector is provided for transmission of fault codes to a dedicated FCR. Retrieval of flash codes by manual means is also possible from Mono-Jetronic, KE-Jetronic, KE-Motronic 1.1 and 1.2 and Mono-Motronic 1.2.1 and 1.1.2 systems. From 1995 onwards, a 16-pin connector is provided in some models for transmission of fault codes to a dedicated FCR alone. It is not possible to retrieve flash codes from vehicles equipped with the 16-pin connector or models equipped with the dual 2-pin connectors (unless specifically indicated).*

Bosch Mono-Jetronic (VW Polo)

In the passenger's side footwell (see illustration 36.1)

Bosch Mono-Jetronic (VW Golf and Jetta)

1-pin connector located near the ignition coil, with yellow or red/white wire.

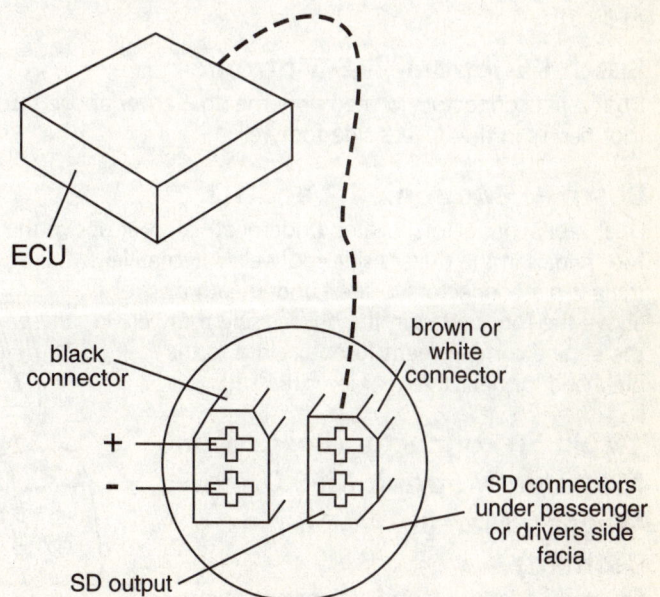

36.1 Location of SD connectors under facia

36.2 Location of SD connectors and initiation of 1-pin codes - Passat

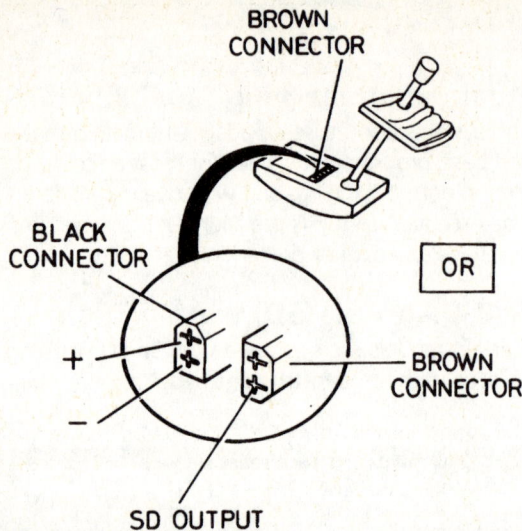

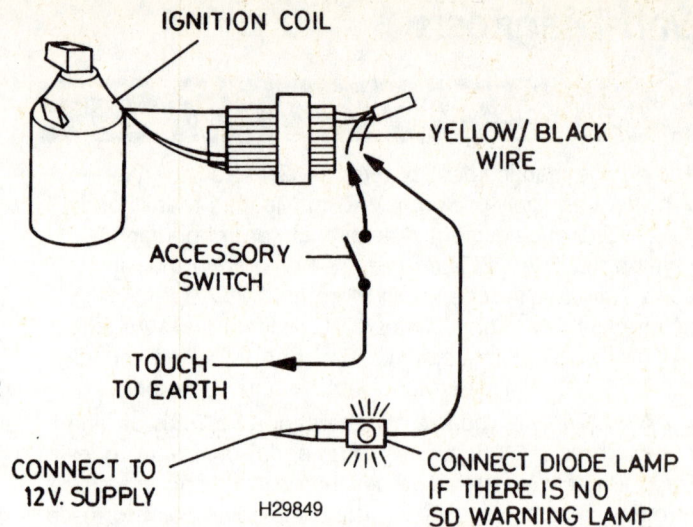

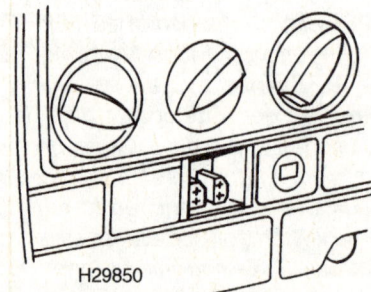

Bosch Mono-Jetronic (VW Passat to 3/89)

1-pin connector located near the ignition coil, with yellow/black wire *(see illustration 36.2)*.

Bosch Mono-Jetronic (VW Passat from 4/89)

Dual 2-pin connectors located near the gear lever *(refer to illustration 36.2)*.

Bosch Mono-Motronic

In the passenger's side footwell *(refer to illustration 36.1)*, or behind a cover under the heating and ventilation controls *(see illustration 36.3)*.

VAG Digifant, Motronic 2.7/2.9

Dual 2-pin connectors located in the passenger's side footwell, behind a cover under the heating and ventilation controls, in the left-hand electrical box close to the bulkhead, or near the gear lever (Passat) *(refer to illustrations 36.1 to 36.3)*.

Bosch KE-Jetronic, KE-Motronic 1.1

Dual 2-pin connectors located underneath a cover above the foot pedals in the driver's side footwell.

Bosch KE-Motronic 1.1 and 1.2

Dual 2-pin connectors located underneath a cover above the foot pedals in the driver's side footwell. Alternatively, triple 2-pin connectors located underneath a cover above the foot pedals in the driver's side footwell, in the engine compartment fusebox close to the bulkhead, or near the gear lever (Passat).

16-pin SD connector (Bosch Mono-Motronic, Motronic MP9.0 and Magneti-Marelli 1AV, 68-pin Digifant)

Situated under the facia heating/ventilation controls adjacent to the ashtray *(see illustration 36.3)*.

36.3 Location of SD connector behind a cover under the heater controls

16-pin SD connector (other models)

Situated under a cover in the rear passenger console, adjacent to the ashtray *(see illustration 36.4)* or in the lower facia to the right of the steering column.

EOBD models

The 16-pin plug is located under the facia - refer to Chapter 38.

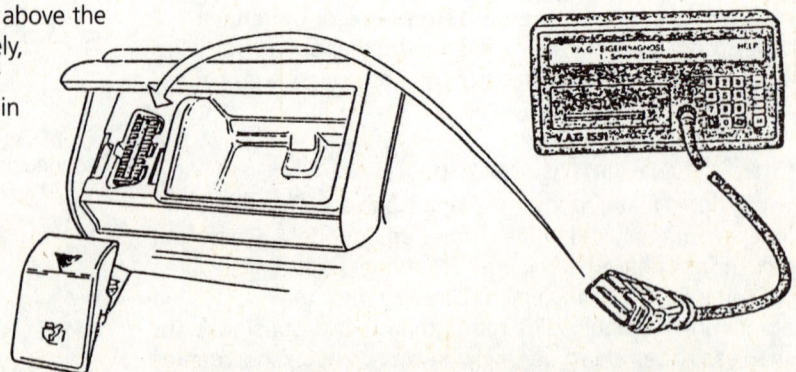

36.4 The 16-pin SD connector is usually situated under a cover in the rear passenger console, adjacent to the ashtray

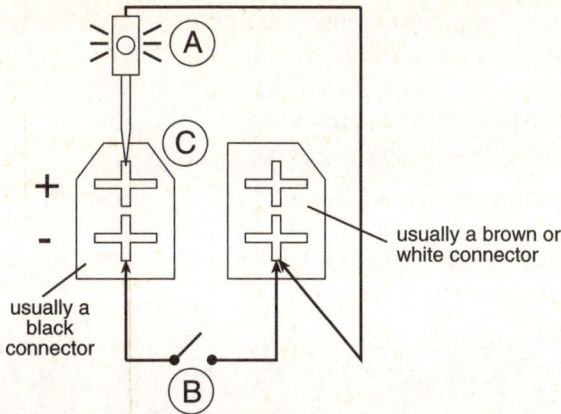

36.5 Initiation of flash codes - dual 2-pin SD connectors
A LED diode light   B Accessory switch   C SD connectors

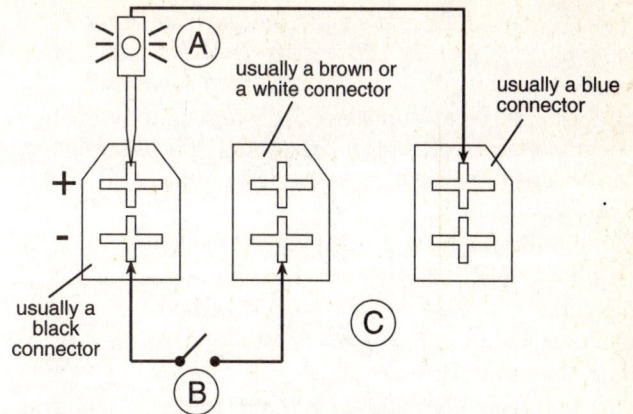

36.6 Initiation of flash codes - triple 2-pin SD connectors
A LED diode light   B Accessory switch   C SD connectors

3 Retrieving fault codes without a fault code reader (FCR) - flash codes

Note 1: *During the course of certain test procedures, it is possible for additional fault codes to be generated. Care must be taken that any codes generated during test routines do not mislead diagnosis. All codes must be cleared once testing is complete.*

Bosch Mono-Jetronic, KE-Jetronic and KE-Motronic 1.1 and 1.2

1 Attach an accessory switch to the single 1-pin *(refer to illustration 36.2)*, dual 2-pin or 3-pin SD connectors *(see illustrations 36.5 and 36.6)*. If the vehicle is not equipped with a facia-mounted SD warning light, connect a diode LED light between the battery (+) supply and the SD connector as shown.

2 Start the engine and allow it to warm up to normal operating temperature. **Note:** *Oxygen sensor (OS) fault codes can only be retrieved after a road test of at least 10 minutes' duration.*

3 Stop the engine and switch on the ignition.

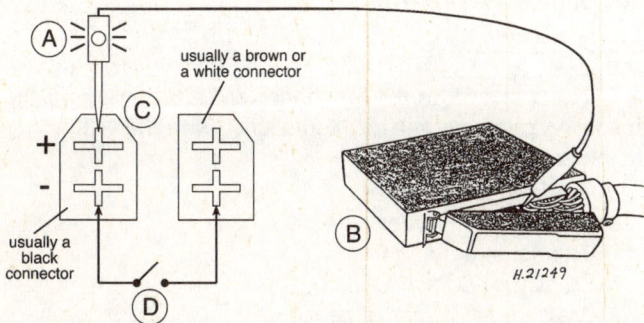

36.7 Initiation of 35-pin and some 45-pin Mono-Motronic flash codes (see text)
A LED diode light   B ECM   C SD connectors   D Accessory switch

4 If the engine will not start, crank the engine for at least 6 seconds, and leave the ignition switched on.

5 Close the accessory switch for at least 5 seconds and then open the switch. The LED light will flash to indicates the 4-digit fault codes as follows:

a) The four digits are indicated by four series of flashes.

b) The first series of flashes indicates the first digit, the second series of flashes indicates the second digit, and so on until all four digits have been flashed.

c) Each series consists of a number of 1- or 2-second flashes, separated by short pauses. Each integer (whole number) in the range 1 to 9 is represented by a number of 1-second flashes, and each zero is represented by 2-second flashes.

d) A 2.5-second pause separates each series of flashes.

e) The code number "1231" is indicated by a 1-second flash, a short pause, two 1-sec-ond flashes, a short pause, three 1-second flashes, a short pause and a 1-second flash. After a 2.5-second pause, the code will be repeated.

6 Count the number of flashes in each series, and record the code. Refer to the table at the end of the Chapter to determine the meaning of the fault code.

7 The code will be repeated until the accessory switch is once more closed for at least 5 seconds. Open the switch and the next code will then be displayed.

8 Continue retrieving codes until code "0000" is transmitted. Code 0000 signifies that no more codes are stored, and is displayed when the light flashes off and on at 2.5-second intervals.

9 If code "4444" is transmitted, no fault codes are stored.

10 Turn off the ignition and remove the accessory switch and LED to end fault code retrieval.

Bosch Mono-Motronic (35-pin version 1.2.1 and 45-pin version 1.2.2)

11 Attach an accessory switch to the dual 2-pin SD connectors *(see illustration 36.7)*. If the vehicle is not equipped with a facia-mounted SD warning light, connect a diode test light between the battery (+) supply and ECM pin number 33 (35-pin or ECM pin number 4 (45-pin) as shown.

Note: *It may be necessary to detach the back of the ECM multi-plugs so that the LED negative probe can back-probe the ECM pin number with the multi-plug connected.*

12 Start the engine and allow it to warm up to normal operating temperature. Note: Oxygen sensor (OS) fault codes can only be retrieved after a road test of at least 10 minutes' duration.

13 Stop the engine and switch on the ignition.

14 If the engine will not start, crank the engine for at least 6 seconds and leave the ignition switched on.

15 Close the accessory switch for at least 5 seconds and then open the switch.

16 The LED light will flash to indicate the 4-digit fault codes as follows:

  a) *The four digits are indicated by four series of flashes.*
  b) *The first series of flashes indicates the first digit, the second series of flashes indicates the second digit, and so on until all four digits have been flashed.*
  c) *Each series consists of a number of 1- or 2-second flashes, separated by short pauses. Each integer (whole number) in the range 1 to 9 is represented by a number of 1-second flashes, and each zero is represented by 2-second flashes.*
  d) *A 2.5-second pause separates each series of flashes.*
  e) *The code number "1231" is indicated by a 1-second flash, a short pause, two 1-sec-ond flashes, a short pause, three 1-second flashes, a short pause and a 1-second flash. After a 2.5-second pause, the code will be repeated.*

17 Count the number of flashes in each series, and record the code. Refer to the table at the end of the Chapter to determine the meaning of the fault code.

18 The code will be repeated until the accessory switch is once more closed for at least 5 seconds. Open the switch and the next code will then be displayed.

19 Continue retrieving codes until code "0000" is transmitted. Code 0000 signifies that no more codes are stored, and is displayed when the light flashes off and on at 2.5-second intervals.

20 If code "4444" is transmitted, no fault codes are stored.

21 Turn off the ignition and remove the accessory switch and LED to end fault code retrieval.

Systems with 16-pin connector or 68 pin ECM multi-plug

22 Flash codes are not available, and a dedicated FCR must be used to retrieve fault codes.

4   Clearing fault codes without a fault code reader (FCR)

Bosch Mono-Jetronic, Mono-Motronic, KE-Jetronic and KE-Motronic

1 Carry out the above procedure to retrieve fault codes (Section 3).

2 Turn off the ignition, then close the accessory switch.

3 Switch on the ignition.

4 Open the accessory switch after a period of 5 seconds. The fault codes should now be cleared.

5 Turn off the ignition on completion.

Clearing fault codes 2341 or 2343 (oxygen sensor)

6 Turn off the ignition. Remove the ECM multi-plug connector from the ECM for at least 30 seconds - see Note below).

> **(!)**   *Warning: Refer to Warning No 3 (in the Reference Section at the end of this book) before disconnecting the ECM multi-plug.*

All systems (alternative method)

7 Turn off the ignition and disconnect the battery negative terminal for a period of approximately 5 minutes.

8 Reconnect the battery negative terminal.

Note: *The first drawback to this method is that battery disconnection (or ECM multi-plug disconnection) will re-initialise all ECM adaptive values (except for Mono-Jetronic systems). Re-learning the appropriate adaptive values requires starting the engine from cold, and driving at various engine speeds for approximately 20 to 30 minutes. The engine should also be allowed to idle for approximately 10 minutes. The second drawback is that the radio security codes, clock setting and other stored values will be initialised, and these must be re-entered once the battery has been reconnected. Where possible, an FCR should be used for code clearing. On models equipped with EOBD, an FCR is essential to retrieve or clear fault codes.*

5   Self-Diagnosis with a fault code reader (FCR)

Note: *During the course of certain test procedures, it is possible for additional fault codes to be generated. Care must be taken that any codes generated during test routines do not mislead diagnosis.*

All Volkswagen models

1 Connect an FCR to the SD connector. Use the FCR for the following purposes, in strict compliance with the FCR manufacturer's instructions:

  a) *Retrieving fault codes.*
  b) *Clearing fault codes.*
  c) *Testing actuators.*
  d) *Displaying Datastream.*
  e) *Making service adjustments.*

2 The FCR may be able to display 4-digit flash codes and/or 5-digit fault codes. Refer to appropriate column in the fault code table at the end of this Chapter.

3 Codes must always be cleared after component testing, or after repairs involving the removal or replacement of an engine management system component.

6 Guide to test procedures

1 Use an FCR to interrogate the ECM for fault codes, or manually gather codes as described in Sections 3 or 5.

Codes stored

2 If one or more fault codes are gathered, refer to the fault code table to determine their meaning.

3 If several codes are gathered, look for a common factor such as a defective earth return or supply.

4 Refer to the component test procedures in Chapter 4, where you will find a means of testing the majority of components and circuits found in the modern EMS.

5 Once the fault has been repaired, clear the codes and run the engine under various conditions to determine if the problem has cleared.

6 Check the ECM for fault codes once more. Repeat the above procedures where codes are still being stored.

7 Refer to Chapter 3 for more information on how to effectively test the EMS.

No codes stored

8 Where a running problem is experienced, but no codes are stored, the fault is outside of the parameters designed into the SD system. Refer to Chapter 3 for more information on how to effectively test the engine management system.

9 If the problem points to a specific component, refer to the test procedures in Chapter 4, where you will find a means of testing the majority of components and circuits found in the modern EMS.

Fault code table

All Volkswagen models (except EOBD)

Note: *Similar codes are generated by each individual system. A small number of codes may suggest alternative meanings depending on which system and what components are fitted. For example, one particular code may indicate an airflow sensor or a MAP sensor, depending on which of those components is fitted. When a code with an alternative meaning is generated, the correct meaning will usually be obvious.*

Flash code	FCR code	Description
4444	00000	No faults found in the ECM. Proceed with normal diagnostic methods
0000	-	End of fault code output
1111	65535	Internal ECM failure
1231	00281	Vehicle speed sensor (VSS) or VSS circuit
1232	00282	Throttle pot sensor (TPS) or TPS circuit
1232	00282	Idle speed stepper motor (ISSM) or ISSM circuit (alternative code)
2111	00513	Engine speed (RPM) sensor or RPM sensor circuit
2112	00514	Top dead centre (TDC) sensor or TDC circuit
2112	00514	Crank angle sensor (CAS)
2113*	00515	Hall-effect sensor (HES) or HES circuit
2114	00535	Distributor
2121	00516	Idle speed stepper motor (ISSM), idle contacts
2121	00516	Ignition control valve circuit fault (alternative code)
2122	-	No engine speed signal
2123	00517	Throttle switch (TS), full-load switch
2141	00535	Knock control 1 (ECM)
2142	00524	Knock sensor (KS) or KS circuit
2142	00545	auto signal missing (alternative code)
2143	00536	Knock control 2 (ECM)
2144	00540	Knock sensor (KS) 2 or KS circuit
2212	00518	Throttle pot sensor (TPS) fault or TPS circuit
2214	00543	Max. engine speed exceeded

Flash code	FCR code	Description
2222	00519	Manifold absolute pressure (MAP) sensor or MAP sensor circuit
2223	00528	Atmospheric pressure sensor (APS) or APS circuit
2224	00544	Turbocharger maximum boost pressure exceeded
2231	00533	Idle control
2232	00520	Vane airflow sensor (AFS) or AFS circuit
2232	00520	Mass airflow (MAF) sensor or MAF sensor circuit (alternative code)
2233	00531	Vane airflow sensor (AFS) or AFS circuit
2233	00531	Mass airflow (MAF) sensor or MAF circuit (alternative code)
2234	00532	Supply voltage incorrect
2242	00521	CO pot or CO pot circuit
2312	00522	Coolant temperature sensor (CTS) or CTS circuit
2314	00545	Engine/gearbox electrical connection
2322	00523	Air temperature sensor (ATS) or ATS circuit
2323	00522	Vane airflow sensor (AFS)
2323	00522	Mass airflow (MAF) sensor (alternative code)
2324	00553	Vane airflow sensor (AFS)
2324	00553	Mass airflow (MAF) sensor (alternative code)
2341	00537	Oxygen sensor (OS) control Inoperative
2342	00525	Oxygen sensor (OS) or OS circuit
2343	00558	Mixture control adjustment, weak
2344	00559	Mixture control adjustment, rich

Flash code	FCR code	Description
2413	00561	Mixture control limits
4332	00750	Electronic control module (ECM)
4343	01243	Carbon filter solenoid valve (CFSV) or CFSV circuit
4411	01244	Injector No. 1 or injector circuit
4412	01247	Injector No. 2 or injector circuit
4413	01249	Injector No. 3 or injector circuit
4414	01250	Injector No. 4 or injector circuit
4421	01251	Injector No. 5 or injector circuit
4431	01253	Idle speed control valve (ISCV) or ISCV circuit
4442	01254	Turbocharger boost pressure solenoid valve (BPSV) or BPSV circuit
-	00527	Intake manifold temperature
-	00530	Throttle pot sensor (TPS) or TPS circuit
-	00532	Supply voltage incorrect
-	00543	Maximum engine speed exceeded
-	00549	Consumption signal
-	00545	Engine gearbox electrical connection
-	00554	Oxygen sensor (OS) control 2
-	00555	Oxygen sensor (OS) or OS circuit
-	00560	Exhaust gas recirculation (EGR) valve or EGR circuit
-	00561	Mixture control 1
-	00575	Manifold absolute pressure (MAP) sensor or MAP sensor circuit
-	00577	Knock control cylinder 1 or circuit
-	00578	Knock control cylinder 2 or circuit
-	00579	Knock control cylinder 3 or circuit
-	00580	Knock control cylinder 4 or circuit
-	00581	Knock control cylinder 5 or circuit
-	00582	Knock control cylinder 6 or circuit
-	00585	Exhaust gas recirculation (EGR) temperature sensor or EGR circuit
-	00586	Exhaust gas recirculation (EGR) valve or EGR circuit
-	00609	Amplifier 1 or amplifier circuit
-	00610	Amplifier 2 or amplifier circuit
-	00611	Amplifier 3 or amplifier circuit
-	00624	Air conditioning (A/C)
-	00625	Vehicle speed sensor (VSS) or VSS circuit
-	00635	Oxygen sensor (OS) heater or OS circuit
-	00640	Oxygen sensor (OS) or OS circuit
-	00670	Idle speed stepper motor (ISSM) pot or ISSM circuit
-	00689	Excessive air in inlet manifold
-	00750	Warning light
-	01025	Self-Diagnosis warning light
-	01087	Basic setting not completed
-	01088	Mixture control 2
-	01119	Gear recognition signal
-	01120	Camshaft timing control
-	01165	Throttle pot sensor (TPS) or TPS circuit
-	01182	Altitude adaptation
-	01235	Secondary air valve
-	01242	Electronic control module (ECM) or ECM circuit
-	01247	Carbon filter solenoid valve (CFSV) or CFSV circuit
-	01252	Injector valve No. 4 or Injector valve circuit
-	01257	Idle speed control valve (ISCV) or ISCV circuit
-	01259	Fuel pump relay or circuit
-	01262	Turbocharger boost pressure solenoid valve (BPSV) or BPSV circuit
-	01264	Secondary air pump
-	01265	Exhaust gas recirculation (EGR) valve or EGR circuit
-	16486	Mass airflow (MAF) sensor or MAF circuit, signal low
-	16487	Mass airflow (MAF) sensor or MAF circuit, signal high
-	16496	Air temperature sensor (ATS) or ATS circuit, signal low
-	16497	Air temperature sensor (ATS) or ATS circuit, signal high
-	16500	Coolant temperature sensor (CTS) or CTS circuit

Flash code	FCR code	Description
-	16501	Coolant temperature sensor (CTS) or CTS circuit, signal low
-	16502	Coolant temperature sensor (CTS) or CTS circuit, signal high
-	16504	Throttle pot sensor (TPS) or TPS circuit
-	16505	Throttle pot sensor (TPS) or TPS circuit, signal implausible
-	16506	Throttle pot sensor (TPS) or TPS circuit, signal low
-	16507	Throttle pot sensor (TPS) or TPS circuit, signal high
-	16514	Oxygen sensor (OS) or OS circuit
-	16515	Oxygen sensor (OS) or OS circuit
-	16516	Oxygen sensor (OS) or OS circuit, signal high
-	16518	Oxygen sensor (OS) or OS circuit
-	16519	Oxygen sensor (OS) or OS circuit
-	16534	Oxygen sensor (OS) or OS circuit
-	16535	Oxygen sensor (OS) or OS circuit
-	16536	Oxygen sensor (OS) or OS circuit, signal high
-	16538	Oxygen sensor (OS) or OS circuit
-	16554	Injector bank 1
-	16555	Injector bank 1, fuel system too lean
-	16556	Injector bank 1, fuel system too rich
-	16557	Injector bank 2
-	16558	Injector bank 2, fuel system too lean
-	16559	Injector bank 2, fuel system too rich
-	16684	Engine misfire
-	16685	Cylinder No. 1 misfire
-	16686	Cylinder No. 2 misfire
-	16687	Cylinder No. 3 misfire
-	16688	Cylinder No. 4 misfire
-	16689	Cylinder No. 5 misfire
-	16690	Cylinder No. 6 misfire
-	16691	Cylinder No. 7 misfire
-	16692	Cylinder No. 8 misfire
-	16705	RPM sensor or circuit
-	16706	RPM sensor or circuit
-	16711	Knock sensor (KS) 1 signal or KS circuit, signal low
-	16716	Knock sensor (KS) 2 signal or KS circuit, signal low
-	16721	Crank angle sensor (CAS) or CAS circuit
-	16785	Exhaust gas
-	16786	Exhaust gas
-	16885	Vehicle speed sensor (VSS) or VSS circuit
-	16989	Electronic control module (ECM)
-	17509	Oxygen sensor (OS) or OS circuit
-	17514	Oxygen sensor (OS) or OS circuit
-	17540	Oxygen sensor (OS) or OS circuit
-	17541	Oxygen sensor (OS) or OS circuit
-	17609	Injector valve No. 1 or injector circuit
-	17610	Injector valve No. 4 or injector circuit
-	17611	Injector valve No. 3 or injector circuit
-	17612	Injector valve No. 4 or injector circuit
-	17613	Injector valve No. 5 or injector circuit
-	17614	Injector valve No. 6 or injector circuit
-	17615	Injector valve No. 7 or injector circuit
-	17616	Injector valve No. 8 or injector circuit
-	17621	Injector valve No. 1 or injector circuit
-	17622	Injector valve No. 2 or injector circuit
-	17623	Injector valve No. 3 or injector circuit
-	17624	Injector valve No. 4 or injector circuit
-	17625	Injector valve No. 5 or injector circuit
-	17626	Injector valve No. 6 or injector circuit
-	17627	Cylinder No. 7 misfire
-	17628	Cylinder No. 8 misfire
-	17733	Knock sensor (KS) control No. 1 cylinder or KS circuit
-	17734	Knock sensor (KS) control No. 2 cylinder or KS circuit

Flash code	FCR code	Description
-	17735	Knock sensor (KS) control No. 3 cylinder or KS circuit
-	17736	Knock sensor (KS) control No. 4 cylinder or KS circuit
-	17737	Knock sensor (KS) control No. 5 cylinder or KS circuit
-	17738	Knock sensor (KS) control No. 6 cylinder or KS circuit
-	17739	Knock sensor (KS) control No. 7 cylinder or KS circuit
-	17740	Knock sensor (KS) control No. 8 cylinder or KS circuit
-	17747	Crank angle sensor (CAS) and vehicle speed sensor (VSS) signals transposed
-	17749	Ignition output 1, short-circuit to earth
-	17751	Ignition output 2, short-circuit to earth
-	17753	Ignition output 3, short-circuit to earth
-	17799	Camshaft sensor (CMP) or CMP circuit
-	17800	Camshaft sensor (CMP) or CMP circuit
-	17801	Ignition output 1
-	17802	Ignition output 2
-	17803	Ignition output 3
-	17808	Exhaust gas recirculation (EGR) valve or EGR circuit
-	17810	Exhaust gas recirculation (EGR) valve or EGR circuit
-	17815	Exhaust gas recirculation (EGR) valve or EGR circuit, signal too small
-	17816	Exhaust gas recirculation (EGR) valve or EGR circuit, signal too large
-	17817	Carbon filter solenoid valve (CFSV) or CFSV circuit
-	17818	Carbon filter solenoid valve (CFSV) or CFSV circuit
-	17908	Fuel pump relay or fuel pump circuit

Flash code	FCR code	Description
-	17910	Fuel pump relay or fuel pump circuit
-	17912	Intake system
-	17913	Idling switch, throttle switch (TS) or TS circuit
-	17914	Idling switch, throttle switch (TS) or TS circuit
-	17915	Idle speed control valve (ISCV) or ISCV circuit
-	17916	Idle speed control valve (ISCV) or ISCV circuit
-	17917	Idle speed control valve (ISCV) or ISCV circuit
-	17918	Idle speed control valve (ISCV) or ISCV circuit
-	17919	Inlet manifold changeover valve (IMCV) or IMCV circuit
-	17920	Inlet manifold changeover valve (IMCV) or IMCV circuit
-	17966	Throttle drive
-	17978	Electronic immobiliser
-	18008	Voltage supply
-	18010	Battery
-	18020	Electronic control module (ECM) incorrectly coded

*Note: *Fault code number 2113 will always be present when the ignition is switched on and the engine is stopped in systems that utilise a Hall sensor as the primary trigger.*

All models with EOBD

For a list of the allocated EOBD codes beginning with P0 (Generic Powertrain), refer to Chapter 1, Section 1.

Notes

Volvo

Index of vehicles

Model	Engine code	Year	System
240 2.0i cat	B200F	1991 to 1993	Bosch LH2.4-Jetronic
240 2.3 cat	B230F	1984 to 1991	Bosch LH2.4-Jetronic
240 2.3i cat	B230F	1989 to 1993	Bosch LH2.4-Jetronic
240 2.3i cat	B230FD	1993 to 1994	Bosch LH2.4-Jetronic
400 1.7i SOHC	B18ED-104	1986 to 1990	Fenix 1 or 3.2
400 1.7i SOHC cat	B18ES-105	1986 to 1990	Fenix 1 or 3.2
400 1.7i SOHC 8V	B18EP-115	1990 to 1994	Fenix 3B
400 1.7i SOHC 8V cat	B18FP-115	1990 to 1995	Fenix 3B
400 1.8i SOHC cat	B18U-103	1992 to 1997	Fenix 3BF SPi
400 1.8i SOHC cat	B18U-103	1996 to 1997	Fenix 3BF SPi
400 2.0i SOHC 8V cat	B20F-116/118	1993 to 1996	Fenix 3B MPi
400 2.0i SOHC 8V cat	B20F-208/209	1994 to 1997	Fenix 3B MPi
440 1.6i SOHC 8V	B16F-109	1991 to 1997	Fenix 3B MPi
460 1.6i SOHC 8V	B16F-109	1991 to 1997	Fenix 3B MPi
740 2.0 cat	B200F	1990 to 1992	Bosch LH2.4-Jetronic
740 2.3i 16V cat	B234F	1989 to 1991	Bosch LH2.4-Jetronic
740 2.3 Turbo cat	B230FT	1985 to 1989	Bosch LH2.4-Jetronic
740 2.3 Turbo cat	B230FT	1990 to 1992	Bosch LH2.4-Jetronic
760 2.3 Turbo cat	B230FT	1985 to 1989	Bosch LH2.4-Jetronic
760 2.3 Turbo cat	B230FT	1990 to 1991	Bosch LH2.4-Jetronic
850 2.0i 20V	B5204S	1992 to 1997	Bosch LH3.2-Jetronic
850 2.5i 20V	B5254S	1992 to 1997	Bosch LH3.2-Jetronic
850 2.0 20V Turbo	B5204T	1994 to 1997	Bosch Motronic M4.3 SEFI
850 T5 DOHC 20V	B5234T	1994 to 1997	Bosch Motronic M4.3 SEFI
850 T-5R	B5234T-5	1994 to 1997	Bosch Motronic M4.3 SEFI
850R	B5234T-5	1994 to 1997	Bosch Motronic M4.3 SEFI
850 2.0i 10V SOHC	B5202S	1995 to 1997	Fenix 5.2 SEFI
850 2.5i 10V SOHC	B5252S	1993 to 1997	Fenix 5.2 SEFI
900 2.3i LPT Turbo	B230FK	1995 to 1998	Bosch LH2.4-Jetronic
940 2.0i cat	B200F	1990 to 1996	Bosch LH2.4-Jetronic
940 2.3i	B230F	1992 to 1994	Bosch LH2.4-Jetronic
940 2.0i Turbo cat	B200FT	1990 to 1996	Bosch LH2.4-Jetronic

Plus All models equipped with EOBD (approximately January 2001-on)

Chapter 37

Self-Diagnosis

1   Introduction

A number of Volvo vehicles are equipped with an Engine Management System that controls primary ignition, fuelling and idle functions from within the same control module. Other Volvo vehicles are equipped with a separate electronic ignition system that controls primary ignition, and an electronic injection system that controls fuelling and idle functions. All of these Volvo engine management, ignition and fuel systems are equipped with Self-Diagnosis, and are capable of generating fault codes.

Engine management systems covered by this Chapter include Bosch Motronic M4.3, and Fenix 3B or 5.2. Electronic fuel injection systems include Bosch LH2.4-Jetronic and LH3.2-Jetronic. Electronic ignition systems with self-diagnosis include Bosch EZ116-K and EZ129-K, and Bendix Rex-1. Generally, a Volvo with Bosch LH2.4-Jetronic will have Bosch EZ116-K or Bendix Rex-1 ignition, while if LH3.2-Jetronic injection is fitted, Bosch EZ129-K ignition will be found.

Some Volvo vehicles are provided with a self-diagnostic unit (SD unit) that contains an LED, a test button, a test lead and six sockets for fault code retrieval. Once the test lead is connected to the appropriate socket, a number of test modes can be initiated, which include retrieving fault codes, clearing fault codes and testing various engine management components. Where the vehicle is equipped with Bosch EZ-K ignition and the LH-Jetronic fuel system, the ignition and fuel systems will generate fault codes separately; these can be retrieved by attaching the test lead to the appropriate socket in the SD unit.

On models equipped with EOBD, the 5-digit fault codes can only be retrieved or cleared using an FCR (Fault Codes Reader).

Self-Diagnosis (SD) function

Each ECM (electronic control module) has a self-test capability that continually examines the signals from certain engine sensors and actuators, and then compares each signal to a table of programmed values. If the diagnostic software determines that a fault is present, the ECM stores one or more fault codes in the ECM memory. Codes will not be stored about components for which a code is not available, or for conditions not covered by the diagnostic software.

Limited operating strategy (LOS)

Volvo systems featured in this Chapter utilise LOS (a function that is commonly called the "limp-home mode"). Once certain faults have been identified (not all faults will initiate LOS), the ECM will implement LOS and refer to a programmed default value rather than the sensor signal. This enables the vehicle to be safely driven to a workshop/garage for repair or testing. Once the fault has cleared, the ECM will revert to normal operation.

Adaptive or learning capability

Volvo systems also utilise an adaptive function that will modify the basic programmed values for most effective operation during normal running, and with due regard to engine wear.

Self-Diagnosis warning light

Most Volvo vehicles are equipped with an SD warning light located within the instrument panel.

2   Self-Diagnostic unit (SD connector) location

Bosch EZ116-K ignition and LH2.4-Jetronic

The SD unit is located in front of the left-hand front suspension strut mounting (see illustration 37.1).

Bosch EZ-129K ignition and LH3.2-Jetronic

There may be two SD units fitted to these vehicles. SD unit "A" is used for engine management fault code retrieval. It is located behind the right-hand headlight in front of the control unit box (see illustration 37.2).

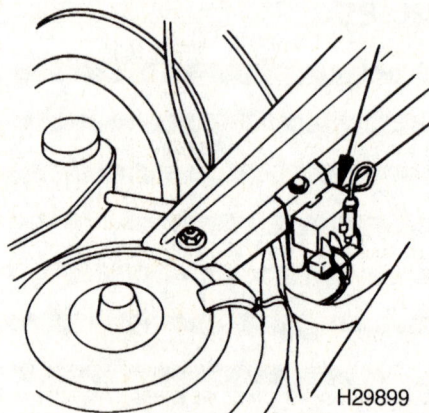

37.1 The SD unit is located in front of the left-hand front suspension strut mounting in the engine compartment

H29899

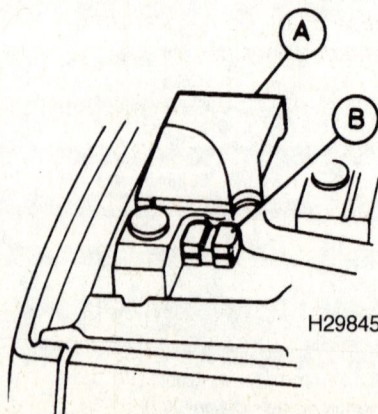

37.2 ECM and SD connector located behind the right-hand side headlight in front of the control unit box in the engine compartment

A The control box contains the ignition, fuel injection and automatic transmission ECMs

B SD unit

H29845

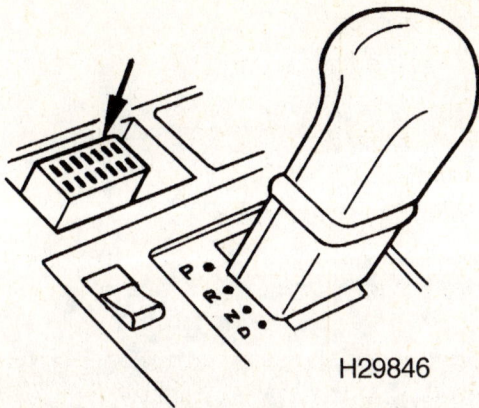

37.3 16-pin SD connector (arrowed) located above the gear selector on the centre console

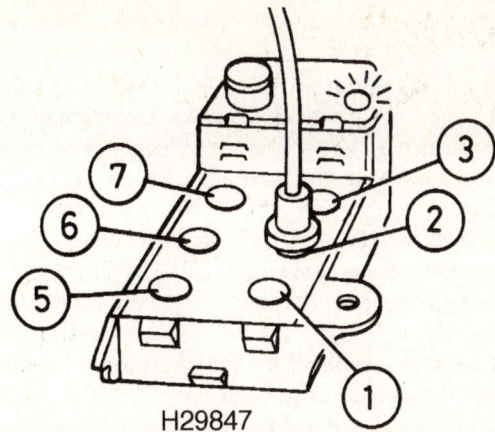

37.4 Retrieval of fuel injection codes with the test lead connected to socket number 2

Bosch Motronic 4.3, Fenix 3B and 5.2

Where two SD units are fitted, SD unit "A" is used for engine management fault code retrieval. It is located behind the right-hand headlight in front of the control unit box *(refer to illustration 37.2)*.

Vehicles built after 1995 are usually fitted with a 16-pin OBD connector, located on the centre console behind a trim panel and above the gear/drive selector *(see illustration 37.3)*.

On models with EOBD, the 16-pin diagnostic connector is located under the facia - refer to Chapter 38.

3   Bosch LH2.4-Jetronic - testing without a fault code reader (FCR)

Note 1: *During the course of certain test procedures, it is possible for additional fault codes to be generated. Care must be taken that any codes generated during test routines do not mislead diagnosis. All codes must be cleared once testing is complete.*

Note 2: *Where applicable, use SD unit "A" for the following test modes (refer to illustration 37.6). Do not start the engine unless the test routine demands it.*

Test mode 1 (retrieving flash codes)

1 Connect the test lead to socket 2 on the SD unit *(see illustration 37.4)*.

2 Switch on the ignition, without starting the engine.

3 Press the test button once, for 1 to 3 seconds.

4 After a pause of 3.5 seconds, the LED on the SD unit will begin flashing to display each 3-digit code as follows:

 a) *The three digits are indicated by three series of flashes.*
 b) *The first series of flashes indicates the first digit, the second series of flashes indicates the second digit, and the third series of flashes indicates the third digit, until all three digits have been flashed.*
 c) *Each series is indicated by 0.5-second flashes, separated by 0.5-second pauses.*
 d) *A 3.5-second pause separates each series of flashes.*
 e) *Code "142" is indicated by one 0.5-second flash, followed by a 3.5-second pause, four 0.5-second flashes, a further 3.5-second pause, and two 0.5-second flashes.*

5 Count the number of flashes in each series, and record each code as it is transmitted. Refer to the tables at the end of the Chapter to determine the meaning of the fault code.

6 Each code is displayed once by the LED.

7 Retrieve the next code by pressing the test button once more for 1 to 3 seconds. After a pause of 3.5 seconds, the code will be displayed. All stored fault codes are transmitted in sequential order. **Note:** *In early versions of Bosch LH 2.4, only the last three codes stored can be retrieved at one time. Before other possible codes can be retrieved, the reason for the first set of faults must be repaired, and the fault codes cleared from memory as described later. In later versions of Bosch LH 2.4, this restriction is lifted, and all stored codes can be retrieved at one time.*

8 Repeat the procedure and continue retrieving codes until all codes have been transmitted.

9 If no codes are stored, the LED will flash code "111".

10 Turn off the ignition to end test mode 1.

Test mode 2 (sensor inputs to the ECM)

11 Connect the test lead to socket 2 on the SD unit.

12 Switch on the ignition, without starting the engine.

13 Press the test button twice to initiate test mode 2. The correct method is as follows:

 a) *Press the test button for approximately 1 to 3 seconds.*
 b) *Pause for 1 to 2 seconds.*
 c) *Press the test button again for approximately 1 to 3 seconds.*

14 The LED will flash continually at approximately 6 flashes per second, indicating that the SD unit is in test mode 2.

15 Perform the sensor tests and observe the behaviour of the LED as follows:

a) *After each test routine, the LED will flash a confirmation code. If the LED does not display a confirmation code, this indicates a faulty component, connection or switch.*

b) *After displaying a confirmation code, the LED will return to flashing at approximately 6 times per second.*

c) *Repeat each test if required.*

16 Open the throttle mid-way. The LED will display confirmation code "332" to signify that the idle switch has opened.

17 Fully open the throttle. If the full-load switch has closed, the LED will display confirmation code "333".

18 Start the engine or, if it does not start, crank the engine for 10 seconds and leave the ignition switched on. If the ECM receives a satisfactory signal from the crank angle sensor, the LED will display confirmation code "331".

19 Ensure that the handbrake is firmly applied. Move the automatic transmission gear selector to the "D" position, and return to the "P" position. If the ECM receives a satisfactory signal from the gear position switch, the LED will display confirmation code "124".

20 Turn the air conditioning (A/C) control switch on. If the ECM receives a satisfactory signal from the A/C switch, the LED will display confirmation code "114". If the ECM receives a satisfactory signal from the A/C compressor, the LED will also display confirmation code "134".

21 Turn off the ignition to end test mode 2.

Test mode 3 (activate selected actuators)

22 Connect the test lead to socket 2 on the SD unit.

23 Switch on the ignition, without starting the engine.

24 Press the test button three times to initiate test mode 3. The correct method is as follows:

a) *Press the test button for approximately 1 to 3 seconds.*

b) *Pause for 1 to 2 seconds.*

c) *Press the test button again for approximately 1 to 3 seconds.*

d) *Pause for 1 to 2 seconds.*

e) *Press the test button again for approximately 1 to 3 seconds.*

25 The ECM will automatically activate each actuator on the actuator list below, one after the other. Listen for an audible sound, or (where appropriate) touch the component to determine whether it has been activated. The LED will flash in time with the audible operation of the actuator.

> ⓘ *Warning: The injectors will actuate during this test routine, and there is a real danger of filling the cylinders with petrol. For this reason, it would be wise to disconnect the fuel pump supply (or remove the fuel pump fuse) before commencing the test. Turn off the ignition at any time to end test mode 3.*

Actuator list

1) *Cooling fan at half-speed.*
2) *Cooling fan at full-speed.*
3) *Injector valves.*
4) *Idle speed control valve.*
5) *Carbon filter solenoid valve.*
6) *Cold start valve.*

26 Turn off the ignition to end test mode 3.

4 Bosch EZ-116K and Bendix Rex-1 ignition systems - testing without a fault code reader (FCR)

Note 1: *During the course of certain test procedures, it is possible for additional fault codes to be generated. Care must be taken that any codes generated during test routines do not mislead diagnosis. All codes must be cleared once testing is complete.*

Note 2: *Do not start the engine unless the test routine demands it.*

Test mode 1 (retrieving flash codes)

1 Connect the test lead to socket 6 on the SD unit *(see illustration 37.5)*.

2 Switch on the ignition, without starting the engine.

3 Press the test button once, for 1 to 3 seconds.

4 After a pause of 3.5 seconds, the LED on the SD unit will begin flashing to display each 3-digit code as follows:

a) *The three digits are indicated by three series of flashes.*

b) *The first series of flashes indicates the first digit, the*

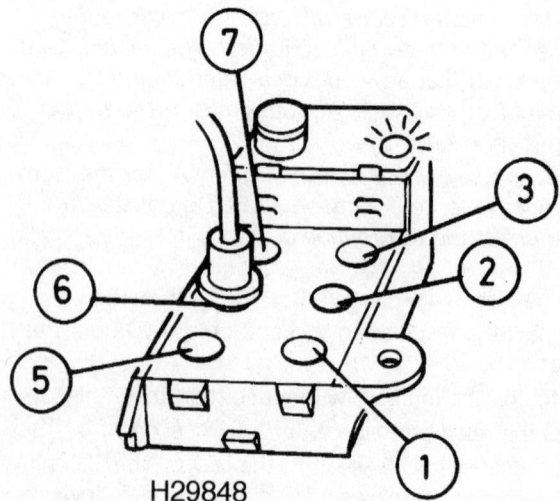

H29848

37.5 Retrieval of ignition codes with the test lead connected to socket number 6

second series of flashes indicates the second digit, and the third series of flashes indicates the third digit, until all three digits have been flashed.

c) Each series is indicated by 0.5-second flashes, separated by 0.5-second pauses.

d) A 3.5-second pause separates each series of flashes.

e) Code "142" is indicated by one 0.5-second flash, followed by a 3.5-second pause, four 0.5-second flashes, a further 3.5-second pause, and two 0.5-second flashes.

5 Count the number of flashes in each series, and record each code as it is transmitted. Refer to the tables at the end of the Chapter to determine the meaning of the fault code.

6 Each code is displayed once by the LED.

7 Retrieve the next code by pressing the test button once more for 1 to 3 seconds. After a pause of 3.5 seconds, the code will be displayed. All stored fault codes are transmitted in sequential order. **Note:** In EZ-116K systems, only the last five codes stored can be retrieved at one time. Before other possible codes can be retrieved, the reason for the first set of faults must be repaired, and the fault codes cleared from memory as described later.

8 Repeat the procedure and continue retrieving codes until all codes have been transmitted.

9 If no codes are stored, the LED will flash code "111".

10 Turn off the ignition to end diagnostic test mode 1.

Test mode 2 (sensor Inputs to the ECM)

11 Connect the test lead to socket 6 on the SD unit.

12 Switch on the ignition, without starting the engine.

13 Press the test button twice to initiate test mode 2. The correct method is as follows:

a) Press the test button for approximately 1 to 3 seconds.

b) Pause for 1 to 2 seconds.

c) Press the test button again for approximately 1 to 3 seconds.

14 The LED will flash continually at approximately 6 flashes per second, indicating that the SD unit is in test mode 2.

15 Perform the sensor tests, and observe the behaviour of the LED as follows:

a) After each test routine, the LED will flash a confirmation code. If the LED does not display a confirmation code, this indicates a faulty component, connection or switch.

b) After displaying a confirmation code, the LED will return to flashing at approximately 6 times per second.

c) Repeat each test if required.

16 Fully open the throttle. If the full-load switch has closed, the LED will display confirmation code "334". Release the throttle.

17 Start the engine or, if it does not start, crank the engine for 10 seconds and leave the ignition switched on. If the ECM receives a satisfactory signal from the crank angle sensor, the LED will display confirmation code "141".

18 Stop the engine.

19 If the test needs to be repeated, switch on the ignition and repeat the procedure from paragraph 13.

5 Bosch LH3.2-Jetronic - testing without a fault code reader (FCR)

Note 1: During the course of certain test procedures, it is possible for additional fault codes to be generated. Care must be taken that any codes generated during test routines do not mislead diagnosis. All codes must be cleared once testing is complete.

Note 2: Do not start the engine unless the test routine requires it.

Test mode 1 (retrieving flash codes)

1 Connect the test lead to socket 2 on the SD unit (see illustration 37.6).

2 Switch on the ignition, without starting the engine.

3 Press the test button once for 1 to 3 seconds.

4 After a pause of 3.5 seconds, the LED on the SD unit will begin flashing to display each 3-digit code as follows:

a) The three digits are indicated by three series of flashes.

b) The first series of flashes indicates the first digit, the second series of flashes indicates the second digit, and the third series of flashes indicates the third digit, until all three digits have been flashed.

c) Each series is indicated by 0.5-second flashes, separated by 0.5-second pauses.

d) A 3.5-second pause separates each series of flashes.

e) Code "142" is indicated by one 0.5-second flash, followed by a 3.5-second pause, four 0.5-second flashes, a further 3.5-second pause, and two 0.5-second flashes.

5 Count the number of flashes in each series, and record each code as it is transmitted. Refer to the tables at the end of the Chapter to determine the meaning of the fault code.

6 Each code is displayed once by the LED.

7 Retrieve the next code by pressing the test button once more for 1 to 3 seconds. After a pause of 3.5 seconds, the

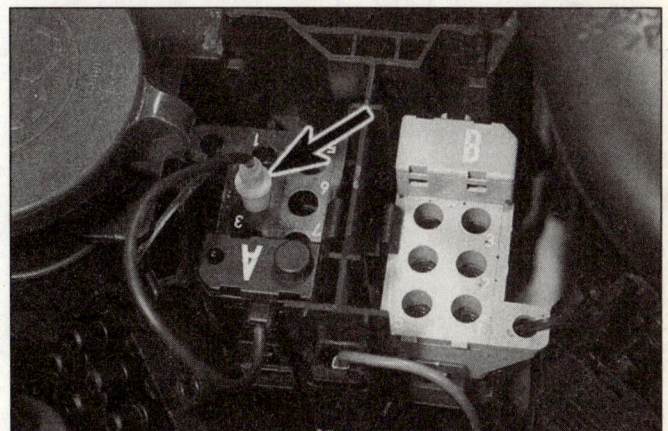

37.6 Where twin SD units are provided, use SD unit "A" for fault code retrieval. The test lead (arrowed) is connected to socket number 2 for retrieval of fuel injection codes

code will be displayed. All stored fault codes are transmitted in sequential order. **Note:** *In Bosch LH 3.2 systems, only the last five codes stored can be retrieved at one time. Before other possible codes can be retrieved, the reason for the first set of faults must be repaired, and the fault codes cleared from memory as described later.*

8 Repeat the procedure and continue retrieving codes until all codes have been transmitted.

9 If no codes are stored, the LED will flash code "111".

10 Turn off the ignition to end test mode 1.

Test mode 2 (sensor inputs to the ECM)

11 Connect the test lead to socket 2 on the SD unit.

12 Switch on the ignition, without starting the engine.

13 Press the test button twice to initiate test mode 2. The correct method is as follows:
  a) *Press the test button for approximately 1 to 3 seconds.*
  b) *Pause for 1 to 2 seconds.*
  c) *Press the test button again for approximately 1 to 3 seconds.*

14 The LED will flash continually at approximately 6 flashes per second, indicating that the SD unit is in test mode 2.

15 Perform the sensor tests, and observe the behaviour of the LED as follows:
  a) *After each test routine, the LED will flash a confirmation code. If the LED does not display a confirmation code, this indicates a faulty component, connection or switch.*
  b) *After displaying a confirmation code, the LED will return to flashing at approximately 6 times per second.*
  c) *Repeat each test if required.*

16 Open the throttle mid-way. The LED will display confirmation code "332" to signify that the idle switch has opened.

17 Fully open the throttle. If the full-load switch has closed, the LED will display confirmation code "333".

18 Start the engine or, if it does not start, crank the engine for 10 seconds and leave the ignition switched on. If the ECM receives a satisfactory signal from the crank angle sensor, the LED will display confirmation code "331".

19 Ensure that the handbrake is firmly applied. Move the automatic transmission gear selector to the "D" position, and return to the "P" position. If the ECM receives a satisfactory signal from the gear position switch, the LED will display confirmation code "124".

20 Turn the air conditioning (A/C) control switch on. If the ECM receives a satisfactory signal from the A/C switch, the LED will display confirmation code "114". If the ECM receives a satisfactory signal from the A/C compressor, the LED will also display confirmation code "134".

21 Turn off the ignition to end test mode 2.

Test mode 3 (activate selected actuators)

22 Connect the test lead to socket 2 on the SD unit.

23 Switch on the ignition, without starting the engine.

24 Press the test button three times to initiate test mode 3.

The correct method is as follows:
  a) *Press the test button for approximately 1 to 3 seconds.*
  b) *Pause for 1 to 2 seconds.*
  c) *Press the test button again for approximately 1 to 3 seconds.*
  d) *Pause for 1 to 2 seconds.*
  e) *Press the test button again for approximately 1 to 3 seconds.*

25 The ECM will automatically activate the injectors and the Idle speed control valve, one after the other with several seconds pause between each actuator. Listen for an audible sound or touch the component to determine whether it has been activated. The LED will flash in time with the audible operation of the actuator.

> ⚠ *Warning: The injectors will actuate for 5 or 10 seconds during this test routine, and there is a real danger of filling the cylinders with petrol. For this reason, it would be wise to disconnect the fuel pump supply (or remove the fuel pump fuse) before commencing the test. Turn off the ignition at any time to end test mode 3.*

26 The test sequence is repeated twice before the procedure ends automatically.

27 Turn off the ignition to end test mode 3.

6 Bosch EZ-129K ignition system - testing without a fault code reader (FCR)

Note 1: *During the course of certain test procedures, it is possible for additional fault codes to be generated. Care must be taken that any codes generated during test routines do not mislead diagnosis. All codes must be cleared once testing is complete.*

Note 2: *Do not start the engine unless the test routine demands it.*

Test mode 1 (retrieving flash codes)

1 Connect the test lead to socket 6 on the SD unit.

2 Switch on the ignition, without starting the engine.

3 Press the test button once for 1 to 3 seconds.

4 After a pause of 3.5 seconds, the LED on the SD unit will begin flashing to display each 3-digit code as follows:
  a) *The three digits are indicated by three series of flashes.*
  b) *The first series of flashes indicates the first digit, the second series of flashes indicates the second digit, and the third series of flashes indicates the third digit, until all three digits have been flashed.*

c) *Each series is indicated by 0.5-second flashes, separated by 0.5-second pauses.*

d) *A 3.5-second pause separates each series of flashes.*

e) *Code "142" is indicated by one 0.5-second flash, followed by a 3.5-second pause, four 0.5-second flashes, a further 3.5-second pause, and two 0.5-second flashes.*

5 Count the number of flashes in each series, and record each code as it is transmitted. Refer to the tables at the end of the Chapter to determine the meaning of the fault code.

6 Each code is displayed once by the LED.

7 Retrieve the next code by pressing the test button once more for 1 to 3 seconds. After a pause of 3.5 seconds, the code will be displayed. All stored fault codes are transmitted in sequential order. **Note:** *In EZ-129K systems, only the last five codes stored can be retrieved at one time. Before other possible codes can be retrieved, the reason for the first set of faults must be repaired, and the fault codes cleared from memory as described later.*

8 Repeat the procedure and continue retrieving codes until all codes have been transmitted.

9 If no codes are stored, the LED will flash code "111".

10 Turn off the ignition to end test mode 1.

Test mode 2 (sensor inputs to the ECM)

11 Connect the test lead to socket 6 on the SD unit.

12 Switch on the ignition, without starting the engine.

13 Press the test button twice to initiate test mode 2. The correct method is as follows:

a) *Press the test button for approximately 1 to 3 seconds.*

b) *Pause for 1 to 2 seconds.*

c) *Press the test button again for approximately 1 to 3 seconds.*

14 The LED will flash continually at approximately 6 flashes per second, indicating that the SD unit is in test mode 2.

15 Perform the sensor tests, and observe the behaviour of the LED as follows:

a) *After each test routine, the LED will flash a confirmation code. If the LED does not display a confirmation code, this indicates a faulty component, connection or switch.*

b) *After displaying a confirmation code, the LED will return to flashing at approximately 6 times per second.*

c) *Repeat each test if required.*

16 Fully open the throttle. If the full-load switch has closed, the LED will display confirmation code "344".

17 Push the vehicle for approximately one metre to produce a signal from the vehicle speed sensor. If the ECM receives a satisfactory signal from the vehicle speed sensor, the LED will display confirmation code "343".

18 Start the engine or, if it does not start, crank the engine for 10 seconds and leave the ignition switched on. If the ECM receives a satisfactory signal from the cylinder identification sensor, the LED will display confirmation code "342".

19 After code 342 is extinguished, the LED will display confirmation code 141 to signify that the ECM has received a satisfactory signal from the crank angle sensor.

20 Turn off the ignition to end test mode 2.

Test mode 3 (activate selected actuators)

21 Connect the test lead to socket 6 on the SD unit.

22 Switch on the ignition, without turning on the engine.

23 Press the test button three times to initiate test mode 3. The correct method is as follows:

a) *Press the test button for approximately 1 to 3 seconds.*

b) *Pause for 1 to 2 seconds.*

c) *Press the test button again for approximately 1 to 3 seconds.*

d) *Pause for 1 to 2 seconds.*

e) *Press the test button again for approximately 1 to 3 seconds.*

24 The ECM will automatically activate each actuator on the appropriate actuator list below, one after the other. Listen for an audible sound or (where appropriate) touch the component to determine whether it has been activated. The LED will flash in time with the audible operation of the actuator.

Actuator list for vehicles before chassis number 30700

1) *Cooling fan at half-speed.*

2) *Cooling fan at full-speed.*

3) *Variable induction sensor valve.*

4) *Rev counter (generating engine speeds of up to 1500 rpm)*

Actuator list for vehicles after chassis number 30700

1) *Variable induction sensor valve.*

2) *Cooling fan at half-speed.*

3) *Exhaust gas regulator.*

4) *Rev counter (generating engine speeds of up to 1500 rpm).*

25 The test sequence is repeated twice before the procedure ends automatically.

26 Turn off the ignition to end test mode 3.

7　Fenix 3B - testing without a fault code reader (FCR)

Note 1: *During the course of certain test procedures, it is possible for additional fault codes to be generated. Care must be taken that any codes generated during test routines do not mislead diagnosis. All codes must be cleared once testing is complete.*

Note 2: *Do not start the engine unless the test routine demands it.*

Test mode 1 (retrieving flash codes)

1 Connect the test lead to socket 2 on the SD unit.

2 Switch on the ignition, without starting the engine.

3 Press the test button once for 1 to 3 seconds.

4 After a pause of 3.5 seconds, the LED on the SD unit will begin flashing to display each 3-digit code as follows:

a) *The three digits are indicated by three series of flashes.*

b) *The first series of flashes indicates the first digit, the second series of flashes indicates the second digit and the third series of flashes indicates the third digit until all three digits have been flashed.*

c) *Each series is indicated by 0.5-second flashes, separated by 0.5-second pauses.*

d) *A 3.5-second pause separates each series of flashes.*

e) *Code "142" is indicated by one 0.5-second flash, followed by a 3.5-second pause, four 0.5-second flashes, a further 3.5-second pause, and two 0.5-second flashes.*

5 Count the number of flashes in each series, and record each code as it is transmitted. Refer to the tables at the end of the Chapter to determine the meaning of the fault code.

6 Each code is displayed once by the LED.

7 Retrieve the next code by pressing the test button once more for 1 to 3 seconds. After a pause of 3.5 seconds, the code will be displayed. All stored fault codes are transmitted in sequential order. **Note:** *In early versions of Fenix 3B, only the last three codes stored can be retrieved at one time. Before any other possible codes can be retrieved, the reason for the first set of faults must be repaired, and the fault codes cleared from memory as described later. In later versions of Fenix 3B, this restriction is lifted, and all stored codes can be retrieved at one time.*

8 Repeat the procedure and continue retrieving codes until all codes have been transmitted.

9 If no codes are stored, the LED will flash code "111".

10 Turn off the ignition to end test mode 1.

Test mode 2 (sensor inputs to the ECM)

Note: *On models with the B18U engine, test mode 2 must always be selected if the throttle cable has been removed and refitted.*

11 Connect the test lead to socket 2 on the SD unit.

12 Switch on the ignition, without starting the engine.

13 Press the test button twice to initiate test mode 2. The correct method is as follows:

a) *Press the test button for approximately 1 to 3 seconds.*

b) *Pause for 1 to 2 seconds.*

c) *Press the test button again for approximately 1 to 3 seconds.*

14 The LED will flash continually at approximately 6 flashes per second, indicating that the SD unit is in test mode 2.

15 Perform the sensor tests, and observe the behaviour of the LED as follows:

a) *After each test routine, the LED will flash a confirmation code. If the LED does not display a confirmation code, this indicates a faulty component, connection or switch.*

b) *After displaying a confirmation code, the LED will return to flashing at approximately 6 times per second.*

c) *Repeat each test if required.*

16 Start the engine or, if it does not start, crank the engine for 10 seconds and leave the ignition switched on. If the ECM receives a satisfactory signal from the crank angle sensor, the LED will display confirmation code "141".

17 Ensure that the handbrake is firmly applied. Move the automatic transmission gear selector to the "D" position, and return to the "P" position. If the ECM receives a satisfactory signal from the gear position switch, the LED will display confirmation code "124".

18 Turn the air conditioning (A/C) control switch on. If the ECM receives a satisfactory signal from the A/C switch, the LED will display confirmation code "114".

19 Turn off the ignition to end test mode 2.

Test mode 3 (activate selected actuators)

20 Connect the test lead to socket 2 on the SD unit.

21 Switch on the ignition, without starting the engine.

22 Press the test button three times to initiate test mode 3. The correct method is as follows:

a) *Press the test button for approximately 1 to 3 seconds.*

b) *Pause for 1 to 2 seconds.*

c) *Press the test button again for approximately 1 to 3 seconds.*

d) *Pause for 1 to 2 seconds.*

e) *Press the test button again for approximately 1 to 3 seconds.*

23 The ECM will automatically activate each actuator on the actuator list below, one after the other, with several seconds' pause between each actuator. Listen for an audible sound or (where appropriate) touch the component to determine whether it has been activated. The LED will flash in time with the audible operation of the actuator.

> ! *Warning: The injectors will actuate for 5 or 10 seconds during this test routine, and there is a real danger of filling the cylinders with petrol. For this reason, it would be wise to disconnect the fuel pump supply (or remove the fuel pump fuse) before commencing the test. Turn off the ignition at any time to end test mode 3.*

Actuator list

1) *Injectors.*
2) *Idle speed regulating valve.*
3) *EVAP valve.*
4) *Air conditioning clutch.*
5) *Main relay.*
6) *Auxiliary relay.*
7) *Water pump.*

24 The test sequence is repeated twice before the procedure ends automatically.

25 Turn off the ignition to end test mode 3.

8 Fenix 5.2 - testing without a fault code reader (FCR)

Note 1: *During the course of certain test procedures, it is possible for additional fault codes to be generated. Care must be taken that any codes generated during test routines do not mislead diagnosis. All codes must be cleared once testing is complete.*

Note 2: *Do not start the engine unless the test routine demands it.*

Test mode 1 (retrieving flash codes)

1 Connect the test lead to socket 2 of the SD unit.

2 Switch on the ignition, without starting the engine.

3 Press the test button once for 1 to 3 seconds.

4 After a pause of 3.5 seconds, the LED on the SD unit will begin flashing to display each 3-digit code as follows:

   a) *The three digits are indicated by three series of flashes.*

   b) *The first series of flashes indicates the first digit, the second series of flashes indicates the second digit, and the third series of flashes indicates the third digit, until all three digits have been flashed.*

   c) *Each series is indicated by 0.5-second flashes, separated by 0.5-second pauses.*

   d) *A 3.5-second pause separates each series of flashes.*

   e) *Code "142" is indicated by one 0.5-second flash, followed by a 3.5-second pause, four 0.5-second flashes, a further 3.5-second pause, and two 0.5-second flashes.*

5 Count the number of flashes in each series, and record each code as it is transmitted. Refer to the tables at the end of the Chapter to determine the meaning of the fault code.

6 Each code is displayed once by the LED.

7 Retrieve the next code by pressing the test button once more for 1 to 3 seconds. After a pause of 3.5 seconds, the code will be displayed. All stored fault codes are transmitted in sequential order. **Note:** *In early versions of Fenix 5.2, only the last three codes stored can be retrieved at one time. Before other possible codes can be retrieved, the reason for the first set of faults must be repaired, and the fault codes cleared from memory as described later. In later versions of Fenix 5.2, this restriction is lifted, and all stored codes can be retrieved at one time.*

8 Repeat the procedure and continue retrieving codes until all codes have been transmitted.

9 If no codes are stored, the LED will flash code "111".

10 Turn off the ignition to end test mode 1.

Test mode 2 (sensor inputs to the ECM)

11 Connect the test lead to socket 2 on the SD unit.

12 Switch on the ignition, without starting the engine.

13 Press the test button twice to initiate test mode 2. The correct method is as follows:

   a) *Press the test button for approximately 1 to 3 seconds.*

   b) *Pause for 1 to 2 seconds.*

   c) *Press the test button again for approximately 1 to 3 seconds.*

14 The LED will flash continually at approximately 6 flashes per second, indicating that the SD unit is in test mode 2.

15 Perform the sensor tests, and observe the behaviour of the LED as follows:

   a) *After each test routine, the LED will flash a confirmation code. If the LED does not display a confirmation code, this indicates a faulty component, connection or switch.*

   b) *After displaying a confirmation code, the LED will return to flash at approximately 6 times per second.*

   c) *Repeat each test if required.*

16 Fully open the throttle. The LED will display confirmation code "333" to signify that the throttle has moved to the full-load position.

17 Release the throttle. The LED will display confirmation code "332" to signify that the throttle position sensor has moved to the idle position.

18 Start the engine, allow it to idle and ensure that the handbrake is firmly applied.

19 Move the automatic transmission gear selector to the "D" position, and return to the "P" position. If the ECM receives a satisfactory signal from the gear position switch, the LED will display confirmation code "124".

20 Turn the air conditioning (A/C) control switch on. If the ECM receives a satisfactory signal from the A/C switch, the LED will display confirmation code "114".

21 Turn off the ignition to end test mode 2.

Test mode 3 (automatic actuator test)

22 Connect the test lead to socket 2 on the SD unit.

23 Switch on the ignition, without starting the engine.

24 Press the test button three times to initiate test mode 3. The correct method is as follows:

   a) *Press the test button for approximately 1 to 3 seconds.*

   b) *Pause for 1 to 2 seconds.*

   c) *Press the test button again for approximately 1 to 3 seconds.*

   d) *Pause for 1 to 2 seconds.*

   e) *Press the test button again for approximately 1 to 3 seconds.*

25 The ECM will automatically activate each actuator on the actuator list below, one after the other, with several seconds' pause between each actuator. Listen for an audible sound or (where appropriate) touch the component to determine whether it has been activated. The LED will flash in time with the audible operation of the actuator.

> *Warning: The injectors will actuate for 5 or 10 seconds during this test routine, and there is a real danger of filling the cylinders with petrol. For this reason, it would be wise to disconnect the fuel pump supply (or remove the fuel pump fuse) before commencing the test. Turn off the ignition at any time to end test mode 3.*

Actuator list

   1) *EGR solenoid valve.*
   2) *Air injection pump.*
   3) *Variable intake manifold solenoid valve.*
   4) *Engine cooling fan (at low speed).*
   5) *Engine cooling fan (at high speed).*
   6) *Injector valve No.1.*
   7) *Injector valve No.2.*
   8) *Injector valve No.3.*
   9) *Injector valve No.4.*
   10) *Injector valve No.5.*
   11) *Air conditioning pump.*
   12) *Main injection relay.*
   13) *Fuel pump relay.*
   14) *ECM box cooling fan.*

26 The test sequence is repeated twice before the procedure ends automatically.

27 Turn off the ignition to end test mode 3.

Test mode 4 (manual actuator test)

28 Connect the test lead to socket 2 on the SD unit.

29 Switch on the ignition, without starting the engine.

30 Press the test button four times to initiate Test Mode 4. The correct method is as follows:

a) Press the test button for approximately 1 to 3 seconds.

b) Pause for 1 to 2 seconds.

c) Press the test button again for approximately 1 to 3 seconds.

d) Pause for 1 to 2 seconds.

e) Press the test button again for approximately 1 to 3 seconds.

f) Pause for 1 to 2 seconds.

g) Press the test button again for approximately 1 to 3 seconds.

31 The LED will illuminate, and wait for input of a 3-digit code.

32 Select a component from the actuator list below, and enter the associated 3-digit code as follows:

a) Press the test button the same number of times as corresponds to the first digit of the 3-digit code for the selected component. The LED will extinguish as the first code is entered. After a few seconds the LED will illuminate again, ready for the second digit.

b) Press the test button the same number of times as corresponds to the second digit of the 3-digit code. The LED will extinguish as the second code is entered. After a few seconds the LED will illuminate again, ready for the third digit.

c) Press the test button the same number of times as corresponds to the third digit of the 3-digit code. The LED will then extinguish as the third code is entered.

33 For example, test the idle speed control valve (actuator code 223). Press the test button twice, and wait until the LED extinguishes and then illuminates. Press the test button twice again, and wait until the LED extinguishes and illuminates. Press the test button three times, and the idle speed control valve will actuate. Listen for an audible sound or (where appropriate) touch the valve to determine whether it has been activated. The LED will flash in time with the audible operation of the valve.

> ⚠ Warning: If testing the injectors, bear in mind that they will each actuate for 5 or 10 seconds during this test routine, and there is a real danger of filling the cylinders with petrol. For this reason, it would be wise to disconnect the fuel pump supply (or remove the fuel pump fuse) before commencing an injector test. Turn off the ignition at any time to end test mode 4.

Codes and actuators

115	Injector valve No.1.
125	Injector valve No.2.
135	Injector valve No.3.
145	Injector valve No.4.
155	Injector valve No.5.
222	Main injection relay
223	Idle speed control valve
235	EGR solenoid valve
342	Air conditioning pump
343	Fuel pump relay
442	Air injection pump
514	Engine cooling fan (at low speed)
515	Engine cooling fan (at high speed)
523	ECM box cooling fan

34 Turn off the ignition to end test mode 4.

9   Motronic 4.3 - testing without a fault code reader (FCR)

Note 1: *During the course of certain test procedures, it is possible for additional fault codes to be generated. Care must be taken that any codes generated during test routines do not mislead diagnosis. All codes must be cleared once testing is complete.*

Note 2: *Do not start the engine unless the test routine demands it.*

Test mode 1 (retrieving fault codes)

1 Connect the test lead to socket 2 of the SD unit.

2 Switch on the ignition, without starting the engine.

3 Press the test button once for 1 to 3 seconds.

4 After a pause of 3.5 seconds, the LED on the SD unit will begin flashing to display each 3-digit code as follows:

a) The three digits are indicated by three series of flashes.

b) The first series of flashes indicates the first digit, the second series of flashes indicates the second digit, and the third series of flashes indicates the third digit, until all three digits have been flashed.

c) Each series is indicated by 0.5-second flashes, separated by 0.5-second pauses.

d) A 3.5-second pause separates each series of flashes.

e) Code "142" is indicated by one 0.5-second flash, followed by a 3.5-second pause, four 0.5-second flashes, a further 3.5-second pause, and two 0.5-second flashes.

5 Count the number of flashes in each series, and record each code as it is transmitted. Refer to the tables at the end of the Chapter to determine the meaning of the fault code.

6 Each code is displayed once by the LED.

7 Retrieve the next code by pressing the test button once more for 1 to 3 seconds. After a pause of 3.5 seconds, the code will be displayed. All stored fault codes are transmitted in sequential order. Note: Depending on the version of Motronic 4.3, only the last eighteen or twenty-eight codes stored can be retrieved at one time. Before other possible codes can be retrieved, the reason for the first set of faults must be repaired, and the fault codes cleared from memory as described later.

8 Repeat the procedure and continue retrieving codes until all codes have been transmitted.

9 If no codes are stored, the LED will flash code "111".

10 Turn off the ignition to end test mode 1.

Test mode 2 (sensor inputs to the ECM)

11 Connect the test lead to socket 2 on the SD unit.

12 Switch on the ignition, without starting the engine.

13 Press the test button twice to initiate test mode 2. The correct method is as follows:

a) *Press the test button for approximately 1 to 3 seconds.*
b) *Pause for 1 to 2 seconds.*
c) *Press the test button again for approximately 1 to 3 seconds.*

14 The LED will flash continually at approximately 6 flashes per second, indicating that the SD unit is in test mode 2.

15 Perform the sensor tests, and observe the behaviour of the LED as follows:

a) *After each test routine, the LED will flash a confirmation code. If the LED does not display a confirmation code, this indicates a faulty component, connection or switch.*
b) *After displaying a confirmation code, the LED will return to flashing at approximately 6 times per second.*
c) *Repeat each test if required.*

16 Fully open the throttle. The LED will display confirmation code "333" to signify that the throttle has moved to the full-load position.

17 Release the throttle. The LED will display confirmation code "332" to signify that the throttle position sensor has moved to the idle position.

18 Start the engine, allow it to idle and ensure that the handbrake is firmly applied.

19 Move the automatic transmission gear selector to the "D" position, and return to the "P" position. If the ECM receives a satisfactory signal from the gear position switch, the LED will display confirmation code "124".

20 Allow the engine to continue idling. Turn the air conditioning (A/C) control switch on.

21 If the ECM receives a satisfactory signal from the A/C switch, the LED will display confirmation code "114". The air conditioning compressor will then be actuated, and the LED will display confirmation code "134".

22 Turn off the ignition to end test mode 2.

Test mode 3 (actuator test)

23 Connect the test lead to socket 2 on the SD unit.

24 Switch on the ignition, without starting the engine.

25 Press the test button three times to initiate test mode 3. The correct method is as follows:

a) *Press the test button for approximately 1 to 3 seconds.*

b) *Pause for 1 to 2 seconds.*
c) *Press the test button again for approximately 1 to 3 seconds.*
d) *Pause for 1 to 2 seconds.*
e) *Press the test button again for approximately 1 to 3 seconds.*

26 The ECM will automatically activate each actuator on the actuator list below, one after the other, with several seconds' pause between each actuator. Listen for an audible sound or (where appropriate) touch the component to determine whether it has been activated. The LED will flash in time with the audible operation of the actuator.

> *Warning: The injectors will actuate for 5 or 10 seconds during this test routine, and there is a real danger of filling the cylinders with petrol. For this reason, it would be wise to disconnect the fuel pump supply (or remove the fuel pump fuse) before commencing the test. Turn off the ignition at any time to end test mode 3.*

Actuator list
1) Engine cooling fan (at low speed).
2) Engine cooling fan (at high speed).
3) Injector valves.
4) Idle speed control valve.
5) Air conditioning pump.

Models up to 1994:
6) Air conditioning compressor.

1995-on models:
7) EGR valve.
8) Air pump.
9) Air conditioning compressor.
10) RPM signal (1500 rpm).

27 The test sequence is repeated twice before the procedure ends automatically.

28 Turn off the ignition to end test mode 3.

10 Clearing fault codes without a fault code reader (FCR)

Note: *On models equipped with EOBD, an FCR is essential for retrieving and clearing fault codes.*

1 Connect the test lead to the relevant socket for the system under test.

2 Switch on the ignition, without starting the engine.

3 Retrieve all flash codes from the ECM by the methods described above. **Note:** *The ECM memory can be cleared only when all the codes have been displayed at least once, and the first displayed code has been repeated.*

4 After all the codes have been displayed, press the test button for at least 5 seconds and then release it.

5 Wait for the LED to illuminate (after a pause of between 3 and 10 seconds).

6 Press the test button a second time for at least 5 seconds.

7 The LED should extinguish, and the fault codes should have been cleared from ECM memory.

8 Repeat the fault code retrieval procedure. Press the test button once for 1 to 3 seconds, and the LED should display code "111", indicating that there are no faults in the ECM memory.

11 Self-Diagnosis with a fault code reader (FCR)

Note: *During the course of certain test procedures, it is possible for additional fault codes to be generated. Care must be taken that any codes generated during test routines do not mislead diagnosis.*

All Volvo models

1 Connect an FCR to the SD unit. Use the FCR for the following purposes, in strict compliance with the FCR manufacturer's instructions:

 a) *Retrieving fault codes.*
 b) *Clearing fault codes.*
 c) *Testing sensor inputs.*
 d) *Testing actuators (automatically).*
 e) *Testing actuators (manually).*
 f) *Datastream.*

Note: *Not all test modes are available on all systems fitted to Volvo vehicles.*

2 Codes must always be cleared after component testing, or after repairs involving the removal or replacement of an engine management system component.

12 Guide to test procedures

1 Use an FCR to interrogate the ECM for fault codes, or gather codes manually using the methods previously described in this Chapter.

Codes stored

2 If one or more fault codes are gathered, refer to the fault code tables at the end of this Chapter to determine their meaning.

3 If several codes are gathered, look for a common factor such as a defective earth return or supply.

4 Refer to the component test procedures in Chapter 4, where you will find a means of testing the majority of components and circuits found in the modern EMS.

5 Once the fault has been repaired, clear the codes and run the engine under various conditions to determine if the problem has cleared.

6 Check the ECM for fault codes once more. Repeat the above procedures where codes are still being stored.

7 Refer to Chapter 3 for more information on how to effectively test the EMS.

No codes stored

8 Where a running problem is experienced, but no codes are stored, the fault is outside of the parameters designed into the SD system. Refer to Chapter 3 for more information on how to effectively test the engine management system.

9 If the problem points to a specific component, refer to the test procedures in Chapter 4, where you will find a means of testing the majority of components and circuits found in the modern EMS.

Fault code tables

Fenix 3B, Fenix 5.2, Bosch Motronic 4.3, and Bosch LH3.2-Jetronic

Flash/FCR code	Description
111	No faults found in the ECM. Proceed with normal diagnostic methods
112	Electronic control module (ECM)
113	Injector or injector circuit
113	Oxygen sensor (OS) or OS circuit (alternative code)
115	Injector No. 1 or injector circuit (850 models)
121	Mass airflow (MAF) sensor signal or MAF sensor circuit
122	Air temperature sensor (ATS) or ATS circuit
123	Coolant temperature sensor (CTS) or CTS circuit
125	Injector No. 2 or injector circuit (850 models)
131	RPM sensor signal or RPM sensor circuit
132	Battery voltage too low/high
133	Coolant temperature sensor (CTS) or CTS circuit
135	Injector No. 3 or injector circuit (850 models)

Flash/FCR code	Description
143	Knock sensor (KS) or KS circuit
144	Load signal absent or faulty
145	Injector No. 4 or injector circuit (850 models)
152	Air pump valve signal or circuit
154	Leak in exhaust gas recirculation (EGR) system (Fenix 5.2)
155	Injector No. 5 or injector circuit (850 models)
211	CO pot or CO pot circuit
212	Oxygen sensor (OS) signal or (OS) circuit
214	RPM sensor signal or RPM sensor circuit
221	Oxygen sensor (OS) control or OS circuit
222	Relay coil
223	Idle speed control valve (ISCV) or ISCV circuit
225	Air conditioning (A/C) pressure sensor or circuit
231	Oxygen sensor (OS) control or OS circuit, mixture rich

Flash/ FCR code	Description
232	Oxygen sensor (OS) control or OS circuit, mixture rich at idle
233	Long-term idle air
235	Exhaust gas recirculation (EGR) signal or EGR circuit
241	Exhaust gas recirculation (EGR) system flow fault or EGR circuit (Fenix 5.2)
243	Throttle pot sensor (TPS) or TPS circuit
244	Knock sensor (KS) or KS circuit
311	Vehicle speed sensor (VSS) signal or VSS circuit
313	Carbon filter solenoid valve (CFSV) or CFSV circuit
314	Camshaft position sensor (CMP) signal or CMP circuit
323	Warning light
324	Auxiliary water pump (relay) or circuit
342	Air conditioning (A/C) relay
343	Fuel pump relay or fuel pump circuit
411	Throttle valve sensor or circuit
412	Full throttle signal or circuit
413	Exhaust gas recirculation (EGR) temperature sensor or EGR circuit (Fenix 5.2)
432	Electronic control module (ECM)
432	Temperature over 95°C
433	Rear knock sensor (KS) signal or KS circuit
442	Air pump relay signal or circuit
511	Oxygen sensor (OS) control or OS circuit, mixture weak at idle
512	Oxygen sensor control or OS circuit, at weak running limit
513	Temperature over 90°C
514	Engine cooling fan
515	Engine cooling fan
521	Oxygen sensor (OS) or OS circuit
523	Electronic control module (ECM)
524	Transmission torque control
535	Turbo regulation (Fenix 5.2)

Bosch LH2.4-Jetronic

Flash/ FCR code	Description
111	No faults found in the ECM. Proceed with normal diagnostic methods
112	Electronic control module (ECM) fault
113	Short-term fuel mixture too weak
121	Manifold absolute pressure (MAP) sensor, signal absent or faulty
123	Coolant temperature sensor (CTS), signal absent or faulty
132	Battery voltage too low or too high
133	Idle adjustment or short-circuit of throttle switch
212	Oxygen sensor (OS) signal absent or faulty or OS circuit
213	Full throttle adjustment, or shorted throttle switch or circuit
221	Long-term fuel mixture too weak
223	Idle speed control valve (ISCV) signal absent or faulty or ISCV circuit
231	Long-term fuel mixture too rich
232	Long-term fuel mixture too weak
233	Idle speed control valve (ISCV) closed, check for air leak
311	Vehicle speed sensor (VSS) signal absent or VSS circuit
312	No signal from knock-related enrichment
321	Mass airflow (MAF) sensor or MAF sensor circuit
322	Mass airflow (MAF) sensor or MAF sensor circuit
344	Exhaust gas temperature controller or circuit
411	Throttle pot sensor (TPS) signal absent or TPS circuit
511	Long-term fuel mixture too rich
512	Short-term fuel mixture too rich

All models with EOBD

For a list of the allocated EOBD codes beginning with P0 (Generic Powertrain), refer to Chapter 1, Section 1.

Notes

EOBD diagnostic plug locations

Index of vehicles

|---|---|---|---|---|---|
Alfa Romeo					
GTE	2001		156	2003	
147	2002				
Audi					
A2	2002		A4	2001	
A3	2001		A6	2002	
BMW					
3 & 5 Series	2002		X5	2002	
730d	2004		Z4	2003	
Citroën					
Berlingo	2004		C8	2004	
C3	2004		Xsara	2003	
C5	2004				
Daewoo					
Kalos	2003		Nubira	2003	
Matiz	2003		Tacuma	2003	
Daihatsu					
Charade	2004		Sirion	2002	
Copen	2004		Terios	2003	
Cuore	2002		YRV	2003	
Fiat					
Doblo	2004		Punto	2003	
Idea	2004		Stilo	2004	
Multipla	2004		Ulysse	2004	
Panda	2004				
Ford					
Fiesta	2003		Galaxy	2003	
Focus	2004		Ka	2003	
Focus C-Max	2004		Mondeo	2002	
Honda					
Accord	2004		HRV	2004	
Civic	2004		S2000	2004	
CRV	2001		Stream	2004	
Jazz	2004				
Hyundai					
Accent	2001		Matrix	2004	
Amica	2004		Santa Fe	2002	
Coupe	2004		Sonata	2004	
Elantra	2004		Terracan	2004	
Getz	2004		Trajet	2004	

Isuzu

Rodeo	2004

Jaguar

X-Type	2002

Kia

Carens	2004		Sedona	2004
Magentis	2002		Sorento	2004
Rio	2004			

Land Rover

Freelander	2004		Defender	2001
Discovery	2004		Range Rover	2004

Lexus

IS200	2002

Mazda

2	2004		6	2004
3	2004		MX5	2004
323F	2001		RX8	2004

Mercedes

A-Class	2001		M-Class	2004
C-Class	2004		S-Class	2001
CLK	2001		SLK	2004

Mini

Cooper	2004

Mitsubishi

Carisma	2004		Grandis	2004
Evolution VII	2004		Shogun Warrior	2004

Nissan

Almera	2004		Terrano	2004
Micra	2004		X-Trail	2004
Primera	2002			

Peugeot

106	2002		406	2001
206	2000		607	2003
307	2003		Partner	2004

Proton

Impian	2004		Satira	2004
Jumbuck	2004		Wira	2004

Renault

Clio	2001		Megane	2004
Espace	2002		Scenic	2004
Kangoo	2004		Vel Satis	2004
Laguna	2004			

Rover/MG

City Rover	2004		75	2001
25 / ZR	2002		TF	2003
45	2003			

Saab

9-3	2003		9-5	2001

SEAT

Alhambra	2004		Ibiza	2004
Arosa	2004		Leon	2003

Skoda

Fabia	2004		Superb	2003
Octavia	2004			

Subaru

Impreza	2004		Legacy	2004
Forrester	2004			

Suzuki

Alto	2004		Swift	2001
Ignis 5-door	2004		Vitara	2004
Ignis 3-door	2004		Wagon-R	2004
Jimny	2004			

Toyota

Avensis	2001		Land Cruiser	2004
Avensis	2004		MR2	2004
Celica	2001		Rav 4	2004
Corolla	2004		Yaris	2004

Vauxhall

Agila	2004		Meriva	2004
Astra-G	2003		Omega	2001
Astra-H	2004		Vectra	2003
Corsa-C	2003		Zafira	2001

VW

Beetle	2003		Polo	2001
Golf	2001		Touran	2004
Passat	2002			

Plug locations

According to the EOBD regulations, all 16-pin diagnostic plugs should be located within reach of the driver's seat, normally under the facia. It may be necessary to remove a cover to expose the plug, but no tools should be needed to remove the cover.

Alfa Romeo GTE 2001

Remove the lower facia panel from the driver's side to expose the 16-pin connector

Alfa Romeo 147 2002

Lower the facia panel to access the 16-pin connector

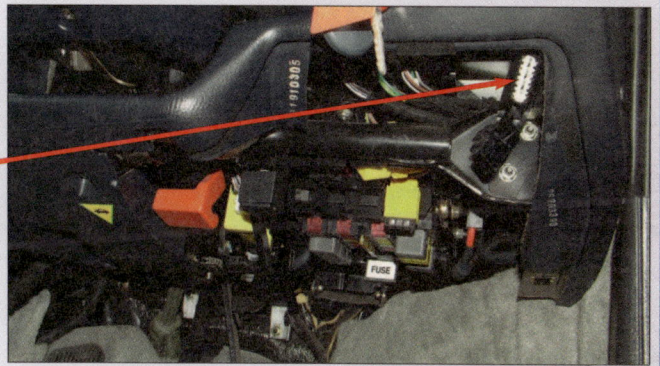

Alfa Romeo 156 2003

Remove the driver's side lower facia panel to access the 16-pin connector

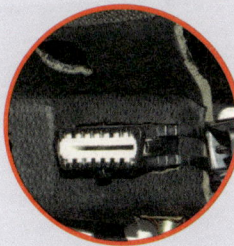

Audi A2 2002

The 16-pin connector is located above the accelerator pedal

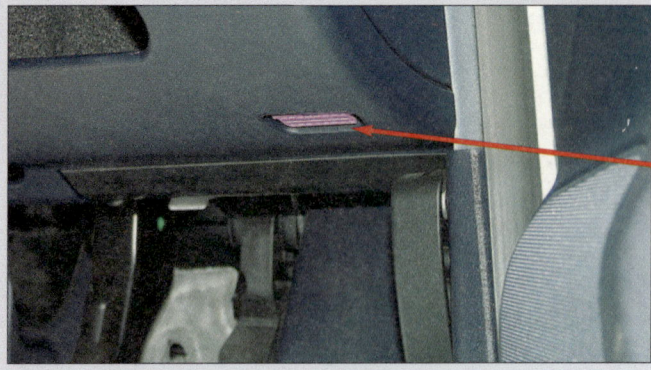
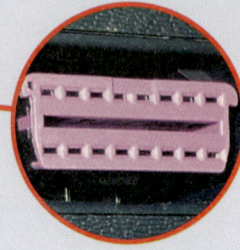

Audi A3 2001
The 16-pin connector is located under the driver's side of the facia

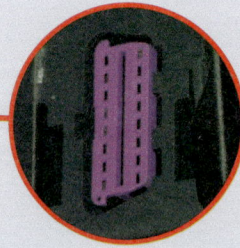

Audi A4 2001
Remove the plastic cover adjacent to the rear ashtray in the centre console to access the 16-pin connector

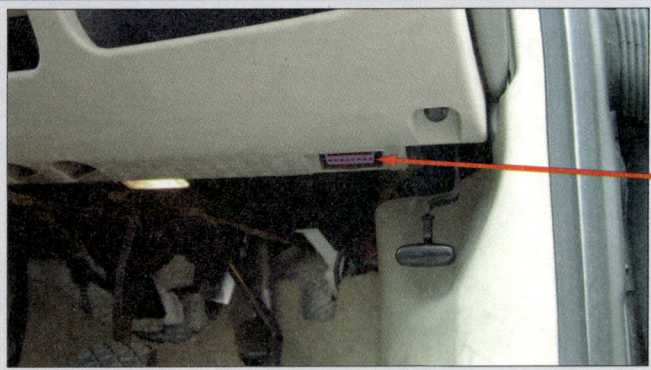
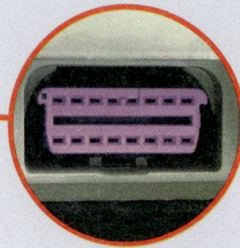

Audi A6 2002
EOBD 16-pin connector under the facia

BMW 3 & 5 Series
Pull down the plastic cover to exposed the 16-pin connector

BMW 730d 2004
Prise of the plastic cover in the driver's side kick panel to access the 16-pin connector

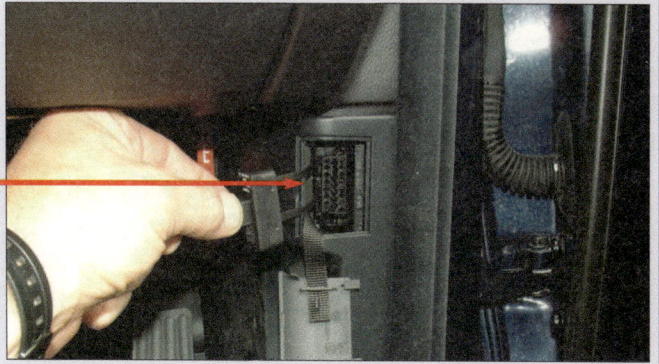

BMW X5 2002
Prise open the plastic cover to access in the driver's side lower facia panel to access the 16-pin connector

BMW Z4 2003
Pull down the plastic cover in the lower facia panel to expose the 16-pin connector

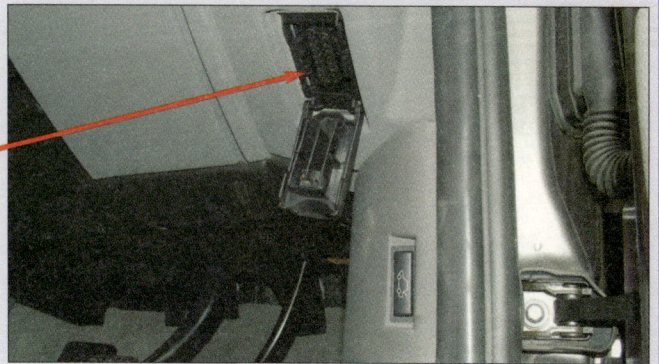

Mini models
EOBD 16-pin connector (note the plastic cover)

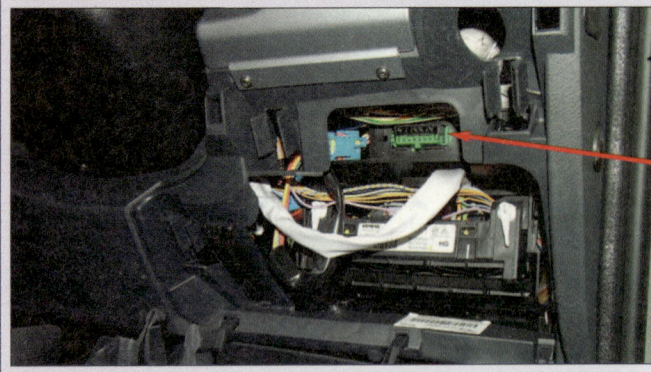

Citroën Berlingo 2004
Pull down the cover to expose the 16-pin connector

Citroën C3 2004
Open the glovebox, and remove the cover to expose the EOBD 16-pin connector

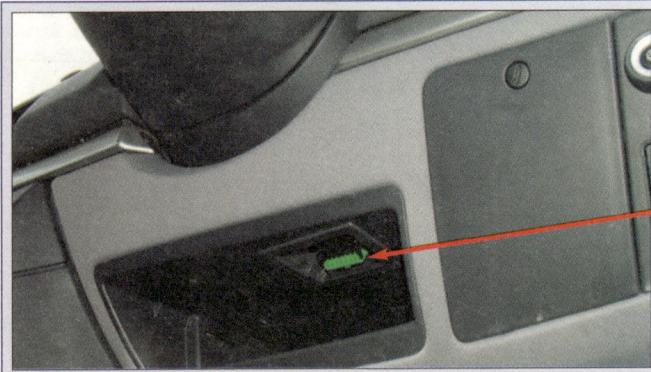

Citroën C8 2004
The 16-pin connector is in the driver's side storage compartment

Citroën Xsara 2003
Open the fuse box cover to access the EOBD 16-pin connector

Citroën C5 2004
Pull out the trim panel from the passenger's side glovebox to expose the 16-pin connector

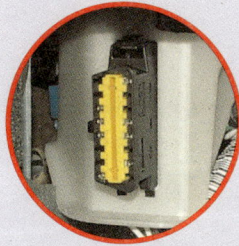

Daewoo Kalos 2003
The 16-pin connector is located under the facia

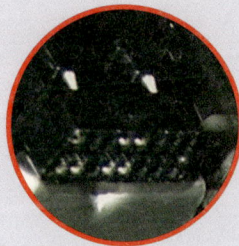

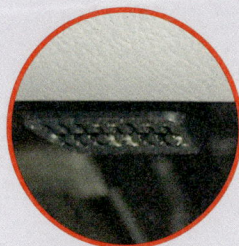

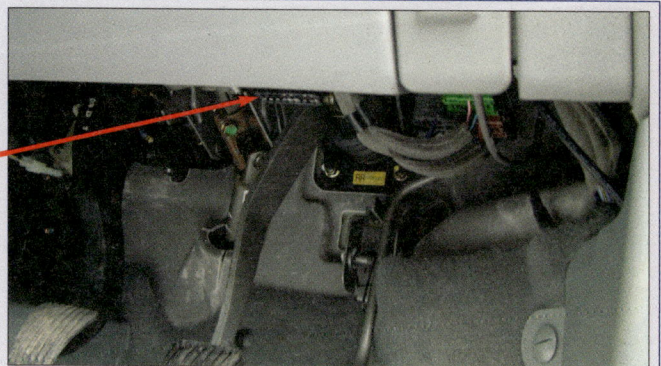

Daewoo Matiz 2003
Reach under the passenger's side facia, and remove the cover to expose the 16-pin plug

Daewoo Nubira 2003
The 16-pin connector is located under the facia

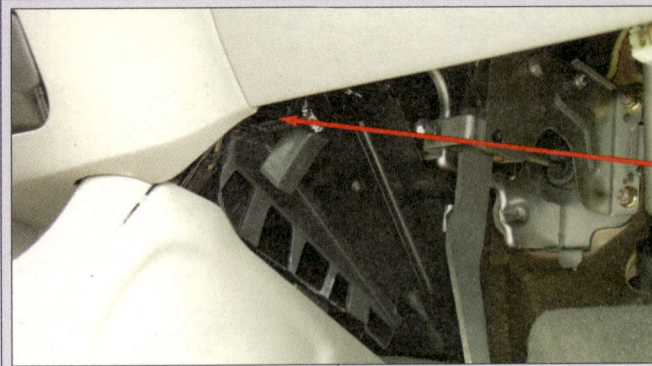

Daewoo Tacuma 2003
Pull of the cover to expose the 16-pin connector

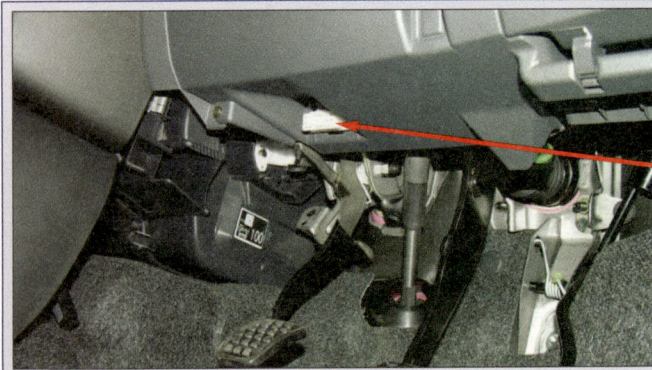

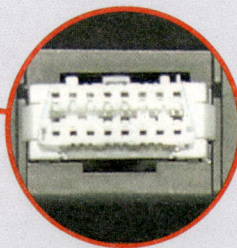

Daihatsu Charade 2004
The 16-pin connector is located under the facia

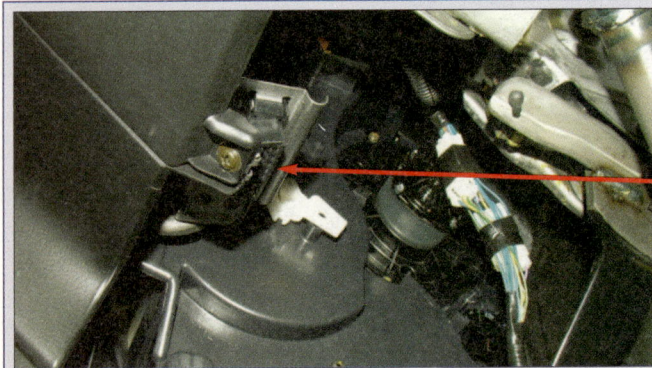

Daihatsu Copen 2004
The 16-pin connector is located under the facia

Daihatsu Cuore 2002
The 16-pin connector is located on the front edge of the centre console

Daihatsu Sirion 2002
The 16-pin connector is located under the facia

Daihatsu Terios 2003
The 16-pin connector is located under the facia

Daihatsu YRV 2003
The 16-pin connector is located under the facia

Fiat Doblo 2004
Remove the fusebox cover from the driver's side of the facia to expose the 16-pin connector

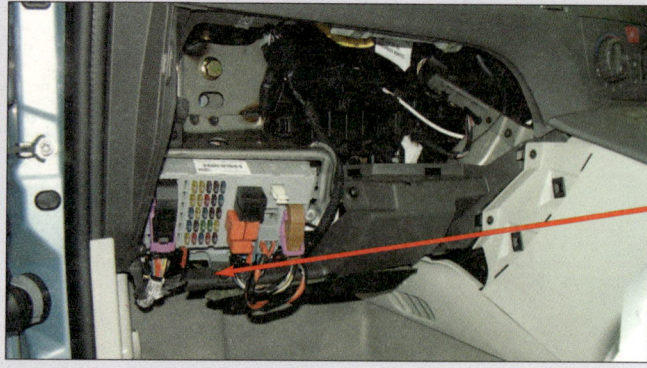

Fiat Idea 2004
Undo the screws, and remove the lower facia panel from the passenger side to access the 16-pin connector

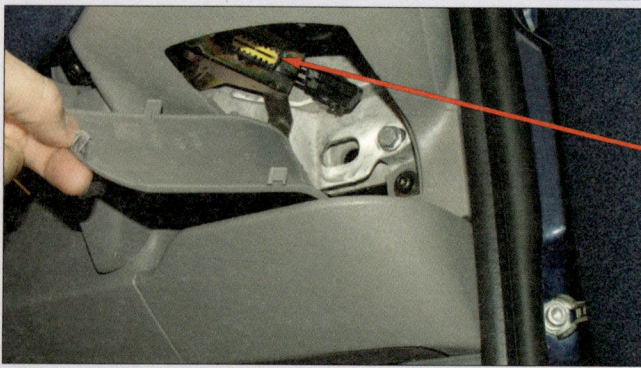

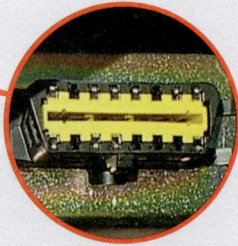

Fiat Multipla 2004
Remove the trim panel from the driver's side of the facia to access the 16-pin connector

Fiat Panda 2004
Undo the fasteners, and remove the trim panel from the driver's side of the facia

Fiat Punto 2003
Remove the lower facia panel to access the 16-pin connector

Fiat Stilo 2004
Remove the fusebox cover from the driver's side of the facia to expose the 16-pin connector

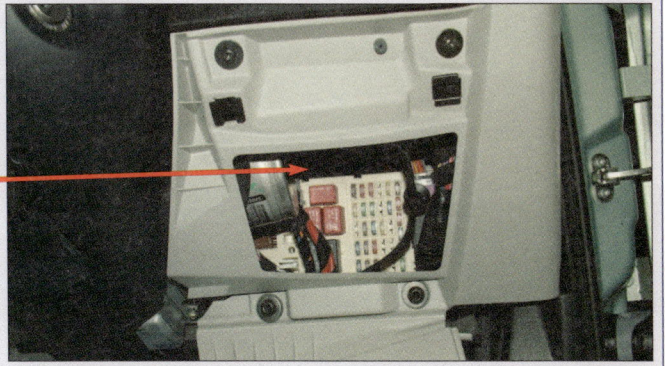

Fiat Ulysse 2004
The 16-pin connector is located in the driver's side facia storage compartment

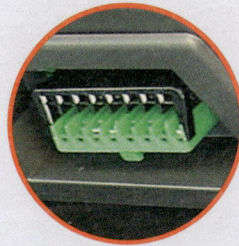

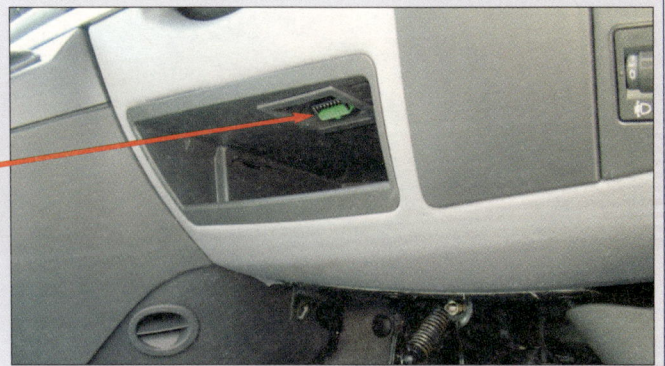

Ford Fiesta 2003
Pull down the flap to access the 16-pin connector

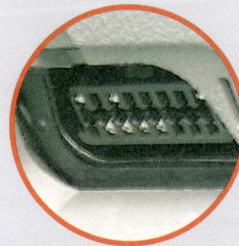

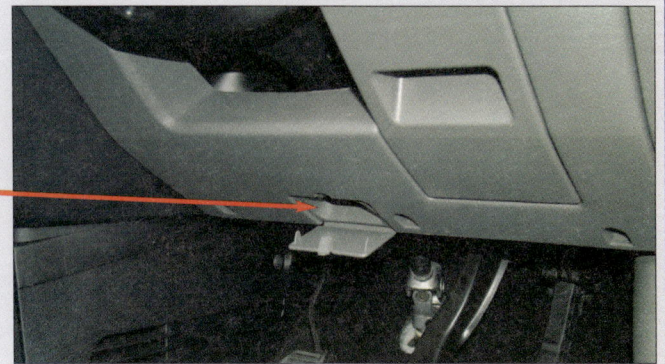

Ford Focus 2004
Pull out the cover to access the EOBD diagnostic connector

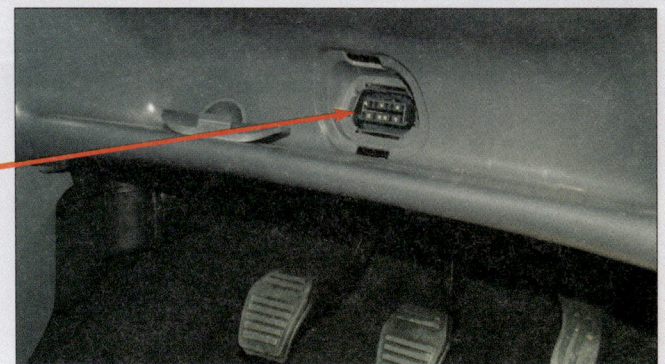

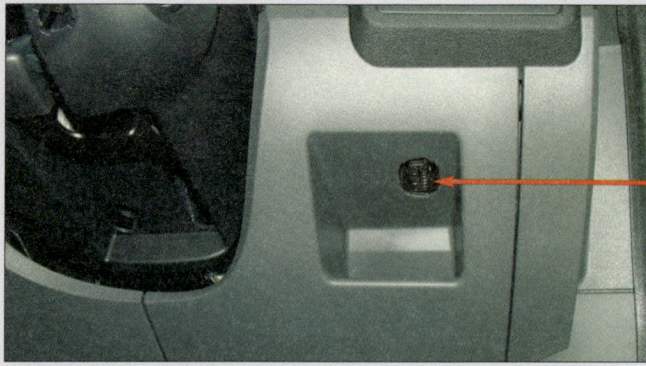

Ford Focus C-Max 2004
The 16-pin connector is located in the driver's side facia storage compartment

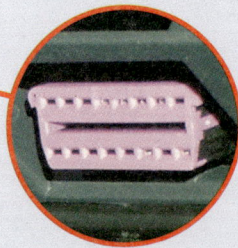

Ford Galaxy 2003
The 16-pin connector is under the driver's side of the facia

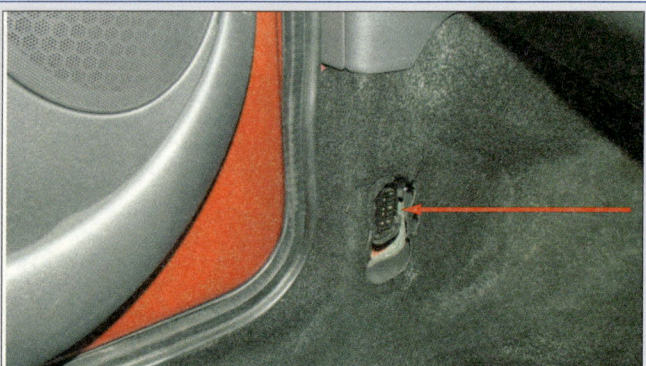

Ford Ka 2003
Pull off the cover to expose the 16-pin connector in the passenger's side footwell

Ford Mondeo 2002
The EOBD 16-pin connector slides down from under the facia

Honda Accord 2004
The 16-pin connector is located under the facia

Honda Civic 2004
The 16-pin connector is located in the driver's side footwell, at the front edge of the centre console

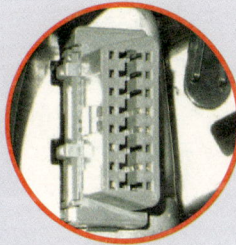

Honda CRV 2001
EOBD 16-pin diagnostic connector in the passenger side footwell

Honda Jazz 2004
The 16-pin connector is located under the facia, adjacent to the centre console

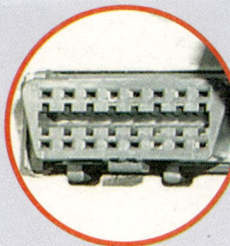

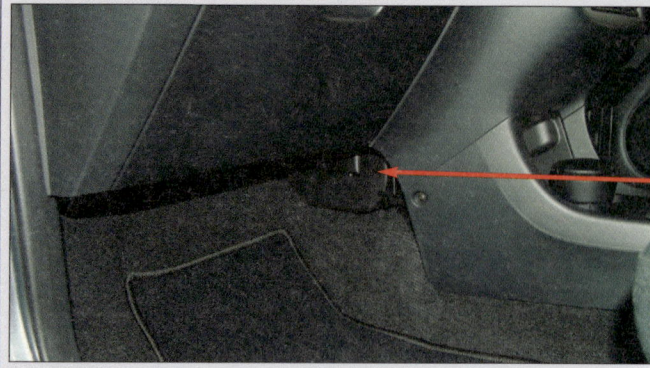

Honda HRV 2004
The 16-pin connector is located in the passenger's side footwell, at the front edge of the centre console

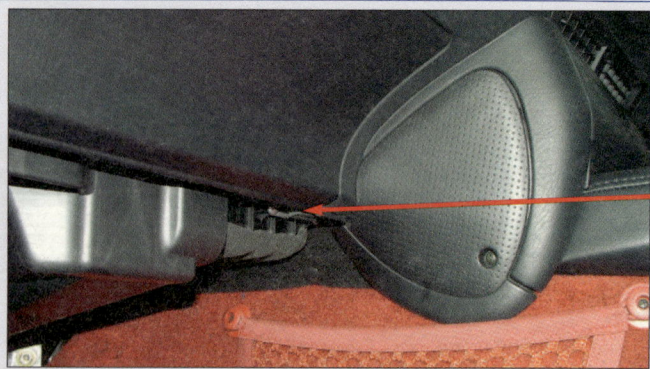

Honda S2000 2004
The 16-pin connector is located in the passenger's side footwell at the front of the centre console

Honda Stream 2004
The 16-pin connector is located under the facia

Hyundai Accent 2001
The 16-pin connector is located under the facia, adjacent to the bonnet release handle

Hyundai Amica 2004
The 16-pin connector is located above the clutch pedal, under the facia

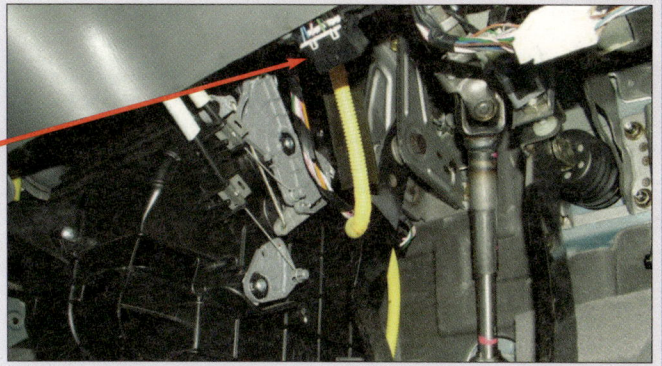

Hyundai Coupe 2004
Remove the fusebox cover from the facia to expose the 16-pin connector

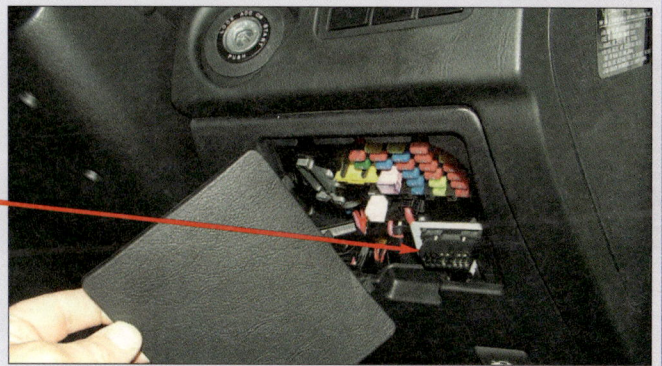

Hyundai Elantra 2004
The 16-pin connector is located under the facia, adjacent to the bonnet release handle

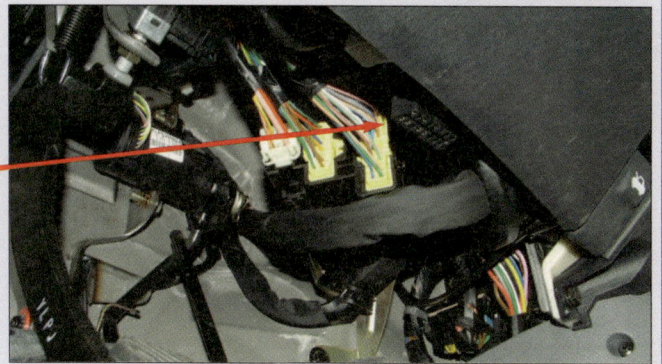

Hyundai Getz 2004
The 16-pin connector is located under the facia, above the driver's pedals

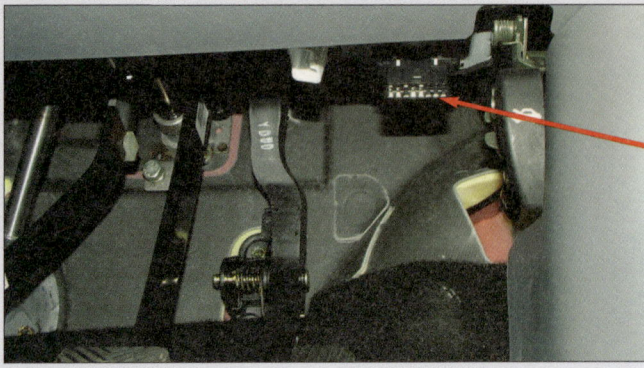

Hyundai Matrix 2004
The 16-pin connector is located under the facia, adjacent to the bonnet release handle

Hyundai Santa Fe 2002
Remove the fusebox cover on the driver's side of the facia to access the 16-pin connector

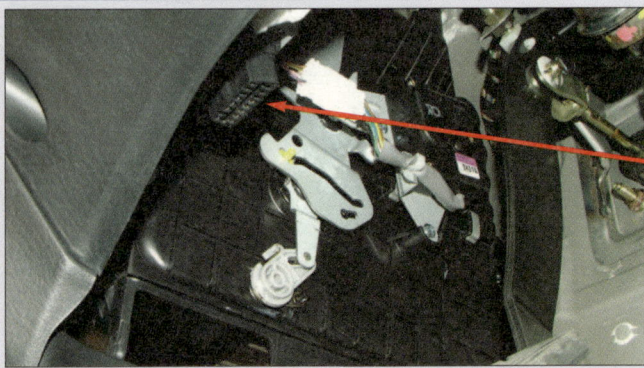

Hyundai Sonata 2004
The 16-pin connector is located under the driver's side of the facia

Hyundai Trajet 2004
The 16-pin connector is located under the facia, above the driver's pedals

Hyundai Terracan 2004
The 16-pin connector is located under the facia, above the driver's pedals

Isuzu Rodeo 2004
The 16-pin connector is located under the facia

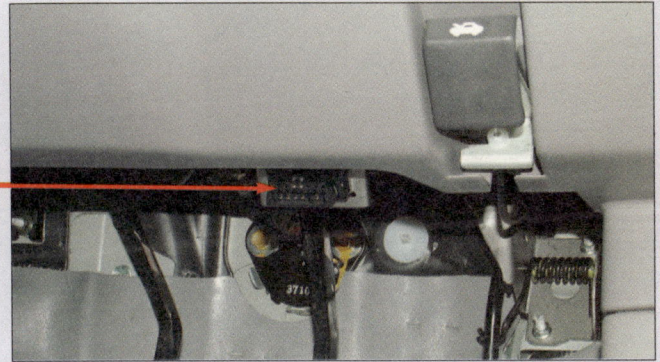

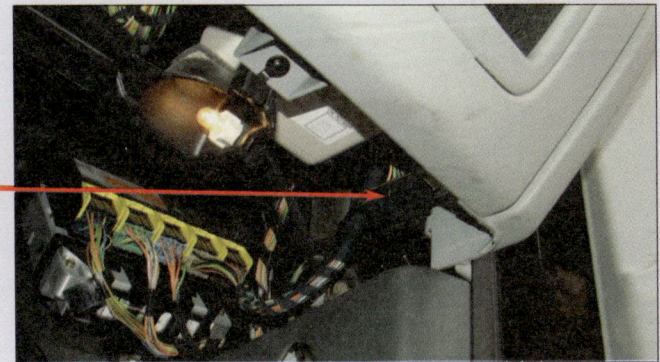

Jaguar X-Type 2002
The 16-pin connector is located under the facia

Kia Carens 2004
The 16-pin connector is located under the driver's side of the facia

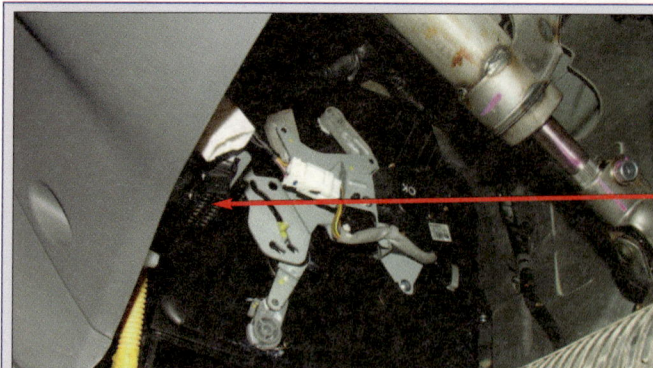

Kia Magentis 2002
The 16-pin connector is up under the facia

Kia Rio 2004
The 16-pin connector is located under the driver's side of the facia

Kia Sedona 2004
The 16-pin connector is located under the driver's side of the facia

Kia Sorento 2004
The 16-pin connector is located under the driver's side of the facia

Land Rover Freelander 2004
EOBD 16-pin connector in the passenger's footwell at the front of the centre console (note the plastic cover)

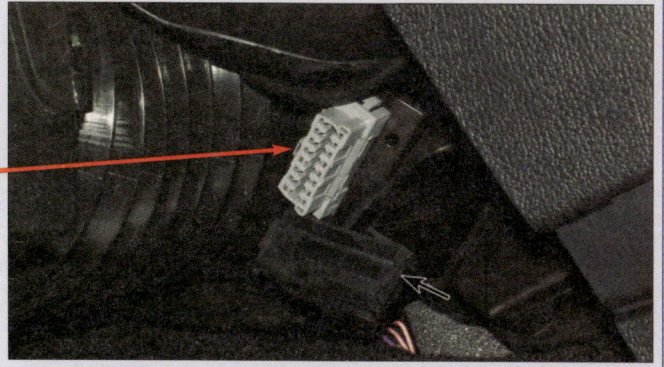

Land Rover Discovery 2004
EOBD 16-pin connector under the facia

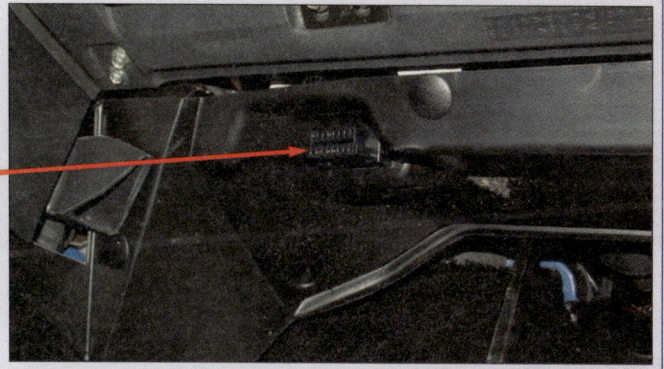

Land Rover Defender 2001
EOBD 16-pin connector between the front seats

Range Rover 2004
EOBD 16-pin connector at the outer edge of the facia

Lexus IS200 2002
The 16-pin connector is located under the facia, adjacent to the bonnet release handle

Mazda 2 2004
Lift the plastic cover in the lower facia panel above the driver's pedals to access the 16-pin connector

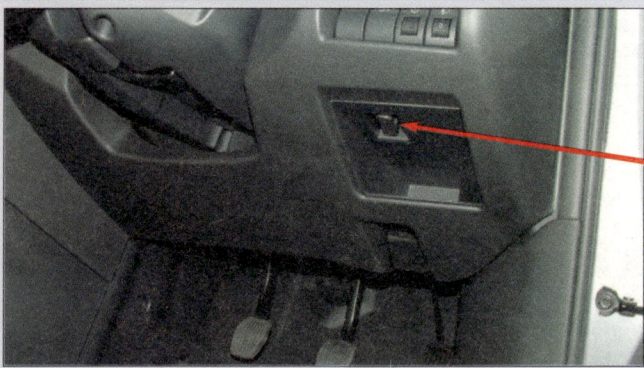

Mazda 3 2004
The 16-pin connector is located in the roof of the storage compartment in the driver's side facia

Mazda 323F 2001
The 16-pin connector is located under the facia on the driver's side

Mazda 6 2004
The 16-pin connector is located above the driver's pedals

Mazda MX5 2004
Remove the fusebox cover above the bonnet release handle to access the 16-pin connector

Mazda RX8 2004
The 16-pin connector is located adjacent to the bonnet release handle

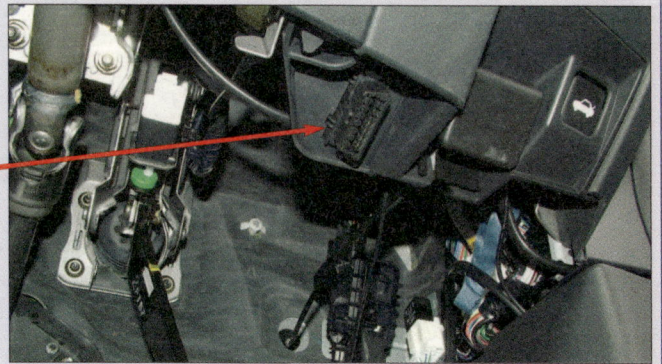

Mercedes A-Class 2001
Pull down the cover to expose the 16-pin connector under the driver's side of the facia

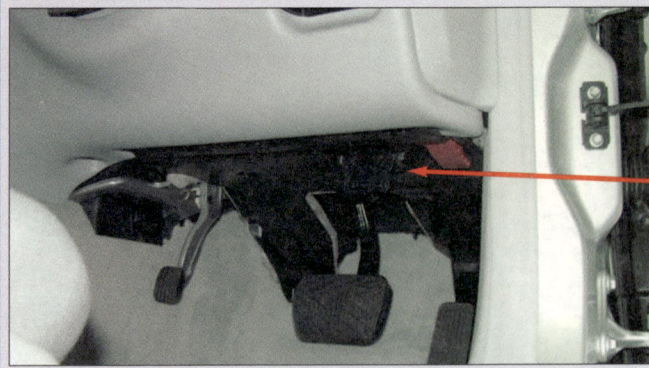

Mercedes C-Class 2004
Pull down the cover to expose the 16-pin connector under the driver's side of the facia

Mercedes CLK 2001
The 16-pin connector is located adjacent to the bonnet release handle

Mercedes M-Class 2004
The 16-pin connector is located under the facia, above the accelerator pedal. Pull down the cover to expose the connector

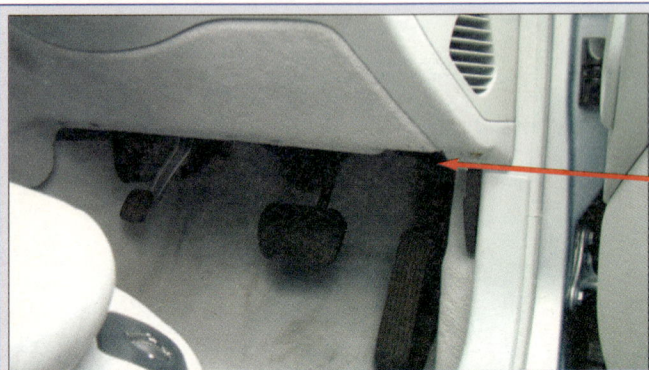

Mercedes S-Class 2001
The 16-pin connector is located adjacent to the bonnet release handle

Mercedes SLK 2004
Pull down the cover to expose the 16-pin connector adjacent to the bonnet release handle

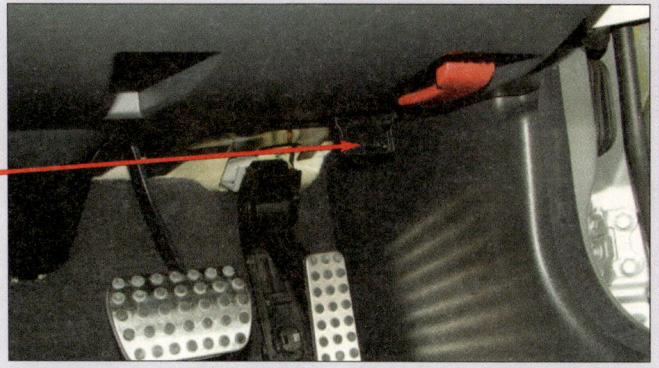

Mitsubishi Carisma 2004
The 16-pin connector is located in the passenger's side footwell, at the front edge of the centre console

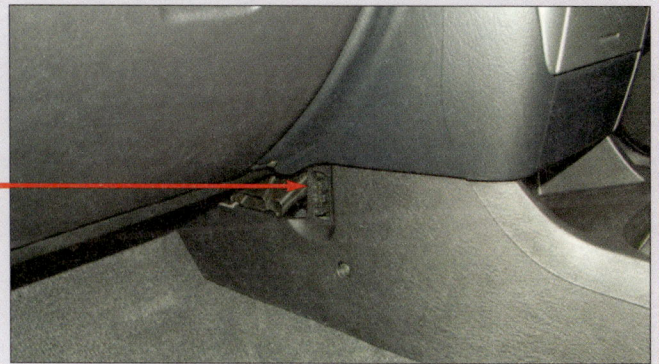

Mitsubishi Evolution VII 2004
The 16-pin connector is located under the facia

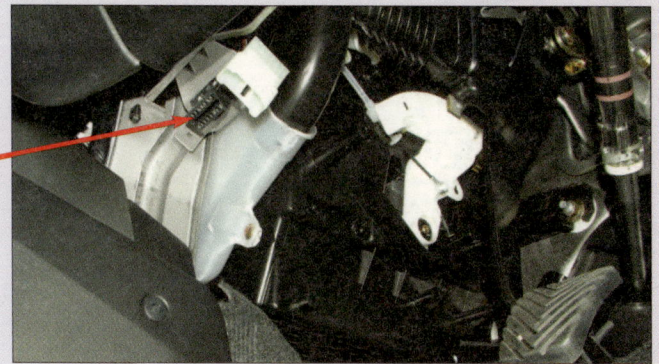

Mitsubishi Grandis 2004
The 16-pin connector is located at the lower edge of the facia

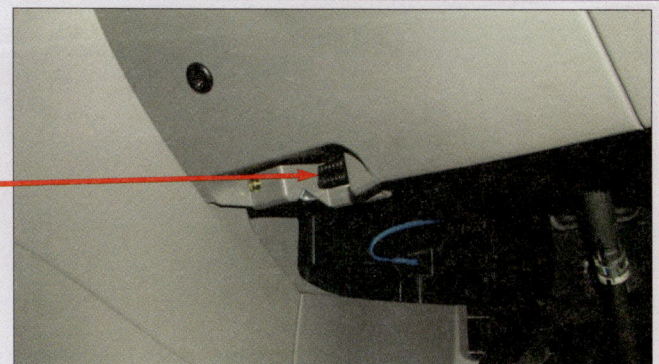

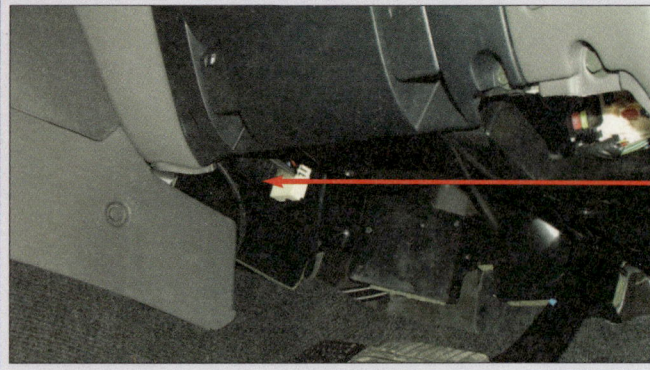

Mitsubishi Shogun Warrior 2004
The 16-pin connector is located under the facia

Nissan Almera 2004
The 16-pin connector is located under the facia

Nissan Micra 2004
Remove the panel on the driver's side of the facia to expose the 16-pin plug

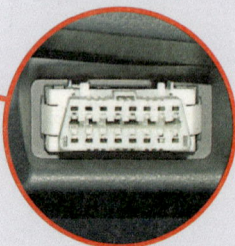

Nissan Primera 2002
The 16-pin connector is located at the lower edge of the facia

Nissan Terrano 2004
The 16-pin plug is under the driver's side of the facia

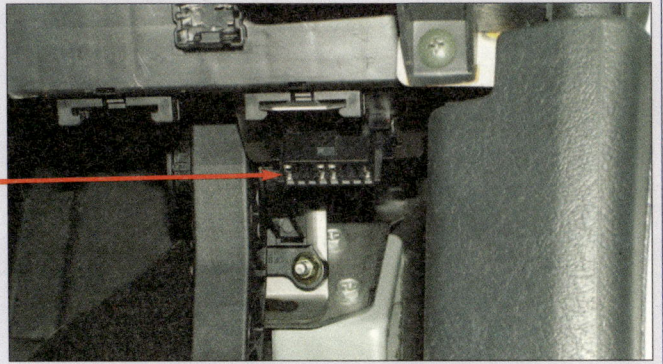

Nissan X-Trail 2004
Remove the trim panel from the lower part of the facia to expose the 16-pin plug

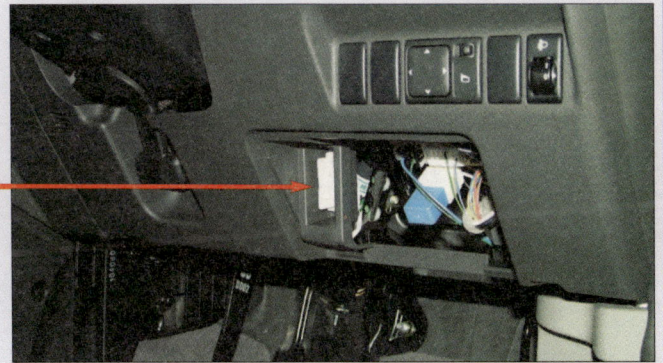

Peugeot 106 2002
The 16-pin connector is located under the facia on the passenger's side

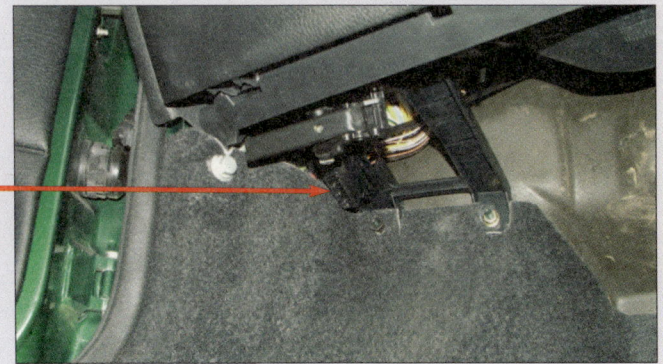

Peugeot 206 2000
EOBD 16-pin connector under the facia, under the fuse box cover

Peugeot 307 2003
Use a coin to undo the fastener, then remove the trim panel from the facia to expose the 16-pin plug

Peugeot 406 2001
To access the 16-pin connector, remove the cover from the driver's side of the facia

Peugeot 607 2003
Pull back the cover in the centre console storage compartment to expose the 16-pin connector

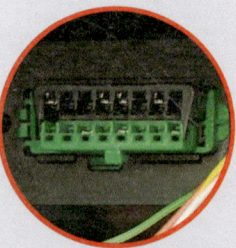

Peugeot Partner 2004
Remove the trim panel from the driver's side of the facia to expose the 16-pin connector

Proton Impian 2004
Pull down the carpet at the front of the centre console to access the 16-pin connector

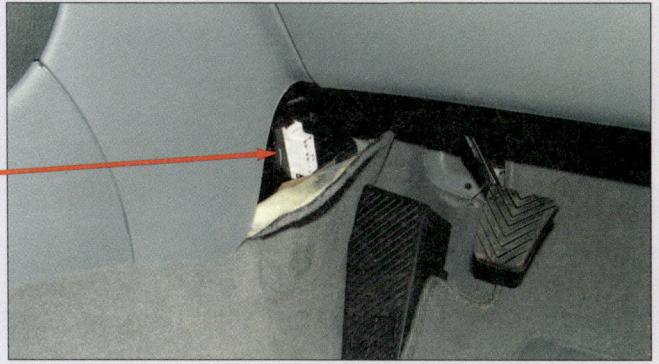

Proton Jumbuck 2004
The 16-pin connector is located immediately below the bonnet release handle

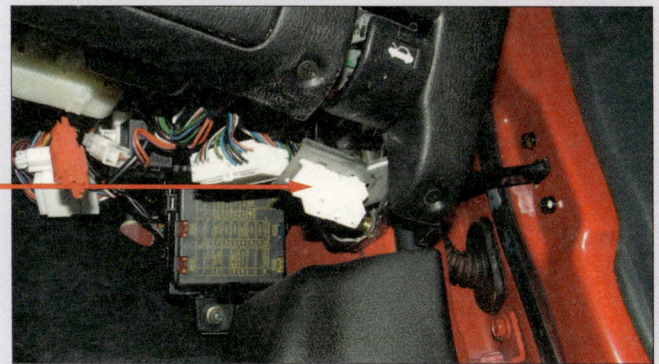

Proton Satira 2004
The 16-pin connector is located immediately below the bonnet release handle

Proton Wira 2004
The 16-pin connector is located immediately below the bonnet release handle

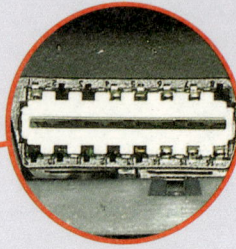

Renault Clio 2001
Remove the ashtray in the centre console to access the 16-pin connector

Renault Espace 2002
Remove the fuse box cover from the passenger's side footwell to expose the 16-pin connector

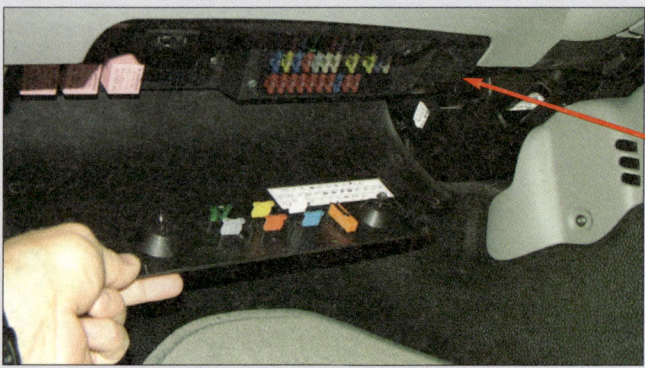

Renault Kangoo 2004
Open the fusebox cover on the passenger's side of the facia to expose the 16-pin connector

Renault Laguna 2004
Remove the ashtray/storage compartment from the centre console, the pull up the plastic cover to access the 16-pin connector

Renault Megane 2004
Remove the trim panel from the front of the centre console to access the 16-pin connector

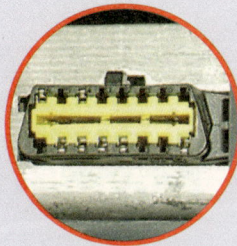

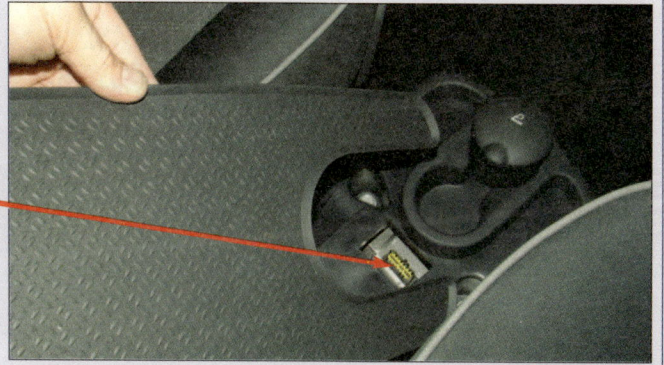

Renault Scenic 2004
Remove the panel from the centre console to access the 16-pin connector

Renault Vel Satis 2004
Remove the ashtray from the centre console to access the 16-pin connector

City Rover 2004
Peel back the flap of carpet ender the front seat to expose the connector

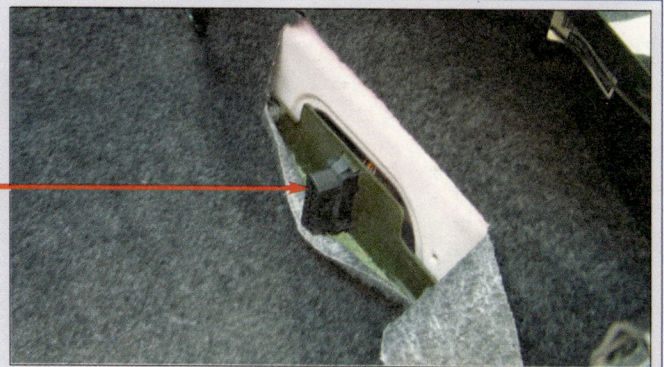

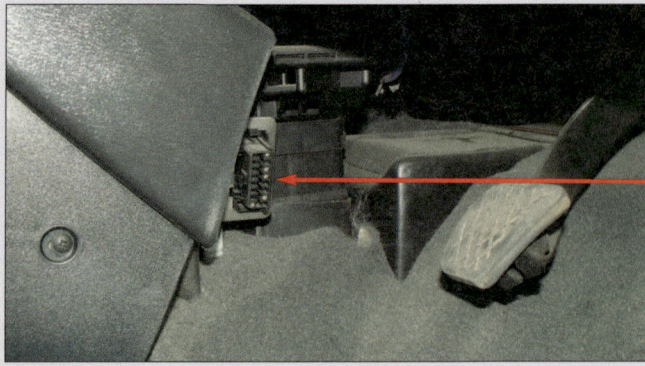

Rover 25 / MG ZR 2002
The 16-pin connector is located in the driver's footwell at the front edge of the centre console

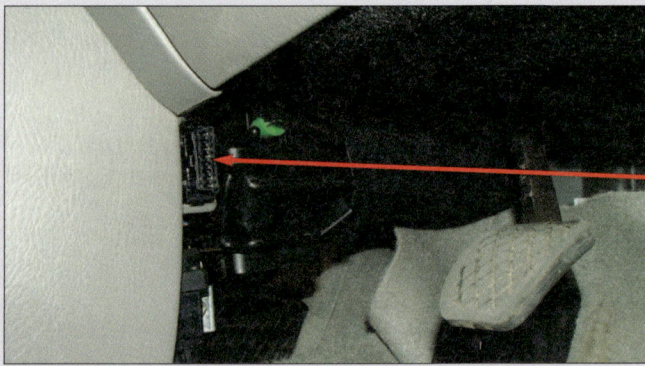

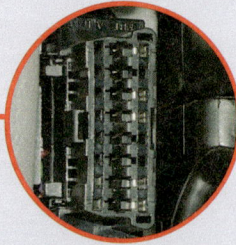

Rover 45 2003
The 16-pin connector is located in the driver's footwell at the front edge of the centre console

Rover 75 2001
EOBD 16-pin connector under the facia

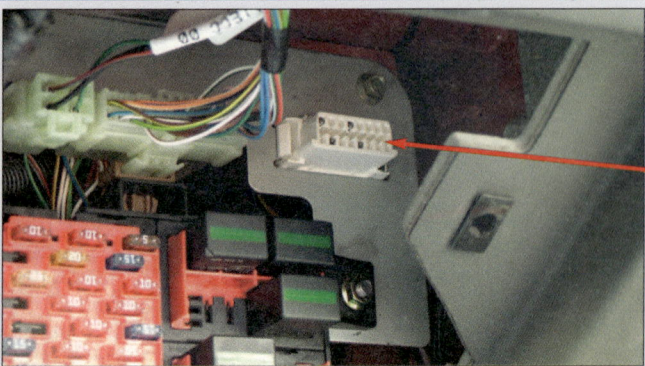

MG TF 2003
Open the fusebox cover under the driver's side of the facia to expose the 16-pin connector

Saab 9-3 2002
Remove the cover to access the 16-pin connector

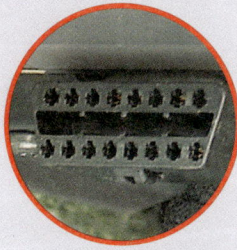

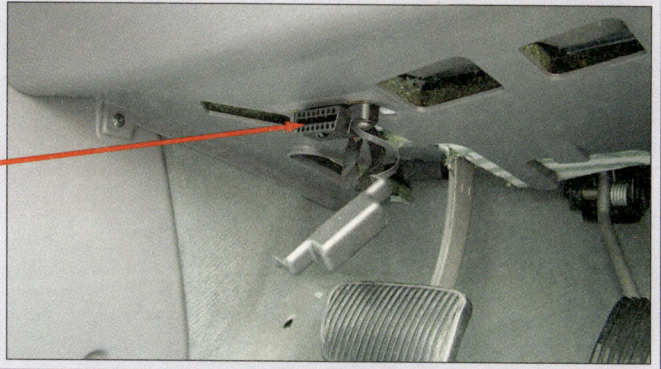

Saab 9-5 2001
Pull down the cover to access the 16-pin diagnostic plug

Seat Alhambra 2004
The 16-pin connector is located under the driver's side of the facia

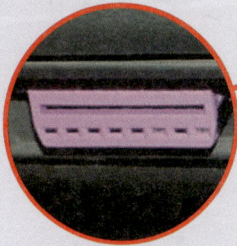

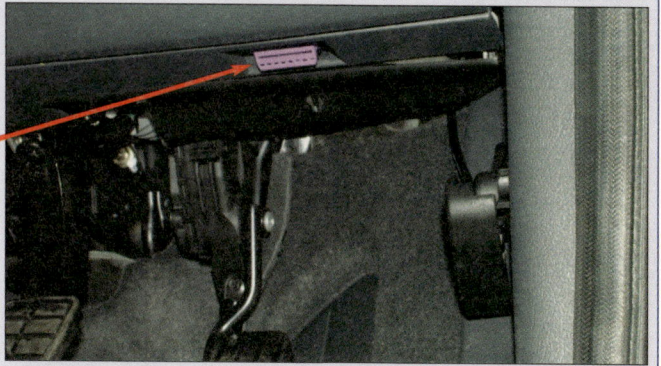

Seat Arosa 2004
Remove the ashtray from the centre console to access the 16-pin connector

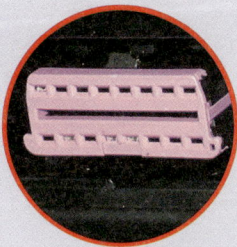

Seat Ibiza 2004
Remove the storage compartment from the driver's side of the facia to expose the 16-pin connector

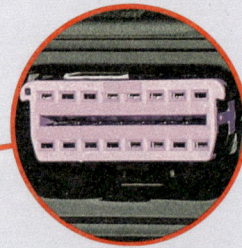

Seat Leon 2003
Pull off the cover to expose the EOBD 16-pin connector

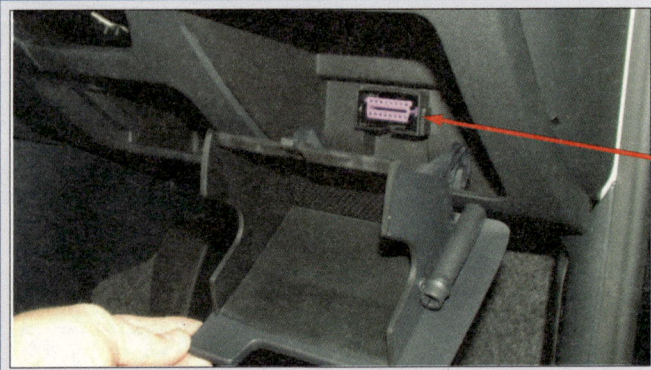

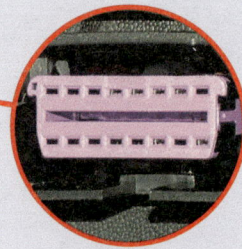

Skoda Fabia 2004
Pull down the storage compartment on the driver's side of the facia to access the 16-pin connector

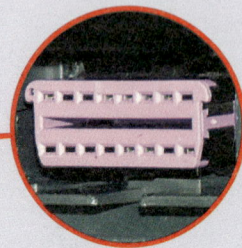

Skoda Octavia 2004
The 16-pin connector is located in the facia storage compartment under the steering column

Skoda Superb 2003
The 16-pin connector is located under the facia, above the brake pedal

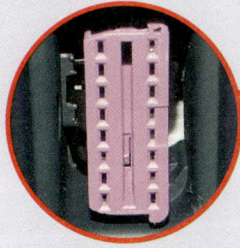

Subaru Impreza 2004
The 16-pin connector is located under the facia

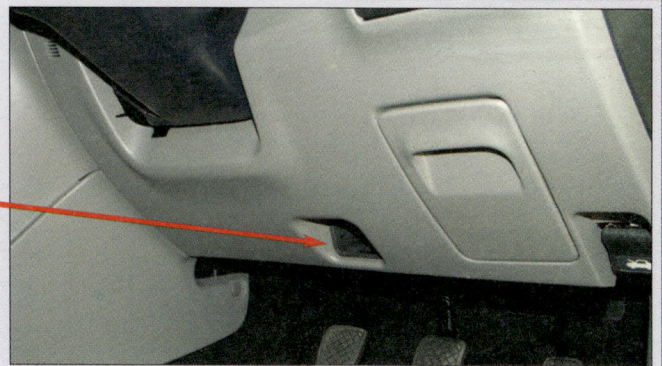

Subaru Forrester 2004
The 16-pin connector is located under the facia

Subaru Legacy 2004
The 16-pin connector is located under the facia

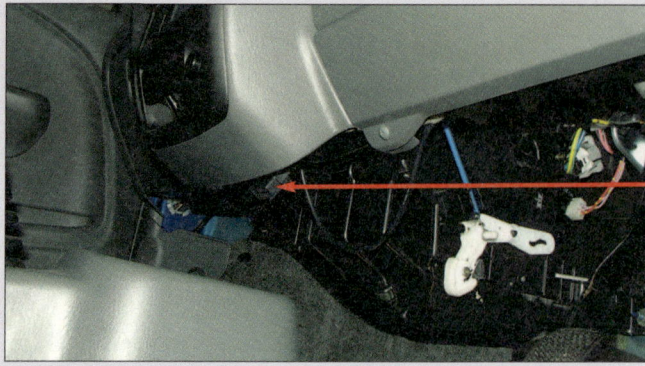

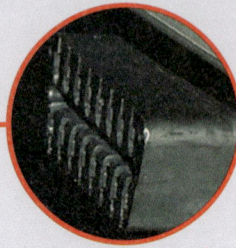

Suzuki Alto 2004
The 16-pin connector is located under the lower edge of the facia centre panel

Suzuki Ignis 5-door 2004
The 16-pin connector is located under the facia, adjacent to the bonnet release handle

Suzuki Ignis 3-door 2004
The 16-pin connector is located under the facia, adjacent to the heater housing

Suzuki Jimny 2004
The 16-pin connector is located under the facia, adjacent to the heater housing

Suzuki Swift 2001
The 16-pin connector is
located under the facia

Suzuki Vitara 2004
The 16-pin connector is
located under the facia,
adjacent to the heater
housing

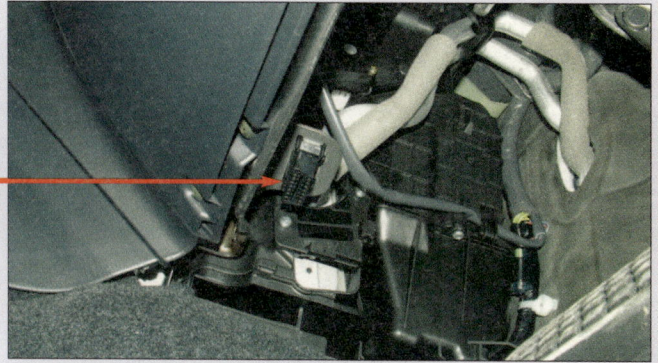

Suzuki Wagon-R 2004
The 16-pin connector is
located under the facia,
adjacent to the bonnet
release handle

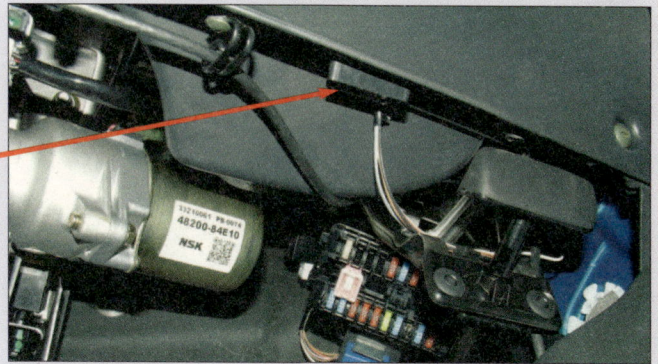

Toyota Avensis 2001
Lift out the storage
compartment on the
driver's side of the facia to
expose the 16-pin
connector

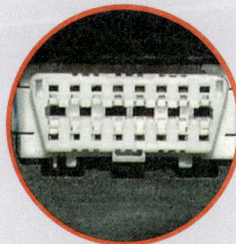

Toyota Avensis 2004
Pull off the plastic cover to expose the 16-pin connector

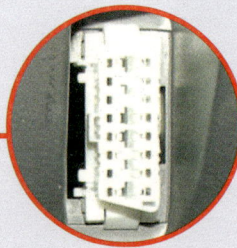

Toyota Celica 2001
The 16-pin connector is located under the driver's side of the facia

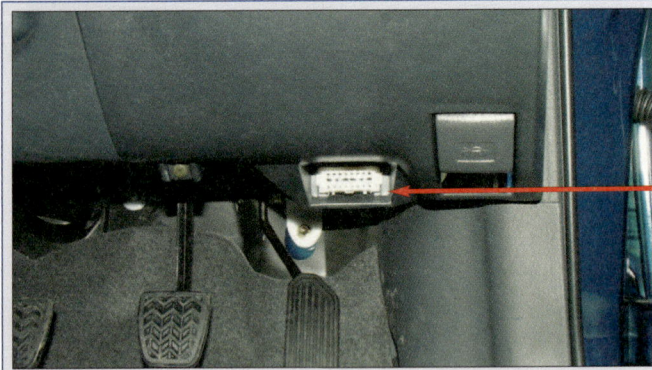

Toyota Corolla 2004
The 16-pin connector is located under the driver's side of the facia

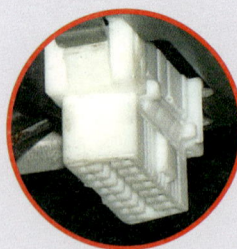

Toyota Land Cruiser 2003
The 16-pin connector is located above the driver's pedals

Toyota MR2 2004
The 16-pin connector is located under the driver's side of the facia

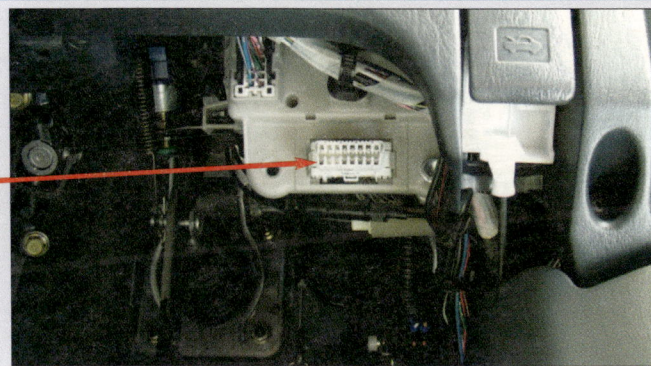

Toyota Rav4 2004
The 16-pin connector is located under the driver's side of the facia

Toyota Yaris 2004
EOBD 16-pin connector

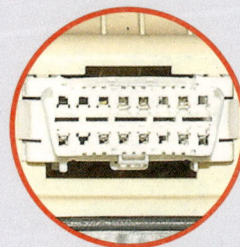

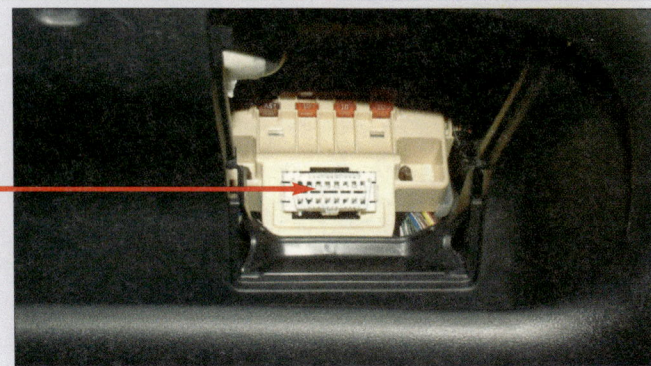

Vauxhall Agila 2004
The 16-pin connector is under the facia adjacent to the bonnet release handle

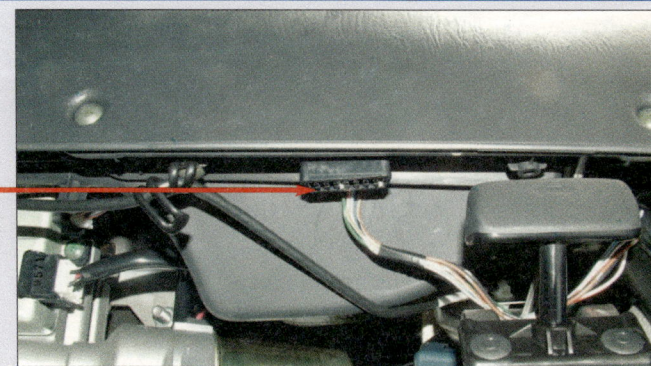

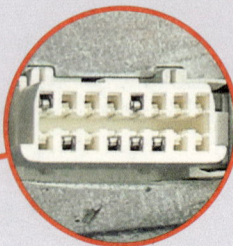

Vauxhall Astra-G 2003
Remove the centre console trim panel to access the EOBD 16-pin connector

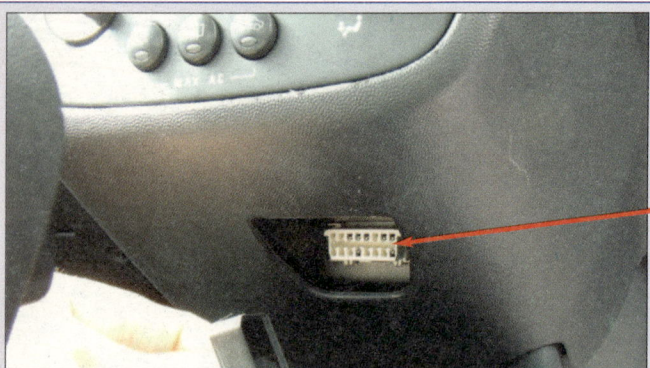

Vauxhall Astra-H 2004
Remove the centre console trim panel to access the EOBD 16-pin connector

Vauxhall Corsa-C 2003
Pull off the cover to expose the 16-pin connector

Vauxhall Meriva 2004
Remove the trim panel from in front of the handbrake lever to access the 16-pin connector

Vauxhall Omega 2001
Open the fusebox cover beneath the steering column to access the 16-pin connector

Vauxhall Vectra 2003
Remove the ashtray to expose the 16-pin connector

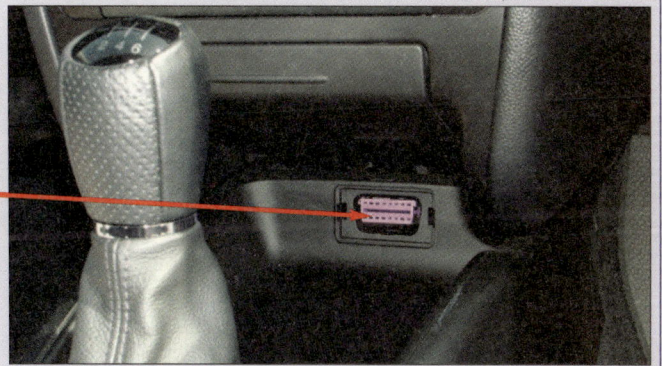

Vauxhall Zafira 2001
Remove the centre console trim panel to access the EOBD 16-pin connector

VW Beetle 2003
The 16-pin connector is located under the facia, adjacent to the bonnet release handle

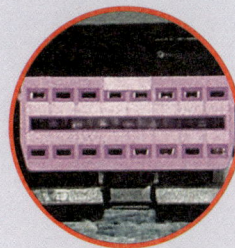

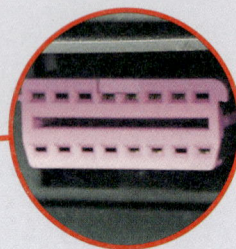

VW Golf 2001
Remove the trim panel beneath the heater controls to expose the 16-pin connector

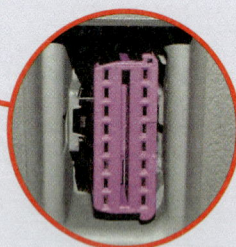

VW Passat 2002
The 16-pin connector is located under the driver's side facia

VW Polo 2001
Remove the ashtray from the centre console to access the 16-pin connector

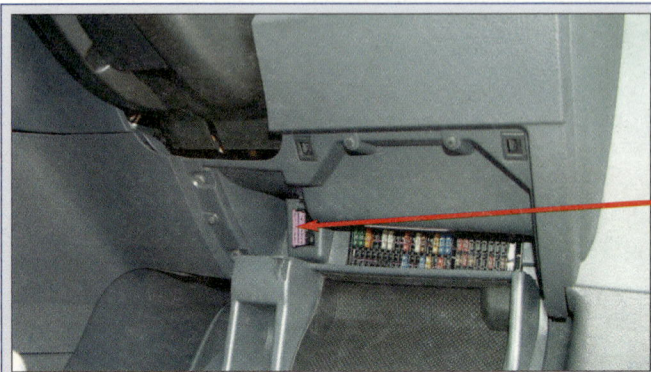

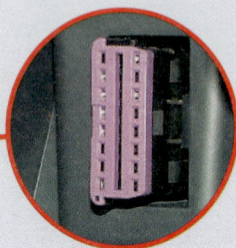

VW Touran 2004
Open the driver's side storage compartment to access the 16-pin connector

Abbreviations and Glossary of technical terms

A

AATS (Ambient Air Temperature Sensor)
AAV (Auxiliary Air Valve)
A/C (Air Conditioning)
AC (Alternating Current) An electric current that first flows in one direction and then the opposite. AC voltage is produced by an alternator or by a pulse generator. AC voltage must be rectified to DC (direct current) before it can be used in the vehicle charging system. AC voltage from a pulse generator is converted to DC by an analogue-to-digital converter.
ACAV (Variable Acoustic Characteristic Induction - PSA term) See Variable Induction system (VIS)
ACC (Air Conditioning compressor Clutch - Ford term)
ACS (Air Conditioning Switch - Ford term)
ACT (Air Charge Temperature - Ford term - see ATS) Usually refers to a totally separate sensor, as distinct to one that is integrated into the airflow sensor.
Actuator A device controlled by the ECM. Examples would be injectors, ISCV etc.
Actuator driver Refer also to driver (actuator), relay driver, control signal and final stage.
ACW (Anti-ClockWise) Direction of rotation.
Adaptive system An EMS that is able to "learn" or relearn the best setting for each application is said to be adaptive.
ADC (Analogue-to-Digital Converter)
Advanced (timing) The opposite to retarded timing. When the ignition timing fires BEFORE the correct moment. Can also be used to describe ignition timing that occurs BTDC. When adjusting the ignition timing to a greater number of degrees BTDC, you are said to be "advancing" the timing.
AEI (Renix) Allumage Electronique Integrale - electronic ignition system fitted to many Renault vehicles.
AFM (AirFlow Meter - see AFS)
AFR (Air/fuel Ratio) Ratio of air to fuel by weight in a vaporised charge, ie 14.7 grammes of air to 1.0 gramme of fuel (see AFR/Lambda

chart). The AFR in carburettor systems varies according to intake air temperature and density. This makes accurate control of the correct mixture strength virtually impossible. In contrast, the electronic fuel injection system uses a number of sensors to monitor all conditions that will affect the AFR. This means that very accurate control of the mixture is possible.

AFR/Lambda chart
AFR = 14.7:1 by weight

AFR	Lambda	
0.7	10.29	
0.8	11.76	
0.9	13.23	
0.97	14.26	) Lambda
1.0	14.70	) "window"
1.03	15.14	)
1.1	16.17	
1.2	17.64	
1.3	19.11	

AFS (AirFlow Sensor) A sensor that measures the volume of air being drawn into the engine, and passes this to the ECM as an electrical signal. The AFS signal determines the engine load, from which the ECM looks-up the appropriate injection duration. Common types of AFS include the mechanical vane or flap type, and the hot-wire or hot-film types.
Air A mixture of nitrogen (79%), oxygen (20%), carbon dioxide (0.04%) and inert gases (0.06%).
ALDL (Assembly Line Diagnostic Link) The name given to the serial data port used mainly on GM vehicles.
ALT (alternator - Ford term)
Alternator A current-generating device used in a vehicle charging system.
Ammeter An instrument for measuring current in amperes.
Amp (abbreviation for ampere) A unit measurement of current flow.
Amp (abbreviation for amplifier)
Amplitude
Square waveform: Difference between the maximum and minimum voltage.

AC waveform: Difference between zero and either the maximum or minimum peak ("positive" or "negative" amplitude). The positive amplitude is likely to be slightly greater than the negative amplitude in crank angle sensor waveforms.
Analogue signal A continuous signal that can change by an infinitely small amount. Any sensor that meets these conditions can also be called an analogue sensor. Typically, an analogue signal is measured by an instrument that uses a needle to progressively sweep across a fixed scale. Any change in the signal will cause the needle to move by a similar amount. One example would be the throttle potentiometer (or "pot"). As the throttle is opened and closed, the voltage output signal from the throttle pot increases and decreases, and an analogue signal is passed to the ECM.
Annular coil A type of signal generator that utilises a coiled wire magnet attached to a stator plate. The plate contains a number of magnetised upright arms, equal to the number of cylinders and also equal to the number of arms on the reluctor.
API (American Petroleum Institute)
APS (Atmospheric Pressure Sensor) A sensor that returns a signal to the ECM to indicate the current atmospheric pressure. The signal varies as the pressure varies.
ASR (Anti-Skid Regulation) Traction control system used on Mercedes models.
ASV (Air Switching Valve) A vacuum switching valve - often found on Japanese vehicles.
Asynchronous Refers usually to an injection system that is not synchronised to the ignition. Asynchronous pulses may occur at a set time interval or be intermittent in operation.
AT (Automatic Transmission)
ATA (Automatic Transmission Actuator - Ford term)
ATDC (After Top Dead Centre) After the piston has reached TDC and is descending. Refers to retarded ignition timing OR measurement of valve timing.

Reference

Atmospheric pressure The weight of atmosphere per unit area. At sea level, the atmospheric pressure is 14.7 psi absolute or 102 kPa. See pressure conversion table under "Pressure".

ATR (Automatic Transmission Relay - Ford term)

ATS (Air Temperature Sensor) A thermistor that changes in resistance according to temperature. As the temperature changes, the thermistor resistance changes, and thus the ECM is able to calculate the air temperature from the level of voltage (or current) that is registered on the sensor signal wire. The ATS may work on the NTC or PTC principle (negative or positive temperature coefficient).

B

Backprobe A method of obtaining a voltage measurement from the multi-plug pin of an electronic component or sensor. The multi-plug must remain connected to the component. The multi-plug insulating boot should be peeled back, and the voltmeter positive probe attached to the relevant pin - ignition key on. **Note:** *In this book, the multi-plug diagrams show the terminals of the harness connector from the "front". When back-probing the multi-plug (or viewing the sensor connector terminals), the terminal positions will be reversed (seen from the "back").*

Ballast resistor A current-compensating device that alters current flow in direct proportion to the temperature of the resistor. When used in the primary ignition circuit, It serves two purposes.

1) *By providing the proper current level to a low primary resistance coil, it promotes cool coil running under all operating conditions.*
2) *When a full 12-volt bypass supply is introduced to the coil under cranking, the coil output will be greater, and starting will therefore be aided.*

The ballast resistor was mainly use in conventional contact breaker ignition systems, to compensate in part for some of the deficiencies of that system. A number of the early electronic ignition systems (not of the constant-energy type) also utilised a ballast resistor for current-control purposes. The ballast resistor can also be found in other circuits where current-compensation is necessary. An example would be the fuel pump circuit on the Lucas LH system fitted to some Rover fuel-injected systems, and in the voltage supply to the fuel injector solenoid on some early systems.

Banked or simultaneous injection Injectors connected in parallel circuits. In some four-cylinder engines, the four injectors may be connected together so that they all open at the same moment. In other four-cylinder systems, the four injectors are connected in two banks of two cylinders. However, all injectors may still be actuated simultaneously. In a six-cylinder engine, the six injectors may be connected in two banks of three cylinders. In an eight-cylinder engine, the eight injectors may be connected in two banks of four cylinders. In a twelve-cylinder engine, the twelve injectors may be connected in four banks of three cylinders.

Bar A unit of pressure. One bar is almost equal to atmospheric pressure. See pressure conversion table under "Pressure".

Barometric pressure Equal to atmospheric pressure. At sea-level, atmospheric pressure is 100 kPa. See pressure conversion table under "MAP sensor".

Battery A storage device for electrical energy in chemical form.

BBDC (Before Bottom Dead Centre)

BDC (Bottom Dead Centre) Piston at exact bottom of stroke.

BHP (Brake Horse Power) Measurement of engine power.

BOB (Break Out Box) A box containing a number of connectors that allows easy access to the ECM input and output signals, without directly probing the ECM pins.

BOO (Brake On / Off switch - Ford term)

BPC (Boost Pressure Control solenoid - turbocharged vehicles - Ford term)

BPSV (Boost Pressure Solenoid Valve - turbocharged vehicles)

BTDC (Before Top Dead Centre) Ascending piston before top of stroke. Refers to advanced ignition timing OR measurement of valve timing.

C

°C (Celsius or Centigrade) Measurement of temperature. Temperature conversion scale.

CAN Communication between system computers.

CANP (Canister Purge solenoid valve)

Capacitor An electronic component capable of storing an electrical charge. May be used as a suppression device, by offering an alternative path for unwanted charge.

CARB (California Air Resources Board)

CAS (Crank Angle Sensor) The CAS works on the same principle as the inductive permanent magnet pick-up. A number of steel pegs or pins are set at regular intervals around the circumference of the flywheel or crankshaft. Typically, a peg may be set at every 10°, with thirty-six in all to make up the 360°. One or more of the pegs may be removed at TDC, BDC or a known distance from these points. The flywheel thus becomes a reluctor.

A permanent magnet inductive signal generator (CAS) is mounted in close proximity to the flywheel. As the flywheel spins, an alternating (AC) waveform is produced, which signals RPM and flywheel position to the ECM. Although most modern systems utilise a single CAS, some of the older systems use two sensors - one for RPM and one for position. The waveform produced by a each type of CAS will be slightly different.

Cat (catalytic converter) Since January 1993, all new UK vehicles are required to be fitted with a catalytic converter. A catalyst is something which promotes a reaction, but itself remains unaffected by the reaction. The catalytic converter consists of a stainless steel housing containing a ceramic monolith, with a honeycomb of passages called cells.

CB (Contact Breaker points) The "primary trigger" in conventional (non-electronic) ignition systems.

CCO (Clutch Converter lock-up solenoid - Ford term)

CEL (Check Engine Light) see SD warning light.

Celsius see °C.

Ceramic block Insulating block used in construction of a certain type of ballast resistor.

CFCOSV (Carbon Filter Cut-off Solenoid Valve) This valve is often fitted to Peugeot and Citroen vehicles. The CFCOSV is actuated by the ignition key, and is used in conjunction with the CFSV. When the ignition is switched off, the valve closes, and fumes are retained in the system.

CFCV (Carbon Filter Control Valve) Mechanically-operated valve used in the evaporation control system, to control recycling of vapours from the carbon canister.

CFSV (Carbon Filter Solenoid Valve) Electrically-operated solenoid valve used in the evaporation control system, to control recycling of vapours from the carbon canister. Sometimes termed a "purge valve".

CFI (Central Fuel Injection - Ford/Vauxhall term - see SPi)

CID (Cylinder IDentification - camshaft sensor - Ford term)

Circuit An electrical path through which current can flow, and that begins and ends at the current source. A circuit is NOT complete unless the current can return to the source. In modern systems, the current flows from the positive terminal of the battery, through wires or cables and switches to the load (ie a starter motor). The return is through earth (usually through the vehicle body or component mounting) to the negative terminal of the battery.

CIS (Continuous Injection System) A Bosch fuel injection system where the injectors spray fuel continuously during running. Another name for Bosch K-Jetronic.

Clear flood Usually, if a fuel-injected vehicle fails to start, continued cranking will result in excessive fuel being injected into the cylinders. Where the fuel injection system has a "clear flood" facility, fully opening the throttle will result in a reduced volume of fuel being injected whilst the engine is cranked.

Closed-loop control An engine with a Lambda sensor is known as a "closed-loop engine". This is because of the measure of tight engine control about the Lambda or stoichiometric point.

CMH or CMHP (Cold Mixture Heater Plate - see "Manifold heater")

CMP (CaMshaft Position sensor)

CO (Carbon monoxide) Carbon monoxide is formed by the partial burning of fuel, due to a lack of oxygen. A low proportion of CO indicates how well the air/fuel ratio is maintained. A high proportion of CO in the exhaust indicates a rich fuel mixture, choked air filter, choked PCV valve, or low idle speed. Low CO would indicate a lean fuel mixture or a vacuum leak, or even an exhaust leak. CO (and HC) emissions decrease as load (heat and temperature) rises to give a more efficient engine.

CO is a very poisonous, tasteless, colourless and odourless gas. It is a serious health hazard in traffic-congested inner cities, and in semi-enclosed areas (workshops or garages). A concentration of 0.3% can be fatal if breathed in continually for 30 minutes. CO combines with the oxygen in red blood cells, and causes suffocation. By weight, CO accounts for about 47% of air pollution, but is thought to have little effect on the environment.

One molecule of CO contains one atom of carbon and one of oxygen and it is measured in % volume. CO is inversely proportional to the air/fuel ratio - the less fuel, the lower the CO.

CO_2 (Carbon dioxide) CO_2 is the product of an efficient engine. With low CO and HC levels, the percentage of CO_2 in the exhaust is likely to be 13 to 15%. Less than 8% CO_2 indicates an incorrect AFR, a misfire, or a leaky exhaust. CO_2 is directly proportional to the air/fuel ratio, but inversely proportional to CO. The less fuel, the higher the CO_2. At speeds over 2000 rpm, the level will be 1 to 2% higher than at idle, due to an increase in engine efficiency.

One molecule of CO_2 contains one atom of carbon and two of oxygen. CO_2 is chemically stable, and does not easily react with other substances. Not poisonous, it is produced by all breathing animals, including fish. Oxygen is inhaled and CO_2 exhaled at a concentration of about 5%. CO_2 is absorbed by all green plants by a process called "photo-synthesis", which only happens in daylight, and which also releases O_2 into the atmosphere.

Any burning process produces CO_2, and the contribution from automotive sources is said to be less than half that of industrial and domestic sources. The contribution from people and animals is insignificant. A heavy concentration of CO_2 is like placing a blanket over the atmosphere, and this prevents heat loss by radiation. At present, more CO_2 is being produced than is being consumed, and the disappearance of the rain forests is another significant factor. As the forests fade away, less CO_2 is absorbed, and the increase in atmospheric concentration is said to contribute towards global warming and the so-called "greenhouse effect".

In the automobile, the only way to produce less CO_2 is to burn less petrol, or even none at all. This means an efficient engine with good economy (a lean-burn engine), or a diesel engine with high economy, or even a car with no engine - ie an electric motor. But electric cars need electricity, and electricity is produced by power stations, and power stations also produce CO_2.

Coil A device that transforms low (battery) voltage into the high voltage required to bridge the rotor and spark plug gaps.

Combustion During the combustion process, oxygen combines with carbon to form carbon dioxide (CO_2), and with hydrogen to form water (H_2O). If the air and fuel were homogenised prior to combustion, and all the petrol was

completely burnt, then the ideal engine would inhale a perfect mixture of fuel and air, and exhale carbon dioxide (CO_2) and water (H_2O). For every gallon of petrol that an engine consumes, a gallon of water is produced. When the engine is at normal operating temperature, this water is exhausted as steam.

Unfortunately, this ideal engine does not exist, and for a number of reasons, incomplete combustion occurs to a degree in even the most efficient engine. In addition to CO_2 and H_2O, the exhaust thus contains varying quantities of CO, HC, O_2 and NO_x. Some of these gases are harmless - CO_2, H_2O and O_2, whilst others - HC, CO and NO_x are atmospheric pollutants. A less efficient engine will exhaust a greater volume of the more harmful pollutants. A regular tune-up and gas analysis should reduce pollution to acceptable levels. However, the more efficient the engine, the more CO_2 will be exhausted.

Compression The charging of a maximum volume of air and fuel into a minimum volume.

Compression tester A gauge to measure the compression pressure of an engine, and usually graduated in bars or psi.

Conductor A material that will pass electrical current efficiently. A good conductor depends on material used, length, cross-sectional area and temperature.

Constant-energy The use of high primary current, limited to a pre-set figure, for efficient electronic ignition operation.

Constant-energy operation (electronic ignition) Electronic ignition, used with a coil of lower primary resistance, produces increased primary current, resulting in increased coil output. Coupled with higher coil energy, this will produce an arc of longer duration at the spark plug, and enable a weaker mixture to be ignited, with a corresponding improvement in economy and exhaust emissions. Improved reliability, better control of timing, and longer periods between "tune-ups" are other benefits over the conventional contact breaker system. Virtually all modern types of electronic ignition use the variable-dwell current-limiting constant-energy system.

Control signal See *"Relay driver"*, *"Driver"* or *"Final stage"*.

Conventional ignition system A system that uses contact breaker points and a condenser to induce ignition. Replaced generally by electronic ignition in recent years.

Conversion tables See Pressure conversion table, Vacuum conversion table, Temperature conversion table.

Coolant A mixture of water, anti-freeze and corrosion inhibitor to allow efficient cooling system operation.

Cooling system The energy produced by combustion generates tremendous amounts of heat. About 25% of this heat energy is turned into the power that drives the roadwheels. A further 50% is expelled with the exhaust gases, which leaves approximately 25%. It is the function of the cooling system to dissipate this excess heat.

All water-cooled engines should use a mixture of anti-freeze and water, known as "coolant". The coolant mixture is usually 40 to 50% anti-freeze to water by volume, and this usually gives protection down to about -40°C. If water alone is used in the engine cooling system, this will affect the temperature rating of all thermal engine temperature sensors, and can cause incorrect metering of fuel in electronic carburettor and electronic fuel injection systems.

Corrected CO reading A calculation that takes improper combustion into consideration. If the corrected CO and CO readings are dramatically different, then the engine has a combustion problem.

Corrosion Deterioration and crumbling of a component by chemical action. Sensor terminals and multi-plugs are particularly susceptible to this complaint, which usually appears as a white or green powdery deposit on metal terminals.

Corrosion inhibitor A preparation to prevent corrosion. Often used to prevent corrosion of the radiator internal channels by water action.

CPS (Crankshaft Position Sensor - see CAS) Ford term corresponding to crank angle sensor (CAS).

CPU (Central processing unit) May be used as an alternative term for ECM.

Cranking Rotating the engine by use of the starter motor. Usually implies that the engine is not to be started, merely turned over.

CTS (Coolant Temperature Sensor) A thermistor that changes in resistance according to temperature. As the temperature changes, the thermistor resistance changes, and thus the ECM is able to calculate the engine coolant temperature from the level of voltage (or current) that is registered on the sensor signal wire. May work on the NTC or PTC principle.

Current The flow of electrons through a conductor, measured in amps.

Current-controlled or pulse modulation injection see EFi systems.

CVH (Compound Valve angle Head - Ford term) Cylinder head with valves arranged in two planes in a V configuration.

CW (ClockWise) Direction of rotation.

Cylinder balance See *"Power balance"*.

Cylinder contribution A method of comparing the relative power output of each cylinder, without removing the spark as in conventional power balance operation. The acceleration time between each pair of ignition sparks is compared. A cylinder that is less efficient will have a lower acceleration time compared with the other cylinders. This method is much safer on catalyst-equipped vehicles.

D

Dashpot A device that enables the throttle to close slowly rather than suddenly snapping shut, thus preventing the removal of droplets of fuel from the inlet manifold walls due to the high vacuum present during deceleration. These fuel droplets would otherwise be emitted as excess hydrocarbons (HCs), adding to pollution and increasing fuel consumption.

Datastream Once the FCR has decoded a fault, a Datastream enquiry (some systems only) is a quick method of determining where the fault might lie. This data may take various forms, but is essentially electrical data on voltage, frequency, dwell or pulse duration, temperature etc, provided by the various sensors and actuators. Unfortunately, such data is not available from all vehicle systems.

Since the data is in "real time", various tests can be made, and the response of the sensor or actuator evaluated.

Actuating the idle control valve, relays and injectors through the ECM is an excellent method of testing effectiveness of the actuators and associated wiring circuits.

DC (Direct Current) An electrical current source which flows in only one direction.

DC - ISC (Throttle plate control motor - Ford term)

Decarbonisation Removing the cylinder head and scraping away the accumulated levels of carbon build-up from the head, valves and tops of pistons.

Deceleration Closing the throttle and allowing the engine speed to reduce to idle. Also known as "overrun".

Decoke Abbreviated term for decarbonisation.

Degree 1/360th part of a circle.

DEI (DE - Ice switch) Ford term.

Detonation Refer to *"Knock"*.

Diaphragm A thin sheet of rubber that is moved by vacuum to actuate a mechanical device.

Diesel engine A fuel injected engine that uses the high temperature generated in compression to ignite the charge. Sometimes referred to as a "compression-ignition" engine.

Dieseling A fault condition where a petrol engine continues running after the ignition has been switched off. Often caused by cylinder hot-spots or carbon deposits that continue to glow and which are hot enough to explode the air/fuel charge. May be cured by a decoke. Often evident on an older engine when ignition timing is retarded for running on unleaded petrol.

Differential pressure The method by which air is drawn through a carburettor and into an engine. By the rules of physics, air will flow from high (atmospheric) pressure to low pressure (depression caused by fall of piston).

Digit A single number from 0 to 9. Compare with *"Integer"*.

Digital signal A digital signal is represented by a code that has two states, on and off. In simple terms, the signal consists of a series of digital pulses when the frequency, pulse width or number of pulses is used to indicate a specific value.

Because the ECM works in a digital fashion, all analogue signals must pass through an analogue-to-digital converter, when the signal will be stored by the ECM in digital format. A digital signal from a digital sensor does not need converting, and processing by the ECM is therefore much faster.

DIN International standard used in the automotive industry.

Diode A transistor that allows current flow in one direction alone.

DIS (Direct Ignition System) - sometimes termed DIStributorless An ignition system where a distributor is not used.

DIS (alternate) Digital Idle Stabiliser

Distributor A component that distributes the secondary voltage to the correct spark plug in firing order. It is also used to house and operate the contact breaker points mechanism in conventional ignition, and the reluctor and stator in some electronic ignition systems. The distributor turns at the same speed as the camshaft, and at half the speed of the flywheel. The distributor can often be adjusted to time the ignition, and distributes the HT spark to the correct spark plug in firing order.

Distributor cam Located in the distributor, it is mounted upon the distributor shaft, and contains a number of peaks (equivalent to the number of cylinders).

Distributor cap An insulated cap with a centre tower and a circular series of terminals, one for each cylinder. The secondary HT pulses travel from the coil to the centre tower and are delivered, in firing order, to each terminal by the rotor.

DME (Digital Motor Electronics) Generic term often used to describe the Bosch Motronic EMS. The term is used in particular by BMW.

DMM (Digital Multi-Meter) An instrument designed for automotive use that can measure voltage, current, and resistance. Sometimes covers other functions such as dwell, duty cycle, frequency, rpm and amperage etc.

DOHC (Double Over Head Camshaft) A set of two camshafts mounted in the cylinder head. Operation is similar to the SOHC type, except that one of the camshafts opens the inlet valves, and the other one opens the exhaust valves. This leads to more efficient valve operation and improved engine efficiency.

DPFE (Delta Pressure Feedback Electronic system - Ford term) An ECM-controlled valve that regulates the flow of exhaust gas to the EGR valve.

Driver (actuator) Refer also to relay driver, control signal and final stage. The system actuators are supplied with a voltage feed, either from the ignition switch or from one of the EFi system relays. The earth connection is then connected to an ECM earth pin. When the ECM actuates the component, it drives the appropriate ECM pin to earth by completing the circuit internally for as long as actuation is required. In general, the earth connection will only be completed after the ECM has received one or more signals from relevant sensors, and either looked up the associated maps or calculated the correct actuator "on" time.

This signal could be termed a "driver" or a "final stage" or a "control" signal. In the this book, we have settled for the "driver" term. Examples of an actuator driver are: injector, relay, ISCV, CFSV, EGR solenoid, etc.

DTR (Distributor - Ford term)

Duty cycle The period of time in % or ms, during which a component is switched on or energised. By connecting the dwell meter between the pulse terminal and earth on actuators such as the coil, ignition module, Hall-effect switch, injector, ISCV or in fact any other switchable device, a duty cycle may be obtained. By comparing this dwell with known operating parameters, correct operation of the device can be determined. Refer to *"Dwell"* for more information.

DVM (Digital VoltMeter)

Dwell Traditionally, a dwell angle is defined as being the number of degrees through which a distributor rotates when the contact breaker points are closed. However, in modern times we should consider the wider context of the meaning of "dwell". A good definition of a dwell angle would be the time or rotational period through which a device passes when it is energised.

Dwell could thus be measured in terms of degrees of rotation, time "on" (or off) as a percentage (%) compared with the total time for one occurrence, or time "on" (or off) in milliseconds (ms). All we need is the appropriate meter. Usually, dwell is measured in degrees, but if we use either (%) or (ms), it is more common to refer to "duty cycle".

To convert dwell degrees to dwell percent and vice versa, use the following formulae:

Dwell° x (Cylinders / 360) x 100 = Dwell%
ie 45° x (4 / 360) x 100 = 50%

(Dwell% / 100) x (360 / Cylinders) = Dwell°
ie (50% / 100) x 360 / 4 = 45°

Dwell angle Number of rotational degrees during which a device is switched "on". Normally used in reference to contact breaker points, refers to the degrees of rotation of the distributor cam whilst the points are closed. See also *"Duty cycle"*.

Dwell meter An instrument used to measure dwell angle.

Dwell variation The difference in dwell reading taken at any two different engine speeds. Normally refers to contact breaker-equipped distributors.

Dynamic testing The testing of a device whilst it is running under load, as opposed to static testing.

Dynamic volt drop In vehicles with electronic ignition, the dynamic volt drop refers to the volt drop over the primary circuit from the coil negative terminal to earth through the amplifier final driver stage. Equivalent to the so-called distributor resistance or distributor volt drop in contact breaker systems. This measurement is only available with the engine cranking or running, because current must be flowing in the circuit before a measurement can be taken. Not all digital multi-meters are capable of measuring this circuit.

E

Earth A path for current to return to the power source. Also known as "ground".

Earthing probe A tool used to test for current leaks. Often used to test for secondary voltage insulation faults.

EACV (Electronic Air Control Valve - Honda, Rover term)

EAI (Electronic Advance Ignition - GM term)

EBCV (Electronic air Bleed Control Valve)

EC (European Community)

ECM (Electronic control module) A computer control unit that assimilates information from various sensors, and computes an output. Can be used to control the engine ignition timing, injection duration, opening of the ISCV, ABS brakes, air bag etc, etc. May be referred to as a CPU, ECU, or PCM.

ECOTEC (Emission Consumption Optimised TECnology) GM term applied to its latest series of engines.

ECR (Electric Choke Resistor - Ford term)

ECT (Engine Coolant Temperature) Ford term corresponding to coolant temperature sensor (CTS).

ECU (Electronic Control Unit) Refer to "ECM".

EDF (Electro Drive Fan - Ford term)

EDIS (Electronic Distributorless Ignition System - Ford term)

EDIS-4 or EDIS-6 Ford term applied to EDIS-equipped 4- or 6-cylinder engines.

EDM (EDIS Diagnostics Monitor Signal - Ford term)

EEC (Electronic Engine Control - Ford term)

EEC IV or EEC V (Electronic Engine Control 4th/5th generation (module) - Ford term)

EFi (Electronic Fuel injection) A fuel injection system where the injectors are opened (pulsed) by an ECM.

EFi pulse duration The period of time that the injector is held open. Can be measured in milliseconds (ms), or by a dwell meter as a duty cycle (%).

EGOS (Exhaust Gas Oxygen Sensor) See "OS (Oxygen sensor)".

EGR (Exhaust Gas Recirculation) A method of recycling a small amount of exhaust gas into the intake system. This leads to lower peak combustion temperature, with a reduction in NOx emissions.

EHPR (Electro-Hydraulic Pressure Regulator - Ford term)

EI (Electronic Ignition) An ignition system that uses a magnetic sensor and transistors to switch the coil negative terminal on and off.

ELCD (Evaporative Loss Control Device)

ELD (Electronic Load Detector)

Electrode An electrical conductor.

Electrolyte A sulphuric acid and water solution used in a lead/acid batteries. Chemical reaction between the acid and battery plates produces voltage and current.

Electronic MAP See mapped timing/injection advance.

Emissions Fumes from the exhaust, breather vent or fuel tank.

Emission control Devices used to control and minimise poisonous fume emissions.

Emission standards

US 79: This standard was set in the USA in 1979, and has been superseded by the US83 standard. The vehicle must be equipped with a regulated three-way catalyst and an oxygen sensor.

US 83: This is the most stringent of the current European emission levels, and the standard was set in the USA in 1983. The vehicle must be equipped with a regulated three-way catalyst, oxygen sensor and evaporative emission control.

US 88 LDT (Light Duty Truck): This standard sets the same requirements as the US83 standard. However, commercial vehicles over a certain weight will fall into this category.

NEEC 5th amendment: This is an European standard for emission control, and vehicles equipped with at least one of the following systems will meet the standard:

Unregulated catalytic converter

Pulse air system

EGR

15.04: This is not a standard, but is a category applied to vehicles that do not meet a particular emission standard. Vehicles without a catalytic converter, EGR, pulse air system or evaporative emission control will fall into this category.

EMR (Engine Management Relay - Ford term)

EMS (Engine Management System) An EMS is essentially an electronic system whereby the engine ignition and fuelling functions are controlled by one or more ECMs. The distributor, when used, is provided purely to distribute the HT spark to the correct cylinder in firing order. When separate ECMs are provided for ignition and fuelling, the two units do not operate independently, and connections are made so that they can communicate with each other. An Ignition ECM would signal the Injection ECM to initiate injection.

Energised The period during which an electrical device is switched on.

Engine sensor see "Sensor".

ENR (ENgine run Relay - Ford term)

EOBD (European On-Board Diagnostics) An emissions related standard set out to standardise vehicles engine management self-diagnosis systems, fault code generation and accessibility. See Chapter 1.

EPT (Electronic Pressure Transducer - Ford term)

ERIC (Electronically Regulated Ignition & Carburettor - Rover term)

ESA (Electronic Spark Advance - Toyota term)

ESC (Electronic Spark Control - Ford term)

ESC II (Electronic Spark Control 2nd generation (module) - Ford term)

EST (Electronic Spark Timing - GM term)

ETV (automatic transmission component - Ford term)

Exhaust gas Burned and unburned gases that are emitted after combustion.

External influences An influence that is not directly attributable to a particular component, but could affect the operation of that component. Could be used to describe driving style or operating conditions, for example.

EVAP (EVAPorative emission control systems - Ford term)

EVR Electronic Vacuum Regulator - Ford term)

F

Fahrenheit (°F) Temperature scale.

Fast codes Digital fault codes emitted by an EMS that are too fast to be displayed on an LED or on a facia-mounted warning light. A digital fault code reader is required for capturing fast codes.

Fault codes Electronics are now extensively used throughout the modern vehicle, and may control functions such as the transmission, suspension, automatic gearbox, ABS brakes, air conditioning and many others besides ignition and fuelling.

Most modern vehicle management systems have the facility of making self-diagnostic checks upon the sensors and actuators that interface with the vehicle ECM(s). A fault in one of the component circuits causes a flag or code to be set in the ECM memory.

The codes may be described as "slow" or "fast", and some ECMs are capable of emitting both types. Slow codes can be captured by an LED, facia-mounted warning light or even an analogue voltmeter (where the codes are read as needle sweeps). Normally, slow codes are output as a series of flashes ("flash codes"), which must then be interpreted by looking up the code in a fault code table.

Fast codes must be captured by a digital FCR. Future EMSs are more likely to utilise fast codes.

If a suitable code reading device is attached to the serial port on the vehicle harness, fast and slow codes can then be read out from the vehicle computer, and displayed in the form of (typically) a three- or four-digit output code.

FCR (Fault Code Reader) A device that can be connected to the vehicle serial (diagnostic port or SD connector) to interrogate the vehicle ECM. Fault codes and Datastream information can then be read from the ECM. In some instances, vehicle actuators can be actuated from the controls on the FCR. A fault code reader is sometimes termed a "scanner".

Where adjustments to the ignition timing or fuel system are possible, for example on some Ford or Rover systems, then these adjustments can sometimes only be made through an FCR. An FCR is often required to set the system into a "service" mode, otherwise altering the settings in the normal way will not be recognised.

FI (fuel injection)

Final stage See "Driver", "Relay driver" or "Control signal".

FIR (Fuel Injection Relay - Ford term)

Firing line The actual firing voltage as represented on an oscilloscope.

Firing order The order in which the cylinders are fired, ie the order in which HT voltage is fed to the spark plugs (typically 1-3-4-2 for a four-cylinder engine).

Reference

Firing voltage The secondary voltage required to overcome the rotor and spark plug gaps.

Flash codes Fault codes of the "slow" variety, that are output on a facia-mounted warning light or via an LED test light.

Flashshield A plastic cover used in the distributor to prevent secondary arcing interfering with primary operation. Usually fitted below the rotor arm.

Flat spot Hesitation or misfiring of the engine under acceleration.

Flow rate Describes (for example) the volume of fuel pumped during a pre-determined period of time, used in order to test fuel system output.

FLW (Fuse Link Wire - Ford term)

Flywheel sensor Another term for crank angle sensor (CAS).

FO (Fuel Octane - Ford term)

FP (Fuel Pump)

FPR (Fuel Pump Relay - Ford term)

Frequency Pulse frequency, usually measured in Hz.

FRS (Fuel Restrictor Solenoid - Rover term)

FRTS (Fuel Rail Temperature Sensor) A sensor to measure the temperature of fuel in the fuel rail.

FSOR (Fuel Shut-Off Relay - Ford term)

FSOS (Fuel Shut-Off Solenoid - Ford term)

FT (Fuel Temperature sensor)

FTS (Fuel Temperature Switch)

FTVV (Fuel Tank Vent Valve) A solenoid valve used to control evaporation emissions in GM vehicles.

Fuel atomisation The process of changing a jet of liquid fuel into a fine spray, to promote proper mixing of air and fuel. Gives improved combustion and reduces emissions.

Fuel injector (EFi systems) The injector is a solenoid-operated valve that delivers an exact amount of fuel according to an opening duration signal from the ECM. A fine filter is used to prevent debris damaging the precision action. However, gums and lacquers can build up on this filter and on the injection pintle, eventually reducing fuel flow and leading to reduced fuel atomisation. Injection fouling is a serious problem on many injection systems.

Fuse A small component containing a sliver of metal that is inserted into a circuit. The fuse will blow at a specified current rating, in order to protect the circuit from voltage overload.

Fuselink (also known as fusible link). A heavy-duty circuit protection component that can burn out if the circuit becomes overloaded.

G

Gas analyser A device used to sample gases at the exhaust pipe, so that an analysis may be made of the exhaust constituents.

Generator An alternator or dynamo that produces voltage and current. See also alternator.

GM (General Motors) Manufacturer of Opel and Vauxhall in Europe. The parent company is based in the USA.

GND (ground)

Ground USA term for earth. See also *Earth*.

H

Hall-effect generator A type of pulse generator which returns a small digital voltage to trigger the coil.

HES (Hall-Effect Switch) A constant 12-volt supply is passed through the Hall-effect switch in the distributor. Opposite the Hall switch is a magnet whose field causes the Hall switch to return a small voltage back to the amplifier. Attached to the distributor shaft is a rotor vane with the same number of cut-outs as cylinders. Passing the rotor between the switch and the magnet will cause the switch to be turned off and on. As the cut-out space proceeds past the switch, a voltage is returned to the amplifier. When the solid portion comes between the switch and magnet, the voltage is turned off as the magnetic field is diverted. The number of voltages returned per four-stroke engine cycle will equal the number of cut-outs.

Hard faults Generally refers to faults logged by an ECM self-diagnosis routine. The faults are usually present at the moment of testing.

HC (High compression (engine))

HC (Hydrocarbons) 15% Hydrogen and 85% carbon. Petrol is almost pure hydrocarbons. HC is a generic term, and refers to unburnt fuel and partially-burnt fuel. It is measured in PPM - parts per million.

There are many different kinds of HC in the exhaust. HC emissions are generally capable of serious damage to eyes, nose and lungs. When mixed with NOx and in the presence of bright sunshine, photochemical smog is formed. HC is also said to be another reason for the death of the forests.

During combustion, the hydrogen (H) atoms combine with the O_2 atoms to produce H_2O. The carbon (C) atoms combine with O_2 atoms to produce CO_2. High levels of HC in the exhaust signifies ignition problems such as defective plugs or HT leads, incorrect timing, vacuum leaks, incorrect air/fuel ratio or engine mechanical faults. In fact, anything that causes inefficient engine operation will increase the level of unburnt HC in the exhaust.

As the air/fuel ratio weakens, the HC emissions increase due to a lean misfire. This is why a black exhaust is often the result of a too-lean idle mixture. Careful design of the combustion chamber can overcome this problem.

HCS (High Compression Swirl - Ford engine term)

Heat range With reference to a spark plug, the operating range in which the plug will safely and effectively operate.

Heat sink A component to dissipate high operating temperatures.

HEDF (High speed Electro Drive Fan - Ford term)

HEGO (Heated Exhaust Gas Oxygen Sensor) See also *"Oxygen sensor (OS)"*.

HEGOG (Heated Exhaust Gas Oxygen sensor Ground - Ford term) See *"HEGOS"*.

HEGOS (Heated Exhaust Gas Oxygen Sensor)

Hg Chemical symbol for measurement of mercury.

HLG (HalL effect Generator)

Hot-film AFS Very similar in operation to the hot-wire airflow sensor.

Hot-wire AFS A type of airflow sensor (AFS) in which the resistance of an electrically-heated wire is measured. The hot-wire AFS is becoming increasingly popular as an alternative to the vane/flap type or MAP sensor type. This is because the volume, temperature and density of air can be more accurately measured at all altitudes.

The hot-wire AFS is mounted in the inlet air trunking between the air filter and the engine. A box containing the electronics for hot-wire operation sits over the AFS body. A voltage of either 5 or 12 volts, according to system, is applied to the AFS unit.

Air passes through the AFS body into the engine. A small quantity of air is drawn into a bypass channel containing two wires. These wires are known as the sensing wire and the compensating wire. A small current is applied to the compensating wire, which remains unheated. As air passes over the wire, its resistance and current change, and the AFS is able to determine the temperature of the incoming air. The sensing wire is heated to a temperature of 100°C above that of the compensating wire. Air passing over the sensing wire causes it to become cooler, and its current and resistance value change. More current is passed through the sensing wire so that it remains 100°C above that of the compensating wire. An output (signal) voltage, proportional to the current applied to the sensing wire, is returned to the ECM.

The value of this voltage is directly related to the volume, temperature and density of air introduced into the engine. The hot-wire system thus allows automatic compensation for altitudes from sea-level to mountain top, and the ECM will accurately calculate the air/fuel ratio under virtually all conditions.

HT (High Tension) High voltage induced in the secondary windings of the ignition coil.

HT lead (High Tension lead) Cable used to distribute secondary ignition to the distributor cap and to the spark plugs.

Hybrid All the semi-conductor modules are densely packed and encased in resin.

Hydrogen Odourless, highly-explosive gas. Forms two-thirds of the chemical make-up of water.

Hz (Hertz) Frequency in cycles per second.

I

IA (Idle Adjust - Ford term)

IBR (Injector Ballast Resistor - Ford term)

ID (Identification)

Idle speed adjustment (EFi systems) Most modern vehicles have fully automatic idle control, with no means of adjustment. Where adjustment is possible, this is usually effected by a bypass idle speed air screw. Turning the screw one way will reduce the air flow and therefore the idle speed. Turning the screw the other way will increase the air flow and therefore the idle speed.

Although most later systems use an ECM-controlled idle speed control valve (ISCV) or stepper motor to maintain idle speed under engine load, some versions of the ISCV or stepper motor may be adjustable. Generally, this only possible with early units.

Idle speed control Idle speed control devices are actuated by the ECM, and are therefore known as actuators - as distinct to sensors. On most modern engines, speed at idle is maintained at a constant value irrespective of engine load or temperature. As idle conditions alter, or a temperature change or electrical load condition occurs, the ECM actuates either a solenoid-controlled ISCV or a stepper motor to maintain the correct idle position - no matter the speed or load. This prevents poor idle and stalling with heavy electrical loads and a lean mixture. Some versions of the ISCV or stepper motor may be adjustable, although generally this only possible with early units.

Idle-up (Far Eastern term) Any mechanical or electronic system that is used to increase the idle speed according to temperature or engine/electrical load could be termed an idle-up system.

IDM (Ignition Diagnostics Monitor signal - Ford term)

IGC (IGnition Coil - Ford term)

IGf (IGnition confirmation signal - Toyota term)

IGN (IGNition switch - Ford term)

Igniter (Ignition module (amplifier)) Term used by Far Eastern vehicle manufacturers to describe the ignition amplifier.

Ignition module Term used to describe the ignition amplifier.

Ignition switch An on-off switch that provides current to the primary ignition circuit. When the switch is closed and the module is switched on, current will flow through the primary circuit and return to the battery via the engine and body earths.

Ignition timing The correct moment to ignite the compressed air/fuel charge for maximum downforce to be exerted upon the piston.

IGt (IGnition trigger signal from the ECM - Toyota term)

IIA (Integrated Ignition Assembly - Toyota term) Ignition module integral with the distributor.

IMA (Idle Mixture Adjuster - Honda, Rover term)

IMCV (Inlet Manifold Changeover Valve) See "VIS".

Impedance Resistance to the flow of current, and often used to describe the resistance of a voltmeter. A minimum 10 megohm impedance is recommended for instruments used to measure values in electronic circuits.

IMPH (Inlet Manifold Pre-Heater) See "Manifold heater".

Inductive (permanent magnet) pick-up The pick-up is a permanent magnet and inductive coil wound around a pole piece. It is usually

fixed securely in the distributor, and radiates a magnetic field. The two most common types in current service are the pick-up limb or the annular coil.

The reluctor or trigger wheel is mounted on the rotating distributor shaft, with a number of triggering lugs equal to the number of engine cylinders. As the rotating lug passes the pick-up, a small alternating voltage is generated that is strongest as the pick-up and lug are exactly opposite. This voltage is the ignition trigger, and is sent to the amplifier for amplification.

Inhibitor switch See *"P/N switch"*.

Injection system See *"MPi"* or *"SPi"*.

Injector fouling Build-up of deposits on the injector internal filter, or on the injector head, so that flow is reduced or disturbed - resulting in improper injector operation.

Insulator A material that will not pass current readily, and therefore used to prevent electrical leakage.

Inst. panel Instrument panel on the vehicle dashboard.

Intake system The components responsible for the intake of the air/fuel mixture, ie air filter, inlet trunking, carburettor (where used), fuel injectors, inlet manifold and inlet valves.

Integer A whole number, not zero.

Intercooler A device for cooling the air charge supplied to the engine from the turbocharger. Cooler air is denser than hot air, and so a greater volume of air is inducted into the engine. The greater the volume of air inducted, the greater will be the horsepower produced by the engine.

IS (Inertia Switch)

ISC (Idle Speed Control - Ford term) See ISCV.

ISC - BPA (Idle Speed Control - By-Pass Air solenoid - Ford term)

ISCV (Idle Speed Control Valve) A gate or rotary valve that is actuated by the ECM to maintain the correct idle speed, no matter the load or temperature. The ISCV is also used to provide a higher idle speed during engine warm-up. Early versions of engines fitted with an ISCV may be adjustable, although generally this is not the case with later units.

The ISCV contains an electro-magnet to open a bypass port, thus allowing a small volume of air to bypass the throttle plate. This air may pass through a hose, or through a port in the inlet manifold. The ISCV is mounted *in situ*, thus allowing the bypass air to pass through the body of the valve. As the temperature decreases, or the load increases, the ECM pulses the valve for longer intervals (the pulse width increases), and the valve is further opened to allow more air to bypass the throttle. This results in a higher idle speed when the engine is cold, or little or no drop in idle speed when the engine is hot.

Early Bosch systems used an ISCV attached to an electric motor that can be rotated clockwise or anti-clockwise by virtue of two opposing circuits. The motor is supplied with a voltage supply and two earth paths that are made through the ECM. When one path is earthed,

the motor will attempt to rotate in one direction. When the other path is earthed, the motor will attempt to rotate in the opposite direction. By varying the time that each circuit is energised, the ECM will place the ISCV in the exact position required. A duty cycle for the time energised can be obtained on each of the ISCV earth terminals, or at the corresponding ECM terminal. The waveform viewed at each terminal on an oscilloscope is that of a square waveform. This type of actuator is characterised by having three wires at the electrical multi-plug (a 12-volt supply and the two earth wires).

Later Bosch systems use a solenoid that is opposed by a strong spring. The solenoid is supplied with a voltage supply and one earth path, made through the ECM. When the ISCV is earthed by the ECM, the solenoid will overcome the spring force and open the ISCV. If the solenoid fails, it will normally fail-safe closed. However, even when closed, a small amount of air will travel through the valve to give a basic (but low) idle speed. The waveform viewed on an oscilloscope is that of a square waveform.

The longer the time that the ECM pulses (holds open) the ISCV, the further open it will become. Pulsing occurs many times a second (the frequency is about 110 Hz), and by varying the time that the circuit is energised, the ECM will place the ISCV in the exact position required. A duty cycle for the time energised can be obtained on the ISCV earth terminal, or at the corresponding ECM terminal.

Ford use an ISCV which is very similar in operation to the later Bosch type. However, the waveform viewed on an oscilloscope is that of a sawtooth waveform.

ISO (International Standards Organisation)

ISSM (Idle Speed Stepper Motor)

ITS (Idle Tracking Switch - Ford term)

IV PWR (Ignition Voltage PoWeR - Ford term)

J

Jumper lead A small electrical cable that is temporarily used to bridge a component or terminals in a connector plug.

J1930 SAE standard for abbreviations and acronyms describing electrical and electronic components.

K

KA PWR (Keep-Alive PoWeR - Ford term)

KAM (Keep-Alive Memory - Ford term) Dynamic memory in the Ford EEC IV control module. This memory retains soft faults and also the vehicle idle speed settings.

KCM (Knock Control Module - Ford term)

KDS (Kick-Down Switch - Ford term)

KEM (KE-Jetronic Module - Ford term)

KEMKE (fuelling module - Ford term)

King HT lead The HT lead/cable that carries secondary ignition voltage from the coil (usually) to the centre terminal of the distributor cap. "King lead" is a slang term in common use.

KNK (KNocK signal, from knock sensor - Ford term)

Knock The spontaneous explosion of the remaining air/fuel charge in the combustion chamber when only a portion of it has burnt progressively. A direct result of excessive combustion chamber temperature. Known also as "detonation".

Knock threshold The moment during engine operation when the onset of knocking is imminent.

KOHMS (Kilohms) A resistance measurement equal to 1000 ohms. Many digital multi-meters and engine analysers display a measurement in kOhms.

kPa (kilopascals) International standard for the measurement of pressure and vacuum. See pressure conversion table and vacuum conversion table.

KS (Knock Sensor) A sensor that outputs a small electrical signal on detecting engine knock. On receiving a knock signal, the ECM will temporarily adjust (retard) the ignition timing to prevent the condition. Some engine systems with KS can detect engine knock in an individual cylinder. Timing for that cylinder alone will be retarded by the ECM until knock ceases.

kV (Kilovolt) A unit of secondary voltage measurement equal to 1000 volts.

L

LAF (Linear AirFlow sensor - Honda term) Digital oxygen sensor (OS).

Lambda Greek word for the "stoichiometric symbol".

As the engine operates, fuel and air are mixed together and drawn into each cylinder. The air/fuel ratio (AFR) at which fuel burns most efficiently is called the "stoichiometric point", and this is where HC and CO are lowest and CO_2 is highest. This air/fuel ratio is 14.7:1 by weight, and it is also called Lambda = 1 which is the Greek word for correct.

A catalyst-equipped engine will attempt to maintain the AFR within the range Lambda = 0.97 to 1.03.

Although Lambda = 1 is not the best point for best fuel consumption, we have already established that it is the best compromise ratio for using a catalytic converter to oxidise CO, HC and NO_x. Therefore, if the engine's AFR can be contained within the "window" of 0.97 to 1.03, the resultant engine emissions will raise the efficiency of the catalytic converter to about 95%. The lower the emissions from the engine, the less work the cat has to do, and the more efficient it will become. Moreover, by reducing the engine emissions, the cat will also last much longer.

Lambda sensor See "OS (Oxygen Sensor)". A sensor that monitors the amount of oxygen in the exhaust gas, and passes a voltage signal back to the ECM. The ECM then alters the amount of fuel passed to the engine. An attempt is therefore made to keep the air/fuel ratio at the most suitable ratio for perfect combustion.

Lb/in² (pounds per square inch, or psi) An Imperial measurement of pressure. See pressure conversion table under "Pressure".

LDT (Light Duty Truck) See "Emission standards". Refers to the US 88 LDT emission standards for commercial vehicles.

Lead A substance (tetra-ethyl lead or TEL) that is added to petrol to assist the fuel's ability to resist knocking and pre-ignition (octane booster). Lead also lubricates the valves and seats in the engine. Lead levels in petrol have gradually been reduced in recent years, and even leaded petrol contains a far smaller concentration than at one time.

Lead is a poisonous substance which progressively and irreversibly reduces the efficiency of the blood to transport oxygen. It functions as cellular poison for blood, bone marrow and nerve cells. Lead also poisons a catalytic converter, clogging the cells and quickly reducing efficiency.

LED (Light Emitting Diode)

LHS (Left-Hand Side) As viewed from the driver's seat.

Limp-home mode See "LOS".

LOS (Limited Operating Strategy) Often called the limp-home mode, this is a safety system that allows the vehicle to be driven to a service area if a fault occurs. Some LOS systems are so smart that the driver may be completely unaware that a fault has occurred, because vehicle operation is so unaffected.

When the system perceives that a sensor is operating outside of its design parameters, a substitute value is used which allows the engine to operate. However, this value is usually that for a hot or semi-hot engine, and this means that the engine may be difficult to start and run badly when it is cold.

When LOS is implemented, the instrument panel warning light (where fitted) may be illuminated to indicate that a fault has occurred.

Some systems (for example Ford) may also lock the timing to a set figure (with no timing advance) and allow the fuel pump to run continuously under LOS.

LT (low tension) Primary ignition circuit.

LUS (Lock-Up Solenoid (clutch of automatic transmission) - Ford term)

M

ma (milli-amperes)

MAF (Mass Air Flow sensor - term for hot-wire) See "Hot-wire AFS".

Magnet A substance that has the ability to attract iron.

Magnetic field The space around a magnet that is filled by invisible lines of magnetic force.

Manifold heater (MH) The inlet manifold heater is sometimes termed a "hedgehog" because of its distinctive "spiky" appearance. The MH may be found in many single-point injection engines or some carburettor-equipped engines, and usually functions on the PTC principle.

The voltage supply to the MH is often made through a thermal switch or a relay when the engine coolant is cold. As the engine coolant rises above a pre-determined temperature, the thermal switch or relay opens and the voltage supply is to the MH is cut. The switch is usually placed in a coolant hose, or located in the coolant passage of the inlet manifold.

MAP sensor (Manifold Absolute Pressure sensor) This is an inexpensive and less accurate alternative to the airflow sensor. The MAP sensor measures the manifold vacuum or pressure, and uses a transducer to pass an electrical signal back to the ECM. The unit may be located in the engine compartment or in the ECM. Used in both simultaneous MPi and SPi systems, the MAP sensor is particularly popular in SPi systems. MAP is calculated from the formula: Atmospheric pressure - vacuum = MAP. Refer to the MAP table below.

Where the manifold is of the "wet" type (such as on single-point injection systems), the changing pressures in the manifold will cause fuel to enter the vacuum hose, where it may eventually reach the MAP sensor. Installation of a fuel trap and careful routing of the vacuum hose may slow down the ingress of fuel. However, once fuel reaches the MAP sensor, its diaphragm may be adversely affected. If the MAP sensor is a separate unit, renewal is comparatively inexpensive.

MAP sensors may take one of two forms. Older generation vehicles use an analogue sensor, where the voltage signal output is proportional to the load. A newer system that is fast gaining popularity is the digital type. Digital MAP sensors send a square waveform in the form of a frequency. As the load increases, the frequency also increases, and the time in ms between pulses becomes shorter. An ECM will respond much faster to a digital signal, because an analogue-to-digital converter is unnecessary in this system.

MAP table

Note: *Atmospheric pressure - Vacuum = MAP.*

Condition		
Pressure	*Vacuum*	*MAP*
Engine off/ignition on		
1.0 ± 0.1	*Zero*	*1.0 ± 0.1*
Idle speed		
1.0 ± 0.1	*0.72 to 0.45*	*0.28 to 0.55*
High load (full-throttle)		
1.0 ± 0.1	*Zero*	*1.0 ± 0.1*
Deceleration		
1.0 ± 0.1	*0.80 to 0.75*	*0.20 to 0.25*

All units are in bars, and are typical rather than definitive. Refer to the Vacuum conversion table and the Pressure conversion table for conversion to/from other units.

Mapped ignition timing or injection Electronic timing advance or injection pulse that is controlled by the ECM from a "map" located within the ECM. A two-dimensional map contains settings for a number of engine load and speed variations. A three-dimensional map contains settings for a number of engine load, speed and temperature variations. The timing and injection settings are usually contained in separate maps within the ECM. Mapping eliminates any need for the ECM to "guess" the most appropriate settings for a particular running condition, as the ECM can simply "look up" the best settings on the map.

Max. Abbreviation for maximum

MEMS (Modular Engine Management System) A type of EMS manufactured by Rover.

MH (Manifold Heater)

MHR (Manifold Heater Relay)

MIL (Malfunction Indicator Light) See *"SD warning light"*.

Mixture adjustment This is a trimming device, and only a small change in CO at the idle condition is generally possible. Once the throttle is opened from its idle stop, the quantity of injected fuel depends upon the pulse duration. Catalyst-equipped vehicles often have no form of CO adjustment. Where CO adjustment is possible, there are two methods of CO adjustment in current use:

1) *An air screw that varies the airflow through an idle passage in the airflow sensor. As the screw position is varied, the airflow acting upon the metering flap varies, causing the flap to change its idle position. The changed position results in an altered voltage signal to the ECM, and the idle mixture will change appropriately. This type is usually fitted to older vehicles.*

2) *A potentiometer with a variable resistance. As the adjustment screw is turned, the resistance varies, causing a change in the voltage signal being returned to the ECM. This sensor may be mounted upon the ECM, on the airflow meter, or even upon the engine compartment inner wing.*

Mixture screw A screw that regulates the flow of fuel or air through a metered channel or orifice.

MKV Engine coding plug - Mercedes term

MLUS (automatic transmission lock-up solenoid - Ford term)

Molecule The smallest particle into which a chemical compound may be divided.

Motronic a type of EMS manufactured by Bosch. "Motronic" usually means a multi-point injection type, while "Mono-Motronic" is a single-point injection version. In BMW applications, Motronic is often referred to as "DME" (Digital Motor Electronics).

MPi (Multi-Point injection) One injector per cylinder. May be triggered in banks (simultaneous injection) or sequentially (typically, in firing order).

MPi (Multi-Point injection - simultaneous) This is the most common type of EFi system in current use. A number of injectors are looped together in a parallel "bank", with a single connection to the ECM. Where an engine has more than one bank, each bank has its own ECM connection.

In a 4-cylinder engine, one bank connects all of the injectors, or they may be grouped in two banks of two. In a 6-cylinder engine, the injectors are placed in two groups of three, and in an 8-cylinder engine the injectors are placed in two groups of four, termed left and right bank. In a 12-cylinder engine, the injectors are placed into four groups of three cylinders. Two power resistors control two groups each.

The injectors are triggered from a reference signal, which may originate from the ignition system, or from a timing pulse at the CAS. Normally, the injectors operate twice per complete engine cycle. Half of the fuel required is injected onto the back of a closed inlet valve, waiting for it to open, and the other half is injected as the valve opens for the intake stroke. Once the valve has opened, the fuel enters the cylinder in the normal way.

This system is fairly effective, and usually works quite well. It is also cheaper to develop than a full-blown sequential system, which makes it very popular amongst vehicle manufacturers.

MPi (Multi-Point injection - sequential) Eventually, both SPi and simultaneous MPi systems are likely to succumb to the sequential MPi system, where the injectors open in cylinder sequence. Emissions can be significantly reduced with this type - particularly if the engine suffers a mechanical or ignition problem. The sequential MPi system uses the same sensors as other injection systems. However, an additional sensor pinpoints the correct cylinder for the sequential system. In some instances, this is a Hall-effect trigger located in the distributor.

ms (millisecond) 1/1000 second.

MSTS-h (Microprocessor Spark Timing System - HES ignition - GM term)

MSTS-i (Microprocessor Spark Timing System - inductive ignition - GM term)

MT (Manual Transmission)

Multi-meter see DMM

Multi-plug A connecting plug in the wiring harness. Often used to connect the harness to a sensor or actuator. In this book, the multi-plug diagram shows the terminals of the harness connector seen from the "front" (with the plug disconnected). When back-probing the multi-plug (or viewing the sensor connector terminals), the terminal positions will be reversed (seen from "behind").

mV (millivolt) 1/1000 of a volt.

MY (Model Year) Most vehicle manufacturers start manufacturing their latest models in the months leading up to the end of a particular year. The actual date when manufacturing commences is usually termed the model year date, and the year used is usually that of the following year. For example, a facelifted or updated vehicle registered new in September 1996 would be called a "1997 model".

N

nbv (nominal battery voltage) Nominally 12 volts, the voltage will vary under engine operating conditions:

a) *Engine stopped: 12 to 13 volts.*
b) *Engine cranking: 9.0 to 12.0 volts.*
c) *Engine running: 13.8 to 14.8 volts.*

NDS (Neutral Drive Switch - Ford term)

Nearside Side nearest to the kerb on any vehicle - irrespective of whether left- or right-hand-drive.

Ne RPM signal from the pick-up coil - Toyota term

NEEC (New European Economic Community)

Newton (N) An international unit of force that is independent of gravity. This unit was introduced because gravity varies in different parts of the world. The Newton is defined as: The force required to accelerate a mass of 1kg at 1 metre per second per second.

Newton units of pressure are measured as N/m^2 and called Pascal units. This unit is very small and measured in megapascals - MPa (1,000,000) or kilopascals - kPa (1,000). See also *"Pascal"*.

Nitrogen An inert gas, forming nearly 80% of the chemical make-up of air.

Non-cat Non-catalyst. Vehicles without a catalytic converter.

Non-sinusoidal Waveforms such as sawtooth (ie Ford idle speed control valve), square wave, ripple wave, etc.

Non-volatile memory ECM memory that is able to retain information - even when the vehicle battery is disconnected.

NO_x (Oxides of Nitrogen) NO_x is a term given to a group of poisonous gases formed due to high temperatures (exceeding 1300°C) and high compression. There are many different kinds of NO_x (ie NO, NO_2, NO_3 etc) and they are all lumped together under the term NO_x. The N represents one nitrogen atom, and O_x represents any number of oxygen atoms.

The nitrogen content of air passes through the combustion process unchanged until high temperatures (over 1300°C) and pressures are reached. Under these conditions, Nitrogen and oxygen react to form nitrogen monoxide - sometimes called nitric oxide - (NO). The breeding conditions for NO_x are wide-open throttle, acceleration and high-speed cruising. When NO is combined with hydrocarbons (HC) in the presence of strong sunshine, NO_2 (nitrogen dioxide), ozone (O_3) and NO_3 (nitrogen nitrate) are the result. NO_2 is a light brown gas commonly called "smog". When combined with hydrogen atoms, NO_3 forms nitric acid (HNO_3) - one of the contributors to "acid rain". Unfortunately, NO_x emissions reach their peak at Lambda = 1, the so-called "perfect combustion" point.

The diesel engine, whilst producing low levels of CO and HC, has a poor record where NO_x is concerned. NO_x is a particular problem due to the high temperature and high pressures present in a diesel engine combustion chamber.

NO_x causes irritation of eyes and respiratory organs, and gives symptoms of poisoning. Inhalation over a long period leads to destruction of lung tissues.

One method of controlling NOx is to recycle a small amount of exhaust gas into the combustion chamber (exhaust gas recirculation, or EGR). This reduces combustion temperature (and power) by recycling the inert exhaust gas.

Reference

NTC (Negative Temperature Co-efficient) A thermistor in which the resistance falls as the temperature rises. An NTC resistor decreases in resistance as the temperature (eg coolant temperature) rises.

O

O_2 (Oxygen) A harmless gas that is present in about 21% of air and is necessary for proper combustion.

O_2 consists of two oxygen atoms, and is measured in % volume. A small proportion of oxygen (1 to 2%) will be left after proper combustion. Too much or too little would indicate an incorrect air/fuel ratio (AFR), ignition or mechanical problems or an exhaust leak.

The amount of O_2 that is expelled into the exhaust is that which is left over after combustion, and is a good indicator of the AFR - so long as the engine is operating correctly.

OA (Octane Adjuster) A device to finely tune the engine timing for fuels of differing octane levels.

OAI (Octane Adjust Input - Ford term)

OBD (On-Board Diagnosis)

OBDI and OBDII Standards for OBD implemented in the USA.

OBDE (OBD Europe) Planned standard for OBD to be implemented in Europe by the year 2000.

Octane level The level of fuel resistance to knock. The higher the octane level, the more resistance to knock.

OHC (Over Head Camshaft)

Ohm A unit of resistance that opposes the flow of current in a circuit.

Ohmmeter An instrument that is used to measure resistance in ohms.

Ohms Law

Volts = Amps x Ohms (V = I x R)
Amps = Volts / Ohms (I = V / R)
Ohms = Volts / Amps (R = V / I)
Also:
Power (Watts) = Volts x Amps

Open circuit A break in an electrical circuit which prevents the flow of current.

Open-loop control When an engine with Lambda control is operating outside of that control, it is in "open-loop". This may occur during acceleration, full-throttle, or during the warm-up period, and when in LOS. Some systems may go into open loop at idle. When the system is under "open-loop" control, a richer mixture is allowed to prevent hesitation or poor driveability.

Optical distributor Alternative type of crank angle sensor that utilises an LED. Mainly used on some Japanese and other Far Eastern vehicles.

OS (Oxygen Sensor) Also refer to *"Lambda"*. An oxygen sensor is a ceramic device placed in the exhaust manifold on the engine side of the catalytic converter for measuring the amount of oxygen that is left in the exhaust after combustion.

Essentially, the OS contains two porous platinum electrodes. The outer surface electrode is exposed to exhaust air, and coated in porous ceramic. The inner surface electrode is exposed to ambient atmospheric air.

The difference in oxygen at the two electrodes generates a voltage signal which is transmitted to the ECM. This voltage is inversely proportional to the amount of oxygen. The quantity of oxygen remaining after combustion is an excellent indicator of a deficit or surplus of air (rich or weak mixture). The oxygen sensor measures the surplus or deficit of air, and sends a signal back to the ECM, which almost instantaneously adjusts the injection duration (within 50 milliseconds). By controlling the engine electronically so that the air/fuel ratio is always in a small "window" around the Lambda point (ie Lambda = 0.97 to 1.03), during most operating conditions, almost perfect combustion could be achieved. Thus the catalyst has less work to do, and it will last longer with fewer emissions at the tailpipe.

The oxygen sensor closed-loop voltage is quite low, and switches between 100 millivolts (weak) to 1.0 volt (rich). The signal actually takes the form of a switch, and switches from weak to rich at the rate of approximately 1 Hz.

Various names have been given to this sensor, and it could equally be called a lambda sensor, oxygen sensor or even an EGOS (exhaust gas oxygen sensor).

OS heater Because the sensor does not operate efficiently below about 300°C, many oxygen sensors incorporate a heater element for rapid warm-up. Such sensors may also be termed HEGOS (heated exhaust gas oxygen sensor).

Oscilloscope A high-speed voltmeter that visually displays a change in voltage against time. Used to display ignition, alternator and engine sensor or actuator waveforms.

OTS (Oil Temperature Sensor)

Overrun See *"Deceleration"*.

OVP (Over-Voltage Protection - Ford term)

Oxidation A chemical change involving the addition of oxygen atoms to other chemical compounds, usually by burning (combustion). In engine management terms, this usually applies to the chemical reactions occurring in the catalytic converter. For example, CO (carbon monoxide) is oxidised to CO_2 (carbon dioxide) by the addition of another oxygen atom. Unburnt hydrocarbons (HCs) are oxidised (burnt) to produce water (H_2O) and carbon dioxide (CO_2). For this reason, catalytic converters are sometimes referred to as "oxidation catalysts".

Oxides of nitrogen Refer to *"NO_x"*.

P

Parade An oscilloscope pattern where all cylinders are displayed in line.

Pascal International standard for the measurement of pressure and vacuum. See pressure conversion table and vacuum conversion table, under *"Pressure"* and *"Vacuum"* respectively. Refer also to *"Newton"*.

PA (Pressure Atmospheric - Honda, Rover term)

PAS (Power Assisted Steering)

PCM (Powertrain Control Module) Alternative term for ECM, ECU or CPU.

PCS (Pressure Control Switch - Ford term)

PCV (Positive Crankcase Ventilation) A control system to recycle crankcase (oil) fumes into the intake system for burning in the combustion chamber. Also known as the breather system.

Percent Parts of a hundred.

Permanent magnet A magnet that has a magnetic field at all times.

Petrol A hydrocarbon-based fuel composed of a mixture of hydrogen and carbons.

Pick-up See also *"Inductive pick-up"*. Used as a trigger in an electronic system. The pick-up generates a small voltage which signals the amplifier or ECM to switch off and thus instigate ignition. The pick-up is usually in the form of a permanent magnet fixed in the distributor or on the flywheel. When a reluctor is rotated in the magnetic field, the signal to switch occurs when the signal is at its strongest.

Pick-up air gap A clearance between the reluctor and pick-up, which is often adjustable.

PIM (MAP sensor signal - Toyota term)

Pinging The audible sound produced by detonation (pre-ignition).

Pinking A commonly-used aberration of pinging.

PIP (Profile Ignition Pick-up - Ford term) Ford term for the basic timing signal.

Plugged exhaust An exhaust blockage causing back-pressure and lack of performance. Can occur in catalyst-equipped vehicles when the catalyst exceeds its normal operating temperature and melts, thus obstructing the exhaust system.

P/N switch (Park/Neutral switch) A safety switch fitted to vehicles with automatic transmission, which cuts the electrical supply to the starter motor and so prevents the engine from being started in any gear other than Park or Neutral.

Polarity A positive or negative state, with reference to two electrical poles.

Pollutants See *"Emissions"*.

Ported vacuum A vacuum source located in front of the throttle valve. The valve must be opened before a vacuum signal is produced.

Pot (short for "potentiometer") A variable resistance.

Power balance For an engine to give maximum power, each cylinder must contribute an equal share to the workload. By cutting the spark to each cylinder in turn, and noting the rpm drop, it is possible to measure the amount of work, or balance, that each cylinder is contributing to the overall power. A weak cylinder will cause less of a drop in rpm than a strong one, when tested in this way.

PPM (Parts Per Million) A measurement value of the concentration of pollutants such as HC.

Pre-emission Engines that do not have emission control devices.

Pre-ignition The premature explosion of the compressed air/fuel charge before proper ignition by the spark plug. Usually caused by excessive combustion temperature.

Pressure conversion table

bar	lb/in²	kPa
0.1	1.45	10
0.2	2.90	20
0.3	4.35	30
0.4	5.80	40
0.5	7.25	50
1.0	14.50	100
1.02	14.75	102**
1.1	15.95	110
1.2	17.40	120
1.3	18.85	130
1.4	20.30	140
1.5	21.75	150
1.6	23.20	160
1.7	24.65	170
1.8	26.10	180
1.9	27.55	190
2.0	29.00	200
3.0	43.50	300
4.0	58.00	400
5.0	72.50	500

**Approximate atmospheric pressure at sea level*

Pressure regulator The fuel pump supplies fuel at a pressure that exceeds the required system pressure. A spring-loaded diaphragm relieves this pressure by allowing excess fuel to flow back to the tank via the fuel return line.

Primary ignition circuit The low voltage circuit required to begin the ignition process. Components are the ignition switch, ballast resistor, ignition coil, CB points and condenser, inductive pick-up or crank angle sensor, amplifier, and the wiring cables between these components. Not all of these components will be found on all systems.

Primary switching The signal provided by the primary ignition circuit which triggers the secondary (HT) circuit.

Primary windings The outer windings (of relatively heavy wire) in an ignition coil in which the primary current flows.

Probe A method of obtaining voltage from the multi-plug pin of an electronic component or sensor. The multi-plug should be disconnected from the component, and the voltmeter positive test lead used to probe the relevant pin.

PROM (programmable read-only memory)
PS (Phase Sensor - Ford term)
PSA (Citroen and Peugeot group)
Psi (Pounds per square inch) an Imperial measurement of pressure. See pressure conversion table under *"Pressure"*.

PSPS (Power Steering Pressure Switch - Ford term)
PTC (Positive Temperature Co-efficient) A thermistor in which the resistance rises as the temperature rises. A PTC resistor increases (positively) in resistance as the temperature (ie coolant temperature) rises.

PU (inductive pick-up coil)
PUA (PULse Air solenoid - Ford term)
Pulse A digital signal actuated by the ECM.
Pulse generator The pulse generator is a trigger used to initiate ignition. It sends a correctly-timed signal to the amplifier, which then amplifies the signal to switch the coil negative terminal. Examples of pulse generators are:
   a) An inductive permanent magnet pick-up located inside the distributor.
   b) An inductive permanent magnet located adjacent to the flywheel (crank angle sensor).
   c) Hall-effect trigger located inside the distributor.

Pulse width The time period during which an electronic component is energised. It is usually measure in milliseconds.
Purge valve refer to CFSV
PVS (Ported Vacuum Switch (valve))

Q

Quad drive module - GM term If the quad driver is actuated, the FCR will test the following circuits and report on which one is faulty:
   a) Warning light circuit
   b) Air conditioning circuit
   c) Engine speed signal to automatic transmission ECM

R

RAM (Random Access Memory - computer term)
Raster Display of all cylinders on an oscilloscope, one below the other in firing order beginning with number one. The order may be from the top down or bottom up, depending on the oscilloscope.
Reference voltage During normal engine operation, battery voltage could vary between 9.5 (cranking) and 14.5 (running). To minimise the effect on engine sensors (for which the ECM would need to compensate), the ECM often supplies a constant voltage to the sensors, known as a reference voltage, of 5.0 volts.
REG (Regulator)
Relay An electro-magnetic switching solenoid controlled by a fine shunt coil. A small current activates the shunt winding, which then exerts magnetic force to close the relay switching contacts. The relay is often used when a low-current circuit is required to connect one or more circuits that operate at high current levels. The relay terminal numbers are usually annotated to the DIN standard, to which most (but not all) European manufacturers subscribe.
DIN standard relay terminal annotation
30   Supply voltage direct from the battery positive terminal.
31   Earth return direct to battery.
85   Relay earth for energising system. May be connected direct to earth, or "driven" to earth through the ECM.
85b Relay earth for output. May be connected direct to earth, or "driven" to earth through the ECM.

86   Energising system supply. May arrive from battery positive or through the ignition switch.
87   Output from first relay or first relay winding. This terminal will often provide power to the second relay terminal 86 and provide voltage to the ECM, injectors, ISCV etc.
87b Output from second relay or second relay winding. Often provides power to the fuel pump and OS.
Relay control See *"Relay driver"*.
Relay driver The system relays are supplied with a voltage feed from either the battery, ignition switch or from another of the EFi system relays. The earth connection is then connected to an ECM earth pin. When the ECM actuates the relay, it drives the appropriate ECM pin to earth by completing the circuit internally for as long as the actuation is required. In general, the relay earth connection will only be completed once the ECM receives a pre-determined sensor input signal.

Depending upon the relay, the input signal may be instigated by switching on the ignition or cranking the engine (ie the crank angle sensor signal). Once the ECM has received the signal, the ECM will "drive" the relay to earth by completing the circuit internally. The signal could be termed a "driver" or a "final stage" or a "control" signal. In this book we have settled for the "driver" term. Examples of other actuator drivers are the idle speed control valve, carbon filter solenoid valve, fuel injectors, etc.
Relays: EFi system One system relay may be used to control the whole fuel injection system. In that instance, the relay will have double contacts. Alternatively, two or more relays may be used to control the system.
Reluctor A metal rotor with a series of tips equal to the number of cylinders.
REMCO (Remote adjustment for CO pot - Ford term)
Remote start A device to operate the starter solenoid directly from under the bonnet, which also enables more efficient turning (or "inching") over of the engine.
Renix A type of EMS used mainly on Renault and Volvo vehicles.
Required voltage The minimum amount of secondary voltage that must be produced to bridge the rotor and spark plug gaps.
Res. abbreviation for resistance
Resistance Opposition to the flow of current.
Retarded timing Opposite to advanced. When the ignition timing fires AFTER the correct moment. Can also be used to describe ignition timing that occurs ATDC. When adjusting the ignition timing to a smaller number of degrees BTDC, you are said to be "retarding" the timing. For example, when adjusting the ignition timing for running on unleaded petrol, it is usual to retard the timing.
Return Term used to describe the earth return path to an ECM or module of typically a sensor or relay, when the return is not directly connected to earth. The ECM or module will internally connect the return to one of its own earth connections. By this method, the number

Reference

of earth connections to the vehicle body is much reduced.

RFI (Radio Frequency Interference) The EMS is susceptible to outside interference. Radiated RFI can be a problem if the levels are high enough, and this can emanate from items such as a faulty secondary HT circuit or a faulty alternator. Excess RFI can disrupt and affect ECM and EMS operation - particularly where both ignition and fuelling are located in the same ECM.

RHS (Right Hand Side) Viewed from the driver's seat.

RMS (Root mean square) AC equivalent to DC voltage. Can be calculated from AC amplitude by the formula: AC amplitude x 0.707 = RMS.

ROM (Read Only Memory - computer term)

Rotor Rotating part of a component such as a rotor arm, or an electro-magnet used in an alternator.

Rotor air gap The space between the rotor tip and the distributor cap terminal.

Rotor arm The rotor arm is a rotating electrical contact, keyed to the distributor shaft so that it points directly at the correct distributor cap terminal to complete the HT circuit and fire the spark plug.

Rotor register The alignment of the rotor tip to the distributor cap terminal. Where the register is misaligned, the resulting large air gap will cause high firing voltages.

RPM (revolutions per minute) A measure of engine speed.

RSS (remote starter switch)

Rubbing block The part of the contact breaker that rubs against the distributor cam. When the cam peak touches the rubbing block, the points will open to instigate ignition.

S

SAE (Society of Automotive Engineers) The Society sets standards for automotive engineering. See also "J1930".

SAW (Spark Advance Word) A Ford term for the modified timing signal passed from the EEC IV ECM to the EDIS module.

Scanner See "FCR". US term for a fault code reader.

Scope Abbreviation for an oscilloscope.

Screen Term usually applied to insulation around a particular wire, to reduce the effects of RFI.

SD (Self-Diagnosis)

SD connector Wiring plug provided for connecting a fault code reader (FCR) for extracting fault codes. It may also be possible on some systems to place a jumper wire between terminals of the SD connector, to extract slow or "flash" codes.

SD warning light A warning light, located upon the instrument panel, that warns of a fault within the EMS. In some systems, the light can be triggered to flash the stored fault codes.

Secondary ignition circuit The high voltage circuit used to distribute secondary voltage to the spark coil. Components are typically the ignition coil, HT leads, distributor cap and rotor arm (where fitted), and the spark plugs themselves.

Secondary voltage Output from ignition coil.

Secondary windings Ignition coil HT windings.

SEFI (Sequential Electronic Fuel Injection) Fuel injection system where the injectors are pulsed in firing order, rather than all at once (simultaneous injection). This makes for improved efficiency and reduced emissions, but its extra cost means that this system is generally only employed in high-performance applications.

Self-diagnosis of serial data See "Fault codes".

Sensor A device that can measure (for example) temperature, position, airflow, pressure, etc, and returns this information to the ECM in the form of a voltage or current signal, for processing by the ECM.

Serial data port The serial port is an output terminal from the ECM. Signals have therefore been processed, and faults or values are output to the terminal as a coded digital signal.

Sequential injection See "SEFI".

SG (Signal Generator) Distributor pick-up coil.

Short-circuit or "short" When an electrical supply to a particular component goes directly to earth, bypassing the component. Because extremely high current values may be present, the condition can cause an electrical fire. Short-circuits are often caused by a breakdown of insulation, typically by a wire's plastic coating rubbing through or melting so that the wire can contact the vehicle body.

Signal generator See "Pulse generator".

Signal voltage A varying voltage returned to the ECM by a sensor so that the ECM can detect load, or temperature.

Simultaneous injection Refer to "MPi". An injection system in which all the injectors are pulsed simultaneously (all fire at the same time).

Sinusoidal A sine wave. ie a CAS or inductive pick-up waveform where the amplitude of the positive part of the waveform is roughly equal to the amplitude of the negative part of the waveform.

Slow codes Fault codes emitted by an EMS that are slow enough to be displayed on an LED light or on a facia-mounted warning light (see "flash codes"). Some systems may be able to display slow codes on an analogue voltmeter, as needle sweeps.

Smog So-called "photo-chemical smog". Formed by combining HC and NO_x in the presence of strong sunshine. A particular problem in car-dense, sunny climates such as California.

Soft faults Generally refers to intermittent faults logged by an ECM self-diagnosis routine. The faults are often not present at the moment of testing, but have been logged at some period in the past.

SOHC (Single OverHead Camshaft) A single rotating camshaft that controls the opening and closing of both inlet and exhaust valves. The camshaft is mounted above the valves in the cylinder head, and acts directly upon them.

Solenoid An electrical device that produces a mechanical effort when energised.

SP (Sensor phase - Ford term)

Spark advance See "Advanced timing".

Spark control Spark advance control by electronic or thermostatic means.

Spark duration The time taken for a spark to bridge the spark plug electrodes. Shown as a spark line on an oscilloscope.

Spark line See "Spark duration". Also known as "burn time".

Spark plug A device screwed into the cylinder head for igniting the compressed air/fuel charge.

Spark plug electrodes
  a) The centre rod passing through the spark plug insulator (positive electrode).
  b) The rod welded to the outer shell (earth electrode).

Spark plug gap The spark plug electrodes can usually be adjusted by (bending open or closing the earth electrode) to an exact gap for the spark to jump across. However, many of the latest vehicles with catalytic converters are being equipped with multi-earth electrode spark plugs, where the plug gap is pre-set, and cannot be adjusted.

SPi (Single-Point injection) Sometimes known as throttle body injection (TBI), the SPi system has gained much popularity over recent years. Essentially less costly, SPi uses the same sensors as MPi (multi-point injection) systems. A single injector (normally of the current-controlled type) injects fuel into a distributing manifold in much the same fashion as a carburettor.

Although the injection of fuel is much more precise, the problems of manifold heating become critical, and the warm-up period must be carefully controlled if driveability is not to be impaired. Furthermore, the manifold is said to be of the "wet" type. This term means that fuel is present in the manifold. An MPi system is said to be of the "dry" type because fuel is injected into the inlet stub to the valve, and thus only air is present in the manifold.

SPOUT Spark Out. A Ford term for the modified timing signal passed from the EEC IV ECM to the TFI module.

Square waveform A waveform that illustrates the switching on and off of a particular circuit. The higher voltage line is at supply voltage, and the lower voltage line is at earth potential. The vertical transition line from supply to earth is straight, and the distance between the transitions defines the time of "switch on" to "switch off" (duration).

SSV (Spool Solenoid Valve) Variable valve timing component found on some Honda models.

STA Starter motor signal - Toyota term.

STAR (Self-Test Automatic Readout (electronic FCR test) - Ford term) Ford scanner or FCR.

Starter motor An electrical motor that rotates the engine to starting speed.

Static ignition This term is often used by European manufacturers to describe a direct (or distributorless) ignition system. Because no distributor is present, there are no moving parts, hence the "static" term.

Stator Used in electronic ignition or an alternator. As the rotating reluctor and stationary stator pass opposite each other, AC voltage is induced.

STC (Self-Test Connector - Ford term) Refer to "SD connector".

Stepper motor The stepper motor is generally used to control idle speed. It may take several forms, but the two most common systems are described below:

a) A motor is used to drive a valve which opens or closes an air bypass passage in the inlet manifold.

b) A motor is used to increment the throttle plate by so many steps, thereby allowing more or less air through the opening.

Usually the motor is supplied with nbv from the fuel system relay. The windings of the motor are then connected to four earth paths. By pulsing the motor using a combination of the earth paths, the ECM can step the motor to the correct position.

STI (Self-Test Input - Ford term)

STO (Self-test Output - Ford term)

Stoichiometric ratio The ideal mixture of fuel and air for most efficient combustion is called the stoichiometric ratio. If this ratio is maintained, the by-products of combustion, HC and CO are lowest and CO_2 is highest. The air/fuel ratio (AFR) by weight at this point is approximately 14.7:1, ie 14.7 grammes of air to 1 gramme of fuel.

Superimposed An oscilloscope display pattern where all cylinder traces are placed on top of each other. Differences between the various cylinders will then tend to "stand out".

Suppression Reduction of radio or television interference generated by the high voltage ignition system. Typical means used are radio capacitors or resistive components in the secondary ignition circuit.

Suppressor Used to prevent radio interference. See "Capacitor".

SVC (SerVice Connector - Ford term) Wiring plug typically used for ignition timing/idle speed adjustment, possibly to allow the use of unleaded petrol.

Synchronised Usually refers to an injection pulse that is synchronised with the ignition system. The injector will be pulsed at a pre-determined time interval before ignition occurs.

System overview A term to describe the technical description of how the system operates.

T

Tacho (tachometer) A device used to indicate engine speed in RPM.

Tachometric relay A relay that requires a speed signal from the ignition to function.

TAD (Thermactor Air Diverter vacuum solenoid valve - Ford term)

TBH (Throttle Body Heater) An PTC device that quickly warms up the throttle area, thereby preventing ice from forming during engine operation in low-temperature, moist conditions.

TBI (Throttle Body Injection) See "SPi".

TBV (Turbo Boost Valve)

TCATS (TurboCharger Air Temperature Sensor)

TDC (Top Dead Centre) Position of the piston at the top of its stroke.

TDCL (Toyota Data Communication Link)

Temp Abbreviation for "temperature".

Temperature conversion table

°C	Value	°F
-17.8	Zero	32
-17.2	1	33.8
-15	5	41.0
-12.2	10	50.0
-9.4	15	59.0
-6.7	20	68.0
-3.9	25	77.0
-1.1	30	86.0
Zero	32	89.6
4.4	40	104.4
7.2	45	113.0
10.0	50	122.0
12.8	55	131.0
15.6	60	140.0
18.3	65	149.0
21.1	70	158.0
23.8	75	166.6
26.7	80	176.0
29.4	85	185.0
32.2	90	194.0
35.0	95	203.0
37.8	100	212.0
40	105	221
43	110	230
46	115	239
49	120	248
52	125	257
54	130	266
57	135	275
60	140	284
63	145	293
66	150	302
68	155	311
71	160	320
74	165	329
77	170	338
79	175	347
82	180	356
85	185	365
88	190	374
91	195	383
93	200	392
96	205	401
99	210	410
102	215	419
149	300	572
204	400	752
260	500	932
316	600	1112
371	700	1292
427	800	1472
482	900	1652
538	1000	1832
743	1370	2500
1206	2202	4000

Conversion formula:

$(°C \times 1.8) + 32 = °F$

$(°F - 32) \times 0.56 = °C$

Terminal An electrical connecting point.

TFI (Thick Film Ignition) Ford term for ignition module.

THA (Air Temperature Sensor - Toyota term) See "ATS".

Thermistor A potentiometer controlled by temperature.

Three-wire sensor The three-wire sensor has a voltage supply of 5 volts, an earth connection (often made through the ECM) and an output (signal) wire. The output wire returns a variable voltage signal to the ECM. The two most common forms of output are by resistance track and wiper arm, or via a transducer. Examples would include the AFS and TPS (wiper arm) and MAP (transducer).

Throttle valve A valve that controls the volume of airflow into the engine. Sometimes known as a "throttle plate" or "throttle disc".

Throttle valve positioner VAG term - see "Stepper motor".

THS 3/4 (Transmission Hydraulic Switch (3rd/4th gear solenoid) - Ford term)

THW Coolant temperature sensor - Toyota term. See "CTS".

Timing light A stroboscopic light used to check and set ignition timing.

Timing marks Two marks, or a scale and a mark, to indicate TDC or the timing point when aligned. These marks may be on the timing case and front pulley, or on the flywheel, often viewed through an inspection hatch.

TN Engine speed signal - Mercedes term.

TP (Throttle plate)

TPS (Throttle Potentiometer Sensor) The throttle potentiometer (or "pot") sends a variable voltage signal to the ECM to indicate (depending on system), throttle position from idle to full throttle, and rate of throttle opening. The throttle pot is adjustable on some models.

The TPS may be used in conjunction with a throttle switch (TS). If so, the TS will indicate the idle position (and possibly full-throttle position), and a non-adjustable throttle pot will be used solely to indicate the rate of throttle opening.

Transducer A device that converts pressure or vacuum etc into an electrical signal, eg manifold vacuum may be fed to a transducer which turns it into an electrical load signal.

Transistor An electronic switching component.

Trigger See "Pulse generator".

Trigger wheel See "Reluctor".

Trouble codes US term for fault codes.

TS (Throttle Switch) The throttle switch informs the ECM when the engine is in idle mode; an additional contact may indicate full-throttle. Additional enrichment may be provided at idle and during full-throttle running. The TS is adjustable on some models. Some systems may support both a TS and a TPS, although most systems support only one of either type.

TSS (Throttle Stop Screw)

TSS (Turbo Speed Sensor)

TTS (Thermo Time Switch) A switch whose operation is dependent on pre-set time and temperature conditions being met.

Turbocharger An exhaust gas-driven compressor that compresses the air inducted by the engine to increase the horsepower for any given engine capacity.

TVS (Thermal Vacuum Switch) Used to control vacuum according to engine temperature. Mainly used in carburettor systems.

TVSV (Thermostatic Vacuum Switching Valve) See "VSV".

Reference

Two-wire sensor The two-wire sensor utilises an earth wire and a 5 volt supply wire in a circuit that begins and ends at the ECM. The supply wire also doubles as the output wire in the following manner. Once the supply and earth wires are connected to the sensor, the resistance value of the sensor causes the voltage value of the supply to vary. Thus, if we take as an example a two-wire coolant temperature sensor (CTS), its supply voltage of 5 volts may drop to 2 or 3 volts when the engine is cold. As the engine warms up, the voltage may fall to less than 1 volt. Most temperature sensors are examples of two-wire sensors.

U

UCL (Upper Cylinder Lubricant)
UESC (Universal Electronic Spark Control (module) - Ford term)
Unleaded petrol A hydrocarbon fuel that is blended without the addition of lead. Even unleaded petrol contains a very small amount of natural lead that is not usually removed during refining. This amount is insignificant from an emissions viewpoint, and has no adverse effect upon the catalytic converter.
Unported vacuum A vacuum source located on the manifold side of the throttle plate. A vacuum signal is produced irrespective of throttle valve position.

V

Vacuum A negative pressure (suction), or a pressure less than atmospheric. Measured in millibars or inches of mercury. A perfect vacuum exists in a space which is totally empty. It contains no atoms or molecules, and therefore has no pressure. In practice, a perfect vacuum cannot be achieved.

A vacuum occurs in the inlet manifold of a petrol engine because the fall of the piston continually attempts to draw air into each cylinder at a greater speed than the partially-closed throttle disc will allow air to flow past it. The level of vacuum will depend on engine speed and throttle opening. The lowest reading will occur with the engine on full load (wide-open throttle), and the highest reading when the throttle is closed with the engine running at high speed (on the overrun, or when descending a hill).

Vacuum conversion table

inHg	mmHg	kPa	millibars
0.5	12.75	1.7	17
1.0	25.395	3.386	33.86
2.0	51.00	6.8	68
3.0	76.50	10.2	102
4.0	102.00	13.6	136
5.0	127.50	17.0	170
6.0	153.00	20.4	204
7.0	178.50	23.8	238
8.0	204.00	27.2	272
9.0	229.50	30.5	305
10.0	255.00	34.0	340
11.0	280.50	37.3	370
12.0	306.00	40.8	408
13.0	331.50	44.2	442
14.0	357.00	47.6	476
15.0	382.50	51.0	510
16.0	408.00	54.0	544
17.0	433.50	57.8	578*
18.0	459.00	61.2	612*
19.0	484.50	64.6	646*
20.0	510.00	68.0	680*
21.0	535.50	71.4	714*
22.0	561.00	74.8	748
23.0	586.50	78.2	782
24.0	612.00	81.6	816
25.0	637.50	85.0	850
26.0	663.00	88.4	884
27.0	688.50	91.8	918
28.0	714.00	95.2	952
29.0	739.50	98.6	986
29.5	750.00	100.0	1000
30.0	765.00	102.0	1020

* normal engine operating range at idle

Vacuum gauge A gauge used to measure the amount of vacuum in the engine intake system.
VAF (Vane AirFlow - Ford term) Refers to a particular type of AFS. See "Vane type AFS".
Valve timing The timing of valve opening and closing in relation to the piston and crankshaft position.
Vane type AFS As air is drawn through the airflow sensor (AFS), the vane or door is pushed open. The vane is attached to a potentiometer that varies as the door position varies. A voltage signal that varies according to the position of the sensor door is thus returned to the ECM. The ECM is therefore able to compute an injection duration that relates to the actual volume of air being drawn into the engine. No recognition is made of air density, so this AFS is less accurate than the hot-wire/hot-film types. This sensor is an example of a three-wire sensor.
VAT (Vane Air Temperature sensor - Ford term)
Vb batt (+) Voltage supplied from the ECM - Toyota term.
Vc Airflow meter reference voltage - Toyota term.
Vcc PIM (MAP sensor) reference voltage - Toyota term.
Vf Feedback voltage
VIN (Vehicle Identification Number) A serial number to identify the vehicle. The number

often contains coded letters to identify model type and date of manufacture.
VIS (Variable Induction System) A control system where the ECM controls the airflow through the inlet manifold, in order to improve torque and power at different engine speeds and loads.
VM (Vehicle Manufacturer)
Volt A unit of electrical "pressure".
Voltage Electrical "pressure".
Voltage drop Voltage drop is voltage expended when a current flows through a resistance. The greater the resistance, the higher the voltage drop. The total voltage drop in any automotive circuit should be no more than 10%.
Voltage regulator A device use to limit the voltage output of a generator such as an alternator or dynamo.
Voltage reserve The ignition system must provide sufficient secondary HT voltage to bridge the rotor and spark plug gaps under normal operating conditions. In addition, an adequate reserve of coil voltage must be maintained to meet the greater demands made by the ignition system during conditions such as hard acceleration or high engine speeds. If at some point during engine operation the coil reserve becomes lower than the voltage demanded by the ignition, misfiring and loss of power will be the result. A low voltage reserve can be caused by poor ignition components (spark plugs, HT leads, etc) or poor primary ignition connections.
Voltmeter An instrument used to measure voltage in a circuit in volts.
Volume screw See "Mixture screw".
VRS (Variable Reluctance Sensor - Ford term)
Vs (Variable signal from the airflow meter to the ECM -Toyota term)
VSS (Vehicle Speed Sensor) A sensor to measure the road speed of the vehicle.
VSTP (Vacuum Solenoid Throttle Plate - Ford term)
VSV (Vacuum Switching Valve - Japanese vehicle manufacturer term)
VTEC (Variable valve Timing and Electronic Control - Honda term)

W

WAC (Wide-open throttle A/C (air conditioning) cut-off)
WCS (Wastegate Control Solenoid - Ford term)
Watt A unit of electrical power. 746 watts are equal to one mechanical horsepower.
Wiggle test With the engine running, a suspect connection is wiggled, gently tapped, or gently heated or cooled. If the engine misfires or otherwise misbehaves, that connection may be suspect.
WOT (Wide-Open Throttle) Throttle position when fully open. Many EFi systems provide more fuel when this condition is met.

Warnings: Precautions to be taken with automotive electronic circuits

1 The electronic ignition high tension (HT) system generates a high secondary voltage. Care must be taken that vulnerable parts of the body, such as the hands or arms, do not contact HT components. Shock or injury may be caused by allowing the HT to pass to earth through the human body. DO NOT work on electronic vehicle systems if you have a heart condition or any form of heart pacemaker. Pacemaker operation can also be disrupted by radiated RFI.

2 The ECM and other electronic components can easily be damaged by an open HT circuit. When HT is faced with an impossible gap to jump, it will look for an alternative path. This path may be via the ECM, and sensitive components such as transistors may be damaged. In addition, spurious electrical signals from the HT circuit or from other sources of RFI (ie the alternator) may disrupt ECM operation.

3 VERY IMPORTANT:
Avoid severe damage to the ECM or amplifier by switching the ignition OFF before disconnecting the multi-plug to these components. It is generally safe to disconnect the multi-plug to other sensors, actuators and components with the ignition switched on, or even with the engine running.

4 Many modern radios are coded as a security measure, and the radio will lose its coding and its pre-selected stations when the battery is disconnected. The code should be obtained from the vehicle owner before disconnecting the battery

5 When taking voltage readings at a multi-plug or terminal block, the use of meter leads with thin probes is strongly recommended. However, it is useful to attach a paper clip or split pin to the terminal, and attach the voltmeter to the clip. Be very careful not to short out these clips. A number of ECMs employ gold-plated pins at the ECM multi-plug. Particular care should be taken that this plating is not removed by insensitive probing. Equally, do not force too large an object into the terminals, or the connection may be broken when the multi-plug is refitted.

6 DO NOT connect an analogue voltmeter, digital voltmeter, or an LED diode light to the ECM (or to the airflow sensor with the ECM in circuit) if the electrical impedance of the test equipment is less than 10 megohms.

7 To prevent damage to a digital multi-meter or to the vehicle electronic system, the appropriate measuring range should be selected before the instrument probes are connected to the vehicle.

8 During resistance tests with an ohmmeter, always ensure that the ignition is OFF, and that the circuit is isolated from a voltage supply. Resistance tests should NOT be made at the ECM pins. Damage could be caused to sensitive components, and in any case results would be meaningless.

9 When removing battery cables, good electrical procedure dictates that the earth (negative) cable is disconnected before the live (positive) cable. This will prevent spurious voltage spikes that can cause damage to electronic components.

10 Use protected jumper cables when jump starting a vehicle equipped with an ECM. If unprotected cables are used, and the vehicle earth cables are in poor condition, a voltage spike may destroy the ECM. Alternatively, separate surge protection devices are available for connecting directly across the battery terminal during jump starting.

11 When a battery is discharged, by far the best course of action is to recharge the battery (or renew the battery if it is faulty), before attempting to start the vehicle. The ECM is put at risk from defective components such as battery, starter, battery cables and earth cables.

12 Do not use a boost charger, nor allow a charging voltage higher than 16 volts, when attempting to start an engine. The battery leads should be disconnected before a boost charger is used to quick-charge the battery.

13 All fuel injection systems operate at high pressure. Keep a fire extinguisher handy, and observe all safety precautions. Before loosening fuel banjos or fuel hoses, it is a good idea to de-pressurise the system. This can be achieved on most vehicles by disconnecting the electrical supply to the fuel pump (or removing the fuel pump fuse), and then running the engine until it stops. Although this should relieve the system pressure, precautions should still be taken against causing a sudden jet of fuel to be emitted. In any case, even when the system pressure has been relieved, fuel will still be present in the system pipes and components, so take precautions against spillage.

14 A number of diagnostic procedures - such as engine cranking and power balance - may result in unburnt fuel passing into the exhaust, and this is potentially harmful to catalyst-equipped vehicles. Each test must be completed quickly, and repeated testing must not be attempted if damage to the catalytic converter is to be avoided. Do not therefore, make repeated cranking or power balance tests with catalyst-equipped vehicles. Always run the engine at a fast idle for at least 30 seconds between such tests to clear the exhaust of the fuel residue. Where the engine is a non-runner, the catalyst may need to be disconnected to allow cranking to continue. If this advice is not followed the petrol in the catalyst may explode once the temperature in the exhaust reaches a certain temperature.

15 Catalyst damage can be caused when the catalyst temperature exceeds 900°C. When unburnt fuel passes into the catalyst, as the result of any engine malfunction or misfire, the catalyst temperature could easily pass the 900°C mark, causing the catalyst to melt. Apart from catalyst destruction, the melted catalyst will usually cause an exhaust blockage with loss of engine power.

16 Disconnect all ECMs (and the alternator/vehicle battery) when welding repairs are to be made upon a vehicle.

17 The ECM must not be exposed to a temperature exceeding 80°C. If the vehicle is to be placed into an oven (such as after paint spraying work), the ECM must be disconnected and removed from the car to a place of safety.

18 Where possible, disable both ignition and injection systems before attempting a compression test. The above advice about avoiding catalyst damage should also be heeded.

19 The following precautions must be taken with vehicles that utilise Hall-effect electronic ignition.
a) Do not connect a suppressor or condenser to the coil negative terminal.
b) If the electronic ignition is suspect, the Hall-effect sensor connection to the distributor and to the amplifier should be disconnected before the vehicle is towed.
c) During engine cranking tests - compression test or otherwise - remove the Hall-effect sensor connection to the distributor.
d) All other precautions, as detailed above, should also be taken.

20 Do not run the fuel pump or bypass the relay when the fuel tank is empty; the pump or pumps will overheat and may be damaged.

21 Some modern vehicles are now equipped with SRS (Supplemental Restraint System), which is an airbag assembly installed in the steering column or passenger compartment. Extreme caution must be exercised when repairing components situated close to the wiring or components of the SRS. In some vehicles, the SRS wiring runs under the facia, and related SRS components are situated in the steering wheel, in and around the under-facia area and adjacent to some components used in the vehicle EMS. Any damage to the SRS wiring must be repaired by renewing the whole harness. Improper removal or disturbance of SRS components or wiring could lead to SRS failure or accidental deployment. Failure to observe these precautions can lead to unexpected deployment of the SRS and severe personal injury. In addition, the SRS must be repaired and serviced according to the procedures laid down by the manufacturer. Any impairment of the SRS could lead to its failure to deploy in an emergency, leaving the vehicle occupants unprotected.

22 Turbochargers generate extremely high temperatures. In the interests of safety, the turbocharger should be allowed to cool before adjustments or checks are attempted.

Preserving Our Motoring Heritage

< *The Model J Duesenberg Derham Tourster. Only eight of these magnificent cars were ever built – this is the only example to be found outside the United States of America*

Almost every car you've ever loved, loathed or desired is gathered under one roof at the Haynes Motor Museum. Over 300 immaculately presented cars and motorbikes represent every aspect of our motoring heritage, from elegant reminders of bygone days, such as the superb Model J Duesenberg to curiosities like the bug-eyed BMW Isetta. There are also many old friends and flames. Perhaps you remember the 1959 Ford Popular that you did your courting in? The magnificent 'Red Collection' is a spectacle of classic sports cars including AC, Alfa Romeo, Austin Healey, Ferrari, Lamborghini, Maserati, MG, Riley, Porsche and Triumph.

A Perfect Day Out

Each and every vehicle at the Haynes Motor Museum has played its part in the history and culture of Motoring. Today, they make a wonderful spectacle and a great day out for all the family. Bring the kids, bring Mum and Dad, but above all bring your camera to capture those golden memories for ever. You will also find an impressive array of motoring memorabilia, a comfortable 70 seat video cinema and one of the most extensive transport book shops in Britain. The Pit Stop Cafe serves everything from a cup of tea to wholesome, home-made meals or, if you prefer, you can enjoy the large picnic area nestled in the beautiful rural surroundings of Somerset.

John Haynes O.B.E., Founder and Chairman of the museum at the wheel of a Haynes Light 12.

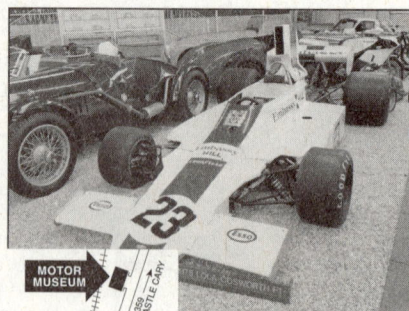

Graham Hill's Lola Cosworth Formula 1 car next to a 1934 Riley Sports.

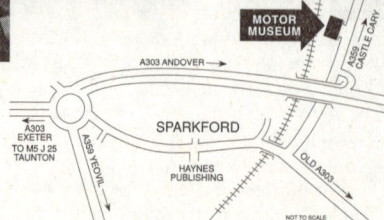

The Museum is situated on the A359 Yeovil to Frome road at Sparkford, just off the A303 in Somerset. It is about 40 miles south of Bristol, and 25 minutes drive from the M5 intersection at Taunton.
Open 9.30am - 5.30pm (10.00am - 4.00pm Winter) 7 days a week, *except Christmas Day, Boxing Day and New Years Day*
Special rates available for schools, coach parties and outings Charitable Trust No. 292048